Robert Markel

EXECUTIVE EDITOR

◆

Susan Waggoner

MANAGING EDITOR

◆

Marcella Smith

RESEARCH AND

RECORDS EDITOR

◆

Foreword by

BILLIE JEAN KING

Preface by

DONNA LOPIANO,
President of the
Women's Sports Foundation

· THE ·

Women's

Sports

ENCYCLOPEDIA

HENRY HOLT AND COMPANY / NEW YORK

Acknowledgments

The authors and editors gratefully acknowledge the assistance they obtained from all the sports associations, federations, clubs and governing bodies. Noble research efforts were made to insure both accuracy and completeness. We do regret that some information was simply not available to us. We hope that our readers will want to supply some of the missing birth dates and places, death dates and, in some cases, records themselves that somehow were never properly recorded or were unverifiable. Thanks again to all. The journey is not over with the publication of this first edition. We hope that there will be more to come over the years and that each succeeding edition will be more comprehensive and complete.

Henry Holt and Company, Inc. / *Publishers since 1866*
115 West 18th Street / New York, New York 10011

Henry Holt ® is a registered trademark of Henry Holt and Company, Inc.

Copyright © 1997 by Markel Enterprises, Inc.
All rights reserved.
Published in Canada by Fitzhenry & Whiteside Ltd.,
195 Allstate Parkway, Markham, Ontario L3R 4T8.

Library of Congress Cataloging-in-Publication Data
    The women's sports encyclopedia / Robert Markel, executive
        editor ; Susan Waggoner, managing editor ; Marcella Smith,
        research and records editor. — 1st ed.
            p.   cm.
        Includes index.
        ISBN 0-8050-4494-9 (alk. paper)
        1. Sports for women—History.   2. Sports for women—Records.
    3. Women athletes—Biography.   I. Markel, Robert.
    II. Waggoner, Susan.   III. Smith, Marcella (Marcella Ann)
    GV709.W589   1997
    796'.082—dc21   97-8850

Henry Holt books are available for special promotions
and premiums. For details contact: Director, Special Markets.

First Edition 1997

Designed by Victoria Hartman

Printed in the United States of America
All first editions are printed on acid-free paper. ∞

10 9 8 7 6 5 4 3 2 1

Contents

◆ ◆ ◆

Foreword

◆ ◆ ◆

As a young girl, no one ever needed to encourage me to "go outside and play." I was almost always outside playing, trying different sports and getting a feel for the thrill of competition and the special bonds forged between human beings who play together. From the start, team sports stood out as something special to me, a unique experience that was replicated nowhere else. My brother, who went on to play pro baseball, was my companion in these explorations. We both loved sports, and I loved the hours I spent playing softball, basketball, and even touch football.

My first experience with tennis came one day at the city park in my hometown. My friend Susan Williams asked me if I wanted to try tennis. "What's tennis?" I asked. I'd never really heard of the game, but I was eager to try it. As soon as the racket was in my hand, I knew that this sport was going to be *my* sport, and that I was going to do everything I could to be the best the world had seen. Before too many volleys had passed over the net, I knew one other thing, too—that I was going to make sure everybody, regardless of class, color, or gender, got a chance to play this wonderful sport.

Neither of my goals was easy. In some ways, the simple wish that everyone have an equal chance to play was more difficult to accomplish than making it to Wimbledon. I wouldn't have succeeded on either count if a lot of people hadn't prepared the way for me. The more I played, the more I fell in love with the game

and the more I wanted to take my place in the chain and improve opportunities for the next generation.

The success I achieved on court provided me with the platform I'd hoped it would, but the going still wasn't easy. The women who stood with me and signed on for the first women's pro tour risked their careers, as I did, to prove that women's tennis could be exciting and commercially viable. Other endeavors I was involved in— the launch of *Women's Sports* magazine, the founding of the Women's Sports Foundation, and WORLDTEAM TENNIS, earth's first major co-educational, equal opportunity team sport—were all considered revolutionary and risky ventures. I'm sure more than one person wondered, probably aloud, why Billie Jean King was "wasting" her time and butting her head against a brick wall.

Luckily, I have a pretty hard head. And there were lots of people who believed, as I did, that it was high time to bring equal opportunity to the world of sports. Title IX, controversial and passionately debated, could never have been passed without the efforts of thousands of parents, high school and college coaches, female athletes, and Washington legislators. Over the years, the combined voices, talents, and efforts of hundreds of women—and men—have indeed transformed the world of sports. Today, the risky position is the one that says only certain sports are "appropriate" for girls and women. In the summer of 1996, it was terrific to see reporters at the Atlanta

Olympics elbowing each other out of the way to cover women's team sports like basketball, softball, and soccer. It's wonderful to wake up in the morning and hear that the Silver Bullets are starting another season and that ticket sales are strong for women's pro basketball and softball events. It's exciting to think that we might soon see a women's pro soccer league, or see another woman make it to the ranks of the NHL.

There is no better way to celebrate this new era than with a book honoring the many gifted and determined women who helped make it possible. In this unique reference book, the biographies, records, and histories of women's sports have for the first time been accorded a place of their own on the bookshelves. I'm happy to have been part of the revolution in women's sports and happy to introduce you to the first edition of *The Women's Sports Encyclopedia*.

—Billie Jean King

Preface

◆   ◆   ◆

"Lights, camera, ACTION!"

Once, girls who dreamed of hearing those words had only one vision in mind—of themselves as Hollywood starlets. Today, they're just as likely to see themselves perched on a diving board, astride a pitcher's mound, or waiting for the starter's pistol to fire. The lights and cameras are poised and ready, but the action has shifted to women's sports.

Over the next decade, more girls and women than ever before are expected to participate in sports. Old records will fall, new benchmarks will be set, and opportunities for women to play professionally will continue to unfold. If this sounds like a revolution, it is. But if you think women's sports are new, you're wrong.

For some women, athletics have always been a natural part of life. As the following pages attest, women's sports are a work in progress. As long as there have been women, there have been women's sports and women who excelled at sports. *The Women's Sports Encyclopedia* is the most comprehensive book ever assembled on these athletes, their lives, and their achievements. On these pages, readers can see how far women have come—and imagine how far we still might go.

—Donna Lopiano
President of the
Women's Sports Foundation

Introduction

◆ ◆ ◆

*I*n 1985, when we began work on *For the Record,* the precursor to *The Women's Sports Encyclopedia,* we firmly believed that women's sports had arrived—or at least had become established enough to warrant a separate record book. Today, it's easy to see how wrong we were. The phenomenon we believed had "arrived" was only in its infancy. In little more than a decade women's sports have catapulted from the limelight to center stage, and female athletes finally are getting the ink—and the laurel wreaths—they deserve.

It wasn't always so. While early Greek and Roman cultures encouraged and celebrated women's athletic achievements, their enthusiasm was the exception rather than the rule. Throughout most of history, society's view of athletic women has been ambivalent at best, critical and exploitative at worst. A mirror of society, sports history offers a reflection of the constrained circumstances in which women lived. From the smock racers of the Renaissance to the dance-hall acrobats of nineteenth-century Paris, female athletes were often viewed as fair game in a kind of soft-core *tableau vivant.*

Fortunately, not all physical activities entailed such a stigma. Hunting, riding, and archery were pursued by many women of the nobility. When Mary Queen of Scots took up golf, it too was added to the list of "appropriate" activities. At the end of the nineteenth century, when the physical fitness movement established a clear link between health and exercise, sports opportunities expanded even further. Women were encouraged to swim and cycle. Colleges led the new movement, both in Europe and America, and soon women

were playing team sports like basketball and baseball. The new freedom brought new concerns. Shows of competitive spirit were looked on as dangerous and definitely suspect. If the smock racers of the 1600s were dismissed as near-prostitutes, serious female athletes of the early twentieth century were dismissed as near-men. It was fine for a woman to play sports, but it was unnatural for her to want to win. While the press and public could openly adore an athlete like Sonja Henie, whose athleticism was masked by fur-trimmed costumes, they had considerable trouble with Babe Didrikson, who made no bones about her desire to beat "everyone in sight."

As women began to resist confining stereotypes in other areas of life, they also began to resist the notion that female athletes must be pretty, married, compliant, grateful, and unpaid. When Billie Jean King took on tennis's notoriously unequal pay scale, it was a watershed moment for women's sports. In the face of hostility, indifference, and hidebound stereotypes, the door of opportunity has been slowly and steadily forced open. Gutsy celebrities like King, parents who have argued for their daughters' right to participate, men and women who have provided training and support for female athletes around the world—all have been instrumental in bringing about a new era of women's sports. In the years since the publication of *For the Record,* there has been a dramatic expansion of women's sports, and an equally dramatic increase in the number of world-class female athletes. Women, who made up less than one-quarter of the athletes at the 1984 Olympics, accounted for more than one-third of the participants in 1996. In the run-up to the 1996 Atlanta games, female athletes dominated the covers of *Newsweek, Sports Illustrated,* and the *New York Times Magazine,* a sustained media blitz that would have been unimaginable just a few years ago.

Today sport still serves as society's reflecting mirror. Female athletes still make up one-third rather than one-half of Olympic participants. They are still faced with challenges men don't have to contend with. Few Muslim men have been harassed into training outside their native country, as runner Hassiba Boulmerka has, and few male basketball players have had to go abroad to earn a living, as Teresa Edwards and other American women have. And no woman's name appeared on *Forbes* magazine's 1996 list of America's forty highest-paid athletes. The changing picture is still changing.

—Bob Markel
Executive Editor

A WORD ABOUT ORGANIZATION, NAMES, DATES, AND RECORDS

We hope you will find *The Women's Sports Encyclopedia* full of information as well as easy to use. For your convenience, you will find information divided by sport. Each sport section includes past and present information about the sport, biographies of prominent athletes, and records for the major competitions. If you are uncertain what sport an athlete might be listed under, please turn to the index on page 328.

When we put together this book, the large number of accomplished female athletes forced us to make many difficult decisions. Since it was impossible to include all the women who deserve to be in this book, we have attempted in the space available to include as many athletes as possible. Where decisions had to be made, we chose to include women who had won titles in the sport's major events, such as the Olympics or world championships. Of course, there were some exceptions to these guidelines, such as athletes who competed before world competition was well organized or who had the misfortune to be at the peak of their careers during years when competitions were canceled due to war or, more recently, Olympic boycott.

We have also attempted to include the most accurate, comprehensive, and up-to-date information available. Unfortunately, the new interest in women's sports hasn't yet been accompanied by a new interest in record keeping. It is our hope in this and future editions of *The Women's Sports Encyclopedia* to standardize and expand information in a field currently fraught with omission and error. We have made every attempt to correct errors found in existing records and books, and to highlight previously overlooked athletes and their achievements.

Since most women first enter the record books under their maiden names, we have listed athletes alphabetically by their maiden names wherever possible. While far from ideal, this system eliminates confusion that arises due to marriage and divorce. If an athlete's maiden name is not well known, you will find a cross-reference under the name by which she is best known, directing you to the appropriate entry. For example, if you look up "Billie Jean King," you will be directed to see "Billie Jean Moffitt King." In the case of Asian athletes who customarily place their last names first, we have followed their custom rather than ours.

We hope you will find *The Women's Sports Encyclopedia* the most comprehensive single volume about female athletes and their sports. We welcome your input as we continue to update and improve our database.

ABBREVIATIONS

AAU   Amateur Athletic Union
AIAW   Association of Intercollegiate Athletics for Women
IOC   International Olympic Committee
NCAA   National Collegiate Athletic Association
USLTA   United States Lawn Tennis Association
USOC   United States Olympic Committee

· T H E ·

Women's
Sports

ENCYCLOPEDIA

Photo credit: Rich Kane

BASKETBALL

◆ *In 1996 basketball celebrated its centennial in a high-growth mode, with attention-getting NCAA drama, renewed efforts to establish a pro league, and all eyes on Olympic gold.*

HISTORY

Without a doubt, basketball was *the* women's sports story of '96. BASKETBALL, one headline screamed, THE NEW CRAZE FOR ATHLETIC YOUNG WOMEN. But the story, featured in the *New York Journal,* didn't mention names like **Rebecca Lobo** or **Sheryl Swoopes.** The year was 1896, and the story described the then-new and, by today's standards, numbingly tame game of basketball. The sport had been invented just five years earlier, the same year that **Senda Beren-son,** a graduate of the highly open-minded and forward-looking Boston Normal School of Gymnastics, adapted it for her students at Smith College. To guard against potentially harmful overexertion, Berenson divided the court into three zones and assigned two players to each zone. The game was an almost instant success. Teams were picked, and practice for a big game began. Due to the immodest nature of the uniforms—bloomers and black stockings—the girls voted unanimously to bar all men from the audience except the school president.

Basketball fever swept East Coast schools and jumped the continent to intoxicate young women in California. Vassar made it a field day event in 1896, and Wellesley officially permitted it in 1898. The women's first intercollegiate game was played at Berkeley, between the University of

California and Stanford. As on the East Coast, men were barred and Armory Hall was filled to the rafters with hundreds of avid, cheering partisans. Such displays of esprit constituted a major threat to the sport's continued acceptance. Competitiveness, stoutly discouraged, was thought to be harmful to tender female psyches, and matches had already been marred by hair-pulling incidents. Nevertheless basketball survived, with influential defenders inside and outside the system. Instructors like Berenson, searching for an antidote to the lethal boredom of calisthenics, found young women more than willing to turn out for drills and practices. Outside academia, feminist author and fitness devotee Charlotte Perkins Gilman publicized the sport by shooting hoops with her teenage daughter. In 1901 philanthropist Phoebe Hearst topped her earlier gift of a gym by giving the women of the University of California an outdoor court.

It's uncertain exactly when basketball crossed the Atlantic, but a generation after its birth it was featured at the 1921 Jeux Olympiques Féminines in Monaco. Teams from Italy, England, France, Norway, and Switzerland played against each other in the Stad du Tir, with the women of Britain emerging victorious. Women's basketball was included in the 1922 and 1928 Olympics but then discontinued. International competitions were not organized again until 1953. In the United States intercollegiate organization lagged even further behind, and a national tournament wasn't initiated until 1966. From its spirited and enthusiastic begining, basketball shrank back into itself. It was perenially popular in the Midwest, where state tournaments drew spectators as well as ink and high-school girls kept the sport alive. So did the lone girls who fought their way into schoolyard pickup games. Women's basketball was biding its time.

THE MODERN ERA

The game we know today—the game that caught fire and vied with the men's for front-page coverage—was not the product of a team, a school, or even a coach. Modern basketball developed in the hands of individual women who ratcheted the game to new levels. It's impossible to think of today's game without thinking of names like **Carol Blazejowski, Ann Meyers,** and **Nancy Lieberman.** The generation born in the mid-1950s wasn't willing to play a tame, ladylike version of the sport. Myers consciously cribbed the moves she saw men make, studying televised games and coming up with her own version of shots and blocks. Blazejowski and Lieberman played schoolyard ball with the boys. When rule changes allowed women to play the same full-court game men had always enjoyed, it unleashed the athletic abilities of players like **Cheryl Miller,** who became the first woman to dunk a ball. The result was a more athletic and aggressive game, a game that offered the same sparks men's basketball did. And of course, from a public relations point of view, it didn't hurt to win a few Olympic medals. When women's basketball was reintroduced at the 1976 games, the United States made it to the finals and came home with a silver medal after losing to a Soviet Union team so formidable that one of its players, **Uljana Semjonova,** was eventually elected to the Basketball Hall of Fame. America had to wait eight years for another Olympic bid, but gold medals in 1984 and '88 salved the disappointment of President Carter's decision to boycott the 1980 games.

One of the most startling and unforeseen developments of the new era was the sudden popularity of college basketball. In 1985 women's Division I games drew just 1.5 million spectators per season. A decade later, attendance topped 4 million. At the end of the 1994–95 season, when no-name U Conn made it to the NCAA Tournament, a new strain of basketball mania—Lobo fever—swept the country. **Rebecca Lobo** and her teammates filled the stands, got national coverage, and helped women's basketball secure a coveted prize—television coverage. ESPN I and II carried more than sixty NCAA games during the 1995–96 season while another cable network, Prime Sports, carried a women's college Game of the Week.

The doubtful spot on the horizon is—and always has been—the challenge of establishing a sta-

---

BACK TO THE FUTURE
How Women's Basketball Became
As Exciting As It Was in the First Place

The game as originally envisioned by Dr. James Naismith was fast, exciting, and often rough. Rule changes were immediately imposed to banish such unsettling elements from the women's game. The decision to confine players to zones, like the decision to restrict guarding and passing, transformed basketball into something midway between Naismith's original game and an exceptionally lively version of Statue Maker. Despite these efforts, life gradually crept back into the game, incrementally at first, then at an accelerating pace during the late 1950s and early 1960s. Listed below, some of the rule changes that have unleashed the women's game.

1918–19. Bounce pass legalized. Basket with an open bottom replaces closed basket with a pull chain.

1932–33. Guarding on any plane replaces vertical guarding.

1938–39. The two-court, six-on-a-side game becomes the rule.

1949–50. The two-bounce dribble with no height restriction becomes legal. Guarding is redefined to permit use of one or both arms, legs, or body in any plane.

1959–60. The ball now remains in play after a missed free goal, introducing the art of rebounding to women's basketball.

1962–63. A watershed year, as two players from each team are now permitted to rove the entire court, and snatching the ball is legalized.

1966–67. The game takes a quantum leap when the unlimited dribble is adopted after a two-year trial period.

1971–72. Dr. Naismith's original game takes shape as the five-player full court is reinstituted.

1987–88. The three-point shot is legalized, as is the interrupted dribble.

---

ble and commercially viable professional league. For years American women have had to go overseas to play professionally, sojourning in Europe, Japan, and South America and racking up, as **Teresa Edwards** told a *Newsweek* reporter, lots of "lonely nights and $1,000 phone bills." Two attempts to establish a pro league at home—the Women's Basketball League and the Women's American Basketball Association—failed in the 1980s, hampered by the lack of a television contract. Women's basketball got smarter in the 1990s. The new Women's National Basketball League enlisted the marketing clout of the NBA, lined up sponsors like pearls on a string, and signed fresh-from-the-Olympics stars. At best, establishing itself will be an uphill struggle for the new league. However popular amateur sports may be, women's pro teams have remained marginalized, a form of emergency sports rations to be consumed only in times of war and national mayhem. And despite the huge growth in audience, the NCAA women's tournament still pulls less than half the audience the men's championship does. On the other hand, the change has all been in the right direction. When there *is* a women's professional sports league in the United States, it isn't likely to be baseball, football, soccer or hockey. It's likely to be basketball.

Hall of Fame

The Naismith Memorial Hall of Fame, in Springfield, Massachusetts, elected its first female members in 1992, when **Lusia Harris** and **Nera White** were inducted. Since then, it has elected several other American women and one Russian, **Uljana Semjonova.**

Major Events and Awards

Team
NCAA Championships
World Championships
Olympic Games

Individual
Naismith Trophy
Wade Trophy
Broderick Award

Going Gold

We don't always do the right things. There are rebounds to be gotten and better defense to be played. But you know the saying, Either you're in or you're out? They're all in.
—Tara VanDerveer, 1996 Olympic team coach, quoted in *Sports Illustrated*

Governing Bodies and Organizations

USA Basketball
5465 Mark Dabling Boulevard
Colorado Springs, Colorado 80918
Phone: 719/590-4800
Fax: 719/590-4811

* * * BIOGRAPHIES * * *

JENNIFER AZZI b. August 31, 1968, Oak Ridge, Tennessee
College team: Stanford University
During Azzi's college seasons (1987–90), Stanford maintained a 101–23 record, won two Pacific-10 Conference titles and made three NCAA tournament appearances. Stanford won the 1990 season championship, and Azzi received the tournament MVP award. After graduation she took her talents to Europe, playing professionally in Italy, France, and most recently, Sweden. A strong believer in "try harder," Azzi wasn't satisfied with a position as alternate on the 1992 Olympic team. She kept training and became a member of several medal-winning national teams, including the 1996 Olympic squad.
Selected championships and honors, team: Gold medal, World Championships, 1990; two gold medals, Goodwill Games, 1990 and '94; NCAA Championship, 1991; bronze medal: Pan American Games, 1991; bronze medal, World Championships, 1994; gold medal, Olympic Games, 1996. *Individual:* Naismith Trophy, 1990; Wade Trophy, 1990; Broderick Award, 1990.

CAROL BLAZEJOWSKI b. September 29, 1956, Elizabeth, New Jersey
College team: Montclair State College, New Jersey
Nicknamed "the Blaze," Blazejowski was a driving force in women's basketball during the late 1970s and a seminal figure in returning U.S. teams to world championship status. A player who patterned her childhood game after the pro men's games she saw on TV, Blazejowksi became one of the leading scorers of all time. During her 1974–77 college career, she set both single-season and career scoring records, with averages of 38.6 and 31.7 points per game respectively. Named all-American three times, she finished college with a record-setting 3,199 points and was the first recipient of the Wade Trophy in 1978. After college she set her sights on the Olympics, maintaining her amateur status by playing for an AAU team from Allentown, Pennsylvania. She was a member of the U.S. Pan American Games team in 1979. That same year, she was the lead scorer on the team that defeated the Soviet Union to win the World Championships, a decisive turning point in U.S. women's basketball history. Picked for the 1980 Olympic team,

Blazejowski lost her chance to play when the United States decided to boycott the Moscow games. Blazejowski quickly gave up her amateur status, signing a three-year contract with the New Jersey Gems for a reported $150,000—paltry by NBA standards, but handsome enough to make her the highest-paid player in the Women's Basketball League. The league's leading scorer and MVP in 1981, Blazejowski's playing days ended when the league disbanded at the end of the season.

Selected championships and honors, team: Gold medal, World Championships, 1979; silver medal, Pan American Games, 1979. *Individual:* Three-time all-American, 1976–78; Wade Trophy, 1978; Basketball Hall of Fame.

RUTH (RUTHIE) BOLTON-HOLIFIELD
b. May 25, 1967, McClain, Mississippi
College team: Auburn University, Alabama
By the time Bolton graduated from college, she had more big game experience than most pro players. During her four seasons (1986–89) Auburn won three championships in the powerful Southeastern Conference and went to four NCAA tournaments, with runner-up finishes in 1988 and 1989. A superb team player, Bolton played professionally in Sweden, Hungary, and Italy and was a member of the 1996 U.S. Olympic squad.

Selected championships and honors, team: Gold medal, Goodwill Games, 1994; bronze medal, World Championships, 1994; gold medal, Olympic Games, 1996. *Individual:* USA Female Basketball Athlete of the Year, 1991.

DENISE CURRY b. August 22, 1959, Davis,
California
College team: UCLA
By the time Curry graduated from UCLA, she'd scored more points than any male or female player in the school's history. Forty-seven of her 3,198 points came in a single game, setting another school record. A forward versatile enough to play any position, Curry was a member of two U.S. Olympic teams (1980 and '84) as well as the 1982 Women's National team.

Selected championships and honors, team: Gold medal, Olympic Games, 1984.

ANNE DONOVAN b. November 1, 1961, Ridge-
wood, New Jersey
College team: Old Dominion University, Virginia

Not many players could have succeeded **Nancy Lieberman** as Old Dominion's star player, but 6'8" Donovan met the test. During her career (1979–82 seasons) she played in all 136 scheduled games and averaged 20 points a game. Her peak came during her junior and senior years, when she led Division I players in rebounding both seasons. The 504 rebounds she pulled down in 1982–83 set a single-season record, and she still holds third place on the all-time season rebound list. Donovan won a clean sweep of individual awards her senior year, a triumph that partially made up for her disappointment over the United States' decision to boycott the 1980 Olympic Games in Moscow. She was a member of the 1983 USA Women's World Championship Team and, after graduation, played professionally in Japan, taking her team to a championship. Donovan returned to the United States in 1984 to coach at her alma mater and set her sights again on the Olympics. She made the team in 1984 and again in 1988, both gold-medal years for the United States.

Selected championships and honors, team: Two gold medals, Olympic Games, 1984 and 1988. *Individual:* Twice all-American, 1981 and '82; Naismith Trophy, 1983; Wade Trophy, 1983; Women's Basketball Coaches Association Player of the Year Award, 1983; Basketball Hall of Fame.

TERESA EDWARDS b. July 19, 1964, Atlanta,
Georgia
College team: University of Georgia
Two-time all-American at the University of Georgia, Edwards was the third woman in the school's history to have her basketball number, 5, retired. Her most remarkable achievement came after her college years, when she became the first (and to date the only) American man or woman ever to play on four U.S. Olympic squads (1984–96), winning a medal in each outing. Edwards also made gold-medal appearances on U.S. World Championship, Pan American Games, and Goodwill Games teams and played professionally in Italy, Japan, and Spain. At the 1996 Olympic Games, which opened on her birthday, Edwards was chosen to take the Olympic oath on behalf of all participating athletes.

Selected championships and honors, team: Two gold medals, Olympic Games, 1984 and '88; two gold medals, World Championships, 1986 and '90; bronze medal, World Championships, 1984; gold medal, Pan American Games, 1987; Two gold medals, Goodwill Games, 1986 and '90. Bronze medal, Pan American

Games, 1991; bronze medal, Olympic Games, 1992; gold medal, Olympic Games, 1996. *Individual:* Two-time all-American, 1985 and '86; two-time USA Basketball Female Athlete of the Year, 1987 and '90.

LUSIA (LUCY) HARRIS-STEWART b. February 10, 1955, Minter City, Mississippi
College team: Delta State University, Mississippi
Harris made waves on and off the court during her four seasons at Delta State (1973–76). The three-time all-American center led her team to three AIAW championships and maintained a 31.2 scoring average during her senior year. Off court, she was the school's first African-American homecoming queen and probably the only homecoming queen to play on U.S. Pan American Games and World University teams during her reign. The next year, Harris played for the United States in the 1976 Olympic Games. In 1977 she received both the Broderick Award and the Broderick Athlete of the Year Award. That same year, she became the first woman ever to be drafted by an NBA team, the New Orleans Jazz. Although she never played for the Jazz, Harris did spend a season in the

---

Woman to Watch: Chamique Holdsclaw

She could be the next **Nancy Lieberman.** Like Lieberman, she's a Queens, New York, native. And, like Lieberman, she learned to play by going one-on-one with boys (usually older and more aggressive than she was) in endless playground games. Despite the similarities, Holdsclaw has her own style and talents. Recruited by Tennessee, the 6'2" Holdsclaw led her team in scoring and rebounds during her freshman (1995–96) season. Her signature talent: tipping offensive rebounds in rather than coming down with the ball and risking a blocked shot from the floor. Tennessee coach Pat Summitt, who's seen lots of talent in her years on and off the court, describes Holdsclaw as "a special talent and a special individual. I've not had a freshman come in and have the numbers across the board that Chamique has."

Women's Basketball League, playing for the Houston Angels in 1980. She discontinued her career to have a family and return to Delta State for a master's degree. *Selected championships and honors, team:* Silver medal, Olympic Games, 1976. *Individual:* Three-time All-American, 1975–77; Broderick Award, 1977; Broderick Athlete of the Year Award, 1977; Basketball Hall of Fame.

PATRICIA HEAD SUMMITT b. June 14, 1952, Clarksville, Tennessee
College team: University of Tennessee-Martin
As a player, and later on as a coach, Summitt was instrumental in transforming women's basketball from an athletic but somewhat predictable game to a swift, aggressive ballet of the air. A standout at the University of Tennessee–Martin, Summitt played for several U.S. teams, including a gold-medal Pan American Games team and the team that won a silver medal at the 1976 Olympics in Montreal. She began her coaching career at the University of Tennessee in the fall of 1974 and quickly established the school as a force to be reckoned with. Summitt-coached teams—marked by a forceful, make-it-happen defense—became regulars at national tournaments and won NCAA championships in 1987, 1989, and 1991. In her first twenty years as a coach, Summitt had a winning average of .808—slightly better than UCLA's legendary John Wooden and enough to put her comfortably on a par with the all-time winningest men's college coaches. Summitt has also coached several medal-winning U.S. teams, including the 1984 team that brought the United States its first Olympic gold medal in basketball.
Selected championships and honors, team: Gold medal, Pan American Games, 1975; silver medal, Olympic Games, 1976. *Coaching:* Gold medal, World Championships, 1979; silver medal, Pan American Games, 1979; silver medal, World Championships, 1983; gold medal, Olympic Games, 1984; three NCAA Championships, 1987, '89, and '91.

PAMELA KELLY b. March 17, 1960, Columbia, Louisiana
College team: Louisiana Tech
Kelly was a starter all four college seasons (1978–81) but peaked in her junior and senior years, when she—along with teammate **Janice Lawrence**—propelled Louisiana Tech to a number-one national ranking. Kelly's greatest talent was shooting from the field, where she racked up an eyebrow-raising .623 average over 153 games. Named all-American in all

but her freshman year, Kelly capped her college career by receiving both the Wade Trophy and the Broderick Award.
Selected championships and honors: Three-time all-American, 1980–82; Wade Trophy, 1982; Broderick Award, 1982.

VENUS LACEY LEVINGSTON b. February 9, 1967, Chattanooga, Tennessee
College team: Louisiana Tech
Lacey's story resembles the bio of another famous American athlete—Wilma Rudolph. Like Rudolph, Lacey spent most of her childhood wearing braces on her legs. As with Rudolph, her physical therapy team consisted of her family. Like Rudolph she dreamed of being "normal," and like Rudolph, she became much more than just normal. When her braces came off, Lacey discovered basketball after being cut from her college volleyball team. She spent her freshman year at Old Dominion, then went to Louisiana Tech on an athletic scholarship. A premier post player, Lacey helped the Lady Techsters to three Final Four appearances and one National Championship. After graduation in 1990, she played six years overseas but returned to be part of the Dream Team fielded for the 1996 Olympics.
Selected championships and honors, team: National Championship, 1988; gold medal, Olympic Games, 1996. *Individual:* All-American, 1990; USBWA Player of the Year, 1990.

JANICE LAWRENCE b. June 7, 1962, Lucedale, Mississippi
College team: Louisiana Tech
Lawrence's career at Louisiana Tech (1980–83) overlapped teammate **Pam Kelly's** by two years, and their combined talents took the team to two number-one rankings. One of the youngest players to ever win a significant award, Lawrence was on fire during the 1982 NCAA playoffs, averaging 22.8 points in tournament play to win an outstanding player award. She was still a sophomore. Lawrence kept up the level of play, being named all-American in her junior and senior years. During her senior year, when she won the Wade Trophy, she averaged 20.7 points per game, pulled down an average 9.1 rebounds, and led her team in steals. She played for two U.S. gold-medal teams—at the 1983 Pan American Games and the 1984 Olympics—and had one pro season with the short-lived Women's American Basketball Association.

Selected championships and awards, team: NCAA Championship, 1982; Gold medal, Pan American Games, 1983; gold medal, Olympic Games, 1984. *Individual:* Two-time all-American, 1983 and 1984; Wade Trophy, 1984; WBCA Division I Player of the Year, 1984.

LISA LESLIE b. July 7, 1972, Inglewood, California
College team: University of Southern California
As a six-foot-tall seventh-grader, Leslie was told by so many people to play basketball that she grew to hate the game. A friend finally convinced her to try for the school team—but that was 5″ of growing and thousands of points in the past. During her four college seasons (1991–94), Southern Cal went to four NCAA tournaments and won one Pacific-10 Conference title. Edwards played professionally in Italy after graduating from college, but returned to play for the U.S. team in the 1996 Atlanta Olympics.
Selected championships and honors, team: Gold medal, Goodwill Games, 1994; bronze medal, World Championship, 1994; gold medal, Olympic Games, 1996. *Individual:* Three-time all-American, 1992–94; Naismith Trophy, 1994; Broderick Award, 1994; WBCA Division I Player of the Year, 1994; USA Basketball Female Athlete of the Year.

NANCY LIEBERMAN CLINE b. July 1, 1958, Brooklyn, New York
College team: Old Dominion University, Virginia
The most famous female player in U.S. history, "Lady Magic" began as a girl in Queens, New York, who wanted to play so badly she was willing to tough it out on the playgrounds against bigger and stronger boys. By the time she was in high school, she was good enough to make the Pan American Games team, and in 1976 she became the youngest member of the U.S. Olympic squad. During her college career at Old Dominion (1976–79), she led her team to national championships in 1979 and '80, years in which she won a clean sweep of Wade Trophies, Broderick Awards, and Broderick Cups. Not noted for height (only 5′10″) or speed, Lieberman dominated her opponents through superior ball handling and shooting. One of the many who missed a chance for Olympic gold due to the 1980 boycott, Lieberman has worked hard to establish women's pro play in the United States. In 1987 she became the first woman to play with the Washington Generals, the team that tours with the Harlem Globetrotters. Married to former pro basketball player Tim Cline, Lieberman broad-

> I make it my little mission to talk history to girls. They need to know about Cheryl Miller and Ann Meyers. They can't be getting their impressions only from Jordan and Malone and Hardaway. Men hand their heroes down to their sons; little boys know all about Mickey Mantle and Jackie Robinson and never saw them play. Women have to do the same thing.
> —Nancy Lieberman Cline

casts for ESPN and Prime Sports during the season, spends her off-season months running basketball camps and publicizing the sport, and still dreams of establishing a pro league for women.

Selected championships and honors, team: Gold medal, Pan American Games, 1975; two National Championships, 1979–80; silver medal, Olympic Games, 1976; silver medal, Pan American Games, 1979. *Individual:* Three-time all-American, 1978–80; two Wade Trophies, 1979 and 1980; two Broderick Awards, 1979 and 1980; two Broderick Cups, 1979 and 1980.

REBECCA LOBO b. October 6, 1973, Southwick, Massachusetts

College team: University of Connecticut

She put U Conn on the map, won thousands of new fans to women's basketball, and spawned a frenzy of hero worship known as Lobo fever. But when it came to the 1996 Olympic team, she was nicknamed "Rookie" by the squad's older members. During her

Neat Feat: Anita Maxwell

When Maxwell became the NCAA's first all-round player to rack up 2,500 points, 1,000 rebounds, and 300 steals in her college career, it was one more sign that women's basketball had come into its own. No other player, male or female, had pulled such impressive numbers. Playing for New Mexico State, Maxwell's 2,500th point came in a February 1996 game against University of New Mexico–Las Vegas.

college career (1992–95), 6′4″ Lobo and 6′7″ teammate **Kara Wolters** were known as "the twin towers." Together, the towers helped power the team to four NCAA tournament berths and Big East Conference championships in 1994 and 1995. U Conn finished the 1994–95 season with a perfect 35–0 record and went on to take the NCAA championship. Lobo played in all thirty-five season games and was named outstanding player of the tournament. The only way to cap a career like that is with Olympic gold, which Lobo earned as a member of the 1996 women's Dream Team.

Selected championships and honors, team: NCAA Championship, 1995; gold medal, Olympic Games, 1996. *Individual:* Naismith Trophy, 1995; Wade Trophy, 1995; Broderick Award, 1995; WBCA Division I Player of the Year, 1995; Naismith Trophy, 1995; Associated Press Female Athlete of the Year, 1995.

KATRINA McCLAIN b. September 19, 1965, Atlanta, Georgia

College team: University of Georgia

Those who think big money has corrupted sports take note: McClain turned down a reported three-hundred-grand offer to spend the 1995–96 season in Europe in order to try for a slot on the 1996 U.S. Olympic team. It wasn't a question of adding another experience to her career but of helping women's basketball establish itself in the United States. The veteran of eleven previous U.S. national teams, McClain is one of the most decorated women in U.S. basketball. The Atlanta games marked her third Olympic appearance, a feat exceeded only by her college teammate **Teresa Edwards,** who played in four Olympics.

Selected championships and honors, team: Two gold medals, World Championships, 1986 and '90; two gold medals, Goodwill Games, 1986 and '90; gold medal, Pan American Games, 1987; two gold medals, Olympic Games, 1988 and '96; bronze medal, Pan American Games, 1991; bronze medal, Olympic Games, 1992; bronze medal, World Championship, 1994; gold medal, Olympic Games, 1996. *Individual:* Broderick Award, 1987; WBCA Division I Player of the Year, 1987; twice named USA Female Basketball Athlete of the Year, 1988 and '92.

NIKKI McCRAY b. December 17, 1971, Collierville, Tennessee

College team: University of Tennessee

McCray's career was threatened before it even began, as a torn ligament caused her to miss the entire

1990–91 season. The ligament healed, and McCray went on to a standout college career. During her years at Tennessee (1992–95) McCray helped her team to three Southeastern Conference titles and one Final Four appearance, in 1995. A combination of toughness and sparkle, McCray once scored 21 points in an upset victory over Stanford—despite the fact that she was playing with a broken hand. There were no broken hands for McCray during the 1996 Olympic Games, just sparkle as the women's Dream Team rolled toward gold.
Selected championships and honors, team: Gold medal, Olympic Games, 1996.

CARLA McGHEE b. March 6, 1968, Peoria, Illinois
College team: University of Tennessee
McGhee had a standout freshman season, playing on a Tennessee team that went all the way to win the NCAA championship title. Then she was in a car accident that broke her jaw and facial bones, fractured her hip, and left her in a coma. When she regained consciousness, doctors told her she was lucky to be alive. As far as basketball went, she would never play again. McGhee disagreed, and got herself through long, difficult months of rehabilitation by vowing to come back better and stronger than ever. McGhee had the last word, and returned to help Tennessee win another NCAA championship. After college, McGhee had several successful pro seasons in Germany, Spain, and France and played on several U.S. national teams, including the gold-medal-winning 1996 Olympic Dream Team.
Selected championships and honors, team: Two NCAA Championships, 1987 and '90; gold medal, Goodwill Games, 1994; bronze medal, World Championships, 1994; gold medal, Olympic Games, 1996.

ANN MEYERS DRYSDALE b. March 26, 1955, San Diego, California
College team: UCLA
A barrier breaker who took women's basketball from margin to mainstream, Meyers is regarded by many as the sport's first superstar. She was the first high-school student to play on a U.S. national team, the first woman to receive a full athletic scholarship at UCLA, and the first woman to sign an NBA contract. Though an unremarkable 5'9" in stature, Meyers early on displayed a talent for high-jumping. At one time she hoped to make her way as a track and field Olympian but focused on basketball after making the U.S. national team in 1974. At the 1976 Olympics she

was team high scorer in the final game, racking up 17 points against the Soviet Union. Meyers's international play was combined with a brilliant college career. UCLA's gamble in offering her a full athletic scholarship paid off big—Meyers was named all-American each of her college seasons and took her team to a national championship in 1978. She made history again after graduation, when the Indiana Pacers signed her to a one-year contract, making her the first woman player ever to receive a paycheck from the NBA. Although Meyers never played for the Pacers, she did sign—and play for—the New Jersey Gems in the Women's Professional Basketball League, tying for MVP honors in the 1979 season. Myers was one of the first women to become a professional commentator, covering the Pacers' televised games, and is one of the few Hall of Fame women married to a Hall of Fame man, the late Dodger pitcher, Don Drysdale.
Selected championships and honors, team: Gold medal, Pan American Games, 1975; gold medal, World Championships, 1975; silver medal, Olympic Games, 1976; NCAA Championship, 1978; gold medal, Pan American Games, 1979. *Individual:* Four-time All-American, 1974–77; Broderick Award, 1978; Broderick Athlete of the Year Award, 1978; Basketball Hall of Fame; International Women's Sports Hall of Fame.

CHERYL MILLER b. January 3, 1964, Riverside, California
College team: University of Southern California
Few players have ever piled up as many points or personal accolades as Miller. As a high schooler she scored 3,026 points—105 of them in a single game—and was the first woman to dunk a basketball in organized competition. Her college career at Southern Cal was equally brilliant. Miller was named all-American each of her four seasons. She took her team to two NCAA championships and was named outstanding tournament player both years, 1983 and '84. Nicknamed "Silk" for her deceptively easy style, Miller was an aggressive point-getter and one of the few women to score more than 3,000 points in college. She wasn't shy about rebounds, either, and ranks in the all-time single-season top ten for grabbing 474 in 50 games in 1985. With **Dawn Staley,** Miller is one of only two women to win consecutive Naismith Trophies and the only woman to win the award three times. She was a top scorer on several U.S. teams she played for, including the 1983 and '84 teams that won gold medals

at the Pan American and Olympic Games. Miller might have had a strong postcollege career but in 1987 sustained a knee injury that ended her career. She was at courtside again in 1996, broadcasting for NBC during the Atlanta Olympics.

Selected championships and honors, team: Two NCAA Championships, 1983 and '84; gold medal, Pan American Games, 1983; gold medal, Olympic Games, 1984; gold medal, World Championship, 1986; gold medal, Goodwill Games, 1984. *Individual:* Four-time all-American, 1982–85; three Naismith Trophies, 1984–86; two Broderick Awards, 1984 and '85; Broderick Cup (shared with swimmer **Tracy Caulkins**), 1984; Wade Trophy, 1985; two-time Women's Basketball Coaches Association Player of the Year, 1985 and '86; Basketball Hall of Fame; International Women's Sports Hall of Fame.

LATAUNYA POLLARD b. July 26, 1960, East Chicago, Indiana

College team: Long Beach State University, California A 5'9" guard with a talent for shooting, Pollard's career was prematurely ended by injury. During her senior year she averaged an astounding 29.3 points per game and was that season's pick for the Wade Trophy. All told, she scored 2,913 points in her four seasons (1978–82)—enough to make her, at the time, the second-highest-scoring woman in college history. Pollard's first piece of bad luck came when the United States decided to boycott the Moscow Olympics in 1980. As a member of the U.S. team in 1983, she injured her ankle at that year's World Championships, which continued to affect her at the Pan American Games later that year. She injured her right knee during trials for the 1984 Olympic team, sustaining cartilage damage that ended her career.

Selected championships and honors, individual: Wade Trophy, 1983; all-American, 1983.

SAUDIA ROUNDTREE b. October 4, 1974, Anderson, South Carolina

College team: University of Georgia Roundtree was National Junior College Player of the Year transferring to Georgia in the fall of 1995—a switch she paid for by earning a scholarship and working overnight factory shifts because she "never liked handouts." In her first year at the school she led her team straight to the NCAA Final Four, where the Bulldogs lost to Southeast Conference rival Tennessee. Roundtree had a phenomenal shooting year, averaging 16.2 points per game and winning the Nai-

smith Trophy. Her goal is to one day coach a Division I men's team, something no woman has ever done. That doesn't bother Roundtree, who explained to a reporter, "If you tell me I can't do it, I'll prove you wrong. I'm one who knows anything is possible."

Selected championships and honors, individual: Naismith Trophy, 1996.

ULJANA SEMJONOVA b. March 9, 1952, Daugavpils, Latvia

In Latvia, she's the most popular athlete in history. In the United States, Semjonova is the only non-American woman ever elected to the Basketball Hall of Fame. In eighteen years of play (1968–84), the 6'10½" Semjonova never lost an international competition. In the 1976 Olympics Semjonova spent half the time on the bench, but she still averaged 19.4 points and 12.4 rebounds per game.

Selected championships and honors, team: Fifteen gold medals, Soviet National Championships; two gold medals, Olympic Games, 1976 and '80; three gold medals, World Championships. *Individual:* Twelve times Latvia's most popular athlete; Basketball Hall of Fame.

DAWN STALEY b. May 4, 1970, Philadelphia, Pennsylvania

College team: University of Virginia If you're only 5'6", you might make your high-school team but you can forget about the big time, right? Wrong. Dawn Staley, who learned the game on the inner-city playgrounds of Philadelphia, not only made it to the big time but got paid for being there, with a scholarship from high-profile Virginia. Few players can steal the ball as deftly as Staley, and her assertive playing style and ability to lead her team have earned her numerous honors, including back-to-back Naismith Trophies and Broderick Awards. One of only three UVA women to have her number, 24, retired, Staley helped the Cavaliers to three NCAA playoffs. In 1991, when Virginia lost the championship to Tennessee in overtime, Staley was named the tournament's outstanding player despite the loss. Like other drop-dead-terrific American players, Staley has mixed overseas pro play with U.S. team play in international competitions and was a member of the 1996 gold-medal Olympic squad.

Selected championships and honors, team: Gold medal, Goodwill Games, 1994; bronze medal, World Championships, 1994; gold medal, Olympic Games, 1996. *Individual:* Outstanding Player, NCAA Tournament, 1991; two Broderick Awards, 1991 and '92; two Naismith Trophies, 1991 and '92; two-time WBCA Division I Player of the Year, 1991 and '92; USA Basketball and United States Olympic Committee Female Athlete of the Year, 1994.

KATY STEDING b. December 11, 1967, Lake Oswego, Oregon

College team: Stanford University

Steding always knew she wanted to play professional basketball. The problem was the same one facing other American women—the lack of a pro league in the United States. Undeterred, Steding worked hard on her game. During her college career at Stanford (1987–90), Steding helped the team to two Pacific-10 Conference crowns and one NCAA championship. Steding was on a hot streak throughout 1990 NCAA tournament play, and on April 1, in a game against Auburn, set Division I and Final Four records for most 3-point field goals scored in a game (6) as well as most 3-point attempts (15). Despite two knee surgeries (in 1990 and '94), Steding has realized her original goal, playing pro ball in Japan and Spain, and was a member of the 1996 gold-medal Olympic squad. Steding also heads her own company—3-Point, Inc.—which runs basketball camps for young women.

Selected championships and honors, team: NCAA Championship, 1990; gold medal, Olympic Games, 1996.

SHERYL SWOOPES JACKSON b. March 25, 1972, Brownfield, Texas

College team: Texas Tech

Swoopes, who learned the game from her two older brothers, transferred to Texas Tech from a junior college and packed four seasons of achievements into her junior and senior years. She helped Tech to two Southwest Conference titles, as well as its first-ever NCAA

championship. During her last season, Swoopes scored 955 points (53 of them in a single game), ending up third on the all-time season scoring list. Swoopes became a household name when Nike christened its first women's "celebrity" basketball shoe after her, calling it "Air Swoopes." Swoopes's membership on the 1996 gold-medal Olympic squad added another coat of luster—sparkle Swoopes hopes will help promote women's basketball in the United States.

Selected championships and honors, team: NCAA Championship, 1993; Goodwill Games, 1994; bronze medal, World Championship, 1994; gold medal, Olympic Games, 1996. *Individual:* All-American, 1992; Naismith Trophy, 1993.

MARGARET WADE b. December 31, 1912, McCool, Mississippi

College Team: Delta State Teachers College, Mississippi

Although Wade played during her college years, captained her team during her sophomore and junior years, and played semi-pro ball for two seasons in the 1930s, her real contributions came as a coach. In 19 seasons as a high school coach, she won 453 games, tied 6, and lost only 89. She returned to her alma in 1959 as director of women's physical education, and in 1973 re-established her sport at the school. Wade coached the Delta State women's team from 1973 through her retirement at the end of the 1978–79 season, racking up 153 wins and 23 losses. In 1992, for her lifetime contribution, she became the first woman ever to receive the James Naismith Basketball Trophy.

Individual: Basketball Hall of Fame, International Women's Sports Hall of Fame, James Naismith Basketball Trophy, 1992.

ORA WASHINGTON. *See entry under Tennis.*

TERESA WEATHERSPOON b. December 6, 1965, Jasper, Texas

College team: Louisiana Tech

A mere 5'8", Weatherspoon couldn't rely on height to boost her game. She succeeded through skills instead and became one of the best defensive players of her day, known for her passing and ball-handling abilities. A starter in each of her college seasons (1983–86), she finished with 958 assists and 411 steals. She helped her team to two NCAA final games, losing to Tennessee in 1987 but beating Auburn for the championship the next year. Weatherspoon also played on

> There's always something every day you can get better at, things you can work on. Of course you get tired, and it's really hard to get out there and to keep going all the time. But you have to remember, in the back of my mind, all I'm thinking of is '96, gold medal . . . I just make myself come out every day and push myself.
>
> —Sheryl Swoopes Jackson

COACHES WHO COUNT

One of the things that separates basketball from other sports is a strong tradition of women coaching women. Below, a few of the women who pass the torch.

Senda Berenson. After reading a description of James Naismith's newly invented game, Berenson introduced it to her students at Smith. Though she has often been criticized for rewriting the rules to make the game tamer and less exciting, her tinkering also made the sport acceptable. Without Berenson's efforts, basketball, like baseball and football, might have been viewed as too rough to be played by women. Basketball Hall of Fame.

Jody Conradt. Three-time National Coach of the Year, Conradt coached her University of Texas Lady Longhorns to a 34–0 record in 1985, becoming the first women's team in history to complete an undefeated season. Conradt's superb record as a coach includes one NCAA championship and, as U.S. National Team coach, a gold medal at the 1987 Pan American Games.

Kerri-Ann McTiernan. When she took over Brooklyn's Kingsborough Community College team in 1995, she became the first—and only—woman to coach a men's college team.

Pat Head Summitt. An outstanding coach, Summitt was also an outstanding player, whose biography can be found on page 8, above.

Vivian Stringer. A winner with a track record to back it up, Stringer made waves when she was hired to take over the Rutgers team in 1995 at a reputed $150,000 per year, making her one of the highest-paid coaches in women's basketball.

Bertha Teague. Teague never played the game herself, but as an elementary teacher and later a high-school coach in Oklahoma, she encouraged thousands of young women to take up the sport. In forty-three years of coaching she fielded five unbeaten teams and eight state championship squads. When she retired in 1969, she left with a winning percentage of .910.

Tara VanDerveer. A college coach with a .781 winning percentage at her schools (Idaho, Ohio, and since 1985, Stanford), VanDerveer has served as U.S. basketball coach since 1990. She coached the 1994 team that won a bronze at the World Championships and a gold at the Goodwill Games, the 1991 gold-medal World University Games team. In 1996 she coached the United States to a gold-medal finish at the Atlanta Olympics.

Margaret Wade. As a high school coach in the 1940s and '50s, Wade's winning percentage topped .800. She spent the 1970s rebuilding women's basketball at her alma mater, Delta State, with even better results. She retired after the 1978–79 season with a record of 157 wins and just 23 losses.

several U.S. national teams, including the 1988 and '92 Olympic squads.

Selected championships and honors, team: Gold medal, World Championships, 1986; gold medal, Goodwill Games, 1986; two-time all-American, 1987 and '88; gold medal, Olympic Games, 1988; bronze medal, Olympic Games, 1992. *Individual:* Wade Trophy, 1988.

NERA WHITE b. November 13, 1935, Macon County, Tennessee

White came of age when opportunities to play were scarce and sometimes nonexistent. The college she went to didn't even have a women's program, so she joined the Nashville Basketball Club in 1954. She was named AAU all-American for the next fifteen consecutive years, played on ten AAU championship teams, and was AAU tournament MVP nine times. A member of the United States' 1957 World Championship team, White had the heady experience of being named best female basketball player in the world that year. Although her basketball career ended in 1969, when the Nashville team broke up, White's award-winning days weren't over. An excellent all-round athlete who could circle the bases in ten seconds flat, White was named to two all-American fast-pitch softball teams and became a slow-pitch all-American player in 1980, at the age of forty-five.

Selected championships and honors, team: Gold medal, World Championships, 1957. *Individual:* Fifteen-time AAU all-American, 1955–69; Best Female Basketball Player in the World, 1957; two-time all-American, fast-pitch softball, 1959 and '65; all-American, slow-pitch softball, 1980; Basketball Hall of Fame.

KARA WOLTERS b. August 15, 1975, Holliston, Massachusetts

College team: University of Connecticut

At 6'7", Wolters's height and genes (her father played for Bob Cousy at Boston College) seemed to make her a natural. But Wolters describes her high-school self as "big, slow, and heavier." To excel, she had to toughen up physically and mentally. At U Conn she shed sixty-five pounds and her "nice girl" image to become one of the most effective post players in the game. Wolters played "twin towers" with elder teammate **Rebecca Lobo,** and had to learn to stand alone when Lobo graduated in 1995. Wolters, class of '97, has played for U.S. international teams. Although she failed to make the final cut for the 1996 Olympic squad, her youth makes her a possible for the year 2000.

Selected championships and honors, team: Bronze medal, World Championships, 1994; NCAA Championship, 1995. *Individual:* All-American, 1996.

LYNETTE WOODARD b. August 12, 1959, Wichita, Kansas

College team: University of Kansas

Scoring, rebounds, steals—at one time or another during her college career (1977–80) Woodard headed the list in each of these categories. She led the nation in rebounding during her freshman year and in steals during her sophomore, junior, and senior seasons. She finished as America's all-time top college scoring champ, with 3,649 points. Not surprisingly, she was named all-American all four years and was recipient of both the Wade Trophy and the Broderick Award. She played for several U.S. national teams, including the doomed-to-disappointment 1980 Olympic squad, and won golds at the 1983 Pan American Games and 1984 Olympics. Woodard spent one season (1981–82) in Italy, where she led the league in scoring, but returned to the United States to volunteer as an assistant coach while getting her master's degree. She played for the Columbus franchise in the short-lived Women's Basketball Association and in 1985 played for the Harlem Globetrotters, the first woman in history to do so.

Selected championships and honors, team: Gold medal, Pan American Games, 1984; gold medal, Olympic Games, 1984. *Individual:* Four-time all-American (1978–81); Wade Trophy, 1981; Broderick Award, 1981.

ZHENG HAIXIA, b. China

When the 1996 U.S. Olympic squad made a list of women to worry about, Zheng, well over 7' tall, was at the top. One of the best players on the international scene, Zheng was named most valuable player of the 1994 World Championships, averaging 26.4 points and 13.1 rebounds per game. After the championships, Zheng shed over thirty pounds and worked to improve her coordination, measures that further increased her scoring average. Her efforts weren't enough to lift her team to victory, however, and China finished the 1996 Olympics in a disappointing ninth place.

Basketball Awards

Broderick Award

Honda has sponsored this award, first presented in 1977 by the late Thomas Broderick, since 1987. The winner is nominated for the Honda Award, which recognizes the collegiate woman athlete of the year.

Wade Trophy

First presented in 1978 by the National Association for Girls and Women in Sport (NAGWS). The trophy is awarded for academics and community service as well as player performance. Named after former Delta State head coach Margaret Wade.

Frances Pomeroy Naismith Award

First presented in 1984 to the outstanding female senior collegian under 5'6" in height. Named by the Basketball Hall of Fame.

Naismith Trophy

First presented in 1983 by the Atlanta Tip-Off Club and voted on by a panel of media and coaches. Named after Dr. James Naismith, inventor of basketball.

Naismith Lifetime Achievement Award
Presented by the Atlanta Tip-Off Club. The 1992 winner was Margaret Wade.

Carol Eckman Award
First presented in 1983 to a coach who has shown spirit, integrity, and courage in coaching women's basketball. The award is named in honor of the late Carol Eckman, former West Chester coach, who died in 1985.

Women's Basketball Coaches Association Player of the Year
Voted on by the Women's Basketball Coaches Association, and first presented by Champion athletic outfitters in 1983.

Association of Intercollegiate Athletics for Women (AIAW)
Before women were admitted as members of the NCAA in 1981–82, most women's programs were under the auspices of the Association of Intercollegiate Athletics for Women. The women listed in the AIAW career records section played all or most of their collegiate careers before the era of official NCAA women's basketball statistics, which began in 1981–82. The AIAW championship served as the national women's large-college playoff for the ten years preceding the NCAA championship in 1982.

Basketball Awards

Broderick Award

Year	Player	Team
1977	Luisa Harris	Delta State
1978	Ann Meyers	UCLA
1979	Nancy Lieberman	Old Dominion
1980	Nancy Lieberman	Old Dominion
1981	Lynette Woodard	Kansas
1982	Pam Kelly	Louisiana Tech
1983	Anne Donovan	Old Dominion
1984	Cheryl Miller	Southern Cal
1985	Cheryl Miller	Southern Cal
1986	Cheryl Miller	Southern Cal
1987	Kamie Ethridge	Texas
1988	Katrina McClain	Georgia
1989	Teresa Weatherspoon	Louisiana Tech
1990	Bridgette Gordon	Tennessee

1991	Dawn Staley	Virginia
1992	Dawn Staley	Virginia
1993	Sheryl Swoopes	Texas Tech
1994	Lisa Leslie	Southern Cal
1995	Rebecca Lobo	Connecticut
1996	Rebecca Lobo	Connecticut

Carol Eckman Award

Year	Coach	Team
1986	Laura Mapp	Bridgewater (Va.)
1987	Jody Conradt	Texas
1988	Kay Yow	North Carolina State
1989	Linda Hill-MacDonald	Minnesota
1990	Maryalyce Jeremiah	Cal State Fullerton
1991	Marian Washington	Kansas
1992	Jill Hutchison	Illinois State
1993	Vivian Stringer	Iowa

Naismith Memorial Hall of Fame

Year	Player
1992	Lucy Harris
1992	Nera White
1993	Ann Meyers
1993	Uljana Semjonova
1994	Carol Blazejowski
1995	Anne Donovan
1995	Cheryl Miller

Wade Trophy

Year	Player	Team
1978	Carol Blazejowski	Montclair State
1979	Nancy Lieberman	Old Dominion
1980	Nancy Lieberman	Old Dominion
1981	Lynette Woodard	Kansas
1982	Pam Kelly	Louisiana Tech
1983	LaTaunya Pollard	Long Beach State
1984	Janice Lawrence	Louisiana Tech
1985	Cheryl Miller	Southern Cal
1986	Kamie Ethridge	Texas
1987	Shelly Pennefeather	Villanova
1988	Teresa Weatherspoon	Louisiana Tech
1989	Clarissa Davis	Texas
1990	Jennifer Azzi	Stanford
1991	Daedra Charles	Tennessee
1992	Susan Robinson	Penn State
1993	Karen Jennings	Nebraska
1994	Carol Ann Shudlick	Minnesota
1995	Rebecca Lobo	Connecticut
1996	Jennifer Rizzotti	Connecticut

Basketball (continued)

Frances Pomeroy Naismith Award

Year	Player	Team
1984	Kim Mulkey	Louisiana Tech
1985	Maria Stack	Georgia
1986	Kamie Ethridge	Texas
1987	Rhonda Windham	Southern Cal
1988	Suzie McConnell	Penn State
1989	Paulette Backstrom	Bowling Green
1990	Julie Dabrowski	New Hampshire
1991	Shanya Evans	Providence
1992	Rosemary Kosiorek	West Virginia
1993	Dena Evans	Virginia
1994	Nicole Levesque	Wake Forest
1995	Amy Dodrill	Johns Hopkins
1996	Jennifer Rizzotti	Connecticut

Naismith Trophy

Year	Player	Team
1983	Anne Donovan	Old Dominion
1984	Cheryl Miller	Southern Cal
1985	Cheryl Miller	Southern Cal
1986	Cheryl Miller	Southern Cal
1987	Clarissa Davis	Texas
1988	Sue Wicks	Rutgers
1989	Clarissa Davis	Texas
1990	Jennifer Azzi	Stanford
1991	Dawn Staley	Virginia
1992	Dawn Staley	Virginia
1993	Sheryl Swoopes	Texas Tech
1994	Lisa Leslie	Southern Cal
1995	Rebecca Lobo	Connecticut
1996	Saudia Roundtree	Georgia

Naismith Lifetime Achievement Award

Year	Recipient
1992	Margaret Wade

Rawlings/WBCA Player of the Year

Year	Division	Player	Team
1983	Div I	Anne Donovan	Old Dominion
	Div II	Jackie White	Cal Poly Pomona
	Div III	Margie O'Brien	Clark (Mass.)
1984	Div I	Janice Lawrence	Louisiana Tech
	Div II	Carla Eades	Central Mo State
	Div III	Page Lutz	Elizabethtown
1985	Div I	Cheryl Miller	Southern Cal
	Div II	Rosie Jones	Central Missouri State
	Div III	Deanna Kyle	Scranton
1986	Div I	Cheryl Miller	Southern Cal
	Div II	Vickie Mitchell	Cal Poly Pomona
	Div III	Jane Meyer	Elizabethtown
1987	Div I	Katrina McClain	Georgia
	Div II	Debra Larsen	Cal Poly Pomona
	Div III	Shelley Parks	Scranton
1988	Div I	Michelle Edwards	Iowa
	Div II	Vanessa Wells	West Texas A&M
	Div III	Jessica Beachy	Concordia-M'head
1989	Div I	Clarissa Davis	Texas
	Div II	Cathy Gooden	Cal Poly Pomona
	Div III	Kirsten Dumford	Cal State Stanislaus
1990	Div I	Venus Lacey	Louisiana Tech
	Div II	Crystal Hardy	Delta State
	Div III	Susan Heidt	Saint John Fisher
1991	Div I	Dawn Staley	Virginia
	Div II	Tracy Saunders	Norfolk State
	Div III	Ann Gilbert	Oberlin
1992	Div I	Dawn Staley	Virginia
	Div II	Mindy Young	Pitt-Johnstown
	Div III	Kathy Beck	Moravian
1993	Div I	Sheryl Swoopes	Texas Tech
	Div II	Yolanda Griffith	Fla Atlantic
	Div III	Laurie Trow	St. Thomas (Minn.)
1994	Div I	Lisa Leslie	Southern Cal
	Div II	Tammy Greene	Phila Textile
	Div III	Laura Schmelzer	Capitol
1995	Div I	Rebecca Lobo	Connecticut
	Div II	Sheri Kleinsasser	North Dakota
	Div III	Emilie Hanson	Central (Iowa)
1996	Div I	Saudia Roundtree	Georgia
	Div II	Jennifer Clarkson	Abilene Christian
	Div III	Wendy Wangerin	Wis-Oshkosh

Basketball (continued)

AIAW Championships

Year	Champions		Year	Champions
1972	Immaculata		1978	UCLA
1973	Immaculata		1979	Old Dominion
1974	Immaculata		1980	Old Dominion
1975	Delta State		1981	Louisiana Tech
1976	Delta State		1982	Rutgers
1977	Delta State			

AIAW Records
Career Records
Scoring Average

Player	Team	Seasons	Pts	Avg
Carol Blazejowski	Montclair State	1975–78	3199	*31.7
Susan Highfill	Roanoke	1976–79	2028	28.6
Carol Menken Schaudt	Oregon State	1979–81	2243	27.7
Kathy Miller	Weber State	1976–79	2746	27.5
Tina Gunn	Brigham Young	1977–80	2759	27.3
Lynette Woodard	Kansas	1978–81	3649	26.3
Lusia Harris	Delta State	1974–77	2981	25.9
Wanda Hightower	UAB	1979–82	2855	25.7
Susie Snider Eppers	Baylor State	1975–77	3137	25.5
Jody Imbrie	Grove City	1980–83	2288	25.1
Cindy Brogdon	Mercer/Tennessee	1976–77, 78–79	3204	25.0
Denise Curry	UCLA	1978–81	3198	24.6
Mary Beth Bowler	King's (Pa.)	1980–82	2024	24.4
Rona Nesbit	Gannon	1978–81	2340	24.4
Susan Taylor	Valdosta State	1977–80	3018	23.6
LaTaunya Pollard	Long Beach State	1980–83	3001	23.4
Valerie Still	Kentucky	1980–83	2763	23.2
Helen Shereda Smith	Oakland	1977–80	2338	23.1
Jody Lavin	Rochester	1979–82	2094	23.0
Donna Hammond Mares	UC Riverside	1980–83	2192	22.8
Queen Brumfield	Southeastern Louisiana	1976–79	2986	22.5
Cindy Stumph	Weber State	1980–83	2690	22.0

*Pre-1982 record.

Rebound Average (minimum 1,000 rebounds)

Player	Team	Seasons	Rebs	Avg
Carla Gadsen	Jersey City State	1981–82	1030	21.5
Gail Koziara	Dartmouth	1979–82	1635	18.4
Anne Gregory	Fordham	1977–80	1999	15.7
Claudette Charney	Saginaw Valley/ Grand Valley State	1977–79, 1980	1796	15.6
Toni Goodman	Hampton	1979–82	1608	15.5
Helen Shereda Smith	Oakland	1977–80	1524	15.1

Basketball (continued)

Rebound Average (minimum 1,000 rebounds)

Player	Team	Seasons	Rebs	Avg
Susie Snider Eppers	Baylor	1975–77	1823	14.8
Maree Jackson	LSU	1977–78	1032	14.7
Tina Gunn	Brigham Young	1977–80	1482	14.7
Anne Donovan	Old Dominion	1980–83	1976	14.5
Lusia Harris	Delta State	1974–77	1662	14.5
Julie Casey	Occidental	1979–82	1114	14.3
Janice Reaves	Fairleigh Dickinson	1980–83	1603	13.9
Pam Cassity	Tennessee Tech	1974–77	1782	13.9
Donna Murphy	Morehead State	1977–80	1439	13.7
Sharon Upshaw	Drake	1977–80	1675	13.2
Mary Kay Babcock	Elmira	1979–82	1084	13.1
Kathy Miller	Weber State	1976–79	1296	13.0
Betty Jackson	Lynchburg	1980–83	1139	12.9
Valerie Still	Kentucky	1980–83	1525	12.8
Doris Felderhoff	Stephen F. Austin	1975–77	1336	12.7
Judy Porter	San Diego State	1980–83	1498	12.5
Lynette Woodard	Kansas	1978–81	1734	12.5
Bev Smith	Oregon	1979–82	1362	12.4
Kim Hansen	Grand Valley State	1976–79	1971	12.3

*Pre-1982 record.

2,000 Points & 1,000 Rebounds

Player	Team	Seasons	Pts	Rebs
Lynette Woodard	Kansas	1978–81	3649*	1734
Cindy Brogdon	Mercer/Tennessee	1976–77, 78–79	3204	1028
Carol Blazejowski	Montclair State	1975–78	3199	1001
Denise Curry	UCLA	1978–81	3198	1310
Susie Snider Eppers	Baylor	1975–77	3137	1823
Queen Brumfield	Southeastern La	1976–79	2986	1586
Lusia Harris	Delta State	1974–77	2981	1662
Pam Kelly	Louisiana Tech	1979–82	2979	1511
Wanda Hightower	UAB	1979–82	2855	1091
Jill Rankin	Wayland Baptist/ Tennessee	1977–79, 80	2851	1101
Valerie Still	Kentucky	1980–83	2763	1525
Tina Gunn	Brigham Young	1977–80	2759	1482
Kathy Miller	Weber State	1976–79	2746	1296
Anne Donovan	Old Dominion	1980–83	2719	1976
Cindy Stumph	Weber State	1980–83	2690	1331
Inge Nissen	Old Dominion	1977–80	2647	1509
Anne Gregory	Fordham	1977–80	2548	1999*
Sharon Upshaw	Drake	1977–80	2513	1675
Julie Gross	LSU	1977–80	2488	1466
Peggie Gillom	Mississippi	1977–80	2486	1271
Nancy Lieberman	Old Dominion	1977–80	2430	1167
Genia Beasley	North Carolina State	1977–80	2367	1245

Basketball (continued)

2,000 Points & 1,000 Rebounds

Player	Team	Seasons	Pts	Rebs
Rosie Thompson	East Carolina	1977–80	2352	1183
Helen Shereda Smith	Oakland	1977–80	2338	1524
Colleen Galloway	California	1978–81	2320	1029
Judy Porter	San Diego State	1980–83	2318	1498
Sheila Foster	South Carolina	1979–82	2266	1427
Margie O'Brien	Clark (Mass.)	1980–83	2215	1392
Linda Street	Memphis	1977–79, 81	2147	1453
Molly McQuire	Oklahoma	1980–83	2147	1071
Adrian Mitchell	Kansas	1976–79	2124	1288
Emma Mumphrey	Mercer	1980–83	2098	1355
Bev Smith	Oregon	1979–82	2063	1362
Donna Murphy	Morehead State	1977–80	2059	1439
Cindy Haugejorde	Iowa	1977–80	2059	1067
Claudette Charney	Saginaw Valley/ Grand Valley State	1977–79, 80	2047	1796
Janice Reaves	Fairleigh Dickinson	1980–83	2016	1603
Cathy Boswell	Illinois State	1979–82	2005	1060

*Pre-1982 record.

NCAA Champions

Division I Champions

Year	Team
1982	Louisiana Tech
1983	Southern Cal
1984	Southern Cal
1985	Old Dominion
1986	Texas
1987	Tennessee
1988	Louisiana Tech
1989	Tennessee
1990	Stanford
1991	Tennessee
1992	Stanford
1993	Texas Tech
1994	North Carolina State
1995	Connecticut
1996	Tennessee

Division II Champions

Year	Team
1982	Cal Poly Pomona
1983	Virginia Union
1984	Central Mo State
1985	Cal Poly Pomona
1986	Cal Poly Pomona
1987	New Haven
1988	Hampton
1989	Delta State
1990	Delta State
1991	North Dakota State
1992	Delta State
1993	North Dakota State
1994	North Dakota State
1995	North Dakota State
1996	North Dakota State

Division III Champions

Year	Team
1982	Elizabethtown
1983	North Central
1984	Rust
1985	Scranton
1986	Salem State
1987	Wis–Stevens Point
1988	Concordia-M'head
1989	Elizabethtown
1990	Hope
1991	St. Thomas (Minn.)
1992	Alma
1993	Central (Iowa)
1994	Capital
1995	Capital
1996	Wis–Oshkosh

Basketball (continued)

Career Records
Scoring Average (Minimum 1,500 points)

Player	Team (Division)	Seasons	Pts	Avg
Jeannie Demers	Buena Vista (III)	1984–87	3171	30.2
Patricia Hoskins	Mississippi Valley (I)	1985–89	3122	28.4
Paulette King	Florida Tech (III)	1992–93	1668	28.3
Sandra Hodge	New Orleans (I)	1981–84	2860	26.7
Lorri Bauman	Drake (I)	1981–84	3115	26.0
Andrea Congreaves	Mercer (II)	1989–93	2796	25.9
Nicole Collins	Angelo State (II)	1994–95	1349	25.5
Valerie Whiteside	Appalachian State (I)	1984–88	2944	25.4
Shannon Williams	Valdosta State (III)	1987–90	2636	25.1
Stacey Cunningham	Shippensburg (III)	1982–84	1763	24.8
Sladja Kovijanic	Middlebury (III)	1990–93	1602	24.6

Rebound Average (Minimum 800 rebounds)

Player	Team (Division)	Seasons	Rebs	Avg
Norma Knight	Norfolk St (II)	1982–83	937	18.4
Sybil Smith	Baruch (III)	1993–95	1033	17.8
Carolina Leary	Middlebury (III)	1989–92	1364	16.8
Tina Shaw	Bishop (III)	1982–84	1168	16.5
Wanda Ford	Drake (I)	1983–86	1887	16.1
Francine Perry	Quinnipiac (II)	1982–85	1626	15.8
Patricia Hoskins	Mississippi Valley (I)	1985–89	1662	15.1
Liza Janssen	Wellesley (III)	1991–94	1403	14.9
Molly Lackman	Immaculata (III)	1991–94	1353	14.4
Sherry Patterson	Wm. Patterson	1984–87	1289	14.3

Olympics

Year	Country	Medals
1896–1972	event not held	
1976	USSR	Gold
	USA	Silver
	BUL	Bronze
1980	USSR	Gold
	BUL	Silver
	YUG	Bronze
1984	USA	Gold
	KOR	Silver
	CHN	Bronze
1988	USA	Gold
	YUG	Silver
	USSR	Bronze
1992	USSR	Gold
	CHN	Silver
	USA	Bronze
1996	USA	Gold
	BRA	Silver
	AUS	Bronze

U.S. Olympic Teams

Year	Location	Result
	Medalists	Home/Team
1976	Montreal	Silver Medal
	Cindy Brogdon	Mercer
	Nancy Dunkle	Cal State Fullerton
	Lusia Harris	Delta State
	Pat Head	Tennessee
	Charlotte Lewis	Illinois State
	Nancy Lieberman	Far Rockaway, Queens, NY
	Gail Marquis	Queens, NY
	Ann Meyers	UCLA
	Mary Anne O'Connor	Southern Conn State
	Patricia Roberts	Emporia State
	Sue Rojcewicz	Southern Conn State
	Julienne Simpson	John F. Kennedy
Coach	Billie Moore	Cal State Fullerton
Asst	Sue Gunter	Stephen F. Austin

Basketball (continued)

U.S. Olympic Teams

Year	Location	Result
	Medalists	Home/Team
1980	Moscow	games boycotted
	Carol Blazejowski	Montclair St
	Denise Curry	UCLA
	Anne Donovan	Old Dominion
	Tara Heiss	Maryland
	Kris Kirchner	Maryland
	Debra Miller	Boston U
	Cindy Noble	Tennessee
	LaTaunya Pollard	Long Beach State
	Jill Rankin	Tennessee
	Rosie Walker	Stephen F Austin
	Holly Warlick	Tennessee
	Lynette Woodard	Kansas
Coach	Sue Gunter	Stephen F Austin
Asst	Pat Head	Tennessee
1984	Los Angeles	Gold Medal
	Cathy Boswell	Illinois State
	Denise Curry	UCLA
	Anne Donovan	Old Dominion
	Teresa Edwards	Georgia
	Lea Henry	Tennessee
	Janice Lawrence	Louisiana Tech
	Pam McGee	Southern Cal
	Cheryl Miller	Southern Cal
	Kim Mulkey	Louisiana Tech
	Cindy Noble	Tennessee
	Carol Menken-Schaudt	Oregon State
	Lynette Woodard	Kansas
Coach	Pat Head Summitt	Tennessee
Asst	Kay Yow	North Carolina State
	Nancy Darsch	Tennessee
1988	Seoul	Gold Medal
	Cynthia Brown	Long Beach State
	Vicky Bullett	Maryland
	Cynthia Cooper	Southern Cal
	Anne Donovan	Old Dominion
	Teresa Edwards	Georgia
	Mary Ethridge	Texas
	Jennifer Gillom	Mississippi
	Bridgette Gordon	Tennessee
	Andrea Lloyd	Texas
	Katrina McClain	Georgia
	Suzie McConnell	Penn State
	Teresa Weatherspoon	Louisiana Tech
Coach	Kay Yow	North Carolina State
Assts	Susan Yow	Drake
	Sylvia Hatchell	North Carolina State
1992	Barcelona	Bronze Medal
	Vicky Bullett	Maryland
	Daedra Charles	Tennessee
	Cynthia Cooper	Southern Cal
	Clarissa Davis	Texas
	Medina Dixon	Old Dominion
	Teresa Edwards	Georgia
	Tammy Jackson	Florida
	Carolyn Jones	Auburn
	Katrina McClain	Georgia
	Suzie McConnell	Penn State
	Vickie Orr	Auburn
	Teresa Weatherspoon	Louisiana Tech
Coaches	Theresa Grentz	Rutgers
	Lin Dunn	Purdue
	Jim Foster	Vanderbilt
	Linda Hargrove	Wichita State
1996	Atlanta, Georgia	Gold Medal
	Jennifer Azzi	Stanford
	Ruth Bolton-Holifield	Auburn
	Teresa Edwards	Georgia
	Venus Lacey	Louisiana Tech
	Lisa Leslie	Southern California
	Rebecca Lobo	Connecticut
	Katrina McClain	Georgia
	Nikki McCray	Tennessee
	Carla McGhee	Tennessee
	Dawn Staley	Virginia
	Katy Steding	Stanford
	Sheryl Swoopes	Texas Tech
Coaches	Tara VanDerveer	Stanford
	Ceal Barry	Colorado
	Nancy Darsch	Ohio State
	Marian Washington	Kansas

The World Basketball Championships for men and women have been played at four-year intervals (give or take a year) since 1970. The men's tournament began in 1950 and the women's in 1953. The Federation Internationale de Basketball Amateur (FIBA), which governs the World and Olympic tournaments, was founded in 1932.

World Championships

Year	Champions	Year	Champions
1953	United States	1979	United States
1957	United States	1983	Soviet Union
1959	Soviet Union	1986	United States
1964	Soviet Union	1990	United States
1967	Soviet Union	1994	Brazil
1971	Soviet Union	1998	at Berlin
1975	Soviet Union		(July)

Photo credit: Louis A. Raynor

BASEBALL AND SOFTBALL

◆ *As historian William Baker has written in his book,* Sports in the Western World, *"Although modern baseball is primarily American, urban and male, its roots are medieval, English, rural and female."*◦

HISTORY

Bat and ball games began on the rolling greens of England, where medieval girls celebrated Shrovetide (the days preceding Ash Wednesday) by playing stoolball, a forerunner of cricket. Stoolball was also played at medieval fairs, and similar

games were played by the women of Germany, Scandinavia, and other European countries. By the mid-eighteenth century, stoolball had given way to cricket. The earliest recorded women's match took place on July 26, 1745, between the neighboring villages of Hambledon and Bramley. The players were distinguished by colored ribbons (red for Hambledon, blue for Bramley), and Hambledon won with 127 notches to Bramley's 119. Reportedly, the match was well attended and the crowd well satisfied—the women, an observer noted, played just as well as men. While the Hambledon-Bramley match is the first we know about, it certainly wasn't the first played. Cricket activity was lively and well organized in England from the 1740s on. In 1747, there were enough village women's cricket teams to convene a tournament in Finsbury.

◦William Baker, *Sports in the Western World* (London: Rowman & Littlefield, 1982).

Who played in these early matches? First of all, they were women, not girls. Records of a 1765 match at Upham, in Hampshire County, note that married women competed against unmarried women, and winners received a large plum cake, barrel of ale, and quantity of tea. While sports such as boxing exploited women trapped in the lower classes and ranked one rung above prostitution, cricket players were middle class—wives, mothers, daughters, and sweethearts, respected by the crowd's male spectators. When the women of Rotherby won an away game against a neighboring village, the men of Rotherby placed them in a triumphant cart, decorated with streamers, and serenaded them all the way home.

Throughout the second half of the eighteenth century, cricket spread from small villages to larger urban areas, and from the middle to the upper classes. In the nineteenth century cricket was exported to Britain's colonial concerns—India, Australia, and the Virgin Islands. In 1890 William Matthews and S. B. Lohman hired twenty-two young women to play cricket professionally. Although the games drew crowds of up to 15,000, Matthews and Lohman ran off with the money, leaving the young women high and dry.

In America, baseball rather than cricket became the sport of the day. In 1866 Vassar College had two women's teams, the Laurel Base Ball Club and the Abenakis Base Ball Club. In 1875 there were three Vassar teams, the Sure-Pops, the Daisy Clippers, and the Royals. At Smith, baseball got off to a more faltering start; the sport was banned in 1878, but the ban was lifted in 1892.

An early effort to establish women's professional ball was made by Harry Freeman in the 1880s. Unfortunately, rumors that he was recruiting shapely young lovelies for prostitution rather than home runs quickly swamped his efforts, and one father sued him in court. Another early effort was made around 1883, when two teams, the Blondes and the Brunettes, toured the eastern seaboard. The most successful attempt was the formation of Bloomer Girls teams, whose heyday lasted from the 1890s through the 1920s. Bloomer teams, based mostly in cities of the Northeast and Midwest, were regional barnstorming organizations that made money playing exhibition ball against local men's teams. Initially, not all Bloomer Girls were girls. In the days before the farm club system was developed, many young men—including future Hall of Famer Rogers Hornsby—joined the teams as a means of gaining playing experience. Early male Bloomer Girls donned wigs and skirts to play, but soon the trend went the other way, and women traded their skirts for short-sleeved tops, knee-length bloomers, and tights. Their scandalously immodest outfits, coupled with the fact that they played against men, earned the Bloomer Girls an unsavory, rough-and-tumble reputation. Not only did "nice girls" not play for Bloomer Girls teams, they did not even attend the games.

Nevertheless, Bloomer Girls teams offered many women opportunities they would not otherwise have had. Most of the players came from factory, mill, or coal-mining towns and seized on baseball as a safer, healthier, better-paying alternative to backbreaking manual labor. Some of the women were able to parlay their talents. In 1898 Lizzie Arlington became the first woman to sign a contract with a men's minor league club. Her salary was a reputed $100 a week, and she pitched one inning before being sent back to the Bloomer Girls circuit. In the 1920s another Bloomer Girl, **Lizzie Murphy,** became the first woman to play major league men's teams in exhibition games. A few Bloomer Girls came off the field to take jobs in the front office. From 1920 through 1933, Margaret Nabel owned and managed the New York Bloomer Girls, one of the league's most successful teams. Another former player, Maud Nelson, created numerous franchises, made them thriving concerns, then sold out at a profit. Still another former Bloomer Girl, Edith Houghton, capitalized on her baseball know-how and, in the years after World War II, became a scout for the Philadelphia Phillies.

The arrival of the Great Depression marked the beginning of the end for the Bloomer Girls, as money for entertainment vanished. Economics weren't the only nail in the coffin, however. By the early 1930s, softball was being heavily promoted as a kinder and gentler game for young women. The last Bloomer Girls team folded in 1934, and with the exception of seventeen-year-old Jackie Mitchell, who pitched an exhibition game against the New York Yankees in 1931, women didn't play hardball again for almost a decade.

A LEAGUE OF THEIR OWN

During World War II, America discovered women could do a lot of things America had never thought women could do. One of them was play baseball. In the early 1940s Congress and the major leagues faced a difficult dilemma. Washington wanted baseball, the *real* symbol of democracy, to continue for the duration. So did club owners, managers, and baseball commissioner Kenesaw Mountain Landis. The problem, logically, was that exempting able-bodied men from the draft while husbands, fathers, and sons risked their lives overseas would almost certainly strike a sour note with the public. The answer: Let women play.

Chicago Cubs owner Philip Wrigley, the motivating force behind the All-American Girls Professional Baseball League, envisioned a league in which "wholesome, normal" girls would embody the fresh-cheeked, bright-eyed, girl-back-home American ideal. Recruitment pamphlets for the league, written by cosmetics entrepreneur Helena Rubenstein, made no bones about the fact that players were "especially chosen for looks, deportment, and feminine charm." Just as African-Americans were excluded from men's play, so were they excluded from women's play. Also excluded were women who might bring a breath of scandal to the endeavor. For girls who made the grade, the rules off the field were almost as involved as the rules of play. They could not smoke or drink in public, could not eat in any restaurant not approved by the team chaperone, and had to have all dates and outings preapproved. Despite these restrictions, there was no shortage of women who were eager to play. At a time when factory work paid $10 a week, the All-American League offered salaries of $50 to $125 plus free room and board. It also offered thousands of women a chance to play ball, a sport many of them had grown up playing.

The league began play in 1943 with four midwestern teams—the Racine Belles, the Kenosha Comets, the Rockford Peaches, and the South Bend Blue Sox. Other franchises came on board later, but league growth was limited by the fact that players had to travel by bus and could not reach farther-flung destinations. A fair portrayal of the era can be viewed in the film *A League of Their Own,* complete down to the short-skirted uniforms that inevitably rolled back during a slide, resulting in endless skin burns for the women. Although men's major league play usurped some of women's popularity when the war ended, the All-American League was able to last until 1954. The problem wasn't only that crowds wanted to see the men again. It was also that, in the rushed return to traditional roles that fueled the baby boom and the growth of suburbia, people *didn't* want to see women in atypical roles. No amount of wholesomeness and charm could offset the public's underlying discomfort. It was time for women to turn in their diamonds.

THE MODERN ERA

With the demise of the All-American League, the focus once again turned from baseball to softball. With one lone exception there has been no concerted effort to reestablish baseball for women. The Colorado Silver Bullets, a Class A minor league baseball team, were initially formed in 1984 in the hope that the cream of the women's crop could give the men in the minors a run for their money. The team didn't quite get off the ground; it was revived in the 1990s by a $3 million infusion from the Coors brewing company, the Bullets finally getting their inaugural season in 1994 under the managership of Phil Niekro.

With few opportunities to play competitive hardball, women have taken what was offered them and made the most of it. Fast-pitch softball, as it has evolved over the years, is a dynamic and exciting game, and one with a growing following. Baseball fans yearning to recapture the traditional feel of the game, fed up with high-tech scoreboards, and yearning for real grass and under-the-sun bleachers have been turning up at unlikely and decidedly unglitzy places, including women's softball parks. National tournaments, played by teams with such colorful names as the Raybestos Brakettes and the Redding Rebels, have grown increasingly popular since they were initiated more than sixty years ago. In the mid-1990s women's softball received a major league shot in the arm when it was included in the 1996 Olympics. The U.S. team, referred to in the press as "the other dream team," made a beeline for the gold. Though NBC's much-criticized television coverage left fans yearning to see a complete game, the fallout of gold dust may well have been enough to boost the sport a notch higher in the public's awareness.

Major Competitions and Awards

National Fast Pitch
Softball Championships

World Championships

Olympic Games

Governing Bodies and Organizations

Amateur Softball Association (ASA)
2801 N.E. 50th Street
Oklahoma City, Oklahoma 73111
(405) 424-5266

* * * BIOGRAPHIES * * *

LAURA BERG b. January 6, 1975, Santa Fe
Springs, California
An accomplished outfielder, Berg won medals in under-eighteen competitions, then moved up to ASA and Olympic Festival medal-winning teams. During the 1994 World Championships, Berg's accurate arm helped the United States win the gold. Two years later Berg was on hand for softball's Olympic debut.
Selected championships and honors: Gold medal, World Championships, 1994; gold medal, Olympic Games, 1996.

GILLIAN BOXX b. September 1, 1973, Torrance,
California
A three-time all-American during her career at the University of California–Berkeley, Boxx went on to taste both World Championship and Olympic gold as a catcher for Team USA. She turned in an especially spectacular performance at the 1994 World Championships, batting .800 for the series, and made history two years later as part of the "other dream team," which rolled into the Olympics with an almost-perfect record.
Selected championships and honors: Gold medal, World Championships, 1994; gold medal, Olympic Games, 1996.

SHEILA CORNELL b. February 26, 1962,
Burbank, California
During her college career at UCLA, Cornell played on two NCAA championship teams, in 1982 and '84. Later, as a member of the famous Raybestos Brakettes, she set a team record for triples in a season (19 in 1988) and was named ASA all-American ten times. Cornell, a right-handed infielder, is noted for her almost-perfect glove, and has played for six medal-winning U.S. squads, including the 1996 gold-medal-winning Olympic team.
Selected championships and honors: Silver medal, Pan American Games, 1983; two gold medals, World Championships, 1990 and '94; two gold medals, Pan American Games, 1991 and '95; gold medal, Olympic Games, 1996.

PAM DAVIS b. September 17, 1974, Mayfield
Heights, Ohio
No sport is as infatuated with records as baseball, and on June 4, 1996, Davis put a new one in the books— she became the first woman to pitch in the minor leagues. It wasn't the first time Davis had bridged the gender gap. Eight years earlier, she was the first girl ever to pitch in the Junior League World Championships, and she went on to pitch for the Colorado Silver Bullets.

PAT DUFFICY b. July 7, 1961, Westerly, Rhode Island

Dufficy spent her teenage years in Connecticut, near the Stratford home of the Raybestos Brakettes, the best-known team in American women's softball. Dufficy, a 5′11″ catcher, joined the Brakettes in 1977 and played with them through 1995. She was part of five national championship teams and became all-time team leader in home runs, hits, runs batted in, runs scored, and number of games played. She also played on several medal-winning Olympic Festival teams, was signed by the Colorado Silver Bullets, and played on medal-winning U.S. World Championship and Pan American Games squads.

Selected championships and honors: Gold medal, World Championships, 1994; gold medal, Pan American Games, 1995.

LAURA ESPINOZA WATSON b. February 5, 1973; Torrance, California

During her college career at the University of Arizona, Espinoza, a right-handed infielder, set ten NCAA records, including most home runs in a season, most career home runs, most runs batted in in a season, most career runs batted in, most total bases per season, and most total bases in a career. In 1993 she helped her team to the NCAA championship and signed to play with the Colorado Silver Bullets after graduating from college.

Selected championships and honors: Gold medal, World Championships, 1991.

BETTY EVANS GRAYSON b. October 9, 1925, Portland, Oregon; d. July 9, 1979

Known as "Bullet Betty" in softball circles, Grayson began her pitching career at age fifteen, as a pitcher for the Portland, Oregon, Florists. She stayed with the team for seventeen years, leading them to a world title in 1943 and a national championship the next year. Along the way she pitched 3 perfect games and, at one point, 125 consecutive scoreless innings. Her career record as an amateur was 465 wins, 11 losses. As a pro with the Chicago Queens, her record was almost as good. In 1950 she pitched 35 winning games and was the losing pitcher just 5 times.

Selected championships and honors: National Fast Pitch Softball Championship; Oregon Florists, 1944; National Softball Hall of Fame.

LISA FERNANDEZ b. February 22, 1971, Long Beach, California

An outstanding pitcher since high school, Fernandez had a record-setting 93 wins and 7 losses during her college career at UCLA and was an NCAA all-American each of her four seasons. She set a college career records for no-hitters pitched, with 11. A phenomenal hitter, Fernandez also set college marks for hits (287), singles (225) and runs scored (142). She has been on various U.S. national teams since 1990 and was a key contributor to the 1996 Olympic gold-medal team.

Selected championships and honors, team: Two gold medals, World Championships, 1990 and '94; two gold medals, Pan American Games, 1991 and '95. *Individual:* ASA SportsWoman of the Year in 1991 and '92; Amoco Softball Player of the Year, 1993.

MICHELE GRANGER b. January 15, 1970, Anchorage, Alaska

A left-handed pitcher, Granger set records before she was out of her teens. In 1987 she became the first (and to date the only) player to compete in the international Junior Girls World Championship, the U.S. Olympic Festival, the Pan American Games, and the ASA National Championship in the same season. As a college standout at University of California–Berkeley, she claimed all but two of the school's twenty-two pitching records. One of Granger's more spectacular outings came at the 1995 Pan American Games, when she pitched four shutouts and one perfect game to help the United States to a gold medal. She was also a starting pitcher for the U.S. squad that won a gold medal at the 1996 Olympic Games in Atlanta.

Selected championships and honors, team: Two gold medals, World Championships, 1986 and '94; ASA National Championships, 1987; two gold medals, Pan American Games, 1991 and '95; gold medal, Olympic Games, 1996. *Individual:* Amateur Athletes Hall of Fame.

LORI HARRIGAN b. September 5, 1970, Las Vegas, Nevada

A 1995 college all-American, Harrigan went on to play for several gold-medal U.S. squads, including the teams that won the 1994 World Championships and 1996 Olympics. Harrigan has also played with the Raybestos Brakettes and the California Commotion of the ASA.

Selected championships and honors: Gold medal, World Championships, 1994; gold medal, Pan American Games, 1995; gold medal, Olympic Games, 1996.

DIONNA HARRIS b. March 4, 1968, Wilmington,
  Delaware
An outfielder with the Raybestos Brakettes, Harris
has been named ASA all-American four times, and
led the league in batting in 1995 with an average of
.611. Harris has also been named to several U.S. national teams, including the 1996 Olympic squad.
Selected championships and honors: Gold medal,
Olympic Games, 1996.

JOAN JOYCE b. August 1, 1940, Waterbury,
  Connecticut
Joyce began playing softball for the Raybestos
Brakettes of Stratford, Connecticut, and helped the
team to eleven national championships over the next
twenty years. As a pitcher, Joyce was phenomenal.
During her career she pitched 105 no-hitters and 33
perfect games, establishing a win-loss record of
509–33. Some of her pitches were clocked at over 110
mph. Joyce also played first base and hit for a career
average of .327, was a three-time all-American in
AAU basketball, and excelled at volleyball and bowling. During her years with the ASA she was named
all-American eighteen times and MVP eight times.
After she retired from softball in 1975, she joined the
LPGA tour and in her best year, 1984, won in excess
of $30,000.
Selected championships and honors, team: Eleven National Fast Pitch Softball Championships, Raybestos
Brakettes. *Individual:* National Softball Hall of Fame;
International Women's Sports Hall of Fame.

DOROTHY (DOTTIE) KAMENSHEK
  b. December 21, 1925, Cincinnati, Ohio
Kamenshek grew up playing softball and joined the
Rockford, Illinois, Peaches when the All-American
Girls Professional Baseball League debuted in 1943.
A first baseman throughout most of her career, Kamenshek often led the AAGPBL in batting, and finished her nine-year career with a batting average of
.292, one of the league's best. After retiring from play,
Kamenshek went went to college and eventually became a physical therapist.

SOPHY KURYS b. May 14, 1925, Flint, Michigan
Often mentioned as the best player in the All-
American Girls Professional Baseball League, Kurys
played with the Racine Belles from 1943 through
1950, when the team folded. She led the league in
stolen bases six seasons and had a career total of 1,114
steals. An all-star second baseman, Kurys was also a

solid hitter. In her best season, 1946, she succeeded
in 201 of 203 steal attempts, batted .286, was walked
93 times, had a fielding percentage of .973, led the
league in runs scored with 117, and was named
league MVP.

DONNA LOPIANO b. September 11, 1946,
  Stamford, Connecticut
By the time she was five, Lopiano knew she wanted
to pitch in the big leagues. She ended up playing nine
seasons with the Raybestos Brakettes and being enshrined in the National Softball Hall of Fame. The
Brakettes won six national championships with Lopiano on the team, and she was named tournament
MVP three times. Lopiano's influence swept far beyond the diamond, however. When she was a child,
her gender cost her a chance to join Little League,
and Lopiano never forgot the disappointment. She
became an enthusiastic coach, college athletic director, and potent activist for women's right to get in the
game. When she took over the women's athletic program at the University of Texas in 1975, the budget
was less than $60,000 a year. When she left seventeen
years later, the budget topped $4 million per annum.
In 1992 she became head of the Women's Sports
Foundation, dedicated to increasing sports opportunities for girls and women throughout the country.

KIM MAHER b. September 5, 1971, Vietnam
Maher, an infielder, grew up in California and started
playing softball in high school. After college, she
joined the Redding Rebels of the ASA and played on
three national championship teams. As a member of
Team USA, she maintained a perfect fielding average
during the 1995 Pan American Games and batted
.375. During the 1996 Olympics she hit a three-run
homer to help America win the first gold medal
awarded in the sport.
Selected championships and honors: Three National
Fast Pitch Softball Championships, Redding Rebels,
1993–95; gold medal, Pan American Games, 1995;
gold medal, Olympic Games, 1996.

ELIZABETH (LIZZIE) MURPHY b. 1894, New
  England
Murphy, a first baseman, was probably the first
woman to have a full-length career in professional
baseball. Although much about her is unknown, what
is known is impressive. From age fifteen until her retirement at forty-one, Murphy played hardball with
the men and made money at it. Most of her playing

years from 1918 on were spent with the Boston All-Stars, a barnstorming team that played exhibition games against major-league teams all over New England. She also played charity exhibition games with several all-star teams drawn from the major leagues.

LEAH O'BRIEN b. September 9, 1974, Chino, California

As a member of the University of Arizona Wildcats, O'Brien pitched her team to two consecutive NCAA World Series Championships (1993 and '94) and was named all-American in 1994 and '95. O'Brien, who later switched her talents to the infield, has played with the Activity A's of the ASA and has twice been named a league all-American. She has played for several U.S. teams, including the 1996 Olympic squad.
Selected championships and honors: Gold medal, Olympic Games, 1996.

DOT RICHARDSON b. September 22, 1961, Orlando, Florida

One of the strongest players on the scene today, Richardson cracked the first home run ever in Olympic softball competition and overnight became one of the hottest stars of the 1996 games. Richardson, an orthopedic surgeon, was an all-round athlete who focused on softball during her college career at UCLA. A shortstop, she was named all-American each of her four years. In the ASA she has played with both the California Commotion and the Raybestos Brakettes and has been named ASA all-American fourteen times. Richardson has played for U.S. teams in a long list of international competitions and has a trail of gold medals stretching back to 1979. In major competitions, her passion for the game and ability to focus unite to create some spectacular performances, as at the 1995 Pan American Games, when she batted .469 and had a perfect fielding percentage.
Selected championships and honors, team: Three gold medals, Pan American Games, 1979, '87, and '95; two gold medals, World Championships, 1986 and '94; gold medal, Olympic Games, 1996. *Individual:* NCAA Player of the Decade, 1980s.

JULIE SMITH b. May 10, 1968, Glendora, California

Smith was a two-time all-American (1990 and '91) during her college career at Fresno State University and played for two different championship ASA teams—the Orange County Majestics and the Redding Rebels. An infielder with a golden glove, Smith

has also played on several medal-winning U.S. teams, including the 1996 Olympic squad.
Selected championships and honors: Three National Fast Pitch Softball Championships (Orange County Majestics, 1987; Redding Rebels, 1993 and '94); gold medal, World Championships, 1994; two gold medals, Pan American Games, 1991 and '95; gold medal, Olympic Games, 1996.

MICHELE SMITH b. June 21, 1967, Plainfield, New Jersey

A left-handed pitcher whose bat is as valuable as her glove, Smith has powered U.S. teams to several gold medals and added at least one gold to her collection every year from 1994 through 1996. As a member of the ASA's Redding Rebels, she was named all-American three times and voted the championship tournament most-valuable-pitcher award four times (1990 and 1993–95).
Selected championships and honors: Three National Fast Pitch Softball Championships, Redding Rebels, 1993–95; gold medal, World Championships, 1994; gold medal, Pan American Games, 1995; gold medal, Olympic Games, 1996.

SHELLY STOKES b. October 26, 1967, Carmichael, California

As a catcher at Fresno State University, Stokes went to the NCAA College World Series all four years. Stokes also plays with the Fresno Force of the ASA and was named league all-American in 1993. She has played with several U.S. teams, including Pan Am Games and Olympics medal teams.
Selected championships and honors: Gold medal, Pan American Games, 1995; gold medal, Olympic Games, 1996.

TONI STONE b. 1921, St. Paul, Minnesota; d. November 2, 1996

Born Alcenia (or Marcenia) Lyle Alberga, the woman who became known as Toni Stone is probably the most obscure "great" in American women's baseball. She was not only a woman but an African-American, and therefore barred from the major leagues on two counts rather than one. Nevertheless, Stone managed a career in men's baseball. After a few seasons in the American Negro League minors, Stone moved up to the San Francisco Sea Lions, a barnstorming team, then took a $300/month job with the New Orleans Creoles. In 1953 she signed with a major Negro League team, the Indianapolis Clowns. Here, as sec-

ond baseman, she filled the spot recently vacated by Henry Aaron and batted a respectable .243. Stone never lost her enthusiasm for the game, and she continued to play amateur ball until she was sixty.
Selected championships and honors: Women's Sports Hall of Fame.

MICKEY STRATTON b. July 12, 1938, Meriden, Connecticut
Stratton, a catcher, played softball with the Raybestos Brakettes of Connecticut from 1958 to 1965 and was with the team for four national championships. Her career batting average was .314, and in her final season she hit .370, a personal best.
Selected championships and honors: Four National Fast Pitch Softball Championships, Raybestos Brakettes; National Softball Hall of Fame.

BERTHA TICKEY b. March 15, 1925, Dinuba, California
With a lifetime pitching record of 757–88 and 162 no-hitters, it isn't hard to see why Tickey was nicknamed "Blazing Bertha" by softball fans. During her twenty-three years in the game she played for two championship clubs, the Orange County Lionettes of California and the Raybestos Brakettes of Connecticut, and was on eleven national championship teams, her first with the Lionettes in 1950 and her last with the Brakettes in 1968. She was named championship tournament MVP eight times, and in her best season, 1950, she struck out 795 batters and pitched 143 consecutive scoreless innings. Tickey retired in 1968.
Selected championships and honors: Eleven National Fast Pitch Softball Championships, Orange County Lionettes and Raybestos Brakettes; National Softball Hall of Fame.

DANI TYLER b. October 23, 1974, Chicago, Illinois
A right-handed infielder, Tyler has been playing softball most of her life. In additional to playing for several U.S. teams in international competitions, she has played for the St. Louis Classics of the ASA. She was also a member of the 1996 team that captured a gold medal in Atlanta.
Selected championships and honors: Gold medal, Olympic Games, 1996.

M. MARIE WADLOW b. April 12, 1917, St. Louis, Missouri; d. April 6, 1979
Batters who faced Wadlow's formidable pitching as a member of the Tabernacle Baptist Church team in

the early 1930s often concluded that God—or perhaps the devil—must be on her side. From 1943 to 1950 she played softball with the Caterpillar Dieselettes of Peoria, whose manager, Charles McCord, pronounced her one of the greatest competitors—male or female—he'd ever seen. Her lifetime record was 341–51, with 42 no-hitters, while her record for the Dieselettes was 103–18—enough to make her the first female player elected to the sport's hall of fame.
Selected championships and honors: National Softball Hall of Fame.

NERA WHITE. *See entry under Basketball.*

CHRISTA WILLIAMS b. February 8, 1978; Houston, Texas
Williams went straight from high school and under-eighteen competitions to the big time—a spot on the 1996 U.S. Olympic team. A right-handed pitcher, Williams was the youngest member on a team already rich in pitching talent. Her two-hitter against the Netherlands, which the United States beat 9–0, helped America claim the gold in the first ever Olympic softball competition.
Selected championships and honors: Gold medal, Olympic Games, 1996.

JOANN WINTER b. 1924; d. 1996
As a member of the All-American Girls Professional Baseball League, Winter pitched for the Racine Belles. Later she exchanged a large ball for a much smaller one and had several successful seasons as a golfer with the LPGA. Winter eventually became a golf coach at Scottsdale Community College, in Arizona, and was a consultant for the movie *A League of Their Own.*

Softball

	Olympics	
Year	Country	Medals
1896–1992		event not held
1996	USA	Gold
	CHN	Silver
	AUS	Bronze

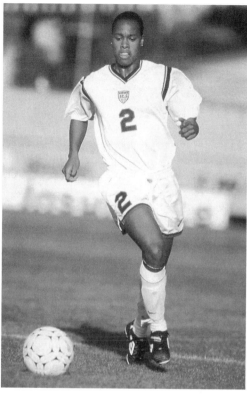

Photo credit: SportsChrome

SOCCER

◆ *Although many Americans consider soccer a European import, early forms of the sport were played all over the world, including pre-Columbian America.*

HISTORY

Ball games, one of the most ancient forms of team sport, are so old their origins are nearly impossible to trace. Games in which players move the ball with their feet are especially old, since they require no additional equipment or technology. There is a good deal of evidence to suggest that football-like games evolved independently in several cultures. We know that they were played in Europe long before Shakespeare, and in the Americas long before Columbus. Native residents of North, South, and Middle America played games in which stone or stuffed leather balls were kicked up and down the playing field. One of the earliest depictions of a ball game comes from China and shows women playing in a garden. Although the women are dressed in elegant silks, they were apparently quite serious about their game, for the artist has taken the trouble to show sweat beading their brows.

In the Western Hemisphere folk football, a forerunner of soccer, was played in England and France as early as the twelfth century. The game was a traditional part of Shrove Tuesday celebrations, and women either played alongside men or competed against each other. In England, matches between single and married women were especially common. Soccer was one of the first sports played by women at Girton College,

Cambridge, which added a women's gymnasium in 1877. The coeds loved the game, but Emily Davies, founder of the college, reportedly commented that "it would certainly shock the world if it were known."

Although soccer-style football was flourishing in England when the Pilgrims set sail for the New World, it's unlikely that the game came along with them. Devout and serious, the Pilgrims eschewed sports and looked instead to hard work, daily prayer, and observation of the Sabbath to fill the void. Instead, European Americans learned the game from Native Americans. Despite the Pilgrims' best efforts, sport soon flourished in the New World as it had in the Old. Ironically, the first soccer club in America was founded just miles from Plymouth Rock. The Boston Oneidas, who played in the years before the Civil War, made Boston Common their home field, and a monument to them still stands there today.

Soccer was also the original American college sport and was widely played by men from the 1820s on. After the Civil War, college play became more organized. Rules, which had been casual and constantly changing, became formalized. The first intercollegiate game, between Princeton and Rutgers, was played on November 6, 1876. Playing on their home field, Rutgers won. The influx of British Isles immigrants during these years also fueled the growth of soccer, and soon mill towns, port towns, and mining towns throughout the Northeast all had a home team, or teams, to root for.

Unfortunately, this surge in popularity served to dampen women's participation in the sport. As soccer became more and more identified with a rough-and-tumble blue-collar set, it became viewed as an inappropriate sport for women. In America colleges were far more likely to promote basketball, archery, and track and field for women and leave soccer out of the mix entirely.

THE MODERN ERA

Although men's World Cup competition began in 1930, women's soccer is a relatively new phenom-

enon, both nationally and internationally. The first U.S. women's national team was organized in 1985 and has fielded squads for international competitions ever since. The 1990s have proven a decade of growth for major international play. Women's World Championship play, the counterpart of the World Cup for men, was inaugurated in 1991 and, like the World Cup, will be held every four years. Soccer, long an Olympic men's sport, debuted as a medal sport for women at the Atlanta games in 1996.

Hall of Fame

The U.S. Soccer Hall of Fame is located in Oneonta, New York.

Major Events and Competitions

World Championships
Olympic Games

Individual awards:
Female Soccer Athlete of the Year
Hermann Trophy

Governing Bodies and Organizations

Federation International de Football Association (FIFA)
Box 85
8030 Zurich
Switzerland
Phone: 41-1/384-9595

U.S. Soccer
Communication Department
1801–1811 South Prairie Avenue
Chicago, Illinois 60616
Phone: 312/808-1300

* * * BIOGRAPHIES * * *

MICHELLE AKERS-STAHL b. February 1, 1966, Santa Clara, California

A four-time all-American while attending the University of South Florida in Orlando, Akers quickly established herself as a world-class offensive player. In Team USA play she holds records for most goals in a match (5), most goals in a season (39), and most points in a season (47)—all recorded in 1991, the year she helped lead the United States to victory in the first ever women's World Championship.

Selected championships and honors, team: Gold medal, World Championships, 1991; bronze medal, World Championships, 1995; gold medal, Olympic Games, 1996. *Individual:* Herman Trophy, 1988; twice named Female Soccer Athlete of the Year, 1990 and '91.

JOY BIEFELD FAWCETT b. February 8, 1968, Inglewood, California

During her career at UC-Berkeley, Fawcett was a three-time all-American (1987–89) and set a record as the school's all-time leading scorer. As a member of Team USA, she has been to both World Championships, and she was the only team member to play every minute of the 1995 tournament. Despite breaking a leg in 1995, Biefeld made a full recovery and was back on track in 1996. In 1993 she was tapped to coach UCLA's first women's soccer team.

Selected championships and honors, team: Gold medal, World Championships, 1991; bronze medal, World Championships, 1995; gold medal, Olympic Games, 1996. *Individual:* Female Soccer Athlete of the Year, 1988.

JULIE FOUDY SAWYERS b. January 23, 1971, Mission Viejo, California

A leading scorer during her college career at Stanford, Foudy was a four-time all-American. She was on the U.S. national team for its first-place finish at the World Championships, but missed the 1995 championships because she was on her honeymoon. Foudy graduated with a B.S. in biology in 1993 and delayed plans to enter medical school to participate in the 1996 Olympics.

Selected championships and honors: Gold medal, World Championships, 1991; bronze medal, World Championships, 1995; gold medal, Olympic Games, 1996.

CARIN JENNINGS GABARRA b. January 9, 1965, East Orange, New Jersey

As a scorer for Team USA, Jennings ranks just behind Mia Hamm and Michelle Akers—no surprise considering that Jennings was an all-American every one of her high school and college seasons. Her alma mater, the University of California at Santa Barbara, voted her female athlete of the decade and retired her jersey. At the first World Championships, she led the United States in scoring and was named outstanding player of the tournament. Jennings remained a key component of the U.S. national team and was on hand for the 1996 Olympic Games.

Selected championships and honors, team: Gold medal, World Championships, 1991; bronze medal, World Championships, 1995; gold medal, Olympic Games, 1996. *Individual:* Twice named Female Soccer Athlete of the Year, 1987 and '92.

MIA HAMM CORY b. March 17, 1972, Selma, Alabama

One of the best players in the world, Hamm is also one of the most versatile—during the 1995 World Championships, she played forward and midfield and even did a stint as goalkeeper. The youngest woman ever to play for the U.S. national team, Hamm was just fifteen when she appeared in her first international match in 1987. During her college career at the University of North Carolina she led her team to four NCAA championships, was a three-time all-American, and became the first woman ever to receive two Hermann Trophies. Only a freight train will prevent Hamm, a key figure in every U.S. medal since joining the team, from nailing down her place in the record books.

Selected championships and honors, team: Gold medal, World Championships, 1991; bronze medal, World Championships, 1995; gold medal: Olympic Games, 1996. *Individual:* Two Hermann Trophies, 1992 and '93; twice named Female Soccer Athlete of the Year, 1994 and '95.

MARY HARVEY b. June 4, 1965, Palo Alto, California

Harvey was a standout goalkeeper for the University of California–Berkeley despite missing most of the 1985 season due to back surgery. She made a full recovery and debuted as a member of the U.S. national team in 1989. At the first World Championships, in 1991, she played every minute in goal and posted three shutouts to help the United States to a first-place finish. Harvey suffered a torn ligament in mid-1993 but rejoined the team in '94 and was on hand for both the second World Championships and the 1996 Olympic Games.

Selected championships and honors: Gold medal, World Championships, 1991; bronze medal: World Championships, 1995; gold medal, Olympic Games, 1996.

KRISTINE LILLY b. July 22, 1971, Wilton, Connecticut

During her four years at the University of North Carolina, Lilly led her team to four NCAA championships (1989–92) and was named the most valuable offensive player of the tournament twice, in 1989 and '90. She has been a top scorer for Team USA since her 1987 debut and has been on hand for all of its medal wins to date.

Selected championships and honors, team: Gold medal, World Championships, 1991; bronze medal, World Championships, 1995; gold medal, Olympic Games, 1996. *Individual:* Hermann Trophy, 1991; Female Soccer Athlete of the Year, 1993.

TIFFANY MILBRETT b. October 23, 1972, Portland, Oregon

A three-time all-American at the University of Oregon, Milbrett helped her team to an NCAA Final Four appearance in 1994 and graduated as the school's all-time scoring leader. At the 1995 World Championships, Milbrett scored six goals to tie with Kristine Lilly and Tisha Venturini as team goal-scoring leader, and she was a member of the 1996 Olympic Games team.

Selected championships and honors: Bronze medal, World Championships, 1995; gold medal, Olympic Games, 1996.

CARLA OVERBECK. *See Carla Werden Overbeck, below.*

BRIANA SCURRY b. September 7, 1971, Minneapolis, Minnesota

Although she didn't join the U.S. team until 1994, goalkeeper Scurry is already on her way to becoming America's number-one shutout queen. During her college years at the University of Massachusetts, she recorded a phenomenal 37 shutouts in 65 starts. Her first season with Team USA was just as good—7 shutouts in 12 starts. Although Scurry sustained a back injury in an auto accident in 1995 and had to miss several games, she was back to start in goal at that year's World Championships. The next year Scurry helped the United States win the first gold ever awarded in women's Olympic soccer.

Selected championships and honors: Gold medal, World Championships, 1991; bronze medal, World Championships, 1995; gold medal, Olympic Games, 1996.

TISHA VENTURINI b. March 3, 1973, Modesto, California

A three-time all-American at the University of North Carolina, Venturini helped her team to four NCAA championships, 1991–94. Outstanding at both offense and defense, Venturini won NCAA tournament MVP awards as both best defensive player (1991) and best offensive player (1994). A member of the U.S. national team since 1992, Venturini played in the 1995 World Championships as well as the 1996 Olympic Games.

Selected championships and honors, team: Bronze medal, World Championships, 1995; gold medal, Olympic Games, 1996. *Individual:* Hermann Trophy, 1994.

CARLA WERDEN OVERBECK b. May 9, 1969, Pasadena, California

Another star in the University of North Carolina crown, Werden played for four NCAA championship teams and was named all-American in all but her freshman year. A member of the U.S. national team since 1988, she has been a key force on a world-class defense that allowed just 5 goals in 6 games during the 1991 championships. In addition to captaining the gold-medal 1996 Olympic squad, she is the assistant women's coach at Duke University.

Selected championships and honors: Gold medal, World Championships, 1991; bronze medal, World Championships, 1995; gold medal, Olympic Games, 1996.

Soccer

Female Athlete of the Year

Year	Winner
1985	Sharon Remer
1986	April Heinrichs
1987	Carin Jennings
1988	Joy Biefeld
1989	April Heinrichs
1990	Michelle Akers-Stahl
1991	Michelle Akers-Stahl
1992	Carin Jennings Gabarra
1993	Kristine Lilly
1994	Mia Hamm
1995	Mia Hamm

Hermann Trophy

Year	Winner	College
1988	Michelle Akers	Central Florida
1989	Shannon Higgins	North Carolina
1990	April Kater	Massachusetts
1991	Kristine Lilly	North Carolina
1992	Mia Hamm	North Carolina
1993	Mia Hamm	North Carolina
1994	Tisha Venturini	North Carolina
1995	Shannon MacMillan	Portland

Olympics

Year	Medalists	Medal	Country
1996	Michelle Akers, Brandi Chastain, Joy Fawcett, Julie Foudy, Carin Gabarra, Mia Hamm, Kristine Lilly, Shannon MacMillan, Tiffeny Milbrett, Carla Overbeck, Cindy Parlow, Tiffany Roberts, Briana Scurry, Tisha Venturini, Staci Wilson	Gold	USA
		Silver	CHN
		Bronze	NOR

World Championships

Year	Site	Champion	Runner-Up
1991	China	USA	Norway
1995	Sweden	Norway	Germany

Photo credit: Ken Regan/Camera 5

VOLLEYBALL

◆ *If you enjoy a casual game of volleyball, you're not alone. More than 800 million earthlings play volleyball every year, making it the planet's most popular participatory sport.*

HISTORY

Say "volleyball" today, and the image of taut, tan California bodies leaps to mind. Ironically, the game was invented for the pale and pasty bodies of middle-aged men who, it was feared, weren't quite up to the exertion of basketball.

The brainchild of William Morgan, a gym instructor at the Holyoke, Massachusetts, YMCA, volleyball was born in 1895. Frustratingly little is known about women's entrance into the game. Unlike basketball, volleyball does not seem to

have been widely played in colleges at the turn of the century—perhaps because even the early, tame version of the game tempted players to jump for the ball, a move thought dangerous to the health of female reproductive organs. Volleyball was exported to foreign countries largely by American soldiers, and organized world competitions for women did not begin until after World War II.

THE MODERN ERA

The first U.S. national championships for women began in 1949, and the World Championships added competition for women in 1952. From its debut as a world sport through the present, women's volleyball has been dominated by teams from the Soviet bloc, China, Japan, and South America. While the United States has fielded some strong teams, it closed the century still looking for its first major world or Olympic gold medal. One reason the U.S. women may have lagged behind is lack of playing opportunity; many of America's top players have gone overseas to play professional volleyball.

The lack of earning opportunities has recently begun to change. During the late 1970s and early '80s, a new version of volleyball evolved. In California, home of so many American inventions, the casual, on-the-beach version was honed from an informal pastime to an exciting new form of competition. Played on the same size court, with the same net and ball, beach volleyball pits teams of two against each other. Playing on sand—much different than hardwood—and having only one partner rather than an entire team has created a

whole new dynamic. In person or as a televised event, beach volleyball is more accessible to spectators than the team version of the sport. And unlike the team sport, it creates individual stars whose skills and personality engage fans' interest. In 1986 the Women's Professional Volleyball Association (WPVA) was formed, with an eye to organizing pro beach volleyball events for women. Four years later the tour opened its inaugural season. Today competitions are staged throughout the United States as well as Puerto Rico and Japan, with annual purses worth more than $1 million and television coverage of several events. The Federation Internationale de Volleyball (FIVB) has also become a proponent of beach volleyball, and since 1992 has overseen a Beach Volleyball World Championship Series. Much has been made of the "jiggle appeal" of beach volleyball, since players compete in everything from

KILLS, SPIKES, AND SILVER BULLETS— IT'S NOT YOUR GRANDMOTHER'S GAME ANYMORE

Today's volleyball—in both the team and beach formats—is a faster-moving, higher-jumping, more strategically sophisticated game than ever before. If you tune in to television coverage, here are a dozen terms to know.

Block. One or more receiving players intercepts the ball before or just after it crosses the net.

Bump. A passing technique in which the ball is played with the forearms, hands together. A bump pass can also be used as a set.

Coverage. Intercepting (or being ready to intercept) a ball that comes glancing back as a result of an effective block by the opposing side.

Cut shot. An offensive shot hit slice fashion to barely clear the net in a parallel trajectory.

Dig. Also called a save. Any part of the body is used in a last-minute move to prevent the ball from hitting the ground.

Dink. A ball played just over the net or hands of the opposing side's blocker. When a dink is successful, the ball passes just out of

reach then abruptly dies, hitting the ground before the opposition can get to it.

Joust. A confrontation in which a hitter from one side and a blocker from the other contest the ball above the net.

Kill. Any action that terminates play in favor of one's own team, either by winning a point or regaining the serve.

Screen. An illegal move in which a player purposely conceals her teammate's serve by interfering with an opponent's line of sight.

Shoot. A two-handed set shot, used to either dink the ball over the net or place it deep in the opponent's court.

Silver bullet. An ace, or serve that scores a point by landing in the opponent's court without ever being touched.

Spike. A ball hit forcibly from net height or higher with a straight-down return trajectory that makes it extremely difficult to save and return. Alternative names for this play are numerous and colorful, and include *crush, hammer, bury, put-away,* and *slam.*

shorts and tank tops to one- and two-piece bathing suits. So far, players have taken a let-them-eat-cake approach to this criticism, pointing out that the sport is, after all, played on a beach. Beach volleyball took another big step forward in 1996, when it made its Olympic debut at the Atlanta Games.

Major Events and Competitions

Team Volleyball
Olympic Games
World Championships
World Cup
World Grand Prix

Beach Volleyball
Olympic Games
Word Championship Series

Governing Bodies and Organizations

USA Volleyball
3595 East Fountain Boulevard, Suite 1-2
Colorado Springs, Colorado 80910-1740

Women's Professional Volleyball Association
840 Apollo, Suite 205
El Segundo, California 90245-4701
Phone: 310/726-0700
Fax: 310/726-0719
Website: http://www.volleyball.org

---

* * * BIOGRAPHIES * * *

PATRICIA ANN (PATTI) BRIGHT b. December 27, 1940, Chicago, Illinois
A member of the U.S. Pan American Games team in 1963, Bright was also a member of two Olympic teams, in 1964 and '68. Though neither team medaled, Bright brought the '68 team its brightest moment when, as server, she aced the Soviet team several times in a row. The victory against the Soviets, who went on to claim the gold medal, was the U.S. team's only win of the tournament.
Selected championships and honors: Silver medal, Pan American Games, 1963.

RITA CROCKETT b. November 2, 1957, San Antonio, Texas
A well-rounded athlete in track, basketball, and volleyball, Crockett decided to focus on volleyball when her junior college team won a national title. She was named all-American that year and in 1978 joined the U.S. team as a hitter/blocker. In the heat of competition, Crockett was an incredible jumper whose high-rise springs made her an effective and powerful spiker. A member of the 1980 and '84 Olympic teams, Crockett helped bring America its first medal in women's volleyball.
Selected championships and honors: Bronze medal, World Championships, 1982; silver medal, Olympic Games, 1984.

TARA CROSS BATTLE b. September 16, 1968, Houston, Texas
One of the most dynamic players in the game today, Cross was an all-American all four of her college years at Long Beach State and led her team to its first-ever Division I title in 1989. An outside hitter, with her kills she helped the United States clinch medals at the 1995 Pan Am Games and World Grand Prix championships, and she was named both Grand Prix tournament MVP and Best Scorer. Cross also played professional volleyball in Italy during the 1992 and '93 seasons.
Selected championships and honors, team: Bronze medal, Olympic Games, 1992; silver medal, Pan American Games, 1995; gold medal, World Grand Prix, 1995. *Individual:* Twice named NCAA Division

I Player of the Year, 1988 and '89; named to 1980s NCAA All-Decade Team; Team USA MVP, 1995.

LORI ENDICOTT VANDERSNICK b. August 1, 1967, Kansas City, Missouri

One of the best setters in the world, with records to prove it, Endicott has won best setter honors at several international competitions, including the 1992 Olympics. Endicott played volleyball throughout her career at the University of Kansas and has started on U.S. teams since 1989.

Selected championships and honors: Bronze medal, Olympic Games, 1992; silver medal, Pan American Games, 1995; gold medal, World Grand Prix, 1995.

DEBBIE GREEN b. June 25, 1958, South Korea

Though she was born in Korea, Green grew up and learned to play volleyball in the United States. At five foot three, Green was always one of the smallest girls on the team—so she compensated by becoming one of the best. A member of the national junior team from 1974 through '78, in 1975 she became the U.S. Volleyball Association's youngest all-American. As a setter Green was nearly unequaled, and she worked on her initially weak serve until she was good enough to make the U.S. national team in 1978. Named to two U.S. Olympic teams, she missed her chance to play at the 1980 games due to the boycott but had the satisfaction of bringing home the silver medal at the L.A. games four years later.

Selected championships and honors: Bronze medal, World Championships, 1982; silver medal, Olympic Games, 1984.

FLORA (FLO) HYMAN b. July 29, 1954; Inglewood, California; d. January 24, 1986

At six foot five, Hyman could have stood still and let the ball come to her. Instead, she pushed herself to go for the ball—and became the greatest American woman ever to play volleyball. Her key skill was hitting, and she was voted best hitter at the World Cup games in Tokyo in 1981. That same year, she became one of a handful of women—and the first American woman—named to the All-World Cup Team. Three years later she helped the U.S. team to its best-ever Olympic finish, a silver medal. A leader who could single-handedly raise her whole team's level of play, Hyman began playing professionally overseas after the Olympics. Tragically, she died in Japan in 1986 of a congenital defect of the aorta, collapsing suddenly while she sat on a bench during a game.

Selected championships and honors, team: three-time all-American, 1974–76; All-World Cup, 1981; silver medal, Olympic Games, 1984. *Individual:* International Women's Sports Hall of Fame.

CAREN KEMNER b. April 16, 1965, Quincy, Illinois

A standout volleyball player throughout high school and college, Kemner joined the U.S. team in 1985 and made her first international appearance at the 1988 Olympics. A 6′1″ dynamo whose all-round skills made her a team standout, Kemner took a much-needed hiatus from her sport after the games but returned to help the United States to bronze-medal finishes at the 1990 World Championships and the 1992 Olympics. Kemner has been named Team USA MVP five times and led the U.S. team with 127 kills and 7 aces at the Barcelona Olympics in 1992. Like many U.S. players, Kemner has had to earn her living abroad, playing professionally in Brazil, Japan, and Italy.

Selected championships and honors, team: Bronze medal, World Championships, 1990; bronze medal, Olympic Games, 1992; silver medal, Pan American Games, 1995; gold medal, World Grand Prix, 1995. *Individual:* Most Valuable Woman Player in the World, 1991; six-time U.S. Olympic Committee Player of the Year, 1986–88 and 1990–92.

MIREYA LUIS HERNANDEZ b. 1967, Camaguey, Cuba

Luis achieved two important firsts in 1986. She gave birth to her first child and, just three months later, played in her first World Championships. Cuba finished second, but Luis made her mark as an up-and-coming star. Since then she has helped her country to several gold medals and more than fulfilled her early promise. Dubbed "the spiker with wings" for her leaping abilities, Luis was voted tournament MVP at the 1995 World Cup and was on the gold-medal-winning 1992 and '96 Cuban Olympic teams.

Selected championships and honors: Silver medal, World Championships, 1994; gold medal, World Championships, 1994; gold medal, Olympic Games, 1996.

KAROLYN KIRBY b. June 30, 1961, Brookline, Massachusetts

A two-time college all-American, Kirby played professionally in Europe and South America before deciding to try her hand at professional beach volleyball.

It wasn't easy, and Kirby says her first year was spent trying to learn the game's basics. By the early 1990s, Kirby was firmly in the wins column, leading the WPVA in earnings in 1991–94. Kirby's most successful, longest-lasting partnership has been with **Liz Maskayan,** with whom she won the FIVB 1994 World Series title and a gold medal at the 1994 Goodwill Games.

TAMMY LILEY. *See Tammy Webb Liley, below.*

LIZ MASKAYAN b. December 31, 1964, Quezon
    City, Philippines
Team volleyball and beach volleyball are described as completely different sports by those who have played both, and Maskayan is one of the few athletes who has triumphed at each one. A member of UCLA's 1984 NCAA Division I championship team, Maskayan played for Team USA from 1986 to 1990. She began playing beach volleyball in 1987, winning just $450 that year and little more than that in the next two. Since 1991, however, it has been a different story, and Maskayan has become one of the sport's stars. Although Maskayan has teamed with six different partners, her most successful alliance has been with **Karolyn Kirby,** with whom she won the FIVB 1994 World Series title and a gold medal at the 1994 Goodwill Games.
Selected championships and honors: Bronze medal, Pan American Games, 1987; bronze medal, World Championships, 1990.

ELAINA ODEN b. March 21, 1967, Orange,
    California
Volleyball runs in Oden's family—both Oden and her sisters Bev and Kim were NCAA all-Americans. During her college career at University of the Pacific, Oden led her team to NCAA championships in 1985 and '86 and was named all-American both years. Playing for the United States in international competition, Oden suffered a major knee injury in 1987 and did not return to competition until 1990. Oden is a phenomenal spiker; her 84 kills during the 1992 Olympics helped the United States to a bronze medal, while her performance during the country's first gold-medal Grand Prix win earned her the Best Spiker of the Tournament award. Oden has also played professionally in Italy.
Selected championships and honors, team: Bronze medal, World Championships, 1990; bronze medal, Olympic Games, 1992; gold medal, World Grand Prix, 1995. *Individual: Volleyball Monthly* Player of the

Year, 1986; named to 1980s NCAA All-Decade Team.

MARY JO PEPPLER b. 1944, Rockford, Illinois
The first world-class player to come out of America, Peppler would have won fame today with her independence, aggressive approach, and skills. At the time, she wasn't always appreciated. After playing on several U.S. teams, including the 1964 and '68 Olympic squads, she was not allowed to try out for the '76 team, and one USVA official described her as a gifted athlete who was nevertheless unmanageable. This despite being voted Best Female Player in the World at the 1970 World Championships. Peppler played with the International Volleyball Association in 1974, the first attempt to organize a professional coed sport, but the venture barely lasted one season.

SANDRA PIRES b. June 16, 1973 and
    JACQUILINE (JACKIE) CRUZ SILVA
    b. February 13, 1962, Rio de Janeiro, Brazil
Although Americans entered the first Olympic beach volleyball competitions with high hopes, none of the U.S. duos finished in the medals. It was Silva and Pires who took the gold by defeating fellow Brazilians Monica Rodrigues and Adriana Samuel. Both Pires and Silva have played on the pro circuit.
Selected championships and honors: Gold medal, beach, Olympic Games, 1996.

INNA RYSKAL b. USSR
Far too little was seen of Ryskal—one of the best players the world has ever produced—in the United States because her career predated the sport's current popularity. She was a member of four consecutive Soviet Olympic teams and, in international competitions, helped her team win more than a half-dozen major medals.
Selected championships and honors: Two silver medals, Olympic Games, 1964 and '76; two gold medals, Olympic Games, 1968 and '72; gold medal, World Championships, 1970; silver medal, World Championships, 1972.

JAQUILINE SILVA. *See Sandra Pires and Jaquiline Cruz Silva, above.*

TAMMY WEBB LILEY b. March 6, 1965, Long
    Beach, California
Webb's combination of quickness and versatility makes her an offensive bundle of dynamite. A starting member of U.S. teams since 1989, Webb's kill performance has helped America to several medal-winning

Team Peru, 1988

If the names Rosa, Gina, Natalia, Denisse, Gabriela, and Cecilia don't ring a bell, you weren't in Peru in 1988. The country, which hadn't won a gold medal since 1948, suddenly saw their chance in the women's volleyball team. Rosa García, Gina Torrealva, Natalia Malaga, Denisse Fajardo, Gabriela Perez Del Solar, and Cecilia Tait, the starters, become so popular they were known by their first names throughout the country. They didn't bring home a gold, but they did provide fans with one of the most exciting matches in volleyball history. Going up against an intimidatingly strong Soviet team in the final, they twice fought ahead from a tie, fended off a match point, and briefly took the lead before ultimately settling for a silver. The Peruvians made the Soviets fight so hard for the gold that medical personnel rushed onto the court after the final point was scored, and several of the women received medical attention before taking the stand at the medal ceremony.

performances, including its first-ever Grand Prix gold in 1995. Webb has also played professional volleyball in France and pro beach volleyball in America.
Selected championships and honors, team: Bronze medal, World Championships, 1990; bronze medal, Olympic Games, 1992; silver medal, Pan American Games, 1995; gold medal, World Grand Prix, 1995. *Individual:* U.S. Olympic Committee Player of the Year, 1993.

PAULA WEISHOFF b. May 1, 1962, Hollywood, California

Weishoff made her U.S. national team debut in 1981 and played on almost every American team through 1996. On the court, few can match Weishoff's skill at blocking and ball control, or her focus-like-a-laser approach to the game, a quality that earned her an outstanding player award at the 1992 Olympics. In addition to U.S. Olympic, Pan American, and World Championship teams, Weishoff has played professionally in Italy, Brazil, and Japan.
Selected championships and honors, team: Bronze medal, World Championships, 1982; silver medal, Pan American Games, 1983; silver medal, Olympic Games, 1984; bronze medal, Olympic Games, 1992; gold medal, World Grand Prix, 1995. *Individual:* U.S. Olympic Committee Player of the Year, 1984; twice named Team USA MVP, 1984 and '92.

TEEE WILLIAMS b. March 28, 1968, Los Angeles, California

Yes, it's really spelled T-e-e-e—possibly as in "T" for tough, since Williams has overcome broken bones, shoulder surgery, and other injuries to stay in the game. Williams, an explosive offensive player, was a standout during her college years at the University of Hawaii and began playing with U.S. national teams in 1990. Despite missing most of the 1993 season due to shoulder surgery, she has managed a full postcollege career, playing overseas in both Italy and Germany and starting for several U.S. medal-winning teams.
Selected championships and honors, team: Bronze medal, World Championships, 1990; bronze medal, Olympic Games, 1992; silver medal, Pan American Games, 1995; gold medal, World Grand Prix, 1995. *Individual:* Twice named NCAA Division I Player of the Year, 1987 and '89; named to 1980s NCAA All-Decade Team.

Volleyball

Olympics

Year	Medalists	Country	Medal
1896–1960	event not held		
1964	Masae Kasai, Emiko Miyamoto, Kinuko Tanida, Yuriko Handa, Yoshiko Matsumara, Sata Isobe, Katsumi Matsumura, Yoko Shinozaki, Setsuka Sasaki, Yuo Fujimoto, Masako Kondo, Ayano Shibuki	JPN	Gold
		USSR	Silver
		POL	Bronze

Volleyball (continued)

Year	Medalists	Country	Medal
1968	Lyudmila Buldakova, Lyudmila Mikhailovska, Vera Lantratova, Vera Galushka, Tatyana Sarycheva, Tatyana Ponyayeva, Nina Smoleyeva, Inna Ryskal, Galina Leontyeva, Roza Salikhova, Valentina Vinogradova (Kamenek)	USSR	Gold
		JPN	Silver
		POL	Bronze
1972	Inna Ryskal, Vera Douiounova (Galushka), Tatyana Tretyakova (Ponyayeva, Nina Smoleyeva, Roza Salikhova, Lyudmila Buldakova, Tatyana Gonobobleva, Lyubov Turina, Galina Leontyeva, Tatyana Sarycheva	USSR	Gold
		JPN	Silver
		PRK	Bronze
1976	Takako Lida, Mariko Okamoto, Echiko Maeda, Noriko Matsuda, Takako Shirai, Kiyami Kato, Yuka Arakida, Katsuko Kanesaka, Mariko Yoshida, Shoko Takayanagi, Hiromi Yano, Juri Yokoyama	JPN	Gold
		USSR	Silver
		KOR	Bronze
1980	Nadezhda Radzevich, Natalya Razumova, Olga Solovova, Yelena Akhaminova, Yelena Andreyuk, Inna Makagonova, Lyubov Kozyreva, Svetlana Nikishina, Lyudmila Chernyshova, Svetlana Badulina, Lidiya Loginova	USSR	Gold
		GDR	Silver
		BUL	Bronze
1984	Lang Ping, Liang Yan, Zhu Ling, Hou Yuzhu, Yang Xilan, Jiang Ying, Li Yanjun, Yang Xiaojun, Zheng Metzhu, Zhang Rongfang	CHN	Gold
		USA	Silver
		JPN	Bronze
1988	Valentina Ogiyenko, Yelena Volkova, Irina Smirnova, Tatyana Sidorenko, Irina Parkhomchuk, Olha Shkurnova, Marina Nikulina, Yelena Ovchinnikova, Olga Krivosheyeva, Marina Kumysh, Tatyana Kravnova, Svetlana Korytova	USSR	Gold
		PER	Silver
		CHN	Bronze
1992	Tania Ortiz Calvo, Marleny Costa Blanco, Mireya Luis Hernandez, Lilia Izquierdo Aguirre, Idalmis Gato Moya, Regla Bell McKenzie, Regla Torres Herrera, Norka Latamblet Daudinot, Mercedes Calderon Martinez, Magaly Carvajal Rivera	CUB	Gold
		USSR	Silver
		USA	Bronze

Volleyball (continued)

World Championships

Year	Champion	Runner-Up
1952	Soviet Union	Poland
1956	Soviet Union	Romania
1960	Soviet Union	Japan
1962	Japan	Soviet Union
1966	Japan	USA
1970	Soviet Union	Japan
1974	Japan	Soviet Union
1978	Cuba	Japan
1982	China	Peru
1986	China	Cuba
1990	Soviet Union	China
1994	Cuba	Brazil
1998	next World Championship	

World Cup

Year	Champion
1973	Soviet Union
1977	Japan
1981	China
1985	China
1989	Cuba
1991	Cuba
1995	Cuba

World Grand Prix Championships

Year	Champion
1993	Cuba
1994	Brazil
1995	USA
1996	Brazil

Olympic Beach Volleyball, Doubles

Year	Medalists	Country
1996	Sandra Pires & Jackie Silva	BRA
	Monica Rodrigues & Adriana Samuel	BRA
	Natalie Cook & Kerri Ann Pottharst	AUS

FIELD HOCKEY

◆ *As the first competitive team sport considered proper for women, field hockey became a cornerstone for all that followed and gave thousands of women a chance to discover their competitive nature.*

HISTORY

Historians believe that stick-and-ball games are the oldest of all sports using equipment, dating back more than four millennia. Men holding curved sticks, with a ball between them, are shown on the tomb wall of Beni-Hasan in the Nile Valley. Evidence abounds that not only Egyptians but Greeks, Romans, Europeans, North and South Americans, and people from many other lands played some version of the game. Although most people think of lacrosse as *the* Native American sport, Arapaho and several other bands played a game far closer to field hockey, using a small ball and a hooked stick.

Field hockey emerged in its modern form in the British Isles and was well established by the 1860s. Women were participating by the late 1890s, when two important trends met head-on. The late-Victorian physical fitness movement, which associated exercise with health and good looks, redefined exercise as a desirable rather than dubious undertaking for women. At the same time, women began to go to college in large numbers, providing an ideal environment for organized participation. Between 1887 and 1900, women's field hockey associations were established in Ireland, England, Scotland, and Wales. When England's Ladies' Hockey Association began publishing *Hockey Field* in October 1901, it marked the first appearance of a periodical devoted solely to women's sport.

During the early years of the twentieth century, women's field hockey spread to Australia, New Zealand, South Africa, Canada, and the United States as well as Switzerland, Germany, and the Netherlands. America's first exposure to the sport came in the summer of 1901, when a British physical education instructor named Constance Appleby staged an exhibition at Harvard University. Appleby spent the next two years teaching the game to women at colleges throughout the eastern seaboard, including Smith, Wellesley, and Mount Holyoke. Field hockey was an instant hit wherever it was tried, and its popularity can hardly be overestimated. Despite the fact that field hockey's first participants competed in heavy petticoats and sweeping skirts, their movements restricted by corsets, high collars, and long, tight sleeves, women loved the sport because it was one of the first venues in which they were allowed to be openly competitive. So widespread was field hockey's popularity and so great was the desire for organized competition that the International Federation of Women's Hockey Associations (IFWHA) was formed in 1927.

THE MODERN ERA

Although field hockey is no longer the only acceptable sport for women, it remains a popular standard. Few women graduate from high school or college without having played the sport in gym class at one time or another. More than 11,000 women now belong to the U.S. Field Hockey Association, the governing organization founded in 1922. In college play, eastern schools remain centers of activity, although good players come all over the country.

Although field hockey has been an Olympic event for men since 1908, an event for women was not included until 1980. When that year's boycott caused the withdrawal of most of the teams slated to compete, the IOC and the host city of Moscow scrambled to find competitors, with the IOC offering to share the expenses involved. Zimbabwe accepted the IOC's offer and, in a field deprived of some of the world's strongest players, ended up with a gold medal. The United States' first and only Olympic medal in the sport, a bronze, was won in 1984.

Major Events and Competitions

NCAA Championship
Olympic Games
World Cup Championship

Governing Bodies and Organizations

U.S. Field Hockey Association (USFHA)
1 Olympic Plaza
Colorado Springs, Colorado 80909

✦ ✦ ✦ BIOGRAPHIES ✦ ✦ ✦

BETH ANDERS b. November 13, 1951,
Norristown, Pennsylvania
Anders was a key player on every U.S. national team for over sixteen years, from 1969 through the end of the 1984 season. She also played on thirteen U.S. World Cup teams, from 1971 through 1983. A leader on the field and off, Anders was a high scorer who consistently took the lead during tournament play.

Few women (or men) have equaled her on penalty corner shot scoring. In her final World Cup tournament she made six shots in seven matches. Anders, picked for the Olympic team during the boycott year of 1980, made the team again in 1984 and was named captain. A veteran with 100 international games under her belt, she led the United States to its highest Olympic finish ever with a bronze medal. In 1980

Anders became field hockey coach at Old Dominion. Through the end of the 1995 season her teams had won seven NCAA Division I championships.
Selected championships and honors: U.S. World Cup Team scoring leader during tournament play, 1971–83; bronze medal, Olympic Games, 1984.

GWEN CHEESEMAN b. August 13, 1951, Harrisburg, Pennsylvania
A diminutive five foot two, Cheeseman had no trouble covering the net and was for several years one of America's top goalkeepers. A member of three World Cup teams (1975, '80, and '83) and two Olympic squads (1980 and '84), she earned her biggest wins after she returned from a two-year retirement in 1983. In the 1984 Four Nations tournament, she allowed only one goal in four matches, helping the United States to a first-place finish. Later that year, she helped America win its first medal in the sport.
Selected championships and honors: Four Nations Championship, 1984; bronze medal, Olympic Games, 1984.

TRACEY FUCHS b. November 3, 1966, Centereach, New York
A USFHA Athlete of the Year, Fuchs joined the U.S. national team in 1987 and played through the 1996 Olympics, when she was team vice captain. Fuchs went on to serve as an assistant coach at her alma mater, the University of Connecticut.
Selected championships and honors, team: Bronze medal, Pan American Games, 1991; bronze medal, World Cup, 1994. *Individual:* USFHA Athlete of the Year, 1990.

KELLI JAMES b. March 16, 1970, Medford, New Jersey
James, a forward, was a two-time all-American at Old Dominion. She won bronze medals on two U.S. national teams and played on the 1996 Olympic squad. She is currently an assistant coach at the University of North Carolina.
Selected championships and honors, team: Bronze medal, Pan American Games, 1991; bronze medal, World Cup, 1994. *Individual:* Broderick Award, 1992.

BARBARA MAROIS b. March 1, 1963, Auburn, Massachusetts
A defender known for her ability to lead, Marois played for her first U.S. national team in 1985 and was still at it more a decade later, when she captained her team to a third-place World Cup finish. Marois

also played on the 1988 Olympic squad and captained the 1996 team.
Selected championships and honors, team: Bronze medal, Pan American Games, 1991; bronze medal, World Cup, 1994. *Individual:* USFHA Athlete of the Year, 1990.

LAUREL MARTIN b. June 8, 1969, Hummelstown, Pennsylvania
Martin joined the U.S. national team in 1986, when she was still a teenager. Ten years later, after a necessary hiatus, she returned just three months after giving birth to play in the 1996 Atlanta Olympics. In between, she played on one NCAA Championship team and two Pan American medal teams and was named all-American in 1991.
Selected championships and honors: NCAA Championship, University of North Carolina team, 1989; bronze medal, Pan American Games, 1991; silver medal, Pan American Games, 1995.

1984 U.S. Bronze Medal Team

Although the U.S. has some excellent college players, it's had a hard time earning medals in international field hockey competitions. This wasn't the case at the Los Angeles games in 1984, when the United States, tied with Australia for third place, defeated the women from Down Under in a 10-5 shootoff. The medal-winning rosters included:

Beth Anders
Leslie Milne
Beth Beglin
Charlene Morett
Regina Buggy
Diane Moyer
Gwen Cheeseman
Marcella Place
Sheryl Johnson
Karen Shelton
Christine Larson Mason
Brenda Stauffler
Kathleen McGahey
Julie Staver
Anita Miller
Julie Strong

MARCIA PANKRATZ b. October 1, 1964, Wakefield, Massachusetts

A two-time all-American while playing for the University of Iowa, Pankratz joined the U.S. national team in 1985 and played for two Olympic squads (1988 and '96) as well as two teams that won bronze medals in international competitions.

Selected championships and honors: Bronze medal, World Cup, 1994.

PATRICIA (PATTY) SHEA b. September 15, 1962, Belmont, Massachusetts

At 5'2", Shea is inches shorter than most of her opponents, but that doesn't inhibit her skill in fending off shots on goal. One of the best goalkeepers in the United States, she was twice named all-American during her college career at the University of Massachusetts and has played on U.S. national teams since 1985, including 1988 and '96 Olympic squads.

Selected championships and honors, team: Bronze medal, World Cup, 1994. *Individual:* USFHA Athlete of the Year, 1988.

ELIZABETH (LIZ) TCHOU b. September 25, 1966, Medford Lakes, New Jersey

Named all-American in 1987 during her college career at the University of Iowa, Tchou was a member of three Big Ten championship teams and helped her team win the NCAA championship in 1986. After graduating from college, she played on several U.S. national teams and is currently an assistant coach at Duke University.

Selected championships and honors: NCAA Championship, University of Iowa, 1986; bronze medal, Pan American Games, 1991; bronze medal, World Cup, 1994.

Field Hockey

Olympics

Year	Medalists	Country	Medal
1896–1976	event not held		
1980	Sarah English, Ann Mary Grant, Brenda Phillips, Patricia McKillop, Sonia Robertson, Patricia Davies, Susan Huggett, Gillian Cowley, Elizabeth Chase, Sandra Chick, Helen Volk, Christine Prinsloo, Arlene Boxhall, Anthea Stewart	ZIM	Gold
		CZE	Silver
		USSR	Bronze
1984	Bernadette de Beus, Alette Pos, Margriet Zegers, Laurien Willemse, Marjolein Eysvogel, Josephine Boekhorst, Carina Benninga, Alexandra le Poole, Francisca Hillen, Marieke van Doom, Sophie von Weiler, Aletta van Manen, Irene Hendriks, Elisabeth Sevens Martine Ohr, Anneloes Nieuwenhuizen	HOL	Gold
		GER	Silver
		USA	Bronze
1988	Kathleen Partridge, Elspeth Clement, Liane Tooth, Loretta Dorman, Lorraine Hillas, Michelle Capes, Sandra Pisani, Deborah Bowman, Lee Capes, Kim Small, Sally Carbon, Jacqueline Pereira, Tracey Belbin, Rechelle Hawkes, Sharon Patmore, Maree Fish	AUS	Gold
		KOR	Silver
		HOL	Bronze
1992	Maria Gonzalez Laguillo, Natalia Dorado Gomez, Virginia Ramirez Merino, Maria del Carmen Barea Cobos, Silvia Manrique Perez, Nagore Gabellanes Marieta, Maria Rodriguez Suarez, Sonia Barrio Gutierrez, Elisabeth Maragall Verge, Teresa Motos Iceta, Maider Telleria Goni, Mercedes Coghen Alberdingo, Nuria Olive Vancells, Ana Maiques Dern, Maria Martinez De Murguia	SPA	Gold
		GER	Silver
		GBR	Bronze
1996	Michelle Andrews, Alyson Annan, Louise Dobson, Renita Farrell, Juliet Haslam, Rechelle Hawkes, Clover Maitland, Karen Marsden, Jenny Morris, Jackie Pereira, Nova Peris-Kneebone, Katrina Powell, Danni Roche, Kate Starre, Liane Tooth	AUS	Gold
		KOR	Silver
		HOL	Bronze

Photo credit: Gerhard Uhl

TEAM HANDBALL

Though men's team handball has been an Olympic sport since the 1930s, the sport is relatively new to women. Most Americans aren't even sure what the sport is, often thinking of individual handball. This is a shame, since team handball is a fast-moving game, satisfying to play and interesting to watch. It is also a game ideally suited to women, since speed and coordination predominate over mass strength. At its heart, team handball is a blend of two better-known sports—soccer and basketball. As in soccer, players attempt to score goals by delivering the ball into a net guarded by a goalie. As in basketball, the ball can be advanced by dribbling down the court, and goals are made by shooting, rather than kicking, into the net. Clearly, the game is begging to be discovered by the same women who've made American basketball one of the world's most exciting games. And just as clearly, the rest of the world is hoping to delay the American discovery as long as possible.

Women's team handball was added to the Olympic roster in 1976 and has been largely dominated by the women of the Soviet Union and South Korea. In recent years the sport's popularity has spread to Scandinavia. The Norwegian team scored a surprise second-place finish at the 1992 games in Barcelona, finishing behind a world-dominant Korean team. In 1996 Denmark's team made its Olympic debut, winning a gold medal when it defeated the Koreans.

Today, team handball is hampered by a lack of publicity and limited opportunities to play. But the picture could well change with a little television coverage and inclusion in school curricula, and tomorrow's dream team might be a whole new story.

Major Events and Competitions

Olympics
World Championships

Governing Bodies and Organizations

U.S. Team Handball Federation (USTHF)
1 Olympic Plaza
Colorado Springs, Colorado 80909
Phone: 719/578-4582

Team Handball

Olympics

Year	Medalists	Country	Medal
1896–1972	event not held		
1976	Natalya Sherstyuk, Rafiga Shabanova, Lyubov Berezhnaya, Tetyana Makarets, Mariya Litoshenko, Lyudmyla Zinaida Turchyna, Bobrus, Tetyana Hluschenko, Lyudmila Shubina, Halyna Zakharova, Aldona Cesaityte, Nina Lobova, Lyudmyla Panchuk, Larysa Karlova	USSR	Gold
		GDR	Silver
		HUN	Bronze
1980	Natayla Tymoshkina (Sherstyuk), Larysa Karlova, Iryna Palchykova, Zinaida Turchyna, Tetyana Kocherhina (Makarets), Lyudmila Poradnyk (Bobrus), Larissa Savkina, Aldona Neneniene (Cesaityte), Yulia Safina, Olha Zubaryeva, Valentyne Lutayeva, Lyubov Odynokova (Berezhnaya), Sigita Strecen	USSR	Gold
		YUG	Silver
		GDR	Bronze
1984	Jasna Ptujec, Mirjana Ognjenovic, Zorica Pavicevic, Ljubinka Jankovic, Svetlana Anastasovski, Svetlana Dasic-Kitic, Emilija Ercic, Alenka Cudeman, Svetlana Mugosa, Mirjana Djurica, Biserka Visnjic, Slavica Djukic, Jasna Kolar-Merdan, Ljijana Mugosa, Dragica Djuric	YUG	Gold
		KOR	Silver
		CHN	Bronze
1988	Song Ji-hyun, Han Hyun-sook, Kim Choon-rye, Kim Myung-soon, Lee Ki-soon, Kim Hyun-mee, Kim Mi-sook, Suk Min-hee, Son Mi-na, Lim Mi-kyung, Kim Kyung-soon, Sung Kyung-hwa	KOR	Gold
		NOR	Silver
		USSR	Bronze
1992	Moon Hyang-ja, Jang Ri-ra, Nam Eun-young, Lee Ho-youn, Lee Mi-young, Hong Jeong-ho, Lim O-kyung, Min Hye-sook, Park Jeong-lim, Oh Sung-ok, Kim Hwa-sook, Park Kap-sook, Cha Jae-kyung	KOR	Gold
		NOR	Silver
		RUS	Bronze
1996	Anja Jul Andersen, Camilla Andersen, Kristine Andersen, Heidi Astrup, Tina Bottzau, Marianne Florman, Conny Hamann, Anja Hansen, Anette Hoffman, Tonje Kjaergaard, Janne Kolling, Susanne Lauritsen, Gitte Madsen, Lene Rantala, Gitte Sunesen, Dorthe Tanderup	DEN	Gold
		KOR	Silver
		HUN	Bronze

Photo credit: Ken Rigan/Camera 5

TENNIS

◆ *For more than a hundred years, tennis has provided a forum for changing attitudes toward women on everything from casual dress to equal pay.*

HISTORY

Although horse racing is universally known as the "sport of kings," tennis could rightfully claim the same title. The sport born on the eve of the Renaissance sprang to life not in peasant camps or village greens but in castle courtyards and was played by contestants freighted with brocades, furs, and jewels. A peasant or worker might speak knowingly of court tennis—or "royal tennis," as it was also known—but he could not play it legally.

At least not in England, where a decree of 1388 expressly forbid servants and laborers to participate. The decree, renewed in 1410, was meant to ensure that tennis, like jousting and hawking, remained the preserve of the upper classes. On the first page of the French novel *The Princess of Cleaves*, set in the 1550s, the author introduces the reader to the lavish court of Henri II with the line, "Every day there were hunting and tennis parties, dances, tournaments, and similar amusements."

Tennis was clearly a social event, and a coed one. However, it is uncertain whether, like jousting, women were cast in the role of admiring spectators or provided with opportunities to play. The ball must have been leaden, the rackets heavy, the volleying slow-going, and the effort enormous. Would women in their yards of fabric, elaborate headdresses, and stiffened panniers have ventured onto the court? It's easy to conclude, as several sources do, that they did not. But this conclusion ignores the obvious—that when the men were off hawking and hunting, when fresh air and sunlight beckoned, women would probably have tried the sport informally, among themselves, dressed in clothes less confining than those worn on more formal occasions. At least one reference attests to the fact that women *did* play. In 1427, history records that the twenty-eight-year-old Margot of Hainault came to Paris and outplayed all male comers.

Just as women inevitably picked up the racket, so did commoners. The nobility's efforts to restrict play only gave tennis the luster of upper-class chic it retains to this day.

THE MODERN ERA

The modern era in tennis dates back over one hundred years, and the sport was celebrating its silver anniversary when the twentieth century was still an infant. Modern tennis was played by upper- and upper-middle-class women and promoted as a women's college sport in England as well as the United States from the late 1870s on. The women of Oxford and Cambridge played tennis, as did women who attended Vassar and the Boston School of Gymnastics.

In 1877 the All-England Croquet Club officially changed its name to the All-England Croquet and Lawn Tennis Club, and the first women's championships were held at the club's headquarters—Wimbledon—in 1884. In a case of unparalleled sibling rivalry, Maud Watson defeated her older sister, Lilian, to win the first Wimbledon. Maud Watson won again the following year, but runner-up Blanche Bingley came back to win in 1886. Bingley, later known as Mrs. G. W. Hillyard, became the first true star of the modern game, winning six Wimbledon singles titles by 1900, often against her archrival, Charlotte ("Lottie") Dod.

In America as in England, tennis preserved its upper-class trappings. Buffered by the irre-

---

Grand Slam Events

Four events make up the grand slam of tennis, and winning each in the course of a year—be it in a single season or in the course of twelve months spread across two seasons—is the Mount Everest of championship play. Each grand slam event features singles, doubles, and mixed doubles play for both women and men.

Australian Open
French Open (also known as the Roland Garros)
U.S. Open
Wimbledon

---

proachable cushions of money and breeding, tennis became instrumental in making the athletic woman more than an oddity but someone whose fitness, health, and competitive spirit were modern and desirable. Eleanora Sears, a descendent of Thomas Jefferson, embodied the new model—in addition to five championships in doubles and mixed doubles tennis, she won the first national squash championship ever held, wore jodhpurs and rode astride, and owned some 240 trophies in a wide-ranging variety of sports. Proof positive that a new era had begun came when one of Coca-Cola's first ads, featured in *Harper's*, depicted a man with golf clubs and a young woman with a tennis racket. In addition to securing new athletic freedoms for women, tennis provided a forum for addressing—and sometimes overcoming—other social inequalities. Along with cycling, tennis revolutionized standards for women's casual dress. It became a tool for breaking racial barriers in the mid-1950s, when **Alice Marble** wrote an open letter to *American Lawn Tennis* magazine protesting **Althea Gibson's** exclusion from grand slam events. Twenty years later, **Billie Jean King** exposed the winked-at practice of awarding "expense" money to amateurs, then took on the great disparity between prize money awarded to men and that offered to women. (*See sidebar,*

THE CLOTHES MAY NOT MAKE THE WOMAN— BUT THEY SOMETIMES MAKE THE GAME

The first sport modern women played out of doors, croquet, required no special clothing. Women of the late 1860s and early 1870s competed in the same hoop skirts, corsets, and confining bodices they took tea in. A few years later two new activities—tennis and cycling—created a new and hitherto unknown demand for a specialized wardrobe for women, and the world has never been the same since.

Women initially attempted to play tennis in ordinary clothing, but the limitations imposed by hobble skirts, starched collars, and tight cuffs soon became obvious. When reigning Wimbledon champion Blanche Bingley was defeated by fifteen-year-old Lottie Dod in 1887, observers noted that Dod's age permitted her to wear shorter, looser skirts, which allowed her to go after balls her opponents couldn't hope to reach. Five years later Ava Willing Astor defied her mother-in-law, Caroline Astor, and took to the polished courts of Newport in bloomers.

Few women have done more to revolutionize the game or its clothing than France's **Suzanne Lenglen.** Rich, eccentric, and brilliant, Lenglen adapted the knee-length, hip-swinging styles of the Jazz Age to the courts, appearing in short pleated skirts (notably sans petticoat), white stockings, sleeveless white silk blouses, and tennis shoes. She was also the first woman to wear a headband—often a bejeweled one—during play.

There is some dispute over when and on whom the first pair of shorts appeared in Wimbledon play. Some sources give the honor to **Helen Hull Jacobs,** who wore them in 1933. Other sources move the date forward to 1931,

when Lili de Alvarez wore "short trousers" to her match. Whether the short trousers bore a greater resemblance to shorts or to trousers is unknown.

The biggest clothing scandal to come out of Wimbledon involved neither shorts nor trousers but a skirt—or rather, the panties beneath the skirt. In 1949 Gussie Moran wore lace panties beneath her typically short tennis dress during doubles competition. Moran and her partner, Pat Todd, faced the formidable American duo of **Louise Brough** and **Margaret Osborne duPont.** Although Brough and duPont disapproved of the costume, Brough reportedly bent almost double to see the flashy lace, and some suggested that Moran's gambit was calculated to unnerve her opponents. If that was the case, the attempt failed, and Moran and Todd went down to defeat.

The last fashion statement to come out of Wimbledon was made by the great Brazilian star, **Maria Bueno.** Bueno, whose court costumes were designed by Ted Tinling, appeared in the 1964 finals in a classic white tennis dress whose skirt was lined with shocking pink. Each time she served, the vibrant crescent of lining winked at the crowd. Bueno's flash wasn't limited to fashion—at the top of her game in the mid-1960s, Bueno won the championship.

Today, all's quiet on the clothing frontier. It's been twenty or thirty years since anyone paid much attention to what women wear on the court. The focus has shifted to how women play, not what they play in—a measure of how far women have come.

page 60.) Above all, tennis has been a beachhead for the cause of equality for all women's sports. After watching a showdown between **Martina Navratilova** and **Chris Evert,** it was no longer possible for even the most chauvinistically inclined to dismiss women's sports as pale, pastel pastimes.

Governing Bodies and Organizations

U.S. Tennis Association (USTA)
70 West Red Oak Lane
White Plains, New York 10604
Phone: 914/696-7000

Corel World Tennis Association Tour
1266 East Main Street, 4th Floor
Stamford, Connecticut 06902-3456

Phone: 203/978-1740
Fax: 203/978-1702
Web site: http://www.corelwtatour.com

❖ ❖ ❖ BIOGRAPHIES ❖ ❖ ❖

JULIETTE ATKINSON b. April 15, 1873, Rahway, New Jersey; d. January 12, 1944

Arguably the first woman to envision the athletic possibilities of women's tennis, Atkinson dominated the American scene at the end of the last century. A self-taught player who frequently paired with her younger sister, Atkinson was the first woman to come to the net and volley, a remarkable achievement in an era of cumbersome costumes. Her 1898 victory over Marion Jones (6–3, 5–7, 6–4, 2–6, and 7–5) still ranks as the longest match in women's national singles play.

Selected championships and honors, singles: Three U.S. Championships, 1895, '97, and '98. *Doubles:* Seven U.S. Championships, 1894–98, 1901, and 1902. *Mixed doubles:* Three U.S. Championships, 1894–96. International Tennis Hall of Fame.

TRACY AUSTIN b. December 12, 1962, Palos Verdes Peninsula, California

It's impossible to read Austin's many records without repeatedly encountering the world "youngest." Eventually her youth caught up with her, and injuries forced her into retirement at the tender age of twenty-one. During her brief career, Austin was seemingly unstoppable. She won twenty-five juniors titles, then at the age of fourteen entered and won her first pro tournament, the Avon Futures. In 1977 she became the youngest player ever to compete in Wimbledon and the U.S. Open. The next year, she became the youngest player to represent the United States in Wightman and Federation Cup play, and when she won the U.S. Open in 1979, she was the youngest player ever to do so. Her physical problems began in 1980, the year she and her brother John became the first siblings ever to capture a Wimbledon mixed doubles crown. Plagued by an injured sciatic nerve, Austin took eight months off. She came back to defeat **Martina Navratilova** for the U.S. Open title in 1981, and assured interviewers she was determined to make a full comeback. Unfortunately, her injuries grew worse. The sciatic problem continued, compounded by a stress fracture to the back and a shoulder injury. Austin sat out much of 1981 and '82 and had to withdraw from Wimbledon in 1983. Although she entered the U.S. indoor championships in 1984, her game was no longer competitive. Austin, immensely popular with fans, became a cautionary role model and an unwitting magnet for debate. Many saw—and continue to see—her as a prime example of protégée-cum-victim, an athlete whose talents were pushed too far, too fast.

Selected championships and honors, singles: Two U.S. Opens, 1979 and '81. *Mixed doubles:* Wimbledon championship, 1980. Twice Associated Press Female Athlete of the Year, 1979 and '81; International Tennis Hall of Fame.

PAULINE BETZ ADDIE b. August 6, 1919, Dayton, Ohio

Betz may have been the first woman to seriously support the idea of a woman's pro tour—a bit of avant-garde feminism that cost her her career and tarnished her otherwise considerable fame. In her prime, Betz was known for her formidable backhand and her agility on court. A natural acrobat whose parents encouraged her to take up the "ladylike" sport of tennis, Betz was able to cover and return shots others couldn't get to. Her game matured during the war years, when international competition was suspended, and Betz had to content herself with a number-one ranking on the home front for several seasons (1942–44 and 1946). She won the first postwar Wimbledon singles and the first postwar French Open doubles, pairing with Patty Budge. Her troubles began soon after that, when the USLTA learned that she and her husband were thinking of organizing a women's pro tour. In a move that had a chilling effect on women players for years to come, Betz was promptly suspended from amateur play, and her career ended. She toured professionally with former rival Sarah Palfrey Cooke in 1947, maintaining a grueling match-a-day schedule, and later toured with Gussie Moran and others. Despite the treatment she received, Betz remained a lifelong proponent of the game. After retiring from active play she conducted clinics for underprivileged children and wrote numerous newspaper and magazine articles on the sport.

Selected championships and honors, singles: Four U.S. Opens, 1942–44, 1946. Wimbledon championship, 1946. *Doubles:* French Open, 1946.

ANNA (MOLLA) BJURSTEDT MALLORY

b. ca. 1893, Oslo, Norway; d. November 21, 1959
Bjurstedt won eight national championships in her native Norway before immigrating to the U.S. in 1914. A player who believed in "always hitting the ball with all my might," Bjurstedt left her mark on American tennis, making it a more aggressive and far more athletic game. Of her many matches, the most famous was a showdown against France's **Suzanne Lenglen** in the course of the 1921 U.S. Open. Lenglen, Europe's great and highly temperamental superstar, lost the first set to Bjurstedt, 6–2, and had lost the first 3 points of the second set when a sudden "illness" forced her off the court. Bjurstedt went on to win the tournament, the sixth of her eight singles titles.
Selected championships and honors, singles: Eight U.S. Opens, 1915–18, 1920–22, and 1926. *Doubles:* Two U.S. Opens, 1916 and '17. *Mixed doubles:* Three U.S. Opens, 1917, '22, and '23. International Tennis Hall of Fame.

ALTHEA LOUISE (LOUISE) BROUGH CLAPP

b. March 11, 1923, Oklahoma City, Oklahoma
Brough grew up in California, where she began playing tennis as a child. As a teenager she played simultaneously in the national juniors championship in Philadelphia and the national women's championship in New York, making numerous round-trip drives with her aunt. Though she won only one U.S. singles championship—in 1947—she gathered three consecutive Wimbledon titles and added a fourth a few years later. She was also a tremendous doubles player, particularly when paired with Margaret Osborne duPont, with whom she won nineteen U.S. Open, Wimbledon, and French Open titles. Brough excelled at mixed doubles as well, winning U.S. Open and Wimbledon championships four times each. Brough retired from competition after she married in 1958 but continued as a tennis coach for two more decades, working with young players and teaching them the game.
Selected championships and honors, singles: U.S. Open, 1947; Four Wimbledon championships, 1948–50 and '55. *Doubles:* Eleven U.S. Opens, 1942–50 and 1955–57; five Wimbledon championships, 1946, 1948–50, and 1954; three French Opens, 1946, '47,

and '49. *Mixed doubles:* Four U.S. Opens, 1942 and 1947–40; Four Wimbledon championships, 1946–48 and '50. International Tennis Hall of Fame.

MARY K. BROWNE b. June 1891, Ventura County, California; d. August 19, 1971
A dominant force in the early days of tennis, Browne is one of the few women ever to have won the U.S. triple crown (singles, doubles, and mixed doubles) three years running. Her doubles partners were Dorothy Green (1912) and Louise Riddell Williams (1913 and '14). Her mixed doubles partner for all three years was the then unknown Bill Tilden. Browne kept playing tennis through World War II and later took up golf as well. Though her career had peaked by 1924, she made it to both the U.S. tennis semifinals and the finals of the national amateur women's golf tournament. In 1926 she was one of the players signed to a professional contract when C. C. Pyle put together the first pro tour.
Selected championships and wins, singles: three U.S. Opens, 1912–14. *Doubles:* Three U.S. Opens, 1912–14. *Mixed doubles:* Three U.S. Opens, 1912–14. International Tennis Hall of Fame.

MARIA BUENO b. October 11, 1939, Sao Paulo, Brazil
Despite the fact that she never took a formal lesson, Bueno won her country's national women's championship at age fourteen, and at seventeen she began playing on the international circuit. During her career, Bueno's graceful-but-powerful volleys and driving ground strokes helped her win three Wimbledons and four U.S. Open singles championships. Partnered with players like **Althea Gibson, Billie Jean King, Margaret Smith Court,** and **Darlene Hard,** she won numerous doubles titles as well. She also won dozens of new fans to the game. A graceful player who once said tennis was as much an art as a sport, Bueno gave it a new dimension with her designer costumes. She was received as a national heroine at home; Brazil issued a postage stamp and erected a statue in her honor.
Selected championships and honors, singles: Three Wimbledon championships, 1959, '60, and '64; four U.S. Opens, 1959, '63, '64, and '66. *Doubles:* Five Wimbledon championships, 1958, '60, '63, '65 and '66; Four U.S. Opens, 1960, '62, '66, and '68; French Open, 1960. *Mixed doubles:* French Open, 1960. Associated Press Female Athlete of the Year, 1959; International Tennis Hall of Fame.

MABEL CAHILL b. April 12, 1863, Ireland
Cahill already knew how to play tennis when she emigrated to the United States in the late 1880s. A two-time U.S. Open singles champion, she was the winner of the first five-set match in women's finals, introduced in 1892. She also won another 1892 innovation—the first-ever U.S. mixed doubles competition.
Selected championships and honors, singles: Two U.S. Opens, 1891 and '92. *Doubles:* Two U.S. Opens, 1891 and '92. *Mixed doubles:* U.S. Open, 1892. International Tennis Hall of Fame.

JENNIFER CAPRIATI b. March 29, 1976, Long
    Island, New York
Capriati turned pro at thirteen, and the next year she was the youngest player ever to reach the semifinals of a grand slam tournament—the 1990 French Open—as well as the youngest person ever to win a match at Wimbledon. Although Capriati defeated **Steffi Graf** to win a gold at the 1992 Olympics, signs of stress had begun to show. She left the tour in '93 and received psychiatric counseling, but continued to have problems, being arrested once for shoplifting and once for drug use. To many, Capriati has become a tragic symbol of what happens when promising players are pushed too hard, too fast, and too far by overreaching parents and coaches. As of 1996, her attempts to make a comeback had proven unsuccessful.
Selected championships and honors, singles: Silver medal, Olympic games, 1988; gold medal, Olympic games, 1992.

ROSEMARY (ROSIE) CASALS b. September 10,
    1948, San Francisco
Though she never won a grand slam singles title, Casals won numerous doubles championships. Paired with **Billie Jean King,** she won five Wimbledon doubles and two U.S. Opens. She also won two U.S. doubles titles (1971 and '82), a U.S. mixed doubles title (1975), and a U.S. indoor doubles (1982). Casals also played and coached several Wightman and Federation Cup teams.
Selected championships and honors, doubles: Five Wimbledon championships, 1967, '68, '70, '71 and '73; two U.S. Opens, 1967 and '74.

MAUREEN CONNOLLY BRINKER b. September
    17, 1934, San Diego, California; d. June 21, 1969
Most girls pout when told, "Honey, we can't afford a horse." Connolly took up a tennis racket instead.

Soon "Little Mo" was winning championships and rewriting the record books. At fourteen, she was the youngest national junior girls champion ever. At sixteen, she was the youngest player ever to win the U.S. women's championship. In 1953 she became the first woman to win all four grand slam events in one year. A baseline player known for her terrific accuracy and tremendous flat drives, Connolly was still developing her game when she won her third Wimbledon title in 1954. It was her last big win, and her career ended two weeks later. Connolly was not yet twenty when she was thrown to the ground in a freak riding accident. Her right leg was severely damaged, and she was never again able to play competitively. Married to Olympic equestrian Norman Brinker, she continued to promote junior tennis through the Maureen Connolly Brinker Foundation. Like her brilliant career, Connolly's life was far too short. She died of cancer at the age of thirty-four.
Selected championships and honors, singles: Three U.S. Opens, 1951–53; three Wimbledon championships, 1952–54; Australian Open, 1953; two French Opens, 1953 and '54. Three times Associated Press Female Athlete of the Year, 1951–53; International Tennis Hall of Fame; International Women's Sports Hall of Fame.

CHARLOTTE (CHATTIE) COOPER STERRY
    b. 1871, Ealing, Middlesex, Great Britain
Cooper, officially the first woman to win a gold medal in the Olympic Games, was a three-time Wimbledon champion by the time she arrived in Paris for the games of 1900. Unusually healthy and virtually tireless, Cooper's secret may have been her attacking game, which few women had at the time. After the Olympics, Cooper returned to her winning ways at Wimbledon, taking her last title in 1908, when she was thirty-seven years old.
Selected championships and honors, singles: Wimbledon championships, 1895, '96, '98, 1901, and 1908; gold medal, Olympic Games, 1900. *Mixed doubles:* Gold medal, Olympic Games, 1900.

CHRISTINE (CHRIS) EVERT LLOYD MILL
    b. December 21, 1954, Fort Lauderdale, Florida
A reserved manner and efficient but untheatrical playing style aren't usually things fans dote on—yet Evert, who possessed both, was one of the most popular players America ever produced. The daughter of tennis pro Jimmie Evert, she had an impressive amateur career

> Many a parent is prejudiced against her daughter having so much freedom, but my mother . . . turned a deaf ear to anyone who advised her not to allow my sister and myself to travel about.
>
> —Charlotte Cooper Sterry

that included a winning streak of forty-six consecutive matches. Evert turned pro on her eighteenth birthday and won her first grand slam title in 1974. On clay or in the midst of a streak, Evert was virtually unbeatable. Between August 1973 and May 1979 she played 125 matches on clay without a single loss. In 1974 she set a modern record by winning 56 consecutive matches. In 1981 she won 72 of 78 matches and took Wimbledon without losing a set. Although their styles were markedly different, Evert's court battles with **Martina Navratilova** raised the level of play to dizzying heights and won thousands of new enthusiasts to the game. The two faced each other in a total of 14 grand slam finals, Evert's consistent ground strokes and well-manicured baseline game proving a nearly equal match for Navratilova's more aggressive style. Although Navratilova won more of the matches (10), Evert won first (1975) and last (1986). Ironically, both finished their careers with the same number of grand slam championships—18. Married first to John Lloyd, a British tennis pro, Evert divorced in 1987 and married skier Andy Mill in 1988. Her last major competition was the 1989 U.S. Open. After more than ten years at the top, she lost in the fifth round to Zina Garrison. As she prepared to leave the court, the crowd cheered and Garrison, moved by the moment, shed tears.

Selected championships and honors, singles: Two Australian Opens, 1982 and '84; seven French Opens, 1974, '75, '79, '80, '83, '85, and '86; three Wimbledon championships, 1974, '75, and '81; six U.S. Opens, 1975–78, '80, and '82. Four times Associated Press Female Athlete of the Year, 1974, '75, '77, and '80; United Press International Female Athlete of the Year, 1981; International Tennis Hall of Fame; International Women's Sports Hall of Fame.

MARY JOE FERNANDEZ b. August 19, 1971, Dominican Republic

Fernandez has yet to win a grand slam event, but she sparkles with three Olympic medals. Her two golds, won in doubles play, were earned with her older sister Gigi.

Selected championships and honors, singles: Bronze medal, Olympic Games, 1992. *Doubles:* Two gold medals, Olympic Games, 1992 and '96.

ALTHEA GIBSON b. August 25, 1927, Silver, South Carolina

Almost everyone knows that Gibson was the first African-American tennis champion to win a grand slam event. Fewer people know that Gibson was also the first woman to take the mike and sing at her Wimbledon Ball. To enjoy that ball, Gibson had to overcome frustrating prejudices and limitations. As a child in Harlem, Gibson learned paddle tennis and won a New York City championship in her age group before moving on to tennis lessons. Barred from public courts because of her race, she was taken in by a well-off African-American doctor so she could practice on his private court. Initially she was barred from public competition as well. Playing in the all-black American Tennis Association, she won her first singles title in 1945 and won consecutive singles titles from 1947 through 1956. Her wins with the ATA and elsewhere should have secured an invitation to Forest Hills, but she was ignored until **Alice Marble** took up her cause in *American Lawn Tennis* magazine. Gibson broke the color barrier and took both the French and Italian titles in 1956. In 1957 she became the first black to win Wimbledon, as well as the first black to be named Associated Press Female Athlete of the Year. An extremely popular player with crowds, press, and her fellow players, Gibson's speed and height (5'10") gave her a tremendous reach, and her ability to return "impossible" shots added excitement to her powerful serve-and-volley game. In 1958 she signed with the Harlem Globetrotters to play exhibitions at half-time, and later she played golf professionally.

Selected championships and honors, singles: French Championship, 1956; two Wimbledon championships, 1956 and '57; two U.S. Opens, 1957 and '58. *Doubles:* Three Wimbledon championships, 1957–58. *Mixed doubles:* U.S. Open, 1957. Twice Associated Press Female Athlete of the Year, 1957 and '58; International Tennis Hall of Fame; International Women's Sports Hall of Fame.

EVONNE GOOLAGONG CAWLEY b. July 31, 1951, Griffith, New South Wales, Australia

Goolagong, a natural and graceful player, was seen as having an instinctive style by some and as untrained by others. During her second year of international competition she won a Wimbledon singles title, but she did not win another until 1980. In the interim she won four Australian and two Virginia Slims titles, married, and took time off to have a baby. Although she returned to competition the year after the birth of her second child, in 1981, she retired soon afterward. Popular with crowds at home and abroad, Australia's first great player of aboriginal ancestry was always interesting to watch, and especially noted for her restless, pacing "walkabouts" during matches.

Selected championships and honors, singles: Two Wimbledon championships, 1971 and '80; French Open, 1971; four Australian Opens, 1974–76 and '77. *Doubles:* Australian Open, 1971. Associated Press Female Athlete of the Year, 1971.

STEPHANIE (STEFFI) GRAF b. June 14, 1969, Bruhl, Germany

After observing Graf's game as a young teenager, **Billie Jean King** predicted that her speed, her power, and her keen tennis instinct would carry her to grand slam competition. King was right, and Graf won her first grand slam singles title, the French Open, in 1987. In 1988 she became the third woman in history to win a "true" grand slam, taking all four events in the same calender year. (**Maureen Connolly** and **Margaret Smith Court** preceded her.) The next year she won all but one of the events, losing the French Open to Mexico's **Arantxa Sanchez Vicario.** From 1987 through 1990, when **Monica Seles** began to dominate, Graf was the WTA's top-ranked player. The Graf-Seles rivalry was intolerable to at least one Graf "fan," who stabbed Seles and forced her out of competition for two years. The attacker didn't do Graf any favors. While she won several tournaments in Seles's absence, she missed her rival and the edge close competition gave her game. Through 1996 Graf had won a total of twenty grand slam singles titles and was second only to **Martina Navratilova** in career winnings, with earnings topping $17 million.

Selected championships and honors, singles: Four Australian Opens, 1988–90 and '94; five French Opens, 1987, '88, '93, '95, and '96; seven Wimbledon championships, 1988, '89, '91–93, '95, and '96; four U.S. Opens, 1988, '89, '93, and '95; gold medal, Olympic Games, 1988; silver medal, Olympic Games, 1992. Associated Press Female Athlete of the Year, 1989; twice United Press International Female Athlete of the Year, 1987 and '89.

DARLENE HARD b. January 6, 1936, Los Angeles, California

Hard once described herself as the "last of the amateurs," noting that her prize for winning the U.S. singles championship consisted of a plane ticket home. Though she won that event twice, and the French title once, her strong serve and inconsistent backhand made her more successful as a doubles player. With eight different partners, she took a total of thirteen doubles titles in grand slam tournaments. Her most amazing achievement may have been her U.S. doubles championship, which she won in 1969—five years after she'd retired from competition to become an instructor.

Selected championships and honors, singles: Two U.S. Opens, 1960 and '61; French Open, 1960. *Doubles:* Six U.S. Opens, 1958–62 and '69; four Wimbledon championships, 1957, '59, '60, and '63; three French Opens, 1955, '57, and '60. International Tennis Hall of Fame.

DORIS HART b. June 20, 1925, St. Louis, Missouri

She had a bad knee, left over from a serious childhood illness, and her mobility was permanently limited. All she knew about tennis was what she saw from her hospital window. But Hart began playing as a means of rehabilitation and made it all the way to the top. Despite her impaired mobility, Hart developed a full-court game and seamless style. Twice ranked number one (1954 and '55) and winner of six grand slam singles titles, Hart, with her excellent serve, also made a sparkling doubles partner. Most of her 25 grand slam doubles victories were won with Shirley Fry, though she also partnered with **Louise Brough Clapp** and others. A member of ten consecutive Wightman Cup teams, she lost only one match from 1946 and 1955. Her last full season of competition was 1956.

Selected championships and honors, singles: Australian Open, 1949. Two French Opens, 1950 and '52; Wimbledon championship, 1951; two U.S. Opens, 1954 and '55. *Doubles:* Four Wimbledon championships, 1947, 1951–53; five French Opens, 1948, 1950–53; Australian Open, 1950; four U.S. Opens, 1951–54. *Mixed doubles:* Six Wimbledon championships, 1951–56; five U.S. Opens, 1951–55. International Tennis Hall of Fame.

MARTINA HINGIS b. September 16, 1980, Kosice, Slovakia

It's no accident that her name is Martina—Hingis's mother, a coach, named her infant daughter after the game's number-one player, Martina Navratilova.

When Hingis was seven, the family moved to Switzerland to provide her with greater opportunities to develop her game. The investment paid off. At sixteen, Hingis became the youngest player ever to achieve a number-one ranking. Despite being named after Navratilova, Hingis's playing style more closely resembles Navratilova's career rival, Chris Evert—a game that succeeds on brains, strategy, and an ability to ferret out her opponent's weak spots rather than on individually brilliant shots. Another difference between the two Martinas—Hingis is known for her outspoken cockiness. Asked by a male reporter whether she was interested in dating any of the men on the pro tour, Hingis responded by asking the reporter if there were any women on the tour *he* was interested in.

Selected championships and honors, singles: Australian Open, 1997; U.S. Open, 1997. *Doubles:* Wimbledon, 1996; Australian Open, 1997.

HAZEL HOTCHKISS WIGHTMAN
b. December 20, 1886, Healdsburg, California; d. December 5, 1974

Hotchkiss won her first national singles title in 1909. Forty-five years later she won her last title, the seniors championships. In between, she won numerous singles, doubles, and mixed doubles titles and two Olympic gold medals in doubles and mixed doubles play, and she was the national squash champion in 1930. A staunch promoter of women's international tennis, she donated a trophy—the Wightman Cup— for international women's team competition.

Selected championships and honors, singles: Four U.S. Opens, 1909–11 and 1919. *Doubles:* Four U.S. Opens, 1909–11 and 1915; gold medal, Olympic Games, 1924. *Mixed doubles:* Four U.S. Opens, 1909–11 and 1915; gold medal, Olympic Games, 1924. International Tennis Hall of Fame; International Women's Sports Hall of Fame.

HELEN HULL JACOBS b. August 8, 1908,
Berkeley, California; d. December 27, 1988

Jacobs won five major singles championships and had a truly superior backhand drive, but today she's remembered for two far more personal aspects of the game—her longtime rivalry with **Helen Wills** and her daring in wearing shorts to Wimbledon in 1933. The rivalry with Wills began in the early 1920s and lasted until 1938. Though Jacobs was far more popular with crowds than the taciturn Wills, she seldom came away victorious. At their final meeting, at Wim-

bledon, Jacobs played to defeat with a torn Achilles tendon rather than default to her rival. Jacobs retired from competition in 1940.

Selected championships and honors, singles: Four U.S. Opens, 1932–35; Wimbledon championship, 1936. *Doubles:* Four U.S. Opens, 1932, '32, '34, and '35. *Mixed doubles:* U.S. Open, 1934. Associated Press Female Athlete of the Year, 1933; International Tennis Hall of Fame.

BILLIE JEAN KING. *See Billie Jean Moffitt King, below.*

SUZANNE LENGLEN b. May 24, 1899,
Compiègne, France; d. July 4, 1938

The grand diva of tennis, and one of the first female athletes to achieve superstar status, Lenglen was equally famous for three things: her temperament, her costumes, and her ability to get to balls that were seemingly out of reach. A wealthy but asthmatic child, Lenglen was encouraged to play by her father and won the first of five consecutive Wimbledon singles titles in 1919. Two years later, on her first trip to America, she claimed illness and defaulted when an exhibition match with **Molla Bjurstedt** was going against her. Lenglen became noted for such gestures, as she became noted for her highly athletic playing style. Crowds disliked her but were also fascinated by her and never failed to turn out to see her play. When she toured the country again in 1926, giving a series of exhibition matches with **Mary K. Browne** and other pros, she received top billing and was the highest paid member of the group. Lenglen was also a phenomenal doubles player and, with partner **Elizabeth Ryan,** won six Wimbledon titles. Lenglen died young, at age thirty-nine, of pernicious anemia.

Selected championships and honors, singles: Five Wimbledon championships, 1919–23; two French Open, 1925 and '26. *Doubles:* Six Wimbledon championships, 1919–23 and '25; two French Open, 1925 and '26. *Mixed doubles:* Three Wimbledon championships, 1920, '22, and '25; two French Open, 1925 and '26. International Tennis Hall of Fame; International Women's Sports Hall of Fame.

ALICE MARBLE b. September 28, 1913, Beckworth, California; d. December 13, 1990

Marble became the first strong serve-and-volley player in women's tennis by default—uncertain of her ground strokes, she sought to compensate by rushing the net. Although her career was initially hampered by a bout of tuberculosis, Marble recovered and began winning major tournaments in 1936. In the years leading up to World War II she was America's top female player, sweeping the U.S. singles, doubles, and mixed doubles titles three years running. After retiring from competition Marble became a coach, numbering among her pupils **Billie Jean King.**

Selected championships and honors, singles: Four U.S. Opens, 1936, 1938–40; Wimbledon championship, 1939. *Doubles:* Four U.S. Opens, 1937–40; two Wimbledon championships, 1938 and '39. *Mixed doubles:* Three U.S. Opens, 1938–40; three Wimbledon championships, 1937–39. Twice Associated Press Female Athlete of the Year, 1939 and '40; International Tennis Hall of Fame.

BILLIE JEAN MOFFITT KING b. November 22, 1943, Long Beach, California

Today she's known by her married name, but when she arrived on the scene to win her first Wimbledon doubles title at age seventeen, in 1961, the press referred to her as "Little Miss Moffitt." She won her first Wimbledon singles title five years later, the first of twelve career singles championships in grand slam competitions. On court King was a trendsetter, and her passionate, aggressive style of play became the prototype for contemporary women's tennis. It also helped attract thousands of new enthusiasts to the sport, and King's grand slam victories proved once and for all that women's tennis could hold its own as a televised sport. King was a key figure off the court as well as on, and a catalyst in women's sports. In the mid-1960s she spoke out against the thinly veiled hypocrisy of awarding "expense" money to "amateur" players. She spoke out just as loudly about the disparity between men's and women's prize money, and was instrumental in establishing a women's professional tour. A pioneer in the game itself and in the cause of women's sports in general, it was only fitting that King became the first female *Sports Illustrated* Sportsman of the Year, making the cover in 1972. In one of the most-watched matches in history, she challenged famous male chauvinist Bobby Riggs to a match and defeated him 6–4, 6–3, and 6–3. The event, which took place on September 20, 1973, drew a record crowd of 30,472 and was seen by 50 million television viewers. King's 1979 doubles victory at Wimbledon, won with **Martina Navratilova,** gave her a total of twenty Wimbledon titles—enough to break the record of **Elizabeth Ryan,** who, ironically, had died the day before at the age of eighty-seven. Shortly be-

fore her death, Ryan was asked to comment on the possibility of seeing her record fall. Her response: "Records are made to be broken. If mine has to go, I would like Billie Jean to have it, because she has so much guts."

Selected championships and honors, singles: Six Wimbledon championships, 1966–68, '72, '73, and '75; four U.S. Opens, 1967, '71, '72, and '74; Australian Open, 1967; French Open, 1972. *Doubles:* Ten Wimbledon championships, 1961, '62, '65, '67, '68, '70–73, '79; five U.S. Opens, 1964, '67, '74, '78, and '80. *Mixed doubles:* Four Wimbledon championships, 1967, '71, '73, and '74; four U.S. Opens, 1967, '71, '73, and '76. Twice Associated Press Female Athlete of the Year, 1967 and '73; *Sports Illustrated* Sportsman of the Year, 1972; International Tennis Hall of Fame; International Women's Sports Hall of Fame.

ELISABETH (BESSIE) MOORE b. March 5, 1876, Brooklyn, New York; d. January 22, 1959

Those who think of Victorian women as frail pastel violets, take note—Moore once played all five sets of a best-three-of-five match and repeated the feat the next day, winning both matches. Two of Moore's four national singles titles came before the 1902 switch to best two of three for women—a rule change she, and many other women of her era, deplored.

Selected championships and honors, singles: Four U.S. Opens, 1896, 1902, 1903, and 1905. *Doubles:* Two U.S. Opens, 1896 and 1903. *Mixed doubles:* Two U.S. Opens, 1902 and 1904. International Tennis Hall of Fame.

MARTINA NAVRATILOVA b. October 18, 1956, Prague, Czechoslovakia

As a child Navratilova had two passions—tennis and America. She ended up with both, and as an American became the winningest tennis champion of all time. No woman has earned more grand slam championships, more money, or more fame on court. None of it came easily. Neither especially tall nor naturally strong, Navratilova early on battled a tendency to gain weight and once, in a *60 Minutes* retrospective, described herself as "the great wide hope" of tennis. One of the first players to employ a personal trainer, she shed the weight and learned to lift weights and follow a regimented diet. One thing she couldn't shed was her glasses. Unable to accustom herself to contact lenses, Navratilova became one of the only players ever to take to the court in glasses. Another potential setback stemmed from a fundamental in-

FROM BASELINE TO FRONTLINE: THE WOMAN WHO PUT THE "PRO" IN WOMEN'S TENNIS

Say the name "Billie Jean King," and most people will respond, "Great tennis player." Few people think of King as whistle-blower, organizer, and pioneer in the struggle for equal pay for women. Yet King was all of these and deserves much of the credit for turning women's tennis into the high-powered, high-stakes game it is today.

King hit the big time in 1965, when she made it to the semifinals at Wimbledon. Despite this success, she had to keep her job as a tennis instructor to pay the rent. In those days, a top woman player might receive a plane ticket home and a free hotel stay, and nonwinners footed their own bills. In addition to being low-paying, the system was also ambiguous. Major events were for amateurs only, but top-ranked players were often funneled money under the guises of "expenses." No one talked about the arrangement until King came along. Flying in the face of the tennis establishment, she decried the arbitrary system that forced honest players to accept under-the-table money and provided male players with larger "expense accounts" than women. King's openness encouraged other players to talk about the situation as well. In the end, there was safety in numbers. The dissenters became too numerous to suspend, the exposure too public to endure. In 1967 major events abandoned the amateur-only policy and became opens, allowing pro and amateurs to compete equally.

King next took on the widespread inequality in men's and women's prize money. A measure of the disparity can be seen in King's own history. In 1968, as Wimbledon singles champion, King received less than $3,000, while the men's champ, Rod Laver, earned $8,000. The next year, she won $600 for winning the Italian Open, while her male counterpart scooped up $3,500. To be officially ranked as a "pro" player was one thing. To earn a living at it was another. In the late 1960s King began working to establish a legitimate pro tour. She persuaded Virginia Slims to sponsor an event and convinced several other players to skip a regular U.S. Lawn Tennis Association event to participate. In 1970 the Virginia Slims Circuit was officially born, with nine women signing symbolic contracts. The nine included Americans King and Rosie Casals as well as Peaches Bartkowitz, Julie Heldman, Kristy Pigeon, Nancy Richie, and Val Zeigenfuss. Two Australian women, Judy Dalton and Kerry Melville, also signed on. Threatened with suspension, the original nine signed on at the risk of their careers. If the venture failed, they might never be permitted to play in grand slam events again. Once again, the establishment lost. King and her cohorts kept playing, and by 1971 the Virginia Slims tour included just shy of thirty events, each worth at least $10,000 in prize money. By 1973 sixty women had signed on to the tour. Over the years, the idea of a pro circuit has become commonplace. All of the once-amateur grand slam events are part of today's dominant circuit, the Corel WTA Tour, which includes sixty events around the world and provides more than 500 women from forty-five countries with opportunities to play for prize money. It's no wonder that the woman who started it all, Billie Jean King, was named one of the 100 most influential Americans of the twentieth century by *Life* magazine in 1989.

ability to hide her personal life. In her autobiography, written with George Vecsey, Navratilova explains that she didn't set out to pioneer for gay rights, it simply didn't occur to her to lie. Although her openness created an initial furor, it died down in the face of her overwhelming popularity. A national champion in her native country, Navratilova defected to the United States in 1975, during the U.S. Open, and became a citizen in 1981. The move was motivated by her feeling that she could not develop under the control of the Czech government, and she credits the United States with providing her the freedom and opportunity to reach her full potential. The potential was realized. In all, Navratilova won fifty-four titles in grand

> My game was rushing the net, playing aggressively, playing for fun, playing to win. My father encouraged it and so did my coach, and the freedom and intensity they endorsed led me to a lot of other choices in my life. I grew up hearing my parents and my coach tell me: "Go for it." And that's exactly what I've done.
>
> —In *Martina*, by Martina Navratilova with George Vecsey

slam singles, doubles, and mixed doubles play. She was the world's number-one-ranked female player in 1978 and '79 and from 1982 to 1986, and she still ranks as the all-time top women's money player, with winnings of over $20 million. A left-handed player who wore down opponents with her aggressive serve-and-volley game, Navratilova made women's tennis more athletic and more dynamic. Her memorable showdowns with **Chris Evert** gained attention for the sport and provided fans with some of the best tennis in history. The two first met at a match in Akron, Ohio, in 1973. Although Navratilova lost that one, she came back to win ten of their fourteen grand slam finals duels. Like her predecessor, **Billie Jean King,** Navratilova has been a tireless champion of women's sports, and she was instrumental in the establishment of the Women's Sports Foundation. Navratilova retired in November 1994 and now spends much of her time at her home in Aspen, Colorado. She is still a tireless promoter of women's sports and donates large amounts of money and personal time to charitable causes.

Selected championships and honors, singles: Eight Wimbledon championships, 1978, '79, '82–87, and '90; three Australian Opens, 1981, '83, and '85; two French Opens, 1982 and '84; four U.S. Opens, 1983, '84, '86, and '87. *Doubles:* Seven Wimbledon championships, 1976, '79, '81–84, and '86, eight Australian Opens, 1980, '82–85, and '87–89; seven French Opens, 1975, '82, and '84–88; nine U.S. Opens, 1977, '78, '80, '83, '84, '86, '87, '89, and '90. *Mixed doubles:* Wimbledon championship, 1985; two French Opens, 1974 and '85; two U.S. Opens, 1985 and '87. Twice Associated Press Female Athlete of the Year, 1983 and '86; United Press Female Athlete of the Year, 1983; International Women's Sports Hall of Fame.

MARGARET OSBORNE DUPONT b. March 4, 1918, Joseph, Oregon

If Osborne hadn't been famous as a doubles champion, she would have been remembered anyway—as a six-time winner in grand slam singles tournaments. On court, Osborne was an excellent volleyer who also had a walloping backhand smash. Her most memorable moments came when she partnered with friend **Louise Brough** to become one of the most successful doubles teams in history. In the fifteen years between 1942 and 1957, they won twenty grand slam doubles titles together. Osborne also won numerous mixed doubles championships, teaming with Bill Tilden and others.

Selected championships and honors, singles: Three U.S. Opens, 1948–50; Wimbledon championship, 1947; two French Opens, 1946 and '49. *Doubles:* Five Wimbledon championships, 1946, '48–50, and '54; fourteen U.S. Opens, 1941–50 and '55–58; Three French Opens, 1946, '47, and '49. *Mixed doubles:* Nine U.S. Opens, 1943–46, '50, '56, and '58–60; Wimbledon championship, 1952. International Tennis Hall of Fame.

SARAH PALFREY COOKE FABYAN b. September 18, 1912, Sharon, Massachusetts

Palfrey won several U.S. titles, but her international success lay in her doubles and mixed doubles play. Each of her mixed doubles titles was won with a different partner, while in doubles play she teamed with **Helen Hull Jacobs,** Betty Nuthall, and **Alice Marble.** Marble was her most successful partner, and together the pair won two Wimbledon and four U.S. doubles titles.

Selected championships and honors, doubles: Two Wimbledon championships, 1938 and '39; nine U.S. Opens, 1930, '32, '34, '35, and '37–41.

ELIZABETH (BUNNY) RYAN b. February 5, 1891, Anaheim, California; d. July 6, 1979

Ryan won nineteen Wimbledon championships, yet few people know her name. The reason may be that Ryan's major victories *all* came in doubles and mixed doubles play, and she had no grand slam singles championships to her credit. Nevertheless, Ryan is known by aficionados as one of the greatest women doubles players in history, and her string of Wimbledon victories stood as a record for forty-five years, until **Billie Jean King** broke it in 1979. Ryan, who once said she didn't want to live to see her record broken, died one day before King's twentieth victory.

That would have been fine with Ryan, who also said that, if her record was going to be broken, she hoped it would fall to Billie Jean.

Selected championships and honors, doubles: Twelve Wimbledon championships, 1914, '19–24, '25–27, '30, '33, and '34; four French Opens, 1930, '32–34. U.S. Open, 1926. *Mixed doubles:* Seven Wimbledon championships, 1919, '21, '23, '27, '28, '30, and '32; U.S. Open, 1933. International Tennis Hall of Fame.

GABRIELA SABATINI b. May 16, 1970, Buenos Aires, Argentina

Sabatini turned pro when she was just fifteen, and though some warned she would soon burn out, she didn't. Instead, she won the U.S. Open at twenty. Her greatest success has been at the Italian Open, where she holds four singles titles. Sabatini also won the Virginia Slims in 1988 and '94. Sabatini announced her retirement in the fall of 1996.

Selected championships and honors, singles: silver medal, Olympic Games, 1988; U.S. Open, 1990.

ARANTXA SANCHEZ VICARIO b. December 18, 1971, Barcelona, Spain

Sanchez's ill luck has been to compete against not one but two superb rivals—**Steffi Graf** and **Monica Seles**—and often to come off the worse for wear. Few players of her caliber have been grand slam runners-up as often. Nevertheless, Sanchez is clearly ranked as one of the best singles and doubles players of her day. In 1995 she became the first woman since **Martina Navratilova** (1987) to hold number-one rankings in singles and doubles play simultaneously.

Selected championships and honors, singles: Two French Opens, 1989 and '94; U.S. Open, 1994; bronze medal, Olympic Games, 1992; silver medal, Olympic Games, 1996. *Doubles:* Two U.S. Opens, 1993 and '94; Wimbledon championship, 1995; two Australian Opens, 1992 and '95.

ELEANORA SEARS b. September 28, 1881, Boston, Massachusetts; d. March 26, 1968

Sears, a society debutante, was one of the great all-round athletes in history. The sports at which she excelled included equestrian events, golf, swimming, tennis, squash, yachting, and long-distance walking. Of the many sports she pursued over the course of her lifetime, the two about which she was most passionate were squash and tennis. She won a national squash title in 1928, when she was forty-six years old. In tennis, she won several titles in doubles and mixed

doubles competition, and her partners included **Hazel Hotchkiss Wightman** and **Molla Bjurstedt Mallory.**

Selected championships and honors, doubles: Three U.S. Opens, 1911, '16, and '17. *Mixed doubles:* U.S. Open, 1916.

MONICA SELES b. December 2, 1973, Novi Sad, Yugoslavia

The left-handed Seles began playing at seven-and-a-half and, at training camp, was so aggressive she played against boys because other girls were afraid to compete with her. Trained by her father and possessed of an unorthodox but highly effective two-handed forehand and backhand, she turned pro in 1987 and vaulted to international attention in 1990 when she won the French, Virginia Slims, Italian, and German Opens in a single season. In both 1991 and '92 she won three of four grand slam events, losing Wimbledon both times to rival **Steffi Graf.** On April 30, 1993, during a changeover at a tournament in Hamburg, Germany, an unemployed, thirty-eight-year-old Graf fan emerged from the crowd and stabbed Seles—then ranked number one—in the back. His aim, he later told police, was to clear the way for Graf. Though the physical wound healed, the psychological wound lingered. Seles dropped out of the tour and did not return to play until 1995. In the interim she became a U.S. citizen and was cheered enthusiastically when she returned to her new home court as a finalist in the 1995 U.S. Open.

Selected championships and honors, singles: Three French Opens, 1990–92; two U.S. Opens, 1991 and '92; two Australian Opens, 1991 and '92. Twice Associated Press Female Athlete of the Year, 1991 and '92; United Press International Female Athlete of the Year, 1991 and '92.

PAM SHRIVER b. July 4, 1962, Baltimore, Maryland

Shriver's career as a singles player was overshadowed by two obstacles: a shoulder injury and **Martina Navratilova.** But in doubles play Navratilova became an ally, and the two formed a nearly unbeatable pair. In 1984 they became the first women's pair to win the grand slam doubles championships in succession. Shriver, whose consistency and powerful serve have made her an ideal doubles player, has also won grand slam titles with Natasha Zvereva and an Olympic gold with Zina Garrison.

Selected championships and honors, doubles: Five Wimbledon championships, 1981–84 and '86; seven

Australian Opens, 1982–85 and '87–89; five U.S. Opens, 1983, '84, '86, '87, and '91; four French Opens, 1984, '85, '87, and '88; gold medal, Olympic Games, 1988.

MARGARET SMITH COURT b. July 16, 1942, Albury, Australia

Critics had a lot to say about Smith. She choked under pressure. She played a competent but uninspired game. She didn't belong in the ethereal ranks of the truly great. The records tell a different story. Between 1960 and 1973, Smith won 26 grand slam singles titles—more than any woman before or since. She also took 21 doubles and 19 mixed doubles championships to lead the all-time grand slam titles roster with an aggregate of 66. In 1966 Smith married Barry Court, a world-class sailor, and retired from competition. Two years and one child later, Court coaxed her out of retirement and became her manager. In 1962 and '65 Smith had come maddeningly close to a grand slam, winning three of the four events. In 1970 she achieved the long-deferred goal, winning in a 46-game final against **Billie Jean King,** the longest in Wimbledon history. Of the countless winning matches Smith played, many people remember her for a single defeat—an exhibition match against fifty-five-year-old Bobby Riggs, played on Mother's Day, 1973. Smith's defeat and Riggs's surfeit of ego prompted Billie Jean King to challenge Riggs (and beat him) later that year. In fairness to Smith's critics, she did succumb to anxiety under pressure, and her style lacked the distinctive flair that makes a player easily memorable. Nevertheless, she had the basics needed of a champion—courage, strength, speed, and unerring coordination.

Selected championships and honors, singles: Eleven Australian Opens, 1960–66, '69–71, and '73; five French Opens, 1962, '64, '69, '70, and '73; three Wimbledon championships, 1963, '65, and '70; five U.S. Opens, 1962, '65, '69, '70, and '73. *Doubles:* Eight Australian Opens, 1961–63, '65, '69–71, and '73; two Wimbledon championships, 1964 and '69; three French Opens, 1964–66; six U.S. Opens, 1963, '68–70, '73, and '75. *Mixed doubles:* Two Australian Opens, 1963–64; four Wimbledon championships, 1963, '65, '66, and '68; four French Opens, 1963–65 and '69; two U.S. Opens, 1969 and '70. International Tennis Hall of Fame; International Women's Sports Hall of Fame.

MAY SUTTON BUNDY b. September 25, 1887, Plymouth, England; d. October 23, 1975

Though born in England, Sutton was raised in California and, with her four sisters, dominated the local tennis scene. The youngest of the Sutton girls, she was also the most talented and the most passionate about the game. On the court, Sutton's assets lay in swiftness, a strong forehand, and a willingness to defy "ladylike" conventions. Sutton didn't hesitate to rush the net, just as she didn't hesitate to literally roll up her sleeves to gain more freedom of movement. She won U.S. singles and doubles titles in 1904 and the next year won the first of two Wimbledon titles, becoming the first American—male or female—to do so. *Selected championships and honors, singles:* Two Wimbledon championships, 1905 and 1907. International Tennis Hall of Fame.

ORA WASHINGTON b. 1898, Philadelphia, Pennsylvania; d. 1971

Washington may be the greatest unknown athlete of all time. An African-American who played in an era when racial discrimination was the norm, Washington was so good at tennis she finally retired for fear of discouraging younger players who were reluctant to play against her. In the all-black American Tennis Association, she won nine singles championships and seven straight doubles titles. She was also a standout at basketball, and played eighteen seasons with the *Philadelphia Tribune* team, a barnstorming squad that toured the country, taking on—and usually beating—all challengers. Since women's sports were hardly a paying profession at the time, Washington worked in domestic service and eventually purchased an apartment building with her savings. A resident of Germantown, Pennsylvania, she was locally famous for giving free clinics and coaching help to youngsters interested in tennis. *Selected championships and honors, singles:* Nine ATA championships, 1924, 1929–35, and 1937.

HELEN WILLS MOODY b. October 6, 1905, Centerville, California

By the time she was fourteen, Wills was good enough to beat her father. By the time she was sixteen, she made it to the U.S. finals. She didn't win that time, but she did the next year—1923. In all, Wills won seven U.S., eight Wimbledon, and four French singles titles. Her total of nineteen singles victories in grand slam events makes her second only to **Margaret Smith Court.** Because she did not smile when she played, Wills was dubbed "Little Miss Poker Face" by the press. Unfazed, Wills pointed out that it wasn't that she didn't enjoy playing, it was simply that she became completely absorbed in the game. Wills applied the same powers of concentration to academic study, graduating from Stanford Phi Beta Kappa. Moody played her last major tournament in 1938, when she defeated longtime rival **Helen Hull Jacobs** at Wimbledon.

Selected championships and honors, singles: Seven U.S. Opens, 1923–25, '27–29, and '31; eight Wimbledon championships, 1927–30, '32, '33, '35, and '38; four French Opens, 1928–30 and 1932; gold medal, Olympic Games, 1924. International Tennis Hall of Fame.

Tennis

U.S. Open Singles

Year	Winner	Finalist
1887*	Ellen Hansell	Laura Knight
1888	Bertha L. Townsend	Ellen Hansell
1889	Bertha L. Townsend	Louise Voorhes
1890	Ellen C. Roosevelt	Bertha L. Townsend
1891	Mabel Cahill	Ellen C. Roosevelt
1892	Mabel Cahill	Elizabeth Moore
1893	Aline Terry	Alice Schultze
1894	Helen Hellwig	Aline Terry
1895	Juliette Atkinson	Helen Hellwig
1896	Elizabeth Moore	Juliette Atkinson
1897	Juliette Atkinson	Elizabeth Moore
1898	Juliette Atkinson	Marion Jones
1899	Marion Jones	Maud Banks
1900	Myrtle McAteer	Edith Parker
1901	Elizabeth Moore	Myrtle McAteer
1902†	Marion Jones	Elizabeth Moore
1903	Elizabeth Moore	Marion Jones
1904	May Sutton	Elizabeth Moore
1905	Elizabeth Moore	Helen Homans
1906	Helen Homans	Maud Barger-Wallach
1907	Evelyn Sears	Carrie Neely
1908	Maud Barger-Wallach	Evelyn Sears
1909	Hazel Hotchkiss	Maud Barger-Wallach
1910	Hazel Hotchkiss	Louise Hammond
1911	Hazel Hotchkiss	Florence Sutton
1912	Mary Browne	Eleanora Sears
1913	Mary Browne	Dorothy Green
1914	Mary Browne	Marie Wagner
1915	Molla Bjurstedt	Hazel Hotchkiss Wightman
1916	Molla Bjurstedt	Louise Hammond Raymond
1917	Molla Bjurstedt	Marion Vanderhoef
1918	Molla Bjurstedt	Eleanor Goss
1919	Hazel Hotchkiss Wightman	Marion Zinderstein
1920	Molla Bjurstedt Mallory	Marion Zinderstein
1921	Molla Bjurstedt Mallory	Mary Browne
1922	Molla Bjurstedt Mallory	Helen Wills
1923	Helen Wills	Molla Bjurstedt Mallory
1924	Helen Wills	Molla Bjurstedt Mallory
1925	Helen Wills	Kathleen McKane
1926	Molla Bjurstedt Mallory	Elizabeth Ryan
1927	Helen Wills	Betty Nuthall
1928	Helen Wills	Helen Jacobs
1929	Helen Wills	Phoebe Holcroft Watson
1930	Betty Nuthall	Anna McCune Harper
1931	Helen Wills Moody	Eileen Whitingstall
1932	Helen Jacobs	Carolin Babcock
1933	Helen Jacobs	Helen Wills Moody
1934	Helen Jacobs	Sarah Palfrey
1935	Helen Jacobs	Sarah Palfrey Fabyan
1936	Alice Marble	Helen Jacobs
1937	Anita Lizane	Jadwiga Jedrzejowska
1938	Alice Marble	Nancye Wynne
1939	Alice Marble	Helen Jacobs
1940	Alice Marble	Helen Jacobs
1941	Sarah Palfrey Cooke	Pauline Betz
1942	Pauline Betz	Louise Brough
1943	Pauline Betz	Louise Brough
1944	Pauline Betz	Margaret Osborne
1945	Sarah Palfrey Cooke	Pauline Betz
1946	Pauline Betz	Patricia Canning
1947	Louise Brough	Margaret Osborne
1948	Margaret Osborne duPont	Louise Brough
1949	Margaret Osborne duPont	Doris Hart

Tennis (continued)

U.S. Open Singles

Year	Winner	Finalist
1950	Margaret Osborne duPont	Doris Hart
1951	Maureen Connolly	Shirley Fry
1952	Maureen Connolly	Doris Hart
1953	Maureen Connolly	Doris Hart
1954	Doris Hart	Louise Brough
1955	Doris Hart	Patricia Ward
1956	Shirley Fry	Althea Gibson
1957	Althea Gibson	Louise Brough
1958	Althea Gibson	Darlene Hard
1959	Maria Bueno	Christine Truman
1960	Darlene Hard	Maria Bueno
1961	Darlene Hard	Ann Haydon
1962	Margaret Smith	Darlene Hard
1963	Maria Bueno	Margaret Smith
1964	Maria Bueno	Carole Graebner
1965	Margaret Smith	Billie Jean Moffitt
1966	Maria Bueno	Nancy Richey
1967	Billie Jean King	Ann Haydon Jones
1968‡	Virginia Wade	Billie Jean King
1969	Margaret Smith Court	Nancy Richey
1970	Margaret Smith Court	Rosie Casals
1971	Billie Jean King	Rosie Casals
1972	Billie Jean King	Kerry Melville
1973	Margaret Smith Court	Evonne Goolagong
1974	Billie Jean King	Evonne Goolagong
1975	Chris Evert	Evonne Goolagong Cawley
1976	Chris Evert	Evonne Goolagong Cawley
1977	Chris Evert	Wendy Turnbull
1978	Chris Evert	Pam Shriver
1979	Tracy Austin	Chris Evert Lloyd
1980	Chris Evert Lloyd	Hana Mandlikova
1981	Tracy Austin	Martina Navratilova
1982	Chris Evert Lloyd	Hana Mandlikova
1983	Martina Navratilova	Chris Evert Lloyd
1984	Martina Navratilova	Chris Evert Lloyd
1985	Hana Mandlikova	Martina Navratilova
1986	Martina Navratilova	Helena Sukova
1987	Martina Navratilova	Steffi Graf
1988	Steffi Graf	Gabriela Sabatini
1989	Steffi Graf	Martina Navratilova
1990	Gabriela Sabatini	Steffi Graf
1991	Monica Seles	Martina Navratilova
1992	Monica Seles	Arantxa Sanchez Vicario
1993	Steffi Graf	Helena Sukova
1994	Arantxa Sanchez Vicario	Steffi Graf
1995	Steffi Graf	Monica Seles
1996	Steffi Graf	Monica Seles

*Results determined by challenge round play.

†Five-set final is abolished.

‡Became open championships (amateurs and professionals).

U.S. Open Doubles

Year	Winners	Finalists
1889	Margarette L. Ballard/Bertha L. Townsend	M. Wright/Laura Knight
1890	Ellen C. Roosevelt/Grace W. Roosevelt	Bertha L. Townsend/Margarette L. Ballard
1891	Mabel Cahill/W. F. Morgan	Grace W. Roosevelt/Ellen C. Roosevelt
1892	Mabel Cahill/A. M. McKinly	A. H. Harris/Amy R. Williams
1893	Aline Terry/Hattie Butler	Alice L. Schultz/Stone
1894	Helen Helwig/Juliette Atkinson	A. C. Wistar/Amy R. Williams
1895	Helen Helwig/Juliette Atkinson	Elizabeth H. Moore/Amy R. Williams
1896	Elizabeth Moore/Juliette Atkinson	A. C. Wistar/Amy R. Williams
1897	Juliette Atkinson/Kathleen Atkinson	F. Edwards/E. J. Rastall
1898	Juliette Atkinson/Kathleen Atkinson	Marie Wiemer/Carrie B. Neely
1899	Jane Craven/Myrtle McAteer	Maud Banks/Elizabeth J. Rastal
1900	Edith Parker/Hallie Champlin	Marie Wiemer/Myrtle McAteer
1901	Juliette Atkinson/Myrtle McAteer	Marion Jones/Elizabeth H. Moore
1902*	Juliette Atkinson/Marion Jones	Maud Banks/Nona Closterman

Tennis (continued)

U.S. Open Doubles

Year	Winners	Finalists
1903	Elizabeth Moore/Carrie B. Neely	Miriam Hall/Marion Jones
1904[†]	May G. Sutton/Miriam Hall	Elizabeth H. Moore/Carrie B. Neely
1905	Helen Homans/Carrie B. Neely	M. F. Oberteuffer/Virginia Maule
1906	Mrs. L. S. Coe/Mrs. D. S. Platt	Helen Homans/Clover Boldt
1907	Marie Wiemer/Carrie B. Neely	Edna Wildey/Natalie Wildey
1908	Evelyn Sears/Margaret Curtis	Carrie B. Neely/Marion Steever
1909	Hazel Hotchkiss/Edith Rotch	Dorothy Green/Lois Moyes
1910	Hazel Hotchkiss/Edith Rotch	Adelaide Browning/Edna Wildey
1911	Hazel Hotchkiss/Eleanora Sears	Dorothy Green/Florence Sutton
1912	Dorothy Green/Mary Browne	Maud Barger-Wallach/Mrs. Frederick Schmitz
1913	Mary Browne/Mrs. R. H. Williams	Dorothy Green/Edna Wildey
1914	Mary Browne/Mrs. R. H. Williams	Louise H. Raymond/Edna Wildey
1915	Hazel Hotchkiss Wightman/Eleanora Sears	Helen H. McLean/Mrs. G. L. Chapman
1916	Molla Bjurstedt/Eleanora Sears	Louise H. Raymond/Edna Wildey
1917	Molla Bjurstedt/Eleanora Sears	Phyllis Walsh/Mrs. Robert Leroy
1918	Marion Zinderstein/Eleanor Gross	Molla Bjurstedt/Mrs. Johan Rogge
1919	Marion Zinderstein/Eleanor Gross	Eleanora Sears/Hazel H. Wightman
1920	Marion Zinderstein/Eleanor Gross	Eleanor Tennant/Helen Baker
1921	Mary Browne/Mrs. R. H. Williams	Helen Gilleaudeau/Mrs. L. G. Morris
1922	Marion Zinderstein Jessup/Helen Wills	Edith Sigourney/Molla B. Mallory
1923	Kathleen McKane/Phyllis Covell	Hazel H. Wightman/Eleanor Goss
1924	Hazel Hotchkiss Wightman/Helen Wills	Eleanor Goss/Marion Z. Jessup
1925	Mary Browne/Helen Wills	May S. Bundy/Elizabeth Ryan
1926	Elizabeth Ryan/Eleanor Goss	Mary K. Browne/Charlotte H. Chapin
1927	Kathleen McKane Godfree/Ermyntrude Harvey	Betty Nuthall/Joan Fry
1928	Hazel Hotchkiss Wightman/Helen Wills	Edith Cross/Anna McCune Harper
1929	Phoebe Watson/Peggy Saunders Michell	Phyllis Covell/Mrs. D. C. Shepherd-Barron
1930	Betty Nuthall/Sarah Palfrey	Edith Cross/Anna McCune Harper
1931	Betty Nuthall/Eileen Fearnly Whitingstall	Helen Jacobs/Dorothy Round
1932	Helen Jacobs/Sarah Palfrey	Edith Cross/Anna McCune Harper
1933	Betty Nuthall/Freda James	Helen Wills Moody/Elizabeth Ryan
1934	Helen Jacobs/Sarah Palfrey Fabyan	Carolin A. Babcock/Dorothy Andrus
1935	Helen Jacobs/Sarah Palfrey Fabyan	Carolin A. Babcock/Dorothy Andrus
1936	Marjorie Gladman Van Ryn/Carolin A. Babcock	Helen Jacobs/Sarah Palfrey Fabyan
1937	Sarah Palfrey Fabyan/Alice Marble	Marjorie G. Van Ryn/Carolin A. Babcock
1938	Sarah Palfrey Fabyan/Alice Marble	Rene Mathieu/Jadwiga Jedrzejowska
1939	Sarah Palfrey Fabyan/Alice Marble	Kay Stammers/Freda Hammersley
1940	Sarah Palfrey Fabyan/Alice Marble	Dorothy Bundy/Marjorie G. Van Ryn
1941	Sarah Palfrey Fabyan/Margaret Osborne	Dorothy Bundy/Pauline Betz
1942	Louise Brough/Margaret Osborne	Pauline Betz/Doris Hart
1943	Louise Brough/Margaret Osborne	Patricia C. Todd/Mary A. Prentiss
1944	Louise Brough/Margaret Osborne	Pauline Betz/Doris Hart
1945	Louise Brough/Margaret Osborne	Pauline Betz/Doris Hart
1946	Louise Brough/Margaret Osborne	Patricia C. Todd/Mary A. Prentiss
1947	Louise Brough/Margaret Osborne	Patricia C. Todd/Doris Hart
1948	Louise Brough/Margaret Osborne	Patricia C. Todd/Doris Hart
1949	Louise Brough/Margaret Osborne	Doris Hart/Shirley Fry
1950	Louise Brough/Margaret Osborne	Doris Hart/Shirley Fry
1951	Shirley Fry/Doris Hart	Nancy Chaffee/Patricia C. Todd
1952	Shirley Fry/Doris Hart	Louise Brough/Maureen Connolly

Tennis (continued)

U.S. Open Doubles

Year	Winners	Finalists
1953	Shirley Fry/Doris Hart	Louise Brough/Margaret Osborne duPont
1954	Shirley Fry/Doris Hart	Louise Brough/Margaret Osborne duPont
1955	Louise Brough/Margaret Osborne duPont	Doris Hart/Shirley Fry
1956	Louise Brough/Margaret Osborne duPont	Betty R. Pratt/Shirley Fry
1957	Louise Brough/Margaret Osborne duPont	Althea Gibson/Darlene Hard
1958	Jeanne Arth/Darlene Hard	Althea Gibson/Maria Bueno
1959	Jeanne Arth/Darlene Hard	Maria Bueno/Sally Moore
1960	Maria Bueno/Darlene Hard	Ann Haydon/Deidre Catt
1961	Darlene Hard/Lesley Turner	Edda Buding/Yola Ramirez
1962	Maria Bueno/Darlene Hard	Karen Hantze Susman/Billie Jean Moffitt
1963	Robyn Ebbern/Margaret Smith	Darlene Hard/Maria Bueno
1964	Billie Jean Moffitt/Karen Hantze Susman	Margaret Smith/Lesley Turner
1965	Carole Graebner/Nancy Richey	Billie Jean Moffitt/Karen Hantze Susman
1966	Maria Bueno/Nancy Richey	Rosemary Casals/Billie Jean King
1967	Rosemary Casals/Billie Jean King	Mary Ann Eisel/Donna Floyd Fales
1968[‡]	Maria Bueno/Margaret Smith Court	Rosemary Casals/Billie Jean King
1969	Francoise Durr/Darlene Hard	Margaret Smith Court/Virginia Wade
1970	Margaret Smith Court/Judy Tegart Dalton	Rosemary Casals/Virginia Wade
1971	Rosemary Casals/Judy Tegart Dalton	Gail Chanfreau/Francoise Durr
1972	Francoise Durr/Betty Stove	Margaret Smith Court/Virginia Wade
1973	Margaret Smith Court/Virginia Wade	Rosemary Casals/Billie Jean King
1974	Rosemary Casals/Billie Jean King	Francoise Durr/Betty Stove
1975	Margaret Smith Court/Virginia Wade	Rosemary Casals/Billie Jean King
1976	Delina Bosnoff/Ilana Kloss	Olgo Morozova/Virginia Wade
1977	Martina Navratilova/Betty Stove	Renee Richards/Bettyann Stuart
1978	Billie Jean King/Martina Navratilova	Kerry M. Reid/Wendy Turnbull
1979	Betty Stove/Wendy Turnbull	Billie Jean King/Martina Navratilova
1980	Billie Jean King/Martina Navratilova	Pam Shriver/Betty Stove
1981	Kathy Jordan/Anne Smith	Rosemary Casals/Wendy Turnbull
1982	Rosemary Casals/Wendy Turnbull	Sharon Walsh-Pete/Barbara Potter
1983	Martina Navratilova/Pam Shriver	Rosalyn Fairbank/Candy Reynolds
1984	Martina Navratilova/Pam Shriver	Anne Hobbs/Wendy Turnbull
1985	Claudia Kohde-Kilsch/Helena Sukova	Martina Navratilova/Pam Shriver
1986	Martina Navratilova/Pam Shriver	Hana Mandlikova/Wendy Turnbull
1987	Martina Navratilova/Pam Shriver	Kathy Jordan/Elizabeth Smylie
1988	Gigi Fernandez/Robin White	Patty Fendick/Jill Hetherington
1989	Hana Mandlikova/Martina Navratilova	Mary Joe Fernandez/Pam Shriver
1990	Gigi Fernandez/Martina Navratilova	Jana Novotna/Helena Sukova
1991	Pam Shriver/Natasha Zvereva	Jana Novotna/Larisa Neiland
1992	Gigi Fernandez/Natasha Zvereva	Jana Novotna/Larisa Neiland
1993	Arantxa Sanchez Vicario/Helena Sukova	Amanda Coetzer/Ines Gorrochategui
1994	Jana Novotna/Arantxa Sanchez Vicario	Katarina Maleeva/Robin White
1995	Gigi Fernandez/Natasha Zvereva	Schultz-McCarthy/Stubbs
1996	Gigi Fernandez/Natasha Zvereva	Arantxa Sanchez Vicario/Jana Novotna

*Five-set final is abolished.

[†]There is some doubt about the accuracy of this result.

[‡]Became open championships (amateurs and professionals).

Tennis (continued)

Wimbledon Singles

Year	Winner	Finalist
1884*	Maud Watson	Lilian Watson
1885	Maud Watson	Blanche Bingley
1886	Blanche Bingley	Maud Watson
1887	Charlotte Dod	Blanche Bingley
1888	Charlotte Dod	Blanche Bingley Hillyard
1889	Blanche Bingley Hillyard	Lena Rice
1890	Lena Rice	M. Jacks
1891	Charlotte Dod	Blanche Hillyard
1892	Charlotte Dod	Blanche Hillyard
1893	Charlotte Dod	Blanche Hillyard
1894	Blanche Hillyard	E. Austin
1895	Charlotte Cooper	H. Jackson
1896	Charlotte Cooper	Mrs. W. H. Pickering
1897	Blanche Hillyard	Charlotte Cooper
1898	Charlotte Cooper	M. Martin
1899	Blanche Hillyard	Charlotte Cooper
1900	Blanche Hillyard	Charlotte Cooper
1901	Charlotte Cooper Sterry	Blanche Hillyard
1902	Muriel Robb	Charlotte Sterry
1903	Dorothea Douglass	E. Thomson
1904	Dorothea Douglass	Charlotte Sterry
1905	May Sutton	Dorothea Douglass
1906	Dorothea Douglass	May Sutton
1907	May Sutton	Dorothea Douglass Lambert Chambers
1908	Charlotte Sterry	A. Morton
1909	Dora Boothby	A. Morton
1910	Dorothea Lambert Chambers	Dora Boothby
1911	Dorothea Lambert Chambers	Dora Boothby
1912	Ethel Larcombe	A. Sterry
1913	Dorothea Lambert Chambers	Mrs. McNair
1914	Dorothea Lambert Chambers	Ethel Larcombe
1915–18	not held	
1919	Suzanne Lenglen	Dorothea Lambert Chambers
1920	Suzanne Lenglen	Dorothea Lambert Chambers
1921	Suzanne Lenglen	Elizabeth Ryan
1922†	Suzanne Lenglen	Molla Mallory
1923	Suzanne Lenglen	Kathleen McKane
1924	Kathleen McKane	Helen Wills
1925	Suzanne Lenglen	Joan Fry
1926	Kathleen McKane Godfree	Lili de Alvarez
1927	Helen Wills	Lili de Alvarez
1928	Helen Wills	Lili de Alvarez
1929	Helen Wills	Helen Jacobs
1930	Helen Wills Moody	Elizabeth Ryan
1931	Cilly Aussem	Hilde Kranwinkel
1932	Helen Wills Moody	Helen Jacobs
1933	Helen Wills Moody	Dorothy Round
1934	Dorothy Round	Helen Jacobs
1935	Helen Wills Moody	Helen Jacobs
1936	Helen Jacobs	Hilde Kranwinkel Sperling
1937	Dorothy Round	Jadwiga Jedrzejowska
1938	Helen Wills Moody	Helen Jacobs
1939	Alice Marble	Kay Stammers
1940–45	not held	
1946	Pauline Betz	Louise Brough
1947	Margaret Osborne	Doris Hart
1948	Louise Brough	Doris Hart
1949	Louise Brough	Margaret Osborne duPont
1950	Louise Brough	Margaret duPont
1951	Doris Hart	Shirley Fry
1952	Maureen Connolly	Louise Brough
1953	Maureen Connolly	Doris Hart
1954	Maureen Connolly	Louise Brough
1955	Louise Brough	Beverly Fleitz
1956	Shirley Fry	Angela Buxton
1957	Althea Gibson	Darlene Hard
1958	Althea Gibson	Angela Mortimer
1959	Maria Bueno	Darlene Hard
1960	Maria Bueno	Sandra Reynolds
1961	Angela Mortimer	Christine Truman
1962	Karen Hantze Susman	Vera Sukova
1963	Margaret Smith	Billie Jean Moffitt
1964	Maria Bueno	Margaret Smith
1965	Margaret Smith	Maria Bueno
1966	Billie Jean King	Maria Bueno
1967	Billie Jean King	Ann Haydon Jones
1968‡	Billie Jean King	Judy Tegart
1969	Ann Jones	Billie Jean King
1970	Margaret Court	Billie Jean King
1971	Evonne Goolagong	Margaret Court
1972	Billie Jean King	Evonne Goolagong
1973	Billie Jean King	Chris Evert
1974	Chris Evert	Olga Morozova

Tennis (continued)

Wimbledon Singles

Year	Winner	Finalist
1975	Billie Jean King	Evonne Goolagong Cawley
1976	Chris Evert	Evonne Goolagong Cawley
1977	Virginia Wade	Betty Stove
1978	Martina Navratilova	Chris Evert
1979	Martina Navratilova	Chris Evert Lloyd
1980	Evonne Goolagong Cawley	Chris Evert Lloyd
1981	Chris Evert Lloyd	Hana Mandlikova
1982	Martina Navratilova	Chris Evert Lloyd
1983	Martina Navratilova	Andrea Jaeger
1984	Martina Navratilova	Chris Evert Lloyd
1985	Martina Navratilova	Chris Evert Lloyd
1986	Martina Navratilova	Hana Mandlikova
1987	Martina Navratilova	Steffi Graf
1988	Steffi Graf	Martina Navratilova
1989	Steffi Graf	Martina Navratilova
1990	Martina Navratilova	Zina Garrison Jackson
1991	Steffi Graf	Gabriela Sabatini
1992	Steffi Graf	Monica Seles
1993	Steffi Graf	Jana Novotna
1994	Conchita Martinez	Martina Navratilova
1995	Steffi Graf	Arantxa Sanchez Vicario
1996	Steffi Graf	Arantxa Sanchez Vicario

*Through 1921, championships decided on challenge round system. If no finalist, hold did not defend.

†Challenge round is abolished.

‡Became open championships (amateurs and professionals).

Wimbledon Doubles

Year	Winners	Finalists
1913*	Winifred McNair/Dora Boothby	Charlotte Sterry/Dorothea Lambert Chambers
1914	Agatha Morton/Elizabeth Ryan	Ethel Hannam/Ethel Thomson Larcombe
1915–18	not held	
1919	Suzanne Lenglen/Elizabeth Ryan	Dorothea Lambert Chambers/Ethel Larcombe
1920	Suzanne Lenglen/Elizabeth Ryan	Dorothea Lambert Chambers/Ethel Larcombe
1921	Suzanne Lenglen/Elizabeth Ryan	Geraldine Beamish/Irene Peacock
1922	Suzanne Lenglen/Elizabeth Ryan	Kathleen McKane/Margaret Stocks
1923	Suzanne Lenglen/Elizabeth Ryan	Joan Austin/Evelyn Colyer
1924	Hazel Wightman/Helen Wills	Phyllis Covell/Kathleen McKane
1925	Suzanne Lenglen/Elizabeth Ryan	Kathleen Bridge/Mary McIlquham
1926	Mary K. Browne/Elizabeth Ryan	Kathleen McKane Godfree/Evelyn Colyer
1927	Helen Wills/Elizabeth Ryan	Bobbie Heine/Irene Peacock
1928	Peggy Saunders/Phoebe Watson	Eileen Bennett/Ermyntrude Harvey
1929	Peggy Saunders/Phoebe Watson	Phyllis Covell/Dorothy Shephard Barron
1930	Helen Wills/Elizabeth Ryan	Edith Cross/Sarah Palfrey
1931	Phyllis Mudford/Dorothy Shepherd Barron	Doris Metaxa/Josane Sigart
1932	Doris Metaxa/Josane Sigart	Helen Jacobs/Elizabeth Ryan
1933	Simone Mathieu/Elizabeth Ryan	Freda James/Billie Yorke
1934	Simone Mathieu/Elizabeth Ryan	Dorothy Andrus/Sylvia Henrotin
1935	Freda James/Kay Stammers	Simone Mathieu/Hilde Sperling
1936	Freda James/Kay Stammers	Sarah Palfrey Fabyan/Helen Jacobs
1937	Simone Mathieu/Billie Yorke	Phyllis Mudford King/Elsie Goldsack
1938	Sarah Fabyan/Alice Marble	Simone Mathieu/Billie Yorke
1939	Sarah Fabyan/Alice Marble	Helen Jacobs/Billie Yorke
1940–45	not held	
1946	Louise Brough/Margaret Osborne	Pauline Betz/Doris Hart
1947	Patricia Todd/Doris Hart	Louise Brough/Margaret Osborne
1948	Louise Brough/Margaret Osborne duPont	Doris Hart/Patricia Todd
1949	Louise Brough/Margaret duPont	Gussy Moran/Patricia Todd

Tennis (continued)

Wimbledon Doubles

Year	Winners	Finalists
1950	Louise Brough/Margaret duPont	Shirley Fry/Doris Hart
1951	Doris Hart/Shirley Fry	Louise Brough/Margaret duPont
1952	Doris Hart/Shirley Fry	Louise Brough/Maureen Connolly
1953	Doris Hart/Shirley Fry	Maureen Connolly/Julia Sampson
1954	Louise Brough/Margaret duPont	Shirley Fry/Doris Hart
1955	Angela Mortimer/Anne Shilcock	Shirley Bloomer/Pat Ward
1956	Angela Buxton/Althea Gibson	Fay Muller/Daphne Seeney
1957	Althea Gibson/Darlene Hard	Mary Hawton/Thelma Long
1958	Maria Bueno/Althea Gibson	Margaret duPont/Margaret Varner
1959	Jeanne Arth/Darlene Hard	Beverly Fleitz/Christine Truman
1960	Maria Bueno/Darlene Hard	Sandra Reynolds/Renee Schuurman
1961	Karen Hantze/Billie Jean Moffitt	Jan Lehane/Margaret Smith
1962	Karen Hantze Susman/Billie Jean Moffitt	Sandra Reynolds Price/Renee Schuurman
1963	Maria Bueno/Darlene Hard	Robyn Ebbern/Margaret Smith
1964	Margaret Smith/Lesley Turner	Billie Jean Moffitt/Karen Hantze Susman
1965	Maria Bueno/Billie Jean Moffitt	Francoise Durr/Jeanine Lieffrig
1966	Maria Bueno/Nancy Richey	Margaret Smith/Judy Tegart
1967	Rosie Casals/Billie Jean Moffitt	Maria Bueno/Nancy Richey
1968†	Rosie Casals/Billie Jean King	Francoise Durr/Ann Jones
1969	Margaret Court/Judy Tegart Dalton	Patty Hogan/Peggy Michel
1970	Rosie Casals/Billie Jean King	Francoise Durr/Virginia Wade
1971	Rosie Casals/Billie Jean King	Margaret Court/Evonne Goolagong
1972	Billie Jean King/Betty Stove	Judy Tegart Dalton/Francoise Durr
1973	Rosie Casals/Billie Jean King	Francoise Durr/Betty Stove
1974	Evonne Goolagong/Peggy Michel	Helen Gourlay/Karen Krantzcke
1975	Ann Kiyomura/Kazuko Sawamatsu	Francoise Durr/Betty Stove
1976	Chris Evert/Martina Navratilova	Billie Jean King/Betty Stove
1977	Helen Gourlay Cawley/JoAnne Russell	Martina Navratilova/Betty Stove
1978	Kerry Reid/Wendy Turnbull	Mima Jausovec/Virginia Ruzici
1979	Billie Jean King/Martina Navratilova	Betty Stove/Wendy Turnbull
1980	Kathy Jordan/Anne Smith	Rosie Casals/Wendy Turnbull
1981	Martina Navratilova/Pam Shriver	Kathy Jordan/Anne Smith
1982	Martina Navratilova/Pam Shriver	Kathy Jordan/Anne Smith
1983	Martina Navratilova/Pam Shriver	Rosie Casals/Wendy Turnbull
1984	Martina Navratilova/Pam Shriver	Kathy Jordan/Anne Smith
1985	Kathy Jordan/Elizabeth Smylie	Martina Navratilova/Pam Shriver
1986	Martina Navratilova/Pam Shriver	Hana Mandlikova/Wendy Turnbull
1987	Claudia Kohde-Kilsch/Helena Sukova	Betsy Nagelsen/Elizabeth Smylie
1988	Steffi Graf/Gabriela Sabatini	Larisa Savchenko/Natasha Zvereva
1989	Jana Novotna/Helena Sukova	Larisa Savchenko/Natasha Zvereva
1990	Jana Novotna/Helena Sukova	Kathy Jordan/Elizabeth Smylie
1991	Larisa Neiland/Natasha Zvereva	Gigi Fernandez/Jana Novotna
1992	Gigi Fernandez/Natasha Zvereva	Jana Novotna/Larisa Neiland
1993	Gigi Fernandez/Natasha Zvereva	Jana Novotna/Larisa Neiland
1994	Gigi Fernandez/Natasha Zvereva	Jana Novotna/Arantxa Sanchez Vicario
1995	Jana Novotna/Arantxa Sanchez Vicario	Gigi Fernandez/Natasha Zvereva
1996	Martina Hingis/Helena Sukova	Meredith McGrath/Larisa Neiland

*Beginning in 1913, women's doubles were officially incorporated into the Wimbledon Championships.
†Became open championships (amateurs and professionals).

Tennis (continued)

Australian Open Singles

Year	Champion	Finalist
1922	Margaret Molesworth	Esna Boyd
1923	Margaret Molesworth	Esna Boyd
1924	Sylvia Lance	Esna Boyd
1925	Daphne Akhurst	Esna Boyd
1926	Daphne Akhurst	Esna Boyd
1927	Esna Boyd	Sylvia Harper
1928	Daphne Akhurst	Esna Boyd
1929	Daphne Akhurst	Louise Bickeron
1930	Daphne Akhurst	Sylvia Harper
1931	Coral Buttsworth	Margorie Crawford
1932	Coral Buttsworth	Kathrine Le Messurier
1933	Joan Hartigan	Coral Buttsworth
1934	Joan Hartigan	Margaret Molesworth
1935	Dorothy Round	Nancye Wynne Bolton
1936	Joan Hartigan	Nancye Wynne Bolton
1937	Nancye Wynne Bolton	Emily Westacott
1938	Dorothy Bundy	D. Stevenson
1939	Emily Westacott	Mrs. N. Hopman
1940	Nancye Wynne Bolton	Thelma Coyne
1941–45	not held	
1946	Nancye Wynne Bolton	Joyce Fitch
1947	Nancye Wynne Bolton	Mrs. N. Hopman
1948	Nancye Wynne Bolton	Marie Toomey
1949	Doris Hart	Nancye Wynne Bolton
1950	Louise Brough	Doris Hart
1951	Nancye Wynne Bolton	Thelma Long
1952	Thelma Long	H. Angwin
1953	Maureen Connolly	Julia Sampson
1954	Thelma Long	J. Staley
1955	Beryl Penrose	Thelma Long
1956	Mary Carter	Thelma Long
1957	Shirley Fry	Althea Gibson
1958	Angela Mortimer	Lorraine Coghlan
1959	Mary Carter-Reitano	Renee Schuurman
1960	Margaret Smith	Jan Lehane
1961	Margaret Smith	Jan Lehane
1962	Margaret Smith	Jan Lehane
1963	Margaret Smith	Jan Lehane
1964	Margaret Smith	Lesley Turner
1965	Margaret Smith	Maria Bueno
1966	Margaret Smith	Nancy Richey
1967	Nancy Richey	Lesley Turner
1968	Billie Jean King	Margaret Smith
1969*	Margaret Smith Court	Billie Jean King
1970	Margaret Court	Kerry Melville Reid
1971	Margaret Court	Evonne Goolagong
1972	Virginia Wade	Evonne Goolagong
1973	Margaret Smith Court	Evonne Goolagong
1974	Evonne Goolagong	Chris Evert
1975	Evonne Goolagong	Martina Navratilova
1976	Evonne Goolagong Cawley	Renata Tomanova
1977 (Jan)	Kerry Melville Reid	Dianne Balestrat
1977 (Dec)	Evonne Goolagong Cawley	Helen Gourlay
1978	Chris O'Neil	Betsy Nagelsen
1979	Barbara Jordan	Sharon Walsh
1980	Hana Mandlikova	Wendy Turnbull
1981	Martina Navratilova	Chris Evert Lloyd
1982	Chris Evert Lloyd	Martina Navratilova
1983	Martina Navratilova	Kathy Jordan
1984	Chris Evert Lloyd	Helena Sukova
1985	Martina Navratilova	Chris Evert Lloyd
1986	not held, moved to Jan '87	
1987	Hana Mandlikova	Martina Navratilova
1988	Steffi Graf	Chris Evert
1989	Steffi Graf	Helena Sukova
1990	Steffi Graf	Mary Joe Fernandez
1991	Monica Seles	Jana Novotna
1992	Monica Seles	Mary Joe Fernandez
1993	Monica Seles	Steffi Graf
1994	Steffi Graf	Arantxa Sanchez Vicario
1995	Mary Pierce	Arantxa Sanchez Vicario
1996	Monica Seles	Anke Huber

*Became open championships (amateurs and professionals).

Tennis (continued)

Australian Open Doubles

Year	Champions	Finalists
1922	Esne Boyd/Marjorie Mountain	Floris St. George/Lorna Utz
1923	Esne Boyd/Sylvia Lance	Margaret Molesworth/Turner
1924	Daphne Akhurst/Sylvia Lance	Kathrine LeMesurier/Meryl O'Hara Wood
1925	Sylvia Lance Harper/Daphne Akhurst	Esne Boyd/Kathrine LeMesurier
1926	Meryl O'Hara Wood/Esne Boyd	Daphne Akhurst/Marjorie Cox
1927	Meryl O'Hara Wood/Louise Bickerton	Esne Boyd/Sylvia Harper
1928	Daphne Akhurst/Esne Boyd	Kathrine LeMesurier/Dorothy Weston
1929	Daphne Akhurst/Louise Bickerton	Sylvia Harper/Meryl O'Hara Wood
1930	Margaret Molesworth/Emily Hood	Marjorie Cox/Sylvia Harper
1931	Daphne Akhurst Cozens/Louise Bickerton	N. Lloyd/Lorna Utz
1932	Coral Buttsworth/Marjorie Cox Crawford	Kathrine LeMesurier/Dorothy Weston
1933	Margaret Molesworth/Emily Hood Westacott	Joan Hartigan/Midge Van Ryn
1934	Margaret Molesworth/Emily Hood Westacott	Joan Hartigan/Ula Valkenburg
1935	Evelyn Dearman/Nancye W. Lyle	Louise Bickerton/Nell Hopman
1936	Thelma Coyne/Nancye Wynne	May Blick/K. Woodward
1937	Thelma Coyne/Nancye Wynne	Nell Hopman/Emily Westacott
1938	Thelma Coyne/Nancye Wynne	Dorothy Bundy/Dorothy Workman
1939	Thelma Coyne/Nancye Wynne	May Hardcastle/Emily Westacott
1940	Thelma Coyne/Nancye Wynne Bolton	Joan Hartigan/Emily Niemeyer
1941–45	not held	
1946	Joyce Fitch/Mary Bevis	Nancye Wynne Bolton/Thelma Coyne Long
1947	Thelma Long/Nancye Wynne Bolton	Mary Bevis/Joyce Fitch
1948	Thelma Long/Nancye Wynne Bolton	Mary Bevis/P. Jones
1949	Thelma Long/Nancye Wynne Bolton	Doris Hart/Marie Toomey
1950	Louise Brough/Doris Hart	Nancye Wynne Bolton/Thelma Long
1951	Thelma Long/Nancye Wynne Bolton	Joyce Fitch/Mary Hawton
1952	Thelma Long/Nancye Wynne Bolton	R. Baker/Mary Hawton
1953	Maureen Connolly/Julia Sampson	Mary Hawton/Beryl Penrose
1954	Mary Hawton/Beryl Penrose	Hazel Redick-Smith/Julie Wipplinger
1955	Mary Hawton/Beryl Penrose	Nell Hopman/Gwen Thiele
1956	Mary Hawton/Thelma Long	Mary Carter/Beryl Penrose
1957	Althea Gibson/Shirley Fry	Mary Hawton/Fay Muller
1958	Mary Hawton/Thelma Long	Lorraine Coghlan/Angela Mortimer
1959	Renee Schuurman/Sandra Reynolds	Lorraine Coghlan/Mary Carter Reitano
1960	Maria Bueno/Christine Truman	Lorraine Coghlan Robinson/Margaret Smith
1961	Mary Carter Reitano/Margaret Smith	Mary Hawton/Jan Lehane
1962	Margaret Smith/Robyn Ebbern	Darlene Hard/Mary Carter Reitano
1963	Margaret Smith/Robyn Ebbern	Jan Lehane/Lesley R. Turner
1964	Judy Tegart Dalton/Lesley Turner	Robyn Ebbern/Margaret Smith
1965	Margaret Smith/Lesley Turner	Robyn Ebbern/Billie Jean King
1966	Carole Graebner/Nancy Richey	Margaret Smith/Lesley R. Turner
1967	Lesley Turner/Judy Tegart Dalton	Lorraine Coghlan Robinson/E. Terras
1968	Karen Krantzcke/Kerry Reid	Judy Tegart Dalton/Lesley R. Turner
1969	Margaret Smith Court/Judy Tegart Dalton	Rosie Casals/Billie Jean King
1970	Margaret Court/Judy Tegart Dalton	Karen Krantzcke/Kerry Reid
1971	Margaret Court/Evonne Goolagong Cawley	Joy Emerson/Lesley Hunt
1972	Kerry Harris/Helen Gourlay	Patricia Coleman/Karen Krantzcke
1973	Margaret Court/Virginia Wade	Kerry Harris/Kerry Reid
1974	Evonne Goolagong Cawley/Peggy Michel	Kerry Harris/Kerry Reid

Tennis (continued)

Australian Open Doubles

Year	Champions	Finalists
1975	Evonne Goolagong Cawley/Peggy Michel	Margaret Court/Olga Morozova
1976	Evonne Goolagong Cawley/Helen Gourlay	Lesley Turner Bowrey/Renata Tomanova
1977 (Jan)	Dianne Balestrat/Helen Gourlay	Betsy Nagelsen/Kerry Reid
1977 (Dec)	Evonne Goolagong Cawley/Helen Gourlay divided with Mona Guerrant/Kerry Reid Finals rained out	
1978	Betsy Nagelsen/Renata Tomanova	Naoko Sato/Pam Whytcross
1979	Judy Chalonet/Dianne Evers	Leanne Harrison/Marcella Mesker
1980	Martina Navratilova/Betsy Nagelsen	Ann Kiyomura/Candy Reynolds
1981	Kathy Jordan/Anne Smith	Martina Navratilova/Pam Shriver
1982	Martina Navratilova/Pam Shriver	Claudia Kohde-Kilsch/Eva Pfaff
1983	Martina Navratilova/Pam Shriver	Anne Hobbs/Wendy Turnbull
1984	Martina Navratilova/Pam Shriver	Claudia Kohde-Kilsch/Helena Sukova
1985	Martina Navratilova/Pam Shriver	Claudia Kohde-Kilsch/Helena Sukova
1986	not held, moved to January 1987	
1987	Martina Navratilova/Pam Shriver	Zina Garrison/Lori McNeil
1988	Martina Navratilova/Pam Shriver	Chris Evert/Wendy Turnbull
1989	Martina Navratilova/Pam Shriver	Patty Fendick/Jill Hetherington
1990	Jana Novotna/Helena Sukova	Patty Fendick/Mary Joe Fernandez
1991	Patty Fendick/M. J. Fernandez	Gigi Fernandez/Jana Novotna
1992	Arantxa Sanchez Vicario/Helena Sukova	Mary Joe Fernandez/Zina Garrison-Jackson
1993	Gigi Fernandez/Natasha Zvereva	Pam Shriver/Elizabeth Smylie
1994	Gigi Fernandez/Natasha Zvereva	Patty Fendick/Meredith McGrath
1995	Jana Novotna/Arantxa Sanchez Vicario	Gigi Fernandez/Natasha Zvereva
1996	Chanda Rubin/Arantxa Sanchez Vicario	Lindsay Davenport/Mary Joe Fernandez

Roland Garros Singles Champions (French Open)

Year	Champion	Finalist
1897*	Adine Masson	P. Girod
1898	Adine Masson	
1899	Adine Masson	
1900	Y. Prevost	
1901	P. Girod	Leroux
1902	Adine Masson	P. Girod
1903	Adine Masson	Katie Gillou
1904	Katie Gillou	Adine Masson
1905	Katie Gillou	Y. De Phoeffel
1906	Katie Gillou Fenwick	MacVeagh
1907	Ctsse. De Kermel	D'Elva
1908	Katie Fenwick	A. Pean
1909	Jeanne Matthey	Gallay
1910	Jeanne Matthey	Marguerite Broquedis
1911	Jeanne Matthey	Marguerite Broquedis
1912	Jeanne Matthey	Marie Daney
1913	Marguerite Broquedis	Jeanne Matthey
1914	Marguerite Broquedis	Suzanne Lenglen
1915–19	not held	
1920	Suzanne Lenglen	Marguerite Broquedis Billout
1921	Suzanne Lenglen	Germaine Golding
1922	Suzanne Lenglen	Germaine Golding
1923	Suzanne Lenglen	Germaine Golding
1924	Diddie Vlasto	Jeanne Vaussard
1925	Suzanne Lenglen	Kathleen McKane
1926	Suzanne Lenglen	Mary K. Browne
1927	Kea Bouman	Irene Peacock
1928	Helen Wills	Eileen Bennett

Tennis (continued)

Roland Garros Singles Champions (French Open)

Year	Champion	Finalist
1929	Helen Wills	Simone Mathieu
1930	Helen Wills Moody	Helen Jacobs
1931	Cilly Aussem	Betty Nuthall
1932	Helen Wills Moody	Simone Mathieu
1933	Margaret Scriven	Simone Mathieu
1934	Margaret Scriven	Helen Jacobs
1935	Hilde Sperling	Simone Mathieu
1936	Hilde Sperling	Simone Mathieu
1937	Hilde Sperling	Simone Mathieu
1938	Simone Mathieu	Nelly Landry
1939	Simone Mathieu	Jadwiga Jedrzejowska
1940–45	not held	
1946	Margaret Osborne	Pauline Betz
1947	Patricia Todd	Doris Hart
1948	Nelly Landry	Shirley Fry
1949	Margaret Osborne duPont	Nelly Adamson
1950	Doris Hart	Patricia Todd
1951	Shirley Fry	Doris Hart
1952	Doris Hart	Shirley Fry
1953	Maureen Connolly	Doris Hart
1954	Maureen Connolly	Ginette Bucaille
1955	Angela Mortimer	Dorothy Knode
1956	Althea Gibson	Angela Mortimer
1957	Shirley Bloomer	Dorothy Knode
1958	Zsuzsi Kormoczy	Shirley Bloomer
1959	Christine Truman	Zsuzsi Kormoczy
1960	Darlene Hard	Yola Ramierez
1961	Ann Haydon	Yola Ramierez
1962	Margaret Smith	Lesley Turner
1963	Lesley Turner	Ann Haydon Jones
1964	Margaret Smith	Maria Bueno
1965	Lesley Turner	Margaret Smith
1966	Ann Jones	Nancy Richey
1967	Francoise Durr	Lesley Turner
1968[†]	Nancy Richey	Ann Jones
1969	Margaret Smith Court	Ann Jones
1970	Margaret Court	Helga Niessen
1971	Evonne Goolagong	Helen Gourlay
1972	Billie Jean King	Evonne Goolagong
1973	Margaret Court	Chris Evert
1974	Chris Evert	Olga Morozova
1975	Chris Evert	Martina Navratilova
1976	Sue Barker	Renata Tomanova
1977	Mima Jausovec	Florenta Mihai
1978	Viginia Ruzici	Mima Jausovec
1979	Chris Evert Lloyd	Wendy Turnbull
1980	Chris Evert Lloyd	Virginia Ruzici
1981	Hana Mandlikova	Sylvia Hanika
1982	Martina Navratilova	Andrea Jaeger
1983	Chris Evert Lloyd	Mima Jausovec
1984	Martina Navratilova	Chris Evert Lloyd
1985	Chris Evert Lloyd	Martina Navratilova
1986	Chris Evert Lloyd	Martina Navratilova
1987	Steffi Graf	Martina Navratilova
1988	Steffi Graf	Natasha Zvereva
1989	Arantxa Sanchez Vicario	Steffi Graf
1990	Monica Seles	Steffi Graf
1991	Monica Seles	Arantxa Sanchez Vicario
1992	Monica Seles	Steffi Graf
1993	Steffi Graf	Mary Joe Fernandez
1994	Arantxa Sanchez Vicario	Mary Pierce
1995	Steffi Graf	Arantxa Sanchez Vicario
1996	Steffi Graf	Arantxa Sanchez Vicario

*Before 1925, the French Championships were reserved to residents of France.

[†]Became open championships (amateurs and professionals).

Roland Garros Doubles Championships (French Open)

Year	Champions	Finalists
1925	Suzanne Lenglen/Didi Vlasto	Evelyn Colyer/Kathleen McKane
1926	Suzanne Lenglen/Didi Vlasto	Evelyn Colyer/Kathleen McKane Godfree
1927	Irene Peacock/Bobbie Heine	Peggy Saunders/Phoebe Watson
1928	Phoebe Watson/Eileen Bennett	Suzanne Deve/Sylvia Lafaurie
1929	Lili de Alvarez/Kea Bouman	Bobbie Heine/Alida Neave
1930	Helen Wills Moody/Elizabeth Ryan	Simone Barbier/Simone Mathieu

Tennis (continued)

Roland Garros Doubles Championships (French Open)

Year	Champions	Finalists
1931	Eileen Bennett Whittingstall/Betty Nuthall	Cilly Aussem/Elizabeth Ryan
1932	Helen Wills Moody/Elizabeth Ryan	Betty Nuthall/Eileen Bennett Whittingstall
1933	Simone Mathieu/Elizabeth Ryan	Sylvia Henrotin/Colette Rosambert
1934	Simone Mathieu/Elizabeth Ryan	Helen Jacobs/Sarah Palfrey
1935	Margaret Scriven/Kay Stammers	Ida Adamoff/Hilde Sperling
1936	Simone Mathieu/Billie Yorke	Susan Noel/Jadwiga Jedzejowska
1937	Simone Mathieu/Billie Yorke	Dorothy Andrus/Sylvia Henrotin
1938	Simone Mathieu/Billie Yorke	Arlette Halff/Nelly Landry
1939	Simone Mathieu/Jadwiga Jedzejowska	Alice Florian/Hella Kovac
1940–45	not held	
1946	Louise Brough/Margaret Osborne	Pauline Betz/Doris Hart
1947	Louise Brough/Margaret Osborne	Doris Hart/Patricia Todd
1948	Doris Hart/Patricia Todd	Shirley Fry/Mary Arnold Prentiss
1949	Margaret Osborne duPont/Louise Brough	Joy Gannon/Betty Hilton
1950	Doris Hart/Shirley Fry	Louise Brough/Margaret Osborne duPont
1951	Doris Hart/Shirley Fry	Beryl Bartlett/Barbara Scofield
1952	Doris Hart/Shirley Fry	Hazel Redick-Smith/Julie Wipplinger
1953	Doris Hart/Shirley Fry	Maureen Connolly/Julia Sampson
1954	Maureen Connolly/Nell Hopman	Maude Galtier/Suzanne Schmidt
1955	Beverly Fleitz/Darlene Hard	Shirley Bloomer/Pat Ward
1956	Angela Buxton/Althea Gibson	Darlene Hard/Dorothy Knode
1957	Shirley Bloomer/Darlene Hard	Yola Ramirez/Rosie Reyes
1958	Rosie Reyes/Yola Ramirez	Mary Hawton/Thelma Long
1959	Sandra Reynolds/Renee Schuurman	Yola Ramirez/Rosie Reyes
1960	Maria Bueno/Darlene Hard	Pat Hales/Ann Haydon
1961	Sandra Reynolds/Renee Schuurman	Maria Bueno/Darlene Hard
1962	Sandra Reynolds Price/Renee Schuurman	Justina Bricka/Margaret Smith
1963	Ann Haydon Jones/Renee Schuurman	Robyn Ebbern/Margaret Smith
1964	Margaret Smith/Lesley Turner	Norma Baylon/Helga Schultze
1965	Margaret Smith/Lesley Turner	Francoise Durr/Jeanine Lieffrig
1966	Maragaret Smith/Judy Tegart	Jill Blackman/Fay Toyne
1967	Francoise Durr/Gail Sheriff	Anette Van Zyl/Pat Walkden
1968*	Francoise Durr/Ann Jones	Rosie Casals/Billie Jean King
1969	Francoise Durr/Ann Jones	Margaret Smith Court/Nancy Richey
1970	Gail Chanfreau/Francoise Durr	Rosie Casals/Billie Jean King
1971	Gail Chanfreau/Francoise Durr	Helen Gourlay/Kerry Harris
1972	Billie Jean King/Betty Stove	Winnie Shaw/Christine Truman
1973	Margaret Court/Virginia Wade	Francoise Durr/Betty Stove
1974	Chris Evert/Olga Morozova	Gail Chanfreau/Katia Ebbinghaus
1975	Chris Evert/Martina Navratilova	Julie Anthony/Olga Morozova
1976	Fiorella Bonicelli/Gail Chanfreau Lovera	Kathleen Harter/Helga Mastoff
1977	Regina Marsikova/Pam Teeguarden	Rayni Fox/Helen Gourlay
1978	Mima Jausovec/Virginia Ruzici	Lesley Bowery/Gail Lovera
1979	Betty Stove/Wendy Turnbull	Francoise Durr/Virginia Wade
1980	Kathy Jordan/Anne Smith	Ivanna Madruga/Adriana Villagran
1981	Rosalyn Fairbank/Tanya Harford	Candy Reynolds/Paula Smith
1982	Martina Navratilova/Anne Smith	Rosie Casals/Wendy Turnbull
1983	Rosalyn Fairbank/Candy Reynolds	Kathy Jordan/Anne Smith
1984	Martina Navratilova/Pam Shriver	Claudia Kohde-Kilsch/Hana Mandlikova
1985	Martina Navratilova/Pam Shriver	Claudia Kohde-Kilsch/Helena Sukova

Tennis (continued)

Roland Garros Doubles Championships (French Open)

Year	Champions	Finalists
1986	Martina Navratilova/Andrea Temesvari	Steffi Graf/Gabriela Sabatini
1987	Martina Navratilova/Pam Shriver	Steffi Graf/Gabriela Sabatini
1988	Martina Navratilova/Pam Shriver	Claudia Kohde-Kilsch/Helena Sukova
1989	Larisa Savchenko/Natasha Zvereva	Steffi Graf/Gabriela Sabatini
1990	Jana Novotna/Helena Sukova	Larisa Neiland/Natasha Zvereva
1991	Gigi Fernandez/Jana Novotna	Larisa Neiland/Natasha Zvereva
1992	Gigi Fernandez/Natasha Zvereva	Conchita Martinez/Arantxa Sanchez Vicario
1993	Gigi Fernandez/Natasha Zvereva	Larisa Neiland/Jana Novotna
1994	Gigi Fernandez/Natasha Zvereva	Lindsay Davenport/Lisa Raymond
1995	Gigi Fernandez/Natasha Zvereva	Jana Novotna/Arantxa Sanchez Vicario
1996	Lindsay Davenport/Mary Joe Fernandez	Gigi Fernandez/Natasha Zvereva

*Became open championships (amateurs and professionals).

Olympic Singles

Year	Medalists	Country	Medal
1996	Lindsay Davenport	USA	Gold
	Arantxa Sanchez Vicario	SPA	Silver
	Jana Novotna	CZE	Bronze

Olympic Doubles

Year	Medalists	Country	Medal
1996	Gigi Fernandez/Mary Joe Fernandez	USA	Gold
	Jana Novotna/Helena Sukova	CZE	Silver
	Conchita Martinez/Arantxa Sanchez Vicario	SPA	Bronze

Photo credit: Courtesy of The Badminton Association

BADMINTON

◆ *Though most of us think of badminton as a tame backyard game, the competitive version is fast, demanding, and in some parts of the world, the sport of the moment.*

HISTORY

Games played with paddles and shuttlecocks date back more than 2,000 years and were played throughout Greece, India, China, and Japan. Such games were equal-opportunity sports, played by men, women, and children without regard to age, sex, or even social class. Similar games were played in Europe from at least the 1500s on. Known as battledore in England and *jeu de volant* in France, badminton's forerunner was played without a net or formal court. The sole purpose

was to keep the shuttlecock aloft. We know from paintings of the era that the sport was deemed appropriate for the well-bred, for we see young women of prerevolutionary France playing in lavish dresses, dainty shoes, and carefully powdered coiffures. We also know, from contemporary art of the day, that the sport crossed the Atlantic and landed in America. Here it became essentially a child's game. A fabric wall hanging from colonial Williamsburg shows children volleying a shuttlecock, while numerous portraits include paddles and shuttlecocks as the expected props of a childhood.

The competitive, adult version of the game came not from Europe but from Asia. With polo, badminton is one of the two modern sports whose roots can be traced to India. Known as *poona*, it was quickly adopted by British Army officers stationed there in the mid-nineteenth century. The first official rules were developed there, and the sport was imported to England by returning officers. When the duke of Gloucester introduced it at a party at his country estate in Gloucestershire, it was an immediate success. Forever after, the English-speaking world called the sport by the name of the duke's estate, Badminton.

In America, badminton became a popular upper-class sport of the 1870s, and the first official organization, the Badminton Club of New York, was founded in 1878. The hourglass-shaped court and high net made the sport leisurely and rather stationary—which probably ensured its continued acceptance as a suitable pastime for women. So stately was the sport at this time that when one gentleman took off his tuxedo jacket during play, a minor scandal ensued. Adoption of a rectangular court and other rule changes in the early 1900s made the game faster and more athletic; formal attire was replaced by tennis clothing, and women—who were still struggling to gain acceptance for bloomers—continued to play.

THE MODERN ERA

Badminton reached its peak of popularity in America in the 1930s. Clubs sprang up across the country, and several Hollywood stars—including Bette Davis, Ginger Rogers, and Sonja Henie—played with enthusiasm. Badminton exhibitions, badminton comedy shows, and even—briefly—badminton on ice toured the country. In 1940 the CBS Silver Bowl was broadcast on national television. By the 1950s, the U.S. women were the best in the world.

Contemporary badminton is a fast, fierce sport that requires top aerobic conditioning and light-

IF YOU'RE IN JAKARTA, DON'T MISS THE BIRDIE!

In Indonesia, there are no movie, television, or MTV stars. There is no annual Super Bowl, Final Four, or World Series—but there is badminton, and the Indonesians roll all the glitz, glamour, and passion of a hundred Super Bowls into their favorite sport. Jakarta, on the island of Java, has become the world capital of *bulutangkis,* as it's called, and winning is serious business. An army general heads the national association. If the national team performs poorly, the country's president voices his personal concern. Indonesia's first-ever Olympic gold medal was won by women's singles champion **Susi Susanti** in 1992. The second was won by her fiancé, Allan Budi Kusuma, at the same games. Susanti and Kusuma, who grew up together in the dormitories of the government-sponsored national training center, are national celebrities. On tiny, crowded Java (the size of Louisiana but with a population of 110 million) they have been showered with fame, perks, and lucrative commercial contracts. For their gold-medal performances each received a $200,000 bonus, a sharp contrast to the average annual Indonesian income of barely $1,000. As the more decorated of the pair, Susanti also received a house.

Just as Americans complain about big money corrupting the purity of baseball, there are Javanese who insist that to see the *real* sport you must leave Jakarta and travel to the country's smaller villages. Here, the sport may be played in traditional bamboo halls—or it may be played outside on informal dirt courts. Matches between local favorites, between neighborhoods, or between teens from rival schools can all be counted on to draw spirited crowds. There are no seating arrangements, and no groundskeepers. Nighttime matches are often lit by extension cords running from nearby houses, or called on account of darkness and resumed at dawn, hours before the work and school day begins. There is hardly an Indonesian who doesn't participate in the national sport, and girls are as likely as boys to utter the unofficial national motto, Badminton is my life.

ning reflexes. Proponents bill it as the world's fastest racket sport—and they're right. In competitive play, the shuttlecock can reach speeds of 150 mph. While matches typically last only half as long as tennis matches, they involve twice as much actual playing time. Though badminton remains a popular recreational sport in America, world dominance has shifted. Today the heart and soul of badminton lies in Asia, and it is the women of Indonesia, Korea, and China who take home the medals.

Major Events and Competitions

Olympic Games
World Championships
All-England Championships
Uber Cup (Women's World Team
Championships)
Sudirman Cup (World Mixed Team
Championships)

Governing Bodies and Organizations

U.S. Badminton Association
One Olympic Plaza
Colorado Springs, Colorado 80909
Phone: 719/578-4808
Fax: 719/578-4507

International Badminton Federation
4 Manor Park, Mackenzie Way
Cheltenham, Gloucestershire, GL51 9TX
U.K.
Phone: 44/1242-234904
Fax: 44/1242-221030

* * * BIOGRAPHIES * * *

BANG SOO-HYUN b. September 13, 1972, Seoul, South Korea

One of the top-ranked women's singles players of the 1990s, Bang was a favorite to win the Olympics' first singles badminton medal but had to settle for a silver behind Indonesia's dynamic **Susi Susanti.** Bang realized her dream four years later, besting both Susanti and Susanti's teammate, sixteen-year-old Mia Audina, who took the silver.

Selected championships and honors: Silver medal, singles, Olympic Games, 1992; gold medal, singles, Olympic Games, 1994.

JUDITH (JUDY) DEVLIN HASHMAN b. 1935, Winnipeg, Manitoba, Canada

A phenomenal athlete, Devlin's name would undoubtedly be a household word if badminton were a more celebrated sport. Devlin learned the game from her father, Frank, a six-time English singles champion. Between 1953 and '67 Devlin won more than fifty national badminton championships in England, Canada, and the United States and garnered assorted national titles in Ireland, Scotland, Sweden, Germany, and the Netherlands. Her string of ten all-England singles titles remains unequaled to this day.

Selected championships and honors: Ten All-England Singles Championships, 1954, '57, '58, '60–64, '66, and '67; nine U.S. National Singles Championships, 1954 and '56–63; twelve U.S. National Doubles Championships, 1953–55, '57–63, '66, and '67; eight U.S. National Mixed Doubles Championships; seven All-England Doubles Championships; International Women's Sports Hall of Fame

LINDA FRENCH b. March 4, 1964, Elmhurst, Illinois

One of America's premiere doubles players, French has twice teamed with Erika Von Heiland to represent the United States in the Olympics. She has also played on World Championship and Uber Cup teams since the mid-1980s. French received her highest international ranking in 1992, when she and partner Joy Kitzmiller were ranked 23rd in women's doubles play.

Selected championships and honors: Bronze medal, doubles, Pan American Games, 1995; bronze medal, mixed doubles, Pan American Games, 1995; five U.S. National Doubles Championships, 1986–89 and '92; seven U.S. National Mixed Doubles Championships, 1987–89 and '92–95.

SUSI SUSANTI b. 1971, Indonesia

A celebrity in Indonesia, her home country, Susanti and fiancé Alan Budi Kusuma won their country's first Olympic gold medals at the 1992 Barcelona games. Susanti, who trains six days a week, has won numerous tournaments throughout Asia, and in the 1990s she consistently ranked among the world's top five women's singles players.

Selected championships and honors: Gold medal, singles, Olympic Games, 1992; four All-England Singles Championships, 1990, '91, '93, and '94; gold medal, singles, World Championships, 1993; bronze medal, singles, Olympic Games, 1996.

ERIKA VON HEILAND b. December 24, 1965, Angeles City, Philippines

Von Heiland, one of America's top singles players, also teams with partner **Linda French** to form one of the country's top contemporary women's doubles teams. Von Heiland holds two Pan American Games medals and made Olympic appearances in 1992 and '96. In a sport where the United States is struggling to reach the level of the play of the women and men of Asia, Von Heiland in 1996 was the top-ranked singles player in the United States, at 106th.

Selected championships and honors: Silver medal, singles, Pan American Games, 1991; bronze medal, doubles, Pan American Games, 1995.

Badminton

All-England Championships/World Badminton Championships

The prestigious All-England Championships, founded in 1899, were considered the unofficial world championships until 1977 when the official World Badminton Championships were instituted. The event is held every odd year, in conjunction with the Sudirman Cup.

Sudirman Cup

The Sudirman Cup competition is the World Mixed Team Badminton Championship, in which countries play five matches (one each in men's singles, women's singles, men's doubles, women's doubles, and mixed doubles) against another country. The event is staged with the World Individual Championships every odd year.

Uber Cup (World Women's Team Championships)

The Uber Cup competition is the Women's World Team Badminton Championships, in which countries play five matches (three women's singles, two women's doubles) against another country. The institution of an international team competition for women, along the lines of the men's Thomas Cup contest, was first introduced in 1950 when the International Badminton Federation received the offer of a trophy from Mrs. H. S. Uber. The first Uber Cup matches took place in 1956–57, with the competition played every even year, along with the men's Thomas Cup.

Badminton

All-England Women's Singles

Year	Champion	Country
1899	no competition	
1900	E. Thomson	ENG
1901	E. Thomson	ENG
1902	M. Lucas	ENG
1903	E. Thomson	ENG
1904	E. Thomson	ENG
1905	M. Lucas	ENG
1906	E. Thomson	ENG
1907	M. Lucas	ENG
1908	M. Lucas	ENG
1909	M. Lucas	ENG
1910	M. Lucas	ENG
1911	M. Larminie	ENG
1912	Mrs. R. C. Tragett	ENG
1913	L. C. Radeglia	ENG
1914	L. C. Radeglia	ENG
1915–19	no competition	
1920	K. McKane	ENG
1921	K. McKane	ENG
1922	K. McKane	ENG
1923	L. C. Radeglia	ENG
1924	K. McKane	ENG
1925	Mrs. A. D. Stockers	ENG
1926	Mrs. F. G. Barrett	ENG
1927	Mrs. F. G. Barrett	ENG
1928	Mrs. R. C. Tragett	ENG
1929	Mrs. F. G. Barrett	ENG
1930	Mrs. F. G. Barrett	ENG
1931	Mrs. F. G. Barrett	ENG

Badminton (continued)

All-England Women's Singles

Year	Champion	Country
1932	L. M. Kingsbury	ENG
1933	A. Woodroffe	ENG
1934	L. M. Kingsbury	ENG
1935	Mrs. H. S. Uber	ENG
1936	T. Kingsbury	ENG
1937	T. Kingsbury	ENG
1938	D. M. C. Young	ENG
1939	Mrs. W. R. Walton, Jr.	CAN
1940–46	no competition	
1947	Marie Ussing	DEN
1948	Kirsten Thorndahl	DEN
1949	A. Schiott Jacobsen	DEN
1950	T. Ahm	DEN
1951	A. Schiott Jacobsen	DEN
1952	T. Ahm	DEN
1953	Marie Ussing	DEN
1954	Judy Devlin	USA
1955	Margaret Varner	USA
1956	Margaret Varner	USA
1957	Judy Devlin	USA
1958	Judy Devlin	USA
1959	H. M. Ward	ENG
1960	Judy Devlin	USA
1961	Judy Hashman	USA
1962	Judy Hashman	USA
1963	Judy Hashman	USA
1964	Judy Hashman	USA
1965	U. Smith	ENG
1966	Judy Hashman	USA
1967	Judy Hashman	USA
1968	E Twedberg	SWE
1969	H. Yuki	JPN
1970	E. Takenake	JPN
1971	E. Twedberg	SWE
1972	N. Nakayama	JPN
1973	M. Beck	ENG
1974	H. Yuki	JPN
1975	H. Yuki	JPN
1976	M. A Gilks	ENG
1977	H. Yuki	JPN
1978	G. M. Gilks	ENG
1979	L. Koppen	DEN
1980	L. Koppen	DEN
1981	Hwang Sun Ai	KOR
1982	Zhang Ailing	CHN
1983	Zhang Ailing	CHN
1984	Li Lingwei	CHN
1985	Han Alping	CHN
1986	Kim Yun-Ja	KOR
1987	K. Larsen	DEN
1988	Gu Jiaming	CHN
1989	Li Lingwei	CHN
1990	Susi Susanti	INA
1991	Susi Susanti	INA
1992	Tang Jiuhong	CHN
1993	Susi Susanti	INA
1994	Susi Susanti	INA
1995	Lim Xiaoqing	SWE
1996	Bang Soo-hyun	KOR

All-England Women's Doubles

Year	Champions	Country
1899	M. Lucas & Graeme	ENG
1900	M. Lucas & Graeme	ENG
1901	St. John & E. M. Moseley	ENG
1902	M. Lucas & E. Thomson	ENG
1903	M. C. Hardy & D. K. Douglass	ENG
1904	M. Lucas & E. Thompson	ENG
1905	M. Lucas & E. Thompson	ENG
1906	M. Lucas & E. Thompson	ENG
1907	M. Lucas & G. L. Murray	ENG
1908	M. Lucas & G. L. Murray	ENG
1909	M. Lucas & G. L. Murray	ENG
1910	A. Gowenlock & D. Cundall	ENG
1911	M. Lucas & M. K. Bateman	ENG
1912	A. Gowenlock & D. Cundall	ENG
1913	H. Hogarth & M. K. Bateman	ENG
1914	Mrs. R. C. Tragett & E. G. Peterson	ENG
1915–19	no competition	
1920	L. C. Radeglia & V. Elton	ENG
1921	K. McKane & M. McKane	ENG
1922	Mrs. R. C. Tragett & H. Hogarth	ENG
1923	Mrs. R. C. Tragett & H. Hogarth	ENG
1924	Mrs. A. D. Stocks & K. McKane	ENG
1925	Mrs. R. C. Tragett & H. Hogarth	ENG
1926	Mrs. A. M. Head & V. Elton	ENG
1927	Mrs. R. C. Tragett & H. Hogarth	ENG
1928	Mrs. F. G. Barrett & V. Elton	ENG
1929	Mrs. F. G. Barrett & V. Elton	ENG
1930	Mrs. F. G. Barrett & V. Elton	ENG
1931	Mrs. H. S. Uber & Mrs. R. J. Horsley	ENG

Badminton (continued)

All-England Women's Doubles

Year	Champions	Country
1932	Mrs. F. G. Barrett & L. M. Kingsbury	ENG
1933	T. Kingsbury & M. Bell	ENG
1934	T. Kingsbury & Mrs. M. Henderson	ENG
1935	T. Kingsbury & M. Bell	ENG
1936	T. Kingsbury & Mrs. M. Henderson	ENG
1937	Mrs. H. S. Uber & D. Doveton	ENG
1938	Mrs. H. S. Uber & D. Doveton	ENG
1939	Mrs. R. Dalsgard & T. Olsen	ENG
1940–46	no competition	
1947	K. Thorndahl & T. Olsen	DEN
1948	K. Thorndahl & T. Ahm	DEN
1949	H. M. Uber & Q. M. Allen	ENG
1950	K. Thorndahl & T. Ahm	DEN
1951	K. Thorndahl & T. Ahm	DEN
1952	A. Jacobsen & T. Ahm	DEN
1953	I. L. Cooley & J. R. White	ENG
1954	S. Devlin & J. Devlin	USA
1955	I. L. Cooley & J. R. White	ENG
1956	S. Devlin & J. Devlin	USA
1957	A. Hammergaard-Hansen & K. Granlund	DEN
1958	M. Varner & H. W. Ward	USA/ENG
1959	W. C. E. Rogers & E. J. Timperley	ENG
1960	S. Devlin & J. Devlin	USA
1961	J. Hashman & S. Peard	USA/IRL
1962	J. Hashman & T. Holst-Christensen	USA/DEN
1963	J. Hashman & S. Peard	USA/IRL
1964	K. Jorgensen & U. Rasmussen	DEN
1965	K. Jorgensen & U. Strand	DEN
1966	J. Hashman & S. Peard	USA/IRL
1967	I. Rietveld & U. Strand	NTH/DEN
1968	Minarni & R. Koestijah	INA
1969	M. B. Boxall & P. E. Whetnall	ENG
1970	M. B. Boxall & P. E. Whetnall	ENG
1971	N. Takagi & H. Yuki	JPN
1972	M Aizawa & E. Takanaka	JPN
1973	M Aizawa & E. Takanaka	JPN
1974	M. Beck & M. A. Gilks	ENG
1975	M Aizawa & E. Takanaka	JPN
1976	M. A. Gilks & P. E. Whetnall	ENG
1977	E. Toganoo & E. Ueno	JPN
1978	A. Tokula & (TK). Takada	JPN
1979	TK. Verawaty & I. Wigoeno	INA
1980	G. M. Gilks & J. P. Perry	ENG
1981	J. P. Perry & J. Webster	ENG
1982	Lin Ying & Wu Dixi	CHN
1983	Xu Rong & Wu Jianqiu	CHN
1984	Lin Ying & Wu Dixi	CHN
1985	Han Aiping & Li Lingwei	CHN
1986	Chung Myung-Hee & Hwang Hye-Young	KOR
1987	Chung Myung-Hee & Hwang Hye-Young	KOR
1988	Chung So Young & Kim Yun-Ja	KOR
1989	Chung Myung-Hee & Chung So Young	KOR
1990	Chung Myung-Hee & Hwang Hye-Young	KOR
1991	Chung Myung-Hee & Hwang Hye-Young	KOR
1992	Lin Yanfen & Yao Fen	CHN
1993	Chung So Young & Gil Young Ah	KOR
1994	Chung So Young & Gil Young Ah	KOR
1995	Gil Young Ah & Jang Hye Ock	KOR
1996	Ge Fei & Gu Jun	CHN

All-England Mixed Doubles

Year	Champions	Country
1899	Oakes & St. John	ENG
1900	Oakes & St. John	ENG
1901	F. S. Collier & E. M. Stawell-Brown	ENG
1902	L. U. Ransford & E. M. Moseley	ENG
1903	G. A. Thomas & E. Thomson	ENG
1904	H. N. Marrett & D. K. Douglass	ENG
1905	H. N. Marrett & H. Hogarth	ENG
1906	G. A. Thomas & E. Thomson	ENG
1907	G. A. Thomas & G. L. Murray	ENG
1908	N. Wood & M. Lucas	ENG
1909	A. D. Prebble & D. Boothby	ENG
1910	G. A. Sautter & D. Cundall	ENG
1911	G. A. Thomas & M. Larminie	ENG
1912	E. Hawthorn & H. Hogarth	ENG
1913	G. A. Sautter & M. E. Mayston	ENG
1914	G. A. Thomas & H. Hogarth	ENG
1915–19	no competition	
1920	G. A. Thomas & H. Hogarth	ENG

Badminton (continued)

All-England Mixed Doubles

Year	Champions	Country
1921	G. A. Thomas & H. Hogarth	ENG
1922	G. A. Thomas & H. Hogarth	ENG
1923	G. S. B. Mack & Mrs. R. C. Tragett	IRE/ENG
1924	J. F. Devlin & K. McKane	IRE/ENG
1925	J. F. Devlin & K. McKane	IRE/ENG
1926	J. F. Devlin & E. G. Peterson	IRE/ENG
1927	J. F. Devlin & E. G. Peterson	IRE/ENG
1928	A. E. Harbot & Mrs. R. C. Tragett	IRE/ENG
1929	J. F. Devlin & Mrs. R. J. Horsley	IRE/ENG
1930	H. S. Uber & Mrs. H. S. Uber	ENG
1931	H. S. Uber & Mrs. H. S. Uber	ENG
1932	H. S. Uber & Mrs. H. S. Uber	ENG
1933	D. C. Hume & Mrs. H. S. Uber	ENG
1934	D. C. Hume & Mrs. H. S. Uber	ENG
1935	D. C. Hume & Mrs. H. S. Uber	ENG
1936	D. C. Hume & Mrs. H. S. Uber	ENG
1937	I. Maconachie & T. Kingsbury	IRE/ENG
1938	R. M. White & Mrs. H. S. Uber	ENG
1939	R. C. F. Nichols & B. M. Staples	ENG
1940–46	no competition	
1947	P. Holm & T. Olsen	DEN
1948	J. Skaarup & K. Thorndahl	DEN
1949	Clinton Stephens & Patsy Stephens	USA
1950	P. Holm & Mrs. G. Ahm	DEN
1951	P. Holm & Mrs. G. Ahm	DEN
1952	P. Holm & Mrs. G. Ahm	DEN
1953	E. L. Choong & Mrs. J. R. White	MAL/ENG
1954	J. R. Best & I. L. Cooley	ENG
1955	F. Kobbero & K. Thorndahl	DEN
1956	A. D. Jordan & E. J. Timperley	ENG
1957	F. Kobbero & K. Granlund	DEN
1958	A. D. Jordan & E. J. Timperley	ENG
1959	P. E. Nielsen & I. B. Hansen	DEN
1960	F. Kobbero & K. Granlund	DEN
1961	F. Kobbero & K. Granlund	DEN
1962	F. Kobbero & U. Rasmussen	DEN
1963	F. Kobbero & U. Rasmussen	DEN
1964	A. D. Jordan & H. J. Pritchard	ENG
1965	F. Kobbero & U. Strand	DEN
1966	F. Kobbero & U. Strand	DEN
1967	S. Andersen & U. Strand	DEN
1968	A. D. Jordan & S. D. Pound	ENG
1969	R. J. Mills & G. M. Perrin	ENG
1970	P. Walsoe & P. Molgaard Hansen	DEN
1971	S. Pri & U. Strand	DEN
1972	S. Pri & U. Strand	DEN
1973	D. Talbot & M. A. Gilks	ENG
1974	J. D. Eddy & P. E. Whetnall	ENG
1975	E. C. Stuart & N. C. Gardner	ENG
1976	D. Talbot & M. A. Gilks	ENG
1977	D. Talbot & M. A. Gilks	ENG
1978	M. G. Tredgett & J. P. Perry	ENG
1979	TK Christian & I. Wigoeno	INA
1980	M. G. Tredgett & J. P. Perry	ENG
1981	M. G. Tredgett & J. P. Perry	ENG
1982	M. C. Dew & G. M. Gilks	ENG
1983	T. Kihlstrom & J. P. Perry	SWE/ENG
1984	M. C. Dew & G. M. Gilks	ENG
1985	W. Gilliland & J. P. Perry	SCO/ENG
1986	Park Joo-Bong & Chung Myung-Hee	KOR
1987	Lee Deuk-Choon & Chung Myung-Hee	KOR
1988	Wang Pengren & Shi Fangjing	CHN
1989	Park Joo-Bong & Chung Myung-Hee	KOR
1990	Park Joo-Bong & Chung Myung-Hee	KOR
1991	Park Joo-Bong & Chung Myung-Hee	KOR
1992	Thomas Lund & Pernille Dupont	DEN
1993	Thomas Lund & Catrine Bengtsson	DEN/SWE
1994	Nick Ponting & Joanne Wright	ENG
1995	Thomas Lund & Marlene Thomsen	DEN
1996	Park Joo-Bong & Ra Kyung-min	KOR

Uber Cup

Year	Country
1956–57	USA
1959–60	USA
1962–63	USA
1965–66	JPN
1968–69	JPN
1971–72	JPN
1974–75	INA
1977–78	JPN
1980–81	JPN
1984	CHN

Badminton (continued)

Uber Cup

Year	Country
1986	CHN
1988	CHN
1990	CHN
1992	CHN
1994	INA
1996	INA

Olympic Doubles

1996	Medalists	Country
	Ge Fei/Gu Jun	CHN
	Gil Young-ah/Jang Hye-ock	KOR
	Yongshu Tang/Yiyuan Qin	CHN

Olympic Singles

1996	Medalists	Country
	Soo Bang Hyun	KOR
	Mia Audina	INA
	Susi Susanti	INA

Olympic Mixed Doubles

1996	Medalists	Country
	Gil Young Ah/Kim Dong Moon	KOR
	Ra Kyung Min/Park Joo Bong	KOR
	Liu Jianjun/Sun Man	CHN

U.S. Hall of Fame

Year	Player
1956	Ethel Marshall
	Del Barkhuff
1958	Evelyn Boldrick Howard
	Zoe S. Yeager
1959	Helen Gibson
1960	Janet Wright
1963	Judy Devlin Hashman
1965	Margaret Varner
1966	Mrs. Hulet Smith
1968	Lois Alston
1969	Beatrice Massman
1971	Helen Tibbetts
1976	Sue Devlin Peard
1981	Pam Brady
1988	Judianne Kelly
1994	Dorothy O'Neil

U.S. Open

Women's Singles

Year	Champion
1983	Sherrie Liu
1984	Luo Yun
1985	Claire Sharpe
1986	Denyse Julien
1987	Suk-Sung Chun
1988	Lee Myeong Hee
1989	no competition
1990	Denyse Julien
1991	Shim Eun Jung
1992	Lim Xiao Qing
1993	Lim Xiao Qing
1994	Liu Guimei
1995	Ye Zhaoying
1996	Mia Audina

Women's Doubles

Year	Champion
1983	Backhouse & Falardeau
1984	Yanahua & Haichen
1985	Sharpe & Skillings
1986	Julien & Falardeau
1987	Ho Kim & So Chung
1988	So Chong & Kim Ja
1989	no competition
1990	Julien & Piche
1991	Shim Eun Jung & Kang Bok Seung
1992	Lim Xiao Qing & C. Magnusson
1993	Young Ah Gil & So Young Chung
1994	Rikke Olsen & Helene Kirkegaard
1995	Gil Young Ah & Jang Hye Ock
1996	Rosiana Zalin & Eliza

Badminton (continued)

U.S. Open Mixed Doubles

Year	Winners
1983	Mika Butler & Claire Backhouse
1984	Pengren & Luo Yun
1985	Mika Butler & Claire Sharpe
1986	Mika Butler & Johanne Falardeau
1987	Deuk Lee & So Chung
1988	Christian Hadinata & Ivana Lie
1989	no competition
1990	Wadood & Britton
1991	Shim Eun Jung & Sang Bok Lee
1992	Thomas Lund & Pernille Dupont
1993	Thomas Lund & Catrine Bengtsson
1994	Jens Eriksen & Rikke Olsen
1995	Kim Dong Moon & Gil Young Ah
1996	Kim Dong Moon & Chung So Young

National Championships

	Women's Singles		Women's Doubles
Year	Champion	Year	Champions
1937	Mrs. Del Barkhuff	1937	D. Barkhuff & Z. Smith
1938	Mrs. Del Barkhuff	1938	R. Bergman & H. Gibson
1939	Mary E. Whitemore	1939	D. Barkhuff & Z. Smith
1940	Evelyn Boldrick	1940	E. Anselm & H. Zabriskie
1941	Thelma Kingbury	1941	T. Kingsbury & J. Wright
1942	Evelyn Boldrick	1942	E. Boldrick & J. Wright
1943–46	no competition	1943–46	no competition
1947	Ethel Marshall	1947	T. Scovil & J. Wright
1948	Ethel Marshall	1948	T. Scovil & J. Wright
1949	Ethel Marshall	1949	T. Scovil & J. Wright
1950	Ethel Marshall	1950	T. Scovil & J. Wright
1951	Ethel Marshall	1951	D. Hann & H. Smith
1952	Ethel Marshall	1952	E. Marshall & B. Massman
1953	Ethel Marshall	1953	J. Devlin & S. Devlin
1954	Judy Devlin	1954	J. Devlin & S. Devlin
1955	Margaret Varner	1955	J. Devlin & S. Devlin
1956	Judy Devlin	1956	E. Marshall & B. Massman
1957	Judy Devlin	1957	J. Devlin & S. Devlin
1958	Judy Devlin	1958	J. Devlin & S. Devlin
1959	Judy Devlin	1959	J. Devlin & S. Devlin
1960	Judy Devlin	1960	J. Devlin & S. Devlin
1961	Judy Devlin Hashman	1961	J. Hashman & S. Peard
1962	Judy Hashman	1962	J. Hashman & P. Stephens
1963	Judy Hashman	1963	J. Hashman & S. Peard
1964	Dorothy O'Neill	1964	M. Barinaga & C. Jensen
1965	Judy Hashman	1965	M. Barrand & J. Pritchard
1966	Judy Hashman	1966	J. Hashman & S. Peard
1967	Judy Hashman	1967	J. Hashman & R. Jones
1968	Tyna Barinaga	1968	M. Barinaga & H. Tibbetts
1969	Tyna Barinaga	1969	R. Koestijah & Minami
1970	Tyna Barinaga	1970	M. Barinaga & C. Hein
1971	Diane Hales	1971	C. Hein & C. Starkey
1972	Pam Brady	1972	P. Bretzke & P. Brady
1973	Eva Twedberg	1973	P. Brady & D. Hales
1974	Cindy Baker	1974	P. Brady & D. Hales
1975	Judianne Kelly	1975	D. Hales & C. Starkey
1976	Pam Stockton	1976	P. Brady & R. Lemon
1977	Pam Brady	1977	D. Osterhues & J. Wilts

Badminton (continued)

National Championships

	Women's Singles		Women's Doubles
Year	Champion	Year	Champions
1978	Cheryl Carton	1978	D. Osterhues & J. Wilts
1979	Pam Brady	1979	P. Brady & J. Kelly
1980	Cheryl Carton	1980	P. Brady & J. Kelly
1981	Utami Kinard	1981	P. Brady & J. Kelly
1982	Cheryl Carton	1982	P. Brady & J. Kelly
1983	Cheryl Carton	1983	P. Brady & J. Kelly
1984	Cheryl Carton	1984	P. Brady & M. Ortez
1985	Judianne Kelly	1985	P. Brady & J. Kelly
1986	Nina Lolk	1986	L. French & N. Lolk
1987	Joy Kitzmiller	1987	L. French & N. Lolk
1988	Joy Kitzmiller	1988	L. French & L. Safarik-Tong
1989	Linda Safarik-Tong	1989	L. French & L. Safarik-Tong
1990	Linda Safarik-Tong	1990	A. French & J. Kitzmiller
1991	Liz Aronsohn	1991	A. French & J. Kitzmiller
1992	Joy Kitzmiller	1992	L. French & J. Kitzmiller
1993	Andrea Andersson	1993	A. Andersson & T. Britton
1994	Joy Kitzmiller	1994	A. Andersson & L. Arohnson
1995	Andrea Andersson	1995	A. Andersson & L. Arohnson
1996	Yeping Tang	1996	Kathy Zimmerman & Ann French

TABLE TENNIS

◆ *Skiing may have more cachet, but table tennis has more participants. Almost 20 million Americans play Ping-Pong each year, versus the 13 million who take to the slopes.*

HISTORY

Prints show boys playing paddle-and-ball games similar to table tennis as early as 1810, but the first adult version of the game is little more than one hundred years old. The balls were probably made of whittled champagne corks, the paddles were cigar-box lids, the net was comprised of stacked books or dishes, the playing ground was the table everyone had just eaten at, and the participants were bored British soldiers posted to South Africa. Not long afterward, ads for "miniature lawn tennis" games began to appear in British and U.S. catalogs. The first manufactured equipment featured rubber balls, but the game took a decisive turn when celluloid balls manufactured in America were exported to Britain in 1900. The celluloid balls not only speeded up the game, the sound they made gave the sport its best-known name, Ping-Pong. Two years later the game took another important step when a British player covered his racquet-style paddle with a textured rubber mat. Ping-Pong, also known as flim-flam and whif-whaf, was immensely popular through the United States and England during the early 1900s. For reasons that are still obscure, its popularity was brief, and Ping-Pong went into a steep decline around 1905.

Major Events and Competitions

Like outdoor tennis, table tennis competitions traditionally feature singles, doubles, and mixed doubles events.

U.S. Nationals
Olympic Games
World Championships
Corbillon Cup (women's team world
   championships)

THE MODERN ERA

Ping-Pong's comeback dates from the early 1920s. The new home of the sport now known as table tennis was not America or Britain but Europe. Women such as **Angelica Adelstein Rozeanu** of Romania and Hungary's **Maria Mednyanszky** dominated the world stage, while

Ruth Hughes Aarons, in the 1930s, became the first—and to date the only—American woman to win a world singles championship. In the wake of World War II the scene changed again, and the seat of power switched to Asia. On the contemporary scene, the women of China have been nearly unbeatable, bringing a new speed and intensity to the game many still think of as a parlor pastime.

Governing Bodies and Organizations

USA Table Tennis
One Olympic Plaza
Colorado Springs, Colorado 80909-5769
Phone: 719/578-4583
Fax: 719/632-6071

International Table Tennis Federation
St. Leonards–on–Sea
East Sussex TN37 6AY, England
Phone: 44/1424-721414
Fax: 44/1424-431871

---

* * * BIOGRAPHIES * * *

ANGELICA ADELSTEIN ROZEANU LOPACKI b. October 15, 1921, Bucharest, Romania

Adelstein, who learned the game on her dining room table, is undoubtedly one of the legends of the sport. She won her first major championship, the Romanian nationals, in 1936, and held the title for the next twenty-one years. Unable to practice throughout World War II because Jews were banned from sports centers, she picked up where she left off when the war was over, winning the first of her six consecutive World Championships in 1950. While still an active player, Adelstein worked as an ambassador of table tennis, coaching and popularizing the sport throughout the Communist world. She and her first husband immigrated to Israel in 1960, where Adelstein continued to play and work as a coach until she retired from the game completely in the mid-1960s.
Selected championships and honors, singles: Six World Championships, 1950–55.

INSOOK BHUSHAN b. South Korea
Bhushan captained the 1973 World Championship South Korea team and shortly afterward moved to the United States, where she won the first of six U.S. Nationals singles championships in 1976. Playing for the United States, she won a total of four gold medals at the 1983 Pan American Games—in singles, doubles, mixed doubles, and team play.
Selected championships and honors, singles: Gold medal, Pan American Games, 1983; U.S. Table Tennis Association Amateur Athlete of the Year, 1983.

AMY FENG b. April 9, 1969, Tianjin, China
Feng began playing at age nine and gained invaluable experience in fourteen years of competitive play in China. In the spring of 1992 she moved to the United States and settled in Wheaton, Maryland. Since the move, Feng has been consistently ranked as America's top female player, winning consecutive national championships from 1992 to 1995.

CHEN JING b. ca. 1967, China
Chen made her Olympic debut in 1988, partly because China's best player, **He Zhili,** was thrown off the team. The pressure was intense, but Chen pulled off a gold-medal win in singles and brought home a silver medal in doubles. Cheng later parted with Chinese officials and moved to Taiwan, for whom she won a silver medal at the 1996 games.

Selected championships and honors, singles: Gold medal, Olympic Games, 1988; silver medal, Olympic Games, 1996. *Doubles:* Silver medal, Olympic Games, 1988.

DENG YAPING b. ca. 1973, China

So diminutive she was twice kept off Chinese teams, Deng let her paddle do the talking, eventually flattening so many opponents that Chinese officials relented. Having reached her adult height of four feet, ten and a half inches, Deng continues to crush all comers. Her speed and concentration are dazzling to watch, and those who have seen Deng play will never again think of table tennis as a mild parlor game.
Selected championships and honors, singles: World Championship, 1991; two gold medals, Olympic Games, 1992 and '96. *Doubles:* Two gold medals, Olympic Games, 1992 and '96.

HE ZHILI b. China

Few women have defied the big red machine of Chinese sports, but He is one of those few. Chinese officials ordered her to throw matches to favored teammates at the 1987 World Championships. She refused, won the title, and became the top-ranked woman in the world. Number one everywhere, that is, except China. As punishment, she was kept off the next year's Olympic team, losing her chance to bring home a gold medal. Later she married a Japanese man and emigrated to Osaka.
Selected championships and honors, singles: World Championship, 1987.

It Pays to Be a Melting Pot

America is famous for lots of things, but table tennis is definitely not one of them. No problem. In addition to the world's tired, poor, and huddled masses, the United States has also welcomed dynamos with paddles. In 1996 the country's five top-ranked women were all born on foreign shores.

Rank	Player	Birthplace
1	Amy Feng	Tianjin, China
2	Lily Yip	Canton, China
3	Wei Wang	Beijing, China
4	Anita Zakharyan	Yerevan, Armenia
5	Virginia Sung	Shanghai, China

RUTH HUGHES AARONS b. 1910, Stamford, Connecticut; d. 1980

Hughes, who never lost a tournament match, ranks as one of the best table tennis players—male or female—America has ever produced. She is the only American woman ever to have won a World Championship singles title, which she took in 1936. She also won four world mixed doubles titles, and in 1937 helped America win the world team championship. At home, Hughes won four national singles titles, 1934–57.
Selected championships and honors, singles: World Championship, 1936. *Mixed doubles:* Four World Championships, 1934–37.

MARIA MEDNYANSZKY b. Hungary

During the fledgling days of table tennis, Mednyanszky was the first truly dominant female player on the world stage. Her skill with a paddle undoubtedly played a role in drawing attention to the sport and winning over new fans. In addition to her singles titles, she won the first doubles championships ever held for women and took six mixed doubles titles with three different partners.
Selected championships and honors, singles: Five World Championships, 1927–31. *Doubles:* Seven World Championships, 1928, '30–35. *Mixed doubles:* Six World Championships, 1927, '28, '30, '31, '33, and '34.

QIAO HONG b. ca. 1970, China

Qiao has had both the good luck and the misfortune to find herself the teammate of one of the best champions in history, **Deng Yaping.** Paired together, the two have proven unbeatable, even at the 1992 Olympics, when Qiao sprained her ankle on the way to the doubles final and played despite the injury. Two days later, when she was pitted against the formidable Deng in the singles final, the injury may have hampered her agility.
Selected championships and honors, singles: Silver medal, Olympic Games, Barcelona; bronze medal, Olympic Games, 1996. *Doubles:* Two gold medals, Olympic Games, 1992 and '96.

LEAH THALL NEUBERGER

One of the top American players of all time, Thall won nine national singles titles between 1949 and 1961, more than any other woman. She also won a dozen U.S. doubles titles—three of them with her sister, Thelma, as partner—and eight mixed doubles championships. Heading north, she won the Canadian singles eleven times before she retired. Internationally, she won a mixed doubles World Championship in

1956 and help American to the Corbillon Cup in 1949. In all she won more than 500 tournaments, and her most treasured trophy may have been her well-earned nickname—Ping.

Selected championships and honors, mixed doubles: World Championships, 1956.

Table Tennis

U.S. Open Singles

Year	Champion	Country
1942	Sally Green	USA
1943	Sally Green	USA
1944	Sally Green	USA
1945	Davida Hawthorne	USA
1946	Bernice Charney	USA
1947	Leah Thall	USA
1948	Peggy McLean	USA
1949	Leah Neuberger	USA
1950	Reba Monness	USA
1951	Leah Neuberger	USA
1952	Leah Neuberger	USA
1953	Leah Neuberger	USA
1954	Mildred Shahian	USA
1955	Leah Neuberger	USA
1956	Leah Neuberger	USA
1957	Leah Neuberger	USA
1958	Susie Hoshi	USA
1959	Susie Hoshi	USA
1960	Sharon Acton	USA
1961	Leah Neuberger	USA
1962	Mildred Shahian	USA
1963	Bernice Chotras	USA
1964	Valeri Bellini	USA
1965	Patty Martinez	USA
1966	Violetta Nesukaitis	CAN
1967	Patty Martinez	USA
1968	Violetta Nesukaitis	CAN
1969	Patty Martinez	USA
1970	Violetta Nesukaitis	CAN
1971	Connie Sweeris	CAN
1972	Wendy Hicks	USA
1973	Violetta Nesukaitis	CAN
1974	Yukie Ohzeki	JPN
1975	Chun Huyn Sook	KOR
1976	Kim Soon Ok	KOR
1977	Insook Bhushan	USA
1978	Hong Ja Park	KOR
1979	Lee Ki Won	KOR
1980	Kayoko Kawahigashi	JPN
1981	Tong Ling	CHN
1982	Kayoko Kawahigashi	JPN
1983	Lee Soo Ja	USA
1984	Kayoko Kawahigashi	JPN
1985	Li Huifen	CHN
1986	Wanhua Xu	CHN
1987	Young Ja Yang	KOR
1988	Jin Xu	CHN
1989	Jin Xu	CHN
1990	Deng Yaping	CHN
1991	Hong Qiao	CHN
1992	Csilla Batorfi	HUN
1993	Chen Jing	TAI
1994	Gao Jun	CHN
1995	Lijuan Geng	CAN
1996	Lee Eun Sil	KOR

Olympic Singles

Year	Medalists	Medal	Country
1896–1984	event not held		
1988	Chen Jing	Gold	CHN
	Li Huifen	Silver	CHN
	Jiao Zhimin	Bronze	CHN
1992	Deng Yaping	Gold	CHN
	Qiao Hong	Silver	CHN
	Hyun Jung-hwa	Bronze	KOR
1996	Deng Yaping	Gold	CHN
	Chen Jing	Silver	TAI
	Qiao Hong	Bronze	CHN

Olympic Doubles

Year	Medalists	Medal	Country
1896–1984	event not held		
1988	Hyjn Jung-hwa/Yang Young-ja	Gold	KOR
	Chen Jing/Jiao Zhimin	Silver	CHN
	Jasna Fazlic/Gordana Perkucin	Bronze	YUG
1992	Deng Yaping/Qiao Hong	Gold	CHN
	Chen Zihe/Gao Jun	Silver	CHN
	Li Bun-hui/Yu Sun-bok	Bronze	PRK
1996	Deng Yaping/Qiao Hong	Gold	CHN
	Liu Wei/Qiao Yunping	Silver	CHN
	Park Hae Jung/Ryu Ji Hae	Bronze	KOR

Photo credit: Culver Pictures, Inc.

TRACK AND FIELD

◆ *In 776 B.C. Coroebus of Elis, a cook, won a 200-yard footrace to become history's first Olympic champion. Many still consider athletics, which concentrate on individual rather than team competitions, the ultimate form of sport.*

HISTORY

The first record of organized athletics comes from Egypt, circa 2000 B.C., where pharaohs were expected to display superior strength and skill as a visible sign of their leadership. In the West, the history of women's participation in sport stretches up the sides of Mount Olympus, where immortals set the example for the mortals below. Greek mythology offers all sorts of athletically inclined women, goddesses, and half-goddesses who tri-

umph through speed, agility, and strategy. The focal point of one of mythology's most famous stories, the race of the Golden Apples, hinges on the heroine's fleetness of foot. The beautiful, adventurous, and athletically powerful Atalanta had no desire to marry and adopted the subterfuge of waiting for a man who could outrace her. Many accepted the challenge, but Atalanta could not be beaten. Finally, Hippomenes turned to Aphrodite for help. The goddess gave him three apples of gold, so beautiful that even the competitive Atalanta could not resist them. Hippomenes tossed them to the ground as he ran, and Atalanta, pausing to retrieve them, lost her lead and ended up married to the clever Hippomenes.

Much has been made of the exclusion of women from the ancient Olympics. This didn't stem from a belief that women were unfit for sports but from a pervasive tendency to divide activities into men's and women's realms. The early Olympics were a kind of male preserve—free and rowdy, with plenty of opportunity for bonding. Originally all women were barred from even observing the games, and being discovered inside the stadium could bring the death penalty. In 396 B.C. Kyniska, a Spartan princess, supplied the horses that won the chariot race, but Kyniska herself was not allowed to watch the race or to participate in the winner's ceremony. Apparently undaunted, she entered the winning horses in the 392 B.C. games as well. The first woman to see the games and live to tell the story may have been Pherenice of Rhodes, who lived sometime before 400 B.C. Her son, a boxer, was to compete in the games, coached by her husband. When her husband died unexpectedly, Pherenice disguised herself as a man and took his place. Luckily her son was victorious, and the Greeks refused to put the mother of a champion to death.

Women were excluded from the Olympics, but they weren't excluded from sports. Sparta, for example, required young women to train in sports, and all-women's games were common throughout Greece. The Heraia, dedicated to the goddess Hera, may be older than the all-male Olympics. These games were held every fourth spring, about a month before the men's games, and like the men's games they were also held at Olympia. The women's race was only slightly shorter than the race run by men—five-sixths of the length of the stade—and the victors received crowns of olive and pieces of the cow sacrificed to Hera. Initially attended by girls from Elis and other nearby towns, the games eventually became famous enough to draw women from the whole Greek world.

Other Greek games also added events for women, and by the first century A.D. there are numerous references to women's races. Like men, women took their athletic achievements seriously and spent considerable time and effort on participation. We know that Tryphosa won an early stade race at the Pythian Games, held at Delphi, and was said to be the first woman to win a race in the Isthmian Games, held at Corinth. Tryphosa's sister, Dionysia, won the stade race at

Alesclepeia, near Epidaurus, while another sister, Hedea, won races at Nemea and at Sycion. These young women hailed from Tralles, in Asia Minor. The distance they traveled to compete, and to compete in races in a variety of locales, suggests that their attitude was indeed serious. It also suggests that their family thought the endeavor a worthy one, for travel arrangements and expenses could not have been undertaken without parental support and approval. To honor the girls' achievements, their proud father, Hermesianax, erected a statue to each of them.

By custom, only virgins could participate in Greek races. There were no events for married women until the tides of history changed, shifting Rome to the center of the world stage. Although Romans were not as eager to include women in athletics as their Greek predecessors, neither did they exclude them. We know from Suetonius's *Lives of the Caesars* that races for girls were a feature of the Capitoline Games. There is also evidence that girls' races were included in the Augustralia, at Naples. The first races for married women were probably also held at Naples, as part of the Sebasteia. The Romans also acknowledged women's participation in other forms of sport. A fourth-century mosaic, known as the "Bikini Mosaic" because its subjects are dressed in bikinilike two-piece costumes, shows young women engaged in a variety of athletic activities, including javelin throw, discus, long jump, a ball game, and a footrace. Since three of the girls are depicted with their prizes, the implication is that all of these events were recognized in formal competitions.

With the decline of Rome, track and field events declined in popularity and remained a marginal feature of life until the waning of the Middle Ages. Why this happened is uncertain, but a number of factors probably fueled the trend. First, the center of civilization shifted north, into climes that hardly favored outdoor events. Unlike the easy pantheism of the Greeks and Romans, which celebrated the body and endorsed its development, Christianity celebrated the life of the spirit while suggesting that the body was frail and untrustworthy. Still another factor may have been that life on earth around the first millennium was simply more difficult. As a species, humans had successfully populated most of Europe and now began competing for resources, territory, and wealth. It's interesting to note that the chief athletic endeavors of the early Middle Ages were all refined elaborations of survival skills, such as hunting, archery, hawking, and horsemanship.

Track and field events reemerged as a feature of European life in the late Middle Ages. They were not city events but a lively feature of rural fairs and festivals, and as such were often staged more for novelty than in the interest of true athletic pursuit. Vestiges of these novelty events can still be seen today, in the guise of one-legged hops or Shrove Tuesday races, where women run holding griddles in one hand and flipping pancakes with the other. Not all events were novelty ones, however. We know that footraces for women were held throughout England, Italy, and Germany from the 1300s on. Yet even the most straightforward races often had a voyeuristic subcurrent that had not been part of the Greek and Roman tradition.

From Pausanias's history of sport, written in the second century A.D., we know that Greek girls raced in special tunics (called *chitons*) that were slightly shorter than knee length and fashioned to leave one shoulder bare. This seemingly skimpy costume was, in fact, a bid for modesty and stood in sharp contrast to men's attire, which consisted of little or nothing at all. We also know from examples like the fleet-footed daughters of Hermesianax that Greek female athletes were generally well-to-do and well respected. This was not the case in Europe, where races were contested by the poor and the disgraced, often for the amusement of the well-off. Smock races were especially popular in England, attracting many contestants whose only hope of new clothing for the season lay in a first-place finish. A race in Basel offered a piece of cloth worth 1½ guldens as its prize. Racers, scantily clad, provided the crowd with a sort of soft-core voyeuristic thrill, and since the contestants were of low class or prostitutes, it was considered good sport for men on the sidelines to attempt to grab or trip them as they sped past.

The growing rowdiness became a matter of controversy, and spurred by the Protestant Refor-

mation of the late sixteenth century, women's races were discontinued. The Cotswold Games, halted in 1642, were revived during the Restoration, and with them the practice of smock races. As can be seen in the novels of Thomas Hardy, such races persisted in rural areas throughout the eighteenth and well into the nineteenth centuries, gradually evolving into a more respectable and less exploitative sport. By the early 1700s women who participated in rural contests were no longer looked down on as prostitutes or prostitutes in the making. According to a 1711 issue of the *Spectator*, Betty Welch's fiancé watched with pride rather than discomfort as his intended held her own in a bar-pitching contest. Around this time, footraces also became a feature of city life. A well-attended race in London's Pall Mall in October 1733 featured prizes of a Holland smock, a cap, embroidered stockings, and laced shoes. A summertime race in Kent Street in 1744 advertised a one-on-one contest between Black Bess of the Mint and a woman known as "the Little Bit of Blue, the Handsome Broom Girl." London's Pall Mall was the venue of another milestone event as well, the first racewalk in history. The lone contestant was an eighteen-month-old girl, whose supporters wagered she could walk the half-mile of the Mall in half an hour. The supporters won, and the tot completed her walk in twenty-three minutes. We know that smock races were exported to the American colonies as well, and the results of one are reported in a June 1753 issue of the Maryland *Gazette*.

THE MODERN ERA

Women's track and field was only partially derailed by the Victorian era. While women could hardly run a marathon in high-buttoned shoes and steel-ribbed corsets, walking was one of the major activities of the day. The Empress Elizabeth of Austria, perhaps the most beautiful and depressed woman in Europe, was noted for her ability to cover miles at a grueling march pace, walking so swiftly her companions frequently could not keep up with her. It should also be remembered that the customs and costumes we associate with Victoriana were largely features of formalized urban life. In the rural reaches of Europe, and along the American frontier, it was a different story altogether. Women's lives and work called for less restrictive clothing, and early photos reveal loose, rolled-up sleeves and an obvious lack of restrictive corsets. Even in the cities, working-class women led vigorous, active lives.

When the Olympics were revived in 1896, a Greek woman named Melpomene sought to enter the marathon. Denied entry, she decided to compete unofficially. Melpomene warmed up out of sight of the officials and ran the beginning of the race off the official course. When the starter was no longer in view, she joined the men and ran alongside them, receiving both taunts and cheers from the surprised spectators. The seventeen male entrants were accompanied by personal aides on bicycles, who supplied them with such niceties as wine, water, raw egg drinks, and alcohol rubdowns. Melpomene, accompanied by no one, stopped only for a glass of water. Only three men finished the race, and Melpomene passed numerous exhausted dropouts on her run to Athens. The race's winner, Spiridon Louis, finished the race in 2 hours, 58 minutes and entered the stadium to wild cheers. Melpomene finished an hour and a half later. By this time the spectators had left and the stadium closed. Unable to enter the stadium, she ran the final lap outside, to no one's cheers but her own.

The fact that Melpomene, with no opportunity for special training or support, was able to run a marathon says much about the physical fitness of the supposedly frail Victorian woman. So do other competitions of the era. A 1903 Parisian race from the Place de la Concord to Nanterre, a distance of 12 kilometers, drew 2,500 contestants. Jeanne Cheminel, the winner, ran the course in an hour and ten minutes, thereby winning the opportunity to perform at a popular music hall. A few weeks later, a series of 300-meter races for shop girls, held in the Parc des Princes, also drew a large field of contestants.

Similar events occurred in America as well. In 1886 the New York Caledonians, an organization for Scottish immigrants, added a 220-yard race for women to its annual athletic festival. A bigger

Major Events and Competitions

In addition to the two major events—the Olympic Games and the World Championships—there are numerous events that loom large in track and field, including the Pan American Games and the many marathons now staged around the world. Some twenty events for women are featured in modern track and field, including:

Track	Field
Individual	*Individual*
100 meters	High jump
200 meters	Long jump
400 meters	Triple jump
800 meters	Shot put
1,500 meters	Discus throw
5,000 meters	Javelin throw
10,000 meters	Heptathlon
Marathon	
100-meter hurdles	
Team	
4 × 100-meter relay	
4 × 400-meter relay	

Discontinued Events

400-meter hurdles	Pentathlon
3,000 meters	
10,000-meter walk	

boost, however, came from the growing movement to include sports in the college curriculum. By the turn of the century track and field were standard in many programs, and any Vassar girl who broke a school record proudly wore a pink "V" on her sweater. At Tuskegee the school athletic director, Cleveland Abbott, took a special lead in promoting women's track and field.

An early track and field festival, the Damensportfest, was held in Berlin in the spring of 1904. Though novelty competitions, such as the broom-in-hand race, had long been part of Carnival, the Damensportfest included only serious events. The winner of the 500-meter event, Gertrude Furkert, raced to victory in a properly modest outfit that covered her arms and legs. Her successors modified the costume, and within five years Germany had provided a model for the first modern sports outfit for women, in which the hem stopped at the knee and the sleeves, at the elbow.

Less than a generation after the Damensportfest, track and field for women made its Olympic debut at the 1928 Amsterdam games. The program included four individual events—100- and 800-meter races, high jump, and discus throw—as well as a 4 × 100-meter relay. As David Wallechinsky reports in his book *The Summer Olympics,* male spectators became flustered when, just before the 100-meter event was run, the three Canadian finalists hugged and kissed each other for luck. Events have been added as well as subtracted from the Olympic roster over the years, and today there are twenty individual and team events for women. It's ironic that one of the most famous Olympic episodes of all time, the 3,000-meter race in which **Mary Decker** clipped the heel of **Zola Budd,** occurred in one of the few events that has since been discontinued. During the games' early years, track events were especially likely to be dominated by the women of North America and Europe. Recently, running has become a truly international sport, with women from South America, the Middle East, Africa, and China claiming their share of the medals.

Hall of Fame

The National Track and Field Hall of Fame, in Indianapolis, Indiana, is noteworthy for the many women included in its rolls.

Governing Bodies and Organizations

USA Track and Field
Box 120
Indianapolis, Indiana 46206
Phone: 317/261-0500

✦ ✦ ✦ BIOGRAPHIES ✦ ✦ ✦

GRETE ANDERSEN WAITZ b. October 1, 1953,
 Oslo, Norway
Although Andersen won her first events as a teenager in Oslo under her maiden name, the world knows her best as Grete Waitz—fittingly so, since it was her husband, Jack Waitz, who encouraged her to enter her first marathon in 1978. Waitz, a solid middle-distance runner, had never run a marathon before, and she followed her husband's suggestion largely because she thought it would be fun to visit America. Her victory in the 1978 New York marathon put Waitz—and women's running—on a new track. A novice at pacing herself through a 26.2-mile distance, Waitz suffered from cramps and dehydration throughout much of the race yet still broke the existing women's world record by a full two minutes, with a time of 2:32:30. It was the first of an unprecedented nine New York wins, and with her victory the next year in 1979, Waitz became the first woman to run an official marathon in under 2½ hours. All in all, Waitz lowered the world record four times between 1978 and 1983, going from 2:32:30 to 2:25:29. Waitz's dominance, modesty, and ever-fresh enthusiasm made her a popular spokesman for running and for physical fitness. Since her retirement from serious competition in 1991, Waitz has continued to promote her sport and to encourage others. When Zoe Koplowitz, a runner with multiple sclerosis who competes on crutches, was the last person to cross the finish line at the 1993 New York Marathon, Waitz was waiting to greet her. *Selected championships and honors:* Five Cross-Country World Championships, 1978–81 and '83; nine New York Marathons, 1978–80, '82–86, and '88; gold medal, marathon, World Track and Field Championships, 1983; silver medal, marathon, Olympic Games, 1984; International Women's Sports Hall of Fame.

JODI ANDERSON b. November 10, 1957,
 Chicago, Illinois
Anderson's serious, laser-focus style helped her set junior high and high school records in long jump, an event she continued to excel in throughout college. As a student at California State–Northridge in the late 1970s, she won a fistful of national indoor, outdoor, and AIAW long jump championships, as well as

the AIAW pentathlon crown in 1979. She finished first in both events at the 1980 Olympic trials but missed her chance for a medal when the United States boycotted the games. Anderson made the team again in 1984 and was scheduled to compete in the heptathlon but was forced to withdraw after injuring herself early in the competition.

EVELYN ASHFORD WASHINGTON b. April 15, 1957, Shreveport, Louisiana

In a sport where longevity is a rare commodity, Ashford's career as a sprinter spanned an entire generation. She was a member of every U.S. Olympic team from 1976 through 1992, winning medals in all but the 1976 games. Ashford was a standout throughout high school, where she was the only girl on her Roseville, California, track and field team. One of the first women to receive a UCLA athletic scholarship, Ashford won AIAW championships in the 100- and 200-meter dashes in 1977 and repeated her 200-meter victory in 1978. But Ashford's real quest was for Olympic gold. As a member of the 1976 U.S. team, she finished fifth in the 100-meter dash, and she dropped out of school in 1978 to train full-time for the 1980 games—a sacrifice that left her all the more disappointed with the United States' decision to boycott. Ashford won the 100- and 200-meter distances in the 1979 World Cup championships, beating world record holders **Marlies Göhr** and **Marita Koch** respectively. She won both events again in 1981. A pulled hamstring during the 1983 World Championships became a chronic problem and threatened to ruin her long-awaited shot at an Olympic medal. At the 1984 games, the hamstring caused her to withdraw from the 200 meter and focus on the 100-meter event. The gamble paid off, and the usually impassive Ashford was in tears as she claimed her medal. As a member of the 400-meter relay team, she won a second gold medal a few days later. Although Ashford's hamstring remained a problem, she continued to compete for another eight years. Her final win was, appropriately, a gold medal, which she won as a member of the U.S. relay team at the 1992 Olympics.

Selected championships and honors, individual: Gold medal, 100 meters, Olympic Games, 1984; silver medal, 100 meters, Olympic Games, 1988. *Team:* Three gold medals, 4 × 100m relay, Olympic Games, 1984, '88, and '92.

IOLANDA BALAS b. December 12, 1936, Timisoara, Romania

High Jump, Low Marks— the 1936 Olympics

Considering the mayhem soon to be unleashed on the world, Hitler's interference in the 1936 Olympics seems trifling. Yet one would have to look long and hard to find a fiasco larger than the Führer's games. During tryouts for the German team, Gretel Bergmann turned in the best high jump performance but was dropped from the team because she was Jewish. Another member of the German team, Dora Ratjen, who finished fourth, was barred from competition as a hermaphrodite in 1938. Thirty years later, Ratjen revealed that he had never been a hermaphrodite, just an ordinary young man who had been forced to compete as a woman in hopes of securing a gold medal for Hitler's showcase. As a consequence, Hungary's Ilona Csak, Britain's Dorothy Odam, and Germany's Elfreide Kaun—who finished first, second, and third—have the odd distinction of being the only women to beat a man in a major international track and field competition.

At six feet, Balas had a distinct advantage in the high jump. She also had a style that for more than a decade made her nearly unbeatable. Although Balas went into the 1956 Olympics as the world record holder, she finished a disappointing fifth and saw her record fall to the United States' **Mildred McDaniel.** It was one of Balas's last losses. Over the next ten years she won her event in 140 consecutive competitions—including two Olympics—and set new world records fourteen times. She was also the first woman to clear the six-foot barrier. Her final record, a 6'3.25" jump in 1961, stood for an entire decade.

Selected championships and honors: Two gold medals, high jump, Olympic Games, 1960 and '64.

KIM BATTEN b. March 29, 1969, McRae, Georgia

A solid multievent athlete in high school, Batten began focusing on 400-meter hurdles while in college at Florida State. She won her first U.S. title in 1991 and made it to fifth place in the World Championships. Her best year, 1995, saw her sweep the nationals, Pan American Games, and World Championships. Prior to the worlds, there had been much talk about a weak field, but Batten's winning time set a new world record. The next year Batten finished second at the Atlanta Olympics.

Selected championships and honors: Gold medal, 400m hurdles, Pan American Games, 1995; gold medal, 400m hurdles, World Championships, 1995; silver medal, 400m hurdles, Olympic Games, 1995.

JOAN BENOIT SAMUELSON b. May 16, 1957, Cape Elizabeth, Maine

A youthful skier who broke her leg on the slopes, Benoit began distance running as a means of rehabilitation. By the time the leg was 100 percent, Benoit was hooked on running. Good enough to qualify for the Junior Olympics during her senior year in high school, Benoit had her first major victory in the 1979 Boston Marathon, which she completed in an American women's record time of 2:35:15. She had both Achilles tendons operated on in 1981 but came back for a second Boston Marathon win in 1983, setting a women's world record with a time of 2:22:43. That same year Benoit set American records in four distances, winning 25-kilometer, 10-kilometer, half-marathon, and 10-mile runs. During her career Benoit often raced against Norway's **Grete Andersen Waitz,** one of the most consistent woman runners of all time. Benoit's knee surgery in April 1984 threatened her Olympic appearance and made Waitz the odds-on favorite to win the games' first women's marathon. During the event, Benoit took a surprise lead at the three-mile mark and never gave it up, beating Waitz by nearly a minute and a half. In a career plagued by difficult and painful injuries, Benoit went on to set another American record in 1985, running the Chicago Marathon in 2:21:21. Benoit has continued to compete well into the mid-1990s despite her injuries, winning points on guts and grit even when a first-place finish eludes her.

Gold Rush

When I came into the stadium and saw all the colors and everything, I told myself, "Listen, just look straight ahead, because if you don't you're probably going to faint."

—Joan Benoit, on winning the first Olympic marathon, Los Angeles, 1984

Selected championships and honors: Two Boston Marathons, 1979 and '83; gold medal, marathon, Olympic Games, 1984; Sullivan Award, 1985.

MARY BIGNAL RAND TOOMEY b. February 10, 1940, Great Britain

The first British woman to earn a track and field gold, Bignal was bitterly disappointed when, favored to win at the 1960 Olympics, she ran through her last two long jump attempts and fell from third place to ninth. It was a different story the next time around, when despite a stiff headwind four of her six jumps were personal bests and the fifth set a new world record. Unused to the metric system, she did not know she had broken the record until consulting a conversion chart. Later in the games, she earned a silver and a bronze as well. At the 1968 games Bignal met U.S. decathlete Bill Toomey, whom she later married.

Selected championships and honors, individual: Gold medal, long jump, Olympic Games, 1964; silver medal, pentathlon, Olympic Games, 1964. *Team:* Bronze medal, 4 × 100m relay, Olympic Games, 1964.

FRANCINCA (FANNY) BLANKERS-KOEN b. April 26, 1918, Amsterdam, the Netherlands

The Babe Didrikson of Europe, Blankers-Koen dominated a half-dozen track and field events, including sprints, relay, hurdles, long jump, and high jump. She had barely begun to compete internationally when World War II broke out. After a sixth-place finish in the long jump at the 1936 games, she had to wait twelve years for another Olympic chance. By 1948 Blankers-Koen was married and the mother of two—and the world record holder in the 100 meters, 80-meter hurdle, long jump, and high jump. Since Olympic rules limited the number of events she could compete in, she entered the 100- and 200-meter sprints and 80-meter hurdles, and ran on the Netherlands' 4 × 100-meter relay team. She won gold medals in each event. Had she been allowed to compete in the long jump and high jump, she would likely have taken golds there as well, since the winners fell short of her past performances. Blankers-Koen attended the 1952 games in Helsinki as well, but had to withdraw from competition due to an infection in her leg. Enormously popular in her home country, Blankers-Koen was admired for her tenacity and modesty as well as for her athleticism.

Selected championships and honors, individual: Gold medal, 100m, Olympic Games, 1948; gold medal,

A Long Way, Baby?

At the 1948 London Olympics, the Netherlands' Fanny Blankers-Koen won four gold medals and proved herself one of the best women athletes in the world. You'd expect her to get a lot of press coverage, and she did, including this headline from the *London Daily Graphic:* FASTEST WOMAN IN THE WORLD IS AN EXPERT COOK. The seemingly sexist headline was in fact an attempt to rescue Blankers-Koen from gossip that she neglected her home and children to pursue her athletic career. Her husband, Jan Koen, went so far as to personally assure the press that "My wife is a real housewife. She cooks, cleans and takes care of our children. She sews and knits their clothes." To the best of our knowledge, there were no press stories on males at the London games who might have stolen time from their wives, children, parents, or jobs in order to train.

200m, Olympic Games, 1948; gold medal, 800m hurdles, Olympic Games, 1948. *Team:* Gold medal, 4 × 100m relay, Olympic Games, 1948. Associated Press Female Athlete of the Year, 1948; International Women's Sports Hall of Fame.

HASSIBA BOULMERKA b. ca. 1968, Constantine, Algeria

Boulmerka's career has mirrored the upheaval of her times. A champion of the 1,500-meter distance, she won the World Championship in 1991, the year the Soviet Union disintegrated. Boulmerka, a devout Muslim, returned home a national heroine—and pariah. While most of her countrymen feted her with flowers and accolades, Muslim fundamentalists denounced her for "running with naked legs" in public. So great was the pressure that Boulmerka went to Germany to train for the 1992 Olympics. Winning the gold by more than 1.5 seconds, her first words across the finish line were "Algérie! Algérie!" She won a third medal for her country, again at 1,500 meters, at the 1995 World Championships.

Selected championships and honors: Two gold medals, 1,500m, World Championships, 1991 and '95; gold medal, 1,500m, Olympic Games, 1992.

VALERIE BRISCO-HOOKS b. July 6, 1960, Greenwood, Mississippi

Known as "VBH" for short, Brisco-Hooks made history at the 1984 Olympic Games as the first athlete ever to win both 200- and 400-meter gold medals at a single Olympics. Her first important win had come just five years earlier when, as a student at the University of California–Northridge, she won the AIAW 200-meter title. She married Philadelphia Eagles wide receiver Alvin Hooks in 1981 and had a son the following year. The pregnancy left her out of shape and forty pounds overweight, but with her husband's encouragement she embarked on a spartan training regime. At the 1984 indoor championships she won the 400-meter event with a time of 49.82, becoming the first American woman to run that distance in less than 50 seconds. Her time was even better for the Olympics later that year, and she shaved almost a full second off her time to win in 48.83, an American record that was still standing a decade later.

Selected championships and honors, individual: Gold medal, 200 meters, Olympic Games, 1984; gold medal, 400 meters, Olympic Games, 1984. *Team:* Two gold medals, 4 × 100m relay, Pan American Games, 1979 and '87; two gold medals, 4 × 100m relay, Olympic Games, 1984 and '87. U.S. Track and Field Hall of Fame.

DORIS BROWN HERITAGE b. September 7, 1942, Tacoma, Washington

An outstanding cross-country runner, Brown earned her first international title in 1967, when she won the first of five world cross-country titles. She set a world record for the 3,000 meters in 1971, was a member of U.S. world teams (including the 1968 and '72 Olympic teams), and won a total of fourteen national titles. Brown, a distance coach at Seattle Pacific University, went on to become the first female member of the Cross Country and Road Running Committee of the International Amateur Athletic Foundation, the sport's world governing body.

Selected championships and honors: Five World Cross-Country Championships, 1967–71; silver medal, 800 meters, Pan American Games, 1971; U.S. Track and Field Hall of Fame.

ZOLA BUDD PIETERSE b. May 26, 1966,
    Bloemfontein, Orange Free State, South Africa
Fairly or not, Budd's name is forever linked with that
of America's **Mary Decker.** In the 3,000-meter finals of the 1984 Olympics, the two somehow became
entangled. Decker fell and could not finish. Despite
the fact that the tangle also cost Budd dearly—she
finished seventh—Decker publicly blamed her for
the mishap. To add to the misfortune, the race was
one of Budd's first "official" competitions. Because of
South Africa's apartheid policy, its athletes had been
barred by the International Amateur Athletic Federation, and none of Budd's wins or records had been
recognized. To remedy the situation, she became a
British citizen in 1984 and ran for the United King-
dom in the Olympics. Like the woman she collided
with in Los Angeles, Budd put the incident behind
her and went on to win two consecutive cross-
country championships. Long-legged and childlike in
appearance, Budd was a barefoot runner with an unusual stride whose power came from a strong finishing kick. Due to circumstances largely beyond her
control, she is not nearly as well remembered as she
should be.
Selected championships and honors: Two Cross-
Country World Championships, 1985 and '86.

TONJA BUFORD BAILEY b. December 13, 1970,
    Dayton, Ohio
Throughout her career at 400-meter hurdles, Buford
has often finished behind fellow American **Kim Batten.** But Buford, the younger of the two, has time on
her side, and her string of medals is nevertheless impressive. At a 1995 meet in Switzerland Buford beat
not only Batten but Jamaica's Deon Hemmings, 1996
Olympic gold medalist.
Selected championships and honors: Silver medal,
400m hurdles, Pan American Games, 1995; silver
medal, 400m hurdles, World Championships, 1995;
bronze medal, 400m hurdles, Olympic Games, 1996.

ETHEL CATHERWOOD b. 1910, Saskatoon,
    Saskatchewan, Canada
Times being what they were, the vote was very much
out on the "appropriateness" of including women's
track and field in the 1928 Olympics. Catherwood,
winner of the first high jump, helped turn the tide.
Eighteen years old, the pretty and unassuming Catherwood—nicknamed "the Saskatoon Lily"—quickly became one of the stars of the games. A huge crowd

celebrated her return to Saskatoon and presented her
with $3,000 to continue her piano lessons. Catherwood
moved to the United States in 1929 and later settled in
San Francisco.
Selected championships and honors: Gold medal,
high jump, Olympic Games, 1928.

CHANDRA CHEESEBOROUGH b. January 10,
    1959, Jacksonville, Florida
Another famous Tigerbelle, Cheeseborough was a
member of two indoor world-record-setting relay
teams at Tennessee State. An unusually versatile runner, good at sprints as well as longer distances, Cheeseborough was a member of three Olympic teams,
including the thwarted 1980 crew. One of her greatest
feats came at her final Olympics, when she became the
first woman ever to win gold medals at both the 4 ×
100- and 4 × 400-meter relay distances, helping her
team to an Olympic record (3:18.29) in the latter.
Selected championships and honors, individual: Silver medal, 400m, Olympic Games, 1984. *Team:* Gold
medal, 4 × 100m relay, Olympic Games, 1984; gold
medal, 4 × 400m relay, Olympic Games, 1984.

ALICE COACHMAN DAVIS b. November 9,
    1923, Albany, Georgia
For an entire decade, Coachman was the AAU outdoor high jump champion. She might have won ten
indoor championships as well, if World War II hadn't
interrupted competition in the 1940s. The war also
cost her her Olympic opportunities, but Coachman
made up for lost time when the games resumed in
1948. Her win in the high jump made her the first
African-American woman ever to win an Olympic
gold medal. Although Coachman is best known for her
dominance in the high jump, she was also a successful
sprinter. In addition to several 50- and 100-meter wins,
she was a member of two national 4 × 100-meter
championship relay teams. Coachman was given a
heroine's welcome home and received a college scholarship, which she used to earn a teaching degree.
Selected championships and honors: Gold medal,
high jump, Olympic Games, 1948; U.S. Track and
Field Hall of Fame; International Women's Sports
Hall of Fame.

LILLIAN COPELAND b. November 25, 1904,
    New York, New York; d. July 7, 1964
Regarded as the first world-class American woman
weight thrower, Copeland won multiple national

championships in javelin (2), discus (2), and shot put (5) in the late 1920s and early '30s. She set world records in the javelin throw three years running (1926–28) and attended the 1928 Olympic Games, the first that included track and field events for women. Although javelin wasn't a recognized women's event at the time, Copeland won a silver in the discus. By the time the next Olympics arrived, Copeland was so immersed in law school she barely made the U.S. team. Nevertheless, she won a gold medal in discus on her final throw.

Selected championships and honors: Silver medal, discus, Olympic Games, 1928; gold medal, discus, Olympic Games, 1932; U.S. Track and Field Hall of Fame.

ELIZABETH (BETTY) CUTHBERT b. 1938,
Ermington, New South Wales, Australia
Part of a brief but, to Australians, memorably sweet dominance in track and field by women from the Land Down Under, Cuthbert followed in the tracks of **Marjorie Jackson** to win the 100 meters at the 1956 Olympics. Quiet and unassuming, Cuthbert later wrote in her autobiography, *Golden Girl,* that she remembered breaking the tape but didn't grasp that she had won until she saw her mother crying with joy. A few days later she won a second gold in the 200 meters, in which she held the current world record, and helped Australia to its first—and only—relay gold. When a pulled hamstring forced her to pull out of the 1960 games, it seemed Cuthbert's career might be over. Remarkably, she came back four years later to win the first Olympic 400-meter event. Describing it as the only perfect race she ever ran, Cuthbert left the Olympic stage, Australia's indisputable golden girl of track.

Selected championships and honors, individual: Gold medal, 100m, Olympic Games, 1956; gold medal, 200m, Olympic Games, 1956; gold medal, 400m, Olympic Games, 1964. *Team:* Gold medal, 4 × 100m relay, Olympic Games, 1956.

DAN SHIN-GEUM b. July 7, 1938, Pyongyang,
North Korea
Dan was a terrific champion and world record holder—yet few know her name and fewer still ever saw her run. In 1963, at a meet in Djakarta, she became the first woman to run an official 800-meter race in under two minutes. The next year, although she held the world records at both 400 and 800 meters, she could not compete in the Olympics because

of the IOC's ban on her country. If she had, she might have been a double medal winner, since both times were comfortably ahead of those of the winners.

HEIKE DAUTE DRECHSLER b. 1965, East
Germany
Daute was co-queen of the long jump for a decade, sharing her throne and alternating top honors with America's **Jackie Joyner-Kersee.** From 1983, when she won her first World Championship, through 1987 she was ranked number one in the world and won at twenty-seven consecutive meets. The eastern bloc boycott of the 1984 Olympics cost her a chance at a gold medal, and her string of wins ended when she injured her knee at the World Championships and finished in third place. She lost to Joyner-Kersee again the following year but finally defeated her at the 1992 games. Ten years after her first World Championship, she won a second gold in 1993.

Selected championships and honors: Silver medal, long jump, Olympic Games, 1988; two gold medals, long jump, World Championships, 1983 and '93; bronze medal, long jump, World Championships, 1987; gold medal, long jump, Olympic Games, 1992.

MARY DECKER SLANEY b. August 4, 1958,
Flemington, New Jersey
Decker began running at an unusually early age, shortly after her family moved to California when she was eleven. Her first international win came at a U.S./USSR track meet in 1973, and by the time she was fifteen, she held world records at 1,000 meters, 880 yards, and 800 meters. But at fifteen, her body had not yet matured, and she began experiencing physical injuries that often sidelined her for months at a time. Over the next years Decker alternated record-setting competitions with sprains, strains, and surgeries. She also began to race longer distances, and in 1980 she set an American record on her first try at the 3,000 meters. One of her most serious injuries, a torn Achilles tendon that required yet another surgery, kept her off the track until 1982, when she returned to her greatest season ever. Racing in the United States and abroad, Decker set world records at 2,000, 3,000, 5,000, and 10,000 meters, and set one-mile records twice. She became the first woman ever to receive the Jesse Owens Award for outstanding track and field athlete of the year. In 1983 she attended the first World Championships and won both the 1,500 and 3,000 meters. All in all, she won ten consecutive 3,000-meter events between 1982 and 1984. Disap-

pointment came soon after, at the 1984 Los Angeles Olympics. With just three laps to go in the 3,000 meters, Decker became entangled with **Zola Budd** and fell, injuring her hip. The spill marked the end of her Olympic hopes. Although Decker set two more world records in 1985, her performance began to decline. She finished tenth in the 3,000 meters at the 1988 Olympics, failed to make the 1992 team, and made her final competitive appearance at the 1996 Olympics, where she failed to advance to the final heat of the 5,000-meter race. Admired by fans and fellow athletes alike, Decker combined exquisite form and gutsy strength with a relentless desire to win.
Selected championships and honors: Gold medal, 1,500m, World Championships, 1983; gold medal, 3,000m, World Championships, 1983; Sullivan Award, 1982; Associated Press Female Athlete of the Year, 1982; Jesse Owens Award, 1982; *Sports Illustrated* Sportsman of the Year, 1983.

GAIL DEVERS b. November 19, 1966, Seattle, Washington
A UCLA alum who competed in sprints, hurdles, and long jump, Devers came to national attention when she won the 100-meter dash at the 1987 Pan American Games and the 1988 NCAA championships. Then she dropped out of sight, and many erroneously assumed she'd retired. In fact, Devers was extremely ill. Her problem was eventually diagnosed as Bright's disease, a serious thyroid disorder. She came perilously close to losing both feet and was not able to compete again until 1992. Healthy once more, Devers was on a roll. In one of the closest races in history, she earned a gold medal in the 100-meter sprint at the 1992 Olympics, coming in just .04 seconds ahead of the fourth-place finisher. The race she's best remembered for in 1992, however, is the one she lost. Leading on the way into the final barrier of the 100-meter hurdles, she lost her rhythm, hit the hurdle with her foot, and fell. Determined to finish, she scrambled up and crossed the line in fifth place. Ironically, it was the heartbreaking fall that cemented her place as one of America's favorite athletes. Devers took both the 100-meter sprint and hurdles titles at the World Championships the next year and repeated as hurdle world champion in 1995. In 1996 she became the first woman since **Wyomia Tyus** to win back-to-back 100-meter sprints at the Olympics.
Selected championships and honors: Gold medal, 100m, Pan American Games, 1987; silver medal, 100m hurdles, World Championships, 1991; two gold med-

als, 100m, Olympic Games, 1992 and '96; gold medal, 100m, World Championships, 1993; two gold medals, 100m hurdles, World Championships, 1993 and '95; gold medal, 100m, Olympic Games, 1996.

MILDRED (BABE) DIDRIKSON ZAHARIAS. *See entry under Golf.*

TATYANA DOROVSKIKH. *See Tatyana Samolenko Dorovskikh, below.*

NAWAL EL MOUTAWAKEL b. April 15, 1962, Casablanca, Morocco
El Moutawakel won the first 400-meter hurdles offered for women at the 1984 Olympics—appropriately, since she was also the first gold medalist from her country and the first woman from an Islamic country to medal at the Olympics. Her road to glory wasn't easy, though. As a college student, soon after arriving in the United States to train, El Moutawakel received word that her father, who had also been her coach and mentor, had died. The next year, El Moutawakel stayed home to study instead of going to a meet. The plane carrying the team crashed, and all of her teammates were killed. El Moutawakel's Olympic victory, carried live in Casablanca, caused a spontaneous round of celebrations in the street, even though it was well after midnight. Today she combines both new and old female roles, coaching the Moroccan Olympic track team, writing for *La Gazette du sport*, and—at home—leading the life of a traditional Muslim wife and mother of two.
Selected championships and honors: Gold medal, 400m hurdles, Olympic Games, 1984.

HERIWENTHA (MAE) FAGGS STARR b. April 10, 1932, Mays Landing, New Jersey
One of many track stars who matured at Tennessee State, Faggs's talents as a sprinter helped her to a dozen national AAU titles, half of which were in the indoor 200 meters. She also ran for the United States on three medal-winning relay teams.
Selected championships and honors, individual: Silver medal, 200m, Pan American Games, 1955. *Team:* Gold medal, 4 × 100m relay, Olympic Games, 1952; gold medal, 4 × 100m relay, Pan American Games, 1955; bronze medal, 4 × 100m relay, Olympic Games, 1956. U.S. Track and Field Hall of Fame.

SANDRA FARMER PATRICK b. August 18, 1962, Kingston, Jamaica

Raised by an aunt in Brooklyn, New York, Farmer Patrick had to choose whether to compete as a Jamaican or as an American. Despite the stiffer competition, Farmer opted for America because, as she told *Track & Field News*, "I feel like an American." She competed in her event, the 400-meter hurdles, against formidably tough competition, both at home—from **Kim Batten** and **Tonja Buford**—and abroad, from British champion **Sally Gunnell.**

Selected championships and honors: Silver medal, 400m hurdles, Pan American Games, 1987; silver medal, 400m hurdles, Olympic Games, 1992; silver medal, 400m hurdles, World Championships: 1993.

SUZY FAVOR HAMILTON b. August 8, 1968, Stevens Point, Wisconsin

An outstanding college runner at the University of Wisconsin, Favor was the first athlete, male or female, to win the NCAA one-mile championship four times. Smaller than most runners (5′3″, 110 pounds), Favor lost only two of the fifty-six events she competed in, taking national championships at the mile, 800 meters, and 1,500 meters.

Selected championships and honors: Broderick Cup, 1990; three times Big Ten Female Athlete of the Year, 1988–90; Big Ten Female Athlete of the Decade, 1981–91.

BARBARA FERRELL EDMONSON b. July 28, 1947, Hattiesburg, Mississippi

Ferrell was one of the world's top sprinters during the late 1960s and might have extended her career through the 1972 Olympics had she not been injured. In addition to several AAU titles, she won two Olympic medals and a gold medal at the Pan American Games. Although she won the trials for the 1972 Olympic Games, injury hampered her performance and kept her out of medal range. Ferrell, who attended the University of Southern California, returned to become the university's women's track and field coach.

Selected championships and honors, individual: Gold medal, 100m, Pan American Games, 1967; silver medal, 100m, Olympic Games, 1968. *Team:* Gold medal, 4 × 100m relay, Olympic Games, 1968. U.S. Track and Field Hall of Fame.

EMMA GEORGE b. 1974, Australia

In the year 2000, the summer Olympics will be held in Sydney, Australia, and if George has her way, her sport, women's pole vault, will at least be featured as a

We Run, We Jump— Now Can We Fly?

Will the next barrier to fall be the "air" ceiling? Very likely. Until recently, the pole vault was a male preserve. It was commonly accepted that women lacked the upper-body strength needed for the sport, and many male vaulters wanted to keep it that way. While it's true that women will never amass the upper-body strength their male counterparts do, it's also true that women have their own advantages—less body weight to launch and a lower center of gravity. The lower center of gravity allows for a freer, wider-arc swing. Women are just beginning to learn how to use these advantages, and as their techniques become more honed, the gap between male and female performance may well narrow dramatically. Another boost may come from increased competition. In the U.S. and many western countries, women don't discover the sport until college. Increased T.V. coverage (the sport will become an official women's event at the Indoor World Championships in 1997) and exciting rivalries like the one between **Emma George** and previous world-record holder Daniela Bartova will help publicize the sport among younger women who may decide that they, too, can learn to fly.

demonstration sport. If it is, it will be fittingly appropriate that it makes its debut in George's homeland. The acrobatic George, whose past includes a stint as a trapeze artist in a children's circus, decided to try pole vault in college because it looked like "fun." By 1995, she was one of the sport's top contenders, along with the Czech Republic's Daniela Bartova. In the summer of 1996, with the world's attention focused on the Olympics, George extended the women's world record to a stunning 4.45 meters (14′7¼″)—more than a quarter of a meter higher than the previous record.

MARLIES GÖHR. *See Marlies Oelsner Göhr, below.*

DELORES (FLORENCE) GRIFFITH-JOYNER

b. December 21, 1959, Los Angeles, California

An athlete whose neon personality and vibrant track suits matched her electrifying speed, "Flo-Jo" captured medals as well as headlines at the 1988 Olympics. Her athletic career actually began at UCLA, when she won NCAA titles in 1982 and '83. She won her first Olympic medal, a silver, at the 1984 games, and by 1988 she had matured into a formidable talent. Her time of 10.49, made during the 100-meter trials, set a women's world record, and she set another world record during the games themselves, running the 200 meters in 21.34. Both records were still standing two Olympiads later. A champion all by herself, Griffith-Joyner was also part of a family dynasty of stars. Her husband's sister, Jackie Joyner, also a multimedalist, married UCLA track coach Bob Kersee.

Selected championships and honors, individual: Silver medal, 200m, Olympic Games, 1984; silver medal, 200m, World Championships, 1987; gold medal, 100m, Olympic Games, 1988; gold medal, 200m, Olympic Games, 1988. *Team:* Gold medal, 4 × 100m relay, World Championships, 1987; gold medal, 4 × 100m relay, Olympic Games, 1988; silver medal, 4 × 400m relay, Olympic Games, 1988. U.S. Track and Field Hall of Fame; Sullivan Award, 1988; Associated Press Athlete of the Year, 1988; United Press International Athlete of the Year, 1988.

SALLY GUNNELL b. July 29, 1966, Chigwell, England

Gunnell, who grew up on a farm in rural Essex, is the first English woman ever to win a gold medal in hurdles. At her specialty, the 400-meter hurdles, she was a world record holder, earning both Olympic and World Championship gold medals. After winning the World Championship in 1993, she shifted to the broadcast booth and covered the 1995 championships for television.

Selected championships and honors: Gold medal, 400m hurdles, Olympics, 1992; gold medal, 400m hurdles, World Championships, 1993.

EVELYN (EVIE) HALL ADAMS b. September 10, 1909, Minneapolis, Minnesota; d. April 20, 1993

An AAU indoor/outdoor champion hurdler and a member of the formidable Illinois Women's Athletic Club of the 1930s, Hall figured in one of the most exciting finishes in Olympic history. At the 1932 games she and teammate Babe Didrikson ran against each other in the 80-meter hurdles. Hall actually led going into the final hurdle, and both women were clocked at a world-record 11.7. Coming out of the hurdle, Didrikson picked up speed and beat Hall to the tape by a distance of two inches. Hall continued to compete and win nationally, but she retired after she failed to make the 1936 Olympic team. She remained active in the sport, however, and coached the women's team at the first Pan American Games in 1951. She also served several years as track and field chairman of the U.S. Olympic Committee.

Selected championships and honors: Silver medal, 80m hurdles, Olympic Games, 1932; U.S. Track and Field Hall of Fame.

HITOMI KINUE b. 1907, Japan; d. 1931

While Asian women are general latecomers to track and field, Hitomi was an early champion whose feats shine all the brighter for the fact that they were so little encouraged. In 1928 Hitomi held world records in the 200-meter sprint and the long jump. Since neither event was included in the Olympics, she entered the 100- and 800-meter races instead, finishing second in the longer distance. At the third Women's World Games, in 1930, Hitomi won a gold in the long jump, a silver in the triathlon, and bronzes in discus and the 60-meter dash. She died the next year, at age twenty-four, of tuberculosis. Most Americans think of Babe Didrikson as the first dynamic all-round female athlete, but Hitomi should rightly share the honor with her.

Selected championships and honors: Silver medal, 800m, Olympic Games, 1928.

Sweet Sullivans

Women who excel at track have won more Sullivan Awards than the women of any other sport, though swimmers come close with a total of four. Five women runners have received the award, one of the most coveted honors in American sports.

Wilma Rudolph, 1961
Mary Decker, 1982
Joan Benoit Samuelson, 1985
Jackie Joyner-Kersee, 1986
Florence Griffith-Joyner, 1988

DANA INGROVA ZATOPKOVA b. 1922, Czechoslovakia

Everyone has heard of runner Emil Zatopek, but few know that his wife was also an Olympic gold-medal winner. A javelin thrower, she competed in four consecutive Olympics—the first in 1948 under her maiden name and the next three as Zatopkova. Carrying her husband's gold medal for luck, she won her event in 1952. When her husband jokingly claimed to have inspired her win with his medal, she suggested he go see if he could inspire some other girl to throw a javelin 50 meters. Although Zatopkova finished out of the medals in 1956, she broke the world record two years later and came back to claim a silver at her final Olympics in 1960. Days shy of her thirty-eighth birthday, Zatopkova became the oldest woman to earn an Olympic medal in track and field.

Selected championships and honors: Gold medal, javelin, Olympic Games, 1952; silver medal, javelin, Olympic Games, 1960.

MARJORIE JACKSON b. September 13, 1931, Lithgow, Australia

Sometimes it isn't what you win but who you beat. Jackson became a national heroine when she beat the unbeatable **Fanny Blankers-Koen** at Australian meets in 1949. A cinder practice track was built for her by her hometown, and Jackson repaid them by equaling Blankers-Koen's 100-meter world record to win a gold at the 1952 Olympics. At the same games, she broke **Stella Walsh's** long-standing record in the 200 meters during trials, then took the gold in the final. Jackson, along with teammate **Shirley Strickland de la Hunty,** became the first women in Australian history to win Olympic track and field golds.

Selected championships and honors: Gold medal, 100m, Olympic Games, 1952; gold medal, 200m, Olympic Games, 1952.

NELL JACKSON b. July 1, 1929, Athens, Georgia; d. April 1, 1988

Jackson, a sprinter who at one time held the American record in the 200 meters, was a member of the U.S. 1948 Olympic team and a medalist at the first Pan American Games in 1951. She went on to became a coach and physical education director at several schools, including her alma mater, Tuskegee. She was the first African-American to serve as head coach on an Olympic team, coaching both the 1956 and '72 teams. A tireless and effective advocate for her sport, she conducted many clinics and served numerous governing bodies, including the U.S. Olympic Committee.

Selected championships and honors, individual: Silver medal, 200m, Pan American Games, 1951. *Team:* Gold medal, 4 × 100m relay, Pan American Games, 1951. U.S. Track and Field Hall of Fame.

LYNN JENNINGS b. July 1, 1960, Princeton, New Jersey

Jennings attracted attention as a superb indoor miler while still in high school, and has had her biggest successes at the World Cross-Country Championships. In addition to three first-place finishes, she placed second in 1986 and third in 1993. Her cross-country success hasn't been matched in Olympic or World Championship competition, however, where she has failed to find her way to a gold or silver.

Selected championships and honors: Three World Cross-Country Championships, 1990–92; bronze medal, 10,000m, Olympic Games, 1992.

JACQUELINE (JACKIE) JOYNER-KERSEE b. March 3, 1962, East St. Louis, Missouri

One of the best multievent track and field stars in U.S. history, Joyner was the first American woman to hold the pentathlon world record. She won her first heptathlon, the national juniors, when she was just fourteen, and focused on the event as her specialty while attending UCLA on a sports scholarship. Instrumental in encouraging her to focus on multievents was Joyner's coach, Bob Kersee, whom she married in 1986. When the Olympic pentathlon was changed to a seven-event heptathlon in 1984, Joyner missed the gold medal by just five points—less than an eyelash compared to a winning score of 6,390. It was the last second-place finish Joyner would suffer for a long time. She won the next nine heptathlons she entered. At the Moscow Goodwill Games, on July 7, 1986, she broke her first world record and became the first woman ever to amass more than 7,000 points in heptathlon. She broke her record three more times, turning in her best performance to win the gold medal at the 1988 Olympics with a score of 7,291. Not only was Joyner one of the best American athletes of her day, she was phenomenally popular. Her extended family not only included her ever-encouraging husband, brother, and sister-in-law **Florence Griffith-Joyner** but reached out to encircle everyone who watched her. Suffering from asthma and recurrent hamstring problems, Joyner became the crowd favorite when she competed in her fourth Olympics in 1996. The injuries forced her out of the heptathlon, but Joyner was able to win a final Olympic medal, a bronze in the long jump. At the close of the games, the world record she set in 1988 had yet to be touched.

Selected championships and honors: Silver medal, pentathlon, Olympic Games, 1984; gold medal, long jump, Pan American Games, 1987; two gold medals, long jump, World Championships, 1987 and '91; two gold medals, heptathlon, World Championships, 1987 and '93; two gold medals, heptathlon, Olympic Games, 1988 and '92; gold medal, long jump, Olympic Games, 1988; two bronze medals, long jump, Olympic Games, 1992 and '96; Broderick Cup, 1985; Sullivan Award, 1986; *Track & Field News* Athlete of the Year, 1986.

TATYANA KAZANKINA b. December 17, 1951, Petrovsk, Russia, USSR

A phenomenal middle-distance runner, Kazankina became known for dropping world records not by fractions but by whole seconds at a time. In 1976 she broke teammate Lyudmila Bragina's existing 1,500-meter record by more than five seconds. Kazankina successively lowered her record, and her best time—3:52.47, set in 1980—stood until **Qu Yunxia** broke it in 1993. Kazankina could also be counted on for spectacular Olympic performances, winning three golds in two games. At a 1980 U.S.-USSR meet, she bested the 3,000-meter record by a stunning 18.3 seconds. Her career, however spectacular, was not without controversy. In 1984, after a 5,000-meter run in Paris, Kazankina was suspended for eighteen months when her coach refused to let her be tested for performance-enhancing drugs.

Selected championships and honors: Gold medal, 800m, Olympic Games, 1976; two gold medals, 1,500m, Olympic Games, 1976 and '80.

IRENA KIRSZENSTEIN SZEWINSKA b. May 24, 1946, Leningrad, USSR

Though born in the Soviet Union, Kirszenstein competed for Poland, her parents' homeland, in each of her five Olympic Games. Few women have had such long or successful track and field careers, and Kirszenstein, who later competed under her married name of Szewinska, won a phenomenal seven medals in five different events—in the 100-, 200-, and 400-meter races, the long jump, and the 4 × 100-meter relay. At her first games, in 1964, she won two silvers and helped Poland to an upset gold in the 4 × 100-meter relay. In 1968, competing under her married name, she won her first individual gold, finishing the 200 meters in world record time. Recently married and competing as Irena Szewinska, she came back to win the 200 meters in the 1968 Olympics, where she also took a bronze in the 100 meters. By the next Olympics, her career was faltering. Now twenty-six and the mother of a two-year-old, Kirszenstein was out of shape and running seconds slower than the new favorite, **Renate Stecher** of East Germany. She finished third in the 200 meters, but astounded everyone when, at her fourth and final Olympics in 1976, she won the gold in the 400 meters, becoming the first woman ever to win Olympic golds twelve years apart. A year later she became the first woman to finish the 400 meters in under 50 seconds. Although Szewinska participated in the 1980 games, she pulled a muscle in the semifinals and for the first time was unable to medal.

Selected championships and honors, individual: Silver medal, 200m, Olympic Games, 1964; silver medal, long jump, Olympic Games, 1964; bronze medal, 100m, Olympic Games, 1968; gold medal, 200m, Olympic Games, 1968; bronze medal, 200m, Olympic Games, 1972; gold medal, 400m, Olympic Games, 1976. *Team:* gold medal, 4 × 100m relay, Olympic Games, 1964.

MARITA KOCH b. February 18, 1957, Wismar, East Germany

Though Koch might have medaled at three Olympics, injury caused her to withdraw from her first, in 1976, and boycott nixed her appearance at a third, in 1984. In between she won a gold in the 400 meters, an event she held the record in. One of her most impressive victories came at the 1978 European Championships, when her win in the 400 meters broke **Irena Kirszenstein Szewinska's** string of thirty-four consecutive wins at that distance.

Selected championships and honors, individual: Gold medal, 200m, World Championships, 1983; gold medal, 400m, Olympic Games, 1980. *Team:* Silver medal, 4 × 400m relay, Olympic Games, 1980; gold medal, 4 × 100m relay, World Championships, 1983.

STEFKA KOSTADINOVA b. March 25, 1965, Plovdiv, Bulgaria

One of the best female high jumpers of all time, Kostadinova entered seventy-seven meets between 1985 and '87 and lost only four times. She set a world record in 1987 that was still standing at the close of the 1996 Olympics—a phenomenal 6'10¼". Although her career slumped in the early 1990s, and she suffered a disappointing fourth-place finish at the 1992 Olympics, she came back strong in the 1995 World Championships and '96 Olympics, winning handily both times. Her world mark has yet to be equaled and, with world-class athletes jumping in the high 6'6"s and low 6'7"s, seems likely to last a while.

Selected championships and honors: Silver medal, high jump, Olympic Games, 1988; two gold medals, high jump, World Championships, 1987 and '95; gold medal, high jump, Olympic Games, 1996.

JARMILA KRATOCHVILOVA b. January 26, 1951, Golcuv Jenikov, Czechoslovakia

Kratochvilova trained almost an entire decade before winning her first world-class medal, an Olympic silver, at age twenty-nine. Finally having tasted success, the Czech middle-distance runner pushed on. Her best career year was still to come, in 1983, when she set a world record at 800 meters, ran undefeated, and won both the 400- and 800-meter events at the World Championships. Still at the top of her stride in 1984, she lost a chance for Olympic gold when Czechoslovakia joined in the boycott of the Los Angeles games. Her 1983 world record remained a monument, lasting for more a dozen years.

Selected championships and honors: Silver medal, 400m, Olympic Games, 1980; gold medal, 400m, World Championships, 1983; gold medal, 800m, World Championships, 1983.

ELZBIETA KRZESINSKA b. 1935, Poland

The greatest long jumper since **Fanny Blankers-Koen,** Krzesinska was a young medical student when she bettered Blankers-Koen's long-standing record by more than three inches. She equaled her record at the 1956 Olympics to win the gold, and took the silver in 1960.

Selected championships and honors: Gold medal, long jump, Olympic Games, 1956; silver medal, long jump, Olympic Games, 1960.

INGRID KRISTIANSEN b. March 21, 1956; Norway

Though Kristiansen was often overshadowed by her fellow countryman, **Grete Waitz,** she was a superb distance runner. At the 1984 Bislett meet in Oslo she became the first woman ever to run 10,000 meters in under 15 minutes. She set a world marathon record in 1985 with a time of 2:21:06 and the next year set

world records at 5,000 and 10,000 meters, thus becoming the only athlete ever to hold the three records simultaneously. Although Kristiansen won the Boston Marathon twice and the New York once, her career was also laced with misfortune. Unaware that she was pregnant, she withdrew from the 1988 Bislett meet with severe stomach cramps and suffered a miscarriage days later. At the Olympics later that year, she was leading the 10,000-meter race when she injured her foot and had to drop out.

Selected championships and honors: Two Boston Marathons, 1986 and '89; gold medals, 10,000m, World Championships, 1987; New York Marathon, 1989; World Cross-Country Championship, 1988.

NATALYA LISOVSKAYA b. July 16, 1962, Alegazy, Russia, USSR

In 1984, when the Soviet bloc boycotted the Los Angeles Olympics, 6'2" Lisovskaya was the world record holder in shot put. In her absence the gold medal went to Germany's Claudia Losch, whose winning throw was more than 6½' short of Lisovskaya's record. Four years later, having extended her record and won a World Championship in the meantime, Lisovskaya got her chance at Olympic competition and turned in one of the best performances in history. Lisovskaya was on such a roll that even the worst of her six throws would have secured the gold. Her 1987 world record, of 74'3", was still intact at the close of the 1996 Olympic Games.

Selected championships and honors: Gold medal, shot put, World Championships, 1987; gold medal, shot put, Olympic Games, 1988.

TECLA LORUPE b. 1973, Kenya (*also spelled "Tegla Loroupe"*)

Before Lorupe, the first black African woman to win a major marathon, could become a national heroine in Kenya, she had to turn the nation's thinking around. Women were to be modest and noncompetitive, and many warned Lorupe that if she continued to run, she'd become sterile. Encouraged by her mother and older sister, Lorupe didn't quit. Instead the 4'11" runner flew through two straight New York Marathons, winning the second just days after the unexpected death of the sister who'd given her so much encouragement. The government, new converts to women's running, rewarded Lorupe with land and livestock, and women in Lorupe's Pokot tribe told her, "You showed that we are like the men—we can do things. We are not useless."

Selected championships and honors: Two New York Marathons, 1994 and '95; bronze medal, 10,000m, World Championships, 1995.

LIA MANOLIU b. 1932, Romania

Known for flickering-flame gymnasts, Romania also produced Manoliu, a discus thrower and the first woman to compete in six consecutive Olympic Games. Manoliu's first outing was in 1952, when she finished sixth. She worked her way to two consecutive bronzes in 1960 and '64, and entered the '68 games with an injured elbow. Certain the injury would flare up, Manoliu put everything into her first throw. Her win made her the oldest woman ever to win a track and field gold—a record she tried to break with a final appearance at the 1972 Games, when she finished ninth.
Selected championships and honors: Gold medal, discus, Olympic Games, 1968.

MADELINE MANNING JACKSON MIMS
b. January 11, 1948, Cleveland, Ohio

The first American woman to win international championships in the 800 meters, Manning came out of retirement three times, adding to her list of wins each time. From 1967—when she set a world record for the 800 meters—through 1981, she won eleven national titles and set several American records. Another famous Tigerbelle from Tennessee State, Manning set an Olympic record in the 800 meters at the 1968 Mexico City games. She was on the silver-medal relay team in the 1972 games and in 1975 came out of her second retirement to become the first American woman to run the 800 meters in under two minutes. She qualified for the Olympic team one more time, in 1980, but did not compete due to the boycott. She retired from competition permanently in 1981.
Selected championships and honors, individual: Gold medal, 800m, Pan American Games, 1967; gold medal, 800m, Olympic Games, 1968. *Team:* Silver medal, 4 × 400m relay, Olympic Games, 1972. International Women's Sports Hall of Fame; U.S. Track and Field Hall of Fame.

MILDRED MCDANIEL SINGLETON
b. November 3, 1933, Atlanta, Georgia

Nicknamed "Tex" and known for her distinctive dribble in basketball, McDaniel's chief fame came in the high jump, where she won seven national titles. Regarded by many as the dominant women's high jumper of the mid-1950s, McDaniel won most of her titles while she was a college student at Tuskegee.

Her best year was 1956, when she beat world record holder **Iolanda Balas** with a world record jump of her own to win the Olympic gold medal. Later that year, she beat her own record with a jump of 5′ 8.75″. She retired from competition in 1957, after her graduation from Tuskegee.
Selected championships and honors: Gold medal, high jump, Pan American Games, 1955; gold medal, high jump, Olympic Games, 1956; U.S. Track and Field Hall of Fame.

EDITH MCGUIRE b. June 3, 1944, Atlanta, Georgia

A Tennessee State sprinter, McGuire had her standout year in 1964, when she won three Olympic medals. Between 1963 and 1965 she won six national titles, including one in the long jump.
Selected championships and honors, individual: Silver medal, 100m, Olympic Games, 1964; gold medal, 200m, Olympic Games, 1964. *Team:* Silver medal, 4 × 100m relay, Olympic Games, 1964. U.S. Track and Field Hall of Fame.

FAINA MELNIK b. June 9, 1945, Bakota, Ukraine, USSR

Discus throwing doesn't get much attention in the United States, but in Eastern Europe, where it does, Melnik was a respected star. Between 1971 and '76 Melnik lowered the world record several times, psyching herself to a perfect throw by yelling at the top of her lungs with each toss. She won a gold medal at the 1972 Olympics and would have won a silver in 1976 had not her best shot been ruled illegal on a technicality.
Selected championships and honors: Gold medal, discus, Olympic Games, 1972.

ULRIKE MEYFARTH b. May 4, 1956, Köln-Rodenkirchen, Germany

Meyfarth holds an unusual Olympic record—she is both the youngest person ever to win an individual track and field gold and the oldest person to win a gold in high jump. She did it with two wins a dozen years apart. In 1972, the 6′½″ highschool student jumped 2¾″ higher than her personal best to win. Twelve years later and 1½″ taller, she was able to jump 4″ higher. Her win made her the second woman in history, behind **Irena Szewinska**, to win Olympic golds twelve years apart, and the first woman to win individual golds twelve years apart.
Selected championships and honors: Two gold medals, high jump, Olympic Games, 1972 and '84.

ROSA MOTA b. ca. 1960, Portugal

Mota was an unexceptional middle-distance runner when her curiosity led her to try marathoning. She won the first race she entered, in 1982, and came in third at the Olympic's debut event two years later, becoming the first Portuguese woman ever to earn an Olympic medal. The diminutive (5'1¾") Mota quickly became a major player, winning marathons by large margins. In her 1987 World Championship victory, she finished more than 11 minutes ahead of the competition. The favorite going into the 1988 Olympics and a sensation in her home country, she won by 75 meters to become Portugal's first female Olympic gold medalist.

Selected championships and honors: Bronze medal, marathon, Olympic Games, 1984; gold medal, marathon, World Championships, 1987; gold medal, marathon, Olympic Games, 1988; three Boston Marathons, 1987, '88, and '90.

MARLIES OELSNER GÖHR b. March 21, 1958, East Germany

A sprinter who finished a disappointing eighth in the 100 meters at the 1976 Olympics, Göhr set a world record the next year and became the first woman to run the event in less than 11 seconds. She held the record for most of the next six years. Her career years coincided with those of **Evelyn Ashford,** and a great rivalry might have developed if bad luck and politics hadn't intervened. The two should have come face-to-face at the 1980 Olympics, which the United States boycotted. They should also have dueled at the 1983 World Championships, but Ashford was injured and had to withdraw. Göhr had one of her best years in 1984, when she consistently ran the 100 meters in under 11 seconds, but again boycotts—this time by the Eastern Bloc—interfered. Ashford won the event with a time of 10.97, fractions of a second slower than Göhr's times that year.

Selected championships and honors, individual: Gold medal, 100m, World Championships, 1983; silver medal, 100m, Olympic Games, 1980. *Team:* Two gold medals, 4 × 100m relay, Olympic Games, 1976 and '80; gold medal, 4 × 100m relay, World Championships, 1983; silver medal, 4 × 100m relay, Olympic Games, 1988.

MICHELINE OSTERMEYER b. 1922, Rang-du-Fliers, France

A successful high school athlete, Ostermeyer set aside athletics to study concert piano, graduating from the Paris Conservatory in 1948. Soon after graduation, French officials pleaded with her to enter the Olympics' first women's discus and shot put. Ostermeyer was reluctant, since she'd only thrown a discus in competition once before, but eventually she was persuaded. After three months of closely coached training, Ostermeyer was able to do far more than avoid embarassment—she was able to win, taking two golds and a bronze. Her athletic career ended in 1951 due to injury, and she resumed her place on the concert stage. Unfortunately, Ostermeyer's athletic excellence hurt her musical career. Intimations of an altogether too masculine style pursued her, in spite of her 1952 marriage. After living abroad in Tunisia and Lebanon, Ostermeyer returned to France to teach music in 1962.

Selected championships and honors: Gold medal, discus, Olympic Games, 1948; gold medal, shot put, Olympic Games, 1948; bronze medal, high jump, Olympic Games, 1948.

SONIA O'SULLIVAN b. 1969, Cobh, Ireland

O'Sullivan began running out of necessity—as a child, ever late in the mornings, she would race from her house to school, half a mile away. The daily training paid off, and O'Sullivan won a scholarship to Villanova University in the United States. O'Sullivan has focused on middle distance and, despite problems with injuries, has had success. After narrowly missing a bronze medal at the 1992 Olympics, O'Sullivan roared back in '95, beating 5,000-meter world record holder **Fernanda Ribeiro** in four races, one of which was the World Championship.

Selected championships and honors: Gold medal, 5,000m, World Championships, 1995; *Track & Field News* Woman Athlete of the Year, 1995.

MERLENE OTTEY b. ca. 1960, Jamaica

One of the most enduring and consistent sprinters of the 1980s and '90s, Ottey was criticized in the late '80s for being unable to nail down important victories at the Olympics and World Championships. Ottey ignored the talk, kept running, and after a dozen years of world competition finally broke the ice with back-to-back World Championship golds in the 200 meters in 1993 and '95 and two silvers in her fifth consecutive Olympic appearance, in 1996.

Selected championships and honors: Two bronze medals, 200m, Olympic Games, 1980, '84, and '92; bronze medal, 100m, Olympic Games, 1984; two bronze medals, 100m, World Championships, 1987 and '91; two gold medals, 200m, World Championships, 1993 and '95; silver medal, 100m, Olympic Games, 1996; silver medal, 200m, Olympic Games, 1996.

ANN PACKER BRIGHTWELL b. March 2, 1942, England

In a reversal of the old cliché about the tough going shopping, Packer *didn't* go shopping during the 1964 Olympics and ended up with a gold medal. A solid but far from unbeatable runner, Packer took the silver in her best event, the 400 meters. Entered in the 800 meters as well, she finished fifth and third in the qualifying rounds and considered skipping the final to go shopping. When her fiancé finished out of the medals in the men's 400 meters, Packer decided to grab the last chance to medal. Seventy yards from the finishing line, Packer powered up a finishing kick, blasted past the favorite, Maryvonne Dupureur, and won by almost two meters.

Selected championships and honors: Gold medal, 800m, Olympic Games, 1964; silver medal, 400m, Olympic Games, 1964.

AUDREY (MICKEY) PATTERSON TYLER b. 1926

Many people think **Alice Coachman** was the first African-American to win an Olympic medal. Actually, Coachman took the gold, but the first medal honors

---

Medal of Honor

Few women have gone through what Mirsada Buric did in order to compete. A hopeful for the 3,000-meter event, Buric trained for the 1992 Olympics in the ravaged, debris-strewn streets of Sarajevo. A Muslim, she was twice fired at by snipers and, two months before the games, taken hostage by Serbs. Held for nearly two weeks and fed one slice of bread and one cup of tea daily, Buric was released only to discover that all of her gear—including her running shoes—had been confiscated. Although she failed to make it to the finals, Buric and her teammates did make it to the Olympics, a feat of spirit and endurance in itself.

---

go to Patterson, whose bronze in the 200 meters came days ahead of Coachman's win. Patterson's achievement is further obscured by the fact that a photo discovered in 1975 revealed that the official fourth-place finisher, Australia's **Shirley Strickland,** had actually been ahead of her. This hardly mattered to Patterson, who, having married and settled in San Diego, found her work as track club founder and youth coach more rewarding than competition.

Selected championships and honors: Bronze medal, 200m, Olympic Games, 1948.

MARIE-JOSÉ PÉREC b. June 9, 1968, Basse-Terre, Guadeloupe

Pérec, born on the island of Guadeloupe, moved with her mother at age sixteen to Paris, where her natural sprinting abilities immediately attracted the attention of French coaches. Although she attended the 1988 Olympics, she did not begin winning major international meets until 1991. In 1996 she became just one of two women in history to win both the 200- and the 400-meter races in the same Olympics (the other was American **Valerie Brisco-Hooks**). At home in France, Pérec's athletic wins and model's body have made her a celebrity with the media.

Selected championships and honors: Gold medal, 400m, World Championships, 1991; two gold medals, 400m, Olympic Games, 1992 and '96, gold medal, 200m, Olympic Games, 1996.

UTA PIPPIG b. September 7, 1965, Leipzig, Germany

With her win in the 1996 Boston Marathon, Pippig become the first woman to win the event three years in a row. The victory was hard-won—Pippig suffered from diarrhea and menstrual cramps throughout the race and went from the winner's circle straight to the hospital, where she spent the next 48 hours being treated for dehydration.

Selected championships and honors: Three Boston Marathons, 1994–96; New York Marathon, 1994.

IRINA PRESS b. March 10, 1939, Leningrad, USSR

The younger of two sisters from the now-renamed St. Petersburg, Press won the first Olympic pentathlon open to women. Like her sister, **Tamara,** she excelled at shot put, where her throw, 2.68 meters farther than her nearest competitor's, gave her a comfortable margin of victory over Britain's **Mary Bignal Rand.** Press, who also won the 100-meter hurdles, did not appear at the next Olympics—possibly due to the fact that sex testing had been made mandatory in the meantime.

Selected championships and honors: Gold medal, pentathlon, Olympic Games, 1964; gold medal, 100m hurdles, 1964.

TAMARA PRESS b. May 10, 1937, Leningrad, USSR

The only woman ever to win consecutive Olympic golds in shot put, Press was virtually unstoppable at the 1960 and '64 games. During her career she extended the world record six times outdoors and three times indoors, and was the first woman to throw more than 60 feet. She was also a world record holder in discus, in which she won Olympic silver and gold. Press stopped competing when sex testing became mandatory—a fact some have suggested is more than mere coincidence.

Selected championships and honors: Two gold medals, shot put, Olympic Games, 1960 and '64; silver medal, discus, Olympic Games, 1960; gold medal, discus, Olympic Games, 1964.

QU YUNXIA b. ca. 1973, China

Qu was trained in the controversial Chinese program, a regimen that drew at least as much attention as her wins. Besides running 150 miles a week, Qu also trained at high altitudes, was forbidden to have romances, and reportedly imbibed an extract made of caterpillars. Whatever the regimen, it worked. After making a bronze-medal appearance at the 1992 Olympics, she took a gold at the World Championships the next year. One of her most noted achievements came at the 1993 Chinese national meet, when she broke **Tatyana Kazankina's** thirteen-year-old record in the 1,500 meters by two full seconds.

Selected championships and honors: Bronze medal, 1,500m, Olympic Games, 1992; gold medal, 3,000m, World Championships, 1993.

ANA QUIROT b. March 23, 1963, Palma Soriano, Cuba

In 1988 Quirot entered thirteen races at 800 meters and placed first in every one of them. Unfortunately, Cuba's decision to boycott that year's Olympics probably cost her a gold medal. Two months pregnant, she won a bronze at the 1992 games. Just five months later, Quirot nearly died when cleaning chemicals ignited while she was doing her laundry. She lost her baby and suffered third-degree burns to her face,

arms, and torso. Four months after the accident Quirot began running again, scheduling practices between rounds of plastic surgery. A gold-medal win at the 1995 World Championships and a silver-medal finish at the Atlanta Olympics helped Quirot feel she'd left the role of patient behind and once again become an athlete.

Selected championships and honors: Bronze medal, 800m, Olympic Games, 1992; gold medal, 800m, World Championships, 1995; silver medal, 800m, Olympic Games, 1996.

KAROLINE (LINA) RADKE b. October 18, 1903, Karlsruhe, Germany; d. February 14, 1983

Radke went into the 1928 Olympics holding the world record at 800 meters and won the race handily, little realizing the event would not be included in another Olympics until 1960. When some runners collapsed at the finish line, a cry of alarm went off around the world. The British press quoted doctors' concerns that such contests would result in premature aging. The Comte de Baillet-Latour, president of the IOC, suggested a return to traditional, all-male games, and the sport's world governing body, the International Amateur Athletic Federation, banned all races for women longer than 200 meters, a ban that remained in effect for thirty-two stifling years. Meanwhile Radke, along with silver and bronze finishers **Hitomi Kinue** of Japan and Inga Gentzel of Sweden, all ran the race in under world record time.

Selected championships and honors: Gold medal, 800m, Olympic Games, 1928.

FERNANDA RIBEIRO b. July 23, 1969, Panafiel, Portugal

One of the flag bearers of the new world running order, Ribeiro is an outstanding middle-distance and distance runner. She announced her arrival on the world stage with first- and second-place finishes at the 1995 World Championships, and continued with an Olympic gold in Atlanta the next year.

Selected championships and honors: Gold medal, 10,000m, World Championships, 1995; silver medal, 5,000m, World Championships, 1995; gold medal, 10,000m, Olympic Games, 1996.

LOUISE RITTER b. February 18, 1958, Dallas, Texas

Winner of ten indoor and outdoor national championships and regarded by most as America's dominant woman high jumper of the 1980s, Ritter seemed doomed to go without an Olympic gold medal. Her first setback came in 1980, when she finished first in the trials but couldn't compete because of the boycott. She won the trials again in 1984 but was hampered by injuries and finished a disappointing eighth in the games. By 1988, when she was competing against an unusually strong field, no one expected her to medal. She surprised the pundits by taking the gold—and setting a new Olympic record—with a jump of 6′8.″

Selected championships and honors: Gold medal, high jump, Pan American Games, 1979; gold medal, high jump, Olympic Games, 1988; U.S. Track and Field Hall of Fame.

FATUMA ROBA b. ca. 1971, Bokeji, Ethiopia
Running in the torrid heat and humidity of Atlanta in the summer of 1996, Roba became the first African woman to win a gold medal in an Olympic marathon. Roba, who began running as a child, was recruited to train seriously when she ran in Ethiopia's national cross-country championships. Coincidentally, Roba's home village of Bokeji has produced another international champion—runner **Derartu Tulu.**

Selected championships and honors: Gold medal, marathon, Olympic Games, 1996.

ELIZABETH (BETTY) ROBINSON
    SCHWARTZ b. August 23, 1911, Riverdale,
    Illinois
The first woman to win an Olympic gold medal in track, Robinson was also the first woman to receive a varsity "N" from Northwestern University. A naturally fast sprinter who tied the world record for the 100 meters in her second race, Robinson won numerous national championships and set several world records in the late 1920s. A plane crash in 1931 left her with a crushed arm, a badly broken leg, and severe head injuries. She was in a coma for nearly two months and needed two years of rehabilitation to fully regain her walking ability. Incredibly, she returned to competition, using a standing start to accommodate her injuries. As a member of the U.S. relay team, she won her second Olympic gold medal in 1936.

Selected championships and honors, individual: Gold medal, 100 meters, Olympic Games, 1928. *Team:* Silver medal, 4 × 100m relay, Olympic Games, 1928; gold medal, 4 × 100m relay, Olympic Games, 1936. U.S. Track and Field Hall of Fame.

WILMA RUDOLPH b. June 23, 1940, Clarksville, Tennessee; d. November 12, 1994

A runner of astonishing beauty in motion, Rudolph burst on the national and international scene in 1960 with the force of a leveling wind. Catapulted to international fame by that year's Olympics, she had already been winning for years. Her first battle was a simple one of survival. Rudolph, the seventeenth of twenty-one children, was a premature baby who fell prey to numerous childhood illnesses, including one that left her leg partially deformed. Determined to restore her daughter's health, Rudolph's mother took her to Nashville, forty-five miles away, twice a week for physical therapy. Rudolph learned how to walk with the aid of a brace, eventually discarding the brace completely. A high-school basketball and track star, she was on the bronze-medal relay team at the Melbourne Olympics in 1956. As a student at Tennessee State she matured from silver to gold, setting a world record in the 200 meters during the Olympic trials in the summer of 1960. At the games she set a world record in the 100 meters and became the first American woman to win three gold medals in track. More than that, she won a generation over to track, making it an acceptable, even glamorous sport. Slim and long-legged (5′11″ and 132 pounds), Rudolph was an elegant sprinter to watch, inspiring such nicknames as "The Black Gazelle," "The Black Pearl," and "The Chattanooga Choo Choo" in the international press. Enormously popular with crowds all over the world, she toured Europe in 1961, the year she beat her own world record in the 100 meters by a tenth of a second. After retiring from track in 1962, she established the Wilma Rudolph Foundation, whose goal is to help underprivileged children explore, enjoy, and compete in sports. Married for several years to Robert Eldridge, with whom she had a daughter, Rudolph later divorced. When she died in 1994, thousands of people around the world were reminded of a single image: Wilma running.

Selected championships and honors, individual: Gold medal, 100m, Olympic Games, 1960; gold medal, 200m, Olympic Games, 1960. *Team:* Bronze medal, 4 × 100m relay, Olympic Games, 1956; gold medal, 4 × 100m relay, Olympic Games, 1960. Sullivan Award, 1961; twice Associated Press Female Athlete of the Year, 1960 and '61; U.S. Track and Field Hall of Fame; International Women's Sports Hall of Fame; U.S. Olympic Hall of Fame.

TATYANA SAMOLENKO DOROVSKIKH
    b. ca. 1961, Ukraine
Known and feared for her finishing kick, Samolenko holds six medals in world and Olympic competition at

1,500 and 3,000 meters. Her first major win, in the 1,500 meters, came when she was twenty-six years old, at the World Championships. Although she won a silver at the 1992 Olympics, her reputation was tarnished the next year, when she tested positive for steroids.

Selected championships and honors: Gold medal, 1,500m, World Championships, 1987; two gold medals, 3,000m, World Championships, 1987 and '91; bronze medal, 1,500m, Olympic Games, 1988; gold medal, 3,000m, Olympic Games, 1988; silver medal, 3,000m, Olympic Games, 1992.

EVELIN SCHLAAK JAHL b. ca. 1956, East Germany

The only woman to repeat as discus throw champion in Olympic or World Championship competition, Schlaak set an Olympic record at the 1976 games and later became world record holder. She lost her record just weeks before the 1980 Olympics, which may have spurred her to outthrow the woman who'd taken it from her, extending her Olympic record by more than eight feet.

Selected championships and honors: Two gold medals, discus, Olympic Games, 1976 and '80.

KATE SCHMIDT b. December 29, 1953, Long Beach, California

Between 1972 and '77 Schmidt won seven national javelin throw championships and set nine American javelin records, raising the mark from 198'8" to 227'5". Twenty years later her record was still intact, and American champions were still throwing under the 200-foot mark. A member of three U.S. Olympic teams (including the ill-fated 1980 team), "Kate the Great" won two bronze medals in a sport usually dominated by Europeans.

Selected championships and honors: Two bronze medals, javelin, Olympic Games, 1972 and '76; U.S. Track and Field Hall of Fame.

ESTHER SHAKHAMOV ROTH b. April 16, 1952, Tel Aviv, Israel

No Israeli woman had ever made it to the finals of an Olympic competition. Shakhamov, a 100-meter hurdler, seemed certain not only to qualify but to contend for a medal. Unfortunately, her dream turned into a nightmare. Esther was with Israel's women's team when their male counterparts were taken hostage at the 1972 Olympics. Among the eleven athletes who lost their lives was Esther's coach, and

Shakhamov withdrew the next day. She stopped competing and married, but came out of retirement for the 1976 games. Although she did not medal, she did succeed in becoming Israel's first finalist, finishing in sixth place. When Israel joined in boycotting the 1980 games, Shakhamov lost her final chance at an Olympic medal.

JEAN SHILEY NEWHOUSE b. November 20, 1911, Harrisburg, Pennsylvania

Shiley appeared at the 1928 Olympics and won several national high jump titles in the early 1930s, but her most memorable moment—and greatest win—came in the 1932 Olympics, when she went head-to-head in a jump-off against teammate Babe Didrikson. Both cleared the bar at a world record height of 5' 5¼", and both failed to clear when the bar was raised to 5'6". The bar was lowered to 5' 5¾", and both again cleared, but Shiley received the gold when Didrikson's technique was ruled illegal. Shiley retired from competition after graduation from Temple University in 1933.

Selected championships and honors: Gold medal, high jump, Olympic Games, 1932; U.S. Track and Field Hall of Fame.

GHADA SHOUAA b. ca. 1974, Syria

Fans of the modern heptathlon could almost feel the shift when, with **Jackie Joyner-Kersee** sidelined by injuries, Shouaa won the heptathlon at the 1995 World Championships. The next year completed the passing of the baton, when Joyner-Kersee withdrew from competition after aggravating a hamstring injury. Shouaa finished 25 points ahead of Belarus's Natasha Sazanovich, becoming the first Syrian, male or female, to win a gold medal for her country.

Selected championships and honors: Gold medal, heptathlon, World Championships, 1995; gold medal, heptathlon, Olympic Games, 1996.

RENATE STECHER b. May 12, 1950, Supitz, East Germany

Stecher dominated 100- and 200-meter events during the early 1970s. In one four-year stretch, from August 1970 through June 1974, she won ninety consecutive outdoor races. Stecher entered the 1972 Olympic Games a clear favorite and did not disappoint, breaking **Wyomia Tyus's** world record by a second to win the 100 meters in 11.07. She won her second Olympic medal, a silver, in the same event in 1976.

Selected championships and honors: Gold medal, 100m, Olympic Games, 1972; silver medal, 100m,

Olympic Games, 1976. *Team:* Silver medal, 4 × 100m relay, Olympic Games, 1972; Gold medal, 4 × 100m relay, Olympic Games, 1976.

HELEN STEPHENS b. February 3, 1918, Fulton, Missouri; d. January 17, 1994
Undefeated in sprint competitions, Stephens is also one of the few women to excel at both track and weight throwing. At the 1936 Olympics she won golds in the individual and relay 100 meters and placed ninth in the discus. That same year she won AAU titles in the 100 meters, shot put, and discus.
Selected championships and honors, individual: Gold medal, 100m, Olympic Games, 1936. *Team:* Gold medal, 4 × 100m relay, Olympic Games, 1936. U.S. Track and Field Hall of Fame.

SHIRLEY STRICKLAND DE LA HUNTY
b. ca. 1925, Australia
Part of a postwar boom in Australian women's track, Strickland won a phenomenal seven medals over three Olympiads, all in sprints, hurdles, and relays. A math and science teacher from western Australia, she made her first Olympic appearance at age twenty-three, in 1948, and went home with two bronzes and a team silver. She came back four years later to win her first gold, setting a world record in the 80-meter hurdles. By 1956 she was an assistant lecturer at Perth Technical College and had had a child—but the increased workload didn't keep her from defending her gold in hurdles and helping her country to its first win in Olympic relay.

> As an athlete, I believe I was popular as long as I was demure, appreciative, decorative, obedient, and winning.
> —Shirley Strickland de la Hunty

Selected championships and honors, individual: Two bronze medals, 100m, Olympic Games, 1948 and '52; bronze medal, 80m hurdles, Olympic Games, 1948; two gold medals, 80m hurdles, 1952 and '56. *Team:* Silver medal, 4 × 100m relay, Olympic Games, 1948; gold medal, 4 × 100m relay, Olympic Games, 1956.

KATHRINE (KATHY) SWITZER b. January 5, 1947, United States
You won't see her name on a marathon winner's list, but the fact that there's a list at all is Switzer's doing.

In 1967 Switzer tried to enter the Boston Marathon and was turned down because she was a woman. She completed the registration as "K. V. Switzer" and ran anyway. During the race, when officials ran in from the sidelines and tried to rip her number off, male runners formed a protective pack around her for the duration of the race. Ironically, Switzer was not the first woman to finish the Boston marathon. The year before, Robin Gibb Bingay ran as a man, wearing a hooded sweatshirt to hide her face and hair, and finished ahead of more than half of the men. The attention gained by these feats started a groundswell of support for women runners. Five years later, women were allowed to enter the Boston Marathon for the first time, and Switzer was one of the nine who did. Years later, the officials who had tried to remove her from the marathon apologized personally. Switzer was also a co-founder of the Mini Marathon for women, which dates from 1971.

IRENA SZEWINSKA *See Irena Kirszenstein Szewinska, above.*

GWEN TORRENCE b. June 12, 1965, Atlanta, Georgia
At a high school practice, Torrence set an unofficial record at 220 yards. She was wearing low-heeled patent leather pumps. Her coach used the incident to persuade her to finally don "real" track gear, which she had avoided for fear of showing off her skinny

---

TIGERBELLISSIMO!

Nashville, Tennessee. Home of country music, big hair, and some of the best athletes ever to burn up a track. For most of this century, Tennessee State has turned out a steady stream of stars. Listed below, a few of the Tigerbelles listed elsewhere in this section:

Chandra Cheeseborough
Mae Faggs
Madeline Manning
Edith McGuire
Wilma Rudolph
Wyomia Tyus
Martha Watson
Willye White

legs. With the right shoes, Torrence's career took off. She often cites 1984 as a turning point year. At that year's Millrose Games, she set a meet record and beat gold medalist **Evelyn Ashford** in the 55-yard dash. Another watershed year came in 1989. Forced to stay months in bed due to complications during pregnancy, Torrence lost muscle tone and, after giving birth, had to relearn the art of running. Though Torrence returned to the winner's circle, controversy has marred her success. After finishing fourth in the 100 meters at the '92 Olympics, she accused other runners of taking performance-enhancing drugs — an unsupported allegation that put Torrence's personality, rather than her performance, at the center of media coverage.

Selected championships and honors: Silver medal, 100m: World Championships, 1991. Silver medal, 200m: World Championships, 1991. Gold medal, 200m: Olympic Games, 1992. *Team wins:* Gold medals, 4 × 100m relay: Olympic Games, 1992. Silver medal: 4 × 400m relay: Olympic Games, 1992.

DERARTU TULU b. 1972, Bokeji, Ethiopia
When Tulu won the 10,000-meter race at the '92 Olympics, she took the hand of South Africa's Ethel Mayer, whom she had just defeated, and ran her victory lap with her. The picture symbolized new African unity as well as a new multicultural order in the running world. When she arrived home, Tulu went to work for her fellow athletes and used her influence to trigger a shake-up at the Ethiopian Athletics Federation, an organization that frequently mislaid athletes' visas, lost track of their money, and even forgot to arrange for food and lodging.

Selected championships and honors: Gold medal, 10,000m: Olympic Games, 1992. Gold medal: World Cross Country Championships, 1995.

WYOMIA TYUS b. August 29, 1945; Griffin, Georgia
A teammate of **Edith McGuire's** at powerful Tennessee State, Tyus was the first to equal the 100-meter world record of another Tennessee State alum, **Wilma Rudolph.** The tie came at the 1964 Olympics, during a preliminary heat for the 100-meters. Although Tyus was .2 second slower in the finals, her 11.4 time gave her the win over McGuire, who ended up with the silver. At home in the United States, Tyus won several national and indoor and out-

door sprint titles. Although her family encouraged her to give up athletics, Tyus set her sights on the 1968 Olympics. No man or woman had ever won the 100 at two consecutive Games, and Tyus would have to face four other world-record holders in the run. Tyus ran the distance in 11.0 to set a new world record and win the gold. Her feat of back-to-back Olympic golds in a sprint has yet to be equaled. Tyus, who later said winning was secondary to the enjoyment of running itself, gave her medals to American teammates Tommy Smith and John Carlos, who were expelled from the Games for giving the Black Power salute during the medal ceremony for the men's 200-meters.

Selected championships and honors: Gold medal, 100-meters: Olympic Games, 1964. Gold medal, 100-meters: Olympic Games, 1968. *Team wins:* Silver medal, 4 × 100: Olympic Games, 1964. Gold medal, 4 × 100: Olympic Games, 1968. U.S. Track and Field of Fame, International Women's Sports Hall of Fame, Olympic Hall of Fame.

GRETE WAITZ *See Grete Andersen Waitz, above.*

STELLA WALSH b. April 3, 1911, Wierzchowina, Poland; d. December 4, 1980
Born Stanisława Walasiewicz, Walsh won over forty U.S. indoor and outdoor titles in sprints, long jump, and discus. She also won numerous Polish titles and represented her native Poland in the 1932 and '36 Olympics. In addition to her exceptionally long career, the "Polish Flyer" set world records in the 100-yard dash, 200 meters, and long jump. Her first and most famous record came at the AAU championships in 1930, when she became the first woman to run the 100-yard dash in under 11 seconds, with a winning time of 10.8. She also won 200-meter and long jump championships that year. Running for Poland in the Olympics, Walsh very nearly became the first woman to win back-to-back 100s, but after her win in the 1932 games, she was beaten in 1936 by American **Helen Stephens.** Back in the United States, she continued to rack up national championships through the late 1940s and won her last title—in long jump—in 1951. A resident of the United States since the age of two, Walsh became a citizen in 1947 and supervised women's recreation programs for the city of Cleveland. Over the years, rumors persisted that Walsh was simply "too strong" to be a woman. When she was shot to death during a

robbery in 1980, an autopsy found that Walsh had male genitals, suggesting that there may have been some truth to the rumors.

Selected championships and honors: Gold medal, 100m, Olympic Games, 1932; silver medal, 100m, Olympic Games, 1936; U.S. Track and Field Hall of Fame.

WANG JUNXIA b. 1973, China

Wang, a distance runner, hit the world scene like a lightning bolt in 1993, when she broke the world record for the 10,000 meters by a 42-second margin. Despite the win, Wang was miserable. Training under the notoriously strict Ma Junren, Wang was forbidden to wear makeup or grow her hair long; she couldn't have boyfriends and was kept from learning of her brother's death in a car accident. In 1994 Wang and several other elites broke with Ma and left his training camp. Her running turned unimpressive, but by 1996 she'd found a new coach and was back on track, storming the Chinese nationals, then taking a gold in the newly added 5,000-meter race and picking up the silver in her old favorite, the 10,000 meters.

Selected championships and honors: Gold medal, 10,000m, World Championships, 1993; gold medal, 5,000m, Olympic Games, 1996; silver medal, 10,000m, Olympic Games, 1996.

MARTHA WATSON b. August 19, 1946, Long Beach, California

A graduate of Tennessee State, Watson made four U.S. Olympic teams (1964, '68, '72, and '76) as a long jumper and ran on the 4 × 100-meter relay team in 1972 and '76. She also won eight national long jump championships and set American records in 1970 and '73.

Selected championships and honors, individual: Silver medal, long jump, Pan American Games, 1975. *Team:* Gold medal, 4 × 100m relay, Pan American Games, 1975; U.S. Track and Field Hall of Fame.

WILLYE (RED) WHITE b. January 1, 1939, Money, Mississippi

A formidable long jump star from Tennessee State, White was the first American woman to compete in five Olympic Games (1956, '60, '64, '68, and '72). Her only individual medal came in her first games, when she won a silver in Melbourne in 1956. She won a second silver as part of the 4 × 100-meter relay team at the

1964 Olympics. She also won one gold and two bronzes in Pan American Games competition. At home, she won a dozen national long jump championships and extended the American record seven times.

Selected championships and honors, individual: Silver medal, long jump, Olympic Games, 1956; two bronze medals, long jump, Pan American Games, 1959 and '67; gold medal, long jump, Pan American Games, 1963. *Team:* Silver medal, 4 × 100m relay, Olympic Games, 1964; U.S. Track and Field Hall of Fame.

SIGRUN WODARS b. ca. 1965, East Germany

Wodars spent most of her career going head-to-head against teammate Christine Wachtel for supremacy at 800 meters. Wachtel won more contests, but Wodars won the big ones, besting Wachtel at the 1987 World Championships and '88 Olympics.

Selected championships and honors: Gold medal, 800m, World Championships, 1987; gold medal, 800m, Olympic Games, 1988.

VALENTINA YEGEROVA b. February 16, 1964, Iziderkino, Russia, USSR

Yegerova's marathon win at the 1992 Olympics was not only one of the hottest ever run (starting temperature 84°F), it was also by the slimmest margin of victory. Through the last 25 kilometers, Yegerova battled Japan's Yuko Arimori for the lead. The final surge went to Yegerova, who won by a mere eight seconds. Four years later, again running in the heat, she finished second in the Atlanta Olympics.

Selected championships and honors: Gold medal, marathon, Olympic Games, 1992; silver medal, marathon, Olympic Games, 1996.

GALINA ZYBINA b. ca. 1932, Russia, USSR

Nobody who met Zybina at the end of World War II would have spotted a future world record holder in shot put. Thin and weak, she had almost died, as her mother and brother did, of cold and malnutrition. Instead Zybina regained her health and went into the 1952 Olympics as the favorite. She broke her own world record to win, and broke it again after the games. She competed in four consecutive Olympics and ended up with a gold, silver, and bronze in her event.

Selected championships and honors: Gold medal, shot put, Olympic Games, 1952; silver medal, shot put, Olympic Games, 1956; bronze medal, shot put, Olympic Games, 1964.

Track and Field

World Records

Event	Perf	Athlete	Country	Site	Date
100m	10.49	Florence Griffith-Joyner	USA	Indianapolis	7/16/88
200m	21.34	Florence Griffith-Joyner	USA	Seoul	9/29/88
400m	47.6	Marita Koch	GDR	Canberra	10/6/85
800m	1:53.28	Jarmila Kratochvilova	CZE	Munich	7/26/83
1,000m	2:29.34	Maria Mutola	MOZ	Brussels	8/25/95
1,500m	3:50.46	Qu Yunxia	CHN	Beijing	9/11/93
Mile	4:12.56	Svetlana Masterkova	RUS	Zurich	8/14/96
2,000m	5:25.36	Sonia O'Sullivan	IRL	Edinburgh	7/8/94
3,000m	8:06.11	Wang Junxia	CHN	Beijing	9/13/93
5,000m	14:36.45	Fernanda Ribeiro	POR	Hechtel	7/22/95
10,000m	29:31.78	Wang Junxia	CHN	Beijing	9/8/93
1 hour	18,084	Silvana Cruciata	ITA	Rome	5/4/81
20,000m	1:06:48.8	Izumi Maki	JPN	Amagasaki	9/19/93
25,000m	1:29:29.2	Karolina Szabo	HUN	Budapest	4/22/88
30,000m	1:47:05.6	Karolina Szabo	HUN	Budapest	4/22/88
100m hurdles	12.21	Yordanka Donkova	BUL	Stara Zagora	8/20/88
400m hurdles	52.61	Kim Batten	USA	Göteborg	8/11/95
High jump	2.09	Stefka Kostadinova	BUL	Rome	8/30/87
Pole vault	4.45	Emma George	AUS	Sapporo	7/14/96
Long jump	7.52	Galina Chistyakova	URS	Leningrad	6/11/88
Triple jump	15.50	Inessa Kravets	UKR	Göteborg	8/10/95
Shot put	22.63	Natalya Lisovskaya	URS	Moscow	6/7/87
Discus	76.80	Gabriele Reinsch	GDR	Neubrandenburg	7/9/88
Hammer	69.42	Mihaela Melinte	ROM	Cluj	5/12/96
Javelin	80.00	Petra Felke	GDR	Potsdam	9/9/88
Heptathlon	7291	Jackie Joyner-Kersee	USA	Seoul	9/23–24/88
5,000m walk	20:13.26	Kerry Saxby	AUS	Hobart	2/25/96
10,000m walk	41:56.23	Nadezhda Ryashkina	URS	Seattle	7/24/90
4×100m relay	41.37	Silke Gladisch, Sabine Rieger, Ingrid Auerswald, Marlies Göhr	GDR	Canberra	10/6/85
4×200m relay	1:28.15	Marlies Göhr, Romy Muller, Barbel Wockel, Marita Koch	GDR	Jena	8/9/80
4×400m relay	3:15.17	Tatyana Ledovskaya, Irina Nazarova, Mariya Pinigina, Olga Bryzgina	USSR	Seoul	10/1/88
4×800m relay	7:50.17	Nadezhda Olizarenko, Lyubov Gurina, Lyudmila Borisova, Irina Podyalovskaya	USSR	Moscow	8/5/84
Marathon	2:21.06	Ingrid Kristiansen	NOR	London	4/21/85

IAAF World Championships

While the summer Olympics have served as the unofficial world outdoor championships for track and field throughout the century, a separate World Championship meet was started in 1983 by the International Amateur Athletic Federation (IAAF). The meet was held every four years from 1983 to 1991, but began an every-other-year cycle in 1993. WR indicates world record; OR indicates Olympic record; CR indicates championship meet record.

Track and Field (continued)

Olympic 100 Meters

Year	Medalists	Country	Time
1896–1924	event not held		
1928	Elizabeth Robinson	USA	12.20
	Fanny Rosenfeld	CAN	12.30
	Ethel Smith	CAN	12.30
1932	Stanislawa Walasiewicz (Stella Walsh)	POL	11.90
	Hilda Strike	CAN	11.90
	Wilhelmina Von Bremen	USA	12.00
1936	Helen Stephens	USA	11.50
	Stanislawa Walasiewicz	POL	11.70
	Kathe Krauss	GER	11.90
1948	Francina "Fanny" Blankers-Koen	HOL	11.90
	Dorothy Manley	GBR	12.20
	Shirley Strickland	AUS	12.20
1952	Marjorie Jackson	AUS	11.50
	Daphne Hasenjager (Robb)	SAF	11.80
	Shirley Strickland de la Hunty	AUS	11.90
1956	Elizabeth Cuthbert	AUS	11.50
	Christa Stubrick	GDR	11.70
	Marlene Matthews	AUS	11.70
1960	Wilma Rudolph	USA	11.00
	Dorothy Hyman	GBR	11.30
	Giuseppina Leone	ITA	11.30
1964	Wyomia Tyus	USA	11.40
	Edith McGuire	USA	11.60
	Ewa Klobukowska	POL	11.60
1968	Wyomia Tyus	USA	11.08 WR
	Barbara Ferrell	USA	11.15
	Irena Szewinska (Kirzenstein)	POL	11.19
1972	Renate Stecher	GDR	11.07 WR
	Raelene Boyle	AUS	11.23
	Silvia Chivas	CUB	11.24
1976	Annegret Richter	GER	11.08
	Renate Stecher	GDR	11.13
	Inge Helten	GER	11.17
1980	Lyudmila Kondratyeva	USSR/Russia	11.06
	Marlies Göhr (Oelsner)	GDR	11.07
	Ingrid Auerswald	GDR	11.14
1984	Evelyn Ashford	USA	10.97 OR
	Alice Brown	USA	11.13
	Merlene Ottey-Page	JAM	11.16
1988	Florence Griffith-Joyner	USA	10.54
	Evelyn Ashford	USA	10.83
	Heike Drechsler (Daute)	GDR	10.85
1992	Gail Devers	USA	10.82
	Juliet Cuthbert	JAM	10.83
	Irina Privalova	RUS	10.84
1996	Gail Devers	USA	10.94
	Merlene Ottey	JAM	10.94
	Gwen Torrence	USA	10.96

Olympic 200 Meters

	Medalists	Country	Time
1896–1936	event not held		
1948	Francina "Fanny" Blankers-Koen	HOL	24.40
	Audrey Williamson	GBR	25.10
	Audrey Patterson	USA	25.20
1952	Marjorie Jackson	AUS	23.70
	Bertha Brouwer	HOL	24.20
	Nadezhda Khnykina	USSR/Georgia	24.20
1956	Elizabeth Cuthbert	AUS	23.40
	Christa Stubnick	GDR	23.70
	Marlene Matthews	AUS	23.80
1960	Wilma Rudolph	USA	24.00
	Jutta Heine	GER	24.40
	Dorothy Hyman	GBR	24.70
1964	Edith McGuire	USA	23.00 OR
	Irena Kirszenstein	POL	23.10
	Marilyn Black	AUS	23.10
1968	Irena Szewinska (Kirzenstein)	POL	22.58 WR
	Raelene Boyle	AUS	22.74
	Jennifer Lamy	AUS	22.88
1972	Renate Stecher	GDR	22.40
	Raelene Boyle	AUS	22.45
	Irena Szewinska (Kirzenstein)	POL	22.74
1976	Barbel Eckert	GDR	22.37 OR
	Annegret Richter	GER	22.39
	Renate Stecher	GDR	22.47
1980	Barbel Wockel (Eckert)	GDR	22.03 OR
	Natalya Bochina	USSR	22.19
	Merlene Ottey	JAM	22.20
1984	Valerie Brisco-Hooks	USA	21.81 OR

Track and Field (continued)

Olympic 200 Meters

Year	Medalists	Country	Time
	Florence Griffith	USA	22.04
	Merlene Ottey-Page	JAM	22.09
1988	Florence Griffith-Joyner	USA	21.34 WR
	Grace Jackson	JAM	21.72
	Heike Drechsler (Daute)	GDR	21.95
1992	Gwendolyn Torrence	USA	21.81
	Juliet Cuthbert	JAM	22.02
	Merlene Ottey	JAM	22.09
1996	Marie-José Pérec	FRA	22.12
	Merlene Ottey	JAM	22.24
	Mary Onyali	NIG	22.38

Olympic 400 Meters

Year	Medalists	Country	Time
1896–1960	event not held		
1964	Elizabeth Cuthbert	AUS	52.00 OR
	Ann Packer	GBR	52.20
	Judith Amoore	AUS	53.40
1968	Colette Besson	FRA	52.03
	Lillian Board	GBR	52.12
	Natalya Pechenkina	USSR	52.25
1972	Monika Zehrt	GDR	51.08 OR
	Rita Wilden (Jahn)	GER	51.21
	Kathy Hammond	USA	51.64
1976	Irena Szewinska (Kirszenstein)	POL	49.28 WR
	Christina Brehmer	GDR	50.51
	Ellen Streidt (Stropahl)	GDR	50.55
1980	Marita Koch	GDR	48.88 OR
	Jamila Kratochvilova	CZE	49.46
	Christina Lathan (Brehmer)	GDR	49.66
1984	Valerie Brisco-Hooks	USA	48.83 OR
	Chandra Cheeseborough	USA	49.05
	Kathryn Cook (Smallwood)	GBR	49.42
1988	Olha Bryzhina	USSR/Ukraine	48.65 OR
	Petra Muller	GDR	49.45
	Olga Nazarova	USSR/Russia	49.90
1992	Marie-José Pérec	FRA	48.83
	Olha Bryzhina	UKR	49.05
	Ximena Restrepo Gaviria	COL	49.64
1996	Marie-José Pérec	FRA	48.25 OR
	Cathy Freeman	AUS	48.63
	Falilat Ogunkoya	NIG	49.1

Olympic 800 Meters

Year	Medalists	Country	Time
1896–1924	event not held		
1928	Karoline "Lina" Radke	GER	2:16.8 WR
	Kinue Hitomi	JPN	2:17.6
	Inga Gentzel	SWE	2:18.8
1932–1956	event not held		
1960	Lyudmyla Shevtsova	USSR/Ukraine	2:04.3
	Brenda Jones	AUS	2:04.4
	Ursula Donath	GDR	2:05.6
1964	Ann Packer	GBR	2:01.1 OR
	Maryvonne Dupureur	FRA	2:01.9
	M. Ann Marise Chamberlain	NZE	2:02.8
1968	Madeline Manning	USA	2:00.9 OR
	Ileana Silai	ROM	2:02.5
	Maria Gommers	HOL	2:02.6
1972	Hildegard Falck	GER	1:58.6 OR
	Nijole Sabaite	USSR/Lithuania	1:58.7
	Gunhild Hoffmeister	GDR	1:59.2
1976	Tatyana Kazankina	USSR/Russia	1:59.94 WR
	Nikolina Shtereva	BUL	1:55.42
	Elfi Zinn	GDR	1:55.60
1980	Nadiya Olizarenko	USSR/Ukraine	1:53.43 WR
	Olga Mineyeva	USSR/Russia	1:54.81
	Tatyana Providokhina	USSR/Russia	1:55.46
1984	Doina Melinte	ROM	1:57.60
	Kimberly Gallagher	USA	1:58.63
	Rafira Fita Lovin	ROM	1:58.83
1988	Sigrun Wodars	GDR	1:56.10
	Christine Wachtel	GDR	1:56.64
	Kimberly Gallagher	USA	1:56.91
1992	Ellen van Langen	HOL	1:55.54
	Lilia Nurutdinova	RUS	1:55.99
	Ana Fidelia Quirot Moret	CUB	1:56.80
1996	Svetlana Masterkova	RUS	1:57.73

Track and Field (continued)

Olympic 800 Meters

Year	Medalists	Country	Time
	Ana Quirot	CUB	1:58.11
	Maria Mutola	MOZ	1:58.71

Olympic 1,500 Meters

Year	Medalists	Country	Time
1896–1968	event not held		
1972	Lyudmila Bragina	USSR/Russia	4:01.4 WR
	Gunhild Hoffmeister	GDR	4:02.8
	Paola Cacchi	ITA	4:02.9
1976	Tatyana Kazankina	USSR/Russia	4:05.48
	Gunhild Hoffmeister	GDR	4:06.02
	Ulrike Klapezynski	GDR	4:06.09
1980	Tatyana Kazankina	USSR/Russia	3:56.6 OR
	Christiane Wartenberg	GDR	3:57.8
	Nadiya Olizarenko	USSR/Ukraine	3:59.6
1984	Gabriella Dorio	ITA	4:03.25
	Doina Melinte	ROM	4:03.76
	Maricica Puica	ROM	4:04.15
1988	Paula Ivan	ROM	3:53.96 OR
	Laimute Baikauskaite	USSR/Lithuania	4:00.24
	Tetyana Samolenko	USSR/Ukraine	4:00.30
1992	Hassiba Boulmerka	ALG	3:56.30
	Lyudmila Rogacheva	RUS	3:56.91
	Qu Yunxia	CHN	3:57.08
1996	Svetlana Masterkova	RUS	4:00.83
	Gabriela Szabo	ROM	4:01.54
	Theresia Kiesl	AUT	4:03.02

Olympic 5,000 Meters

Year	Medalists	Country	Time
1996	Wang Junxiá	CHN	14:59.88
	Pauline Konga	KEN	15:03.49
	Roberta Bruney	ITA	15:07.52

Olympic 10,000 Meters

Year	Medalists	Country	Time
1896–1984	event not held		
1988	Olga Bondarenko	USSR/Russia	31:05.21 OR
	Elizabeth McColgan	GBR	31:08.44
	Olena Zhuplyova	USSR/Ukraine	31:19.82
1992	Derartu Tulu	ETH	31:06.02
	Elana Meyer	SAF	31:11.75
	Lynn Jennings	USA	31:19.89
1996	Fernanda Ribeiro	POR	31:01.63 OR
	Wang Junxia	CHN	31:02.58
	Gete Wami	ETH	31:06.65

Olympic Marathon

Year	Medalists	Country	Time
1896–1980	event not held		
1984	Joan Benoit	USA	2:24:52
	Grete Waitz	NOR	2:26:18
	Rosa Mota	POR	2:26:57
1988	Rosa Mota	POR	2:25:40
	Lisa Martin	AUS	2:25:53
	Kathrin Dorre	GDR	2:26:21
1992	Valentina Yegorova	RUS	2:32:41
	Yuko Arimori	JPN	2:32:49
	Lorraine Moiler	NZE	2:33.59
1996	Fatuma Roba	ETH	2:26.05
	Valentina Yegorova	RUS	2:28.05
	Yuko Arimori	JPN	2:28.39

Olympic 100-Meter Hurdles

Year	Medalists	Country	Time
1896–1928	event not held		
1932	Mildred "Babe" Didrikson	USA	11.7 WR
	Evelyne Hall	USA	11.7
	Marjorie Clark	SAF	11.8
1936	Trebisonda Valla	ITA	11.7
	Anni Steuer	GER	11.7
	Elizabeth Taylor	CAN	11.7
1948	Francina "Fanny" Blankers-Koen	HOL	11.2 OR
	Maureen Gardner	GBR	11.2
	Shirley Strickland	AUS	11.3
1952	Shirley Strickland de la Hunty	AUS	10.9 WR
	Maria Golubnichaya	USSR/Russia	11.1
	Maria Sander	GER	11.1
1956	Shirley Strickland de la Hunty	AUS	10.7 OR
	Gisela Kohler	GDR	10.9
	Norma Thrower	AUS	11.0
1960	Iryna Press	USSR/Ukraine	10.8
	Carole Quinton	GBR	10.9
	Gisela Birkemeyer (Kohler)	GDR	11.0

Track and Field (continued)

Olympic 100-Meter Hurdles

Year	Medalists	Country	Time
1964	Karin Balzer	GDR	10.54w
	Teresa Clepia-Wieczorek	POL	10.55
	Pamela Kilborn	AUS	10.56
1968	Maureen Caird	AUS	10.39 OR
	Pamela Kilborn	AUS	10.46
	Chi Cheng	TAI	10.51
1972*	Anneliese Ehrhardt	GDR	12.59 WR
	Valeria Bufanu	ROM	12.84
	Karin Balzer	GDR	12.90
1976	Johanna Schaller	GDR	12.77
	Tatiana Anisimova	USSR/Russia	12.78
	Natalya Lebedeva	USSR/Russia	12.80
1980	Vera Komisova	USSR/Russia	12.56 OR
	Johanna Klier (Schaller)	GDR	12.63
	Lucyna Langer	POL	12.65
1984	Benita Fitzgerald-Brown	USA	12.84
	Shirley Strong	GBR	12.88
	Michele Chardonnet	FRA	13.06
1988	Yordanka Donkova	BUL	12.38 OR
	Gloria Siebert	GDR	12.61
	Claudia Zackiewicz	GER	12.75
1992	Paraskevi "Voula" Patoulidou	GRE	12.64
	LaVonna Martin	USA	12.69
	Yordanka Donkova	BUL	12.70
1996	Ludmila Enquist	SWE	12.58
	Brigita Bukovec	SLO	12.59
	Patricia Girard Leno	FRA	12.65

*From 1932 to 1968 the length of the race was 80 meters; beginning in 1972 the race was run at 100 meters.

Olympic 400-Meter Hurdles

Year	Medalists	Country	Time
1896–1980	event not held		
1984	Nawal El Moutawakel	MOR	54.61 OR
	Judi Brown	USA	55.20
	Cristina Cojocaru	ROM	55.41
1988	Debra Flintoff-King	AUS	53.17 OR
	Tatyana Ledovskaya	USSR/Belarus	53.18
	Ellen Fiedler	GDR	53.63
1992	Sally Gunnell	GBR	53.23
	Sandra Farmer-Patrick	USA	53.69
	Janeene Vickers	USA	54.31
1996	Deon Hemmings	JAM	52.82 OR
	Kim Batten	USA	53.08
	Tonja Buford-Bailey	USA	53.22

Olympic 4 × 100-Meter Relay

Year	Medalists	Country	Time
1896–1924	event not held		
1928	Fanny Rosenfeld, Ethel Smith, Florence Bell, Myrtle Cook	CAN	48.4 WR
		USA	48.80
		GER	49.00
1932	Mary Carew, Evelyn Furtsch, Annette Rogers, Wilhelmina VonRemen	USA	46.9 WR
		CAN	47.00
		GBR	47.60
1936	Harriet Bland, Annette Rogers, Elizabeth Robinson, Helen Stephens	USA	46.90
		GBR	47.60
		CAN	47.80
1948	Xenia Stad-de Jong, Jeanette Witziers-Timmer, Gerda van der Kade-Koudijs, Francina "Fanny" Blankers-Koen	HOL	47.50
		AUS	47.60
		CAN	47.80

Track and Field (continued)

Olympic 4 × 100-Meter Relay

Year	Medalists	Country	Time
1952	Mae Faggs, Barbara Jones, Janet Moreau, Catherine Hardy	USA	45.9 WR
		GER	45.9 WR
		GBR	46.20
1956	Shirley Strickland de la Hunty, Norma Croker, Fleur Mellor, Elizabeth Cuthbert	AUS	44.5 WR
		GER	44.70
		USA	44.90
1960	Martha Hudson, Lucinda Williams, Barbara Jones, Wilma Rudolph	USA	44.50
		GER	44.80
		POL	45.00
1964	Teresa Ciepla (Wieczorek), Irena Kirszenstein, Halina Gorecka (Richter), Ewa Klobukowska	POL	43.60
		USA	43.90
		GBR	44.00
1968	Barbara Ferrell, Margaret Bailes, Mildrette Netter, Wyomia Tyus	USA	42.88 WR
		CUB	43.36
		USSR/Russia	43.41
1972	Christiane Krause, Ingrid Mickler (Becker), Annegret Richter, Heidemarie Rosendahl	GER	42.81 WR
		GDR	42.95
		CUB	43.36
1976	Marlies Oelsner, Renate Stecher, Carla Bodendorf, Barbel Eckert	GDR	42.55 OR
		GER	42.59
		USSR	43.09
1980	Romy Muller, Barbel Wockel (Eckert), Ingrid Auerswald, Marlies Göhr (Oeisner)	GDR	41.60 WR
		USSR/Russia	42.10
		GBR	42.43
1984	Alice Brown, Jeanette Bolden, Chandra Cheeseborough, Evelyn Ashford	USA	41.65
		CAN	42.77
		GBR	43.11
1988	Alice Brown, Sheila Echols, Florence Griffith-Joyner, Evelyn Ashford (Dannette Young)	USA	41.98
		GDR	42.09
		USSR/Russia	42.75
1992	Evelyn Ashford, Esther Jones, Carlette Guidry, Gwendolyn Torrence (Michelle Finn)	USA	42.11
		RUS	42.16
		NGR	42.81
1996	Chryste Gaines, Gail Devers, Inger Miller, Gwendolyn Torrence	USA	41.95
		BAH	42.14
		JAM	42.24

Track and Field (continued)

Olympic 4 × 400-Meter Relay

Year	Medalists	Country	Time
1896–1968	event not held		
1972	Dagmar Kasling, Rita Kuhne, Helga Seidler, Monika Zehrt	GDR	3:23.0 WR
		USA	3:25.2
		GER	3:26.5
1976	Doris Maletzki, Brigitte Rohde, Ellen Streidt, Christina Brehmer	GDR	3:19.23 WR
		USA	3:22.81
		USSR	3:24.24
1980	Tetyana Prorochenko, Tatyana Goistchik, Nina Zyuskova, Irina Nazarova (Olga Mineyeva, Lyudmila Chernoval)	USSR	3:20.2
		GDR	3:20.4
		GBR	3:27.5
1984	Lillie Leatherwood, Sherri Howard, Valerie Brisco-Hooks, Chandra Cheeseborough (Diane Dixon, Denean Howard)	USA	3:18.29 OR
		CAN	3:21.21
		GER	3:22.98
1988	Tatyana Ledovskaya, Olga Nazarova, Marlya Pinihina, Olha Bryzhina (Lyudmila Dzhigalova)	USSR	3:15.17 WR
		USA	3:15.51
		GDR	3:18.29
1992	Yelena Ruzina, Lyudmila Dzhigalova, Olga Nazarova, Olha Bryzhina (Marina Shmonina, Lilia Nurudtinova)	USSR	3:20.20
		USA	3:20.92
		GBR	3:24.23
1996	Rochelle Stevens, Maicel Malone, Kim Graham, Jearl Miles	USA	3:20.91
		NGR	3:21.04
		GER	3:21.14

Olympic 10,000-Meter Walk

Year	Medalists	Country	Time
1896–1988	event not held		
1992	Chen Yueling	CHN	44:32
	Yelena Nikolayeva	RUS	44:33
	Li Chunxiu	CHN	44:41
1996	Yelena Ninikolayeva	RUS	41:49
	Elisabetta Perrone	ITA	42:12
	Wang Yan	CHN	42:19

Track and Field (continued)

Olympic High Jump

Year	Medalists	Country	Meters	Ft-In
1896–1924	event not held			
1928	Ethel Catherwood	CAN	1.59	5-2½
	Carolina Gisolf	HOL	1.56	5-1¼
	Mildred Wiley	USA	1.56	5-1¼
	Jean Shiley	USA	1.51	4-11½
1932	Jean Shiley	USA	1.657	5-5¼ WR
	Mildred "Babe" Didrikson	USA	1.657	5-5¼ WR
	Eva Dawes	CAN	1.60	5-3
	Carolina Gisolf	HOL	1.58	5-2¼
1936	Ibolya Csak	HUN	1.60	5-3
	Dorothy Odam	GBR	1.60	5-3
	Elfriede Kaun	GER	1.60	5-3
1948	Alice Coachman	USA	1.68	5-6 OR
	Dorothy Tyler (Odam)	GBR	1.68	5-6 OR
	Micheline Ostermeyer	FRA	1.61	5-3¼
1952	Esther Brand	SAF	1.67	5-5¾
	Sheila Lerwill	GBR	1.65	5-5
	Aleksandra Chudina	USSR/Russia	1.63	5-4¼
1956	Mildred McDaniel	USA	1.76	5-9¼ WR
	Thelma Hopkins	GBR	1.67	5-5¾
	Maria Pissaryeva	USSR/Russia	1.67	5-5¾
1960	Iolanda Balas	ROM	1.85	6-0¾ OR
	Jaroslawa Jozwiakowska	POL	1.71	5-7¼
	Dorothy Shirley	GBR	1.71	5-7¼
1964	Iolanda Balas	ROM	1.90	6-2¾ OR
	Michele Brown (Mason)	AUS	1.80	5-11
	Taisa Chenchyk	USSR/Ukraine	1.78	5-10
1968	Miloslava Rezkova	CZE	1.82	5-11½
	Antonina Okorokova	USSR/Russia	1.80	5-10¾
	Valentyna Kozyr	USSR/Ukraine	1.80	5-10¾
1972	Ulrike Mayfarth	GER	1.92	6-3½
	Yordanka Blagoyeva	BUL	1.88	6-2
	Ilona Gusenbauer	AUT	1.88	6-2
1976	Rosemarie Ackermann (Wischas)	GDR	1.93	6-4 OR
	Sara Simeoni	ITA	1.91	6-3¼
	Yordanka Blagoyeva	BUL	1.91	6-3¼
1980	Sara Simeoni	ITA	1.97	6-5½ OR
	Urszula Kielan	POL	1.94	6-4¼
	Jutta Kirst	GDR	1.94	6-4¼
1984	Ulrike Meyfarth	GER	2.02	6-7½ OR
	Sara Simeoni	ITA	2.00	6-6¾
	Joni Huntley	USA	1.97	6-5½
1988	D. Louise Ritter	USA	2.03	6-8 OR
	Stefka Kostadinova	BUL	2.01	6-7¼
	Tamara Bykova	USSR/Russia	1.99	6-6¾
1992	Heike Henkel	GER	2.02	6-7½
	Galina Astafel	ROM	2.00	6-6¾
	Ioamnet Quintero Alvarez	CUB	1.97	6-5½
1996	Stefka Kostadinova	BUL	2.05	6-8¾ OR
	Niki Bakogianni	GRE	2.03	6-8
	Inga Babakova	UKR	2.01	6-7

Track and Field (continued)

Olympic Long Jump

Year	Medalists	Country	Meters	Ft-In
1896–1936	event not held			
1948	Olga Gyarmati	HUN	5.695	18-8¼
	Noemi Simonetto De Portela	ARG	5.60	18-4½
	Ann-Britt Leyman	SWE	5.575	18-3½
1952	Yvetta Williams	NZE	6.24	20-5¾ OR
	Aleksandra Chudina	USSR/Russia	6.14	20-1¾
	Shirley Gawley	GBR	5.92	19-5¼
1956	Elzbieta Krzesinska	POL	6.35	20-10 WR
	Willye White	USA	6.09	19-11¾
	Nadezhda Dvalischvili (Khnykina)	USSR/Georgia	6.07	19-11
1960	Vira Krepkina	USSR/Ukraine	6.37	20-10¾ OR
	Elzbieta Krzesinska	POL	6.27	20-7
	Hildrun Claus	GDR	6.21	20-4½
1964	Mary Rand (Bignal)	GBR	6.76	22-2¼ WR
	Irena Kirszenstein	POL	6.60	21-8
	Tatyana Schelkanova	USSR/Russia	6.42	21-0¾
1968	Viorica Viscopoleanu	ROM	6.82	22-4½ WR
	Sheila Sherwood	GBR	6.68	21-11
	Tatyana Talisheva	USSR/Russia	6.66	21-10¼
1972	Heidemarie Rosendahl	GER	6.78	22-3
	Diana Yorgova	BUL	6.77	22-2½
	Eva Suranova	CZE/SLV	6.67	21-10¾
1976	Angela Voight	GDR	6.72	22-0¾
	Kathy McMillan	USA	6.66	21-10¼
	Lidiya Alfeyeva	USSR/Ukraine	6.60	21-8
1980	Tatyana Kolpakova	USSR/KYR	7.06	23-2 OR
	Brigitte Wujak	GDR	7.04	23-1¼
	Tetyana Skachko	USSR/Ukraine	7.01	23-0
1984	Anisoara Cusmir-Stanciu	ROM	6.96	22-10
	Valeria Ionescu	ROM	6.81	22-4¼
	Susan Hearnshaw	GBR	6.80	22-3¾
1988	Jacqueline Joyner-Kersee	USA	7.40	24-3¼ OR
	Heike Drechsler (Daute)	GDR	7.22	23-8¼
	Regina Cistjakova	USSR/Lithuania	7.11	23-4
1992	Heike Drechsler	GER	7.14	23-5¼
	Inessa Kravets	UKR	7.12	23-4½
	Jacqueline Joyner-Kersee	USA	7.07	23-2½
1996	Chioma Ajunwa	NGR	7.12	23-4½
	Fiona May	ITA	7.02	23-0½
	Jacqueline Joyner-Kersee	USA	7.00	22-11¾

Olympic Triple Jump

1996	Inessa Kravets	UKR	15.33	50-3½
	Inna Lasovskaya	RUS	14.98	49-1¾
	Sarka Kasparkova	CZE	14.98	49-1¾

Track and Field (continued)

Olympic Shot Put

Year	Medalists	Country	Meters	Ft-In
1896–1936	event not held			
1948	Micheline Ostermeyer	FRA	13.75	45-1½
	Amelia Piccinini	ITA	13.09	42-11½
	Ine Schaffer	AUT	13.08	42-11
1952	Galina Zybina	USSR/Russia	15.28	50-1¾ WR
	Marianne Werner	GER	14.57	47-9¾
	Klavdia Tochenova	USSR/Russia	14.50	47-7
1956	Tamara Tyshkevich	USSR/Russia	16.59	54-5 OR
	Galina Zybina	USSR/Russia	16.53	54-2¾
	Marianne Wernere	GER	15.61	51-2¾
1960	Tamara Press	USSR/Ukraine	17.32	56-10 OR
	Johanna Luttge	GDR	16.61	54-6
	Earlene Brown	USA	16.42	53-10½
1964	Tamara Press	USSR/Ukraine	18.14	59-6¼
	Renate Garisch-Culmberger	GDR	17.61	57-9½
	Galina Zybina	USSR/Russia	17.45	57-3
1968	Margitta Gummel (Heimboldt)	GDR	19.61	64-4 WR
	Marita Lange	GDR	18.78	61-7½
	Nadezhda Chizhova	USSR/Russia	18.19	59-8¼
1972	Nadezhda Chizhova	USSR/Russia	21.03	69-0 WR
	Margitta Gummel (Heimboldt)	GDR	20.22	66-4¼
	Ivanka Hristova	BUL	19.35	63-6
1976	Ivanka Hristova	BUL	21.16	69-5¼ OR
	Nadezhda Chizhova	USSR/Russia	20.96	68-9¼
	Helena Fibingerova	CZE	20.67	67-9¾
1980	Ilona Stupianek (Schoknecht)	GDR	22.41	73-6¼ OR
	Svetlana Krachevskaya (Esfir) Dolzhenko	USSR/Russia	21.42	70-3½
	Margitta Pufe (Droese)	GDR	21.20	69-6¾
1984	Claudia Losch	GER	20.48	67-2¼
	Mihaela Loghin	ROM	20.47	67-2
	Gael Martin	AUS	19.19	62-11½
1988	Natalya Lisovskaya	USSR/Russia	22.24	72-11¾
	Kathrin Neimke	GDR	21.07	69-1½
	Li Meisu	CHN	21.06	69-1¼
1992	Svetlana Krivelyova	RUS	21.06	69-1¼
	Huang Zhihong	CHN	20.47	67-2
	Kathrin Neimke	GER	19.78	65-2¾
1996	Astrid Kumbernuss	GER	20.56	67-5½
	Sui Xinmei	CHN	19.88	65-2¾
	Irina Khudorozhkina	RUS	19.35	63-6

Olympic Discus Throw

Year	Medalists	Country	Meters	Ft-In
1896–1924	event not held			
1928	Halina Konopacka	POL	39.62	129-11¾ WR
	Lillian Copeland	USA	37.08	121-8
	Ruth Svedberg	SWE	35.92	117-10
1932	Lillian Copeland	USA	40.58	133-2 OR

Track and Field (continued)

Olympic Discus Throw

Year	Medalists	Country	Meters	Ft-In
1936	Ruth Osburn	USA	40.12	131-7
	Jadwiga Wajs	POL	38.74	127-1
	Gisela Mauermayer	GER	47.63	156-3 OR
1948	Jadwiga Wajs	POL	46.22	151-8
	Paula Mollenhauer	GER	39.80	130-7
	Micheline Ostermeyer	FRA	41.92	137-6
1952	Edera Cordiale Gentile	ITA	41.17	135-0
	Jacqueline Mazeas	FRA	40.47	132-9
	Nina Romaschkova	USSR/Russia	51.42	168-8 OR
1956	Yelisaveta Bagryantseva	USSR/Russia	47.08	154-5
	Nina Dumbadze	USSR/Georgia	46.29	151-10
	Olga Fikotova	CZE	53.69	176-1 OR
1960	Irina Beglyakova	USSR/Russia	52.54	174-4
	Nina Ponomaryeva (Romaschkova)	USSR/Russia	52.02	170-8
	Nina Ponomaryeva (Romaschkova)	USSR/Russia	55.10	180-9 OR
1964	Tamara Press	USSR/Ukraine	52.59	172-4
	Lia Manoliu	ROM	52.36	171-9
	Tamara Press	USSR/Ukraine	57.27	187-10 OR
1968	Ingrid Lotz	GDR	57.21	187-8
	Lia Manoliu	ROM	56.97	186-10
	Lia Manoliu	ROM	58.28	191-2 OR
1972	Liesel Westermann	GER	57.76	189-6
	Jolan Kleiber	HUN	54.90	180-1
	Faina Melnik	USSR/Ukraine	66.62	218-7 OR
1976	Argentina Menis	ROM	65.06	213-5
	Vassilka Stoyeva	BUL	64.34	211-1
	Evelin Schlaak	GDR	69.00	226-4 OR
1980	Maria Vergova	BUL	67.30	220-9
	Gabriele Hinzmann	GDR	66.84	219-3
	Evelin Jahl (Schlaak)	GDR	69.96	229-6 OR
1984	Maria Pelkova (Vergova)	BUL	67.90	222-9
	Tatyana Lesovaya	USSR/KAZ	67.40	221-1
	Ria Stalman	HOL	65.36	214-5
1988	Leslie Deniz	USA	64.86	212-9
	Florenta Craciunescu (Tacu)	ROM	63.64	208-9
	Martina Hellmann	GDR	72.30	237-2½ OR
1992	Diana Gansky	GDR	71.88	235-10
	Tzvetanka Hristova	BUL	69.74	228-10
	Maritza Marten Garcia	CUB	70.06	229-10
1996	Tzvetanka Khristova	BUL	67.78	222-4
	Daniela Costian	AUS	66.24	217-4
	Ilke Wyludda	GER	69.65	228-6
	Natalya Sadova	RUS	66.47	218-1
	Ellina Zvereva	BLR	65.63	215-4

Olympic Javelin Throw

Year	Medalists	Country	Meters	Ft-In
1896–1928	event not held			
1932	Mildred "Babe" Didrikson	USA	43.68	143-4 OR
	Ellen Braumuller	GER	43.49	142-8
	Ottilie "Tilly" Fleischer	GER	43.00	141-1

Track and Field (continued)

Olympic Javelin Throw

Year	Medalists	Country	Meters	Ft-In
1936	Ottilie "Tilly" Fleischer	GER	45.18	148-3 OR
	Luise Kruger	GER	43.29	142-8
	Maria Kwasniewska	POL	41.80	137-2
1948	Hermine "Herma" Bauma	AUT	45.57	149-6 OR
	Kaisa Parviainen	FIN	43.79	143-8
	Lily Carlstadt	DEN	42.08	138-1
1952	Dana Zatopkova (Ingrova)	CZE	50.47	165-7 OR
	Aleksandra Chudina	USSR/Russia	50.01	164-0
	Yelena Gorchakova	USSR/Russia	49.76	163-3
1956	Inese Jaunzeme	USSR/Latvia	53.86	176-8 OR
	Marlene Ahrens	CHI	50.38	165-3
	Nadiya Konyayeva	USSR/Ukraine	50.28	164-11½
1960	Elvira Ozolina	USSR/Russia	55.98	183-8 OR
	Dana Zatopkova (Ingrova)	CZE	53.78	176-5
	Birute Kalediene	USSR/Lithuania	53.45	175-4
1964	Mihaela Penes	ROM	60.54	198-7
	Marta Rudas	HUN	58.27	191-2
	Yelena Gorchakova	USSR/Russia	57.06	187-2
1968	Angela Nemeth	HUN	60.36	198-0
	Mihaela Penes	ROM	59.92	196-7
	Eva Janko	AUT	58.04	190-5
1972	Ruth Fuchs	GDR	63.88	209-7 OR
	Jacqueline Todten	GDR	62.54	205-2
	Kathryn Schmidt	USA	59.94	196-8
1976	Ruth Fuchs	GDR	65.94	216-4 OR
	Marion Becker	GER	64.70	212-3
	Kathryn Schmidt	USA	63.96	209-10
1980	Maria Colon Ruenes	CUB	68.40	224-5 OR
	Saida Gunba	USSR/Georgia	67.76	222-2
	Ute Hommola	GDR	66.56	218-4
1984	Theresa "Tessa" Sanderson	GBR	69.56	228-2 OR
	Ilse "Tina" Lillak	FIN	69.00	226-4
	Fatima Whitbread	GBR	67.14	220-3
1988	Petra Felke	GDR	74.68	245-0 OR
	Fatima Whitbread	GBR	70.32	230-8½
	Beate Koch	GDR	67.30	220-10
1992	Silke Renk	GER	68.34	224-2
	Natalya Shikolenko	BLR	68.26	223-11
	Karen Forkel	GER	66.86	219-4
1996	Heli Rantanen	FIN	67.94	222-11
	Louise McPaul	AUS	65.53	215-0
	Trine Hattestad	NOR	64.97	213-2

Olympic Heptathlon/Pentathlon

Year	Medalists	Country	Score
1896–1960	event not held		
1964	Iryna Press	USSR/UKR	5246 WR
	Mary Rand (Bignal)	GBR	5035.00
	Galina Bystrova	USSR/Russia	4956.00

Track and Field (continued)

Olympic Heptathlon/Pentathlon

Year	Medalists	Country	Score
1968	Ingrid Becker	GER	5098.00
	Elisabeth "Liese" Prokop	AUT	4966.00
	Annamaria Toth	HUN	4959.00
1972	Mary Peters	GBR	4801 WR
	Heidemarie Rosendahl	GER	4791.00
	Burglinde Pollak	GDR	4768.00
1976	Siegrun Siegl	GDR	4745.00
	Christine Laser (Bodner)	GDR	4745.00
	Burglinde Pollak	GDR	4740.00
1980	Nadiya Tkachenko	USSR/UKR	5083 WR
	Olga Rukavishnikova	USSR/Russia	4937.00
	Olga Kuragina	USSR/Russia	4875.00
1984	Glynis Nunn	AUS	6390 OR
	Jacqueline Joyner	USA	6385.00
	Sabine Everts	GER	6363.00
1988	Jacqueline Joyner-Kersee	USA	7291 WR
	Sabine John (Paetz)	GDR	6897.00
	Anke Behmer	GDR	6858.00
1992	Jacqueline Joyner-Kersee	USA	7044.00
	Irina Belova	RUS	6845.00
	Sabine Braun	GER	6649.00
1996	Ghada Shouaa	SYR	6780.00
	Natasha Sazanovich	BLR	6563.00
	Denise Lewis	GBR	6489.00

Olympic 3,000 Meters (Discontinued Event)

1896–1980	event not held		
1984	Maricica Pulca	ROM	8:35.96 OR
	Wendy Sly	GBR	8:39.47
	Lynn Williams	CAN	8:42.14
1988	Tetyana Samolenko	USSR/UKR	8:26.53 OR
	Paula Ivan	ROM	8:27.15
	Yvonne Murray	GBR	8:29.02
1992	Yelena Romanova	RUS	8:46.04
	Tetyana Dorovskikh (Samolenko)	UKR	8:46.85
	Angela Chalmers	CAN	8:47.22

World Championship 100 Meters

Year	Champion	Country	Time
1983	Marlies Göhr	GDR	10.97
1987	Silke Gladisch	GDR	10.9
1991	Katrin Krabbe	GER	10.99
1993	Gail Devers	USA	10.81 CR
1995	Gwen Torrence	USA	10.85

World Championship 200 Meters

1983	Marita Koch	GDR	22.13
1987	Silke Gladisch	GDR	21.74 CR
1991	Katrin Krabbe	GER	22.09
1993	Merlene Ottey	JAM	21.98
1995	Merlene Ottey	JAM	22.12

Track and Field (continued)

World Championship 400 Meters

Year	Champion	Country	Time
1983	Jarmila Kratochvilova	CZE	47.99 WR
1987	Olga Bryzgina	USSR	49.38
1991	Marie-José Pérec	FRA	49.13
1993	Jearl Miles	USA	49.82
1995	Marie-José Pérec	FRA	49.28

World Championship 800 Meters

1983	Jarmila Kratochvilova	CZE	1:54.68 CR
1987	Sigrun Wodars	GDR	1:55.26
1991	Lilia Nurutdinova	USSR	1:57.50
1993	Maria Mutola	MOZ	1:55.43
1995	Ana Quirot	CUB	1:56.11

World Championship 1,500 Meters

1983	Mary Decker	USA	4:00.90
1987	Tatyana Samolenko	USSR	3:58.56 CR
1991	Hassiba Boulmerka	ALG	4:02.21
1993	Liu Dong	CHN	4:00.50
1995	Hassiba Boulmerka	ALG	4:02.42

World Championship 5,000 Meters
(held as 3,000-meter race 1983–93)

1983	Mary Decker	USA	8:34.62
1987	Tatyana Samolenko	USSR	8:38.73
1991	Tatyana Dorovskikh (Samolenko)	USSR	8:35.82
1993	Qu Yunxia	CHN	8:28.71 CR
1995	Sonia O'Sullivan	IRE	14:46.47 CR

World Championship 10,000 Meters

1983	event not held		
1987	Ingrid Kristiansen	NOR	31:05.85
1991	Liz McColgan	GBR	31:14.31
1993	Wang Junxia	CHN	30:49.30 CR
1995	Fernanda Ribeiro	POR	31:04.99

World Championship Marathon

1983	Grete Waitz	NOR	2:28:09
1987	Rose Mota	POR	2:25:17 CR
1991	Wanda Panfil	POL	2:29:53
1993	Junko Asari	JPN	2:30:03
1995	Manuela Machado	POR	2:25:39

World Championship 100-Meter Hurdles

1983	Bettine John	GDR	12.35
1987	Ginka Zagorcheva	BUL	12.34 CR
1991	Lyudmila Narazhilenko	USSR	12.59
1993	Gail Devers	USA	12.46
1995	Gail Devers	USA	12.68

World Championship 400-Meter Hurdles

1983	Yekaterina Fesenko	USSR	54.12
1987	Sabine Busch	GDR	53.62
1991	Tatiana Ledovskaya	USSR	53.11
1993	Sally Gunnell	GBR	52.74 WR
1995	Kim Batten	USA	52.61 WR

World Championship 4 × 100-Meter Relay

1983		GDR	41.76
1987		USA	41.58
1991		JAM	41.94
1993		RUS	41.49 CR
1995		USA	42.12

World Championship 4 × 400-Meter Relay

1983		GDR	3:19.73
1987		GDR	3:18.63
1991		USSR	3:18.43
1993		USA	3:16.71 CR
1995		USA	3:22.39

World Championship 10-Kilometer Walk

1983	event not held		
1987	Irina Strakhova	USSR	44:12
1991	Alina Ivanova	USSR	42:57
1993	Sari Essayah	FIN	42:59
1995	Irina Stankina	RUS	42:13 CR

World Championship High Jump

			Ft-In
1983	Tamara Bykova	USSR	6-7
1987	Stefka Kostadinova	BUL	6-10¼ WR
1991	Heike Henkel	GER	6-8¾
1993	Ioamnet Quintero	CUB	6-6¼
1995	Stefka Kostadinova	BUL	6-7

World Championship Long Jump

1983	Heike Daute	GDR	23-10¼
1987	Jackie Joyner-Kersee	USA	24-1¾ CR
1991	Jackie Joyner-Kersee	USA	24-0¼
1993	Heike Drechsler	GER	23-4
1995	Fiona May	ITA	22-10¾

Track and Field (continued)

World Championship Triple Jump

Year	Champion	Country	Ft-In
1983	event not held		
1987	event not held		
1991	event not held		
1993	Ana Biryukova	RUS	46-6¼ WR
1995	Inessa Kravets	UKR	50-10¾ WR

World Championship Shot Put

1983	Helena Fibingerova	CZE	69-0
1987	Natalia Lisovskaya	USSR	69-8 CR
1991	Huang Zhihong	CHN	68-4
1993	Huang Zhihong	CHN	67-6
1995	Astrid Kumbernuss	GER	69-7½

World Championship Discus

1983	Martina Opitz	GDR	226-2
1987	Martina Opitz Hellmann	GDR	235-0 CR
1991	Tsvetanka Khristova	BUL	233-0
1993	Olga Burova	RUS	221-1
1995	Ellina Zvereva	BLR	225-2

World Championship Javelin

1983	Tiina Lillak	FIN	232-4
1987	Fatima Whitbread	GBR	251-5 CR
1991	Xu Demei	CHN	225-8
1993	Trine Hattestad	NOR	227-0
1995	Natalya Shikolenko	BLR	221-8

World Championship Heptathlon

1983	Ramona Neubert	GDR	6770
1987	Jackie Joyner-Kersee	USA	7128 CR
1991	Sabine Braun	GER	6672
1993	Jackie Joyner-Kersee	USA	6837
1995	Ghada Shouaa	SYR	6651

Photo credit: Ken Regan/Camera 5

GYMNASTICS

◆ *Catapulted to popularity by Olga Korbut's tears at the 1972 Olympics, women's gymnastics outshines men's—with a larger following and more participants—in much of the world, including the United States.*

HISTORY

Women's gymnastics didn't grow out of men's gymnastics but descended from theater and dance. And while men's gymnastics are woven firmly into the Western tradition, the women's sport owes more to the traditions of the East.

The earliest gymnasts were entertainers, lower-class citizens or slaves, who incorporated acrobatics into dance. Troupes of dancer-acrobats entertained the pharaohs of Egypt, and later the

Caesars of Rome. By the Middle Ages no great European court was without its retinue of acrobats, actors, jugglers, and jesters—but by then the role of women was much reduced. In the West, tumblers and acrobats became almost exclusively male as women became increasingly constrained by notions of modesty, frailty, and virtue. Women could play the lute and dance through the complex patterns of the Renaissance, but only in the privacy of their own homes. To stand on their heads or perform for strangers was unthinkable. This was not so in the East, where Chinese acrobatic troupes continued to include both men and women. In Asia such troupes were not joined by society's wealthiest individuals, but neither were they on the fringes of civilized society. Chinese acrobatic troupes formed a respectable tradition. For a woman, being a performer in the East did

131

◆ ◆

RUSSIAN GOLD: THE YEARS OF SOVIET GLORY

In 1952 the Soviet women's team took home its first Olympic gold medal. Over the next forty years they took home ten more, a string of consecutive wins broken only by their boycott of the Los Angeles games in 1984. The string of victories ended with the dissolution of the Soviet Union. In 1996 former teammates attended the games under separate flags, clearing the way for America's first gold in team gymnastics. However flawed the Soviet system was at producing tractors, automobiles, or housing, there's little doubt that it succeeded brilliantly in producing the world's greatest gymnasts.

Gold-medal team of 1952*: Maria Gorokhovskaya, Nina Bocharova, Galina Minaicheva, Galina Urbanovich, Pelageya Danilova, Galina Shamrai, and Yekaterina Kalinchuk.

Gold-medal team of 1956: Larissa Latynina, Sofia Muratova, Tamara Manina, Lyudmila Yegorova, Polina Astakhova, and Lidiya Kalinina.

Gold-medal team of 1960: Larissa Latynina, Sofia Muratova, Polina Astakhova, Margarita Nikolayeva, Lidiya Kalinina Ivanova, and Tamara Lyukhina.

---

* Team members are listed in scoring order, highest scorers first.

Gold-medal team of 1964: Larissa Latynina, Polina Astakhova, Yelena Volchetskaya, Tamara Lyukhina Zamotailova, Tamara Manina, and Lyudmila Gromova.

Gold-medal team of 1968: Zinaida Voronina, Natalya Kuchinskaya, Larissa Petrik, Olga Karasseva, Lyudmila Tourischeva, and Lyubov Burda.

Gold-medal team of 1972: Lyudmila Tourischeva, Olga Korbut, Tamara Lazakovitch, Lyubov Burda, Elvira Saadi, and Antonina Koshel.

Gold-medal team of 1976: Nelli Kim, Lyudmila Tourischeva, Olga Korbut, Elvira Saadi, Maria Filatova, and Svetlana Grozdova.

Gold-medal team of 1980: Natalya Shaposhnikova, Yelena Davydova, Nelli Kim, Maria Filatova, Stella Zakharova, and Yelena Naimushina.

Gold-medal team of 1988: Yelena Shushunova, Svetlana Boginskaya, Natalya Lashchenova, Svetlana Baitova, Yelena Shevchenko, and Olga Strazheva.

Gold-medal team of 1992: Svetlana Boginskaya, Tatyana Lysenko, Rozalya Galiyeva, Tatyana Gutsu, Yelena Grudneva, and Oksana Chusovitina.

not carry the stigma of near-prostitution it did in the West.

Nor did the West consider troupe performers—even the most skillful male tumblers—serious athletes. From the earliest times, Western civilization saw men's gymnastics as a thing apart from acrobatic entertainment. First in Greece, and later in Rome, gymnastics were a standard and necessary part of a young man's schooling, pursued as a means of building strength and enhancing overall physical health. Though ancient gymnastics declined with the fall of Greece and Rome, these essential themes remained in place. When Germany's Frederick Jahn (b. 1788) popularized the notion of building strength by working out on apparatus, he spoke only to men. The

equipment he invented and promoted—the parallel bars, vault, and horizontal bar—were used exclusively by men, and gymnastic training became de rigeur for German soldiers. Again, whatever gymnastics were performed by women were performed in the context of theater—and therefore linked to libertinism and titillation. In belle epoque Europe, women's gymnastics could be seen in dance halls and circuses every night of the week. Georges Seurat's final—and unfinished—painting, *The Circus*, depicts a male tumbler in mid-flip and a female tumbler balancing on one foot atop a running horse. A poster for the infamous Folies-Bergère shows a troupe of shapely female acrobats taking the stage while another of their number performs a trapeze act overhead. At another Paris nightspot, the Moulin Rouge, the splits were incorporated into the naughty sensation of the moment, the cancan.

Far from the jubilant netherworld of circus and cabaret, "serious" gymnastics for women took its first tentative steps. Touted as part of the physical health movement of the late nineteenth century, gymnastics were seen for the first time as beneficial to women as well as men. Early gymnastics were not designed to delight an audience or create an artistic impression. Apparatuses were seen as aids in the body's battle against disease, particularly tuberculosis. Gradually, gymnastics, cycling, and other turn-of-the-century activities lost their medical trappings and became valued as worthwhile in their own right. Once they crossed the ledger and moved into the arena of sport, the stage was set. Gymnastics rapidly mutated from exercise for the masses to sport–cum–art for the gifted and dedicated few.

THE MODERN ERA

Individual gymnastics for men were included in the first modern Olympic Games, held in 1896, and a team event was added in 1904. There were no events for women until 1928, when team competition was included. The first women's gold medal went to the team from Holland: Petronella van Randwijk, Jacomina van den Berg, Anna Polak, Helena Nordheim, Alida van den Bos, Hendrika van Rumt, Anna van der Vegt, Elka de Levie, Jacoba Stelma, and Estella Agsteribbe. Four of these women, plus one alternate, were Jewish. Helena Nordheim, Anna Polak, and alternate Judikje Simons were killed, along with their children, at Sobibor. Estella Agsteribbe and her children died in an Auschwitz gas chamber. Elka de Levie was the only Jewish member to survive.

International individual competitions for women began in 1934 with the World Championship all-arounds. Medals for individual apparatus were added in 1950. The Olympics soon followed suit, adding individual competition for women with the Helsinki games in 1952. That year also

marked the beginning of another Olympic phenomenon—the dominance of Soviet women's teams, who won gold medals for the next four decades and produced such incomparable athletes as **Larissa Latynina** and **Lyudmila Tourischeva.**

Despite the excellence of these and other eastern bloc champions, such as Czechoslovakia's **Vera Cáslavská,** gymnastics remained a minor sport in the West. The obscurity ended almost overnight when **Olga Korbut** burst on the scene, altering the future of the sport for years to come.

RHYTHMIC GYMNASTICS

Unlike regular gymnastics, flips, handsprings, and other acrobatic moves are forbidden in rhythmic competition. Instead, contestants perform with

---

Major Events and Competitions

World Championships
Olympic Games
World Cup
Pan American Games
European Championship

Apparatus

There are four apparatus in women's gymnastics:

Balance beam: 12cm high × 500cm long × 10cm wide.

Vault: 120cm high × 160cm long × 35cm wide. The runway is a maximum of 25m long.

Uneven (or asymmetrical) parallel bars: high bar is 235–240cm high; low bar is 140–160cm high; the width between (adjustable by each gymnast) can be a maximum of 143.5cm.

Floor: space measuring 40 × 40 feet is supported by springs below and covered with synthetic material.

LITTLER, LIGHTER, RISKIER:
HOW WOMEN'S GYMNASTICS BECAME A LITTLE GIRLS' SPORT

Agnes Keleti, the first great gymnast of the modern era, won the first of her ten Olympic medals at age thirty-one, the last at age thirty-five. Her successor, **Larissa Latynina,** medaled in three consecutive Olympics and retired at age thirty-two. A few decades later, such careers would be unthinkable. When **Shannon Miller** made her final competitive appearance at the 1996 Olympics, she was considered a veteran whose time may well have come and gone. Miller was twenty-one—the age Latynina had been when she made her Olympic debut. What happened in the space of thirty years to transform women's gymnastics into gymnastics for girls?

The turning point came in 1972, at the Munich Olympics, with a girl named **Olga Korbut.** During the team competition, Korbut performed so badly on the bars that she sat down in tears. Millions of people watched the event on television, and millions of people were captivated by Korbut. At seventeen, standing an inch under five feet tall and weighing 85 pounds, Korbut looked and acted younger than her years. When she came back the next night to medal in individual events, her tears turned into an open, unself-conscious smile. Her pigtails, tied with bright, fat coils of yarn, bounced as she waved to the audience. Within a year, gym clubs around the world were awash in little girls who showed up with the same yarn-tied pigtails, saying they wanted to be "just like Olga."

At the 1976 Olympics, Korbut was again in tears—but this time there was no happy ending as she was upstaged by fourteen-year-old **Nadia Comaneci.** Tiny and fearless, Comaneci became the youngest champion in the history of Olympic gymnastics. Another star of the games, the Soviet Union's **Nelli Kim,** was older than Comaneci but no taller, while Kim's teammate, Maria Filatova, was nicknamed "the Siberian Sparrow" because she stood four foot five and weighed just sixty-six pounds. Clearly, smallness and youth had become the new trend to follow. In 1976, the tallest girl on the

Soviet team, Elvira Saadi, stood five foot three and a half. Four years later, no one on the team was even five feet tall. In 1984 America fielded its own small superstar, four-foot-eight-and-three-quarters **Mary Lou Retton.** At ninety-four pounds, Retton, visibly heavier than the Eastern Europeans, was often described—without apparent irony—as "solid" and "muscular."

The penchant for ever smaller and younger girls was more than a matter of subliminal Humbert Humbert-ism. Younger girls, who had not yet faced the growth spurts and mandatory weight gains of puberty, were lighter. They could move around the apparatus more easily, launch themselves higher into the air, and perform more somersaults on the way down. No matter how much talent they had, no matter how many hours of training they were willing to put in, older, taller, and heavier girls found themselves unable to keep up. Encumbered by breasts, hips, and height, they could not master the moves now necessary to win.

In 1972 Korbut used her small stature to push the envelope of her sport. Performing on the bars, she did a back flip off the high bar, then recaught it on her way down. Even riskier was her back salto on the beam. By the time the 1976 Olympics rolled around, millions of TV viewers waited with bated breath to see what new stunts were in store.

The watchers weren't disappointed. Picking up where Korbut's back flip left off, Comaneci pushed back off the high bar, whirled through the air in a front salto, and, with legs in a straddle position, recaught the bar with breathtaking deftness. Such innovations, which became known as release moves, quickly became standard in world-class competitions. Comaneci also revolutionized the dismount, launching her body off the bar and performing a half twist and back salto on the way down. Other innovations at the 1976 games were introduced by Nelli Kim, whose double back salto in floor exercise was the first ever done in Olympic competition. On vault, Kim's performance was also revolutionary. Previously, vaults had consisted of a simple handspring accompanied by a body twist or pike. Kim did a back salto with a body twist dismount—and girls around the world knew they would have to match the standard if they hoped to win.

As competitors shrank in size and weight, coaches noted that, if the uneven bars were just a few more inches apart, the girls could perform "giants"—circles around the bar with body fully extended. Though giants are a staple of men's competition, they were not possible for women, whose feet would hit the lower bar—until, of course, those women of 5'3" became girls of 4'10". In the late 1970s manufacturers made it possible to increase the space between the bars, and little girls did giant circles. In themselves, giants are not especially difficult or dangerous. They are important because they allow the gymnast to gather force and momentum, to launch herself higher into the air, giving her more time to execute complex tumbling moves in midair.

The explosive increase in difficulty on apparatus resulted in more problems for competitors. For many, the need to remain light led to compulsive dieting, poor nutrition, and eating disorders. Failure to increase weight and bone mass resulted in amenorrhea and osteoporosis. Injuries became more common, as well as more debilitating. Two weeks before the 1980 Olympics, defending world champion **Yelena Mukhina** broke her spine practicing floor exercises and was permanently paralyzed from the neck down. Americans **Kim Zmeskal** and **Dianne Durham** became just two of many girls to suffer career-ending injuries, and even "survivors" had long medical records. When **Kerri Strug** performed a medal-winning vault with torn ligaments at the 1996 Olympics, audiences applauded her courage. But Strug had already experienced far worse —years earlier, at a minor competition in Florida, she fell off the bars and was so badly injured doctors weren't sure she would ever walk again.

By the mid-1990s the high rate of injury, combined with the decline in average age and the much-publicized demands of the sport itself, cast serious shadows over gymnastics. The little girls who had seemed so glamorous two decades earlier began to seem more like exploited Dickensian waifs. In America, USA Gymnastics initiated programs to educate girls, parents, and coaches about nutrition and eating disorders. Internationally, Olympic policy raised the age limits for the sport. Beginning with the Sydney Olympics in 2000, girls would not be allowed to compete unless they were sixteen years old. For the time being, there would be no more Nadias or Mary Lous.

various props—hoops, clubs, ribbons, rope, and balls. The focus is on grace rather than strength, and routines are performed to music. Historically, rhythmic gymnastics predate modern gymnastics by several centuries. They are the direct descendent of Chinese acrobatic theater, in which performers often balanced delicate pieces of crockery or used lengths of brightly colored cloth to dramatic effect. In the West, dances that used props were an early precursor to the sport. A decoration on an eleventh-century Hungarian crown depicts in enamel and gold cloisonné a female dancer swinging a graceful arc of ribbon over her head, jump-rope fashion. Despite the sport's history and the considerable skill required, rhythmic gymnastics have never achieved widespread acceptance or respect. The Olympics in particular have had an on-again, off-again relationship with the sport, including it in 1952, then dropping it, reintroducing it in 1984, and adding a team event in 1996.

Governing Bodies and Organizations

USA Gymnastics
Pan American Plaza, Suite 300
201 South Capitol Avenue
Indianapolis, Indiana 46225
Phone: 317/237-5050 or 1-800-345-4719
Fax: 317/237-5069
E-mail: USGF@delphi.com
Web site: http://www.usa-gymnastics.org/usag

✴ ✴ ✴ BIOGRAPHIES ✴ ✴ ✴

POLINA ASTAKHOVA b. October 30, 1936,
Donetsk, Ukraine, USSR

Often overshadowed by her contemporary and team-mate **Larissa Latynina,** Astakhova was a brilliant and enduring gymnast in the great Soviet tradition. With Latynina, Astakhova appeared at three Olympic Games (1956–64) and helped her team to three consecutive wins. Individually, she won one World Championship and two Olympic gold medals—all of them on the uneven bars—and was a two-time bronze medalist in Olympic all-arounds.

Selected championships and honors, individual: Two gold medals, bars, Olympic Games, 1960 and '64; two silver medals, floor exercise, Olympic Games, 1960 and '64; two bronze medals, all-around, Olympic Games, 1960 and '64. *Team:* Three gold medals, Olympic Games, 1956, '60, and '64.

SVETLANA BOGINSKAYA b. February 9, 1973,
Minsk, Belarus, USSR

Boginskaya's long, graceful lines earned her the appelation "Goddess of Gymnastics," and her perseverance earned her a spot in three Olympiads (1988–96), an almost unheard-of feat in the modern era. Initially a figure skater, Boginskaya switched to gymnastics in 1981. In Olympic and World Championship competition, she medaled in every event except the uneven bars and is best remembered for her dramatic floor routines. Boginskaya, who moved to the United States in 1994, competed for her native Belarus in her last Olympic appearance.

Selected championships and honors, individual: Gold medal, vault, Olympic Games, 1988; silver medal, floor exercise, Olympic Games, 1988; gold medal, all-around, World Championships, 1989; gold medal, floor exercise, World Championships, 1989; silver medal, all-around, World Championships, 1991; gold medal, vault, World Championships, 1991. *Team:* Two gold medals, Olympic Games, 1988 and '92; two gold medals, World Championships, 1989 and '91.

AMANDA BORDEN b. May 10, 1977, Cincinnati,
Ohio

Borden wasn't the best known of the Mag Seven, as the U.S. 1996 Olympic squad was known, but her drive for perfection and quiet leadership made her the choice for team captain. During the team competitions in Atlanta she performed on the beam and

Mag Seven—As in Magnificent

Team titles were part of the Eastern European empire, a laurel wreath passed back and forth between the old Soviet Union and Romania. The best U.S. finish was a silver, earned at the 1984 Olympics in the absence of the Soviets. Going into the 1996 games, there was much hometown hype about the U.S. squad being the strongest ever. But, hype aside, could they do it? The answer came on a hot night in July. Points away from victory, the gold medal would be decided on the last two performances of the final rotation, the vault. Going second-to-last, Dominique Moceanu missed both landings. The final competitor, Kerri Strug, not only missed her first landing but injured her ankle. The American team was stunned. The girls who never missed *had* missed, and missed badly. But there was one more vault, and Strug was determined to do it. Her gutsy performance secured the gold, and the Mag Seven more than lived up to the hype that preceded them. Below, the golden girls and the contribution each made to their medal-winning performance:

Amanda Borden, 19: beam, floor, and vault; team captain.
Amy Chow, 18: bars and vault.
Dominique Dawes, 19: bars, beam, floor, and vault.
Shannon Miller, 19: bars, beam, floor, and vault.
Dominique Moceanu, 14: bars, beam, floor, and vault.
Jaycie Phelps, 16: bars, beam, floor, and vault.
Kerri Strug, 18: bars, beam, floor, and vault.

floor exercises, events in which she had won gold and silver medals at the Pan American Games the year before.

Selected championships and honors, individual: Gold medal, beam, Pan American Games, 1995; silver medal, all-around, Pan American Games, 1995; silver medal, floor exercise, Pan American Games, 1995. *Team:* Gold medal, Pan American Games, 1995; gold medal, Olympic Games, 1996.

VERA CÁSLAVSKÁ b. May 3, 1942, Prague, Czechoslovakia

It was a bittersweet moment when Cáslavská defeated the incomparable **Larissa Latynina** at the 1966 World Championships. In a single competition, the reigning queen of women's gymnastics was deposed. As subsequent competitions revealed, Cáslavská was a more than worthy successor. Originally trained as a figure skater, the graceful and accomplished Cáslavská also had the expressive sparkle that transforms a technically correct routine into a work of art. During her ten year career, Cáslavská won titles on every apparatus and at all levels of competition. Individually, she collected seven Olympic golds and a silver. As a member of the Czechoslovakian team, she helped her country capture three team silvers. Cáslavská's career ended, as it had begun, on a bittersweet note. Her greatest triumph came at her last international competition, the 1968 Olympics, when she won two silvers and a gold. Saddened by the Soviet Union's invasion of her country earlier that year, she gave all her medals to the leaders of the Czech nationalist movement. During the 1968 games she married Josef Odlozil, a Czech track star, whom she divorced in 1972. Cáslavská retired from competition soon after the 1968 games. After the fall of communism in 1989, Cáslavská was named to her country's Olympic committee.

Selected championships and honors, individual: Two gold medals, all-around, Olympic Games, 1964 and '68; gold medal, all-around, World Championships, 1966; two gold medals, vault, World Championships, 1962 and '66. *Team:* Three silver medals, Olympic Games, 1960, '64, and '68.

AMY CHOW b. May 15, 1978, San Jose, California

As part of the Magnificent Seven of 1996, Chow's strong performance on uneven bars helped the United States nail down its first team gold in Olympic gymnastics. The same routine won her a silver in event finals. The year before, Chow had missed the

World Championships due to a sprained ankle. She did appear at the Pan American Games that year, where she took home a team gold as well as an individual gold (vault) and bronze (all-around).

Selected championships and honors, individual: Gold medal, vault, Pan American Games, 1995; silver medal, bars, Pan American Games, 1995; bronze medal, all-around, Pan American Games, 1995; silver medal, bars (tie with Bi Wenjiing), Olympic Games, 1996. *Team:* Gold medal, Olympic Games, 1996.

NADIA COMANECI CONNER b. November 12, 1961, Gheorghiu-Dej, Romania

Comaneci wasn't widely known when she took the 1976 Olympics by storm. At 4'11" and 86 pounds, Comaneci seemed even younger than her fourteen years, and her unprepossessing attitude toward her perfect score on the uneven parallel bars—the first 10 in Olympic history—earned her a place in the world's heart. So great was her popularity that her theme music, from the American soap opera *The Young and the Restless,* became an instant hit and was redubbed "Nadia's Theme." Comaneci left Montreal with three golds and one bronze. At home in Romania, she was hailed as a Hero of Socialist Labor. Her performance at the 1980 games was only slightly less spectacular, with two golds, one silver, and a team silver. Comaneci's last major international appearance was in 1981. She retired in 1981, and defected to the United States in December 1989. In 1996 she married American gymnast Bart Conner. Today Comaneci and Conner run gymnastic camps and clinics and hope to elevate their sport to the status of figure skating in America.

Selected championships and honors, individual: Gold medal, all-around, Olympic Games, 1976; gold medal, bars, Olympic Games, 1976; two gold medals, beam, Olympic Games, 1976 and '80; bronze medal, floor exercise, Olympic Games, 1976; gold medal, vault, World Championships, 1978; silver medal, all-around (tie, with East Germany's Maxi Gnauk), Olympic Games, 1980; gold medal, floor exercise, Olympic Games, 1980. *Team:* Silver medal, Olympic Games, 1980.

MURIEL DAVIS GROSSFIELD b. 1941, Indianapolis, Indiana

A member of three U.S. Olympic teams (1956, '60, and '64) and winner of seventeen national titles, Davis might have been better known if there had been more television coverage during her career.

There wasn't, and Davis had to make her fame as a coach. Trained in ballet as a child, Davis stressed gracefulness and discipline. She was national all-around champion in 1957 and '63, and national champion on the uneven bars in 1960 and '63. Her true expertise lay in floor exercise, where she won eight national titles (1956–58, 1960–64) and beam, in which she won five national titles (1957, '59, '62–64). Davis married fellow gymnast Abie Grossfield in 1960, began coaching her own club in 1962, and coached U.S. women's teams bound for the Pan American Games and North American championships. A performer and coach before gymnastics had a following in America, Davis was a true pioneer, and she is honored in the International Women's Sports Hall of Fame.

DOMINIQUE DAWES b. November 20, 1976,
Silver Spring, Maryland
Known in gymnastic circles as "Awesome Dawesome," Dawes was part of the "Magnificent Seven" squad that brought the United States its first Olympic team gold in 1996. Four years earlier she was on the bronze-medal team, the first U.S. squad to medal at a fully attended Olympic Games. Noted for her powerful tumbling abilities, Dawes's final competitive appearance was the event finals of the games, where she won a bronze for her floor exercise.
Selected championships and honors, individual: Silver medal, bars, World Championships, 1993; silver medal, beam, World Championships, 1993; bronze medal, floor exercise, Olympic Games, 1996. *Team:* Bronze medal, Olympic Games, 1992; gold medal, Olympic Games, 1996.

DIANNE DURHAM b. June 7, 1968, Gary, Indiana
Although Durham's career ended prematurely due to injury, in 1983 she was one of America's brightest hopes for the 1984 Olympics. The first African-American to win a national gymnastics title, Durham won four of five events in the 1983 nationals and tied for second on the uneven parallel bars. That same year she won the gold and silver medals at the McDonald's International Championships before suffering the knee injury that ended her career.

MARCIA FREDERICK b. January 4, 1963,
Massachusetts
Frederick is not nearly as well known as she deserves to be, but her moment of glory was great. At the 1978 World Championships, fifteen-year-old Frederick became the first American woman ever to win a gold in World Championship competition. Her medal came on the uneven bars, her strongest event.
Selected championships and honors: Gold medal, bars, World Championships, 1978.

KARIN JANZ b. February 17, 1952,
Hartmannsdorf, East Germany
At age six months, Janz attempted her first pull-up. Ten months later her gymnast father taught her to hang by her knees from a bar. The head start paid off, and during her career Janz won five individual and two team Olympic medals. Today she is remembered as an innovator whose willingness to try new and difficult moves in major competitions often cost her vital points. Janz would undoubtedly have been more famous had she not been the exact contemporary of **Lyudmila Tourischeva,** the Soviet gymnast who finished a rung ahead of her in competition after competition. Unlike gymnasts who neglected their education during their careers, Janz kept up with her studies and entered medical school after her final competition in 1972. She eventually specialized in orthopedic surgery, headed a clinic near Berlin, and with another doctor developed an artificial disc used in replacement surgery.
Selected championships and honors, individual: Silver medal, bars, Olympic Games, 1968; gold medal, bars, World Championships, 1970; silver medal, vault, World Championships, 1970; silver medal, all-around, Olympic Games, 1972; gold medal, bars, Olympic Games, 1972; gold medal, vault, Olympic Games, 1972; bronze medal, beam, Olympic Games, 1972. *Team:* Bronze medal, Olympic Games, 1968; silver medal, Olympic Games, 1972.

AGNES KELETI b. January 9, 1921, Budapest,
Hungary
Keleti had to wait twelve years and survive Hitler's persecution to win her medals, but she managed both. A hopeful for the canceled 1940 Olympics, Keleti barely survived the war. Her father was sent to Auschwitz, her mother and sister went into hiding, and Keleti lived on forged papers. Unwilling to give up her original dream, Keleti retained her passion for gymnastics. Unable to compete in 1948 due to injury, she finally got her chance—at age thirty-one—at the 1952 Olympics, the first to feature individual competition for women. Keleti won a gold medal in floor exercises, a bronze on the uneven bars, and a team silver. Four years later, at the age of thirty-five, she

returned to win gold in all but the vault, in which she failed to place, and the all-around, where she settled for a silver behind newcomer **Larissa Latynina.** Her strongest event was the bars, on which she won a World Championship gold in 1954. The 1956 games, which were held in Sydney, provided Keleti with the opportunity to defect. She remained behind in Australia and eventually emigrated to Israel.

Selected championships and honors, individual: Bronze medal, bars, Olympic Games, 1952; gold medal, bars, World Championships, 1954; silver medal, all-around, Olympic Games, 1956; gold medal, beam, Olympic Games, 1956; two gold medals, floor exercise, Olympic Games, 1952 and '56. *Team:* Two silver medals, Olympic Games, 1952 and '56.

NELLI KIM b. July 29, 1957, Chimkent, Kazakhstan, USSR

Kim was the star of the gold-medal 1976 Soviet Olympic team in 1976, and won individual golds—with perfect 10s—on both the vault and floor exercises. But in 1976, gold wasn't good enough. Kim, who should have become a superstar, had the misfortune to perform her perfect routines minutes after **Nadia Comaneci** became the first gymnast in history to do so. At the 1980 games, she tied with Comaneci for first in floor exercises but finished fifth in the all-around. Kim, who also won a gold in vault at the 1978 World Championships, never quite achieved the fame she deserved. In 1996, living in Minnesota's Twin Cities area and seeking entrée to the business side of gymnastics, Kim described herself to an interviewer as living in a "vacuum," her name utterly devoid of the door-opening power owned by her Romanian rival.

Selected championships and honors, individual: Silver medal, all-around, Olympic Games, 1976; gold medal, vault, Olympic Games, 1976; gold medal, floor exercise, Olympic Games, 1976; gold medal, floor exercise (tie with Yelena Mukhina), World Championships, 1978; gold medal, vault, World Championships, 1978; silver medal, all-around, World Championships, 1978; gold medal, all-around, World Championships, 1979. *Team:* Two gold medals, Olympic Games, 1976 and '80.

OLGA KORBUT b. May 16, 1955, Grodno, Belarus, USSR

A bright spark of light burned against the tragedy of the 1972 Munich Olympics, and that spark was Korbut. She caught the public's eye with a brilliant performance on the uneven bars during team competition. Two days later, competing for the all-around, she performed the routine badly and sat down in tears. The next night she took two golds and a silver in individual apparatus competitions and the audience cheered wildly, setting aside nationalism in favor of Olga-ism. Korbut won a gold on vault at the 1974 World Championships and appeared at the 1976 Olympics as well, where she was overshadowed by her sport's new star, **Nadia Comaneci.** Yet during those brief days in Munich Korbut won something worth more than gold—she won a permanent place on the world stage for women's gymnastics. After her career, Korbut married Leonid Bortkevich, a famous singer. She was living in Grodno, near Chernobyl, when disaster struck the nuclear power plant. She eventually emigrated to the United States with her husband and son, settled near Atlanta, and founded a foundation for victims of Chernobyl.

Selected championships and honors, individual: Gold medal, beam, Olympic Games, 1972; gold medal, floor exercise, Olympic Games, 1972; silver medal, bars, Olympic Games, 1972; gold medal, vault, World Championships, 1974. *Team:* Two gold medals, Olympic Games, 1972 and '76. International Women's Sports Hall of Fame.

LARISSA LATYNINA b. December 27, 1934, Kherson, Ukraine, USSR

It's impossible to know about modern women's gymnastics without knowing something about Latynina. During her twelve-year career she won eleven individual golds in World Championship and Olympic competition. She attended three Olympics (1956–64) and helped her team to three consecutive gold medals—despite twice interrupting her career for the birth of her children. In her strongest event, floor exercises, her artfully choreographed and flawlessly executed transitions from move to move set new standards for grace and pointed women's gymnastics in a fresh direction. Her last international competition was the 1966 World Championships, where she failed to medal. The next year she became the head coach of the Soviet women's team, a position she held until 1977. Here again, Latynina left a dramatic imprint on her sport, creating the 1972 team that won the Olympic gold in Montreal.

Selected championships and honors, individual: Two gold medals, all-around, Olympic Games, 1956 and '60; gold medal, vault, Olympic Games, 1956; two gold medals, bars, Olympic Games, 1956 and '60; silver medal, floor exercise, Olympic Games, 1956; two gold medals, all-around, World Championships, 1958 and '62; gold medal, bars, World Championships, 1958; gold medal, beam, World Championships, 1958; gold medal, vault, World Championships, 1958; two gold medals, floor exercise, Olympic Games, 1960 and '64; silver medal, beam, Olympic Games, 1960; bronze medal, vault, Olympic Games, 1960; gold medal, floor exercise, World Championships, 1962; silver medal, all-around, Olympic Games, 1964; silver medal, vault, Olympic Games, 1964; bronze medal, bars, Olympic Games, 1964; bronze medal, beam, Olympic Games, 1964. *Team wins:* Three gold medals, Olympic Games, 1956–64.

JULIANNE McNAMARA b. October 6, 1966, Flushing, New York

McNamara made the 1980 Olympic team when she was thirteen but missed her chance to compete due to the boycott. Thereafter, her career was often overshadowed by that of her younger teammate, **Mary Lou Retton.** Nevertheless, McNamara was a superb all-around gymnast. At the 1981 World Championships she finished the all-around in seventh place, the highest finish to date for an American woman. At the Los Angeles games in 1984 she tied for a gold on her favorite event, the uneven parallel bars, and missed a bronze in the all-around by one-quarter of a point.

Selected championships and honors, individual: Gold medal, bars (tie with Mah Yanhonjg), Olympic Games, 1984. *Team:* Silver medal, Olympic Games, 1984.

SHANNON MILLER b. March 10, 1977, Rolla, Missouri

Studious and somewhat camera-shy even in her hometown of Edmond, Oklahoma, Miller was never as famous as Nadia, Olga, or Mary Lou—but she won more medals than any of them and ranks as the most accomplished gymnast the United States has ever produced. At the 1992 Olympics Miller came heartbreakingly close to winning the all-around gold medal but had to settle for a silver when she finished just .012 points behind Tatyana Gutsu. Miller went on to win two consecutive all-around golds in World Championship competition, but wanted one final try at Olympic gold. The 1996 Games were an emotional roller-coaster as Miller led the U.S. squad to its first Olympic team gold, then finished a disappointing eighth in the all-around, then had one last chance for individual gold in the event finals. In the last routine of her competitive career, Miller performed a near-

flawless routine on the beam and earned the medal that had so long eluded her.

Selected championships and honors, individual: Silver medal, beam (tie), World Championships, 1991; silver medal, all-around, Olympic Games, 1992; silver medal, beam, Olympic Games, 1992; bronze medal, bars, Olympic Games, 1992; bronze medal, floor exercise, Olympic Games, 1992; two gold medals, all-around, World Championships, 1993 and '94; gold medal, bars, World Championships, 1993; gold medal, floor exercise, World Championships, 1993; gold medal, beam, World Championships, 1994; gold medal, beam, Olympic Games, 1996. *Team:* Bronze medal, Olympic Games, 1992; bronze medal, World Championships, 1995; gold medal, Olympic Games, 1996.

DOMINIQUE MOCEANU b. September 30, 1981, Hollywood, California

The American-born daughter of Romanian gymnast immigrants, Moceanu's uncanny likeness to an earlier champion, **Nadia Comaneci,** drew almost as much attention as her extreme youthfulness at the 1996 Olympics. At ten, Moceanu became the youngest gymnast ever to make the U.S. Junior National team. At thirteen, she became the youngest Senior National Champion in history. At fourteen, she helped the U.S. squad win its first ever Olympic team gold.

Selected championships and honors, individual: Silver medal, beam (tie with **Lilia Podkopayeva**), World Championships, 1995. *Team:* Bronze medal, World Championships, 1995; gold medal, Olympic Games, 1996.

YELENA MUKHINA b. 1961, Moscow, USSR

In 1977 Mukhina dazzled spectators at the World Cup and European championships. The next year, at the World Championships, she won two individual golds, two silvers, and a team gold. Noted for her fearlessness—she pioneered a difficult twisting somersault on the uneven bars—Mukhina seemed ordained to be the next great Soviet star. Instead, tragedy struck. A few weeks before the 1980 Olympics, while practing her floor exercise, Mukhina missed a one-and-one-half salto with one-and-one-half twist. The fall broke her spine, paralyzing her from the neck down.

Selected championships and honors, individual: Gold medal, all-around, World Championships, 1978; gold medal, floor exercise (tie with Nelli Kim), World Championships, 1978; silver medal, beam, World Championships, 1978; silver medal, bars, World Championships, 1978. *Team:* Gold medal, World Championships, 1978.

JAYCIE PHELPS b. September 26, 1979,
     Indianapolis, Indiana
Phelps, who started gymnastics at age four, was somewhat overshadowed by her teammates on the Magnificent Seven. Nevertheless, she performed on all four apparatuses to help the United States win its first Olympic team gold.
Selected championships and honors, team: Bronze medal, World Championships, 1995; gold medal, Olympic Games, 1996.

LILIA PODKOPAYEVA b. 1979, Donetsk, Ukraine
Nicknamed "Lilipod" by her coaches and teammates, Podkopayeva's unusual grace may have been genetic—her grandmother was a ballerina. At the 1996 Olympics her dance abilities sparkled. In her floor routine, set to an Irish jig, she earned the games' highest score—a 9.887—to win the event final. The same routine cemented her bid for the all-around gold.
Selected championships and honors: Gold medal, all-around, World Championships, 1995; silver medal, vault, World Championships, 1995; silver medal, bars (tie with Mo Huilan), World Championships, 1995; Silver medal, beam (tie with Dominique Moceanu), World Championships, 1995; gold medal, all-around, Olympic Games, 1996; gold medal, floor exercise, Olympic Games, 1996; silver medal, beam, Olympic Games, 1996.

MARY LOU RETTON b. January 24, 1968,
     Fairmont, West Virginia
In contrast to the small, elfin gymnasts of the eastern bloc, Retton burst on the scene with the force of a compact, muscular firecracker. Eight years after earning a 1.0 in her first competition, Retton became the star of the 1984 Olympics. It was her first international competition and came just six weeks after arthroscopic surgery to remove torn cartilage from her knee. During the all-around competition, Retton scored a perfect 10 on floor exercises, then flew down the mats twice to score two more perfect 10s on the vault. Retton was the first American to earn a perfect score, and her energy, determination, and smile made her one of the best-known athletes of her era.
Selected championships and honors, individual: Gold medal, all-around, Olympic Games, 1984; silver medal,

vault, Olympic Games, 1984; bronze medal, bars, Olympic Games, 1984; bronze medal, floor exercise, Olympic Games, 1984. *Team:* Silver medal, Olympic Games, 1984.

CATHY RIGBY McCOY b. December 12, 1952,
     Los Alamitos, California
Rigby never won a World Championship or Olympic gold medal, but that hardly matters to millions of Americans who remember her as the first U.S. gymnast to medal in world-class competition. Rigby began gymnastics at age eleven and was the high scorer on the 1968 Olympic team. At the World Championships two years later, her silver-medal performance on balance beam was televised to millions of Americans. Suddenly and somewhat unfairly, Rigby was seen as a gold-medal shoo-in for the 1972 Olympics. Americans had never had a medal contender before, and now, oblivious to the eastern bloc powerhouse, they expected nothing short of a first-place finish. Pitted against a field that included **Lyudmila Tourischeva, Olga Korbut,** and **Karin Janz,** Rigby managed to finish tenth in the all-around, the highest place ever achieved by an American woman. She also led the U.S. squad to a best-ever finish in fourth place. After retiring from competition, Rigby openly discussed two pervasive problems in gymnastics: eating disorders and the depression of finding oneself a "has-been" at the age of twenty. Though Rigby personally suffered from the first pitfall, she escaped the second. After retiring from competition, she covered her sport for network television and enjoyed a career on the stage. With her second husband, Tom McCoy, Rigby produces theatrical and video events for McCoy Rigby Entertainment.
Selected championships and honors: Silver medal, beam, World Championships, 1970.

YELENA SHUSHUNOVA b. Russia, USSR
Viewers of the 1988 Olympics witnessed two of the greatest floor exercises of all time. Shushunova's performance was letter-perfect, and earned a score of 10. Minutes later, **Daniela Silivas** performed an even more perfect routine—but the judges could only give her a 10 as well. The twist of fate was crucial, as Shushunova won the gold by a mere .025 of a point.
Selected championships and honors, individual: Gold medal, all-around (tie with Oksana Omeliantchik), World Championships, 1985; gold medal, floor exer-

cise (tie with Daniela Silivas), World Championships, 1987; two gold medals, vault, World Championships, 1985 and '87; gold medal, all-around, Olympic Games, 1988; silver medal, beam, Olympic Games, 1988; bronze medal, bars, Olympic Games, 1988. *Team:* Gold medal, Olympic Games, 1988.

DANIELA SILIVAS b. Romania

One of the premier gymnasts of the late 1980s, Silivas isn't as well known as she deserves to be. Between 1985 and 1989 she won five individual World Championships and Olympic gold medals. She also lost a memorable heartbreaker at the 1988 Olympics. Although she performed a better floor exercise routine than **Yelena Shushunova,** the judges had already awarded Shushunova the highest possible mark, a 10. Silivas lost the gold by an eyelash, finishing just .025 of a point behind her rival. She had the last word on the matter a few nights later, when she came back to win three individual event golds, while Shushunova won none.

Selected championships and honors, individual: Two gold medals, beam, World Championships, 1985 and '89; two gold medals, floor exercise (tie with Elena Shushunova, tie with Svetlana Boginskaya), World Championships, 1987 and '89; gold medal, bars (tie with Doerte Thuemmier), World Championships, 1987; silver medal, all-around, Olympic Games, 1988; gold medal, bars, Olympic Games, 1988; gold medal, beam, Olympic Games, 1988; gold medal, floor exercise, Olympic Games, 1988; bronze medal, vault, Olympic Games, 1988. *Team:* Silver medal, Olympic Games, 1988.

KERRI STRUG b. November 19, 1977, Tucson, Arizona

How do you injure yourself, miss the individual competitions, and still end up the star of the Olympics? Strug didn't plan it that way, but that's what happened at the 1996 games. The competition for the team gold was so close, it all came down to Strug's vault performance. She missed her first landing and badly injured her ankle. Ignoring the pain of torn ligaments, she performed her final vault, stuck the landing, and fell to the mat in pain. Her vault was enough to win gold, and Strug, with a taped ankle, was helped to the medal stand by her teammates and coach Bela Karolyi. The injury, made much of in the press, was minor for Strug, who once fell from the bars so badly that it was uncertain if she would even walk again.

Selected championships and honors: Silver medal,

World Championships, 1991; bronze medal, Olympic Games, 1992; gold medal, Olympic Games, 1996.

LYUDMILA TOURISCHEVA BORZOV
b. October 7, 1952, Grozny, Russia

Despite winning fifteen individual medals in Olympic and World Championship competition, Tourischeva never quite received the fame that should have been hers. A member of the gold-medal-winning Soviet team at the 1968 Olympics, Tourischeva's first wins in individual events came at the 1970 World Championships, where she took the all-around as well as floor exercise titles. Poised to dominate the 1972 Olympics, she won the all-around gold but was upstaged by teammate **Olga Korbut,** who took the gold to Tourischeva's silver on floor exercises and the beam. Back in the Soviet Union, Tourischeva also played a supporting role to the more popular but less talented Korbut—on the eve of the 1976 Olympics, Tourischeva was reportedly stunned and embittered when the Soviet Training Council removed her from the role of team captain and gave the position to Korbut. Tourischeva married Valery Borzov in 1977 and in 1978 received a postgraduate degree in education. Perhaps not surprisingly, her dissertation was entitled "A Study of the Emotional State of Qualified Female Gymnasts."

Selected championships and honors, individual: Two gold medals, all-around, World Championships, 1970 and '74; two gold medals, floor exercise, World Championships, 1970 and '74; silver medal, bars, World Championships, 1970; bronze medal, vault (tie with Lyubov Burda), World Championships, 1970; gold medal, all-around, Olympic Games, 1972; two silver medals, floor exercise, Olympic Games, 1972 and '76; bronze medal, vault, Olympic Games, 1972; gold medal, beam, World Championships, 1974; silver medal, vault, World Championships, 1974; bronze medal, bars, World Championships, 1974; bronze medal, all-around, Olympic Games, 1976; silver medal, vault (tie with Carola Dombeck), Olympic Games, 1976. *Team:* Three gold medals, Olympic Games, 1968–76.

MARIAN TWINING BARONE b. March 18, 1924, Philadelphia, Pennsylvania

An early national gymnastics champ, Twining was a member of the U.S. team that won a bronze medal at the 1948 Olympic Games. Twining took national titles in her strongest event, the uneven bars, in 1945 and '51, tied for national vault champion in 1945 with Clara

Schroth, and had the vault title all to herself in 1950. One of the few women to win championships in two sports, Twining also won four national titles in a now-extinct track and field event, the basketball free throw. *Selected championships and honors, team:* Bronze medal, Olympic Games, 1948.

KIM ZMESKAL b. February 6, 1976, Houston, Texas

Although her career ended early due to injury, Zmeskal has an enduring place in gymnastics as the first American woman to win the all-around gold medal in a major international competition. Firmly in the tradition of small, light, and young competitors, Zmeskal stood just 4′7″ and weighed only 80 pounds when she won the all-around at the 1991 World Championships. The next year, she won golds in balance beam and floor exercise as well. Favored to do well in the 1992 Olympics, she misfired on the beam, her first event, and finished a disappointing tenth. Unable to come back after an injury in 1993, she retired without another chance at competition. *Selected championships and honors:* Gold medal, all-around, World Championships, 1991; gold medal, floor exercise, World Championships, 1992; gold medal, beam, World Championships, 1992.

Gymnastics

Olympic All-Around

Year	Medalists	Points	Country
1896–1948	event not held		
1952	Maria Horokhovska	76.78	UKR
	Nina Bocharova	75.94	UKR
	Margit Korondi	75.82	HUN
1956	Larissa Latynina	74.933	UKR
	Agnes Keleti	74.633	HUN
	Sofia Muratova	74.466	UKR
1960	Larissa Latynina	77.031	UKR
	Sofia Muratova	76.696	RUS
	Polina Astakhova	76.164	UKR
1964	Vera Cáslavská	77.564	CZE
	Larissa Latynina	76.998	UKR
	Polina Astakhova	76.965	UKR
1968	Vera Cáslavská	78.25	CZE
	Zinaida Voronina	76.85	RUS
	Natalya Kuchinskaya	76.75	RUS
1972	Lyudmila Tourischeva	77.025	RUS
	Karen Janz	76.875	GDR
	Tamara Lazakovich	76.85	BLR
1976	Nadia Comaneci	79.275	ROM
	Nelli Kim	78.675	KAZ
	Lyudmila Tourischeva	78.625	RUS
1980	Yelena Davydova	79.15	RUS
	Nadia Comaneci	79.075	ROM
	Maxi Gnauck	79.075	GDR
1984	Mary Lou Retton	79.175	USA
	Ecaterina Szabo	79.125	ROM
	Simona Pauca	78.675	ROM
1988	Yelena Shushunova	79.662	RUS
	Daniela Silivas	79.637	ROM
	Svetlana Boginskaya	79.4	BLR
1992	Tatyana Gutsu	39.737	UKR
	Shannon Miller	39.725	USA
	Lavinia Milosovici	39.687	ROM
1996	Lilia Pokopayeva	39.255	UKR
	Gina Gogean	39.075	ROM
	Simona Amanar	39.067	ROM
	Lavinia Milosovici	39.067	ROM

Olympic Side Horse Vault

Year	Medalists	Country
1896–1948	event not held	
1952	Yekaterina Kalinchuk	RUS
	Maria Horokhovska	UKR
	Galina Minaicheva	RUS
1956	Larissa Latynina	UKR
	Tamara Manina	RUS
	Ann-Sofi Colling-Pettersson	SWE
1960	Marharyta Nikolayeva	UKR
	Sofia Muratova	RUS
	Larissa Latynina	UKR
1964	Vera Cáslavská	CZE
	Larissa Latynina	UKR
	Birgit Radochia	GDR
1968	Vera Cáslavská	CZE
	Erika Zuchold	GDR
	Zinaida Voronina	RUS
1972	Karin Janz	GDR
	Erika Zuchold	GDR
	Lyudmila Tourischeva	RUS
1976	Nelli Kim	KAZ
	Carola Dombeck	GDR
	Lyudmila Tourischeva	RUS
1980	Natalya Shaposhnikova	RUS
	Steffi Kraker	GDR
	Melita Ruhn	ROM
1984	Ecaterina Szabo	ROM
	Mary Lou Retton	USA
	Lavinia Agache	ROM
1988	Svetlana Boginskaya	BLR
	Gabriela Potorac	ROM
	Daniela Silivas	ROM

Gymnastics (continued)

Olympic Side Horse Vault

Year	Medalists	Country
1992	Lavinia Milosovici	ROM
	Henrietta Onodi	HUN
	Tatyana Lysenko	UKR
1996	Simona Amanar	ROM
	Mo Huilan	CHN
	Gina Gogean	ROM

Olympic Asymmetrical (Uneven) Bars

Year	Medalists	Country
1896–1948	event not held	
1952	Margit Korondi	HUN
	Maria Gorokhovskaya	UKR
	Agnes Keleti	HUN
1956	Agnes Keleti	HUN
	Larissa Latynina	UKR
	Sofia Muratova	RUS
1960	Polina Astakhova	UKR
	Larissa Latynina	UKR
	Tamara Lyukhina	RUS
1964	Polina Astakhova	UKR
	Katalin Makray	HUN
	Larissa Latynina	UKR
1968	Vera Cáslavská	CZE
	Karin Janz	GDR
	Zinaida Voronina	RUS
1972	Karin Janz	GDR
	Olga Korbut	BLR
	Erika Zuchold	GDR
1976	Nadia Comaneci	ROM
	Teodora Ungureanu	ROM
	Marta Egervari	HUN
1980	Maxi Gnauck	GDR
	Emilia Eberle	ROM
	Maria Filatova	RUS
1984	Ma Yanhong	CHN
	Julianne McNamara	USA
	Mary Lou Retton	USA
1988	Daniela Silivas	ROM
	Dagmar Kersten	GDR
	Yelena Shushunova	RUS
1992	Lu Li	CHN
	Tatyana Gutsu	UKR
	Shannon Miller	USA
1996	Svetlana Chorkina	RUS
	Amy Chow	USA
	Bi Wenjiing	CHN

Olympic Balance Beam

Year	Medalists	Country
1896–1948	event not held	
1952	Nina Bocharova	UKR
	Maria Ghorokhovskaya	UKR
	Margit Korondi	HUN
1956	Agnes Keleti	HUN
	Eva Bosakova (Vechtova)	CZE
	Tamara Manina	RUS
1960	Eva Bosakova (Vechtova)	CZE
	Larissa Latynina	UKR
	Sofia Muratova	RUS
1964	Vera Cáslavská	CZE
	Tamara Manina	RUS
	Larissa Latynina	UKR
1968	Natalya Kuchinskaya	RUS
	Vera Cáslavská	CZE
	Larissa Petrik	BLR
1972	Olga Korbut	BLR
	Tamara Lazakovich	BLR
	Karin Janz	GDR
1976	Nadia Comaneci	ROM
	Olga Korbut	BLR
	Teodora Ungureanu	ROM
1980	Nadia Comaneci	ROM
	Yelena Davydova	BLR
	Natalya Shaposhnikova	BLR
1984	Simona Pauca	ROM
	Ecaterina Szabo	ROM
	Kathy Johnson	USA
1988	Daniela Silivas	ROM
	Yelena Shushunova	RUS
	Phoebe Mills	GDR
1992	Tatyana Lysenko	UKR
	Lu Li	CHN
	Shannon Miller	USA
1996	Shannon Miller	USA
	Lilia Podkopayeva	UKR
	Gina Gogean	ROM

Olympic Floor Exercise

Year	Medalists	Country
1896–1948	event not held	
1952	Agnes Keleti	HUN
	Maria Gorokhovskaya	UKR
	Margit Korondi	HUN
1956	Agnes Keleti	HUN
	Larissa Latynina	UKR
	Elena Leustean	ROM

Gymnastics (continued)

Olympic Floor Exercise

Year	Medalists	Country
1960	Larissa Latynina	UKR
	Polina Astakhova	UKR
	Tamara Lyukhina	RUS
1964	Larissa Latynina	UKR
	Polina Astakhova	UKR
	Aniko Janosi-Ducza	HUN
1968	Vera Cáslavská	CZE
	Larissa Petrik	BLR
	Natalya Kuchinskaya	RUS
1972	Olga Korbut	BLR
	Lyudmila Tourischeva	RUS
	Tamara Lazakovich	BLR
1976	Nelli Kim	KAZ
	Lyudmila Tourischeva	RUS
	Nadia Comaneci	ROM
1980	Nadia Comaneci	ROM
	Nelli Kim	KAZ
	Maxi Gnauck	GDR
1984	Ecaterina Szabo	ROM
	Julianne McNamara	USA
	Mary Lou Retton	USA
1988	Daniela Silivas	ROM
	Svetlana Boginskaya	BLR
	Diana Dudeva	BUL
1992	Lavinia Milosovici	ROM
	Henrietta Onodi	HUN
	Cristina Bontas	ROM
1996	Lilia Podkopayeva	UKR
	Simona Amanar	ROM
	Dominique Dawes	USA

Olympic Team Combined Exercises

Year	Medalists	Points	Country
1896–1924	event not held		
1928	Petronella van Randwijk, Jacomina van den Berg, Anna Polak, Helena Nordheim, Alida van den Bos, Hendrika van Rumt, Anna van der Vegt, Elka de Levie, Jacoba Stelma, Estella Agsteribbe	316.75	HOL
		289	ITA
		258.25	GBR
1932	event not held		
1936	Trudi Meyer, Erna Burger, Kathe Sohnemann, Isolde Frolian, Anita Barwirth, Paula Pohlsen, Friedel Iby, Julie Schmitt	506.5	GER
		503.6	CZE
		499	HUN
1948	Zdenka Honsova, Miloslava Misakova, Vera Ruzickova, Bozena Smcova, Milena Mullerova, Zdenka Vermirovska, Olga Silhanova, Marie Kovarova	445.45	CZE
		440.55	HUN
		422.63	USA
1952	Maria Gorokhovskaya, Nina Bocharova, Galina Minaicheva, Galina Urbanovich, Pelageya Danilova, Galina Shamrai, Yekaterina Kalinchuk	527.03	USSR
		520.96	HUN
		503.32	CZE
1956	Larissa Latynina, Sofia Muratova, Tamara Manina, Lyudmila Yegorova, Polina Astakhova, Lidiya Kalinina	444.8	USSR
		443.5	HUN
		438.2	ROM

Gymnastics (continued)

Olympic Team Combined Exercises

Year	Medalists	Points	Country
1960	Larissa Latynina, Sofia Muratova, Polina Astakhova, Margarita Nikolayeva, Lidiya Ivanova (Kalinina), Tamara Lyukhina	382.32	USSR
		373.323	CZE
		372.053	ROM
1964	Larissa Latynina, Polina Astakhova, Yelena Volchetskaya, Tamara Zamotailova (Lyukhina), Tamara Manina, Lyudmila Gromova	380.89	USSR
		379.969	CZE
		377.889	JPN
1968	Zinaida Voronina, Natalya Kuchinskaya, Larissa Petrik, Olga Karasyova, Lyudmila Tourischeva, Lyubov Burda	382.82	USSR
		382.2	CZE
		379.1	GDR
1972	Lyudmila Tourischeva, Olga Korbut, Tamara Lazakovich, Lyubov Burda, Elvira Saadi, Antonina Koshel	380.5	USSR
		376.55	GDR
		368.25	HUN
1976	Nelli Kim, Lyudmila Tourischeva, Olga Korbut, Elvira Saadi, Maria Filatova, Svetlana Grozdova	466	USSR
		462.35	ROM
		459.3	GDR
1980	Natalya Shaposhnikova, Yelena Davydova, Nelli Kim, Maria Filatova, Stella Zakharova, Yelena Naimushina	394.9	USSR
		393.5	ROM
		392.55	GDR
1984	Ecaterina Szabo, Laura Cutina, Simona Pauca, Cristina Grigoras, Mihaela Stanulet, Lavinia Agache	392.02	ROM
		391.2	USA
		388.6	CHN
1988	Yelena Shushunova, Svetlana Boginskaya, Natalya Lashchenova, Svetlana Baitova, Yelena Shevchenko, Olga Strazheva	395.475	USSR
		394.125	ROM
		390.875	GDR
1992	Svetlana Boginskaya, Tatyana Lysenko, Rozalya Galiyeva, Tatyana Gutsu, Yelena Grudneva, Oksana Chusovitina	395.666	USSR
		395.079	ROM
		394.704	USA
1996	Amanda Borden, Amy Chow, Dominique Dawes, Shannon Miller, Dominique Moceanu, Jaycee Phelps, Kerri Strug	389.225	USA
		388.404	RUS
		388.246	ROM

Gymnastics (continued)

Olympic Team Exercise with Portable Apparatus
(Discontinued Event)

Year	Country	Medal
1952	SWE	Gold
	USSR	Silver
	HUN	Bronze
1956	HUN	Gold
	SWE	Silver
	POL	Bronze

Olympic Rhythmic All-Around

Year	Winners	Medal	Country
1984	Lori Fung	Gold	CAN
	Doina Staiculescu	Silver	ROM
	Regina Weber	Bronze	GDR
1988	Marina Lobach	Gold	USSR/Belarus
	Adriana Dunavska	Silver	BUL
	Oleksandra Tymoshenko	Bronze	USSR/Ukraine
1992	Oleksandra Tymoshenko	Gold	USSR/Ukraine
	Carolina Pascual Gracia	Silver	SPA
	Oksana Skaldina	Bronze	UKR
1996	Ekaterina Serebryanskaya	Gold	UKR
	Ianina Batyrchina	Silver	RUS
	Elena Vitrichenko	Bronze	UKR

Olympic Rhythmic Team

Year	Winners	Medal	Country
1996	Marta Baldo, Nuvia Cabanillas, Estela Gimenez, Lorena Guvendez, Tania Lamarca, Estiboliz Martinez	Gold	SPA
		Silver	BUL
		Bronze	RUS

World Championship All-Around

Year	Champion	Country
1934	Vlasta Dekanova	Czechoslovakia
1938	Vlasta Dekanova	Czechoslovakia
1950	Helena Rakoczy	Poland
1954	Galina Roudiko	USSR
1958	Larissa Latynina	USSR
1962	Larissa Latynina	USSR
1966	Vera Cáslavská	Czechoslovakia
1970	Lyudmila Tourischeva	USSR
1974	Lyudmila Tourischeva	USSR
1978	Yelena Mukhina	USSR
1979	Nelli Kim	USSR
1981	Olga Bicherova	USSR
1983	Natalia Yurchenko	USSR
1985	Yelena Shushunova	USSR
	Oksana Omeliantchik	USSR
1987	Aurelia Dobre	Romania
1989	Svetlana Boginskaya	USSR
1991	Kim Zmeskal	USA
1993	Shannon Miller	USA
1994	Shannon Miller	USA
1995	Lilia Podkopayeva	Ukraine
1996	event not held	

World Championship Floor Exercise

Year	Champion	Country
1950	Helena Rakoczy	Poland
1954	Tamara Manina	USSR
1958	Eva Bosakava	Czechoslovakia
1962	Larissa Latynina	USSR
1966	Natalia Kuchinskaya	USSR
1970	Lyudmila Tourischeva	USSR
1974	Lyudmila Tourischeva	USSR
1978	Nelli Kim	USSR
	Yelena Mukhina	USSR
1979	Emilia Eberle	Romania
1981	Natalia Ilenko	USSR
1983	Ecaterina Szabo	Romania
1985	Oksana Omeliantchik	USSR
1987	Yelena Shushunova	USSR
	Daniela Silivas	Romania
1989	Svetlana Boginskaya	USSR
	Daniela Silivas	Romania
1991	Cristina Bontas	Romania
	Oksana Tchusovitina	USSR
1992	Kim Zmeskal	USA
1993	Shannon Miller	USA
1994	Dina Kochetkova	Russia
1995	Gina Gogean	Romania
1996	Gina Gogean	Romania
	Yuanyuan Kui	China

Gymnastics (continued)

World Championship Uneven Bars

Year	Champion	Country
1950	Gretchen Kolar	Austria
	Anna Pettersson	Sweden
1954	Agnes Keleti	Hungary
1958	Larissa Latynina	USSR
1962	Irina Pervuschina	USSR
1966	Natalia Kuchinskaya	USSR
1970	Karin Janz	E. Germany
1974	Annelore Zinke	E. Germany
1978	Marcia Frederick	USA
1979	Ma Yanhong	China
	Maxi Gnauck	E. Germany
1981	Maxi Gnauck	E. Germany
1983	Maxi Gnauck	E. Germany
1985	Gabriele Fahnrich	E. Germany
1987	Daniela Silivas	Romania
	Doerte Thuemmier	E. Germany
1989	Fan Di	China
	Daniela Silivas	Romania
1991	Gwang Suk Kim	N. Korea
1992	Lavinia Milosivici	Romania
1993	Shannon Miller	USA
1994	Luo Li	China
1995	Svetlana Chorkina	Russia
1996	Svetlana Chorkina	Russia
	Yelena Tiskiun	Belarus

World Championship Balance Beam

Year	Champion	Country
1950	Helena Rakoczy	Poland
1954	Keiko Tanaka	Japan
1958	Larissa Latynina	USSR
1962	Eva Bosakova	Czechoslovakia
1966	Natalia Kuchinskaya	USSR
1970	Erika Zuchold	E. Germany
1974	Lyudmila Tourischeva	USSR
1978	Nadia Comaneci	Romania
1979	Vera Cema	Czechoslovakia
1981	Maxi Gnauck	E. Germany
1983	Olga Mostepanova	USSR
1985	Daniela Silivas	Romania
1987	Aurelia Dobre	Romania
1989	Daniela Silivas	Romania
1991	Svetlana Boginskaya	USSR
1992	Kim Zmeskal	USA
1993	Lavinia Milosivici	Romania
1994	Shannon Miller	USA
1995	Mo Huilan	China
1996	Dina Kochetkova	Russia

World Championship Vault

Year	Champion	Country
1950	Helena Rakoczy	Poland
1954	Tamara Manina	USSR
	Anna Pettersson	Sweden
1958	Larissa Latynina	USSR
1962	Vera Cáslavská	Czechoslovakia
1966	Vera Cáslavská	Czechoslovakia
1970	Erika Zuchold	E. Germany
1974	Olga Korbut	USSR
1978	Nelli Kim	USSR
1979	Dumitrita Turner	Romania
1981	Maxi Gnauck	E. Germany
1983	Boriana Stoyanova	Bulgaria
1985	Yelena Shushunova	USSR
1987	Yelena Shushunova	USSR
1989	Olesia Durnik	USSR
1991	Lavinia Milosovici	Romania
1992	Henrietta Onodi	Hungary
1993	Elena Piskun	Belarus
1994	Gina Gogean	Romania
1995	Lilia Podkopayeva	Ukraine
	Simona Amanar	Romania
1996	Gina Gogean	Romania

Pan American Games Team

Year	Team	Place
1995	USA	First
	Cuba	Second
	Argentina	Third

Pan American Games All-Around

Year	Winner	Place	Country
1995	Shannon Miller	First	USA
	Amanda Borden	Second	USA
	Amy Chow	Third	USA

Pan American Games Vault

Year	Winner	Place	Country
1995	Amy Chow	First	USA
	Shannon Miller	Second	USA
	Annia Portuondo	Third	Cuba

Pan American Games Uneven Bars

Year	Winner	Place	Country
1995	Shannon Miller	First	USA
	Amy Chow	Second	USA
	Annia Portuondo	Third	Cuba

Gymnastics (continued)

Pan American Games Balance Beam

Year	Winner	Place	Country
1995	Amanda Borden	First	USA
	Annia Portuondo	Second	Cuba
	Leyanet Gonzalez	Third	Cuba

Pan American Games Floor Exercise

Year	Winner	Place	Country
1995	Shannon Miller	First	USA
	Amanda Borden	Second	USA
	Leyanet Gonzalez	Third	Cuba

Pan American Games Rhythmic Team

Year	Team	Place
1995	USA	First
	Cuba	Second
	Argentina	Third

Pan American Games Rhythmic All-Around

Year	Winner	Place	Country
1995	Yardania Corrales	First	Cuba
	Tamara Levinson	Second	USA
	Jessica Davis	Third	USA

Pan American Games Rhythmic Rope

Year	Winner	Place	Country
1995	Yardania Corrales	First	Cuba
	Kirenia Ruiz	Second	Cuba
	Tamara Levinson	Third	USA

Pan American Games Rhythmic Ball

Year	Winner	Place	Country
1995	Alejandra Unsain	First	Argentina
	Cecilia Schutman	Second	Argentina
	Tamara Levinson	Third	USA

Pan American Games Rhythmic Clubs

Year	Winner	Place	Country
1995	Yardania Corrales	First	Cuba
	Jessica Davis	Second	USA
	Tamara Levinson	Third	USA

Pan American Games Rhythmic Ribbon

Year	Winner	Place	Country
1995	Tamara Levinson	First	USA
	Jessica Davis	Second	USA
	Luciana Eslava	Third	Argentina

Pan American Games Rhythmic Group

Year	Team	Place
1995	Cuba	First
	USA	Second
	Brazil	Third

SWIMMING

◆ *One of the first strenuous sports in which women were seen as serious athletes, swimming has long been a proving ground for women's strength, skill, and tenacity.*

HISTORY

It isn't hard to imagine how swimming began, with bathers in a lake or stream exploring their watery environment, testing the limits of their buoyancy, and modifying their movements to increase their navigational capabilities. Opportunities to swim, embedded as they were in daily routine, were at least as available to women as to men, and it is probable that women began swim-

ming at the same time that men did. Egyptian artifacts dating from the Eighteenth Dynasty, 3,500 years ago, clearly depict women swimming—an indication that Egyptians considered swimming not only an acceptable activity for women but a worthy subject for art.

After this promising beginning, women's swimming vanishes from the records of Western history. One reason may be that as technology advanced and brought hygiene indoors, contact with pools, rivers, and lakes was restricted. We know, for example, that both Greeks and Romans considered swimming an essential skill for men, but there are no corresponding references concerning women. Over the next centuries, swimming declined in popularity even among men. This may have been part of a general cultural shift, as society's focus shifted first to the spirit, during the Middle Ages, then to the mind, during the Renaissance. Enthusiasm for swimming may also have been dampened by shifts in climate and locale. As world trade and power shifted from Greece and Rome to Europe, world temperatures dropped precipitously. Just as bathing became onerous in the damp, chilly climate of northern Europe, so swimming must have seemed anything but inviting.

The resurgence of swimming in the West was triggered by a highly unlikely benefactor, the Viennese scientist-cum-hypnotist-cum-fraud Anton Mesmer. Hounded out of Austria, Mesmer arrived in Paris in 1778, at the height of the Enlightenment, and quickly became a sensation. Fundamental to Mesmer's hypnotherapy was the idea that water was therapeutic, and dipping oneself in water became a sensation among fashionable Parisians. Throughout Europe, women as well as men "took the waters" at famous spas, wading toga-clad into chest-high pools of warmed mineral springs to stand, gossiping and sipping herbal potions, for innumerable hours. Though this was hardly swimming, the toe was definitely in the water. When the physical fitness movement took hold in the late nineteenth century, swimming finally reappeared in Western civilization.

Somewhat surprisingly, Victorians didn't protest the idea of women swimming as they protested female participation in many other sports. In 1885, when Parisians organized a race from the Pont de Passy to the Pont de Grenelle on the Seine, women as well as men were invited to compete. Needless to say, they were modestly clad in—and undoubtedly weighed down by— full-skirted, knee-length costumes and woolen socks. Protecting women from lascivious male eyes was a challenge to fin de siècle culture. In the 1890s men were initially prevented from watching women's competitions in Germany. A few years later, they were allowed in but seated at least thirty yards from the contestants. As late as 1919, **Ethelda Bleibtrey** was ticketed for nude bathing when she took off her stockings at a New York beach.

STROKES, THE BIRTH OF THE FREESTYLE, AND SWIMMING'S HIDDEN HISTORY

While the West all but turned its back on swimming for long centuries, people in other cultures continued to have fun in the water. The real history of modern swimming is a hidden one, whose origins lie far outside Western tradition. European explorers noted the impressive swimming skills of men and women in Hawaii, Tahiti, West Africa, and South America. Native Americans were also swift and expert swimmers. Competitive swimming, which began in England in 1837, entered a new era when two Native Americans, Tobacco and Flying Gull, competed in a London meet in 1844. The crowd, used to the genteel sidestroke and breaststroke, was astonished to see the men "thrashing" the water and churning their arms "like a windmill" while kicking with their feet. Flying Gull defeated Tobacco by swimming 130 feet in 30 seconds. He shocked the crowd with his "totally un-European" performance—and he won the first freestyle event ever staged in Europe.

Impressive as it was, Flying Gull's style did not catch on. Since 1696, when the French author Thevenot published his *Art of Swimming*, the breaststroke had been the preferred stroke for serious swimmers. Even after Flying Gull's performance, the breaststroke remained the stroke of choice throughout Europe until the late 1870s, when Jack Trudgen introduced a "new" stroke to England. Trudgen's stroke wasn't new at all, but a modification of a method he'd seen used by native South Americans—and probably very similar to Flying Gull's. Nevertheless, it was Trudgen's success in teaching the stroke to others that finally established the "crawl" as the dominant competitive stroke. The backstroke was added shortly afterward, but it was not until the 1930s that the final modern competitive stroke, the butterfly, was added. The butterfly grew out of the breaststroke, when swimmers discovered they could gain speed with an over-the-water recovery. Originally considered a novelty, too strenuous to be taken seriously, the butterfly did not become a competitive event until the 1950s.

THE MODERN ERA

Swimming, one of the first sports in which women were viewed as serious competitors, has always been a wonderful showcase for women's athletic potential. When **Fanny Durack** won the first women's 100-meter Olympic freestyle in 1912, her time of 1:22.2 was identical to that of Alfred Hajos, the winner of the first men's event in 1896. The inaugural Olympic competition underscored women's grit in another way, when world record holder Daisy Curwen of Great Britain managed to make it all the way through the semifinals before acute appendicitis forced her to undergo emergency surgery. From one single freestyle event in the 1912 Olympics, swimming expanded to include a range of distances and strokes. With the addition of a 4 × 200-meter freestyle relay in 1996, Olympic swimming grew to include sixteen events.

In America, Britain, and Australia, swimming was the glamour sport of the 1920s and '30s. F. Scott Fitzgerald's Jazz Age opus *Tender Is the Night* opens on a beach in the French Riviera, where the earnest young actress Rosemary Hoyt emerges from "a choppy little four-beat crawl" to encounter the novel's other heroine, Nicole Diver, whose swimsuit, tan, and athletic beauty are set off by a string of carelessly dangling pearls. In *Tender Is the Night*, Rosemary's success as an actress earns her a berth among the privileged swimmers. In real life, it was often the other way around, and women who won in the water emerged at least as famous as—and often more famous than—men. Long before Esther Williams appeared in the lush, if often silly, aquatic extravaganzas that made her world famous, she was a national freestyle champion. Even swimmers who didn't go on to a Hollywood career were celebrated. When **Gertrude Ederle** became the first woman to cross the English Channel in 1926, her hometown—New York City—welcomed her back with a ticker tape parade.

From the glamour sport of the 1930s, swimming became the high-tech sport of the postwar world. Research actually began years earlier, when swimmers were photographed in action and their techniques carefully studied. The Japanese were among the first to use this research to improve athletic performance, and the Japanese men's teams dominated the 1932 and '36 Olympics. The real breakthrough, however, came at the 1956 Olympics. Led by **Dawn Fraser,** the Australians claimed a lion's share of medals and swept both the men's and women's team relays. The Australians' "secret" was cardiovascular conditioning. The world took notice, and swimmers ever since have excelled through a combination of stroke mechanics and cross-training techniques. In 1956, Dawn Fraser, Faith Leech, Sandra Morgan, and **Lorraine**

Major Events and Competitions

Olympic Games
Pan American Games
World Championships

As of 1996, the above international meets all included the sixteen events listed below:

Individual
Freestyle: 50-, 100-, 200-, 400-, and 800-meter distances.
Backstroke: 100- and 200-meter distances.
Breaststroke: 100- and 200-meter distances.
Butterfly: 100- and 200-meter distances.
Individual Medley: 200- and 400-meter distances. (In both individual medleys, the stroke order is the same—butterfly, backstroke, breaststroke, and freestyle.)

Team
Freestyle: 4 × 100- and 4 × 200-meter distances.
Medley: 4 × 100-meter distances. (In medley relay, the stroke order is backstroke, breaststroke, butterfly, and freestyle.)

Crapp swam the 4 × 100-meter freestyle relay in a world record time of 4:17.1. Less than twenty years later, at the 1992 Olympics, the U.S. team of **Nicole Haislett,** Dara Torres, Angel Martino, and **Jenny Thompson** won with a time of 3:39.46.

Hall of Fame

Women swimmers have been enshrined in the Olympic Hall of Fame, the International Women's Sports Hall of Fame, and the International Swimming Hall of Fame in Fort Lauderdale, Florida.

Governing Bodies and Organizations

United States Swimming
One Olympic Plaza
Colorado Springs, Colorado 80909-5707
Phone: 719/578-4578
Fax: 719/578-4669
Website: http://www.usswim.org

FINA
Federation Internationale de Natation Amateur
Avenue de Beaumont 9
1012 Lausanne
Switzerland

* * * BIOGRAPHIES * * *

GRETA ANDERSEN b. May 1, 1927, Copenhagen, Denmark

As a member of the Danish swim team, Andersen won a gold medal at the 1948 Olympic games, set a world 100-meter freestyle record, and won numerous Danish national and European titles before moving to the United States in 1953. With a glorious swimming career behind her, Andersen settled down to become a coach—only to launch a second and even more impressive career as a distance swimmer. She entered her first open-water race in 1956, a 10.5-mile dip in the Salton Sea. Several men beat her, but Andersen was the first woman to finish, with a time of 4 hours, 25 minutes. Over the next decade she consistently defeated other women and often finished ahead of the men. In a race across the English Channel in 1957 she was one of only two swimmers to finish in a field of twenty-four, beating Britain's Ken Ray by more than two hours. The next year she completed a double crossing of the Catalina Channel and won three major competitions another English Channel crossing, an eighteen-mile crossing of Quebec's Lake St. John, and a twenty-six-mile race off the coast of Guaymas, Mexico. In 1962 she became the first person ever to break the fifty-mile barrier by crossing Lake Michigan. Physically strong and mentally tough, Andersen was never able to complete a double crossing of the English Channel. She made three attempts, always finishing the first leg and once, in 1964, setting an England-to-France record.

Selected championships and honors: Gold medal, 100m freestyle, Olympic Games, 1948; two first-place English Channel races, 1957–58; second place, Guaymas, Mexico, race, 1957; first place, Guaymas, Mexico, race, 1958; first place, Lake St. John, Quebec, 1958; world record, mainland United States to Catalina Island in 11:7, 1959; world record, England-to-France crossing of the English Channel in 13:14, 1964; International Swimming Hall of Fame.

THERESA ANDREWS b. Santa Clara, California

Just as America's absence left a clear field for the East Germans at the 1980 Olympics, so the Soviet bloc boycott left the West unchallenged at Los Angeles in 1984. Andrews took the gold in the 100-meter backstroke, while **Betsy Mitchell** finished just eight-hundredths of a second behind her for a silver. Both times were more than 1.5 seconds slower than that of future medal-winner **Kristin Otto** during the trials. *Selected championships and honors:* Gold medal, 100m backstroke, Olympic Games, 1984.

SHIRLEY BABASHOFF b. January 31, 1957, Whittier, California

Although Babashoff never won an individual Olympic gold medal, her total of eight medals earned in the 1972 and '76 games places her in the three-way tie (with **Dawn Fraser** and **Kornelia Ender**) for most-decorated female Olympian. A freestyler who was strong at every recognized distance, Babashoff's most exciting race may have been the 100-meter freestyle at the 1972 Olympics. In seventh place at the turn, she managed to finish second, beating Australian superwoman **Shane Gould** by three-hundredths of a second. During her career Babashoff set six individual world records, won twenty-seven national championships, and was a member of five world-record-setting relay teams.

Selected championships and honors, individual: Two silver medals, 100m freestyle, World Championships, 1973 and '75; silver medal, 200m freestyle, World Championships, 1973; gold medal, 200m freestyle, World Championships, 1975; gold medal, 400m freestyle, World Championships, 1975; bronze medal, 800m freestyle, World Championships, 1975; two silver medals, 100m freestyle, Olympic Games, 1972 and '76; two silver medals, 200m freestyle, Olympic Games, 1972 and '76; silver medal, 400m freestyle, Olympic Games, 1976; silver medal, 800m freestyle, Olympic Games, 1976; silver medal, 400m individual medley, Olympic Games, 1976. *Team:* Two gold medals, 4 × 100m relay, Olympic Games, 1972 and '76. U.S. Olympic Hall of Fame.

SYBIL BAUER b. September 18, 1903, Chicago, Illinois; d. January 3, 1927

Bauer's event, the backstroke, was relatively new to world competition during her competitive years and made its Olympic debut (with just one distance) in 1924. Nevertheless, Bauer set twenty-three world records during her six years of swimming and won ten national titles between 1921 and 1926. At an unofficial meet in Bermuda in 1922 she swam a 440-yard backstroke in 6:24.8—four seconds faster than the recognized men's record for that distance. In 1924 she held records at every backstroke distance and easily won the only backstroke distance offered at that year's Olympics. A student at Northwestern University, she also played basketball and field hockey. At the time of her early death from cancer she was engaged to sportswriter Ed Sullivan, who went on to become a well-known television host.

Selected championships and honors: Gold medal, 100m backstroke, Olympic Games, 1924; International Swimming Hall of Fame.

MELISSA BELOTE b. October 10, 1956, Washington, D.C.

Belote, who specialized in the backstroke because she hated getting chlorine in her eyes, was relatively unknown when she entered the 1972 U.S. Olympic tri-

als at the age of fifteen. She beat favorite Susie Atwood in the 100-meter distance and set a world record in the 200 meters. She set another 200-meter record at the Olympics later that year, where she also won the 100-meter distance and helped the United States to a team gold in the 4 × 100-meter medley relay. After the games, Belote won three national backstroke championships, in 1973 and '75.

Selected championships and honors, individual: Gold medal, 100m backstroke, Olympic Games, 1972; gold medal, 200m backstroke, Olympic Games, 1972; silver medal, 100m backstroke, World Championships, 1973. *Team:* Gold medal, 4 × 100m medley relay, Olympic Games, 1972.

BROOKE BENNETT b. May 6, 1980, Tampa, Florida

Bennett came to international attention as a distance swimmer at the age of fourteen, when she won a bronze in the 800-meter freestyle at the 1994 World Championships. She won a gold and silver at the Pan American Games the following year. Though her qualifying times made her a favorite to win at the 1996 Olympics, Bennett was overshadowed by the publicity given to teammate **Janet Evans.** Bennett let her stroke do the talking and became, with Evans's retirement, the next great American distance swimmer.

Selected championships and honors: Bronze medal, 800m freestyle, World Championships, 1994; gold medal, 400m freestyle, Pan American Games, 1995; silver medal, 800m freestyle, Pan American Games, 1995; gold medal, 800m freestyle, Olympic Games, 1996.

ETHELDA BLEIBTREY b. February 27, 1902, Waterford, New York; d. May 6, 1978

Bleibtrey began swimming to strengthen her body after a bout of polio and started competing in 1918. She was never defeated in amateur competition and held national titles in every distance open to women, from 100 meters to 3 miles. In addition to the eleven national freestyle championships she won between 1919 and 1922, Bleibtrey won a national backstroke title in 1920. At the Antwerp Olympics that year she swept all three swimming events open to women even though the backstroke, in which she held the world record, was not included in the games. Owing to the lack of swimming facilities, the competitions were held in an estuary, and Bleibtrey later described the experience as akin to swimming in mud. Nevertheless, her time of 1:13.6 in the 100-meter freestyle set a world record. Bleibtrey's most notable wins weren't in chlorine but in the court of public opinion. At Manhattan Beach in 1919, she peeled off her stockings before entering the water and was ticketed for "nude bathing." A public outcry on her behalf lead to a relaxation of the rules for women's swimwear. In 1928 she again ran afoul of the law—this time for swimming in Central Park's Reservoir to publicize the lack of city facilities. Again, Bleibtrey had public opinion on her side, and the city soon opened its first public pool.

Selected championships and honors, individual: Gold medal, 100m freestyle, Olympic Games, 1920; gold medal, 300m freestyle, Olympic Games, 1920. *Team:* Gold medal, 4 × 100m freestyle relay, Olympic Games, 1920. International Swimming Hall of Fame.

BETH BOTSFORD May 21, 1981, Baltimore, Maryland

Botsford, a backstroker, rocketed from promising rookie in 1994 to the world stage in 1996. At the first international meet of her life Botsford came up big, winning a gold in the 100-meter backstroke at the Atlanta Olympics and swimming the backstroke lap to help the U.S. team to victory in the medley relay.

Selected championships and honors: Gold medal, 100m backstroke, Olympic Games, 1996. *Team:* Gold medal, 4 × 100m medley relay, Olympic Games, 1996

LYNN BURKE b. 1943, Laurel Hollow, New York

American women had a strong history in freestyle events but had never won a gold in Olympic backstroke competition until Lynn Burke came along. In July 1960 Burke broke Cornelia Kint's twenty-one-year-old world record in the event, lowered it twice during the Olympic trials, then won the gold medal at the Rome games.

Selected championships and honors: Gold medal, 100m backstroke, Olympic Games, 1960.

CATHERINE CARR

Carr is one of only two American women ever to win an Olympic gold medal in breaststroke events. (The other is **Sharon Wichman.**) Carr's victory at Munich in 1972 broke the existing world record for the 100-meter breaststroke with a time of 1:13.58. Carr also won two national championships in the 100-meter breaststroke.

Selected championships and honors, individual: Gold medal, 100m breaststroke, Olympic Games, 1972.

Team: Gold medal, 4 × 100m medley relay, Olympic Games, 1972.

TRACY CAULKINS b. January 11, 1963, Winona, Minnesota

Arguably the most versatile woman swimmer America has ever produced, Caulkins could swim—and win—any event at virtually any distance. Between 1977 and 1984, she won forty-eight national championships, two Olympic medals, and three world championship golds, not counting her team wins. She set sixty-one American and five world records, and in 1978 she was the youngest recipient of the Sullivan Award to date. Her career was not a cakewalk to victory, however. Caulkins hit her prime as a swimmer at what seemed a perfect time—on the eve of the 1980 Olympics. Although she kept swimming despite the United States' decision to boycott, many doubted that Caulkins could hold her edge for another four years. At the 1982 World Championships the best she could manage were bronzes, and her times had begun to slow. Caulkins staged a fortuitous comeback and played to her strength—versatility—to win both the 200- and 400-meter individual medleys at the Los Angeles Olympics. Having gained her Olympic medals at last, Caulkins retired from competition following the games.

Selected championships and honors, individual: Gold medal, 200m butterfly, World Championships, 1978; gold medal, 200m individual medley, World Championships, 1978; Gold medal, 400m individual medley, World Championships, 1978; silver medal, 100m breaststroke, World Championships, 1978; two gold medals, 200m individual medley, Pan American Games, 1979 and '83; two gold medals, 400m individual medley, Pan American Games, 1979 and '83; bronze medal, 200m individual medley, World Championships, 1982; bronze medal, 400m individual medley, World Championships, 1982; gold medal, 200m individual medley, Olympic Games, 1984; gold medal, 400m individual medley, Olympic Games, 1984; Sullivan Award, 1978; two Broderick Cups, 1982 and '84. *Team:* Gold medal, 4 × 100m medley relay, World Championships, 1978; gold medal, 4 × 100m freestyle relay, World Championships, 1978; gold medal, 4 × 100m medley relay, Olympic Games, 1984. International Women's Sports Hall of Fame; U.S. Olympic Hall of Fame.

FLORENCE CHADWICK b. November 9, 1918, San Diego, California; d. March 15, 1995

An ocean swimmer who never won a major pool event and failed to make the 1936 Olympic team, Chadwick was determined to play to her strength—distance and endurance. In 1950 she made her first crossing of the English Channel in record time and greeted reporters at Dover with the famous comment, "I feel fine. I am quite prepared to swim back." The next year she became the first woman to make the more difficult England-to-France crossing, swimming against winds and tides so heavy she had to take seasickness medicine en route. She made the same crossing in 1953 and '55, bettering her time with each attempt to a personal best of 13 hours, 55 minutes in 1955. In 1952 she became the first woman to swim the Catalina Channel, and in 1953 she swam across the Straits of Gibraltar. In both cases, her times broke records set by male swimmers. When not in the water, Chadwick worked as a stenographer.

Selected championships and honors: World record, Catalina Island to Palos Verde, California, 13:47:32, 1952; world record, Straits of Gibraltar, 5:6:0, 1953; International Swimming Hall of Fame.

TIFFANY COHEN b. June 11, 1966, Culver City, California

As a junior swimmer, Cohen's record was impressive but uneven. A few years of seasoning and a lot of hard work turned her into a consistent winner. Taller and lighter than most swimmers (5′8″ and 120 pounds), Cohen was America's best distance racer throughout the 1980s. Between 1981 and 1986 she won sixteen national freestyle titles at distances ranging from 200 to 1,500 meters. She also won a national title in butterfly (1986). She won two gold medals at the 1983 Pan American Games and picked up two more golds at the Olympics the following year. Cohen retired in 1988 after finishing second to rising star **Janet Evans** in the 400- and 800-meter nationals.

Selected championships and honors: Bronze medal, 400m freestyle, World Championships, 1982; gold medal, 800m freestyle, Pan American Games, 1983; gold medal, 400m freestyle, Olympic Games, 1984; gold medal, 800m freestyle, Olympic Games, 1984.

LYNNE COX b. January 2, 1957, Manchester, New Hampshire

Cox made her first big swim at the age of fifteen—when she crossed the English Channel in a time that shattered both the men's and women's existing record. Over the next few years she won so many swimming trophies that she tired of them and began looking for a deeper meaning in her sport. She found it in a simple cause—world peace. Ever since, Cox has used her talents to prick the world's conscience. In 1994 she swam fourteen miles across the Gulf of Aqaba to draw neighbors Jordan, Israel, and Egypt symbolically together. When the Berlin Wall fell, Cox promptly swam the Spree River. Cox's most challenging swim, however, was a literal cold war event. In 1987 she swam the Bering Strait—a distance of just 2.7 miles, but life-threatening and difficult due to the 40° temperatures. Cox, who in peak condition carries 10 percent more body fat than the average woman and whose normal temperature is a degree below normal, was able to complete the swim without experiencing hypothermia or cardiac difficulties.

LORRAINE CRAPP b. October 1, 1938, Foster, New South Wales, Australia

Not nearly as well known as her teammate, **Dawn Fraser,** Crapp defeated Fraser in the 400-meter freestyle at the 1956 Olympics to win the gold. Crapp went into the event as world record holder, having become, just ten weeks earlier, the first woman ever to swim 400 meters in less than five minutes.

Selected championships and honors, individual: Gold medal, 400m freestyle, Olympic Games, 1956. *Team:* Gold medal, 4 × 100m relay, Olympic Games, 1956.

ANN CURTIS CUNEO b. March 6, 1926, Rio Vista, California

The first woman in history to receive the Sullivan Award for outstanding athlete of the year, Curtis learned to swim in elementary school and won her first title—the AAU girls' freestyle—when she was only eleven years old. Age restrictions kept her out of senior competitions until 1943, but she began to win the minute she hit the water. Between 1943 and '48 she won national indoor and outdoor championships in virtually every freestyle distance from 100 yards to one mile. Her total of thirty-one national titles set a women's record that was not broken until **Tracy Caulkins** came along four decades later. World War II deprived Curtis of a chance to win Olympic gold in 1944, but she kept swimming—and winning—in national events. When the games resumed in 1948, Curtis won an individual gold and silver. She also gained a team gold, swimming the anchor leg of the freestyle relay. Curtis retired after the Olympics and later opened a swimming school.

Selected championships and honors, individual: Gold medal, 400m freestyle, Olympic Games, 1948; silver medal, 100m freestyle, Olympic Games, 1948; Sullivan Award, 1944; Associated Press Female Athlete of the Year, 1944. *Team:* Gold medal, 4 × 100m freestyle, Olympic Games, 1948. International Women's Sports Hall of Fame.

DONNA DE VARONA b. April 26, 1947, San Diego, California

The first female sportscaster on network television, de Varona was also the first woman to do Olympic coverage, in 1968. Before her broadcast career began, de Varona was one of America's most versatile swimmers. Between 1960 and '64 de Varona won a baker's dozen national titles—two backstroke, one butterfly, and ten individual medley. She swam on the 1960 Olympic team and made the team again four years later, when she won the 400-meter individual medley and swam on the winning 4 × 100-meter freestyle relay team. She retired after the games and entered the broadcast booth the next year. A wonderful advocate for women's participation in sports, de Varona served on President Carter's Commission on Olympic Sports and was a cofounder of the Women's Sports Foundation.

Selected championships and honors, individual: Gold medal, 400m individual medley, Olympic Games, 1964. *Team:* Gold medal, 4 × 100m freestyle relay, Olympic Games, 1964. International Swimming Hall of Fame; U.S. Olympic Hall of Fame; International Women's Sports Hall of Fame.

VIRGINIA (GINNY) DUENKEL b. March 7, 1947, West Orange, New Jersey

Duenkel was an expert in both the freestyle and the backstroke—as she proved at the 1964 Olympics in Tokyo. She won the gold in a 1-2-3 American finish in the 400-meter freestyle, then finished behind teammate **Cathy Ferguson** and France's Kiki Caron to win a bronze in the 100-meter backstroke.

Selected championships and honors: Gold medal, 400m freestyle, Olympic Games, 1964; bronze medal, 100m backstroke, Olympic Games, 1964.

SARAH (FANNY) DURACK b. 1891, Australia; d. 1955

When Australian officials decided not to send a women's swim team to the 1912 Olympics, Durack waged a publicity campaign to change their minds. Public opinion favored Durack, and she became the first woman to medal in the sport, winning the only individual event offered, the 100-meter freestyle. In

When 2 × 2 Doesn't Equal Four

At the 1912 Olympics, the Australian team consisted of just two women—Fanny Durack and Mina Wylie, who nailed the gold and silver medals in the freestyle race. Eager to compete in the relay, they volunteered to alternate slots, swimming two legs each. The judges nixed their proposal, and the event was won by Isabella Moore, Jennie Fletcher, Annie Speirs, and Irene Steer of England.

those days of infrequent international competition, when swimmers' abilities were measured against the clock, Durack set records at distances from 50 yards to one mile and held them for years at a time.

Selected championships and honors: Gold medal, 100m freestyle, Olympic Games, 1912; world record, 100yd, 1912–21; world record, 110m, 1912–20; world record, 220yd, 1915–21; world record, 500m, 1915–17; world record, mile, 1914–26; International Swimming Hall of Fame.

GERTRUDE EDERLE b. October 23, 1906, New York, New York

The first woman ever to swim the English Channel, Ederle was a champion at virtually every distance she swam. She set her first world record, in the 880-yard freestyle, when she was twelve years old, and went on to win several national indoor and outdoor titles as well as a bronze medal at the 1924 Olympics. Her most impressive achievements, however, came at greater distances, and Ederle seemed to gather strength and speed as she swam. She won the first distance race she entered, defeating fifty other swimmers in a three-mile swim in 1921. The next year, at Brighton Beach, New York, she broke seven world records in the course of a single 500-meter swim. She won three national freestyle championships in 1923 and '24, turned pro in 1925, and in 1926 set her sights on the English Channel. Only five other people had made the swim before, none of them women. Moreover, it was widely believed that women weren't capable of such a feat. Ederle made the France-to-England crossing on August 6, 1926. Her time of 14 hours, 31 minutes beat the existing men's record by more than two hours and stood as a woman's record for almost four decades, until **Greta Andersen** broke it in 1964. Ederle returned to a hero's welcome in New York, complete with a ticker tape parade attended by two million cheering fans. The moment of fame came at a heavy price. Damage sustained during the crossing cost Ederle her hearing, while a back injury sustained later caused her to wear a cast for over four years. Perhaps as a result, Ederle suffered severe mental problems in 1928. Her recovery was slow, and undoubtedly more difficult than any swim she ever made. Yet Ederle, whose coach had once described her as lacking confidence, regained her equilibrium and in 1933 began teaching swimming to hearing-impaired children.

Selected championships and honors, individual: Bronze medal, 100m, Olympic Games, 1924; two National Outdoor Championships, 440yd, 1922 and '23; world record, English Channel crossing, 14:31, 1923. *Team:* Gold medal, 4 × 100m relay, Olympic Games, 1924. International Swimming Hall of Fame; International Women's Sports Hall of Fame.

KRISZTINA EGERSZEGI b. ca. 1974, Budapest, Hungary

When Egerszegi went to her first Olympics, in 1988, she was only fourteen years old and weighed just 99 pounds—more than 40 pounds less than her opponents. But she swam the 100-meter backstroke just a second slower than gold medalist **Kristin Otto.** It was a fitting beginning for the woman who would replace Otto as the reigning star from Eastern Europe. Egerszegi went on to win the 200-meter backstroke, the first of five individual Olympic golds over the next eight years. No swimmer in history, male or female, had ever won as many individual golds, and Egerszegi, who earned four of her medals in backstroke, became known as the greatest backstroker of all time. She retired from competition after the 1996 games.

Selected championships and honors: Gold medal, 200m backstroke, Olympic Games, 1988; silver medal, 100m backstroke, Olympic Games, 1988; gold medal, 100m backstroke, World Championships, 1991; gold medal, 200m backstroke, World Championships, 1991; gold medal, 100m backstroke, Olympic Games, 1992; gold medal, 200m backstroke, Olympic Games, 1992; gold medal, 400m individual medley, Olympic Games, 1992; gold medal, 200m backstroke, Olympic Games, 1996.

KORNELIA ENDER b. October 25, 1958, Halle, East Germany

A powerhouse from East Germany, Ender was the first woman to swim 200 meters in less than two minutes and the first woman to win four golds at a single Olympics. Speed was only one of Ender's attributes. The other was strength, and she won most of her honors in freestyle, butterfly, and individual medley. As a child, Ender began swimming as therapy for orthopedic problems. A member of the 1972 East German Olympic team, she won one individual and two team silvers despite the fact that, at age thirteen, she had not yet developed the power she would eventually be known for. That began to change the next year, and Ender began winning European and world championships. She had a phenomenal 1976 Olympics, winning three individual golds and setting a new world record with each win. After the games she married fellow countryman and champion backstroker Roland Matthes, whom she later divorced. During her career Ender lowered the world record for the 100-meter freestyle ten times, and her total of eight Olympic medals and eight world titles made her one of the most decorated swimmers in the world. When the iron curtain dissolved in 1989, Ender told the press that throughout her career she had often received injections whose contents were never revealed to her.

Selected championships and honors, individual: Silver medal, 200m individual medley, Olympic Games, 1972; silver medal, 200m individual medley, World Championships, 1973; two gold medals, 100m freestyle, World Championships, 1973 and '76; silver medal, 200m freestyle, World Championships, 1975; two gold medals, 100m butterfly, World Championships, 1973 and '75; gold medal, 100m freestyle, Olympic Games, 1976; gold medal, 200m freestyle, Olympic Games, 1976; gold medal, 100m butterfly, Olympic Games, 1976; three times World Swimmer of the Year, 1973, '75, and '76. *Team:* Silver medal, 4 × 100m, Olympic Games, 1972; silver medal, 4 × 100m medley, Olympic Games, 1972; gold medal, 4 × 100m medley, Olympic Games, 1976; silver medal, 4 × 100m relay, Olympic Games, 1976; two World Championships, 4 × 100m medley relay, 1973 and '75; two World Championships, 4 × 100m freestyle relay, 1973 and '75. International Swimming Hall of Fame.

JANET EVANS b. August 28, 1971, Placentia, California

A freestyler who specialized in 400-meter and longer events, Evans was the first woman to break the 16-minute barrier in the 1,500 meters. Evans was a true

SWIMMING, STRENGTH, STEROIDS, AND SPORTSMANSHIP

Produced naturally, corticosteroids manufactured in the adrenal cortex play a vital role in protein and carbohydrate production, cardiopulmonary action, kidney function, and muscle coordination. Ingested or injected, steroids—the artificial equivalent of corticosteroids—have proven to be a headache to organized sports and an individual nightmare to athletes who take them. In contests where wins are often worth millions and the difference between first place and last is measured in tenths of a second, steroids are devil's candy. There's no doubt that they can enhance strength and boost performance—just as there's no doubt that they can trigger mood swings and leave women with deepened voices, facial hair, acne, and perilously unbalanced hormones. Though external side effects subside when the drug is withdrawn, internal damage may be permanent, and the victorious athlete may be left with a shortened life span.

While most other sports responded to steroids by instituting rigorous policies, FINA, swimming's international governing body, was slow to respond. Instead of testing all top finishers in an event, FINA's guidelines called for only random testing of two of the top four finishers. The policy's flaws became all too apparent at the 1992 Barcelona Olympics, when China's **Yong Zhuang** could not be tested after her win in the 100-meter freestyle. Were American, Australian, and other coaches right in alleging that Yong's deep voice and heavy muscles were symptoms of steroid abuse—or was it simply a case of nationalistic bickering? In the wake of the controversy the United States and Australia both continued to push for more stringent testing and harsher punishment for steroid use—only to find themselves embarrassed by having their own swimmers fail important drug tests. U.S. freestyler Jessica Foschi tested positive for steroids and was banned from swimming for two years. Protesting that she had been sabotaged with steroid-spiked Gatorade or otherwise given the drugs without her knowledge, Foschi took her case to arbitration and eventually won. Although the ban was lifted in time for her to compete in trials for the 1996 Olympics, her times weren't good enough to win a berth on the team. In Australia, breaststroker Samantha Riley had better luck after testing positive for dextropropoxyphene, ingested in a prescription headache medication. Because the drug has no known performance-enhancing effect, Riley was given a personal warning but allowed to compete. Her coach, who gave her the medication, was given a two-year suspension by FINA.

Despite efforts to correct the problem, drugs and drug testing remained the talk of the pool deck throughout the 1996 Olympic Games. FINA publicized newly tightened testing requirements and the Chinese, who vowed to arrive drug-free, fell short of their performance at the 1992 Games. The other side of the controversy raged as well, when **Michelle Smith** of Ireland took multiple individual golds. A virtual unknown, ranked below the world's top forty swimmers, Smith was suspected of using drugs—even though she'd been repeatedly tested before competition and came up clean in the postrace test. Smith supporters said the accusations were examples of poor sportsmanship on the part of Americans, whose golden girl, **Janet Evans,** had failed to qualify for the 400 freestyle. It was another ugly, drug-induced moment in sports—and probably not the last.

water baby, whose natural affinity for the water was in evidence when she was still in diapers. At 5'5" and just 102 pounds, Evans was substantially lighter than most of her competitors. She also had an unorthodox, awkward-looking stroke that drew its share of criticism—until she began winning. Between 1987 and '95 she won fifteen national freestyle championships and four national championships in individual medley. In 1987 Evans broke long-standing records at 400, 800, and 1,500 meters. The next year she broke the 16-

minute barrier in the 1,500-meters, with a time of 15:52.10. Later that year she set another world record by swimming 400 meters in 4:03.85, and in 1989 she swam 800 meters in 8:16.22 for another world record. All three records were still standing at the end of the 1995 season. Evans is best remembered for her Olympic appearances, especially the 1988 Seoul games, at which she won three individual gold medals. Winner of numerous national titles, Evans was the Sullivan Award recipient in 1990. She left Stanford in 1991 when the NCAA imposed a rule limiting swimmers to twenty hours of practice time per week. Winner of two World Championship titles in 1991, she returned to the '92 Olympics for a second gold and a silver. Evans's final competition was the 1996 Olympic Games. She didn't win any medals but crowned her career another way—as the penultimate bearer of the Olympic torch, it was Evans who handed the flame to Muhammad Ali.

Selected championships and honors: Gold medal, 400m freestyle, Olympic Games, 1988; two gold medals, 800m freestyle, Olympic Games, 1988 and '92; gold medal, 400m individual medley, Olympic Games, 1988; gold medal, 400m freestyle, World Championships, 1991; gold medal, 800m freestyle, World Championships, 1991; silver medal, 200m freestyle, World Championships, 1992; silver medal, 400m freestyle, Olympic Games, 1992; Sullivan Award, 1990.

CATHY FERGUSON

The backstroke competition at the 1964 Olympic Games was truly an all-star event, bringing together six world record holders in the event. Favored were France's Kiki Caron, who held the record until America's **Ginny Duenkel** broke it just weeks before the games. Ferguson, world record holder in the 200-meter backstroke, finished ahead of them in a new world record time of 1:07.7.

Selected championships and honors, individual: Gold medal, 100m backstroke, Olympic Games, 1964. *Team:* gold medal, 4 × 100m medley relay, Olympic Games, 1964.

DAWN FRASER b. September 4, 1937, Balmain, New South Wales, Australia

A fabulous sprint swimmer who was able to maintain her edge over the course of three Olympiads, Fraser is the only swimmer to win the same event at three consecutive games. She was also the first woman ever to swim 100 meters in less than a minute. The youngest of eight children, Fraser didn't begin swimming competitively until she was sixteen. A year

later, she won the Australian 100-meter title in world record time. At her first international event—the 1956 Olympics—she won gold and silver individual medals as well as a team gold. Her gold medal came in her signature event, the 100-meter freestyle, which set a new world record. She held onto the record for another fifteen years, lowering the time on nine different occasions. Immensely popular with her fellow Australians, Fraser was both high-spirited and brash. She was also able to pull against the odds when it mattered. At twenty-five, an age when most swimmers have peaked, she broke the one-minute barrier for 100 meters. A little over a year later, just months before the 1964 Olympics, she was seriously injured and her mother killed in an automobile accident. Fraser came back in time for the games and won her third 100-meter gold with her fastest Olympic performance yet. Though she was smooth as silk in the water, the rough edges of Fraser's personality remained a problem. The same year she was named Australian Athlete of the Year, she was suspended by the Australian Swimming Association. However the authorities frowned on her, her fellow Australians remained firmly in the Fraser camp—a feeling they reaffirmed when they elected Fraser to the parliament of New South Wales in 1990.

Selected championships and honors, individual: Three gold medals, 100m freestyle, Olympic Games, 1956, '60, and '64; silver medal, 400m freestyle, Olympic Games, 1956. *Team:* Gold medal, 4 × 100m freestyle, Olympic Games, 1956.

HEIKE FRIEDRICH b. ca. 1970, East Germany

A fabulous, very nearly unbeatable freestyler, Friedrich came to international attention at age fifteen, when she won five golds at the 1985 European championships. At the next year's World Championships she added two individual and two team golds to her record, and she took the 200-meter freestyle gold in the 1988 Olympics. Here Friedrich's chain of fourteen undefeated finals came to an abrupt end, and she finished second to the United States' **Janet Evans** in the 400-meter event.

Selected championships and honors, individual: Gold medal, 200m freestyle, World Championship, 1986; gold medal, 400m freestyle, World Championship, 1986. *Team:* Gold medal, 4 × 100m freestyle relay, World Championship, 1986; gold medal, 4 × 200m freestyle relay, World Championship, 1986; gold medal, 200m freestyle, Olympic Games, 1988; silver medal, 400m freestyle, Olympic Games, 1988.

SHANE GOULD b. November 23, 1956, Brisbane, Queensland, Australia

One of the best all-round women swimmers in history, Gould set freestyle records at every distance from 100 to 1,500 meters and swam all strokes well enough to win an Olympic gold medal in the individual medley. Between July 1971 and January 1972 Gould achieved a world record sweep, setting record times in the 100, 200, 400, 800, and 1,500 meters. The only other woman ever to hold five concurrent world swimming records was the United States' **Helene Madison.** By the time the 1972 Olympics arrived, Gould was so formidable that the U.S. team armed itself with T-shirts reading "All that glitters is not Gould." The slogan was hardly effective. Gould more than lived up to her name, winning three golds—each in world record time—and taking a silver and a bronze as well. The next year, with little left to achieve, Gould retired from competition.

Selected championships and honors: Gold medal, 200m freestyle, Olympic Games, 1972; gold medal, 400m freestyle, Olympic Games, 1972; gold medal, 200m individual medley, Olympic Games, 1972; silver medal, 800m freestyle, Olympic Games, 1972; bronze medal, 100m freestyle, Olympic Games, 1972; International Swimming Hall of Fame.

NICOLE HAISLETT b. December 16, 1962, St. Petersburg, Florida

Haislett's talent as freestyler was evident in high school, when she became the fastest female in that age group ever to swim a hundred meters. She went on to win thirteen national titles and Olympic as well as World Championship gold medals. At the 1992 Olympics Haislett was in a dead heat for first in the 200-meter freestyle with fourteen-year-old Franziska van Almsick of Germany. When she realized that van Almsick, swimming next to her, was too close to the lap line, she moved closer to ride the wake—and ended up winning by a tenth of a second.

Selected championships and honors, individual: Gold medal, 100m freestyle, World Championships, 1991; gold medal, 200m freestyle, Olympic Games, 1992. *Team:* Gold medal, 4 × 100m freestyle relay, World Championships, 1991; gold medal, 4 × 100m medley relay, World Championships, 1991; gold medal, 4 × 100m freestyle relay, Olympic Games, 1992.

KAYE HALL b. May 15, 1951, Tacoma, Washington

Hall was an unlikely pick for a backstroke victory at the Mexico City games in 1968. Even though the world record holder, South African **Karen Muir,** was out of the picture because of the ban imposed on her country by the IOC, Canada's Elaine Tanner had the best qualifying times. She had also defeated Hall in several preliminary rounds. Although Tanner swam her personal best in the final, so did Hall, who won the event in 1:06.2 to set a new world record.

Selected championships and honors: Gold medal, 100m backstroke, Olympic Games, 1968; bronze medal, 200m backstroke, Olympic Games, 1968.

JAN HENNE b. August 11, 1947, Oakland, California

Henne was a virtual unknown in U.S. swimming, with no national championships in freestyle, when she made the 1968 Olympic team. At the games, she led a U.S. sweep of the 100-meter freestyle, finishing ahead of teammates Susan Pederson and Linda Gustavson.

Selected championships and honors: Gold medal, 100m freestyle, Olympic Games, 1968; silver medal, 200m freestyle, Olympic Games, 1968.

NANCY HOGSHEAD b. April 17, 1962, Iowa City, Iowa

A swimmer who specialized in the butterfly much of her career, Hogshead didn't seriously pursue the freestyle until she was nearly twenty-two years old. By this time she had several years of competition, one retirement, and one comeback behind her. Hogshead began swimming competitively in 1976 and won three national titles in butterfly in 1977 and '78. Foiled by the 1980 Olympic boycott, Hogshead didn't return to competitive swimming until 1983, when she finished third in the 200 meters at both the indoor and outdoor nationals. Her coach urged her to work on her freestyle, and in 1984 Hogshead swam to a first-place finish in the 200-meter event at the long-course nationals. She made the Olympic team once more, and this time she wasn't disappointed. In the 100-meter freestyle she and teammate Carrie Steinseifer swam to the only dead-even tie in Olympic swimming history. In addition to her shared gold, Hogshead won two team golds and an individual silver.

Selected championships and honors, individual: Silver medal, 200m butterfly, World Championships, 1978; gold medal, 100m freestyle (tie, with Carrie Steinseifer), Olympic Games, 1984; silver medal, 200m individual medley, Olympic Games, 1984. *Team:* Gold medal, 4 × 100m relay, Olympic Games, 1984; gold medal, 4 × 100m medley relay, Olympic Games, 1984.

ELEANOR HOLM b. December 6, 1913,
New York, New York

A national individual medley and backstroke champion, Holm attended her first Olympics in 1928, when she was only fourteen. That year she finished fifth in her event, the backstroke, but returned to take the gold in 1932. By that time she had won several of what would turn out to be twenty national championships—nine in individual medley (1927–32) and eleven in backstroke (1929–36). Holm made the Olympic team again in 1936 but was suspended for drinking in an event that made national headlines. Whether the incident was the drunken debauch the officials depicted or the innocent glass of champagne Holm described was never clarified. The glamorous scandal sounded a keynote for Holm's later career. After retiring from competition in 1936, she embarked on a swimming-and-show-business career. During her second marriage, to showman Billy Rose, she starred in his Aquacade and appeared at the 1939 New York World's Fair. The marriage later ended in a messy and much-publicized divorce.

Selected championships and honors: Gold medal, 100m backstroke, Olympic Games, 1932; International Swimming Hall of Fame; International Women's Sports Hall of Fame.

RAGNILD HVEGER ANDERSON
b. December 10, 1920, Denmark

One of the great freestylers, Hveger's peak years were overshadowed by World War II, which interrupted world competition. Hveger attended her first Olympics at age fifteen, in 1936, and her second when she was more than twice that old, in 1952. She won a silver the first time out and, swimming on the Danish relay team, came home from her second empty-handed. But in the interim she set more than forty world records at various distances. Four of the records she set in 1938—at 200, 400, 800, and 1,500 meters—stood until 1953. Had the Olympics been held in 1940 and '44, Hveger would almost certainly have won multiple golds.

Selected championships and honors: Silver medal, 400m freestyle, Olympic Games, 1936; International Swimming Hall of Fame.

ANNETTE KELLERMAN b. July 6, 1888, Sydney,
Australia; d. November 5, 1975

What Esther Williams was to Americans, Kellerman was to Australians—years earlier. There was virtually no form of swimming Kellerman didn't excel at, and her feats included racing, distance swimming, diving, and synchronized acrobatics in shows that toured the world. She starred and swam in several Hollywood movies, and was the subject of a film biography, *Million Dollar Mermaid*, in which her part was played by Esther Williams.

Selected championships and honors: International Swimming Hall of Fame.

CLAUDIA KOLB b. December 14, 1949, Santa
Clara, California

At fourteen, Kolb won both long- and short-course national breaststroke championships, then was the surprise silver medalist at that year's Olympics. Kolb's signature event, however, was the individual medley, in which she held world records and won eight of her dozen national championships. She swept both individual medley races at the 1968 Olympics, finishing the 400-meter race 20 meters and 13.7 seconds ahead of her nearest opponent.

Selected championships and honors: Silver medal, 200m breaststroke, Olympic Games, 1964; gold medal, 200m individual medley, Olympic Games, 1968; gold medal, 400m individual medley, Olympic Games, 1968.

Yes, Yes, Annette

Bikinis come and bikinis go, but serious swimmers have long preferred the traditional tank, the one-piece that fits like a skin. They owe it all to Annette Kellerman, who not only came up with the suit but dared to wear it. Even with long black stockings underneath, she was roundly criticized for her exhibitionism when she took a dip in Boston Harbor in 1910. A picture of Kellerman in the suit indeed shows a vast improvement over the water-absorbing skirts and puffed elbow-length sleeves of the fashionable bathing costumes of the era—a simple affair with V-neck, cap sleeves, and bermuda-length legs, it was just begging for the addition of water and, ultimately, Lycra. Criticized as she may have been, Kellerman kept wearing her suit—and thousands of women soon joined her.

BARBARA KRAUSE b. July 7, 1959, Potsdam, East Germany

Like her countryman and predecessor **Kornelia Ender,** Krause began swimming as therapy for orthopedic problems. By the time the 1976 Olympics rolled around, she was East Germany's leading sprint swimmer, but an attack of angina forced her to miss the games. She made up her mind to swim another four years, and won the 100-meter World Championship in 1978. She finally got her Olympic chance in 1980, taking golds in both the 100- and 200-meter freestyles. Krause was the first woman to swim 100 meters in less than 55 seconds, a record she eventually lowered to 54.79.

Selected championships and honors: Gold medal, 100m freestyle, World Championships, 1978; silver medal, 200m freestyle, World Championships, 1978; gold medal, 100m freestyle, Olympic Games, 1980.

ETHEL LACKIE WATKINS b. October 27, 1907, Chicago, Illinois

Lackie was the first woman to swim 100 yards in less than a minute and the first woman to swim 100 meters in less than 1 minute, 10 seconds. At the 1924 Paris Olympics, she finished first in an all-American sweep of the 100-meter freestyle and was on the gold-medal-winning U.S. relay team.

Selected championships and honors, individual: Gold medal, 100m freestyle, Olympic Games, 1924. *Team:* Gold medal, 4 × 100m freestyle relay, Olympic Games, 1924.

LE JINGYI b. 1975, Shanghai, China

As a child, Le was so thin and lanky that her nickname was "Bean Sprout." She wasn't a very good freestyler, either, but her coach saw something no one else did—a passion for swimming so strong she put up with exhausting commutes to reach the pool and swam even when in pain. His gamble on Le paid off, and the onetime Bean Sprout became known on pool decks around the world as "the Human Harpoon." At the 1996 games, when the Chinese pledge to arrive steroid-free resulted in disappointing showings, Le took the gold in the 100-meter freestyle.

Selected championships and honors, individual: Gold medal, 50m freestyle, World Championships, 1994; gold medal, 100m freestyle, World Championships, 1994; gold medal, 100m freestyle, Olympic Games, 1996. *Team:* Silver medal, 4 × 100m freestyle relay, Olympic Games, 1992; gold medal, 4 × 100m freestyle relay, World Championships, 1994.

LI LIN b. May 4, 1970, Natung, China

In an age of specialization, Li, one of a new crop of powerful Chinese athletes, is versatile enough to medal in multiple events. At the 1991 World Championships, Li edged out American **Summer Sanders** in the 200-meter individual medley, and beat her again in the 400-meter event. The two met again at the next year's Olympics, and Li finished ahead of Sanders two more times, though Hungarian **Krisztina Egerszegi** finished ahead of both of them in the 400-meter distance.

Selected championships and honors: Gold medal, 200m individual medley, World Championships, 1991; gold medal, 400m individual medley, World Championships, 1991; gold medal, 200m individual medley, Olympic Games, 1992; silver medal, 400m individual medley, Olympic Games, 1992.

HELENE MADISON b. June 19, 1913, Madison, Wisconsin; d. November 27, 1970

At 5'10" and 154 pounds, Madison was invariably described as "shapely"—but she cut the water like a rapier, and in one spectacular 16½-month period (1930–31) broke all sixteen world records, at distances from 100 yards to one mile. Between 1930 and '32 she won fourteen national championships at a variety of freestyle distances. Favored to win a medal in the 1932 Olympics, Madison did not disappoint, winning two individual golds and swimming on the world-record-setting relay team. The attractive Madison seemed a shoo-in for Hollywood, but her one role, in *The Warrior's Husband* (1933), was unsuccessful, as was her career as a nightclub entertainer. Thrice married and divorced, Madison died of cancer at the age of fifty-seven.

Selected championships and honors, individual: Gold medal, 100 meters, Olympic Games, 1932; gold medal, 400 meters, Olympic Games, 1932. *Team:* Gold medal, 4 × 100m freestyle relay, Olympic Games, 1932. Associated Press Female Athlete of the Year, 1931; International Swimming Hall of Fame; U.S. Olympic Hall of Fame.

SHIRLEY MANN b. October 15, 1937, New York, New York

Mann began swimming to strengthen her limbs after a bout of polio. By the time she was twelve she was strong enough to compete, and by her mid-teens she was nailing down national championships. Between 1954 and '56 Mann won thirteen national championships—two backstroke, six butterfly, three individual medley, and two freestyle. In fact, Mann's "strengthening program" was so successful that she ended up winning an Olympic gold medal in the butterfly, the most strength-demanding of all strokes. At the 1956 games she also helped the U.S. freestyle relay team swim to a second-place finish.

Selected championships and honors: Bronze medal, 100m butterfly, Pan American Games, 1955; gold medal, 200m butterfly, Olympic Games, 1956.

SUSIE MARONEY b. ca. 1975, Australia

On May 12, 1997, Maroney stepped ashore at Key West and became the first person to swim from Cuba to Florida, one of the last unconquered open-water challenges. A childhood asthma sufferer, Maroney was encouraged to swim as a means of strengthening her lungs. At age 14, she won the U.S. 25km Long Distance Championship with a time of 4 hours and 58 minutes. The next year she swam the English Channel and the year after that completed a double Channel crossing. At the time of her Cuba-to-Florida swim, she held several world distance records, including the fastest Channel single crossing and the women's speed record for a double Channel crossing. Her Florida swim, a distance of 112 miles, was completed in just under 24 hours.

ANGEL MARTINO *See Angel Meyers Martino, below.*

HENDRIKA (RIE) MASTENBROECK

b. February 26, 1919, Rotterdam, the Netherlands

The Netherlands' hopes for the 1936 Olympics were pinned on their world record holder, Willy den Ouden. But it was den Ouden's teammate, Mastenbroeck, who supplied the fireworks, winning two individual golds in come-from-behind finishes. Mastenbroeck's career wasn't long, but during it she set nine world records, three in freestyle and six in backstroke. Later, after her troubled marriage ended in divorce, Mastenbroeck worked fourteen hours a day cleaning houses to support her children. In 1972 she told a *Sports Illustrated* interviewer that she felt completely forgotten; "No one remembers who I was."

Selected championships and honors, individual: Gold medal, 100m freestyle, Olympic Games, 1936; gold medal, 400m freestyle, Olympic Games, 1936; silver medal, 100m backstroke, Olympic Games, 1936. *Team:* Gold medal, 4 × 100m freestyle, Olympic Games, 1936.

MARY T. MEAGHER PLANT b. October 27, 1964, Louisville, Kentucky

One of the best butterfly swimmers the United States has ever produced, "Mary T." set her first world record in the event when she was fourteen years old, at the 1979 Pan American Games. The next year she qualified for both Olympic relay teams and three individual events but missed her chance to compete due to the U.S. boycott. Each of Meagher's qualifying times was good enough to have won a gold medal, and her disappointment was so intense she considered retiring from competition. Instead she decided to train for the 1984 games. Competing at the national long-course championships in 1981, Meagher lowered her own world records in both the 100- and 200-meter butterfly. Her new records stood for more than a dozen years. At the 1984 Los Angeles Olympics Meagher swept both butterfly events and swam on the first-place U.S. medley relay team. She continued to swim and win for another four years. As a student at the University of California she won several NCAA titles, and in 1987 she was named Outstanding Female College Athlete of the Year. Between 1981 and '85 she won six national championships in butterfly and one national freestyle championship. At the 1988 games she won her final Olympic medal, a bronze in the 200-meter butterfly.

Selected championships and honors, individual: Gold medal, 200m butterfly, Pan American Games, 1979; gold medal, 100m butterfly, World Championships, 1982; silver medal, 200m butterfly, World Championships, 1982; gold medal, 100m butterfly, Olympic Games, 1984; gold medal, 200m butterfly, Olympic Games, 1984; gold medal, 200m butterfly, World Championships, 1986; silver medal, 100m butterfly, World Championships, 1986; bronze medal, 200m freestyle, World Championships, 1986; bronze medal, 100m butterfly, World Championships, 1986; bronze medal, 200m butterfly, Olympic Games, 1988; Broderick Award, 1987; Broderick Cup, 1987. *Team wins:* Gold medal, 4 × 100 medley relay, Olympic Games, 1984.

DEBORAH (DEBBIE) MEYER b. August 14, 1952, Annapolis, Maryland

Meyer began swimming in California, where her family had moved in hopes of improving her asthma. She swam her first race in 1965 and was a national champion within two years. Between 1967 and 1971 Meyer won seventeen national championships at various freestyle distances, as well as two individual medley titles. Her record-setting performance at the 1967 Pan American Games prompted the Soviet news agency TASS to name her female athlete of the year. At the Olympics the next year, Meyer's performance was hampered by the thin air of Mexico City and a case of dysentery. She won three golds nevertheless, and became the first swimmer to win triple golds in one Olympiad. She might have returned for more, but persistent bursitis forced her to retire after the 1971 season. In her five seasons of competition Meyer set twenty-four American and fifteen world records, and broke time barriers at four different distances.

Selected championships and honors: Gold medal, 400m freestyle, Pan American Games, 1967; gold medal, 800m freestyle, Pan American Games, 1967; gold medal, 200m freestyle, Olympic Games, 1968; gold medal, 400m freestyle, Olympic Games, 1968; gold medal, 800m freestyle, Olympic Games, 1968; Sullivan Award, 1968; Associated Press Female Athlete of the Year, 1969; World Swimmer of the Year, 1967–69; International Women's Sports Hall of Fame; U.S. Olympic Hall of Fame.

ANGEL MEYERS MARTINO b. 1967, Americus, Georgia

At the 1996 Olympics, much was made of **Janet Evans's** status as the grande dame of the pool—but Martino, who swims under her married name, had five years on Evans. Raised in the small town of Americus, Martino swam for Division II Furman University in college. Thrown off the 1988 Olympic team after a positive drug test, Martino decided the only way to prove the test was inaccurate was to keep swimming—and winning. She did, and her best swimming came in the wake of the 1988 fiasco.

Debbie Meyer, Barrier Breaker

Most swimmers count themselves lucky if they break one significant time barrier in their careers. Debbie Meyer broke four of them. During her five years of competition, Meyer was the first woman to—

Swim 1,500 meters in less than 18 minutes.
Swim 400 meters in less than 4.5 minutes.
Swim 500 yards in less than 5 minutes.
Swim 1,650 yards in less than 17 minutes.

Selected championships and honors, individual: Bronze medal, 50m freestyle, Olympic Games, 1992; gold medal, 100m freestyle, Pan American Games, 1995; bronze medal, 100m butterfly, Olympic Games, 1996. *Team:* Two gold medals, 4 × 100m freestyle relay, Olympic Games, 1992 and '96; gold medal, 4 × 100m medley relay, Olympic Games, 1996.

KAREN MOE THORNTON b. January 22, 1953, Moraga, California

Moe's competitive career wasn't long, but she swept both long- and short-course national championships in the 200-meter butterfly in 1972, when she set a world record at that distance. Later that year, at the Munich Olympics, she lowered her record and won a gold medal. Moe also competed at the 1976 Olympics.

Selected championships and honors: Gold medal, 200m butterfly, Olympic Games, 1972.

KAREN MUIR b. September 16, 1962, Kimberly, South Africa

Muir, a South African backstroker, was not allowed to compete in the Olympics due to IOC policy, which banned her country because of apartheid. Muir was nevertheless a presence in the sport during the late 1960s and early '70s, when she frequently held the world record for this event at both 100 and 200 meters.

MARTHA NORELIUS WRIGHT b. January 20, 1908, Stockholm, Sweden; d. September 23, 1955

Norelius immigrated to America at a young age and grew up in New York City, where she began competing. She made her Olympic debut in 1924, at the age of fifteen, and defeated teammates **Helen Wainwright** and **Gertrude Ederle** in the 400-meter freestyle event. Between 1926 and 1928 she won twelve national championships in a variety of freestyle distances. She repeated her Olympic victory in 1928, becoming the first woman ever to win the same swimming event at two Olympics. Sandwiched between her golds were several national championships and two official world records. In 1929 she gave an exhibition with professional swimmers, sharing the pool space but not the profits. This, by the stringent standards of the day, cost her her amateur status. Norelius had the last word, however. She turned professional and promptly won $10,000 dollars in the Wrigley Marathon in Toronto. Here she met Canadian double sculls champion Joe Wright, whom she later married.

Selected championships and honors, individual: Two gold medals, 400m freestyle, Olympic Games, 1924 and '28. *Team:* Gold medal, 4 × 100m freestyle, Olympic Games, 1928.

DIANA NYAD b. August 22, 1949, New York, New York

She never won a national title or went to the Olympics—but she's still one of the best known swimmers in America. A promising teenager who won several Florida state backstroke championships, Nyad dreamed of going to the 1968 Olympics. During her junior year in high school, Nyad developed endocarditis, a serious infection of the heart. After three months in bed and a period of recuperation she returned to the pool, only to discover a permanent loss in speed that signaled the end of her Olympic hopes. Despite the void this left in her life, Nyad might have given up swimming for good had not Buck Dawson, then director of the International Swimming Hall of Fame, encouraged her to try marathon swimming in 1970. Nyad took his advice and set a woman's record in her first race, a 10-mile swim in Lake Ontario. Between 1971 and 1974 Nyad competed in numerous marathon races around the world, then began solo marathoning. She set a women's record for the 22-mile distance from Capri to Naples and broke the existing male record for a north-to-south crossing of Lake Ontario. Some of her most spectacular feats were technical failures. In 1974 she attempted a double crossing of Lake Ontario, something no one had ever done before. Although she finished the first 32-mile crossing in 18 hours and 20 minutes, she lost consciousness on the return trip and had to be pulled from the water. In 1977 she again set out to do the impossible—a 130-mile swim from Havana to the Florida Keys. Although that attempt failed, Nyad set a new distance record the following year, swimming 89 miles from the Bahamas to Florida in 27 hours and 38 minutes. Nyad retired from competition in 1978 but went on to write a book on fitness as well as *Other Shores,* a book about her marathon experiences.

ALBINA OSIPOWICH b. United States

By 1928 freestylers like Osipowich had begun to whittle their times considerably. Osipowich's time of 1:11.0 in the 100-meter event was 11.2 seconds faster than the time swum by **Fanny Durack** in the inaugural race sixteen years earlier. By the next Olympics, **Helene Madison** would lower the Olympic record by another 3.2 seconds.

Selected championships and honors, individual: Gold medal, 100m freestyle, Olympic Games, 1928. *Team:* Gold medal, 4 × 100m freestyle, Olympic Games, 1928.

KRISTIN OTTO b. February 7, 1966, Leipzig, East Germany

The golden woman of the 1980s, 6'1" Otto's reputation was subsequently tarnished when declassified documents showed that her East German coaches had boosted her performance with testosterone and other banned substances—a shame, since Otto would have been a superb athlete without them. Between 1982 and 1988 Otto won eight individual gold medals in World Championship and Olympic competition, even though her country's decision to boycott the 1984 games robbed her of a chance to compete. Her medals reflect her versatility as a swimmer, and the only event she didn't excel in was the breaststroke.

Selected championships and honors, individual: Gold medal, 100m backstroke, World Championships, 1982; gold medal, 200m individual medley, World Championships, 1986; gold medal, 100m freestyle, World Championships, 1986; gold medal, 200m individual medley, World Championships, 1986; silver medal, 50m freestyle, World Championships, 1986; silver medal, 100m butterfly, World Championships, 1986; gold medal, 50m freestyle, Olympic Games, 1988; gold medal, 100m freestyle, Olympic Games, 1988; gold medal, 100m backstroke, Olympic Games, 1988; gold medal, 100m butterfly, Olympic Games, 1988. *Team:* Two gold medals, 4 × 100m freestyle relay, World Championships, 1982 and '86; two gold medals, 4 × 100m medley relay, World Championships, 1982 and '86; gold medal, 4 × 100m freestyle relay, Olympic Games, 1988; gold medal, 4 × 100 medley relay, Olympic Games, 1988.

Extra! Extra! Poll Sisters Corner the Precious Metals Market!

Between them, Claudia and Silvia Poll have a lock on the total Olympic medal tally for their country, Costa Rica. In 1988 Silvia Poll won a silver in the 200-meter freestyle. Eight years later, at the Atlanta games, younger sister Claudia took the gold in the same event.

HALINA PROZUMENSHCHYKOVA STEPANOVA b. ca. 1949, Sevastopol, Ukraine
Prozumenshchykova ranks as one of the all-time great breaststrokers. She won five medals over the course of three Olympiads and was the first woman ever to win a breaststroke gold for her country. A determined competitor, she pushed herself so hard in the 200-meter breaststroke in 1968 that she had to be given oxygen when she emerged from the water.
Selected championships and honors: Gold medal, 200m breaststroke, Olympic Games, 1964; two silver medals, 100m breaststroke, Olympic Games, 1968 and '72; two bronze medals, 200m breaststroke, Olympic Games, 1968 and '72.

KATHERINE RAWLS THOMPSON b. June 14, 1918, Nashville, Tennessee; d. April 8, 1982
A phenomenally versatile athlete, Rawls won national championships in both swimming and springboard diving and came home from the 1936 Olympics with medals in each. Though born in Tennessee, she grew up in water-rich Florida, where she began swimming and diving. At the age of thirteen, in 1931, she won a national championship in breaststroke and placed second in a national diving competition. From 1932 through 1938 Rawls dominated American swimming and diving. In addition to two silvers in Olympic springboard competition, she earned a career total of more than two dozen national championships, taking titles in diving, breaststroke, freestyle, and individual medley. Rawls retired from competition in 1939 and went on to another form of fame, as one of the first twenty-one female pilots chosen to ferry planes to combat zones during World War II.
Selected championships and honors: Two silver medals, 3m springboard, Olympic Games, 1932 and '36; Associated Press Athlete of the Year, 1937; International Swimming Hall of Fame.

AILEEN RIGGIN. *See entry under Diving.*

KEENA ROTHHAMMER b. February 26, 1957, Canoga Park, California
It sometimes seemed Rothhammer, a talented middle-distance freestyler, had an almost conscious desire to do the unexpected. At her two highest-level meets—the 1972 Olympics and '73 World Championships—she lost events she was heavily favored in but won events no one expected her to. After retiring from competition, Rothhammer covered swim competitions for CBS Television.

Selected championships and honors: Gold medal, 800m freestyle, Olympic Games, 1972; bronze medal, 200m freestyle, Olympic Games, 1972; gold medal, 200m freestyle, World Championships, 1973; silver medal, 400m freestyle, World Championships, 1973.

SUMMER SANDERS b. ca. 1973, Roseville, California
A national champion in both butterfly and individual medley, Sanders's usual strategy was to take an early lead and hold on. At the 1992 Olympics, after losing both individual medleys with this strategy, she radically altered her strategy for the 200-meter butterfly, her last chance at a medal. Sanders swam behind the leaders until the final lap, then pulled ahead for the gold. Although no one broke **Mary Meagher's** world record, it was a breakneck race in which the top seven finishers all swam personal best times.
Selected championships and honors: Gold medal, 200m butterfly, World Championships, 1991; gold medal, 200m butterfly, Olympic Games, 1992; silver medal, 200m individual medley, Olympic Games, 1992; bronze medal, 400m individual medley, World Championships, 1991; bronze medal, 100m individual medley, Olympic Games, 1992.

CAROLYN SCHULER b. United States
The 1960 Olympic butterfly event came down to a heat between two Americans—Schuler and her fourteen-year-old teammate Carolyn Wood. Wood had bested Schuler in the trials but swallowed too much water during the race and became so disoriented she ceased swimming. Schuler finished first, and Wood never touched the wall.
Selected championships and honors, individual: Gold medal, 100m butterfly, Olympic Games, 1960. *Team:* Gold medal, 4 × 100m medley relay, Olympic Games, 1960.

MICHELLE SMITH DE BRUIN b. ca. 1970, Ireland
Despite winning gold medals in the 200-meter individual medley and 200-meter butterfly at the 1995 European championships, Smith wasn't listed with the world's top-ranked swimmers. On July 20, 1996, she was still virtually unknown. Five days later, she was the greatest Irish Olympian of all time, in possession of three individual gold medals. No other woman of her country had ever won one gold medal, and no man had won two. Smith's decisive wins left many other swimmers stunned, and some accused her of

using performance-boosting drugs. Smith attributed her wins to her training program, and her tests, which repeatedly came up clean, made her accusers look like bad sports.

Selected championships and honors: Gold medal, 200m individual medley, Olympic Games, 1996; gold medal, 400m individual medley, Olympic Games, 1996; gold medal, 400m freestyle, Olympic Games, 1996.

JILL STERKEL b. May 27, 1961, United States
Winner of fifteen national titles in freestyle and butterfly, Sterkel was the first woman ever to swim on four U.S. Olympic teams. Unfortunately, her strongest years were the later 1970s and early '80s, and the U.S. decision to boycott the 1980 games may have cost her an Olympic medal. Although Sterkel retired after the 1984 Olympics, she returned in 1987 and won a berth on the '88 team when Angel Meyers tested positive for steroids.

Selected championships and honors, individual: Gold medal, 100m butterfly, Pan American Games, 1979; two silver medals, 100m freestyle, Pan American Games, 1975 and '79; bronze medal, 100m freestyle, World Championships, 1982; bronze medal, 50m freestyle (tie with East Germany's Katrin Meissner), Olympic Games, 1988; Broderick Award, 1981. *Team:* Gold medal, 4 × 100m freestyle medley, Olympic Games, 1976.

SHARON STOUDER b. November 9, 1948,
    Altadena, California
Although her international career lasted only two years, Stouder distinguished herself as a dynamic freestyle and butterfly champion. In 1964, her key year, she won four national championships, two in freestyle and two in butterfly, as well as an Olympic gold in the butterfly and a silver in freestyle. In the freestyle 100-meter event she finished just four-tenths of a second behind **Dawn Fraser.** Fraser's time of 59.5 made her the first woman to swim 100 meters in less than a minute. Stouder, with a time of 59.9, became the second. The next year, Stouder won another national championship in the butterfly, but a series of series of injuries hampered her performance and forced her to retire soon after.

Selected championships and honors, individual: Gold medal, 100m butterfly, Olympic Games, 1964; silver medal, 100m freestyle, Olympic Games, 1964. *Team:* Gold medal, 4 × 100m freestyle relay, Olympic Games, 1964; gold medal, 4 × 100m medley relay, Olympic Games, 1964.

EVA SZEKELY GYARMATI b. April 3, 1927,
    Budapest, Hungary
Szekely showed early promise as a swimmer, but in 1941, a fourteen-year-old Jewish girl, she was thrown off the team. She and her family survived the war by hiding, and Szekely realized her dream of swimming in the Olympics in 1948. In 1951 she broke the world breaststroke record at 100 meters. That same year she married Hungarian water polo star Dezso Gyarmati. She won her first Olympic medal, a breaststroke gold, at the 1952 Olympics, and the next year she broke the world record for the 400-meter individual medley. In all, Szekely set ten world and five Olympic records. During the 1956 Olympics, Szkeley and her husband learned of the bloody Russian crackdown taking place in their absence. Frantic with worry over her young daughter and family, Szekely could not sleep and lost over ten pounds. She still managed to win a silver, not learning until later that everyone was safe. Her daughter, Andrea Gyarmati, won a silver medal in 100-meter backstroke and a bronze in the 100-meter butterfly at the Munich Olympics in 1972.

Selected championships and honors: Gold medal, 200m breaststroke, Olympic Games, 1952; silver medal, 200m breaststroke, Olympic Games, 1956; International Swimming Hall of Fame

JENNY THOMPSON b. February 26, 1973, Dover,
    New Hampshire
In March 1992 Thompson set a world record for 100 meters—the first non–East German to do so in twenty years. She lowered her time during the qualifying rounds at that year's Olympics but finished the finals second to China's controversial **Yong Zhuang.** Thompson's most impressive performances often came in relays, where her leadership and freestyle skills combined to give her five gold medals.

Selected championships and honors, individual: Gold medal, 50m freestyle, Pan American Games, 1987; bronze medal, 100m freestyle, Pan American Games, 1987; silver medal, 100m, Olympic Games, 1992. *Team:* Two gold medals, 4 × 100m freestyle relay, Olympic Games, 1992 and '96; two gold medals, 4 × 100m medley relay, Olympic Games, 1992 and '96; gold medal, 4 × 200m freestyle relay, Olympic Games, 1996.

PETRA THÜMER b. 1961, East Germany
Weeks before the 1976 Olympics, teammate **Barbara Krause** fell ill, and fifteen-year-old Thümer

learned that she would have to swim the 400-meter freestyle as well as her own event, the 800 meters. She filled in with a solid gold performance, and a time fast enough to win the silver in the men's event that year. Thümer also won her own event in world record time.

Selected championships and honors: Gold medal, 400m freestyle, Olympic Games, 1976; gold medal, 800m freestyle, Olympic Games, 1976.

AMY VAN DYKEN b. February 15, 1973,
   Englewood, Colorado

At the 1996 Olympics, Van Dyken took two individual and two team golds and became the first female swimmer in history to win four golds at a single Olympic competition. As a child Van Dyken suffered from severe asthma, and she began swimming at age six to strengthen her lungs. She wasn't a natural phenom in the water, and it took another six years for her to be able to swim the length of a 50-meter pool. Incredibly perseverant, Van Dyken worked to improve her speed and developed a powerful butterfly as well. Her determination paid off at the 1996 Olympics, when she won golds in both strokes and became one of the stars of the games.

Selected championships and honors, individual: Gold medal, 100m butterfly, Pan American Games, 1995; gold medal, 100m butterfly, Olympic Games, 1996; gold medal, 50m freestyle, Olympic Games, 1996; Swimmer of the Year, 1994. *Team:* Gold medal, 100m freestyle relay, Olympic Games, 1996; Gold medal, 100m medley relay, Olympic Games, 1996.

SUSAN CHRISTINA (CHRIS) VON SALTZA
   b. January 3, 1944, San Francisco, California

In the late 1950s, the AAU instituted age-group swimming in hopes of reestablishing U.S. women as world competitors. The plan worked, and von Saltza was its first product. Though her career lasted just six years, von Saltza brought new confidence and enthusiasm to the U.S. program. She won the first of her nine national freestyle titles in 1957 and came home from the 1959 Pan American Games with four individual gold medals. The next year she became the first American woman to swim 400 meters in less than five minutes and was the leader of the U.S. women's Olympic team. Dubbed the Water Babies, the team turned in the best U.S. performance since 1932. Von Saltza finished her competitive career in 1961, with two national wins, one a freestyle and the other backstroke. After retirement she continued to

promote the sport she loved, taking a year off during college to teach swimming abroad on behalf of the U.S. State Department.

Selected championships and honors, individual: Gold medal, 100m freestyle, Pan American Games, 1959; gold medal, 200m freestyle, Pan American Games, 1959; gold medal, 400m freestyle, Pan American Games, 1959; gold medal, 400m freestyle, Olympic Games, 1960; silver medal, 100m freestyle, Olympic Games, 1960. *Team:* Gold medal, 4 × 100m freestyle relay, Olympic Games, 1960; gold medal, medley relay, Olympic Games, 1960.

HELEN WAINWRIGHT b. March 15, 1906

With **Aileen Riggin** (listed under Diving), Wainwright is one of only two American women to win Olympic medals in both swimming and diving. Her first medal, a silver in springboard diving, came at the 1920 games. Four years later she won a bronze in the 400-meter freestyle. Wainwright also won double titles at home, although her strongest events were freestyle races. Between 1922 and 1925 she won eight national freestyle titles, as well as a national springboard title in 1925. Wainwright retired from competition the next year and, like other famous swimmers of her era, performed professionally with various water shows. She eventually married a career army officer and during World War II donated her medals and trophies to the government so they could be melted down as scrap metal.

Selected championships and honors: Silver medal, springboard diving, Olympic Games, 1920; bronze medal, 400m freestyle, Olympic Games, 1924; International Swimming Hall of Fame.

LILLIAN (POKEY) WATSON b. Honolulu,
   Hawaii

A versatile swimmer, Watson swam on the medal-winning U.S. freestyle relay team at the 1964 Olympics. After the games, she shifted her focus to the backstroke. At the 1968 games she became the first woman to win the newly added 200-meter backstroke. Sorely missed from the competition was world record holder **Karen Muir,** who could not compete because her country, South Africa, had been banned by the IOC.

Selected championships and honors, individual: Bronze medal, 100m freestyle, Pan American Games, 1967; gold medal, 200m backstroke, Olympic Games, 1968. *Team:* Gold medal, 4 × 100m freestyle relay, Olympic Games, 1964.

MARY WAYTE b. United States

In 1980, U.S. athletes chafed over missing the Olympics. In 1984 it was eastern bloc athletes who had to miss their chance. Wayte finished ahead of teammate **Sippy Woodhead** to win a gold in the 200-meter freestyle, but her time was more than a full second behind the record set by **Kristin Otto** in May.

Selected championships and honors: Gold medal, 200m freestyle, Olympic Games, 1984.

SHARON WICHMAN b. May 13, 1952,
   Churubusco, Indiana

Breaststroke became an Olympic event in 1924, but the United States had to wait until 1968 for its first gold. With **Catherine Carr,** Wichman remains one of only two American women to finish first in Olympic breaststroke competition. Wichman also won three national breaststroke championships.

Selected championships and honors: Gold medal, 200m breaststroke, Olympic Games, 1968.

TRACEY WICKHAM b. November 24, 1962,
   Keperra, Queensland, Australia

U.S. athletes weren't the only ones deprived of a chance to compete at the 1980 Olympic Games. Wickham, an Australian, was the reigning world champion and record holder at 400 and 800 meters. Winning times at the Moscow games were 2.48 and 4.28 seconds behind Wickham's records, respectively. Although Wickham didn't compete in the next Olympics, her records stood until 1987, when **Janet Evans** broke both of them.

Selected championships and honors: Gold medal, 400m freestyle, World Championships, 1978; gold medal, 800m freestyle, World Championships, 1978.

ESTHER WILLIAMS b. August 8, 1923,
   Inglewood, California

She never won an Olympic medal, but she might have had not World War II canceled the 1940 games. A national freestyle champion who made the U.S. team easily, Williams didn't let global warfare thwart her swimming career. She toured one year with Billy Rose's Aquacade and then went on to make the splashy MGM movies she is best known and remembered for. Her considerable personal charm, like her ability to smile underwater, fascinated the public and helped popularize swimming throughout America.

CYNTHIA (SIPPY) WOODHEAD b. February 7,
   1964, Riverside, California

Winner of ten national championships in various freestyle events, Woodhead was considered one of the world's best freestylers in 1978 and '79 and seemed poised for Olympic glory in 1980—until the U.S. boycott dashed her hopes. The boycott was the first in a series of disappointments, and although Woodhead continued to compete in the face of illness and injury, she was never again at her peak. Woodhead past her peak was still world class, and she managed to win a gold at the 1983 Pan American Games and a silver in the Olympics the next year.

Selected championships and honors: Gold medal, 200m freestyle, World Championships, 1978; silver medal, 400m freestyle, World Championships, 1978; silver medal, 800m freestyle, World Championships, 1978; gold medal, 100m freestyle, Pan American Games, 1979; two gold medals, 200m freestyle, Pan American Games, 1979 and '83; gold medal, 400m freestyle, Pan American Games, 1979; gold medal, 200m freestyle, Pan American Games, 1983; silver medal, 200m freestyle, Olympic Games, 1984.

New Kids on the Block— and Fastest, Too

Chinese women began claiming their share of medals in the late 1980s, but a team win eluded them until 1992, when Yong Zhuang led them to a silver in a 4 × 100-meter freestyle. Two years later, at the 1994 World Championships, they swept all three team events, and the too-small handful of countries who compete for team medals increased by one.

1992 Olympic silver-medal 4 × 100m freestyle team: Yong Zhuang, Lu Bin, Yang Wenyi, Le Jingyi.

1994 World Championship gold-medal 4 × 100m freestyle team: Le Jingyi, Ying Shan, Le Ying, Lu Bin.

1994 World Championship gold-medal 4 × 200m freestyle team: Le Ying, Yang Alhua, Zhou Guabin, Lu Bin.

1994 World Championship gold-medal 4 × 100m medley relay team: He Cihong, Dai Guohong, Liu Limin, Lu Bin.

ZHUANG YONG b. August 10, 1972, China
Yong's silver medal in the 100-meter freestyle slipped into history at the 1988 Olympics, but when she came back to win the gold in Barcelona four years later, a controversy erupted. Coaches from other countries charged that Yong's swift time, deep voice, and heavy muscles were steroid-produced. Since swimming's governing body enforced only random testing at the time, Yong could not be tested after her win—but the cloud over her remained.
Selected championships and honors, individual: Silver medal, 100m freestyle, Olympic Games, 1988; gold medal, 50m freestyle, World Championship, 1991; gold medal, 100m freestyle, Olympic Games, 1992. *Team:* Silver medal, 4 × 100m freestyle relay, Olympic Games, 1992.

Swimming

World Records

Event	Time	Champion	Country	Site	Date
50m freestyle	24.51	Le Jingyi	CHN	Rome, ITA	9/11/94
100m freestyle	54.01	Le Jingyi	CHN	Rome, ITA	9/5/94
200m freestyle	1:56.78	Franziska van Almsick	GER	Rome, ITA	9/6/94
400m freestyle	4:03.85	Janet Evans	USA	Seoul, KOR	9/22/88
800m freestyle	8:16.22	Janet Evans	USA	Tokyo, JPN	8/20/89
1500m freestyle	15:52.10	Janet Evans	USA	Orlando, FL	3/26/88
100m backstroke	1:00.16	He Cihong	CHN	Rome, ITA	9/10/94
200m backstroke	2:06.62	Krisztina Egerszegi	HUN	Athens, GR	8/25/91
100m breaststroke	1:07.69	Samantha Riley	AUS	Rome, ITA	9/9/94
200m breaststroke	2:24.76	Rebecca Brown	AUS	Queensland, AUS	3/16/94
100m butterfly	57.93	Mary T. Meagher	USA	Brown Creek, WI	8/16/81
200m butterfly	2:05.96	Mary T. Meagher	USA	Brown Creek, WI	8/13/81
200m indiv. medley	2:11.65	Li Lin	CHN	Barcelona, ESP	7/30/92
400m indiv medley	4:36.10	Petra Schneider	GDR	Guayaquil, ECU	8/1/82
4 × 100m freestyle relay	3:37.91	Le Jingyi, Ying Shan, Le Ying, Bin Lu	CHN	Rome, ITA	8/7/94
4 × 200m freestyle relay	7:55.47	Manuella Stellmach, Astrid Strauss, Anke Mohring, Heike Friedrich	GDR	Strasbourg, FRA	8/18/87
4 × 100m medley relay	4:01.67	He Cihong, Dai Guohong, Liu Limin, Le Jingyi	CHN	Rome, ITA	9/10/94

Olympic 50m Freestyle

Year	Medalists	Country	Time
1896–1984	event not held		
1988	Kristin Otto	GDR	25.49 OR
	Yang Wenyi	CHN	25.64
	Katrin Meissner	GDR	25.71
1992	Yang Wenyi	CHN	24.79 WR
	Yong Zhuang	CHN	25.08
	Angelina Martino	USA	25.23
1996	Amy Van Dyken	USA	24.87
	Le Jingyi	CHN	24.90
	Sandra Volker	GER	25.14

Olympic 100m Freestyle

Year	Medalists	Country	Time
1896–1908	event not held		
1912	Sarah "Fanny" Durack	AUS	1:22.2
	Wilhelmina Wylie	AUS	1:25.4
	Jennie Fletcher	GBR	1:27.0

Swimming (continued)

Olympic 100m Freestyle

Year	Medalists	Country	Time
1920	Ethelda Bleibtrey	USA	1:13.6 WR
	Irene Guest	USA	1:17.0
	Frances Schroth	USA	1:17.2
1924	Ethel Lackie	USA	1:12.4
	Mariechen Wehselau	USA	1:12.8
	Gertrude Ederle	USA	1:14.2
1928	Albina Osipowich	USA	1:11.0 OR
	Eleanor Garatti	USA	1:11.4
	Margaret Joyce Cooper	GBR	1:13.6
1932	Helene Madison	USA	1:06.8 OR
	Willemijntje den Ouden	HOL	1:07.8
	Eleanor Saville (Garatti)	USA	1:09.3
1936	Hendrika "Rie" Mastenbroek	HOL	1:05.9 OR
	Jeanette Campbell	ARG	1:06.4
	Gisela Arendt	GER	1:06.6
1948	Greta Andersen	DEN	1:06.3
	Ann Curtis	USA	1:06.5
	Marie-Louise Vaessen	HOL	1:07.6
1952	Katalin Szöke	HUN	1:06.8
	Johanna Termeulen	HOL	1:07.0
	Judit Temes	HUN	1:07.1
1956	Dawn Fraser	AUS	1:02.0 WR
	Lorraine Crapp	AUS	1:02.3
	Faith Leech	AUS	1:05.1
1960	Dawn Fraser	AUS	1:01.2 OR
	S. Christina von Saltza	USA	1:02.8
	Natalie Steward	GBR	1:03.1
1964	Dawn Fraser	AUS	59.5 OR
	Sharon Stouder	USA	59.9
	Kathleen Ellis	USA	1:00.8
1968	Jan Henne	USA	1:00.0
	Susan Pedersen	USA	1:00.3
	Linda Gustavson	USA	1:00.3
1972	Sandy Neilson	USA	58.59 OR
	Shirley Babashoff	USA	59.02
	Shane Gould	AUS	59.06
1976	Kornelia Ender	GDR	55.65 WR
	Petra Priemer	GDR	56.49
	Enith Brigitha	HOL	56.65
1980	Barbara Krause	GDR	54.79 WR
	Caren Metschuck	GDR	55.16
	Ines Diers	GDR	55.65
1984	Carrie Steinseifer (tie for gold)	USA	55.92
	Nancy Hogshead (tie for gold)	USA	55.92
	Annemarie Verstappen	HOL	56.08
1988	Kristin Otto	GDR	54.93
	Yong Zhuang	CHN	55.47
	Catherine Piewinski	FRA	55.49
1992	Yong Zhuang	CHN	54.64 OR
	Jennifer Thompson	USA	54.84
	Franziska van Almsick	GER	54.94
1996	Le Jingyi	CHN	54.50
	Sandra Volker	GER	54.88
	Angel Martino	USA	54.93

Olympic 200m Freestyle

Year	Medalists	Country	Time
1896–1964	event not held		
1968	Debbie Meyer	USA	2:10.5 OR
	Jan Henne	USA	2:11.0
	Jane Barkman	USA	2:11.2
1972	Shane Gould	AUS	2:03.56 WR
	Shirley Babashoff	USA	2:04.33
	Keena Rothhammer	USA	2:04.92
1976	Kornelia Ender	GDR	1:59.26 WR
	Shirley Babashoff	USA	2:01.22
	Enith Brigitha	HOL	2:01.40
1980	Barbara Krause	GDR	1:58.33 OR
	Ines Diers	GDR	1:59.64
	Carmela Schmidt	GDR	2:01.44
1984	Mary Wayte	USA	1:59.23
	Cynthia Woodhead	USA	1:59.50
	Annemarie Verstappen	HOL	1:59.69
1988	Heike Friedrich	GDR	1:57.65 OR
	Silvia Poll Ahrens	CRC	1:58.67
	Manuela Stellmach	GDR	1:59.01
1992	Nicole Haislett	USA	1:57.90
	Franziska van Almsick	GER	1:58.00
	Kerstin Kielgass	GER	1:59.67
1996	Claudia Poll	CosRica	1:58.16
	Franziska van Almsick	GER	1:58.57
	Dagmar Hase	GER	1:59.56

Swimming (continued)

Olympic 400m Freestyle

Year	Medalists	Country	Time
1896–1912	event not held		
1920	Ethelda Bleibtrey	USA	4:34.0 WR
	Margaret Woodbridge	USA	4:42.8
	Frances Schroth	USA	4:52.0
1924	Martha Norelius	USA	6:02.2 OR
	Helen Wainwright	USA	6:03.8
	Gertrude Ederle	USA	6:04.8
1928	Martha Norelius	USA	5:42.8 WR
	Maria Braun	HOL	5:57.8
	Josephine McKim	USA	6:00.2
1932	Helene Madison	USA	5:28.5 WR
	Lenore Kight	USA	5:28.6
	Jennie Maakal	SAF	5:47.3
1936	Hendrika "Rie" Mastenbroek	HOL	5:26.4 OR
	Ragnild Hveger	DEN	5:27.5
	Lenore Wingard (Kight)	USA	5:29.0
1948	Ann Curtis	USA	5:17.8 OR
	Karen-Margrete Harup	DEN	5:21.2
	Catherine Gibson	GBR	5:22.5
1952	Valeria Gyenge	HUN	5:12.1 OR
	Eva Novak	HUN	5:13.7
	Evelyn Kawamoto	USA	5:14.6
1956	Lorraine Crapp	AUS	4:54.6 OR
	Dawn Fraser	AUS	5:02.5
	Sylvia Ruuska	USA	5:07.1
1960	S. Christina von Saltza	USA	4:50.6 OR
	Jane Cederqvist	SWE	4:53.9
	Catharina Lagerberg	HOL	4:56.9
1964	Virginia Duenkel	USA	4:43.3 OR
	Marilyn Ramenofsky	USA	4:44.6
	Terri Stickles	USA	4:47.2
1968	Debbie Meyer	USA	4:31.8 OR
	Linda Gustavson	USA	4:35.5
	Karen Moras	AUS	4:37.0
1972	Shane Gould	AUS	4:19.04 WR
	Novella Calligaris	ITA	4:22.44
	Gudrun Wegner	GDR	4:23.11
1976	Petra Thümer	GDR	4:09.89 WR
	Shirley Babashoff	USA	4:10.46
	Shannon Smith	CAN	4:14.60
1980	Ines Diers	GDR	4:08.76 OR
	Petra Schneider	GDR	4:09.16
	Carmela Schmidt	GDR	4:10.86
1984	Tiffany Cohen	USA	4:07.10 OR
	Sarah Hardcastle	GBR	4:10.27
	June Croft	GBR	4:11.49
1988	Janet Evans	USA	4:03.85 WR
	Heike Friedrich	GDR	4:05.94
	Anke Mohring	GDR	4:06.62
1992	Dagmar Hase	GER	4:07.18
	Janet Evans	USA	4:07.37
	Hayley Lewis	AUS	4:11.22
1996	Michelle Smith	IRE	4:07.25.2
	Dagmar Hase	GER	4:08.30
	Kirsten Vlieghuis	HOL	4:09.83

Olympic 800m Freestyle

Year	Medalists	Country	Time
1896–1964	event not held		
1968	Deborah Meyer	USA	9:24.0 OR
	Pamela Kruse	USA	9:35.7
	Maria Teresa Ramirez	MEX	9:38.5
1972	Keena Rothhammer	USA	8:53.68 WR
	Shane Gould	AUS	8:56.39
	Novella Calligaris	ITA	8:57.46
1976	Petra Thümer	GDR	8:37.14 WR
	Shirley Babashoff	USA	8:37.59
	Wendy Weinberg	USA	8:42.60
1980	Michelle Ford	AUS	8:28.90 OR
	Ines Diers	GDR	8:32.55
	Heike Dahne	GDR	8:33.48
1984	Tiffany Cohen	USA	8:24.95 OR
	Michele Richardson	USA	8:30.73
	Sarah Hardcastle	GBR	8:32.60
1988	Janet Evans	USA	8:20.20 OR
	Astrid Strauss	GDR	8:22.09
	Julie McDonald	AUS	8:22.93
1992	Janet Evans	USA	8:25.52
	Hayley Lewis	AUS	8:30.34
	Jana Henke	GER	8:30.99
1996	Brooke Bennett	USA	8:27.89
	Dagmar Hase	GER	8:29.91
	Kirsten Vlieghuis	HOL	8:30.84

Olympic 100m Backstroke

Year	Medalists	Country	Time
1896–1920	event not held		
1924	Sybil Bauer	USA	1:23.2 OR
	Phyllis Harding	GBR	1:27.4
	Aileen Riggin	USA	1:28.2
1928	Maria Braun	HOL	1:22.0
	Ellen King	GBR	1:22.2
	Margaret Joyce Cooper	GBR	1:22.8

Swimming (continued)

Olympic 100m Backstroke

Year	Medalists	Country	Time
1932	Eleanor Holm	USA	1:19.4
	Philomena "Boony" Mealing	AUS	1:21.3
	Elizabeth Valerie Davies	GBR	1:22.5
1936	Dina "Nida" Senff	HOL	1:18.9
	Hendrika "Rie" Mastenbroek	HOL	1:19.2
	Alice Bridges	USA	1:19.4
1948	Karen-Margrete Harup	DEN	1:14.4 OR
	Suzanne Zimmerman	USA	1:16.0
	Judith Davies	AUS	1:16.7
1952	Joan Harrison	SAF	1:14.3
	Geertje Wielema	HOL	1:14.5
	Jean Stewart	NZE	1:15.8
1956	Judith Grinham	GBR	1:12.9 OR
	Carin Cone	USA	1:12.9
	Margaret Edwards	GBR	1:13.1
1960	Lynn Burke	USA	1:09.3 OR
	Natalie Steward	GBR	1:10.8
	Satoko Tanaka	JPN	1:11.4
1964	Cathy Ferguson	USA	1:07.7 WR
	Christine Caron	FRA	1:07.9
	Virginia Duenkel	USA	1:08.0
1968	Kaye Hall	USA	1:06.2 WR
	Elaine Tanner	CAN	1:06.7
	Jane Swagerty	USA	1:08.1
1972	Melissa Belote	USA	1:05.78 OR
	Andrea Gyamati	HUN	1:06.26
	Susan Atwood	USA	1:06.34
1976	Ulrike Richter	GDR	1:01.83 OR
	Birgit Treiber	GDR	1:03.41
	Nancy Garapick	CAN	1:03.71
1980	Rica Reinisch	GDR	1:00.86 WR
	Ina Kleber	GDR	1:02.07
	Petra Riedel	GDR	1:02.64
1984	Theresa Andrews	USA	1:02.55
	Betsy Mitchell	USA	1:02.63
	Jolanda de Rover	HOL	1:02.91
1988	Kristin Otto	GDR	1:00.89
	Krisztina Egerszegi	HUN	1:01.56
	Cornelia Sirch	GDR	1:01.57
1992	Krisztina Egerszegi	HUN	1:00.68 OR
	Tonde Szabo	HUN	1:01.14
	Lea Loveless	USA	1:01.43
1996	Beth Botsford	USA	1:01.19.2
	Whitney Hedgepeth	USA	1:01.47
	Marianne Kriel	SAR	1:02.12

Olympic 200m Backstroke

Year	Medalists	Country	Time
1896–1964	event not held		
1968	Lillian "Pokey" Watson	USA	2:24.8 OR
	Elaine Tanner	CAN	2:27.4
	Kaye Hall	USA	2:28.9
1972	Melissa Belote	USA	2:19.19 WR
	Susan Atwood	USA	2:20.38
	Donna Gurr	CAN	2:23.22
1976	Ulrike Richter	GDR	2:13.43 OR
	Birgit Treiber	GDR	2:14.97
	Nancy Garapick	CAN	2:15.60
1980	Rica Reinisch	GDR	2:11.77 WR
	Cornelia Polit	GDR	2:13.75
	Birgit Treiber	GDR	2:14.14
1984	Jolanda de Rover	HOL	2:12.38
	Amy White	USA	2:13.04
	Aneta Patrascoiu	ROM	2:13.29
1988	Krisztina Egerszegi	HUN	2:09.29 OR
	Kathrin Zimmerman	GDR	2:10.61
	Cornelia Sirch	GDR	2:11.45
1992	Krisztina Egerszegi	HUN	2:07.06 OR
	Dagmar Hase	GER	2:09.46
	Nicole Stevenson (Livingstone)	AUS	2:10.20
1996	Krisztina Egerszegi	HUN	2:07.83
	Whitney Hedgepeth	USA	2:11.98
	Cathleen Rund	GER	2:12.06

Olympic 100m Breaststroke

Year	Medalists	Country	Time
1896–1964	event not held		
1968	Djurdjica Bjedov	YUG/CRO	1:15.8 OR
	Halina Prozumensh-chykova	UKR	1:15.9
	Sharon Wichman	USA	1:16.1

Swimming (continued)

Olympic 100m Breaststroke

Year	Medalists	Country	Time
1972	Catherine Carr	USA	1:13.56 WR
	Halina Stepanova (Prozumensh-chykova)	UKR	1:14.99
	Beverley Whitfield	AUS	1:15.73
1976	Hannelore Anke	GDR	1:11.16
	Lyubov Rusanova	RUS	1:13.04
	Marina Koshevaia	RUS	1:13.30
1980	Ute Geweniger	GDR	1:10.22
	Elvira Vasilkova	RUS	1:10.41
	Susanne Nielsson	DEN	1:11.16
1984	Petra van Staveren	HOL	1:09.88 OR
	Anne Ottenbrite	CAN	1:10.69
	Catherine Poirot	FRA	1:10.70
1988	Tania Dangalakova (Bogomilova)	BUL	1:07.95 OR
	Antoaneta Frenkeva	BUL	1:08.74
	Silke Horner	GDR	1:08.83
1992	Yelena Rudkovskaya	BLR	1:08.00
	N. Anita Hall	USA	1:08.17
	Samantha Riley	AUS	1:09.25
1996	Penelope Heyns	SAF	1:07.73
	Amanda Beard	USA	1:08.09
	Samantha Riley	AUS	1:09.18

Olympic 200m Breaststroke

Year	Medalists	Country	Time
1896–1920	event not held		
1924	Lucy Morton	GBR	3:33.2 OR
	Agnes Geraghty	USA	3:34.0
	Gladys Carson	GBR	3:35.4
1928	Hildegard Schrader	GER	3:12.6
	Mietje "Marie" Baron	HOL	3:15.2
	Lotte Muhe	GER	3:17.6
1932	Clare Dennis	AUS	3:06.3 OR
	Hideko Maehata	JPN	3:06.4
	Else Jacobsen	DEN	3:07.1
1936	Hideko Maehata	JPN	3:03.6
	Martha Geneger	GER	3:04.2
	Inge Sorensen	DEN	3:07.8
1948	Petronella van Vliet	HOL	2:57.2
	Beatrice Lyons	AUS	2:57.7
	Eva Novak	HUN	3:00.2
1952	Eva Szekely	HUN	2:51.7 OR
	Eva Novak	HUN	2:54.4
	Helen "Elenor" Gordon	GBR	2:57.6
1956	Ursula Happe	GER	2:53.1 OR
	Eva Szekely	HUN	2:54.8
	Eva-Maria ten Elsen	GDR	2:55.1
1960	Anita Lonsbrough	GBR	2:49.5 WR
	Wiltrud Urselmann	GER	2:50.0
	Barbara Gobel	GDR	2:53.6
1964	Halina Prozumensh-chykova	UKR	2:46.4 OR
	Claudia Kolb	USA	2:47.6
	Svetlana Babanina	RUS	2:48.6
1968	Sharon Wichman	USA	2:44.4 OR
	Djurdjica Bjedov	YUG/CRO	2:46.4
	Halina Prozumensh-chykova	UKR	2:47.0
1972	Beverley Whitfield	AUS	2:41.71 OR
	Dana Schoenfield	USA	2:42.05
	Halina Stepanova (Prozumensh-chykova)	UKR	2:42.36
1976	Marina Koshevaia	RUS	2:33.35 WR
	Maryna Yurchenya	UKR	2:36.08
	Lyubov Rusanova	RUS	2:36.22
1980	Lina Kaciusyte	LIT	2:29.54 OR
	Svetlana Varganova	RUS	2:29.61
	Yulia Bogdanova	RUS	2:32.39
1984	Anne Ottenbrite	CAN	2:30.38
	Susan Rapp	USA	2:31.15
	Ingrid Lempereur	BEL	2:31.40
1988	Silke Homer	GDR	2:26.71 WR
	Huang Xiaomin	CHN	2:27.49
	Antoaneta Frenkeva	BUL	2:28.34
1992	Kyoko Iwasaki	JPN	2:26.65 OR
	Li Lin	CHN	2:26.85
	N. Anita Nall	USA	2:26.88
1996	Penelope Heyns	SAF	2:25.41.2
	Amanda Beard	USA	2:25.75
	Agnes Kovacs	HUN	2:26.57

Olympic 100m Butterfly

Year	Medalists	Country	Time
1896–1952	event not held		

Swimming (continued)

Olympic 100m Butterfly

Year	Medalists	Country	Time
1956	Shelly Mann	USA	1:11.0 WR
	Nancy Ramey	USA	1:11.9
	Mary Sears	USA	1:14.4
1960	Carolyn Schuler	USA	1:09.5 OR
	Marianne Heemskerk	HOL	1:10.4
	Janice Andrew	AUS	1:12.2
1964	Sharon Stouder	USA	1:04.7 WR
	Ada Kok	HOL	1:05.6
	Kathleen Ellis	USA	1:06.0
1968	Lynette McClements	AUS	1:05.5
	Ellie Daniel	USA	1:05.8
	Susan Shields	USA	1:06.2
1972	Mayumi Aoki	JPN	1:03.34 WR
	Roswitha Beier	GDR	1:03.61
	Andrea Gyarmati	HUN	1:03.73
1976	Kornelia Ender	GDR	1:00.13
	Andrea Pollack	GDR	1:00.98
	Wendy Boglioli	USA	1:01.17
1980	Caren Metschuck	GDR	1:00.42
	Andrea Pollack	GDR	1:00.90
	Christiane Knacke	GDR	1:01.44
1984	Mary T. Meagher	USA	59.26
	Jenna Johnson	USA	1:00.19
	Karin Seick	GER	1:01.36
1988	Kristin Otto	GDR	59.00 OR
	Birte Weigang	GDR	59.45
	Qian Hong	CHN	59.52
1992	Qian Hong	CHN	58.62 OR
	Christine Ahmann-Leighton	USA	58.74
	Catherine Piewinski	FRA	59.01
1996	Amy Van Dyken	USA	59.13.2
	Liu Limin	CHN	59.14
	Angel Martino	USA	59.23

Olympic 200m Butterfly

Year	Medalists	Country	Time
1896–1964	event not held		
1968	Ada Kok	HOL	2:24.7 OR
	Helga Lindner	GDR	2:24.8
	Ellie Daniel	USA	2:25.9
1972	Karen Moe	USA	2:15.57 WR
	Lynn Colella	USA	2:16.34
	Ellie Daniel	USA	2:16.74
1976	Andrea Pollack	GDR	2:11.41 OR
	Ulrike Tauber	GDR	2:12.50
	Rosemarie Gabriel (Kother)	GDR	2:12.86
1980	Ines Geissler	GDR	2:10.44 OR
	Sybille Schonrock	GDR	2:10.45
	Michelle Ford	AUS	2:11.66
1984	Mary T. Meagher	USA	2:06.90
	Karen Phillips	AUS	2:10.56
	Ina Beyermann	GER	2:11.91
1988	Kathleen Nord	GDR	2:09.51
	Brite Weigang	GDR	2:09.91
	Mary T. Meagher	USA	2:10.80
1992	Summer Sanders	USA	2:08.67
	Wang Xiaohong	CHN	2:09.01
	Susan O'Neill	AUS	2:09.03
1996	Susan O'Neill	AUS	2:07.76
	Petria Thomas	AUS	2:09.82
	Michelle Smith	IRE	2:09.91

Olympic 200m Individual Medley

Year	Medalists	Country	Time
1896–1964	event not held		
1968	Claudia Kolb	USA	2:24.7 OR
	Susan Pedersen	USA	2:28.8
	Jan Henne	USA	2:31.4
1972	Shane Gould	AUS	2:23.07 WR
	Kornelia Ender	GDR	2:23.59
	Lynn Vidali	USA	2:24.06
1976–1980	event not held		
1984	Tracy Caulkins	USA	2:12.64 OR
	Nancy Hogshead	USA	2:15.17
	Michele Pearson	AUS	2:15.92
1988	Daniela Hunger	GDR	2:12.59 OR
	Yelena Dendeberova	RUS	2:13.31
	Noemi Lung	ROM	2:14.85
1992	Li Lin	CHN	2:11.65
	Summer Sanders	USA	2:11.91
	Daniela Hunger	GER	2:13.92
1996	Michelle Smith	IRE	2:13.93
	Marianne Limpert	CAN	2:14.35
	Li Lin	CHN	2:14.74

Olympic 400m Individual Medley

Year	Medalists	Country	Time
1896–1960	event not held		
1964	Donna De Varona	USA	5:18.7 OR
	Sharon Finneran	USA	5:24.1
	Martha Randall	USA	5:24.2

Swimming (continued)

Olympic 400m Individual Medley

Year	Medalists	Country	Time
1968	Claudia Kolb	USA	5:08.5 OR
	Lynn Vidali	USA	5:22.2
	Sabine Steinbach	GDR	5:25.3
1972	Gail Neall	AUS	5:02.97 WR
	Leslie Cliff	CAN	5:03.57
	Novella Calligaris	ITA	5:03.99
1976	Ulrike Tauber	GDR	4:42.77 WR
	Cheryl Gibson	CAN	4:48.10
	Becky Smith	CAN	4:50.48
1980	Petra Schneider	GDR	4:36.29 WR
	Sharron Davies	GBR	4:46.83
	Agnieszka Czopek	POL	4:48.17
1984	Tracy Caulkins	USA	4:39.24
	Suzanne Landells	AUS	4:48.30
	Petra Zindler	GER	4:48.57
1988	Janet Evans	USA	4:37.76
	Noemi Lung	ROM	4:39.46
	Daniela Hunger	GDR	4:39.76
1992	Krisztina Egerszegi	HUN	4:36.54
	Li Lin	CHN	4:36.73
	Summer Sanders	USA	4:37.58
1996	Michelle Smith	IRE	4:39.18
	Allison Wagner	USA	4:42.03
	Krisztina Egerszegi	HUN	4:42.53

Olympic 4 × 100m Freestyle Relay

Year	Medalists	Country	Time
1896–1908	event not held		
1912	Isabella Moore, Jennie Fletcher, Annie Speirs, Irene Steer	GBR	5:52.8 WR
		GER	6:04.6
		AUT	6:17.0
1920	Margaret Woodbridge, Frances Schroth, Irene Guest, Ethelda Bleibtrey	USA	5:11.6 WR
		GBR	5:40.8
		SWE	5:43.6
1924	Gertrude Ederle, Euphrasia Donnelly, Ethel Lackie, Mariechen Wehselau	USA	4:58.8 WR
		GBR	5:17.0
		SWE	5:35.6
1928	Adelaide Lambert, Eleanor Garatti, Albina Osipowich, Martha Norelius (Josephine McKim, Susan Laird)	USA	4:47.6 WR
		GBR	5:02.8
		SAF	5:13.4
1932	Josephine McKim, Helen Johns, Eleanor Saville (Garatti), Helene Madison	USA	4:38.0 WR
		HOL	4:47.5
		GBR	4:52.4
1936	Johanna Selbach, Catherina Wagner, Willemijntje den Ouden, Hendrika "Rie" Mastenbroek	HOL	4:36.0 OR
		GER	4:36.8
		USA	4:40.2
1948	Marie Corridon, Thelma Kalama, Brenda Heiser, Ann Curtis	USA	4:29.2 OR
		DEN	4:29.6
		HOL	4:31.6
1952	Ilona Novak, Judit Temes, Eva Novak, Katalin Szoke (Maria Littomericzky, Ilona Novak)	HUN	4:24.4 WR
		HOL	4:29.0
		USA	4:30.1

Swimming (continued)

Olympic 4 × 100m Freestyle Relay

Year	Medalists	Country	Time
1956	Dawn Fraser, Faith Leech, Sandra Morgan, Lorraine Crapp (Margaret Gibson)	AUS	4:17.1 WR
		USA	4:19.2
		SAF	4:25.7
1960	Joan Spillane, Shirley Stobs, Carolyn Wood, S. Christine von Saltza (Donna De Varona, Susan Doerr, Sylvia Ruuska, Molly Botkin)	USA	4:08.9 WR
		AUS	4:11.3
		GDR/GER	4:19.7
1964	Sharon Stouder, Donna De Varona, Lillian "Pokey" Watson, Kathleen Ellis (Jeanne Hallock, Ericka Bricker, Lynne Allsup, Patience Sherman)	USA	4:03.8 WR
		AUS	4:06.9
		HOL	4:12.0
1968	Jane Barkman, Linda Gustavson, Susan Pedersen, Jan Henne	USA	4:02.5 OR
		GDR	4:05.7
		CAN	4:07.2
1972	Sandra Neilson, Jennifer Kemp, Jane Barkman, Shirley Babashoff (Kim Peyton, Lynn Skrifvars, Ann Marshall)	USA	3:55.19 WR
		GDR	3:55.55
		GER	3:57.93
1976	Kim Peyton, Wendy Boglioli, Jill Sterkel, Shirley Babashoff (Jennifer Hooker)	USA	3:44.82 WR
		GDR	3:45.50
		CAN	3:48.81
1980	Barbara Krause, Caren Metschuck, Ines Diers, Sarina Hulsenbeck (Carmela Schmidt)	GDR	3:42.71 WR
		SWE	3:48.93
		HOL	3:49.51
1984	Jenna Johnson, Carrie Steinseifer, Dara Torres, Nancy Hogshead (Jill Sterkel, Mary Wayte)	USA	3:43.43
		HOL	3:44.40
		GER	3:45.56
1988	Kristin Otto, Katrin Meissner, Daniela Hunger, Manuela Stellmach (Sabina Schulze, Heike Friedrich)	GDR	3:40.63 OR
		HOL	3:43.39
		USA	3:44.25
1992	Nicole Haislett, Dara Torres, Angelina Martino, Jennifer Thompson (Ashley Tappin, Christine Ahmann-Leighton)	USA	3:39.46 WR
		CHN	3:40.12
		GER	3:41.60
1996	Jenny Thompson, Catherine Fox, Angel Martino, Amy Van Dyken	USA	3:39.29 OR
		CHN	3:40.48
		GER	3:41.48

Swimming (continued)

Olympic 4 × 200m Freestyle Relay

Year	Medalists	Country	Time
1896–1992	event not held		
1996	Trina Jackson, Sheila Taormina, Cristina Teuscher, Jenny Thompson	USA	7:59.87
		GER	8:01.55
		AUS	8:05.47

Olympic 4 × 100m Medley Relay

Year	Medalists	Country	Time
1896–1956	event not held		
1960	Lynn Burke, Patty Kempner, Carolyn Schuler, S. Christine Von Saltza (Anne Warner, Carolyn Wood, Joan Spillane)	USA	4:41.1 WR
		AUS	4:45.9
		GDR/GER	4:47.6
1964	Cathy Ferguson, Cynthia Goyette, Sharon Stouder, Kathleen Ellis (Nina Harmar, Judith Reeder, Susan Pitt, Lillian "Pokey" Watson)	USA	4:33.9 WR
		HOL	4:37.0
		USSR	4:39.2
1968	Kaye Hall, Catie Ball, Ellie Daniel, Susan Pedersen (Jane Swagerty, Suzy Jones, Susan Shields, Jan Henne)	USA	4:26.3 OR
		AUS	4:30.0
		GER	4:36.4
1972	Melissa Belote, Catherine Carr, Deena Deardurff, Sandra Neilson (Susan Atwood, Judith Melick, Dana Shrader, Shirley Babashoff)	USA	4:20.75 WR
		GDR	4:24.91
		GER	4:26.46
1976	Ulrike Richter, Hannelore Anke, Andrea Pollack, Kornelia Ender (Birgit Treiber, Carola Nitschke, Rosemarie Gabriel)	GDR	4:07.95 WR
		USA	4:14.55
		CAN	4:15.22
1980	Rica Reinisch, Ute Geweniger, Andrea Pollack, Caren Metschuck (Sarina Hulsenbeck)	GDR	4:06.67 WR
		GBR	4:12.24
		USSR	4:13.61
1984	Theresa Andrews, Tracy Caulkins, Mary T. Meagher, Nancy Hogshead (Betsy Mitchell, Susan Rapp, Jenna Johnson, Carrie Steinseifer)	USA	4:08.34
		GER	4:11.97
		CAN	4:12.98
1988	Kristin Otto, Silke Horner, Birte Weigang, Katrin Meissner (Cornelia Sirch, Manuela Stellmach)	GDR	4:03.74 OR
		USA	4:07.90
		CAN	4:10.49
1992	Lea Loveless, N. Anita Nall, Christine Ahmann-Leighton, Jennifer Thompson (Elizabeth "Janie" Wagstaff, Megan Kleine, Summer Sanders, Nicole Haislett)	USA	4:02.54 WR
		GER	4:05.19
		USSR	4:06.44

SYNCHRONIZED SWIMMING

◆ *It looks so easy many don't consider it a sport—but maneuvering in nine feet of water without ever touching the bottom requires not only grace but a unique combination of aerobic and anaerobic strength.*

Although synchronized swimming was developed in the early years of the twentieth century, it has had a difficult time establishing itself as a serious sport. The first known public demonstration of "water ballet," as it was originally called, was performed by Australian swimmer **Annette Kellerman**[*] at the New York Hippodrome in 1907. The first American proponent of synchronized swim-

ming was Olympic champion **Eleanor Holm,** who performed at the New York World's Fair in 1939. She set the stage for **Esther Williams,** whose aquatic acrobatics were seen by millions of moviegoers around the world. Nevertheless, national competitions weren't organized until 1945, and international competition didn't begin for another decade.

A survey conducted on the eve of the 1996 Olympics revealed that numerous sports enthusiasts wished synchronized swimming—along with rhythmic gymnastics and a few other competitions—would simply go away. The enthusiasts didn't get their wish, but they did get a new approach to the sport. Solo and duet competitions, introduced at the 1984 Olympics, were dropped after 1992. In their place, team competition made its debut at the 1996 games. The move, de-

---

[*] The biographies of Kellerman, Holm, and Williams can be found under Swimming.

signed to earn respect for synchronized swimming, got off to an inauspicious start when the French team had to be told that its intended routine, depicting the arrival of Jewish women in concentration camps during World War II, was not considered appropriate.

Despite the bad press, the team strategy may eventually work. While synchronized swimming has thus far failed to ignite public passion, there's no reason why it can't. The French team's misstep in judgment was no tackier than Tonya Harding's attack on fellow skater Nancy Kerrigan, and thus far synchronized swimming has been free of the drug and steroid controversies that have plagued other sports. The chief criticism leveled against synchronized swimming—that it's too "pretty" to be taken seriously—might just as easily be leveled at figure skating, diving, or dressage.

Unlike skating, whose difficult moves take place in midair, synchronized swimming purposely hides its difficult moves. A swimmer emerges from the water poised on the shoulders of two other swimmers who appear to be standing solidly on the pool's bottom. But the pose is an illusion—no one is touching bottom, and the women who form the solid base of the pyramid are actually treading water, making constant adjustments to maintain their seemingly fixed position. It's entirely possible that spectators may yet come to appreciate synchronized swimming, just

---

Major Events and Competitions

Pan American Games
World Aquatic Championships
FINA World Cup
Olympic Games

---

as they came to appreciate skating, gymnastics, basketball, and other sports that used to merit little more than a sigh of disinterest. To get on the map, synchronized swimming may need nothing more than a Carol Heiss, a Nadia Comaneci, or a Nancy Lieberman—and a golden moment when it all comes together.

Governing Bodies and Organizations

U.S. Synchronized Swimming
201 South Capitol Avenue, Suite 510
Indianapolis, Indiana 46225
Phone: 317/237-5700
Fax: 317/237-5705

FINA
Federation Internationale de Natation Amateur
Avenue de Beaumont 9
1012 Lausanne, Switzerland

---

* * * BIOGRAPHIES * * *

CANDY COSTIE b. March 12, 1963, Seattle, Washington

Costie began performing with partner **Tracie Ruiz** in 1975 and with her had a spectacular career in duet events. Together the two set the tone for American synchronized swim, creating a powerful, athletic, and seamless style. Their years of hard work together were rewarded with a gold medal in the first Olympic duet ever held.

Selected championships and honors: Gold medal, duet, Olympic Games, 1984.

BECKY DYROEN LANCER b. February 19, 1971, San Jose, California

With nine gold medals in solo and duet competitions, no woman has won more international competitions than Becky Dyroen, a strong performer whose hobby is masters competitive swimming, and whose hallmark has become flawless execution. In the course of qualifying for the 1996 Olympic team, she scored perfect 10s—the first ever awarded in the sport. Though Dyroen's younger sister, Suzannah Bianco, is also a synchronized swimmer, the two have never paired together. Dyroen's partner in all of her four duet wins has been Jill Sudduth. All three women were on the U.S. team that competed at the 1996 Olympics.

Selected championships and honors, solo: Gold medal, World Aquatic Championships, 1994; two gold medals,

FINA World Cup, 1993 and '95; two gold medals, Pan American Games, 1991 and '95. *Duet:* Gold medal, World Aquatic Championships, 1994; two gold medals, FINA World Cup, 1993 and '95; gold medal, Pan American Games, 1995. *Team:* Gold medal, Olympic Games, 1996.

KAREN AND SARAH JOSEPHSON b. January 10, 1964, Bristol, Connecticut

Identical twins, the Josephsons began working together at the age of eight. Giving the lie to the notion that synchronized swimming is a lightweight endeavor, their training program included distance and interval swimming, weight training, yoga, and dance. After finishing behind Michelle Cameron and Carolyn Waldo in the 1988 Olympics, they entered the 1992 Games with fifteen straight victories behind them—and added a gold medal to make their winning streak sixteen.

Selected championships and honors, duet: Gold medal, Pan American Games, 1987; silver medal, Olympic Games, 1988; gold medal, World Aquatic Championships, 1991; gold medal, FINA World Cup, 1991; gold medal, Olympic Games, 1992.

TRACIE RUIZ-CONFORTO b. February 4, 1963, Honolulu, Hawaii

Both as a soloist and in duet, Ruiz was one of the most successful synchronized swimmers in history. In major international competitions she won both solo and duet competitions, in which she paired with **Candy Costie.**

Selected championships and honors, solo: Gold medal, World Aquatic Championships, 1982; two gold medals, Pan American Games, 1983 and '87; gold medal, Olympic Games, 1984; silver medal, Olympic Games, 1988. *Duet:* Gold medal, Pan American Games, 1983; gold medal, Olympic Games, 1984.

CAROLYN WALDO b. December 11, 1964, Kanata, Ontario, Canada

Synchronized swimming has been dominated by two countries—the United States and Canada—with the women of Japan poised to make a three-way competition for the gold. The dominant Canadian performer of the 1980s, both in solo and duet events, was undoubtedly Waldo. With partner Michelle Cameron, also of Canada, Waldo won four gold medals in major international competitions. Alone, she won four golds and a silver. Waldo's toughest competitor was America's Tracie Ruiz—just as Ruiz's toughest competitor was Waldo. At the 1984 Olympics, Waldo finished behind Ruiz in solo competition. At the 1988 games they reversed the order.

1996 Gold Medal Olympic Team USA

In 1996 the Olympics dispensed with solo and duet synchronized swimming events in favor of teams. Although there may seem to be safety in numbers, team competition is actually considered the most difficult form of the sport, since eight women in the water at one time multiplies the need for precision and vastly expands the possibility of error. In solo events, a competitor can cover a mistake with an improvised move. In duet, partners are often able to compensate for each other's errors. In team competition there's no such cover. Going into the 1996 games, the U.S. team had been ranked number one for five straight years, and all members had been on the team for six or more years. All but one of the women were Californians, as were co-coaches Chris Carver and Gail Emery. The lone "alien," Emily Porter LeSeuer, hailed from Mesa, Arizona. As they performed their gold-medal-winning routine, the commentator stated the obvious: the women of the U.S. team had taken the sport to a whole new level. Women who raised the bar included:

Suzannah Bianco
Tammy Cleland
Becky Dyroen Lancer
Heather Pease
Emily Porter LeSeuer
Jill Savery
Natalie Schneyder
Heather Simmons Carrasco
Jill Sudduth
Margot Thien

Selected championships and honors, solo: Two gold medals, FINA World Cup, 1985 and '87; silver medal, Olympic Games, 1984; gold medal, World Aquatic Championships, 1986; gold medal, Olympic Games, 1988. *Duet:* Two gold medals, FINA World Cup, 1985 and '87; gold medal, World Aquatic Championships, 1986; gold medal, Olympic Games, 1988.

Synchronized Swimming

Olympic Solo

Year	Gold	Silver	Bronze
1984	Tracie Ruiz/USA	Carolyn Waldo/CAN	Miwako Motoyoshi/ JPN
1988	Carolyn Waldo/CAN	Tracie Ruiz-Conforto/USA	Mikako Kotani/JPN
1992*	Kristen Babb-Sprague/USA Sylvie Frechette/CAN		Fumiko Okuna/JPN

Olympic Duet

Year	Gold	Silver	Bronze
1984	Candy Costie/Tracie Ruiz/ USA	Sharon Hambrook/ Kelly Kryczka/CAN	Saeko Simura/ Miwako Motoyoshi/ JPN
1988	Michelle Cameron/ Carolyn Waldo/CAN	Sarah & Karen Josephson/USA	Miyako Tanaka/ Mikako Kotani/JPN
1992	Karen & Sarah Josephson/USA	Penny & Vicky Vilagos/CAN	Fumiko Okuno/ Aki Takayama/JPN

Olympic Team

1996	USA	CAN	JPN
	Suzannah Bianco	Christine Larsen	Miya Tachibana
	Tammy Cleland	Karen Clark	Akiko Kawase
	Becky Dyroen Lancer	Valerie Hould Marchand	Rei Jimbo
	Emily Le Sueur	Sylvie Frechette	Miho Takedo
	Heather Pease	Janice Bremner	Kaori Takahashi
	Jill Savery	Karen Fonteyne	Raika Fuji
	Nathalie Schneyder	Erin Woodley	Junko Tanaka
	Heather Simmons Carrasco	Cari Read	Riho Nakajima
	Jill Sudduth	Kasia Kulesga	Miho Kawabe
	Margot Thien	Lisa Alexander	Mayoko Fujiki

* Disputed scoring for gold.

International Competitions World Aquatic Championships

Year	Solo	Duet	Team
1973	Teresa Andersen/USA	Teresa Andersen/Gail Johnson/USA	USA
1975	Gail Johnson/USA	Robin Curren/Amanda Norriah/USA	USA
1978	Helen Vanderburg/CAN	Calkins/Helen Vanderburg/CAN	USA
1982	Tracie Ruiz/USA	Sharon Hambrook/Kelly Kryczka/CAN	CAN
1986	Carolyn Waldo	Carolyn Waldo/Michelle Cameron/CAN	CAN
1991	Sylvie Frechette/CAN	Karen & Sarah Josephson/USA	USA
1994	Becky Dyroen-Lancer/USA	Becky Dyroen-Lancer/Jill Sudduth/USA	USA

International Competitions FINA World Cup

Year	Solo	Duet	Team
1985	Carolyn Waldo/CAN	Carolyn Waldo/Michelle Cameron/CAN	CAN
1987	Carolyn Waldo/CAN	Carolyn Waldo/Michelle Cameron/CAN	USA
1989	Tracy Long/USA	Tracy Long/Michelle Svitenko/USA	USA
1991	Sylvie Frechette/CAN	Karen & Sarah Josephson/USA	USA
1993	Becky Dyroen-Lancer/USA	Becky Dyroen-Lancer/Jill Sudduth/USA	USA
1995	Becky Dyroen-Lancer/USA	Becky Dyroen-Lancer/Jill Sudduth/USA	USA

Synchronized Swimming (continued)

International Competitions Pan American Games

	Solo	Duet	Team
1955	Beulah Gundling/USA	E. Richard/Connie Todoroff/USA	USA
1959	Demonstration Sport (USA only)		
1963	Roberta Armstrong/USA	B. Burke/J. Schaack/USA	USA
1967	Demonstration Sport (CAN only)		
1971	Heidi O'Rourke/USA	J. Lang/Heidi O'Rourke/USA	USA
1975	Gail Johnson Buzonas/USA	Robin Curren/Amanda Norriah/USA	USA
1979	Helen Vanderburg/CAN	Kelly Kryszka/Helen Vanderburg/CAN	USA
1983	Tracie Ruiz/USA	Candy Costie/Tracie Ruiz/USA	CAN
1987	Tracie Ruiz-Conforto/USA	Karen & Sarah Josephson/USA	USA
1991	Becky Dyroen-Lancer/USA	D. Urlich/T. Harding	USA
1995	Becky Dyroen-Lancer/USA	Becky Dyroen-Lancer/Jill Sudduth/USA	USA

Photo credit: Ken Regan/Camera 5

DIVING

♦ *Though diving is always grouped with swimming because of its watery venue, it actually has more in common with gymnastics, from which it originated.*

HISTORY

The earliest display diving was probably performed in natural settings by local people—predominantly men—as an exhibition of skill and courage. And it was probably performed first by people living far outside the European culture loop. There is virtually no tradition of diving in any Western country before the eighteenth century. The early version of the sport, known as "plunging," consisted of a plain (swan) dive into the water below. The first organized diving championships, held in Europe, took place in 1893 and continued through 1937.

Diving took a decisive turn when the hot sport of the era—gymnastics—escaped its indoor confines and headed for the great outdoors. Eager to enjoy the brief, bright summer months, German and Swedish gymnasts moved their equipment to the beach. It didn't take long for someone to position the equipment over the water itself, a move that not only provided a built-in mat but greatly increased the acrobatic possibilities. No longer required to land on their feet, gymnasts found themselves tumbling, rotating, and spinning into the water. Gymnastic apparatus soon vanished, replaced by diving platforms and springboards.

They Did It First—and Often Best

Mary Ellen Clark. First woman to win U.S. Diving Athlete of the Year Award.
Georgia Coleman. First woman to complete a forward 2½ somersault.
Victoria Draves. First woman to win both golds at a single Olympics, 1948.
Marjorie Gestring. First thirteen-year-old to win a gold medal in Olympic diving, 1936.
Patty McCormick. First diver, man or woman, to win both golds at two consecutive Olympics. First (and only) female diver to win the Sullivan Award.
Dorothy Poynton Hill. First woman to win an Olympic medal at age thirteen—a silver in the 1928 springboard.
Aileen Riggin. First athlete, male or female, to win Olympic medals in both swimming and diving.

THE MODERN ERA

The first diving competition to be included as a women's Olympic event was platform diving. It made its debut in 1912, eight years after men's platform competition was included. The 3-meter springboard competition was added at the 1920 games, a dozen years after men's competition began. Today, while most other international competitions have also added a 1-meter springboard event, the Olympics steadfastly has not.

Throughout most of the twentieth century, American women and men have dominated Olympic diving, winning more than half of the available gold medals and producing the first diver ever to sweep both golds in two consecutive Olympics, **Pat Keller McCormick.** American Olympic dominance ended in 1976, with **Jennifer Chandler's** win in the 3-meter springboard. Beginning in the 1980s, the women to watch became the Chinese, who took the lead in Olympic as well as World Championship competitions.

While the elements of diving—board, height, and air—have not changed much over the years, the degree of athleticism has. At the 1912 Olympics diving consisted of a straightforward plunge into the water. Today, divers hoping to medal consider the reverse 3½ somersault a "must" in their repertoire. How much further the envelope can be pushed remains to be seen. Some suggest the limits have already been reached. But those same suggestions were made decades ago, with just as much certitude, only to be proved wrong. The definite new wrinkle in the sport is synchronized diving. Performed by pairs from a 3-meter platform, synchronized diving for women as well as men was added to several international competitions in the mid-1990s, though the Olympics was not one of them.

Hall of Fame

Women divers have been enshrined in the Olympic Hall of Fame, the International Women's Sports Hall of Fame, and the International Swimming Hall of Fame. Nearly half of the divers and diving coaches in the International Swimming Hall of Fame in Fort Lauderdale are women, a parity rare in the sports world. Two women, **Pat McCormick** and **Micki King,** can be found on all three honor roles.

Major Events and Awards

Olympic Games
World Championships
Diving World Cup
Pan American Games
U.S. Indoor Nationals
U.S. Outdoor Nationals

Individual Awards
U.S. Diving Athlete of the Year
World Diver of the Year

Governing Bodies and Organizations

U.S. Diving
Pan American Plaza
201 South Capital Avenue, Suite 430
Indianapolis, Indiana 46225
Phone: 317/237-5252
Fax: 317/237-5257

FINA
Federation Internationale de Natation Amateur
Avenue de Beaumont 9
1012 Lausanne, Switzerland

* * * BIOGRAPHIES * * *

ELIZABETH BECKER PINKSTON b. March 6, 1903, Philadelphia, Pennsylvania; d. April 6, 1988 With **Pat Keller McCormick,** Becker is one of only two women in Olympic history to win gold medals in both springboard and platform diving. A U.S. national indoor champion, Becker had a spectacular 1924 Olympics, winning the gold medal for springboard and the silver for platform diving. She also met diving medalist Clarence Pinkston, whom she married the following year and who retired from competition to become her coach. Becker won another national indoor title in 1926, the same year she gave birth to twins. At the 1928 Olympics, Becker won a second gold medal, this time for the platform event.
Selected championships and honors: Four national championships, 3-meter springboard, 1922–24 and '26; gold medal, springboard, Olympic Games, 1924; silver medal, platform, Olympic Games, 1924; gold medal, platform, Olympic Games, 1928; International Swimming Hall of Fame.

SYLVIE BERNIER b. January 31, 1964, Rosmere, Quebec, Canada
Bernier, who'd never won a major international competition, wasn't expected to medal in the 1984 Olympic springboard competition. The Americans and Chinese were expected to sweep the medals, and Bernier was noted for choking under pressure. To ease her jitters, she refused to follow the standings during the event, blotting out the PA system by listening to the sound track from *Flashdance* on her walkman. Only after her final dive did she learn she was in first place—and the winner of a gold medal.
Selected championships and honors: Gold medal, springboard, Olympic Games, 1984.

LESLEY BUSH b. September 17, 1947, Orange, New Jersey

Bush was a virtual unknown with no national championships when she represented the United States at the 1964 Olympics. Germany's **Ingrid Kramer Engel** was favored to win, but Bush went ahead of her on the first dive and held the lead on successive dives to capture the gold. She came home to win several indoor and outdoor championships, and won a gold at the 1967 Pan American Games. She failed to win a medal at the 1968 Olympics and retired shortly afterward.
Selected championships and honors: Three National Championships, platform, 1965, '67, '68; two National Championships, springboard, 1967, '68; gold medal, platform, Olympic Games, 1964; gold medal, platform, Pan American Games, 1967; International Swimming Hall of Fame.

JENNIFER CHANDLER JONES b. June 13, 1959, Langdale, Alabama
No one really expected Chandler, holder of two national indoor titles, to beat East German world champion Christine Koehler in the springboard event at the 1976 Olympics. But Chandler had a superb first dive and hung on to take the gold. Although injuries forced her into early retirement from competition, Chandler went on to work as a diving commentator on television.
Selected championships and honors: Six national championships, springboard, 1974–78; gold medal, springboard, Pan American Games, 1975; gold medal, springboard, Olympic Games, 1976; bronze medal, 3m springboard, World Championships, 1978; International Swimming Hall of Fame.

CHI BIN b. China
With teammate **Fu Mingxia,** Chi is one of the top platform divers of the 1990s, and a major part of the Chinese rise to supremacy. A medalist at World

Championship as well as World Cup competitions, Chi also won the platform event at the FINA/USA Diving Grand Prix in 1994. That same year, Chi set an unofficial record for highest-scoring platform performance at a single meet, racking up 516.31 points on eight dives at the China Open.

Selected championships and honors: Silver medal, platform, World Championships, 1994; two gold medals, platform, World Cup, 1993 and '95.

MARY ELLEN CLARK b. December 25, 1962, Abington, Pennsylvania

A force in contemporary American diving, Clark managed a solid career despite bouts of vertigo in 1988, '90, and '95. At the 1992 Olympics she won the bronze in platform diving to become, at age twenty-nine, the oldest American woman to win an Olympic diving medal. In an era of single-event specialization, Clark has been a remarkably versatile diver, sweeping all three events at the 1994 U.S. Indoor Nationals. The next year her dizziness became so severe she missed the entire season. Tough and determined, Clark made the 1996 Olympic team and won another bronze to become, at thirty-three, the oldest diver ever to medal in the Olympics.

Selected championships and honors: Two national championships, springboard, 1994; five national championships, platform, 1987, '92–94; two bronze medals, platform, Olympic Games, 1992 and '96; two-time U.S. Diving Athlete of the Year, 1993 and '94.

STEFANIE CLAUSEN FRYLAND b. Denmark

Clausen competed against fourteen other women to win a gold medal in platform diving at the 1920 Olympic Games. Among the competitors was American **Aileen Riggin,** who won that year's springboard gold but could only manage a fifth-place finish in platform.

Selected championships and honors: Gold medal, platform, Olympic Games, 1920.

GEORGIA COLEMAN b. January 23, 1912, St. Maries, Idaho; d. September 14, 1940

When Coleman won her first Olympic medals, at the 1928 games, she had been diving all of six months. Four years later she came back for two more, including a gold. What Coleman lacked in experience she made up for in athleticism, and she is the first woman to do a 2½ forward somersault in competition. She also won eleven national championships between 1929 and 1932. Coleman died at age twenty-eight, as an aftermath of polio contracted three years earlier.

Selected championships and honors: Seven national championships, springboard, 1929–32; three national championships, platform, 1929–31; two silver medals, platform, Olympic Games, 1928 and '32; bronze medal, springboard, Olympic Games, 1928; gold medal, springboard, Olympic Games, 1932; International Swimming Hall of Fame.

HELEN CRIENKOVICH MORGAN b. United States

A versatile diver who won national titles in both springboard and platform events, Crienkovich would have been a world contender had not World War II called a halt to international competition. As it was, Crienkovich had to settle for competing against fellow American and springboard champion **Ann Ross.** It was a fine rivalry, with Crienkovich taking seven 3-meter springboard championships and Ross taking five between 1939 and 1945.

Selected championships and honors: Seven U.S. Indoor National championships, springboard, 1939–42, '45; two national championships, platform, 1941, '45; International Swimming Hall of Fame.

MILENA DUCHKOVÁ b. 1952, Czechoslovakia

Czechoslovakia had never won a medal in diving when sixteen-year-old Duchková represented her country at the 1968 Olympic Games. The platform finals took on added drama as diminutive, sixteen-year-old Duchková battled for the lead with Natalya Lobanova of the Soviet Union. Months earlier the Soviet Union had occupied Duchková's country, and the partisan crowd cheered when she went ahead of Lobanova on her last two dives to win the gold. Duchková won a second Olympic medal, a silver in platform, at the 1972 Olympics, and remains the only Czech ever to medal in the sport.

Selected championships and honors: Gold medal, platform, Olympic Games, 1968; silver medal, platform, Olympic Games, 1972.

JANET ELY THORBURN b. United States

In contrast to the many excellent divers who won more often at home than in international competitions, Ely is best remembered for her international performances. Holder of three silver medals won at the Pan American Games of 1975 and '79, Ely's biggest day came at the World Championship finals in 1975. Diving against reigning world champion **Ulrike Knape,** Ely turned in a spectacular series of dives to bring America its first-ever World Championship gold.

Selected championships and honors: Three national championships, platform, 1972, '74, '75; gold medal, platform, World Championships, 1975; silver medal, 3m springboard, Pan American Games, 1979; two silver medals, platform, Pan American Games, 1975 and '79.

JANE FAUNTZ b. December 19, 1910
A spectacular diver in the age before television, Fauntz is often overlooked because her name only makes two appearances in the record books, as the winner of the U.S. Indoor Nationals on the 1-meter springboard in 1929 and '30. Unfortunately for Fauntz, the 1-meter competition was slow to catch on, and to this day has yet to be included as an Olympic event. At the time Fauntz competed, the Indoor Nationals were literally the only game in town.
Selected championships and honors: Two U.S. Indoor National championships, springboard, 1929 and '30; International Swimming Hall of Fame

FU MINGXIA b. ca. 1979; China
Part of the "Chinese revolution" in world diving, Fu came to international attention in 1990, when—at age eleven—she took first place in platform diving at both the Goodwill Games and the FINA/USA Diving Grand Prix. The next year she won the World Championship, and the year after that she came home from her first Olympics with a gold medal. Originally a platform specialist, Fu competed in both the platform and 3-meter springboard in the 1996 Atlanta games. Fu's formula for success? Practice, practice, practice. Interviewed before the 1996 Olympics, Fu's coach said his pupil had been training a minimum of ten hours a day, packing more than a thousand board exercises into each practice session. Practice made her perfect, or nearly so. At the 1996 games she took golds in both the platform and springboard, becoming the only female diver since **Pat Keller McCormick** to win golds in two consecutive Olympiads, and the first since **Ingrid Kramer** (1980) to win both springboard and platform events.
Selected championships and honors: Two gold medals, platform, World Championships, 1991 and '94; two gold medals, platform, Olympic Games, 1992 and '96; silver medal, platform, World Cup, 1995; gold medal, springboard, Olympic Games, 1996.

GAO MIN b. Zigong, Sichuan Province, China
Arguably the greatest women's springboard diver of the modern era, Gao burst on the international scene in 1986, when she won her first World Championship. For the next six years, until her retirement in 1992, she was undefeated in international competition, winning three World Championships, two World Cups, and two Olympic golds. In 1988 Gao became the first woman to break the 600-point barrier in diving, a feat she performed three times that year. Her highest score—614.07 points on ten dives at that year's Dive Canada—remains a record for women's springboard competition. Gao's reign might have ended there, as shoulder injuries and recurrent pain threatened her 1992 Olympic performance. Despite the pain, Gao went ahead on her sixth dive and won by an even larger margin than she had in 1988. Gao also won two 3-meter FINA/USA Grand Prix springboard championships, in 1988 and '92.
Selected championships and honors: Two gold medals, 3m springboard, World Championships, 1986 and '91; two gold medals, 3m springboard, World Cup, 1987 and '89; two gold medals, springboard, Olympic Games, 1988 and '92; gold medal, 1m springboard, World Championships, 1991.

MARJORIE GESTRING b. November 18, 1922, Los Angeles, California
Three months short of her fourteenth birthday, Gestring became the youngest person ever to win an Olympic gold medal, an honor she still retains. She won the springboard event at the 1936 games, and might well have captured more medals had World War II not curtailed international competitions. At home Gestring won several national championships in both springboard and platform diving.
Selected championships and honors: Six U.S. Outdoor National championships, 3m springboard, 1936–38, '40; two national championships, platform, 1939, '40; gold medal, springboard, Olympic Games, 1936; International Swimming Hall of Fame.

SUE GOSSICK b. November 12, 1947, Chicago, Illinois
Gossick specialized in the 3-meter springboard, winning her first national championship in 1966. Diving for the United States at the 1964 Olympics, she narrowly missed a medal and finished fourth. The story was similar at the 1968 games, but this time Gossick was on the winning end. Russian diver Tamara Pogosheva led after seven rounds, had a bad eighth dive, and barely struggled back to win the silver, leaving Gossick the gold.

How to Bronze a Baby Shoe: Juno Stover Irwin

Among other things, diving requires impeccable balance and a daily willingness to tumble through the air—skills not usually associated with pregnancy. When American platform diver Juno Stover Irwin became pregnant with her second child in the spring of 1952, she continued to train, hoping for a berth on the Helsinki-bound Olympic team. She got her chance and, three and a half months pregnant, dove well enough to win the bronze medal, finishing ahead of a dozen nonpregnant competitors. Four years later, as a twenty-eight-year-old mother of three, she returned to win the silver.

Selected championships and honors: Three national championships, 3m springboard, 1966 and '67; gold medal, 3m springboard, Pan American Games, 1967; gold medal, springboard, Olympic Games, 1968; International Swimming Hall of Fame.

MARGARETA (GRETA) JOHANSON b. 1895, Sweden

The first Olympic diving medal, for platform, went to Johanson, whose stiffest competition came from her own countrywomen. Of the top eight finishers that year, only British bronze medalist Isobel White wasn't Swedish.

Selected championships and honors: Gold medal, platform, Olympic Games, 1912.

PATRICIA (PAT) KELLER McCORMICK b. May 12, 1930, Seal Beach, California

Few people know McCormick by her maiden name, Keller, because she was already married by the time she won her first national title in 1949. It was the first of many wins for McCormick, who won a silver at the Pan American Games two years later, and the year after that became the first woman to sweep both diving golds at a single Olympics. Though McCormick continued to win U.S. championships, she was far from a shoo-in for a medal at the 1956 Olympics. She was twenty-six and had had a baby just eight months before. She won the springboard handily but was in a close three-way contest for the platform finals. McCormick later recalled telling herself, "You can't go out now after so many years of hard work without a fight." She did fight—by performing two of the best dives of her life. Her final gold made her the first diver in history to sweep golds at two consecutive Olympics. McCormick's success came through a combination of grueling practice and gutsy risk-taking. Her training schedule called for eight hours a day, six days a week, twelve months a year. In her choice of dives, McCormick eschewed "pretty" acrobatics in favor of difficult and challenging dives, the kind done by men—but seldom by women—of her day. Such ambition had its price. When a doctor examined McCormick in 1951, he found healed fractures and lacerations, a loosened jaw, and fresh welts and bruises on her back, arms, and legs. None of these were of particular concern to McCormick, who only wanted help for the exhaustion caused by her 100-dive-a-day schedule. Although McCormick retired from competitive diving after the 1956 Olympics, she has remained a superstar whose name is synonymous with American diving. When the International Swimming Hall of Fame was established in 1965, she and **Katherine Rawls** were chosen as inaugural inductees. She participated in the opening ceremonies of the 1984 Olympics as a member of the U.S. flag escort—the same games at which her daughter, **Kelly McCormick,** won a silver medal in springboard competition.

Selected championships and honors: Sixteen national championships, springboard, 1950–56; three national championships, platform, 1949–51, '54, '56; silver medal, 3m springboard, Pan American Games, 1951; two gold medals, platform, Pan American Games, 1951 and '55; gold medal, 3m springboard, Pan American Games, 1955; two gold medals, springboard, Olympic Games, 1952 and '56; two gold medals, platform, Olympic Games, 1952 and '56; Associated Press Female Athlete of the Year, 1956; Sullivan Award, 1956; International Women's Sports Hall of Fame; International Swimming Hall of Fame; Olympic Hall of Fame.

MAXINE (MICKI) KING b. July 26, 1944, Pontiac, Michigan

King began diving as a child and was an all-American water polo goalie in college when her coach urged her to take up diving again. With national titles in springboard as well as platform events, King was favored to medal in the 1968 Olympics. She led the competition after eight dives, but on her ninth, attempting a reverse 1½ somersault, she broke her arm on the board. Although she returned to perform her tenth dive, she finished in fourth place. King returned to diving as soon as her arm healed, winning the 3-meter FINA/USA Diving Grand Prix in 1970. Two years later she got another chance to win an Olympic medal at the 1972 Munich games. Again she led after eight dives, and again she chose a reverse 1½ for her ninth dive. This time she executed perfectly, kept the lead, and won the gold. King retired after the Munich games but remained a powerhouse in diving as well as women's sports. An air force officer, she became the first woman ever to coach at the Air Force Academy and was a founding member of the Women's Sports Foundation.

Selected championships and honors: Six national championships, 3m springboard, 1965, '67, '69, and '70–72; three National Championships, platform, 1965, '69, and '71; two silver medals, 3m springboard, Pan American Games, 1967 and '71; International Swimming Hall of Fame; Women's Sports Hall of Fame; Olympic Hall of Fame.

ULRIKE KNAPE b. April 26, 1955, Karlskoga, Sweden

Better known in Europe than in the United States, Knape came to American attention when she took first place in both springboard and platform events at the FINA/USA Grand Prix in 1972. Later that year she won gold and silver medals at the 1972 Olympics, a feat she repeated at the first World Championships the following year. In four brief years (1972–76) Knape won three Olympic and three World Championships medals, as well as six FINA/USA Grand Prix championships. Her daughter Anna Lindberg also became a diver and at age fourteen, was a finalist at the 1996 Olympic Games.

Selected championships and honors: Gold medal, platform, Olympic Games, 1972; silver medal, springboard, Olympic Games, 1972; gold medal, platform, World Championships, 1973; silver medal, 3m springboard, World Championships, 1973; bronze medal, platform, World Championships, 1975; silver medal, platform, Olympic Games, 1976; International Swimming Hall of Fame.

INGRID KRAMER ENGEL GULBIN b. July 29, 1943, Dresden, Germany

In the United States, Kramer is remembered as the woman who broke the "golden chain" of American Olympic dominance. She did it by winning both the springboard and platform events at the 1960 Olympics in Rome. Four years later, diving under her married name, she returned for two more medals, one gold and one silver. A superb diver, Kramer's best performance was reputed to have come at the 1962 European championships, where she won both events with the most spectacular dives of her career. Kramer also competed at the 1968 Olympics, managing only a fifth-place finish on the springboard.

Selected championships and honors: Two gold medals, springboard, Olympic Games, 1960 and '64; gold medal, platform, Olympic Games, 1960; silver medal, platform, Olympic Games, 1964.

VICTORIA MANOLO DRAVES b. December 31, 1924, San Francisco, California

Manolo became the first woman to win both Olympic golds in diving, but to do it she had to overcome a formidable roadblock—prejudice. Her surname barred her, as the daughter of a Filipino father, from swim clubs of the time, a problem that ended when she married coach Lyle Draves and adopted his irreproachably neutral surname. Primarily a platform diver, Draves won gold medals in both springboard and platform events at the 1948 Olympics, her last competition before retiring.

Selected championships and honors: Three national championships, platform, 1946–48; national championship, springboard, 1948; gold medal, platform, Olympic Games, 1948; gold medal, springboard, Olympic Games, 1948; International Swimming Hall of Fame.

KELLY McCORMICK b. February 13, 1960, Anaheim, California

McCormick was born four years after her mother retired from competitive diving and had the difficult task of diving in her mother's footsteps. Often criticized for being inconsistent, McCormick nevertheless won nine national titles, two Pan American golds, a World Cup bronze, and silver and bronze Olympic medals. In her ability to withstand unprecedented scrutiny with grace and good humor, McCormick demonstrated that she was at least as tough as her mother, **Pat Keller McCormick.**

Selected championships and honors: Silver medal, springboard, Olympic Games, 1984; two gold medals, 3m springboard, Pan American Games, 1983 and '87; nine national championships, springboard, 1979–82, '84, '85, '87, and '89; bronze medal, springboard,

> ## Me 'n' Mom
>
> She showed me her gold medals when I was a little girl. I made a bet with her that someday I'd make an Olympic team and win.
>
> —Kelly McCormick

Olympic Games, 1988; bronze medal, 3m springboard, World Cup, 1989.

PATRICIA McCORMICK. *See Patricia (Pat) Keller McCormick, above.*

HELEN MEANY b. December 15, 1904, New York City; d. July 21, 1991
Meany went to two Olympics (1920 and '24) before finally winning a medal in 1928, making her the first American diver to compete in three Olympics. Shortly after her Olympic victory, Meany performed in a Miami Beach water show with fellow champions Pete DesJardins and Johnny Weissmuller. The show wasn't sanctioned by the AAU, and Meany's appearance cost her her amateur status.
Selected championships and honors: Nine national championships, springboard, 1921, '22, and '25–28; five national championships, platform, 1921–23, '25, and '28; gold medal, springboard, Olympic Games, 1928; International Swimming Hall of Fame.

MICHELE MITCHELL ROCHA b. January 10, 1962, Tucson, Arizona
One of the best American platform divers of recent times, Mitchell managed two silver-medal performances against the formidable Chinese women at the 1984 and '88 Olympic Games. Her best performance, however, came at a 1985 McDonald's U.S.–China meet and was seen by relatively few people. Mitchell was near perfect that day, setting an American women's platform scoring record with 479.40 points on eight dives. She set another American record that day as well, for most points on a single dive. Her score of 92.80 was won on an inward 3½ somersault tuck. A versatile diver, Mitchell won national championships in all three events and won the FINA/USA Grand Prix platform championship three times, in 1983, '85, and '86.
Selected championships and honors: Two national championships, springboard, 1985, '86; six national championships, platform, 1983–87; two silver medals,

platform, Olympic Games, 1984 and '88; gold medal, platform, World Cup, 1985; gold medal, platform, Pan American Games, 1987; World Diver of the Year, women's platform, 1985; International Swimming Hall of Fame.

PAULA JEAN MYERS POPE b. November 11, 1934, LaVerne, California
Holder of eleven national championships, Myers medaled at three Olympics, winning her first just out of high school and her last as the married mother of two. In fact, her best years came as she matured. In 1959, the year before she retired, she took both golds at the Pan American Games. The next year, her final year of competition, she won double silvers at the Olympics. Myers's total of four Olympic medals is an impressive feat considering that she often dove against two of the best divers in history, **Pat Keller McCormick** and **Ingrid Kramer Engel.**
Selected championships and honors: Seven national championships, springboard, 1953, '57, and '58; four national championships, platform, 1953, '57–'59; two silver medals, platform, Olympic Games, 1952 and '60; bronze medal, platform, Olympic Games, 1956; gold medal, 3m springboard, Pan American Games, 1959; gold medal, platform, Pan American Games, 1959; silver medal, springboard, Olympic Games, 1960; International Swimming Hall of Fame.

MEGAN NEYER b. United States
One of the best springboard divers of the 1980s, Neyer won a total of fifteen national titles in 1- and 3-meter events. Between 1981 and '88 she won five FINA/USA Grand Prix springboard competitions, taking two 1-meter competitions (1987 and '88) and three 3-meters (1981, '82, and '86). Neyer is also the only American to have won a gold medal in World Championship springboard competition.
Selected championships and honors: Silver medal, 3m springboard, World Cup, 1981; gold medal, 3m springboard, World Championships, 1982; silver medal, 3m springboard, Pan American Games, 1987; fifteen national championships, springboard, 1981–84 and '86–88; World Diver of the Year, women's springboard, 1981 and '82.

ZOE ANN OLSEN JENSEN b. February 11, 1931, Stuart, Florida
Fourteen was a lucky number for Olsen, who won her first national titles at that age and ended up winning a total of fourteen national titles in springboard competitions. She also medaled at both the 1948 and '52

Olympics, the only female diver to do so. In 1949 Olsen married professional baseball player Jackie Jensen and began diving under her married name.
Selected championships and honors: Fourteen national championships, springboard, 1945–49; silver medal, springboard, Olympic Games, 1948; bronze medal, springboard, Olympic Games, 1952; International Swimming Hall of Fame.

CYNTHIA POTTER McINGVALE b. August 27, 1950, Houston, Texas
More than two decades after her retirement, Potter still holds the record for most national diving championships, with a total of twenty-eight, won in all three events. Her strongest event was the 1-meter springboard, in which she won seventeen of her titles. Potter might easily have won Olympic medals as well, had not bad luck dogged her international career. Favored to win a gold in 1972, she sustained a serious injury during a practice session and was able to place no higher than seventh. She won a bronze medal at the next games and was picked for the 1980 team that never dove due to the boycott. After retiring from competition, Potter coached for Southern Methodist University and the University of Arizona.
Selected championships and honors: Twenty-six national championships, springboard, 1968–78; two national championships, platform, 1970, '71; bronze medal, springboard, Olympic Games, 1976; bronze medal, 3m springboard, Pan American Games, 1975; silver medal, 3m springboard, World Championships, 1978; International Swimming Hall of Fame.

DOROTHY POYNTON HILL b. July 17, 1915, Salt Lake City, Utah
Poynton's competitive career began early—at age eleven, when she finished third in the national indoor 3-meter springboard championships. The next year she won her first Olympic medal, a springboard silver. She went on to compete in two more Olympics and win three more medals, including back-to-back springboard golds in 1932 and '36. Poynton won seven national titles and retired after the 1936 Olympics. She continued to promote her sport by giving exhibitions and operating an aquatic club in Los Angeles.
Selected championships and honors: Three national championships, platform, 1933–35; four national indoor championships, 1m springboard, 1933, '34, and '36; International Swimming Hall of Fame.

AILEEN RIGGIN SOULE b. May 2, 1906, Newport, Rhode Island

At 4'8" and 70 pounds, Riggin was predictably nicknamed Tiny, a monicker that belied her ultimate impact on American swimming and diving. She won her first Olympic medal, a gold, when she was just fourteen and added two more medals at the 1924 games, a diving silver and a bronze in the backstroke. Her double-medal performance made her the first person ever to medal in both swimming and diving. Riggins also won several national championships and starred in the first slow-motion and underwater coaching films ever made. She turned professional in 1926, diving in exhibitions, helping to organize Billy Rose's Aquacade, and even appearing in Hollywood musicals. She wrote numerous articles on diving and was one of the earliest women sportswriters in America. In her eighties she was still swimming and winning, setting age group records in masters competitions. Riggin celebrated her ninetieth birthday at her home in Hawaii in 1996.
Selected championships and honors: Four national championships, springboard, 1923–25; gold medal, springboard, Olympic Games, 1920; silver medal, springboard, Olympic Games, 1924; bronze medal, 100m backstroke, Olympic Games, 1924; International Women's Sports Hall of Fame; International Swimming Hall of Fame.

ANN ROSS b. November 28, 1923, Troy, New York
A seven-time U.S. springboard champion, Ross might well have become an international diving star had her career not exactly coincided with World War II. Winning her first national title in 1941 and her last three years later, Ross had retired by the time international competitions resumed after the war. Her diving was spectacular nonetheless, and Ross deserved far more recognition than she received.

CAROLINE SMITH b. July 21, 1906, Cairo, Illinois
Smith never won a national title, largely because her specialty—platform diving—wasn't an event during her career. Nevertheless, she was the first American woman to win an Olympic gold medal in the event, placing first at the 1924 games. Her teammate **Elizabeth Becker** took the silver. Smith's win was a harbinger of things to come. America won the event in each of the next seven Olympiads, always taking the gold and silver and twice (in 1932 and '56) taking gold, silver, and bronze.
Selected championships and honors: Gold medal, platform, Olympic Games, 1924; International Swimming Hall of Fame.

ELENA VAYTSEHOVSKAYA b. ca. 1958, Moscow, Russia

Vaytsehovskaya wasn't expected to medal at the 1976 Montreal Olympics. Sweden's Ulrika Knape had dominated international competition for the past four years and was still strong. Vaytsehovskaya, in fifth place midway through the competition, executed her fifth dive, a backward 2½ piked somersault, almost flawlessly and jumped to first place. The lead was enough to carry her through the last rounds, and she finished four points ahead of Knape.

Selected championships and honors: Gold medal, platform, Olympic Games, 1976.

HELEN WAINWRIGHT. *See entry under Swimming.*

WENDY LIAN WILLIAMS b. United States

A specialist in platform diving, Williams swept indoor and outdoor national platform titles in '88 and '90. Williams also won medals in numerous international competitions, including bronzes at the '88 Olympics and '91 World Championships. She took top platform honors at the 1989 World Cup and was named women's platform World Diver of the Year.

Selected championships and honors: Bronze medal, platform, Olympic Games, 1988; gold medal, platform, World Cup, 1989; bronze medal, platform, World Championships, 1991; two national indoor championships, platform, 1988 and '90; two national outdoor championships, platform, 1988 and '90; World Diver of the Year, women's platform, 1989.

WENDY WYLAND b. United States

Along with **Janet Ely,** Wyland is one of only two American women to win a gold medal in World Championship platform diving. A specialist in platform events, Wyland medaled in numerous international competitions, holds seven national platform titles, and won the FINA/USA Grand Prix in platform in 1984.

Selected championships and honors: Six national championships, platform, 1981–84, '89; bronze medal, platform, World Cup, 1981; gold medal, platform, World Championships, 1982; gold medal, platform, Pan American Games, 1983; bronze medal, platform, Olympic Games, 1984; two-time World Diver of the Year, women's platform, 1982 and 83.

XU YANMEI b. 1971, China

Xu, a platform dynamo, was favored to win the gold medal easily at the 1988 Olympics. But with just one dive left to go, she led American **Michele Mitchell** by only .27 of a point. For her final dive, Xu performed an excellent back 2½ pike, while Mitchell did a forward 3½ tuck and lost points on a less-than-perfect entry. The final round gave Xu the gold by a slim seven-point margin.

Selected championships and honors: Gold medal, platform, World Championships, 1988; gold medal, platform, Olympic Games, 1988; bronze medal, platform, World Championships, 1989.

ZHOU JIHONG b. 1965, Hubei Province, China

Zhou was nineteen when she competed in the Barcelona Olympics in 1992, though—at 5'1" and just 92 pounds—she looked younger than her years when balanced on the edge of a platform. A diver who fought off jitters by listening to piano concertos on her Walkman between dives, Zhou finished ahead of Americans **Michele Mitchell** and **Wendy Wyland** to take the gold.

Selected championships and honors: Gold medal, platform, World Championships, 1983; gold medal, platform, Olympic Games, 1984.

Diving

US Olympic Hall of Fame

Year	Inductee
1985	Pat McCormick
1992	Micki King

International Swimming Hall of Fame

1965	Pat McCormick
	Katherine Rawls
1966	Georgia Coleman
1967	Elizabeth Becker Pinkston
	Aileen Riggin Soule
1968	Dorothy Poynton
1969	Victoria Draves
1971	Helen Meany
	Helen Wainwright
1976	Marjorie Gestring
1978	Micki King
1979	Paula Jean Meyers Pope
1981	Helen Crienkovich
1984	Ann Ross
1986	Lesley Bush
1987	Jennifer Chandler
	Cynthia Potter
1988	Caroline Smith
	Sue Gossick
1989	Zoe-Ann Olsen
1991	Jane Fauntz
1995	Michele Mitchell-Rocha

Diving (continued)

International Women's Sports Hall of Fame

1983	Micki King
1984	Pat McCormick
1988	Aileen Riggin Soule

Olympic 3m Springboard

Year	Medalists	Country
1896–1912	event not held	
1920	Aileen Riggin	USA
	Helen Wainwright	USA
	Thelma Payne	USA
1924	Elizabeth Becker	USA
	Aileen Riggin	USA
	Caroline Fletcher	USA
1928	Helen Meany	USA
	Dorothy Poynton	USA
	Georgia Coleman	USA
1932	Georgia Coleman	USA
	Katherine Rawls	USA
	Jane Fauntz	USA
1936	Marjorie Gestring	USA
	Katherine Rawls	USA
	Dorothy Poynton Hill	USA
1948	Victoria Draves	USA
	Zoe Ann Olsen	USA
	Patricia Elsener	USA
1952	Patricia McCormick	USA
	Madeleine Moreau	FRA
	Zoe Ann Jensen Olsen	USA
1956	Patricia McCormick	USA
	Jeanne Stunyo	USA
	Irene MacDonald	CAN
1960	Ingrid Kramer	GER
	Paula Jean Pope (Myers)	USA
	Elizabeth Ferris	GBR
1964	Ingrid Kramer Engel	GDR
	Jeanne Collier	USA
	Mary "Patsy" Willard	USA
1968	Sue Gossick	USA
	Tamara Pogosheva (Fyedosova)	RUS
	Keala O'Sullivan	USA
1972	Maxine "Micki" King	USA
	Ulrika Knape	SWE
	Marina Janicke	GDR
1976	Jennifer Chandler	USA
	Christa Kohler	GDR
	Cynthia Potter	USA
1980	Irina Kalinina	RUS
	Martina Proeber	GDR
	Karin Guthke	GDR
1984	Sylvie Bernier	CAN
	Kelly McCormick	USA
	Christina Seufert	USA
1988	Gao Min	CHN
	Li Qing	CHN
	Kelly McCormick	USA
1992	Gao Min	CHN
	Irina Lashko	RUS
	Brita Baldus	GER
1996	Fu Mingxia	CHN
	Irina Lashko	RUS
	Annie Pelletier	CAN

Olympic Platform Diving

1896–1908	event not held	
1912	Margareta Johanson	SWE
	Lisa Regnell	SWE
	Isobel White	GBR
1920	Stefanie Clausen	DEN
	B. Eileen Armstrong	GBR
	Eva Ollivier	SWE
1924	Caroline Smith	USA
	Elizabeth Becker	USA
	Hjördis Töpel	SWE
1928	Elizabeth Becker Pinkston	USA
	Georgia Coleman	USA
	Lala Sjöquist	SWE
1932	Dorothy Poynton	USA
	Georgia Coleman	USA
	Marion Roper	USA
1936	Dorothy Poynton Hill	USA
	Velma Dunn	USA
	Käthe Köhler	GER
1948	Victoria Draves	USA
	Patricia Elsener	USA
	Birte Christoffersen	DEN
1952	Patricia McCormick	USA
	Paula Jean Myers	USA
	Juno Irwin (Stover)	USA
1956	Patricia McCormick	USA
	Juno Irwin (Stover)	USA
	Paula Jean Myers	USA
1960	Ingrid Krämer	GER
	Paula Jean Pope Myers	USA
	Ninel Krutova	USSR
1964	Lesley Bush	USA
	Ingrid Kramer Engel	GDR
	Galina Alekseyeva	USSR
1968	Milena Duchková	CZE
	Natalya Lobanova (Kuznetsova)	USSR
	Ann Peterson	USA
1972	Ulrika Knape	SWE
	Milena Duchková	CZE
	Marina Janicke	GDR

Diving (continued)

Olympic Platform Diving

Year	Medalists	Country
1976	Elena Vaytsehovskaya	USSR
	Ulrika Knape	SWE
	Deborah Wilson	USA
1980	Martina Jäschke	GDR
	Servard Emirzyan	ARM
	Liana Tsotadze	GEO
1984	Zhou Jihong	CHN
	Michele Mitchell	USA
	Wendy Wyland	USA
1988	Xu Yanmei	CHN
	Michele Mitchell	USA
	Wendy Lian Williams	USA
1992	Fu Mingxia	CHN
	Yelena Miroshina	RUS
	Mary Ellen Clark	USA
1996	Fu Mingxia	CHN
	Annika Walter	GER
	Mary Ellen Clark	USA

World Championship 1m Springboard

Year	Champion	Country
1991	Gao Min	CHN
1994	Chen Lixia	CHN

World Championship 3m Springboard

1973	Christa Kohler	GDR
1975	Irina Kalinina	URS
1978	Irina Kalinina	URS
1982	Megan Neyer	USA
1986	Gao Min	CHN
1991	Gao Min	CHN
1994	Tan Shuping	CHN

World Championship Platform

1973	Ulrike Knape	SWE
1975	Janet Ely	USA
1978	Irina Kalinina	URS
1982	Wendy Wyland	USA
1986	L. Chen	CHN
1991	Fu Mingxia	CHN
1994	Fu Mingxia	CHN

World Cup 1m Springboard

1989	Gao Min	CHN
1991	Yu Xiaoling	CHN
1993	Tan Shuping	CHN
1995	Vera Ilyina	RUS

World Cup 3m Springboard

1979	Valerie McFarlane	AUS
1981	Shi Mei Qin	CHN
1983	Li Yihua	CHN
1985	Li Yihua	CHN
1987	Gao Min	CHN
1989	Gao Min	CHN
1991	Brita Baldus	GER
1993	Tan Shuping	CHN
1995	Fu Mingxia	CHN

World Cup 3m Synchronized

1995	Guo/Deng	CHN

World Cup Platform

1979	Irina Kalinina	URS
1981	Chen Xiao Xia	CHN
1983	Zhou Ji Hong	CHN
1985	Michele Mitchell	USA
1987	Xu Yanmei	CHN
1989	Wendy L. Williams	USA
1991	Elena Mirochina	URS
1993	Chi Bin	CHN
1995	Chi Bin	CHN

World Cup Platform Synchronized

1995	Guo/Deng	CHN

Pan American Games 1m Springboard

Year	Winner	Country
1991	A. Jill Schlabach	USA
1995	Mayte Garbey	CUB

Pan American Games 3m Springboard

1951	Mary Cunningham	USA
1955	Pat McCormick	USA
1959	Paula Pope	USA
1963	Barbara McAlister	USA
1967	Sue Gossick	USA
1971	Elizabeth Carruthers	CAN
1975	Jennifer Chandler	USA
1979	Denise Christensen	USA
1983	Kelly McCormick	USA
1987	Kelly McCormick	USA
1991	Karen LaFace	USA
1995	Annie Pelletier	CAN

Pan American Games Platform

1951	Pat McCormick	USA
1955	Pat McCormick	USA
1959	Paula Pope	USA
1963	Linda Cooper	USA
1967	Lesley Bush	USA
1971	Nancy Robertson	CAN
1975	Janet Nutter	CAN
1979	Barb Weinstein	USA
1983	Wendy Wyland	USA
1987	Michele Mitchell	USA
1991	Eileen Richetelli	USA
1995	Anne Montminy	CAN

Photo credit: Ken Regan/Cameras

GOLF

◆ *One of the oldest modern sports, golf is also—thanks to the LPGA—one of the first sports to provide women with professional career opportunities.*

HISTORY

Though most people associate golf with Scotland and Britain, the sport was very nearly an early casualty of the strife between the two nations. Scottish soldiers learned the game from Flemish soldiers early in the fifteenth century, and they soon became so devoted to the game that it interfered with military training. Since Scotland was almost continually at war with Britain at the time, such interference was not to be tolerated, and golf was banned by successive acts of the Scottish parliament. The last ban, enacted under James IV, was lifted when Britain and Scotland signed a peace treaty in 1502. Shortly after the ban was lifted, James himself ordered a set of clubs from a bow maker in Perth. Golf flourished in England as well, becoming so popular that a scant decade after the treaty Queen Catherine mentioned it in a letter to Cardinal Wolsey.

Exactly when women took up the clubs is not known. Mary Queen of Scots and Catherine of Aragon were both enthusiasts, and other women of the upper classes must have golfed as well. Two hundred years later, by the late 1700s, the sport had trickled down to the masses, and Scottish peasant women and commoners began golfing. The women of Scotland were especially eager to compete, and the Royal Musselburgh Golf Club of Scotland offered prizes to women

197

golfers as early as 1810. The first golf club known to include women, the North Berwick Club, was founded in 1832. In 1867 the Ladies' Golf Club, the first exclusively for women, was founded at St. Andrews, and two British women's clubs were formed the next year. By the end of the century one-third of all Scotland's golf club members were women. The end of the century also saw the formation of the Ladies' Golf Union in England and the initiation, in 1893, of a British women's amateur competition. In 1901 the Ladies' Golf Union was denied permission to hold a tournament at Scotland's St. Andrews golf course, but permission was granted just seven years later, marking the beginning of the British Women's Open.

Golf caught on in other English-speaking countries as well. In the United States the sport was popular enough to cause problems—in 1659 the city government of Albany, New York, stopped the practice of playing in the streets. The first U.S. Women's Amateur competition was held in 1895, and ten years later the women of Britain defeated an American team in international competition. In Australia the first national championships for women, held in 1894, actually preceded the first men's national by a year.

THE MODERN SCENE

Modern women's golf begins in 1908, at Princes Ladies Golf Course, when Mrs. Gordon Robinson becomes the first woman to make money playing. The rise of women's golf coincided with women's suffrage and the new emphasis on women's fitness, and the image of the lady pro golfer was sprinkled with the stardust of glamour and modernity. Sleek, healthy, and independent, a woman who could earn a living without resorting to the factory line, the sales counter, or the public schoolroom was clearly someone to be reckoned with. In F. Scott Fitzgerald's Jazz Age gem *The Great Gatsby,* golfer Jordan Baker is very much a part of the rich and glittering world of Long Island's Gold Coast. Yet Baker, like Gatsby himself, is also an ambivalent figure. If she is rich, she is also reckless and insensitive—

the kind of woman, Fitzgerald explains, who would borrow a car and leave the top down during a rainstorm. Her name is also ambivalent, a unisexual handle that stands in sharp relief to that of the novel's wiltingly feminine heroine and love object, Daisy Buchanan. In the character of Jordan Baker, Fitzgerald aptly captures the public's conflicted feelings toward the independent female athlete.

The first efforts to establish a professional tour for women began on the heels of World War II, when Hope Seignious, Betty Hicks, and Ellen Griffin founded the Women's Professional Golf Association (WPGA). The tour struggled along until the early 1950s, when it was replaced by the Ladies Professional Golf Association (LPGA). Although the LPGA eventually became one of the strongest and most successful women's sports organizations in the world, its early days were extremely tenuous. Tournaments were sparse, financial rewards minimal or nonexistent, and the founders—women like **Patty Berg, Betty Jameson,** and **Louise Suggs**—often had to set up and administer the same matches they played in, logging long hours for little reward. The biggest thing the fledgling tour had going for it was its players. Throughout the 1950s, stars like Berg, Jameson, and Suggs, along with **Babe Didrikson Zaharias** and **Betsy Rawls,** attracted a good deal of attention and, by the sheer excellence of their game, established the LPGA's credentials. The tour continued to draw attention when new stars—including **Mickey Wright** and **Kathy Whitworth**—joined the tour in the 1960s. The high quality of play created enough demand to interest television, and the final rounds of the LPGA tournament were first televised in 1963. Television gave the tour a healthy boost and a visibility that helped entice sponsors. During the 1960s the tour prize money neatly tripled, from $200,000 to $600,000. In 1975 the LPGA went big-time, switching from a player-run organization to a business concern and hiring its first commissioner. At each turn of the calendar, as the old guard retires, the LPGA has seen a fresh influx of talent. Few women's sports can boast such an unbroken chain of superstars, from Patty Berg in the 1950s to **Nancy Lopez** in the

ON PAR?

In 1950, Babe Didrikson Zaharias led the LPGA in season's winnings with earnings of $14,800. Forty years later, Beth Daniel was the season high leader with $863,758. Wow? Wow, you bet. An increase of almost $850,000 is nothing to sneeze at . . . but it isn't exactly the whole story, is it?

Season Money Leaders*

Year	Men's Tour	Winnings	Women's Tour	Winnings	+/– Differential
1950	Sam Snead	$ 35,759	Babe Didrikson	$ 14,800	$ –20,959
1951	Lloyd Mangrum	26,089	Babe Didrikson	15,087	–11,002
1952	Julius Boros	37,033	Betsy Rawls	14,505	–12,528
1953	Lew Worsham	34,002	Louise Suggs	19,816	–14,286
1954	Bob Toski	65,820	Patty Berg	16,011	–49,808
1955	Julius Boros	63,122	Patty Berg	16,492	–46,630
1956	Ted Kroll	72,836	Marlene Hagge	20,235	–52,601
1957	Dick Mayer	65,835	Patty Berg	16,272	–49,563
1958	Arnold Palmer	42,607	Beverly Hanson	12,639	–29,968
1959	Art Wall	53,158	Betsy Rawls	26,774	–26,384
	Decade Average Disparity				**$ –31,373**
1960	Arnold Palmer	75,263	Louise Suggs	16,892	–58,371
1961	Gary Player	64,540	Mickey Wright	22,236	–42,304
1962	Arnold Palmer	81,448	Mickey Wright	21,641	–59,807
1963	Arnold Palmer	128,230	Mickey Wright	31,269	–96,961
1964	Jack Nicklaus	113,284	Mickey Wright	29,800	–83,484
1965	Jack Nicklaus	140,752	Kathy Whitworth	26,658	–94,094
1966	Billy Casper	121,945	Kathy Whitworth	33,517	–88,428
1967	Jack Nicklaus	188,998	Kathy Whitworth	32,937	–156,061
1968	Billy Casper	205,169	Kathy Whitworth	48,379	–156,790
1969	Frank Beard	164,707	Carol Mann	49,152	–115,555
	Decade Average Disparity				**$ –79,579**
1970	Lee Trevino	157,038	Kathy Whitworth	30,235	–126,803
1971	Jack Nicklaus	244,490	Kathy Whitworth	41,181	–203,309
1972	Jack Nicklaus	320,542	Kathy Whitworth	65,063	–255,389
1973	Jack Nicklaus	308,362	Kathy Whitworth	82,864	–225,389
1974	Johnny Miller	353,022	JoAnne Carner	87,094	–265,928
1975	Jack Nicklaus	298,149	Sandra Palmer	76,374	–211,775
1976	Jack Nicklaus	266,439	Judy Rankin	150,734	–115,706
1977	Tom Watson	310,653	Judy Rankin	122,890	–187,763
1978	Tom Watson	362,429	Nancy Lopez	189,814	–172,615
1979	Tom Watson	462,646	Nancy Lopez	197,489	–265,157
	Decade Average Disparity				**$ –180,444**

---

*Rounded to the nearest dollar.

Continued on next page.

Year	Men's Tour	Winnings	Women's Tour	Winnings	+/– Differential
1980	Tom Watson	530,808	Beth Daniel	231,000	–299,808
1981	Tom Kite	375,699	Beth Daniel	206,998	–168,691
1982	Craig Stadler	446,462	JoAnne Carner	310,400	–136,062
1983	Hal Sutton	426,668	JoAnne Carner	291,404	–135,264
1984	Tom Watson	476,260	Betsy King	266,771	–209,489
1985	Curtis Strange	542,321	Nancy Lopez	416,472	–126,300
1986	Greg Norman	653,296	Pat Bradley	492,021	–161,275
1987	Curtis Strange	925,941	Ayako Okamoto	466,034	–459,907
1988	Curtis Strange	1,147,644	Sherri Turner	350,851	–796,793
1989	Tom Kite	1,395,278	Betsy King	654,132	–741,146
		Decade Average Disparity			**$ –323,473**
1990	Greg Norman	1,165,477	Beth Daniel	863,578	–301,899
1991	Corey Pavin	979,430	Pat Bradley	763,118	–216,312
1992	Fred Couples	1,344,188	Dottie Motchie	693,335	–650,853
1993	Nick Price	1,478,557	Betsy King	595,992	–552,565
1994	Nick Price	1,499,927	Laura Davies	687,201	–812,726
1995	Greg Norman	1,654,959	Annika Sorenstam	666,533	–988,425
		1990–95 Average Disparity			**$ –587,163**

1970s, **Beth Daniel** in the 1980s, and countless others. As golf becomes a more and more global sport and women from other countries offer hard competition to the traditionally dominant Americans, the chain is likely to glitter brighter than ever. As of 1996, the tour that began as a labor of love offered over $25 million in winnings.

Governing Bodies and Organizations

Ladies Professional Golf Association (LPGA)
2570 W. International Speedway Boulevard, Suite B
Daytona Beach, Florida 32114
Phone: 914/254-8800

U.S. Golf Association
Box 708 Golf House
Library Corner Road
Far Hills, New Jersey 07931-0708
Phone: 908/234-2300

Major Events and Competitions

The Grand Slam of Women's Golf
LPGA Championship
U.S. Women's Open
du Maurier Classic (formerly the Peter Jackson Classic)
Dinah Shore

Individual Awards
Vare Trophy
LPGA Player of the Year
LPGA Rookie of the Year

Halls of Fame

The LPGA Hall of Fame, located in Daytona Beach, Florida, is the only major all-women's hall of fame dedicated to a single sport in the United States. The World Golf Hall of Fame is located in Pinehurst, North Carolina.

MARGARET ABBOTT DUNNE b. June 15, 1878, Calcutta, India; d. June 10, 1955
Not only is Abbott, the first American woman to win an Olympic medal, unknown to most Americans, she herself never knew she'd won a medal. A socialite who was studying art in Paris in 1900, she entered a nine-hole golf tournament held there largely for fun. After her studies, she returned to the United States and married political satirist Finley Peter Dunne. Despite her protestations that she played only for amusement, Abbott in fact seems to have taken the game seriously. She sought coaching from top male amateurs, was a fierce competitor on the links, and was noted for her stylish—and effective—backswing. Neither she nor any of the other women in the Paris tournament knew they had taken part in an Olympic event, and only recently did research disclose that it was indeed on the program.
Selected championships and honors: Gold medal (awarded posthumously), Olympic Games, 1900.

AMY ALCOTT b. February 22, 1956, Kansas City, Missouri
As a mere teenager Alcott had the heady experience of breaking a record set by **Babe Didrikson Zaharias—** the women's course record at Pebble Beach, which Alcott took with a score of 70. Alcott turned pro in 1975, and consistent winning soon became her trademark. From her debut season onward, Alcott won at least one tournament a year and averaged 1.5 tournament wins per season. As of 1995 she ranked sixth on the all-time earnings list, with more than $3 million.
Selected championships and honors: Twenty-nine pro career wins, including du Maurier Classic, 1979, and U.S. Women's Open, 1980; three-time Dinah Shore winner, 1983, '88, and '91; Vare Trophy, 1980.

MARLENE BAUER HAGGE b. February 16, 1934, Eureka, South Dakota
A diminutive (5'2") player who developed an economical but powerful swing, Bauer earned her first amateur win at the Long Beach Boys Junior competition in 1944. In 1949, still an amateur champion, she was named Golfer of the Year and Associated Press Female Athlete of the Year. The next year she joined the LPGA and became the youngest member in its history. Bauer married and, as Marlene Hagge, won

the 1956 LPGA championship in a dramatic sudden-death playoff against **Patty Berg.** She finished in the top-ten earnings category in a total of eight seasons, and in 1971 she became the first woman to shoot 9 holes in 29 strokes, a record that stood for thirteen years.
Selected championships and honors: LPGA Championship, 1956; Associated Press Female Athlete of the Year, 1949; Golfer of the Year, 1949.

PATRICIA (PATTY) BERG b. February 13, 1918, Minneapolis, Minnesota
When Berg began quarterbacking for an all-boys neighborhood football squad, her parents persuaded her to switch to the more ladylike sport of golf. The next year Berg won the first of more than two dozen amateur tourneys. Despite the fact that there was no organized pro tour at the time, and only a handful of tournaments, Berg turned pro in 1940. She earned money giving workshops and clinics and had a contract with Wilson Sporting Goods, who manufactured golf clubs bearing her name. Sidelined by a car accident in 1941, Berg then joined the marines. Berg returned to golfing full-time after the war and won the first U.S. Women's Open. Over the next eleven years, Berg won over three dozen pro tournaments, was named Associated Press Female Athlete of the Year three times, received three Vare Trophies, and was the leading money winner in 1954, '55, and '57. With 57 career wins, she ranks third on the all-time win list, just behind **Kathy Whitworth** (88) and **Mickey Wright** (82). Even more important than Berg's wins were her pioneer efforts on behalf of women's golf. In 1948 she helped found the Ladies Professional Golf Association and served as the organization's first president. Berg is one of a handful of athletes to have an award created in her honor—the Patty Berg Award, established by the LPGA in 1979 to honor women who have made an outstanding contribution to the sport.
Selected championships and honors: Fifty-seven pro wins, including U.S. Women's Open Championship, 1946; three Vare Trophies, 1953, '55, and '56; three-time Associated Press Female Athlete of the Year, 1938, '43, and '55; LPGA Hall of Fame; World Golf Hall of Fame; International Women's Sports Hall of Fame.

SUSAN (SUSIE) BERNING MAXWELL b. July 22, 1941, Pasadena, California

Despite a promising debut in 1964, Berning cut back her tournament play when she married four years later. Never a major LPGA force, Berning is nevertheless memorable for being one of only four women to win more than two U.S. Women's Open championships. (The other multiple winners are **Betsy Rawls, Mickey Wright,** and **Hollis Stacy.**)

Selected championships and honors: Eleven pro career wins, including three U.S. Women's Open Championships, 1968, '72, and '73; Rookie of the Year, 1964.

JANE BLALOCK b. September 19, 1945, Portsmouth, New Hampshire

Sometimes overlooked because she only won one "major" tournament, Blalock nevertheless had an impressive LPGA career, with 29 wins. From 1969, her rookie season, through 1980, she made the cut to play in 299 consecutive LPGA tournaments. In 1977–80 Blalock became the first woman to earn more than $100,000 four years in a row. She retired from competition in 1986 and now heads her own sports consulting firm.

Selected championships and honors: Twenty-nine pro career wins, including Dinah Shore, 1972.

PATRICIA (PAT) BRADLEY b. March 24, 1951, Westford, Massachusetts

The only woman to win the "grand slam" of golf, Bradley was a competitive skier before she switched to golf in college. Bradley turned pro in 1974 and won her first tournament two years later. She had a stellar 1986 season, winning the Dinah Shore, du Maurier, and LPGA Championship titles and setting a single-season earnings record with $492,000. Bradley, the first woman to top the $2 million mark, passed the $3 million mark in 1990 and the $4 million mark in '91.

Selected championships and honors: Thirty-one pro career wins, including U.S. Women's Open, 1981, Dinah Shore, 1986, three du Mauriers, 1980, '85 and '86, and LPGA Championship, 1986; twice LPGA Golfer of the Year, 1986 and '91; Vare Trophy, 1986.

DONNA CAPONI YOUNG b. January 29, 1945, Detroit, Michigan

A member of the LPGA since 1965, Caponi's first tour win was a blockbuster—the U.S. Women's Open, a victory she repeated the following year. Her best years came in 1979, '80, and '81, when she won two LPGA Championships (1979 and '81) and garnered

over $200,000 in season winnings ($220,619 in 1980). Caponi began to cut back her play in the late 1980s, when she began as a commentator for ESPN and, later, an analyst on the Golf Channel. Her last year of play was 1992.

Selected championships and honors: Twenty-four pro career wins, including two U.S. Women's Open Championships, 1969 and '70, du Maurier, 1976, and two LPGA Championships, 1979 and '81.

JOANNE CARNER See JoAnne Gunderson Carner, below.

GLENNA COLLETT VARE b. June 20, 1903, New Haven, Connecticut; d. February 10, 1989

Long before the LPGA was formed, Collett was making waves on the green. Despite taking two seasons off (1933 and '34) to raise her children, she won a record six U.S. amateur championships, along with Canadian amateur titles in 1923 and '24. Fluid and accurate, Collett was praised by Bobby Jones, to whom she was often likened, as an exceptionally well rounded golfer. Her winning ways made her a celebrity, drawing large crowds and winning support for her sport. Although she retired after her sixth amateur championship in 1935, she played recreationally all her life and was reportedly still shooting in the high 80s at age eighty-five. The Vare Trophy, donated in 1952 by **Betty Jameson,** was named in her honor.

Selected championships and honors: Six U.S. Amateur Championships, 1922, '25, '28–'30, and '35; World Golf Hall of Fame; International Women's Sports Hall of Fame.

ELIZABETH (BETH) DANIEL b. October 14, 1956, Charleston, South Carolina

As a student at Furman University, Daniel sandwiched two U.S. Women's Amateur titles in between studies and joined the LPGA shortly after graduating. She was named Rookie of the Year in 1979 and heralded by sports writers as "the next Nancy Lopez." Although Daniel led in earnings the next two seasons, she clearly felt the pressure, and earned a reputation for throwing equipment and yelling at caddies during play. Back problems and a bout of mononucleosis in 1988 have also interfered with her game. At 5'11", Daniel boasts a powerful swing. Another asset is sheer persistence, and after suffering through a four-and-a-half year drought between 1985 and '89, she came back to win the LPGA Championship in 1990. She led the tour in earnings again that year and became the first woman to take home more than $800,000 in a single season. In 1994 she joined a select handful of women to total more than $4 million in career earnings.

Selected championships and honors: Thirty-two pro career wins, including LPGA Championship, 1990; Rookie of the Year, 1979; three times LPGA Player of the Year, 1980, '90, and '94; three Vare Trophies, 1989, '90, and '94; United Press International Female Athlete of the Year, 1990.

LAURA DAVIES b. October 5, 1963, Coventry, England

Davies won the U.S. Women's Open in 1987 and was granted automatic LPGA pro status as a result. The next year she received the high honor of being named Member of the British Empire by Queen Elizabeth. Davies has never failed to have at least one first- or second-place finish since turning pro in 1988, and has earned more than $2 million on the tour.

Selected championships and honors: U.S. Women's Open, 1987; ten pro career wins, including LPGA Championship, 1994.

MILDRED (BABE) DIDRIKSON ZAHARIAS
b. June 26, 1914, Port Arthur, Texas;
d. September 27, 1956

She was the most versatile female athlete of all time, competitive at almost every sport, and lived out two hall-of-fame careers before she died of cancer at the youthful age of forty-two. She was also a pioneer who refused to fit the stereotype of the pretty, polite, and acceptably "feminine" athlete. Married in 1938 to professional wrestler George Zaharias, whom she later divorced, Didrikson took little trouble to hide her rough edges or her fiercely competitive nature. Out of the arena, she could play poker, brag, and talk trash with the men. In the arena, she could beat them. The child of Norwegian immigrants, Didrikson began performing gymnastics on backyard equipment. She soon moved on to neighborhood softball games, and one story claims she earned her nickname for her Ruth-like ability to belt the ball out of the sandlot. In 1931 she led the Employers Casualty Insurance Company's basketball team to an AAU championship. The next year she won five AAU track and field events and three Olympic medals. For the innocuous but then-brazen act of allowing an auto manufacturer to use her picture in an ad, she was suspended from future AAU competition. No problem—Didrikson toured the country with her own basketball team,

A Few Words on the Fabulous Babe

She is beyond all belief until you see her perform. Then you finally understand that you are looking at the most flawless section of muscle harmony, of complete mental and physical coordination, that the world of sport has ever seen.

—Grantland Rice on The Babe

For even if some yet unborn games queen matches her talent, versatility, skill, patience and will to practice, along with her flaming competitive spirit . . . there still remains the little matter of courage and character, and in these departments the Babe must be ranked with the champions of all times.

—Paul Gallico on The Babe

The first female athlete to make people confront issues of femininity: how much muscle is too much? how much is unfeminine?

—Adrianne Blue on The Babe

I am out to beat everybody in sight, and that is just what I'm going to do.

—The Babe on The Babe

as well as playing exhibition baseball, billiards, and golf. As an amateur golfer, she won the Texas Women's Championship in 1935 and became one of the first female athletes to have equipment named after her—Babe Didrikson golf clubs. For her role in promoting the clubs, she was suspended from amateur golf competitions until 1943. Over the next four years Didrikson won forty tournaments. Then, in the late 1940s, she helped found the Ladies Professional Golf Association (LPGA), one of the first and most successful professional organizations for women athletes. Although she was only able to play for another eight years (1947–55), Didrikson nevertheless won thirty-one tour victories. She was diagnosed with cancer and underwent a colostomy in 1953, but came back to win her third U.S. Women's Open championship in 1954. In an era when cancer was a terrifying, even unmentionable, word, Didrikson went public, telling people her win proved that cancer was "nothing to be afraid of." She predicted a long future for herself on the links, one of the few expectations she was not able to live up to. She underwent a second cancer operation in 1956 and died later that year. In the early days of her career, Didrikson's lack of charm and her outright braggadocio often caused reporters and fans to side with her rivals. By the time she died, there was no one who wasn't on her side.

Selected championships and honors: Gold medal, 100m hurdles, Olympic Games, 1932; gold medal, javelin, Olympic Games, 1932; silver medal, high jump, Olympic Games, 1932; thirty-one pro career wins in golf, including three U.S. Women's Opens, 1948, '50, and '54; six-time Associated Press Female Athlete of the Year, 1932, 1945–47, and '54; Associated Press Outstanding Woman Athlete of the Half Century, 1950; Vare Trophy, 1954; U.S. Track and Field Hall of Fame; LPGA Hall of Fame; World Golf Hall of Fame; International Women's Sports Hall of Fame; Olympic Hall of Fame.

JANE GEDDES February 5, 1960, Huntington, New York

Geddes turned pro in 1983 and played sixty-five tournaments before she won her first victory, the Women's Open in 1986. It was the start of a dynamite decade, in which Geddes had at least one first- or second-place finish in all but two seasons. The next year she won the LPGA Championship and four other tour events, and she crossed the million-dollar earnings mark in 1989.

Selected championships and honors: Eleven pro career wins, including U.S. Women's Open, 1986, and LPGA Championship, 1987.

JOANNE GUNDERSON CARNER b. April 4, 1939, Kirland, Washington

Though most fans know her by her married nickname, "Big Mama" Carner was known as "The Great Gundy" during her single days on the amateur circuit, where she won five national titles before joining the LPGA in 1970. She won a pro tournament her first year out, followed it with a U.S. Open title the next year, and captured a second U.S. Open title in a playoff against Sandra Palmer in 1976. But Carner's best years were still to come. In her forties she became the first woman to break the $200,000 mark three years in a row, and in 1981 she was the first woman ever to top $300,000 in season's earnings. Assured and aggressive in competition, Carner's openness and friendliness off the links made her a favorite with fans. Though Carner's last first-place finish was in 1985, she continued to play—and finish in the top ten—through the 1995 season.

Selected championships and honors: Forty-two pro career wins, including five U.S. Amateur Championships, 1957, '60, '62, '66, and '68, U.S. Women's Open, 1971 and '76, and two du Mauriers, 1975 and '78; LPGA Player of the Year, 1974; five Vare Trophies, 1974, '75, and 1981–83; three times Golf Writers Association of America Player of the Year, 1981–82; LPGA Hall of Fame; World Golf Hall of Fame; International Women's Sports Hall of Fame.

SANDRA HAYNIE b. June 4, 1943, Ft. Worth, Texas

Haynie turned pro at the tender age of seventeen and in 1974 became the second woman in history to win the U.S. Women's Open and the LPGA Championship in the same year. By 1976 she had won thirty-nine tournaments, but between 1977 and 1980 arthritis limited her play to a few tournaments a year. She returned to full-time competition in 1981 and in 1988 broke the million-dollar mark in career earnings.

Selected championships and honors: Forty-two pro career wins, including U.S. Women's Open, 1974, du Maurier, 1982, and LPGA Championship, 1974; LPGA Hall of Fame.

JULI INKSTER *See Julie Simpson Inkster, below.*

ELIZABETH (BETTY) JAMESON b. May 19, 1919, Norman, Oklahoma

A highly successful amateur, Jameson joined with **Patty Berg, Babe Didrikson, Louise Suggs,** and others to form the LPGA in 1948. She also conceived the idea of presenting an annual award to the woman with the lowest average strokes per round and donated a trophy for that purpose, naming it after **Glenna Collett Vare.** A 5'8" blond with brown eyes, Jameson was sometimes portrayed as a glamour girl by sportswriters. But there was plenty of power behind the glamour, and her winning score of 295 in the 1947 Women's Open made her the first woman in history to shoot under 300 in a 72-hole tournament.

Selected championships and honors: Ten pro career wins, including U.S. Women's Open, 1947; LPGA Hall of Fame.

ELIZABETH (BETSY) KING b. August 13, 1955, Reading, Pennsylvania

A promising amateur who turned pro in 1977, King's first seven seasons were an uphill battle. By 1980, King was desperate enough to attempt the impossible—to rebuild her game from the ground up, including her swing. Few people can accomplish such a feat, and for a time King's game was worse then ever. Her phenomenal will paid off, and King won her first pro tournament in 1984. She's been on a winning streak ever since, and in 1995 turned in her thirtieth victory—the requisite number for automatic induction into the LPGA Hall of Fame.

Selected championships and honors: Thirty pro career wins, including two Dinah Shores, 1987 and '90, two U.S. Women's Opens, 1989 and '90, and an LPGA Championship, 1992; three-time LPGA Player of the Year, 1984, '89, and '93; two Vare Trophies, 1987 and '93.

CATHERINE LACOSTE b. June 27, 1945, Paris, France

The daughter of French golf champion Simone Thion de la Chaume and tennis star René Lacoste, the question was never "sports" but *"which* sport." The answer soon became clear. Lacoste quickly became one of the most successful French amateurs, winning the French Closed twice and the French Open three times. She also won British and U.S. amateur titles and, in 1967, became just the second foreign-born woman in history to win the U.S. Women's Open.

Selected championships and honors: U.S. Women's Open, 1967.

SALLY LITTLE b. October 12, 1951, Capetown, South Africa

Named Rookie of the Year after she turned pro in 1971, Little had to wait five years for her first tour victory. She won a pro event each year from 1971 to 1982, then suffered a setback when she underwent both abdominal and arthroscopic knee surgeries in 1983. Although she didn't win another event until 1988, her in-the-money finishes helped her become the tour's twelfth million-dollar earner in 1985. In 1986 Little narrowly missed winning the U.S. Women's Open, losing an 18-hole playoff to Jane Geddes, and finally broke her winless streak by taking the du Maurier Classic in 1988. Granted U.S. citizenship in 1982, Little now lives in West Palm Beach, Florida.

Selected championships and honors: Fifteen pro career wins, including LPGA Championship, 1980, Dinah Shore, 1982, and du Maurier, 1988; LPGA Rookie of the Year, 1971.

NANCY LOPEZ KNIGHT b. January 6, 1957, Torrance, California

The premier women's golfer of the 1970s and '80s and one of the most popular players of all time, Lopez grew up in New Mexico, where her father taught her to golf at age eight. She won the state's amateur women's championship at twelve and turned pro in 1977, winning her first Vare Trophy in 1978 with a record-setting average of 71.76. The record stood just one year—until 1979, when Lopez broke it with an average of 71.20 strokes per round. These feats, along with her 1978 LPGA Championship, made Lopez a national celebrity. As with Chris Evert in tennis, Lopez's combination of excellence, enthusiasm, and congeniality spilled over onto her sport, and women's golf enjoyed a surge of popularity. She married baseball player Ray Knight in 1983, which became an especially lucky year when she passed the million-dollar winnings mark and gave birth to the first of her three children. With forty-seven tour victories—three of them LPGA Championships—Lopez ranks sixth on the all-time wins list and has earned over $4 million at the sport she loves. Her game is fluid and remarkably natural. Not only does Lopez look relaxed, she *plays* relaxed, and she once told a *Newsday* reporter, "It's not a job. It's a Game." Fellow Hall of Fame golfer **Carol Mann,** whose record for average strokes per round Lopez broke, said, "She plays by feel. All her senses come into play. That's when golf is an art."

Selected championships and honors: Forty-seven pro career wins, including three LPGA Championships, 1978, '85, and '89; LPGA Rookie of the Year, 1978; three-time LPGA Player of the Year, 1978, '79, and '85; three Vare Trophies, 1978, '79, and '85; Associated Press Female Athlete of the Year, 1978; LPGA Hall of Fame; World Golf Hall of Fame.

CAROL MANN HARDY b. February 3, 1941, Buffalo, New York

At model height (6'3"), Mann struck a fashion-conscious note on the course—a note that was wasted on opponents, who strove to overcome her controlled drives and never-flinch putts. Mann turned pro in 1960 and won multiple events in eight of her twenty seasons. She won the Vare Trophy in 1968 with a

72.04-strokes-per-round average, a record that stood until **Nancy Lopez** broke it in 1978. Mann cut back on tour events in the late 1970s and began doing television commentary. She retired in 1981 but has remained active in sports, both with the Women's Sports Foundation and with substance abuse outreach programs for male and female athletes.
Selected championships and honors: Thirty-eight career wins, including U.S. Women's Open, 1965; Vare Trophy, 1968; LPGA Hall of Fame; Women's Sports Hall of Fame.

MEG MALLON b. April 14, 1963, Natick, Massachusetts
Mallon turned pro in 1986 and has been a consistent top-ten finisher since 1990, passing the $2 million mark in 1995. Her best finishes came in 1991, when she won the LPGA Championship and the U.S. Women's Open in a three-week stretch.
Selected championships and honors: Six pro career wins, including LPGA Championship, 1991, and U.S. Women's Open, 1991.

DOROTHY (DOTTIE) MOCHRIE PEPPER b. August 17, 1965, Saratoga Springs, New York
A champion amateur, Pepper turned pro in 1987 and had a terrific rookie season, with seven top-ten finishes and earnings topping $130,000. She has had at least one first- or second-place finish every season since 1989 and has racked up more than $3 million in winnings. Her best season to date was 1992, when she led the tour in earnings and took the Dinah Shore in a dramatic sudden-death playoff against Juli Inkster.
Selected championships and honors: Ten pro career wins, including Dinah Shore, 1992; Vare Trophy, 1992; LPGA Player of the Year, 1992.

SANDRA PALMER b. March 10, 1941, Ft. Worth, Texas
An avid golfer since working as a caddie at age thirteen, Palmer turned pro in 1964 and was still playing, on a reduced schedule, thirty-two years later. Even more astonishing, she had at least one top-ten finish every season from 1964 to 1989 and in 1986 became the LPGA's thirteenth pro to pass the million-dollar earnings mark.
Selected championships and honors: Twenty-one pro career wins, including U.S. Women's Open, 1975; LPGA Player of the Year, 1975.

JUDY RANKIN See *Judy Torluemke Rankin, below.*

ELIZABETH (BETSY) RAWLS b. May 4, 1928, Spartanburg, South Carolina
Rawls didn't take up golf until she was seventeen and living in Texas. Once the club was in her hand, she quickly made up for lost time, turning pro in 1951 and winning at least one event each season for the next fifteen seasons. With fifty-five tour victories, she ranks fourth on the all-time win list behind **Kathy Whitworth, Mickey Wright,** and **Patty Berg.** A Phi Beta Kappa grad of the University of Texas, Rawls may have used her math and physics knowhow on the green, for she was a first-rate putter and seldom failed to sink the shot. After retiring from the tour in 1975, she went to work for the LPGA and played a major role in lifting women's pro golf to its current high-profile status. Among her other achievements, Rawls became known as "the Circuit Judge" for her voluminous knowledge of the game, and in 1970 she became the first woman to serve on the U.S. Men's Open rules committee.
Selected championships and honors: Fifty-five pro career wins, including four U.S. Women's Opens, 1951, '53, '57, and '60, and two LPGA Championships, 1959 and '69; Vare Trophy, 1959; LPGA Hall of Fame; World Golf Hall of Fame.

PATRICIA (PATTY) SHEEHAN b. October 27, 1956, Middlebury, Vermont
Had Sheehan's family not moved to Nevada in the early 1970s, the world might have been down one golfer—and up one skier. Sheehan's father, a noted ski instructor, taught his daughter the sport, and as a junior Sheehan showed promise. In Nevada she discovered golf, and she began winning state championships in 1975. Sheehan turned pro in 1980 and has had a stellar career despite being troubled with arthritis in her hands throughout most of her playing years. From 1981 through 1995, Sheehan failed to have at least one first-place finish in only season, 1987, when her best finish was a second. She is one of the golden circle who has earned more than $4 million at her sport, with nearly $4.8 million at the end of 1995. Keenly interested in course layout, she was a design consultant for the Green Horn Creek course at Angels Camp, California.
Selected championships and honors: Thirty-four pro career wins, including three LPGA Championships, 1983, '84, and '93, and two U.S. Women's Opens, 1992 and '94; Vare Trophy, 1984; one of eight "Athletes Who Care" *Sports Illustrated* Athletes of the Year, 1987; LPGA Player of the Year, 1993.

JULI SIMPSON INKSTER b. June 24, 1960, Santa
   Cruz, California

Before turning pro in late 1983, Inkster became the
third woman in history (along with **Glenna Collet
Vare** and Virginia Van Wie) to win the U.S. Women's
Amateur Championship three years in a row (1980–
82). In 1984, her first full season, Inkster became the
first rookie in history to win two major tournaments,
the Dinah Shore and the du Maurier Classic. On the
greens, Inkster is an unusually complete player, with
no weaknesses in her game.

Selected championships and honors: Fifteen pro career
wins, including two Dinah Shores, 1984 and '89, and
du Maurier Classic, 1984; Rookie of the Year, 1984.

MARILYN SMITH b. April 13, 1929, Topeka,
   Kansas

As a University of Kansas student Smith had a terrific
amateur career, winning three consecutive state amateur championships as well as the national collegiate
title. Like other women of her day, she saw the need
for a pro tour and rose to the occasion. Smith became
a charter member of the LPGA and eventually won
twenty-two events. She also became one of the best
ambassadors women's golf could ask for. So likable
and outgoing she was routinely called "Miss Personality," Smith has given demonstrations in all fifty states
and three dozen foreign countries. She served as
LPGA president from 1958 to 1960, and in 1973 she
became the first female commentator to cover a televised men's tournament. She organized the Marilyn
Smith Founders Classic, the first senior-circuit pro
tournament for women. Smith is still involved in her
sport today, as a teacher at the Firewheel Club in
Dallas.

ANNIKA SORENSTAM b. October 9, 1970,
   Stockholm, Sweden

Sorenstam began playing golf in her native Sweden
and made waves as an amateur while attending college in America. After touring in Europe, she joined
the LPGA in 1993, and in 1994 she won the Women's
Open. Sorenstam divides her time between the Old
World and the New, living in both Stockholm and San
Diego and playing professionally in the United States,
Europe, and Australia. Her younger sister, Charlotta,
is also a promising amateur golfer.

Selected championships and honors: Three pro career
victories, including U.S. Women's Open, 1995; LPGA
Rookie of the Year, 1993; LPGA Player of the Year,
1994; Vare Trophy, 1995.

The Viking Invasion

After a century of near dominance, Americans and Brits are facing a new challenge—
the women of Sweden. Though it doesn't
quite fit the stereotype, golf is big in Sweden, and many Swedes, living in the tem-
perate regions of the south, are able to golf
most of the year. An early invader was
Liselotte Neumann, who won the Women's
Open in 1988. Following in her wake came
Helen Alfredsson, with a win in the 1993
Dinah Shore, and Annika Sorenstam, pro-
filed above.

HOLLIS STACY b. March 16, 1954, Savannah,
   Georgia

A three-time winner of the USGA Junior Girls Championship (1969–71), Stacy turned pro in 1974 and
won her first victories in 1977. One of them was the
U.S. Women's Open, which she won two more times,
making her one of only four golfers (along with **Susie
Berning Maxwell, Betsy Rawls,** and **Mickey
Wright**) to win the event more than twice. From
1977 through 1985, the year she crossed the million-
dollar mark in earnings, Stacy had at least one first-
place finish each season. Still very active on the tour,
Stacy is also involved in golf course design and works
as an assistant golf coach at the University of Southern California. The Blackhawk Golf Course in Austin,
Texas, is her creation.

Selected championships and honors: Eighteen pro career wins, including three U.S. Women's Opens,
1977, '78, and '84, and du Maurier Classic, 1983.

JAN STEPHENSON b. December 22, 1951,
   Sydney, Australia

Stephenson had a successful amateur career in her native country and turned pro there before transferring
her talents and joining the LPGA tour in 1974. In two
decades of play, Stephenson has failed to have at least
one top-four finish in only one season—1990, the year
a mugger broke her left ring finger and she had to cut
her play back to thirteen events. One of the tour's $2
million winners, Stephenson was also the first woman
pro to become involved in golf course design.

Selected championships and honors: Sixteen pro career wins, including du Maurier Classic, 1981, and

LPGA Championship, 1982; LPGA Rookie of the Year, 1974.

MAE LOUISE (LOUISE) SUGGS b. September 7, 1923, Atlanta, Georgia

Suggs began playing at age ten and had a stunning amateur career that lasted from 1940 through 1948 and included both U.S. and British amateur titles, in 1947 and '48 respectively. A founding member of the LPGA, Suggs racked up fifty pro wins, placing her fifth on the all-time win list. In forty-four years of amateur and professional play, Suggs never failed to have at least one top-ten finish and usually finished far higher, winning at least one event a year from 1946 through 1962. Her unhurried, methodical playing style caused many to liken her to Ben Hogan, while Bob Hope dubbed her "Miss Slugs" for her long drives. In addition to helping found the LPGA, she also served three terms as president. Her last year of play was 1984.

Selected championships and honors: Fifty pro career wins, including U.S. Women's Open, 1949 and '51, and LPGA Championship, 1957; Vare Trophy, 1957; LPGA Hall of Fame; World Golf Hall of Fame; International Women's Sports Hall of Fame.

JUDY TORLUEMKE RANKIN b. February 18, 1945, St. Louis, Missouri

Rankin won her first tournament—the St. Louis Peewee—at age eight and turned pro just nine years later. Her prime playing years were the mid-1970s, when she won three Vare Trophies and, in 1976, became the first LPGA member to earn more than $100,000 in a single season. The next year she set a tour record, with twenty-five finishes in the top ten. Rankin suffered a back injury in the late 1970s, which limited her schedule and interfered with the consistency of her play.

Selected championships and honors: Twenty-six pro career wins, including Dinah Shore, 1976, and du Maurier Classic, 1977; three Vare Trophies, 1973, '76, and '77; twice LPGA Player of the Year, 1976 and '77.

GLENNA VARE *See Glenna Collett Vare, above.*

JOYCE WETHERED HEATHCOAT-AMORY b. November 17, 1901, Maldon, Surrey, England

Wethered's matches were like Leonardo da Vinci's paintings—few, precise, and perfect. Though a celebrity in her day and considered by many who saw her to be the best woman golfer ever, Wethered is not well known today because she shunned rather than embraced the spotlight. During her main playing years, 1920–26, she won four British Opens and five English Ladies' Championships. Her coolheadedness and ability to focus under pressure became legendary. According to one anecdote, a train roared by just as she was about to sink the winning putt. Asked about the incident later, she inquired, "What train?" Private to the point of shy, Wethered retired in 1926 but returned for one final match in 1929, when it was announced that the amateur championship would be played at St. Andrews, in Scotland. St. Andrews is not only the world's oldest course, but also one of the most difficult, and Wethered couldn't pass up the challenge. The match became one of the greatest in golf history, coming down to a nip-and-tuck finish in which Wethered defeated American **Glenna Collett.** Soon after the legendary match, Wethered took a job in the golf department of a London store, a move that cost her her amateur status. Her only American appearance was a series of exhibition events in 1935, when she toured the country with **Babe Didrikson** and Gene Sarazen. In 1937 Wethered married Sir John Heathcoat-Amory and, as lady of a Devonshire estate, became a respected horticulturist.

KATHRYNE (KATHY) WHITWORTH b. September 27, 1939, Monahans, Texas

Few athletes have matched Whitworth's drive for excellence at a sport, and few have matched her achievements. Growing up in New Mexico, Whitworth tried golf at the local country club when she was fifteen. She wasn't especially good at it, but became obsessed with improving her game. Three years later she won the state amateur championship. She turned pro in 1958, feeling she would learn more on the tour than as a college scholarship player, and did not win a tournament until 1962. That win was the start of a phenomenal streak. In 1981 she became the first woman ever to pass the million-dollar mark in earnings, and in 1984 she broke Sam Snead's record of eighty-four wins to become the winningest professional golfer in history. No other golfer has had more pro wins (88), led the tour in earnings more seasons (8), won more Vare Trophies (7), or been named Player of the Year more times (7). More than an exceptional athlete, Whitworth won respect from reporters everywhere with her professional—if sometimes passionate—approach and left no doubt that women's golf was a serious sport. Whitworth served as LPGA presi-

dent several times, did much to help the tour grow to its present status, and—not surprisingly—was named 1968–77 Golfer of the Decade by *GOLF Magazine.*
Selected championships and honors: Eighty-eight pro career wins, including three LPGA Championships, 1967, '71, and '75; seven-time LPGA Player of the Year, 1966–69, and 1971–73; seven Vare Trophies, 1965–67 and 1969–72; two-time Associated Press Athlete of the Year, 1965 and '66; LPGA Hall of Fame; World Golf Hall of Fame.

MARY KATHRYN (MICKEY) WRIGHT

b. February 14, 1935, San Diego, California
Wright came from a follow-your-dreams family, with a grandfather who was an inventor and a grandmother who was Illinois's first female pharmacist. So when she showed an early interest in golf, she was encouraged and given lessons, and she won her first important amateur girls' championship at age thirteen. Early training, combined with Wright's willingness to practice hours every day, paid off. Wright, who turned pro in 1955, not only became one of the best golfers of the 1950s and '60s, she developed a swing that is still regarded as technical perfection. Perfectly timed and generating terrific speed, the swing made her a joy to watch and won new fans to women's golf. Well aware of her importance to the still-young tour, Wright felt the pressure keenly, once saying that the drive to win wasn't nearly as compelling as "the total rejection and horror of doing it badly." In a quarter century of play, Wright rarely did it badly, even when plagued by wrist and foot injuries in the mid-1960s. With eighty-two career victories, she was number one on the all-time win list until **Kathy Whitworth** passed her in 1982. Although Wright stopped playing full-time after 1969, she continued to enter occasional tournaments, made several appearances in the Legends of Golf tournament in the 1980s, and in 1994 finished second in the Senior Sprint Challenge.

> The main emotion going into any new season was fear. . . . It was the fear that no matter how good the previous year had been, this year would not be as good, and the pressure to win the first tournament was unbelievable.
>
> —Mickey Wright, quoted in *The Illustrated History of Women's Golf*

Selected championships and honors: Eighty-two pro career wins, including four LPGA Championships, 1958, '60, '61, and '63, and four U.S. Women's Opens, 1958, '59, '61 and '64; five Vare Trophies, 1960–64; LPGA Hall of Fame; Golf Hall of Fame; International Women's Sports Hall of Fame; two-time Associated Press Athlete of the Year, 1963 and '64.

Golf Competitions/Awards

Solheim Cup

The Solheim Cup is a biennial transatlantic team match play competition between European members of the Women Professional Golfers' European Tour (WPGET) and the U.S. members of the Ladies Professional Golf Association (LPGA). The first Solheim Cup competition was staged in November 1990 at Lake Nona Golf Club in Orlando, Florida.

The event comprises three days of competition. The first two days feature two sessions of matches, one of foursome/alternate shot format, and one of foursome format. The third day features twelve singles matches. One point is awarded for each match won, and half a point for halved matches.

Bob Jones Award

Since 1955, the USGA has presented an award honoring a person who, by a single act or over the years, emulates Bob Jones's sportsmanship, respect for the game and its rules, generosity of spirit, and sense of fair play, self-control, and perhaps even sacrifice.

Curtis Cup Match

The Curtis Cup is played for by women amateur golfers, one team from the United States and one team comprising England, Ireland, Northern Ireland, Scotland, and Wales. Each team consists of not more than eight players and a captain. Victory in a match scores one point. When a match goes 18 holes without a decision, one-half point is awarded to each side.

The match is held every two years, alternately in the United States and Great Britain/Ireland. The country winning the cup takes custody for the ensuing two years. In case of a tie, the cup remains with the previous winner until the next match is played. The inscription on the silver rose bowl, of Paul Revere design, reads, "To stimulate friendly rivalry among the women golfers of many lands."

Golf

Bob Jones Award

Year	Player
1957	Mildred D. Zaharias
1958	Margaret Curtis
1963	Patty Berg
1965	Glenna Collett Vare
1981	JoAnne Gunderson Carner
1983	Maureen Ruttle Garrett
1990	Peggy Kirk Bell
1996	Betsy Rawls

Curtis Cup Match

Year	Finish	Scores
1932	United States	5½
	Great Britain & Ireland	3½
1934	United States	6½
	Great Britain & Ireland	2½
1936	United States	4½
	Great Britain & Ireland	4½
1938	United States	5½
	Great Britain & Ireland	3½
1948	United States	6
	Great Britain & Ireland	2½
1950	United States	7
	Great Britain & Ireland	1½
1952	Great Britain & Ireland	5
	United States	4
1954	United States	6
	Great Britain & Ireland	3
1956	Great Britain & Ireland	5
	United States	4
1958	Great Britain & Ireland	4½
	United States	4½
1960	United States	6
	Great Britain & Ireland	2½
1962	United States	8
	Great Britain & Ireland	1
1964	United States	10½
	Great Britain & Ireland	7½
1966	United States	13
	Great Britain & Ireland	5
1968	United States	10½
	Great Britain & Ireland	7½
1970	United States	11½
	Great Britain & Ireland	6½
1972	United States	10
	Great Britain & Ireland	8
1974	United States	13
	Great Britain & Ireland	5
1976	United States	11½
	Great Britain & Ireland	6½
1978	United States	12
	Great Britain & Ireland	6
1980	United States	13
	Great Britain & Ireland	5
1982	United States	14½
	Great Britain & Ireland	3½
1984	United States	9½
	Great Britain & Ireland	8½
1986	Great Britain & Ireland	13
	United States	5
1988	Great Britain & Ireland	11
	United States	7
1990	United States	14
	Great Britain & Ireland	4
1992	Great Britain & Ireland	10
	United States	8
1994	United States	9
	Great Britain & Ireland	9
1996	Great Britain & Ireland	11½
	United States	6½

LPGA Hall of Fame

Year	Player	Career Victories
1951	Patty Berg	57
1951	Betty Jameson	10
1951	Louise Suggs	50
1951	Babe Didrikson Zaharias	31
1960	Betsy Rawls	55
1964	Mickey Wright	82
1975	Kathy Whitworth	88
1977	Sandra Haynie	42
1982	JoAnne Carner	42*
1987	Nancy Lopez	47*
1991	Pat Bradley	31*
1993	Patty Sheehan	34*
1994	Dinah Shore	Honorary
1995	Betsy King	30*

*Denotes player still on Tour.

Golf (continued)

McDonald's LPGA Championship

Year	Champion	Score
1955	Beverly Hanson	220
1956	Marlene Hagge	291
1957	Louise Suggs	285
1958	Mickey Wright	288
1959	Betsy Rawls	288
1960	Mickey Wright	292
1961	Mickey Wright	287
1962	Judy Kimball	282
1963	Mickey Wright	294
1964	Mary Mills	278
1965	Sandra Haynie	279
1966	Gloria Ehret	282
1967	Kathy Whitworth	284
1968	Sandra Post	294
1969	Betsy Rawls	293
1970	Shirley Englehorn	285
1971	Kathy Whitworth	288
1972	Kathy Ahern	293
1973	Mary Mills	288
1974	Sandra Haynie	288
1975	Kathy Whitworth	288
1976	Betty Burfeindt	287
1977	Chako Higuchi	279
1978	Nancy Lopez	275
1979	Donna Caponi	279
1980	Sally Little	285
1981	Donna Caponi	280
1982	Jan Stephenson	279
1983	Patty Sheehan	279
1984	Patty Sheehan	272
1985	Nancy Lopez	273
1986	Pat Bradley	277
1987	Jane Geddes	275
1988	Sherri Turner	281
1989	Nancy Lopez	274
1990	Beth Daniel	280
1991	Meg Mallon	274
1992	Betsy King	267
1993	Patty Sheehan	275
1994	Laura Davies	279
1995	Kelly Robbins	274
1996	Laura Davies	213

LPGA Championship Records
9 Hole

Year	Player	Score
1984	Hollis Stacy	31
	Patty Sheehan	

1985	Nancy Lopez	
1989	Sandra Haynie	
1990	Chris Johnson	

18 Hole

| 1984 | Patty Sheehan | 63 |

36 Hole

| 1983 | Alexandra Reinhardt | 135 |

54 Hole (Par 72)

| 1984 | Patty Sheehan | 204 |

54 Hole (Par 71)

| 1992 | Betsy King | 201 |

72 Hole (Par 71)

| 1992 | Betsy King | 267 |

72 Hole (Par 72)

| 1984 | Patty Sheehan | 272 |

U.S. Open

Year	Champion	Score
1946	Patty Berg	5 & 4*
1947	Betty Jameson	295
1948	Babe Didrikson Zaharias	300
1949	Louise Suggs	291
1950	Babe Didrikson Zaharias	291
1951	Betsy Rawls	293
1952	Louise Suggs	284
1953	Betsy Rawls	302
1954	Babe Didrikson Zaharias	291
1955	Fay Crocker	299
1956	Kathy Cornelius	302
1957	Betsy Rawls	299
1958	Mickey Wright	287
1959	Mickey Wright	287
1960	Betsy Rawls	292
1961	Mickey Wright	293
1962	Murle Breer	301
1963	Mary Mills	289
1964	Mickey Wright	290
1965	Carol Mann	290
1966	Sandra Spuzich	297
1967	Catherine LaCoste	294

Golf (continued)

U.S. Open

Year	Champion	Score
1968	Susie Berning	289
1969	Donna Caponi	294
1970	Donna Caponi	287
1971	JoAnne Carner	288
1972	Susie Berning	299
1973	Susie Berning	290
1974	Sandra Haynie	295
1975	Sandra Palmer	295
1976	JoAnne Carner	292
1977	Hollis Stacy	292
1978	Hollis Stacy	289
1979	Jerilyn Britz	284
1980	Amy Alcott	280
1981	Pat Bradley	279
1982	Janet Anderson	283
1983	Jan Stephenson	290
1984	Hollis Stacy	290
1985	Kathy Baker	280
1986	Jane Geddes	287
1987	Laura Davies	285
1988	Liselotte Neumann	277
1989	Betsy King	278
1990	Betsy King	284
1991	Meg Mallon	283
1992	Patty Sheehan	280
1993	Lauri Merten	280
1994	Patty Sheehan	277
1995	Annika Sorenstam	278
1996	Annika Sorenstam	272

*5 up with 4 holes to play.

Nabisco Dinah Shore

Year	Champion	Score
1972	Jane Blalock	213
1973	Mickey Wright	284
1974	Jo Ann Prentice	289
1975	Sandra Palmer	283
1976	Judy Rankin	285
1977	Kathy Whitworth	289
1978	Sandra Post	276
1979	Sandra Post	276
1980	Donna Caponi	275
1981	Nancy Lopez	277
1982	Sally Little	278
1983	Amy Alcott	282
1984	Juli Inkster	280

1985	Alice Miller	275
1986	Pat Bradley	280
1987	Betsy King	283
1988	Amy Alcott	274
1989	Juli Inkster	279
1990	Betsy King	283
1991	Amy Alcott	273
1992	Dottie Mochrie	279
1993	Helen Alfredsson	284
1994	Donna Andrews	276
1995	Nanci Bowen	285
1996	Patty Sheehan	281

Dinah Shore Records
9 Hole

1980	Sandra Palmer	30

18 Hole

1981	Nancy Lopez	64
1982	Sally Little	64

36 Hole

1989	Juli Inkster	135

54 Hole

1988	Amy Alcott	203

72 Hole

1991	Amy Alcott	273

du Maurier Ltd. Classic

Year	Champion	Score
1973	Jocelyne Bourassa	214
1974	Carole Jo Callison	208
1975	JoAnne Carner	214
1976	Donna Caponi	212
1977	Judy Rankin	214
1978	JoAnne Carner	278
1979	Amy Alcott	285
1980	Pat Bradley	277
1981	Jan Stephenson	278
1982	Sandra Haynie	280
1983	Hollis Stacy	277
1984	Juli Inkster	279
1985	Pat Bradley	278
1986	Pat Bradley	276

Golf (continued)

du Maurier Ltd. Classic

Year	Champion	Score
1987	Jody Rosenthal	272
1988	Sally Little	279
1989	Tammie Green	279
1990	Cathy Johnson	276
1991	Nancy Scranton	279
1992	Sherri Steinhauer	277
1993	Brandie Burton	277
1994	Martha Nause	279
1995	Jenny Lidback	280
1996	Laura Davies	277

du Maurier Classic Records
9 Hole

1990	Beth Daniel	30
	Patti Rizzo	

18 Hole

1978	JoAnne Carner	64
1985	Jane Geddes	64
1993	Dawn Coe-Jones	64

36 Hole

1978	JoAnne Carner	135
1990	Cathy Johnston	135

54 Hole

1978	JoAnne Carner	205
1990	Cathy Johnston	205

72 Hole (Par 72)

1987	Jody Rosenthal	272

72 Hole (Par 73)

1990	Cathy Johnston	276

ARCHERY

◆ *With its classical links to Diana, goddess of the hunt, archery served as an early and enduring image of women's athletic nature, persisting even in eras that discouraged physical activity.*

HISTORY

Some of the world's most famous women have been archers. In classical mythology, the sport was associated with a goddess rather than a god— Diana, a huntress rather than a warrior, took up the bow for sustenance, not conquest. It's likely that women throughout history did much the same, taking up the bow to provide their families with small game. Archery contests for men were standard fare at medieval festivals, and contests for women were occasionally added as a kind of

novelty event. Women were barred from the sport during the Renaissance, but then, as now, convention bowed to wealth and power. The infamously chic Diane de Poitiers, mistress of France's Henri III, was an avid archer who often posed with a bow and arrow. Anne Boleyn pursued the sport so enthusiastically that Henry VIII complained of the costs. Her daughter Elizabeth I became an excellent huntress with the crossbow, the standard equipment of the era. Archery flourished throughout England and France but was also pursued in the Germanic countries. In 1570 the wife of Ferdinand II of Tyrol won a silver drinking cup with her crossbow skills. Women were admitted to many archery guilds in Flanders, and annual contests were held for both men and women. One of the first organized clubs, England's Toxon Society, founded in 1781, lasted only six years as an all-male institution. In 1788 Miss Harriet Boycott won their first women's tournament.

Popularized by goddesses, queens, and royal mistresses, archery has always been associated with the upper classes and pageantry. This gilt-edged image undoubtedly contributed to its survival, sparing it the condemnations usually aimed at women's competitive sports. Archery was also helped by the fact that it was a stationary sport, requiring none of the rapid movements viewed with such suspicion by Victorians. It was one of the few sports that Queen Victoria looked on with any favor at all, and archery clubs could be quite elitist. In the mid-nineteenth century, Josiah Wedgwood's granddaughter noted proudly that her daughter had won a "beautiful pair of earrings" in an archery contest. It's hard to imagine her writing with similar pride of her daughter winning a footrace or weight-throwing contest, just as it's hard to imagine her describing a cheap or tasteless pair of earrings as "beautiful." From this small personal entry we learn that archery was accepted in the upper classes, and prizes were genuinely valuable. Victorian archery clubs emphasized the pageantry of the sport, and dressing in lavish historical garb was often part of the allure. That did not disguise the fact that many women were serious about their skills, however. In 1844 eleven women competed in England's second Grand National Archery Meeting, aiming at targets 60 yards away. The club initiated regular annual national contests for women in 1880.

Archery also became a stylish upper-class pursuit in America. Vassar, which led the way in women's college athletics, introduced coeds to archery and several other sports. May Welland, the well-bred but thoroughly contemporary young American woman in Edith Wharton's *Age of Innocence*, was an archer. In the 1870s, the all-women's Crescent City Archery Club of New Orleans was formed. The National Archery Association came about as an indirect consequence of the Civil War. Barred from gun ownership, ex-Confederate soldiers took up the bow as a hunting tool and became accomplished marksmen. The NAA was founded as a coeducational organization in 1879, and championships for both men and women have always been included. The first

winner of the women's event was Mrs. S. Brown. In 1883, **Lida Scott Howell** won the first of her record seventeen national titles.

Archery was included in the Olympic games of 1900, 1904, 1908, and 1920. However, lack of standardized international rules led to widespread confusion, and each host country imposed its own method of play. After the 1920 games, archery was deleted from the program.

THE MODERN ERA

In 1931, the Federation Internationale de Tir (FITA) was formed with an eye to standardizing rules and competitions. It organized the first World Championships, held that year, and encouraged countries to adopt the international system.

After years of patient effort, archery was reinstated as an Olympic sport in 1972. Since 1979, women's archery has also been selected as an event in the Pan American Games. Although U.S. women dominated the first Olympic competitions, the women of Korea began to excel at target events in the mid-1980s. Field archery, in which contestants compete on a varied-terrain course, has been firmly in the hands of the women of Scandinavia and western Europe since its introduction to world competition.

Archery today is an extremely dynamic sport. In the 1990s World Championship competitions diversified to include events with both the recurve (or Olympic) bow and the compound bow. In addition to the three more-established forms of competition (target, field, and flight), two new events are gaining popularity. Ski-archery, called

---

Major Events and Awards

World Target Championships
World Field Championships
World Indoor Championships
Olympic Games
Pan American Games
Shenk Award

ski-arc for short, combines cross-country skiing with field archery. Arcathlon, a summer sport, combines archery with cross-country running.

Governing Bodies and Organizations

National Archery Association
One Olympic Plaza
Colorado Springs, Colorado 80909

Phone: 719/578-4576
Fax: 719/632-4722

National Field Archery Association
31407 Outer I-10
Redlands, California 92373
Phone: 909/794-2133
Fax: 909/794-8512

* * * BIOGRAPHIES * * *

JUDI ADAMS b. July 12, 1959, Phoenix, Arizona
Adams won the intercollegiate championship title in 1981 and was a member of eleven U.S. teams between 1982 and 1996. She has competed internationally in Russia, as well as in the Chinese and Mexican nationals.
Selected championships and honors: Gold medal, Championships of the Americas, 1978; silver medal, World Target Championships, 1979; bronze medal, Pan American Games, 1979; two bronze medals, Championships of the Americas, 1980 and '92; bronze medal, World Field Championships, 1992; National Field Championship, 1992; National Target Championship, 1994; Shenk Award, 1989 and '92; Female Archery Athlete of the Year, 1980.

JANET DYKMAN b. January 17, 1954, Monterey Park, California
Three-time winner of the national field championships, Dykman had a sparkling performance at the 1995 Pan American Games, where she took the individual gold and helped the United States to a team first.
Selected championships and honors, individual: Three National Field Championships, 1990, '92, and '94; gold medal, Pan American Games, 1995. *Team:* Gold medal, Pan American Games, 1995.

LIDA SCOTT HOWELL b. August 23, 1859; d. December 20, 1933
Howell won her first major competition, the Ohio state championship, in 1881, when she was still Lida Scott. She repeated the next year, and the year after that, competing under her married name, she won her first national title. Howell won seventeen national championships in all, the last in 1907. She also took

two Olympic gold medals, in the 1904 games. The dominant archer of her time, Howell would have stood her ground with today's field, and scoring records she set in 1895 stood until 1931.
Selected championships and honors: Seventeen national championships, 1893, '85, '86, '90–93, '95, '96, '98–1900, 1902–1905, and 1907; two gold medals, Olympic Games, 1904.

KIM JIN-HO b. South Korea
Kim's win in the 1979 World Target Championships ushered in a new era in archery, as women from Korea became a force to be reckoned with. She repeated her win two meets later, in 1983. Kim was also a favorite at the 1984 Olympics, but finished third behind teammate Seo Hyang-soon and China's Li Lingjuan.
Selected championships and honors: Two gold medals, World Target Championships, 1979 and '83; bronze medal, Olympic Games, 1984.

Olympic First: Neroli Fairhall

A motorcycle accident severely damaged Fairhall's spinal cord, and doctors told her she would not walk again. They said nothing about her arms, however, or her strength and coordination. New Zealander Fairhall represented her country at the 1984 Olympics and, shooting from her wheelchair, became the first paraplegic athlete ever to compete in the Olympics.

Silver Belles

Indonesia had never won an Olympic medal in any sport when team archery was introduced at the 1988 Olympic Games. No one expected the women of Indonesia—competing against strong competitors from the United States, China, and the Soviet Union—to turn in more than a respectable performance. But Lilies Handayani, Nurfitriyana Saiman, and Kusumu Wardhani won a 72–67 shootout against the Americans to win the silver and give their country its first-ever Olympic medal.

KIM SOO-NYUNG b. 1971, South Korea
Kim was only seventeen when she won her first Olympic medal, a gold at the 1988 games, which her country hosted. She also helped Korea win the first team gold ever offered in the sport. She went on to win two World Target Championships and two more Olympic medals, an individual silver and a team gold at the 1992 games.
Selected championships and honors, individual: Two gold medals, World Target Championships, 1989 and '91; gold medal, Olympic Games, 1988; silver medal, Olympic Games, 1992. *Team:* Two gold medals, Olympic Games, 1988 and '92.

ANGELA MOSCARELLI b. September 11, 1981, Vallijo, California
Just put the words "youngest to" after Moscarelli's name in the record books. In 1995, at age thirteen, she became the youngest archer ever on a U.S. world team, the youngest archer on a U.S. gold medal team, and the youngest archer to win a world title in her event, the compound bow. Moscarelli and teammates set new world scoring records for compound bow in Olympic round play at both the World Target Championships and the World Indoor Championships in 1995. Prior to 1995, Moscarelli won numerous junior, intermediate, and cadet titles.
Selected championships and honors, individual: Gold medal, World Target Championships, compound bow, 1995. *Team:* Gold medal, World Target Championships, compound bow, 1995; gold medal, World Indoor Championships, compound bow, 1995.

DEBBIE OCHS b. January 30, 1966, Howell, Michigan
Ochs had a peak year in 1988, winning the national target championship, shooting for the bronze-medal-winning U.S. Olympic team, receiving the Shenk Award, and being named Female Archery Athlete of the Year. She repeated her target title in 1989.
Selected championships and honors, individual: Silver medal, Pan American Games, 1983; bronze medal, Championships of the Americas, 1988; two National Target Championships, 1988–89; Shenk Award, 1988; Female Archery Athlete of the Year, 1988. *Team:* Bronze medal, Olympic Games, 1988.

DENISE PARKER b. December 12, 1973, South Jordan, Utah
Winner of multiple national championships, Parker has often made her best performances at the Pan American Games. A two-time individual gold medalist, she set several meet records and was a member of three U.S. gold-medal-winning teams. Parker also set numerous national records and one world record, for the indoor 18-meter target competition.
Selected championships and honors, individual: Two gold medals, Pan American Games, 1987 and '91; four National Target Championships, 1989–91 and '93; seven National Indoor Championships, 1988–92, '94, and '95; Female Archery Athlete of the Year, 1987 and '89. *Team:* Three gold medals, Pan American Games, 1987, '91, and '95; bronze medal, Olympic Games, 1988.

CAROL PELOSI b. March 12, 1946, Greenbelt, Michigan
One of the few American women to specialize in crossbow, Pelosi is one of the world's best. She has won twenty-two national crossbow target titles since 1973, as well as twenty national indoor championships. She has won a half dozen medals in world championship competition, half of them gold.
Selected championships and honors: Twenty-two National Target for Crossbow Championships, 1972–95; three gold medals, World Crossbow Championships, 1982, '84, and '86; two bronze medals, World Crossbow Championships, 1988 and '90; silver medal, World Crossbow Championships, 1994.

RUTH ROWE b. November 3, 1947, Pittsburgh, Pennsylvania
Rowe won her first major event, the national target title, in 1972. Twenty-three years later she was still

competing—and winning, with an individual silver in the 1995 Pan American Games. In between Rowe won numerous national and international events, turning in one of her best performances at the 1983 Pan American Games, where she set three meet records and won individual and team gold medals.

Selected championships and honors: Two National Target Championships, 1972 and '84; three National Indoor Championships, 1982, '83 and '93; three National Field Championships, 1981–83; Female Archery Athlete of the Year, 1983 and '84; gold medal, Pan American Games, 1983; silver medal, Pan American Games, 1995.

LUANN RYON b. January 13, 1953, Riverside, California

Ryon's first international competition was definitely the big time—the 1976 Olympics. Ryon shot her personal best during the trials to make the team, then surpassed it with a score of 2,499 to win the gold medal. The next year, she won the World Target Championship with a woman's world record score of 2,515. Winner of multiple international and U.S. championships, Ryon was also a two-time collegiate all-American.

Selected championships and honors: Four National Target Championships, 1976–78 and '82; National Field Championship, 1976; three gold medals, Championships of the Americas, 1976, '80, and '82; National Indoor Championship, 1977; gold medal, World Target Championships, 1977; bronze medal, Pan American Games, 1983.

MELANIE SKILLMAN b. September 23, 1954, Lauderdale, Pennsylvania

A member of the 1988 U.S. Olympic squad, Skillman helped her team to a bronze-medal finish and won an individual gold at that year's Championships of the Americas. Skillman previously won a national field title and finished second in the national target competitions in 1987 and '88.

Selected championships and honors, individual: National Field Championship, 1985; gold medal, Championships of the Americas, 1988. *Team:* Bronze medal, Olympic Games, 1988.

DOREEN WILBUR b. January 8, 1930, Jefferson, Iowa

Wilbur scores a "first" on several counts. The first woman to score 1,200 in a FITA round in a national championship and the first amateur woman to score 500 in a field round of a national championship, she's also the first female archer to have her Olympic uniform enshrined in the Smithsonian. Wilbur didn't pursue the sport seriously until she was in her early thirties and didn't compete in the nationals until 1965. Her first major win was the national field title in 1967, and she took her first national target championship in 1969. Her gold-medal-winning score of 2,424 at the 1972 Olympics set a world record.

Selected championships and honors: National Field Championship, 1967; two silver medals, World Target Championships, 1969 and '71; three National Target Championships, 1969, '71 and '74; gold medal, Olympic Games, 1972.

Archery Awards

The Shenk Award

The Shenk Award is given each year to the male and female archer with the highest accumulated score from the U.S. Indoor, U.S. Field, and National Target Championships. The award originated in 1980 to recognize former NAA president and executive secretary Clayton Shenk for his dedication and contributions to the sport of archery.

Olympic Games

Archery was included in the 1900, 1904 (U.S. gold for Lida Howell), 1908, and 1920 Olympic Games, with each host country using its own rules and format. The resulting confusion caused the sport to be dropped until international rules were adopted in 1972.

Archery

Shenk Award

Year	Player
1982	Ruth Rowe
1983	Ruth Rowe
1984	Rebecca Wallace
1985	Eileen Pylypchuk
1986	Kitty Frazier
1987	Terry Quinn
1988	Debra Ochs
1989	Judi Adams
1990	Julie Nelson
1991	Janet Dykman
1992	Judi Adams
1993	Julie Nelson
1994	Courtney Kane
1995	Janet Barrs
1996	Teresa Kuhloney

Olympics

Year	Medalists	Country
1972	Doreen Wilbur	USA
	Irena Szydlowska	POL
	Emma Gapchenko	USSR
1976	Luann Ryon	USA
	Valentina Kovpan	USSR
	Zebinsio Rustamova	USSR
1980	Keto Losaberidze	USSR
	Natalya Butuzova	USSR
	Paivi Meriluoto	FIN
1984	Seo Hyang-soon	KOR
	Li Lingjuan	CHN
	Kim Jin-ho	KOR
1988	Kim Soo-nyung	KOR
	Wang Hee-kyung	KOR
	Yun Young-sook	KOR
1992	Cho Youn-jeong	KOR
	Kim Soo-nyung	KOR
	Natalia Valveeva	Moldova Republic
1996	Kim Kyung-wook	KOR
	He Ying	CHN
	Olena Sadovnycha	UKR

Team

1996	Kim Jo-sun, Yoon Hye-young, Kim Kyung-wook	KOR
		GER
		POL

World Target Championships

Year	Champion	Country
1959	Ann Weber Corby	USA
1961	Nancy Vonderheide	USA
1963	Victoria Cook	USA
1965	Marie Lindholm	Finland
1967	Maria Maczynska	Poland
1969	Dorothy Lidstone	Canada
1971	Emma Gapchenko	Russia
1973	Linda Myers	USA
1975	Zeiniso Rustamova	Russia
1977	Luann Ryon	USA
1979	Kim Jin-ho	Korea
1981	Natalia Boutousova	Russia
1983	Kim Jin-ho	Korea
1985	Irina Soldatova	Russia
1987	Ma Xiangjun	China
1989	Kim Soo-nyung	Korea
1991	Kim Soo-nyung	Korea
1993	**Recurve (Olympic) Bow** Kim Hyo-jung	Korea
1995	**Compound Bow** Angela Moscarelli	USA
	Recurve (Olympic) Bow Natalia Valveeva	Moldova Republic

World Indoor Championships

1991	**Recurve (Olympic) Bow** Natalie Valveeva	Moldova Republic
	Compound Bow Lucia Panico	Italy
1993	**Recurve (Olympic) Bow** Natalia Valveeva	Moldova Republic
	Compound Bow Glenda Penaz	USA

Archery (continued)

World Field Championships

Year	Recurve (Olympic) Bow	Compound Bow	Barebow
1969	Irma Danielsson (Sweden)		Rae Dabelow (USA)
1970	Sonia Johansson (Sweden)		Eunice Schewe (USA)
1972	Maureen Bechdolt (USA)		Ingegerd Granquist (Sweden)
1974	Lucille Lessard (Canada)		Eunice Schewe (USA)
1976	Annemarie Lehmann (Germany)		Shirley Sandiford (Grt Britain)
1978	Annemarie Lehmann (Germany)		Suizuko Kobuchi (Japan)
1980	Carita Jussila (Finland)		Sirpa Kontilla (Finland)
1982	Carita Jussila (Finland)		Annie Dardenne (France)
1984	Lisa Buscombe (Canada)		Giuseppina Meini (Italy)
1986	Carita Jussila (Finland)		Annie Dardenne (France)
1988	Liselott Andersson (Sweden)		Giuseppina Meini (Italy)
1990	Carole Ferriou (France)	Ann Shepherd (Grt Britain)	Nadine Visconti (France)
1992	Carole Ferriou (France)	Susanne Kessler (Denmark)	Nadine Visconti (France)
1994	Jenny Sjouall (Sweden)	Michelle Ragsdale (USA)	Odile Boussiere (France)
1996	Carole Ferriou (France)	Petra Ericsson (Sweden)	Odile Boussiere (France)

Pan American Games

Year	Medalists	Country
1979	Lynette Johnson	USA
	Carol Strausberg	USA
	Joan McDonald	CAN
1983	Ruth Rowe	USA
	Debra Ochs	USA
	Linda Kazienko	CAN
1987	Denise Parker	USA
	Trena King	USA
	Eva Bueno	CUB
1991	Denise Parker	USA
	Jennifer O'Donnell	USA
	Aurora Breton	MEX
1995	Janet Dykman	USA
	Ruth Rowe	USA
	Marisol Breton	MEX

BOWLING

◆ *With a membership of more than 2 million bowling enthusiasts, the Women's International Bowling Congress is the largest single sports membership organization in the world.*

HISTORY

The sport that originated in Egypt around 5200 B.C. had to wait seven centuries for women to discover it. Female bowlers made their debut in Gilded Age America, but organized competition didn't begin until the early twentieth century. The first tourney, held in Cincinnati in 1908, was organized by wives tired of watching while their husbands vied for prizes in American Bowling Congress tournaments. Pivotal during the early days was Ellen Kelly, who formed the St. Louis

Women's Bowling Association in 1915 and promoted the formation of similar leagues across the country. In 1916 Kelly, joined by local bowling alley proprietor Dennis Sweeney, organized the first women's competition. Held in St. Louis on the heels of the men's annual ABC tournament, the event attracted eight five-woman teams whose members hailed from eleven different cities. The prize money—$222—was shared by winners of four events. The team title went to the Progress of St. Louis. Mrs. Roy Acker and Mrs. Jack Reilly took the doubles event, and Mrs. A. J. Koester won both the singles and all-events titles. These ladies, whose first names were never officially recorded, were the first real money winners in the history of women's bowling. Before returning to their homes, the participants met at Sweeney's to form a national league. Though the league's name changed several times over the years, the purpose and spirit did not. The association that eventually became known as the Women's International Bowling Congress was born in Dennis Sweeney's Washington Recreation Parlor in St. Louis, Missouri, in 1918.

THE MODERN ERA

Women's bowling enjoyed a meek half-century, and world-class women bowlers were hard-pressed to find venues worthy of their skills. Such was the case for Floretta Doty McCutcheon, one of the best of the century. In 1927, at her peak at age thirty-nine, she challenged men's champion Jimmy Smith to a three-game match and beat him by four points. Such attention-getting feats kept the women's game alive, but organized professional competition didn't gain a significant toehold until 1960, when the Professional Women Bowlers Association (renamed the Women's Professional Bowling Association in 1978) was formed. The PWBA Championship and the WIBC Queens tournament, which began in 1961, gave the sport two showcase competitions. Under the aegis of these organizations, and later the Ladies Professional Bowlers Tour (LPBT), events and purses increased nationwide. The sport got another boost in the mid-1970s, when competitions began to be televised. Bowling in the 1990s is no longer a TV ratings-getter, and fewer people are bowling recreationally than in the past. Nevertheless, women's bowling is alive and well. In the United States, the LPBT administers a host of extremely competitive events, with purses worth over $1.5 million each season. The bowling scene also includes numerous youth, collegiate, and amateur events. Team USA, formed in 1987, consists of two six-member teams (women's and men's) and represents the United States in national and international play. Popular in many countries throughout the world, bowling was a demonstration sport at the 1988 summer Olympics in Seoul and has been eligible for inclusion as a medal event in the Pan American Games since 1986. World Championships, presided over by the Federation Internationale

des Quillers, began in 1954 but offered no events for women until 1963. Today, approximately 200 women from four dozen countries participate in team as well as individual World Championship events. Though America is widely thought of as the home of contemporary bowling, it by no means dominates the sport. Women from the Scandinavian countries, Korea, and Japan are especially likely to be found at the top of the charts.

Halls of Fame

Two halls of fame honor women bowlers in the United States. In 1984 the WIBC, in conjunction with the men's ABC, opened a hall of fame and museum in downtown St. Louis. Over one hundred women have been inducted, either for superior performance or for service to the WIBC. In 1995 a hall of fame was established by the LPBT at Sam's Town Bowling Center in Las Vegas, Nevada. The ten charter inductees included PWBA founder Georgia Veatch, pioneer enthusiast Helen Duval, and performers **Patty Costello, Millie Martorella Ignizio, Donna Adamek, Dorothy Fothergill, Marion Ladewig,** and **Betty Morris.**

Major Events and Awards

BPAA U.S. Open
WIBC Queens
Sam's Town Invitational
WPBA (PWBA) National Championship
BWAA Bowler of the Year
LPBT Player of the Year
WPBA and LPBT Rookie of the Year

Governing Bodies and Organizations

Women's International Bowling Congress (WIBC)
5301 South 76th Street
Greendale, Wisconsin 53129-1127
Phone: 414/421-9000
Fax: 414/421-4420

Ladies Professional Bowlers Tour (LPBT)
7171 Cherry Vale Boulevard
Rockford, Illinois 61112

Phone: 815/332-5756
Fax: 815/332-9636

* * * BIOGRAPHIES * * *

DONNA ADAMEK b. February 1, 1957, Duarte, California

Known as "Mighty Mite," Adamek dominated bowling in the late 1970s and early '80s and was the first woman to win bowling's triple crown—the BPAA Open, WIBC Queens, and Sam's Town Invitational. She also won the WPBA Championship in its final year and remains the only woman to win Australia's Melbourne Cup.

Selected championships and honors: Two BPAA U.S. Opens, 1978 and '81; two Queens, 1979 and '80; WPBA Championship, 1980; Sam's Town Invitational, 1988; four-time BWAA Bowler of the Year, 1978–81; LPBT Hall of Fame.

PATTY COSTELLO b. January 31, 1947, Scranton, Pennsylvania

One of the most exciting rookies in bowling history, Costello won three pro titles in her debut season (1970), two the next year, and five the year after that. She holds the record for individual pro titles won in a single season (seven, in 1976). By the time she retired, her pro titles numbered over two dozen, making her one of just four women to break the twenty-title career mark.

Selected championships and honors: Two BPAA U.S. Opens, 1974 and '76; Sam's Town Invitational, 1985; three WPBA Championships, 1971, '72, and '76; two-time BWAA Bowler of the Year, 1972 and '76; LPBT Player of the Year, 1985; WIBC Hall of Fame; LPBT Hall of Fame.

DOROTHY FOTHERGILL b. April 10, 1945, Lincoln, Rhode Island

Her career was abbreviated due to an arm injury, but from 1967 through the late 1970s Fothergill was one of the preeminent bowlers on the women's tour. She was the tour's top money winner two years in a row (1968 and '69) and won major championships through the mid-1970s. Her game began to decline in the late 1970s due to arthritis, and she retired in 1978.

Selected championships and honors: Two BPAA U.S. Opens, 1968 and '69; two WPBA Championships, 1968 and '69; two WIBC Queens, 1972 and '73; two-time BWAA Bowler of the Year, 1968 and '69.

MILLIE IGNIZIO *See Millie Martorella Ignizio, below.*

PATRICIA (TISH) JOHNSON b. June 8, 1962, Oakland, California

A self-taught left-hander, Johnson joined the pro tour in 1980 and is one of the dominant bowlers on the scene today. In 1995 she became one of only four women to register more than twenty pro title career wins. Johnson holds records for perfect games in a season (seven, in 1993) and is one of only two women to top the $700,000 career earning mark.

Selected championships and honors: BPAA U.S. Open, 1992; three Sam's Town Invitationals, 1989, '92, and '94; three-time BWAA Bowler of the Year, 1990, '92, and '95; two-time LPBT Bowler of the Year, 1992 and '95.

MARION LADEWIG b. October 30, 1918, Grand Rapids, Michigan

As a teenager, Ladewig earned money from her very first day at the lanes—$2.50, her salary as a cashier, cleaner, and sometimes pinsetter. The job sparked her interest in the sport, and Ladewig went on to become bowling's first superstar. She dominated the sport throughout the fifties, was the first woman ever to be named International Bowler of the Year (1957), and won a record fifth World Invitational title in 1965, the year she retired. To win the BPAA title in 1951 she averaged 247.5 over an eight-day period—a higher average than the BPAA men's tournament winner the same year. Named Greatest Woman

> I have loved bowling all my life. It has always gotten me through the rough times by helping me stay focused and giving me a goal to accomplish.
>
> —Tish Johnson

FEATS AND FIRSTS

Rose Jacobs was the first woman credited with a perfect 300 game. She did it in Schenectady, New York, in 1929.

Everyone's choice for top bowler of all time, **Marion Ladewig** was the first woman to be named International Bowler of the Year (1957) and is the only bowler in the International Women's Sports Hall of Fame.

Proving that age doesn't count but pins do, pioneer pro Helen Duval rolled a perfect game at age sixty-five.

Proving that age doesn't count at the rookie end of the spectrum either, Wendy Macpherson rolled a 300 game at just fourteen, four years before becoming the LPBT's Rookie of the Year in 1986.

No woman has ever won as many pro titles in a season as **Patty Costello,** three of whose seven 1976 titles were won back to back.

Although no woman has ever bowled a perfect game in televised play, Paula Drake of DeSoto, Texas, came the closest with a 299 game in August 1987.

In 1988 **Donna Adamek** became the first and only woman to win Australia's Melbourne Cup.

The first woman to break the gender barrier and bowl in the ABC Masters tournament was Linda Wallace, in 1995.

Bowler of All Time in a 1973 poll, Ladewig remains the experts' pick as best of the best and is the only bowler in the International Women's Sports Hall of Fame, inducted 1984.
Selected championships and honors: Nine BPAA Championships, 1949–52, '54, '56, '59, and '63; WPBA Championship, 1960; nine times BPAA Bowler of the Year, 1950–54, '57–'59, '63; International Women's Sports Hall of Fame; WIBC Hall of Fame; LPBT Hall of Fame.

MILLIE MARTORELLA IGNIZIO b. January 11, 1947, Rochester, New York

Martorella took off like a rocket in 1967, when she was just twenty. That year she garnered both the Alberta Crow Star of Tomorrow and BWAA Bowler of the Year Awards. Over the next seven years, bowling both as Millie Ignizio and Millie Martorella, she became known best as "Marvelous Millie," winner of three WIBC Queens titles and one BPAA U.S. Open championship. Debilitating arthritis forced Martorella to retire in the mid-1970s, but in a few short seasons she built a gilt-edged reputation as one of the all-time best.
Selected championships and honors: Three WIBC Queens, 1967, '70, and '71; BPAA U.S. Open, 1973; BWAA Bowler of the Year, 1967; LPBT Hall of Fame.

BETTY MORRIS b. May 10, 1948, Sonora, California

Although *Bowler's Journal* and *Bowling Illustrated* named her 1970s Bowler of the Decade, Morris has actually won titles in four decades—the 1960s, '70s, '80s, and '90s. Morris's best year may have been 1974, when she scored a first- or second-place finish in eleven of the fifteen tournaments she entered. She is the only woman credited with two perfect games in the same day, bowled on June 2, 1976, during a BPAA Open in which she finished second. After a slump in the 1980s, Morris came roaring back in 1987 to lead the tour in season's earnings and be named bowler of the year by the BWAA and LPBT.
Selected championships and honors: BPAA U.S. Open, 1977; WPBA Championship, 1973; three-time BWAA Bowler of the Year, 1974, 1977, and '87; LPBT Player of the Year, 1987; WIBC Hall of Fame; LPBT Hall of Fame.

LISA RATHGEBER WAGNER b. May 19, 1961, Hillsboro, Illinois

The winningest woman in pro bowling, Wagner tops the charts with twenty-nine pro titles as of December 31, 1995. Named 1980s Bowler of the Decade by *Woman Bowler* and *Bowling Magazine*, Wagner became familiar as the most televised woman on the tour, setting records for most career TV appearances

(83), most games bowled on television (142), and most televised match wins (83). Wagner was the first woman to earn more than $100,000 in a season (1988) and ranks third in all-time career earnings.
Selected championships and honors: BPAA Open, 1988; four-time BWAA Bowler of the Year, 1983, '86, '88, and '93; twice LPBT Player of the Year, 1988 and '93.

ALETA RZEPECKI SILL b. September 9, 1962, Detroit, Michigan
We don't know if Sill has a theme song, but if she does it might well be "We're in the Money." Sill has topped the LPBT season's earning charts a record six times and holds the record for most money earned in a season ($126,325, in 1994). She is one of only two women to earn more than $700,000 in her career and is one of only four women to have won more than twenty pro titles.
Selected championships and honors: BPAA U.S. Open, 1996; two WIBC Queens, 1983 and '85; two Sam's Town Invitational, 1984 and '86; two-time BWAA Bowler of the Year, 1984 and '85; LPBT Player of the Year, 1984; WIBC Hall of Fame.

LISA WAGNER *See Lisa Rathberger Wagner, above.*

Bowling

WIBC Queens

Year	Winner	Runner-Up
1961	Janet Harman	Eula Touchette
1962	Dorothy Wilkinson	Marion Ladewig
1963	Irene Monterosso	Georgette DeRosa
1964	D. D. Jacobson	Shirley Garms
1965	Betty Kuczynski	LaVerne Carter
1966	Judy Lee	Nancy Peterson
1967	Millie Martorella Ignizio	Phyllis Massey
1968	Phyllis Massey	Marian Spencer
1969	Ann Feigel	Millie Martorella Ignizio
1970	Millie Martorella Ignizio	Joan Holm
1971	Millie Martorella Ignizio	Katherine Brown
1972	Dotty Fothergill	Maureen Harris
1973	Dotty Fothergill	Judy Soular
1974	Judy Soular	Betty Morris
1975	Cindy Powell	Patty Costello
1976	Pam Buckner	Shirley Sjostrom
1977	Dana Stewart	Vesma Grinfelds
1978	Loa Boxberger	Cora Fiebig
1979	Donna Adamek	Shinobu Saitoh
1980	Donna Adamek	Cheryl Robinson
1981	Katsuko Sugimoto	Virginia Norton
1982	Katsuko Sugimoto	Nikki Gianulias
1983	Aleta Sill	Dana Miller-Mackie
1984	Kazue Inahashi	Aleta Sill
1985	Aleta Sill	Linda Graham
1986	Cora Fiebig	Barbara Thorberg
1987	Cathy Almeida	Lorrie Nichols
1988	Wendy Macpherson	Leanne Barrette
1989	Carol Gianotti	Sandra Jo Shiery
1990	Patty Ann	Vesma Grinfelds
1991	Dede Davidson	Jeanne Maiden
1992	Cindy Coburn-Carroll	Dana Miller-Mackie
1993	Jan Schmidt	Pat Costello
1994	Anne Marie Duggan	Wendy Macpherson-Papanos
1995	Sandra Postma	Carolyn Dorin
1996	Lisa Wagner	Tammy Turner

BPAA U.S. Open

Year	Winner	Runner-Up
1949	Marion Ladewig	Catherine Burling
1950	Marion Ladewig	Stephanie Balogh
1951	Marion Ladewig	Sylvia Wene
1952	Marion Ladewig	Shirley Garms
1953	not held	
1954	Marion Ladewig	Sylvia Wene
1955	Sylvia Wene	Sylvia Fanta
1955	Anita Cantaline	Doris Porter
1956	Marion Ladewig	Marge Merrick
1957	not held	
1958	Marie Matthews	Marion Ladewig
1959	Marion Ladewig	Donna Zimmerman
1960	Sylvia Wene	Marion Ladewig
1961	Phyllis Notaro	Hope Riccilli
1962	Shirley Garms	Joy Abel
1963	Marion Ladewig	Bobbie Shaler
1964	LaVerne Carter	Evelyn Teal
1965	Ann Slattery	Sandy Hooper
1966	Joy Abel	Bette Rockwell
1967	Gloria Bouvia	Shirley Garms
1968	Dotty Fothergill	Doris Coburn
1969	Dotty Fothergill	Kayoka Suda
1970	Mary Baker	Judy Cook
1971	Paula Carter	June Llewellyn
1972	Lorrie Nichols	Mary Baker

Bowling (continued)

BPAA U.S. Open

Year	Winner	Runner-Up
1973	Millie Martorella	Patty Costello
1974	Patty Costello	Betty Morris
1975	Paula Carter	Lorrie Nichols
1976	Patty Costello	Betty Morris
1977	Betty Morris	Virginia Norton
1978	Donna Adamek	Vesma Grinfelds
1979	Diana Silva	Bev Ortner
1980	Pat Costello	Shinobu Saitoh
1981	Donna Adamek	Nikki Gianulias
1982	Shinobu Saitoh	Robin Romeo
1983	Dana Miller-Mackie	Aleta Sill
1984	Karen Ellingsworth	Lorrie Nichols
1985	Pat Mercatani	Nikki Gianulias
1986	Wendy Macpherson	Lisa Wagner
1987	Carol Norman	Cindy Coburn
1988	Lisa Wagner	Lorrie Nichols
1989	Robin Romeo	Michelle Mullen
1990	Dana Miller-Mackie	Tish Johnson
1991	Anne Marie Duggan	Leanne Barrette
1992	Tish Johnson	Aleta Sill
1993	Dede Davidson	Dana Miller-Mackie
1994	Aleta Sill	Anne Marie Duggan
1995	Cheryl Daniels	Tish Johnson
1996	Liz Johnson	Marianne DiRupo

BWAA Bowler of the Year

Year	Winner
1948	Val Mikiel
1949	Val Mikiel
1950	Marion Ladewig
1951	Marion Ladewig
1952	Marion Ladewig
1953	Marion Ladewig
1954	Marion Ladewig
1955	Sylvia Wene
1956	Anita Cantaline
1957	Marion Ladewig
1958	Marion Ladewig
1959	Marion Ladewig
1960	Sylvia Wene
1961	Shirley Garms
1962	Shirley Garms
1963	Marion Ladewig
1964	LaVerne Carter
1965	Betty Kuczynski
1966	Joy Abel
1967	Millie Martorella
1968	Dotty Fothergill
1969	Dotty Fothergill
1970	Mary Baker
1971	Paula Sperber
1972	Patty Costello
1973	Judy Soular
1974	Betty Morris
1975	Judy Soular
1976	Patty Costello
1977	Betty Morris
1978	Donna Adamek
1979	Donna Adamek
1980	Donna Adamek
1981	Donna Adamek
1982	Nikki Gianulias
1983	Lisa Rathgeber
1984	Aleta Sill
1985	Aleta Sill
1986	Lisa Wagner
1987	Betty Morris
1988	Lisa Wagner
1989	Robin Romeo
1990	Tish Johnson
1991	Leanne Barrette
1992	Tish Johnson
1993	Lisa Wagner
1994	Anne Marie Duggan
1995	Tish Johnson
1996	Wendy Macpherson

LPBT Player of the Year

Year	Winner
1983	Lisa Rathgeber
1984	Aleta Sill
1985	Patty Costello
1986	Jeanne Maiden
1987	Betty Morris
1988	Lisa Wagner
1989	Robin Romeo
1990	Leanne Barrette
1991	Leanne Barrette
1992	Tish Johnson
1993	Lisa Wagner
1994	Anne Marie Duggan
1995	Tish Johnson
1996	Wendy Macpherson

Bowling (continued)

PWBA Champion

Year	Winner
1960	Marion Ladewig
1961	Shirley Garms
1962	Stephanie Balogh
1963	Janet Harman
1964	Betty Kuczynski
1965	Helen Duval
1966	Joy Abel
1967	Betty Mivalez
1968	Dotty Fothergill
1969	Dotty Fothergill
1970	Bobbe North
1971	Patty Costello
1972	Patty Costello
1973	Betty Morris
1974	Patty Costello
1975	Pam Buckner
1976	Patty Costello
1977	Vesma Grinfelds
1978	Toni Gilliard
1979	Cindy Coburn
1980	Donna Adamek

Bowling Rookie of the Year

Year	Winner
1978	Toni Gillard
1979	Nikki Gianulias
1980	Lisa Rathgeber
1981	Cindy Mason
1982	Carol Norman
1983	Anne Marie Pike
1984	Paula Vidad
1985	Dede Davidson
1986	Wendy Macpherson
1987	Paula Drake
1988	Mary Martha Cerniglia
1989	Kim Terrell
1990	Debbie McMullen
1991	Kim Kahrman
1992	Marianne DiRupo
1993	Kathy Zielke
1994	Tammy Turner
1995	Krissy Stewart
1996	Liz Johnson

Sam's Town Invitational

Year	Winner	Runner-Up
1984	Aleta Sill	Cheryl Daniels
1985	Patty Costello	Robin Romeo
1986	Aleta Sill	Dina Wheeler
1987	Debbie Bennett	Lorrie Nichols
1988	Donna Adamek	Robin Romeo
1989	Tish Johnson	Dede Davidson
1990	Wendy Macpherson	Jeanne Maiden
1991	Lorrie Nichols	Dana Miller-Mackie
1992	Tish Johnson	Robin Romeo
1993	Robin Romeo	Tammy Turner
1994	Tish Johnson	Carol Gianotti
1995	Michelle Mullen	Cheryl Daniels
1996	Carol Gianotti	Leanne Barrette

BILLIARDS

◆ *There's no Olympic medal for it, but there is a pro women's tour—and a surprising number of women play for fun and relaxation.*

HISTORY

Have you ever wondered why the playing surface of the pool table is green? The answer lies in the origins of the game. Billiards evolved from a fifteenth-century sport similar to modern croquet. It was played outside, on a green sweep of lawn, with balls and mallets. When the game was miniaturized and brought indoors, the green of the playing surface was retained. Although billiards probably originated in France, it quickly became popular throughout Europe. Shakespeare mentions the sport anachronistically in *Antony and Cleopatra*, and by the late 1600s most towns in England had a public pool table. Around this time, mallets were replaced by pool cues, since the head of the mallet made it difficult to play balls that lay near the edge of the table.

For billiards, the "great leap forward" came in the nineteenth century. Improvements in equipment, made possible by the industrial revolution, introduced new opportunities for skilled players. Adding a leather tip to the cue, for example, made it possible to use spin, a technique called "English" by Americans and "side" by everyone else. Billiard parlors flourished, including the famous Bassford's, a New York establishment that catered to the Wall Street crowd. The sport retained its popularity into the early years of the twentieth century, and variations of the game that have now become standard established themselves. Eight ball appeared shortly after the turn of the century, while straight pool (also known as 14.1) dawned with the Roaring Twenties.

Women's participation in the sport has been heavily influenced by socioeconomics. Billiard tables have been largely found either in pubs and taverns or in clubs. For many years this made the sport effectively off-limits for most women. Not only were "nice" women supposed to steer clear of bars and clubs but the men who patronized them would hardly have welcomed a female onslaught. As a result, only two types of women had access to tables: those whose husbands were wealthy enough to have a billiard room in the home, and those who were willing to flout convention. Despite these limitations, each generation can point to at least one woman who could wield a cue with the best of men, including turn-of-the century trick shot artist May Kaarlus and the 1930s' Ruth McGinnus, who toured the country with male champion Willie Mosconi.

THE MODERN ERA

In America two movies—*The Hustler* in 1961 and *The Color of Money* in 1986—sparked widespread interest in the sport and created a new demand for public tables. For women, the release of the Paul Newman–Jackie Gleason classic was especially well timed. Pool's new popularity coincided with the early stages of the feminist move-

Major Events and Competitions

World Championships
U.S. Open

ment, and women suddenly saw no reason to be kept out of the sport. Women played in local bars alongside their husbands and boyfriends, as well as in the many family billiard parlors that were built to meet the new demand. By 1967 there were enough top-class women players for the sport's governing body, the Billiard Congress of America, to initiate women's division championships. World championships for women began in the 1970s, and a professional tour, under the aegis of the Women's Professional Billiard Association, was organized in 1976. The release of *The Color of Money* in the middle of the 1980s refueled America's interest in billiards, this time producing a wave of upscale parlors in urban centers across the country—and introducing another generation of young women to the sport.

Governing Bodies and Organizations

Women's Professional Billiard Association
1411 Pierce Street
Sioux City, Iowa 51105
Phone: 712/252-4789
Fax: 712/252-4799

* * * BIOGRAPHIES * * *

JEAN BALUKAS b. 1959, Brooklyn, New York
Balukas began competing before separate championships for women even existed, entering her first U.S. Open when she was nine years old and finishing a respectable seventh. She eventually won the Open seven times, took six women's world championships, and was named Player of the Year five times. In 1985 Balukas became the youngest member named to the Billiard Congress of America's Hall of Fame.
Selected championships and honors: Seven U.S. Opens, 1972–77 and '83; six World Championships, 1977–80, '82, and '83.

ROBIN BELL DODSON b. May 30, 1956, Garden Grove, California
Bell began playing pool as a teenager and by 1972 had won the first of three consecutive state championships in California. Bell retired from amateur competition in the late 1970s and, after a five year break, joined the pro tour in 1984. In addition to winning dozens of individual events, Bell has won two world championships and finished the 1995 season as the number-one-ranked woman on the tour.
Selected championships and honors: Two World Championships, 1990 and 1991.

LOREE JON OGONOWSKI JONES
b. November 6, 1965, Hillsborough, New Jersey
Four-year-old Ogonowski started fooling around in her father's billiard room, and twelve years later, at the tender age of fifteen, became the youngest-ever world champion in her sport. In addition to four World Championships and two U.S. Opens, Ogonowski had a terrific 1995 season, earning just under $100,000 despite taking several months off to have her third child. *Selected championships and honors:* Four World Championships, 1981, '84, '86, and '93; two U.S. Opens, 1989 and '92.

DOROTHY WISE b. 1914, Spokane, Washington
A pioneer in women's billiards, Wise began playing when there were few organized tournaments. However, she won so many state and local tournaments in America that she made a name for herself despite the lack of official accolades. When Wise began referring to herself as the unofficial women's world champion, no one disputed her. In the late 1960s she finally got a chance to earn an official spot in the record books. When the Billiard Congress of America initiated a U.S. Open championship for women in 1967, Wise entered and won five consecutive titles. In 1981 she became the first woman ever inducted into the Billiard Congress's Hall of Fame.
Selected championships and honors: Five U.S. Opens, 1967–71.

Billiards

World Championships

Year	Tournament	Player
1974	World 14.1 Championship	Meiko Harada
1977	World 14.1 Championship	Jean Balukas
1978	World 14.1 Championship	Jean Balukas
1979	World 14.1 Championship	Jean Balukas
1980	World 14.1 Championship	Jean Balukas
1981	World 14.1 Championship	Loree Jon Jones
1982	World 14.1 Championship	Jean Balukas
1983	World 14.1 Championship	Jean Balukas
1984	World 9-Ball Open	Loree Jon Jones
1985	World 14.1 Championship	Belinda Bearden
1986	World 14.1 Championship	Loree Jon Jones
1987	not held	
1988	not held	
1989	not held	
1990	WPA World Championship	Robin Bell
1991	WPA World Championship	Robin Bell
1992	WPA World Championship	Franziska Stark
1993	WPA World 9-Ball Championship	Loree Jon Jones
1994	WPA World 9-Ball Championship	Ewa Mataya-Laurance
1995	WPA World 9-Ball Championship	Gorda Hofstatter
1996	WPA World 9-Ball Championship	Allison Fisher

WPBA Hall of Fame

Year	Player	Country
1976	Ruth McGinnis	USA
1980	Dorothy Wise	USA
1990	Masako Katsura	Japan

Photo credit: Ken Regan/Camera 5

SHOOTING

♦ *Although some think of marksmanship as a man's sport, America's first great celebrity athlete was a shooter and a woman—Annie Oakley.*

HISTORY

An odd fact of sports history is that, while women were often discouraged from enjoying relatively tame pursuits such as running and cycling, they were seldom discouraged from blood sports that revolved around hunting. Women were admired as archers and routinely rode to hound, perched on precarious sidesaddles. When the gun was introduced and women took it up as well, there was little noticeable outcry. Though women in cities had little exposure to firearms, women in less settled regions probably learned to shoot at a young age. Chronicles of the American frontier are especially rich in references to women who could hunt and shoot, and their abilities rise far above the amateur marksman level. Although a family might own just one rifle, and that one rifle might belong chiefly to the head of the household, it was also a shared possession, and women developed their skills by hunting small game for food.

Early rifles, which required both laboriously hand-fashioned ammunition and manual loading, hardly lent themselves to sport. But as equipment became standardized and ammunition grew more abundant, casual competitions became common. Fancy marksmanship and stunt shooting also became popular, especially along the rough-and-tumble American frontier, and here, in a haze of blue smoke, America's first female sports superstar rose to fame.

THE MODERN ERA

Organized world shooting competition began in 1907, when eight nations formed the International Shooting Union. The United States joined the organization the next year. Women did not begin participating in major international shooting events until much later, however. Women's World Championship competition dates from 1966. Women entered Olympic shooting in 1968, competing equally with men. Beginning in 1984, some events were broken out as exclusive men's or women's events, and as of 1996 all events were separated by gender. Both Olympic and World Championship competition include rifle as well as pistol events.

Governing Bodies and Organizations

USA Shooting
One Olympic Plaza
Colorado Springs, CO 80909
Telephone: (719) 578-4670

Major Events and Competitions

The major events in international shooting are the Olympic Games and the World Championships. Both include four competitive events:

Small-bore rifle
Air rifle
Sport pistol
Air pistol

Annie Moses, Better Known As Oakley

Born in Ohio on the eve of the Civil War, Annie Moses developed her talents to help feed her family. Her marksmanship was so good that soon she was shooting for profit as well, supplying restaurants with quail and other game birds. Moses was the pride of Greenville, Ohio, and in 1895 her neighbors raised money to send her to Cincinnati to compete in a shooting match against Frank Butler, who had his own traveling show. Moses defeated Butler, who promptly hired her for the show and changed her name to Oakley. The two eventually married, and Butler had no qualms about playing second fiddle to his wife, who became one of America's best-known celebrities of the day. He also had no qualms about placing his life in his wife's hands—one of Oakley's stunts involved shooting a cigarette from Butler's lips. Oakley's other feats involved hitting a playing card at thirty paces, hitting a dime tossed in the air, and—using three double-barreled shotguns—breaking six glass balls thrown in the air before any touched the ground. Few people who met Oakley failed to be charmed by her. Sitting Bull, who traveled with Oakley and Butler in Buffalo Bill Cody's Wild West Show, referred to her as "Little Sureshot." Irving Berlin found her intriguing enough to write a musical about her, *Annie Get Your Gun*. Oakley, who outlived her husband, continued to shoot long after her retirement. At the age of sixty-two, just four years before she died, she was still an accomplished trapshooter who could hit 100 targets in a row.

* * * BIOGRAPHIES * * *

MARINA DOBRANCHEVA LOGVINENKO
b. Rostov-on-Don, Russia

Through the 1980s and early 1990s, Dobrancheva was one of the best female pistol shooters in the world, always at or near the top of her sport. In Olympic and World Championship competitions she won six golds, three in air pistol and three in sport pistol.

Selected championships and honors: Two gold medals, air pistol, World Championships, 1982 and '85; bronze medal, air pistol, Olympic Games, 1988; two gold medals, sport pistol, World Championships, 1986 and '90; gold medal, sport pistol, Olympic Games, 1992; gold medal, air pistol, Olympic Games, 1992.

VESSELA LETCHEVA b. Bulgaria
Letcheva never won an Olympic gold medal, but she nevertheless is one of the premier riflists of the modern era. At the 1988 Seoul Olympics, Letcheva's performance was hindered by media mayhem. Reporters found her irresistibly beautiful, and dogged her every step. Unused to the attention, Letcheva crumbled under the pressure and finished in seventeenth place in the air rifle competition. A few days later she regained her composure and came from behind to finish second in the small-bore competition. Her best performances were in the World Championships, where she won five titles—two in small-bore and three in air rifle.

Selected championships and honors: Two gold medals, small-bore rifle, World Championships, 1986 and '90; three gold medals, air rifle, World Championships, 1986–89; silver medal, small-bore, Olympic Games, 1988.

LAUNI MEILI b. United States
A keen eye is one aspect of shooting, and an ability to quell nerves is another. At the 1988 Olympics Meili was in first place two-thirds of the way through the small-bore rifle competition. On the third leg of the event, jitters overcame Meili, and she slipped from first place to seventh. She also finished out of the medals in her other event, air rifle. Four years later, Meili again was in first place after the first two rounds of the small-bore rifle competition, leading by just two points. This time Meili was able to ignore her jitters and hang on to win the gold.

Selected championships and honors: Gold medal, small-bore rifle, Olympic Games, 1992.

MARGARET MURDOCK. *See Margaret Thompson Murdock, below.*

KIM RHODE b. July 16, 1979, El Monte, California
Rhode had just turned seventeen when she became the youngest person ever to win a medal in Olympic shooting, taking a gold in double trap at the Atlanta games. Rhode, who had placed first in the same event at the national championships the year before, became interested in shooting after accompanying her family on hunting trips. She began competing at age eleven and joined the U.S. team in 1994. In her event, Rhode missed only 19 of 160 shots.

Selected championships and honors: Bronze medal, double trap, World Cup, 1995; gold medal: double trap, Olympic Games, 1996. *Team wins:* Gold, skeet, World Cup, 1995.

MARGARET THOMPSON MURDOCK
b. August 25, 1942, Topeka, Kansas

At the 1967 Pan American Games, Murdock set a world record in small-bore rifle competition by shooting a score of 391. This event, barely noticed by the media, was the first time in sports history that a women's world record had surpassed a men's record in any sport. Nine years later, at the Montreal Olympics, Murdock competed in the same event, then a coed competition. When she finished in a tie with American teammate Lanny Basham, the judges awarded the gold to Basham on rules technicalities. At the award ceremony, Basham reached down and drew Thompson up to him, and the two shared the top platform together as the anthem was played. As a marksman, Thompson didn't receive the attention she might have if her sport had been a more publicized one, but she remains a groundbreaking champion in women's sports.

Selected championships and honors: Two gold medals, small-bore rifle, World Championships, 1966 and '70; silver medal, small-bore, three positions, Olympic Games, 1976; Women's Sports Hall of Fame.

PAT SPURGIN b. ca. 1966, Billings, Montana
Spurgin was a teenager from Montana when she competed at the Los Angeles Olympics in 1984. Her event, air rifle, was being staged for the first time, and Spurgin faced fierce competition, especially from

China's Wu Xiaoxuan, small-bore rifle gold medalist. Just before the competition, a friend advised Spurgin to think of ducks on a pond—calm on the surface, paddling like hell underneath. Spurgin took the advice and finished two points ahead of Italy's Edith Gufler, hitting 393 of 400 shots. Xiaoxuan finished in third place.

Selected championships and honors: Gold medal, small-bore rifle, Olympic Games, 1984.

Shooting

Olympic Sport Pistol

Year	Medalists	Country	Points
1896–1980	event not held		
1984	Linda Thom	CAN	585/198
	Ruby Fox	USA	585/197
	Patricia Dench	AUS	583/196
1988	Nino Salukvadze	GEO	690
	Tomoko Hasegawa	JPN	686
	Jasna Sekaric	YUG	686
1992	Marina Logvinenko (Dobrancheva)	RUS	684
	Li Duihong	CHN	680
	Dorzhsuren Munkhbayar	MGL	679
1996	Li Duihong	CHN	687.9
	Diana Yorgova	BUL	684.8
	Marina Logvinenko	RUS	684.2

Olympic Air Pistol

Year	Medalists	Country	Points
1896–1984	event not held		
1988	Jasna Sekaric	YUG	489.5 WR
	Nino Salukvadze	GEO	487.9
	Marina Dobrancheva	RUS	485.2
1992	Marina Logvinenko (Dobrancheva)	RUS	486.4/99.4
	Jasna Sekaric	YUG	486.4/97.4
	Maria Grozdeva	BUL	481.6
1996	Olga Klochneva	RUS	490.1
	Marina Logvinenko*	RUS	488.5
	Mariya Grozdeva	BUL	488.5

*Won shootoff.

Shooting (continued)

Olympic Small-Bore Rifle, Three Positions

Year	Medalists	Country	Points
1896–1980	event not held		
1984	Wu Xiaoxuan	CHN	581
	Ulrike Homer	GER	578
	Wanda Jewell	USA	578
1988	Sylvia Sperber	GER	685.6
	Vessela Letcheva	BUL	683.2
	Valentina Cherkasova	RUS	681.4
1992	Launi Meili	USA	684.3
	Nonka Matova	BUL	682.7
	Malgorzata Ksiazkiewicz	POL	681.5
1996	Aleksandra Ivosev	YUG	686.1
	Irina Gerasimenok	RUS	680.1
	Renata Mauer	POL	679.8

Olympic Air Rifle

Year	Medalists	Country	Points
1896–1980	event not held		
1984	Pat Spurgin	USA	393
	Edith Gufler	ITA	391
	Wu Xiaoxuan	CHN	389
1988	Irina Shilova	BLR	498.5
	Sylvia Sperber	GER	497.5
	Anna Malukhina	RUS	495.8
1992	Yeo Kab-soon	KOR	498.2
	Vessela Letcheva	BUL	495.3
	Aranka Binder	YUG	495.1
1996	Renata Mauer	POL	497.6
	Petra Horneber	GER	497.4
	Aleksandra Ivosev	YUG	497.2

Olympic Double Trap

Year	Medalists	Country	Points
1896–1992	event not held		
1996	Kim Rhode	USA	141
	Susanne Kiermayer*	GER	139
	Deserie Huddleston	AUS	139

*Won shootoff.

Photo credit: Bongarts

CYCLING

◆ *Cycling, which wheeled to popularity as women were breaking free of Victorian constraints, offers a unique window on women's shifting role over the past hundred years.*

HISTORY

Among the sketches left in the notebooks of Leonardo da Vinci is a prototype for something remarkably akin to the modern bicycle. As far as we know, it was never built. But in the nineteenth century the velocipede—as early machines were called—became the rage of western Europe and, eventually, the world.

From the start, the bicycle was seen as both a recreational and a sports vehicle, and women's desire not only to ride sedately but to compete touched off storms of controversy. In allowing women to race without objection, the French win the blue ribbon for sportsmanship. As early as 1868, young women raced through the Bois de Boulogne to a cheering crowd. The next year, in a race from Paris to Rouen, four women competed with the men. Across the channel, things were not so sanguine. In 1893 Tessie Reynolds, sixteen, rode from Brighton to London and back in 8.5 hours. Reynold's 120-mile ride ignited a national debate. Never mind that Reynolds accomplished the ride in good health; her countrymen had but one question to ask: *should* women be allowed to undertake such rides? Unfortunately for the naysayers, the genie was already out of the bottle. Women would continue to compete, even as events became more and more grueling.

From the late 1880s right through the 1930s, six- and even eight-day races were cycling's most popular event. In 1895 sixteen-year-old Frankie Nelson won a tortuous six-day race in New York City. She went on to compete in Europe, the mecca of the cycling world. The same year Nelson won her New York race, French world champion Hélène Dutrier set a record by covering 39.19 kilometers in an hour. The next year Amélie LeGall, who rode under the name "Lisette," rode a 100-kilometer race against Scotland's Clara Grace and won with a time of 2 hours, 41 minutes, and 12 seconds. The immensely popular Lisette went on to compete against men, beating renowned cyclist Albert Champion in a 25-kilometer race.

Despite these successes, the ride for most women was far from smooth. Cycling arrived during a time of immense transition, as the physically tepid Victorian damsel was making her final bow and the fit and energetic girl of the new century was waiting in the wings. Victorian society recognized cycling as a healthful—and therefore desirable—activity for women. An advertisement for the ill-fated *Titanic*, for example, shows a woman using a stationary cycle in the ship's gymnasium. On the other hand, cycling differed from other sports of the era in that it required neither organization nor supervision. Basketball, field hockey, tennis, and other activities all placed women within a secure arena. But cycling did not, and that was the problem. Frances Willard, champion of women's rights, grasped the significance of cycling as early as 1895 when she proclaimed, "She who succeeds in gaining the mastery of the bicycle will gain the mastery of life." For many, this was precisely the problem. Mounted on a bicycle, capable of covering great distances on her own, dependent on no one for permission and needing nothing but the power of her own legs—there was no telling where such a woman might end up.

Proof that the road to hell could be ridden on a bicycle came in the machine's configuration and the demands it made upon the female user. The sweeping skirts of the era, distinctly unsuitable for cycling, were replaced by bloomers. The idea of wearing bloomers in public—scandalous enough when worn in the privacy of a gymnasium—in public shocked the Victorians. A *New York Times* column of the 1890s chided that a woman in bloomers "does not stand the glare of sunshine well." In Chicago young women who wore bloomers to a dance were threatened with arrest, and the dance itself was shut down by the police. Moreover, women who cycled were risking their sexual health and purity. Dozens of medical articles appeared attacking cycling because the saddle design, combined with pedaling, was thought to produce genital friction. This, of course, would lead to moral degeneration and general sexual promiscuity. Manufacturers responded by modifying the machine (see "The Cycle: A Brief History," sidebar on page 238) to eliminate such dangers. These modifications ultimately led to the wide-saddled, high-handlebarred bike that dominated most of the twentieth century. It was a morally wholesome, sexually safe, societally approved machine that not only discouraged promiscuity—it made racing nearly impossible.

THE MODERN ERA

U.S. men's championships began in 1899, and national women's events were added in 1937. Despite this, cycling did not capture the public imagination until the 1980s. The early popularity of cycle racing died out as the automobile took over and car races became the public's favorite. While long-established events such as the Tour de France continued, they did not gain appreciably in popularity until after World War II. Bicycles seemed tame, emblems of a slower, bygone era.

Then, beginning in the early 1970s, bicycle culture underwent a dynamic change. Racing-style bikes, previously used only by aficionados and eccentrics, began to be mass marketed. The light and streamlined frame, range of gears, and low handlebars encouraged what the Victorians had tried so hard to suppress—racing for speed. New crops of consumers grew up with these bikes rather than the heavy-bodied bikes of the past. They also grew up in an era that placed

◆ ◆

THE CYCLE: A BRIEF HISTORY

Around 1500, Leonardo da Vinci entered a sketch in his notebooks for a two-wheeled vehicle—complete with chains and gears—remarkably like today's bicycle. The machine was never produced, and the bicycle had to wait more than 300 years to be officially invented. Unfortunately, early models weren't nearly as ingenious as da Vinci's sketch. There were no gears or chains, not even a way of propelling the thing. The first bicycles, in fact, resembled hobbyhorses with wheels. The rider could coast and steer, but could not make the thing go. When a Scottish blacksmith named Kirkpatrick MacMillan added pedal power in 1834, it was hailed as a great innovation.

The first bicycles offered anything but a smooth and comfortable ride. The U.S. patent granted to Pierre Lallement and James Carroll in 1866, for example, depicts a wooden body whose wooden wheels were covered with iron for durability. A decade later, cycling took a surrealistic turn when a new model was exhibited at the Centennial Exposition in Philadel-phia. The new machine, with an enormous front wheel, high-above-the-ground seat, and small back wheel, was quite literally out of reach of women. A far tamer vehicle—an adult-sized version of a tricycle—was provided for ladies, and one can only imagine the thrill of cruising along at a brisk few miles an hour.

Ten more years brought another evolution in bicycle design, when Englishman James Starley introduced the "safety bicycle." Starley restored sanity to wheel size, made both wheels of equal size, and added gears. Two years later, in 1888, an Irish veterinary surgeon named John Dunlop developed the pneumatic tire. Dunlop's invention was quickly adapted to Starley's, and the prototype for the modern bicycle was born. Over the past 100 years, endless improvements, experiments, and modifications have been made. Today's racing bike is a tribute to aerodynamic design, craftsmanship, and man-made materials, and new designs are likely to be guarded as closely and unveiled with as much fanfare as racing yachts.

fresh emphasis on fitness. Aerobic activities weren't just for "professional" athletes—they were for everyone. Like running, cycling was rescued from the tar pits of sport history to become chic. A movie such as *Breaking Away,* made in the mid-1970s, gave racing more publicity than it had received since Hemingway's "A Pursuit Race," written fifty years earlier.

For women, the watershed year in the new era was 1984, the inaugural year for the Tour de France Féminin. More important, however, was the inclusion of women's cycling in the Olympics. The 70-kilometer road race introduced at the Los Angeles games was won by American **Connie Carpenter Phinney,** with teammate **Rebecca Twigg** taking the silver. A 1,000-meter sprint was added in 1988, a 3,000-meter individual pursuit premiered in 1992, and 1996 saw the addition of a road time trial as well as a cross-country race.

Major Events and Awards

Professional cycling is structured much like golf, with tours and circuits that include dozens of individual events. The major international competitions, open to professionals and amateurs alike, are the Olympic Games and the World Championships. The number of events for women cyclists has increased dramatically since the mid-1980s, and medal events at the 1996 Olympics included:

1,000-meter match sprint road race
3,000-meter individual pursuit road time trial
Points race
Cross-country race

Governing Bodies and Organizations

U.S. Cycling Federation
One Olympic Plaza
Colorado Springs, CO 80909
Phone: 719/578-4581
Fax: 719/578-4628

Bicycle Federation of America
1818 R Street, NW
Washington, D.C. 20009

* * * BIOGRAPHIES * * *

BERYL BURTON b. 1937, England.
One of the greatest cyclists of all time, Burton beat the men's top distance as well as the women's with her 277.27-mile performance in a 12-hour distance race in 1967. During her career she won more than eighty British titles, including twenty-three straight Women's Best British All-Rounder championships (1958–1980). Burton also won seven World Championships, excelling in both pursuit and road racing.
Selected championships and honors: Five gold medals, pursuit, World Championships, 1959, '60, '62, '63, and '66; two gold medals, road, World Championships, 1960 and '67.

CONNIE CARPENTER PHINNEY b. February 26, 1957, Madison, Wisconsin
Put the word "first" after Carpenter's name, and you won't go wrong. In 1984 she became the first woman ever to compete in both winter and summer Olympics, after making her debut as a speed skater in 1972. Because '84 was the year cycling became an Olympic sport for women, Carpenter was also first to bring the United States a woman's cycling gold. Carpenter switched to competitive cycling after a serious ankle injury in 1976. She won three national cycling titles, then suffered a concussion in 1979. She returned to competition in 1981 and began winning national titles once again. Carpenter's first international victory, the World Championship in pursuit racing, came less than eight weeks after she broke her arm. Her most exciting win was in the 79-kilometer road race at the 1984 Olympics. Just three meters from the tape and dead even with U.S. teammate **Rebecca Twigg,** Carpenter rose out of the saddle and threw her arms forward, using her weight to propel her bike across the finish line—a tactic learned from husband Davis Phinney. Carpenter retired after the '88 games and since has worked on the Olympic Committee,

served on the U.S. Cycling Federation board, coached, and worked to promote women's athletics.
Selected championships and honors: Gold medal, pursuit, World Championship, 1983; gold medal, road, Olympic Games, 1984; International Women's Sports Hall of Fame.

JULI FURTADO b. United States
When Furtado was born, mountain biking (also known as cross-country racing) didn't exist. A California-born sport, mountain biking and Furtado have shaped each other's lives and futures. When the first mountain bike World Championships were held in 1990, Furtado won. By 1995 she was able to pull down an estimated $400,000 a year in prize money and endorsements.

BETH HEIDEN. *See entry under Speed Skating.*

JEANNIE LONGO CIPRELLI b. ca. 1958, France
Men's sports are loaded with bad boys, but in women's sports a bad girl is bound to get attention—and Longo does. A brilliant pursuit cyclist, Longo's penchant for changing coaches at will and refusal to race in team competitions or wear sponsors' products has been much publicized. She was so certain France would expel her from the 1992 Olympic team that she threatened to ride for Luxembourg or Morocco. In the end she rode for France, taking a silver in the road race. Winner of multiple World Championships as well as the women's Tour de France, Longo said she had all the medals she wanted. Nevertheless she was back for the 1996 Olympics and earned the one medal that had eluded her, an Olympic gold.
Selected championships and honors: Three gold medals, pursuit, World Championships, 1986, '88, and '89; silver medal, road, Olympic Games, 1992; gold medal, road, Olympic Games, 1996.

SUE NOVARA REBER November 22, 1955, Flint, Michigan

Novara began as a sprint cyclist and ended her career as a road racer. In 1975, at nineteen, she became the youngest competitor ever to win the women's World Sprint Championship. She repeated the win in 1980, then revamped her style and training program to make the transition from the track to road racing. She had several top finishes in important races but failed to win another international event and retired in 1984. *Selected championships and honors:* Two gold medals, World Sprint Championships, 1975 and '80.

CONNIE PARESKEVIN YOUNG b. United States

A match sprint dynamo who competed under her married name, Young won three consecutive World Championships between 1982 and '84. When her event was included in the Olympics for the first time, in 1988, Young was on hand to win the bronze. She closed out her international career with a typically terrific finishing kick—a fourth World Championship, won in 1990.

Selected championships and honors: Four gold medals, match sprint, World Championships, 1982–84, 1990; bronze medal, match sprint, Olympic Games, 1988.

Hands Across the Water

When the Soviet Union crumbled, Estonia resolved to field its own team at the 1992 Olympic Games, something it had not been able to do since being annexed by the USSR in 1940. The goal often seem unreachable. Funding was hard to come by, and athletes were hard-pressed to find training facilities, coaching, and support. Cyclist **Erika Salumäe** got a helping hand from American rival **Connie Young,** who'd finished third to Salumäe's first in the match sprint event at Seoul. Young oversaw the arrangements that made it possible for Salumäe to train part of each year in the United States. When thirty-six athletes marched under the Estonian flag in the opening ceremonies at Barcelona, Salumäe was one of them.

CHRISTA ROTHENBURGER LUDING. *See entry under Speed Skating.*

ERIKA SALUMÄE b. Tallinn, Estonia

If Salumäe was American, her story would have become a made-for-TV movie by now. Raised in an orphanage, Salumäe won her first cycling medal as a member of the Soviet team. She was welcomed home by cheering crowds—and one hopeful placard that read OUR OWN TEAM IN BARCELONA IN 1992. The dream became reality when the Soviet Union fell. Salumäe defended her match sprint medal in Barcelona, competing despite a painful back injury against a tough field that included world record holder Galina Yenyokhina. Because of Salumäe's win, the Estonian flag was raised at the Olympics for the first time in more than half a century.

Selected championships and honors: Two gold medals, match sprint, Olympic Games, 1988 and '92; gold medal, match sprint, World Championships, 1989.

REBECCA TWIGG b. March 26, 1963, Honolulu, Hawaii

She's smart, she cycles, and she may be America's best-known female cyclist ever. That's what most people know about Twigg. Born in Hawaii and raised in Seattle, *acceleration* is the keyword in Twigg's life. She was a college freshman at age fourteen and a world champion at nineteen, when she won the first of an eventual six gold medals in World Championship pursuit competitions. Finishing second to teammate **Connie Carpenter** in the 1984 Olympic Games road race, Twigg retired after failing to make the 1988 Olympic team. Life in the slow track proved intolerable, however, and she unretired in 1991. She was soon back in gear, winning two more World Championships. Although Twigg made the '96 U.S. Olympic squad, she had a disappointing showing in the quarterfinals, and after a dispute with the team coach over her training methods, Twigg abruptly packed her bags and returned to her home in Colorado Springs.

Selected championships and honors: Six gold medals, pursuit, World Championships, 1982, '84, '85, '87, '93, and '95; silver medal, road race, Olympic Games, 1984; gold medal, pursuit, Pan American Games, 1987; gold medal, road, Pan American Games, 1987; bronze medal, individual pursuit, Olympic Games, 1992.

KATHRYN WATT b. ca. 1965; Warrgul, Australia
Growing up in a small Australian town, Watt had
plenty of space to practice in as a child. It paid off, and
Watt came home from the 1992 Olympics with gold
and silver in her pocket, the first woman from Down
Under to medal in cycling. Watt's speed and small
stature—just 5'½"—may have factored into one of the
most unusual finishes in Olympic history. With a full
ten-mile circuit left to go in the '92 road race, Watt
slipped away from the pack unnoticed and overtook
the leaders. When world champion **Jeannie Longo**
crossed the finish line, the French team cheered—
only to discover that Watt had crossed the line 20 seconds before, forcing Longo to settle for a silver.
Selected championships and honors: Gold medal,
road, Olympic Games, 1992; silver medal, pursuit,
Olympic Games, 1992.

CONNIE YOUNG. *See Connie Pareskevin Young,
above.*

SHEILA YOUNG OCHOWICZ. *See entry under
Speed Skating.*

Cycling

Olympic Road Race

1896–1980	event not held		Time
1984	Connie Carpenter Phinney	USA	2:11.14
	Rebecca Twigg	USA	2:11.14
	Sandra Schumacher	GER	2:11.14
1988	Monique Knol	HOL	2:00.52
	Jutta Niehaus	GER	2:00.52
	Laima Ziporite	LIT	2:00.52
1992	Kathryn Watt	AUS	2:04.42
	Jeannie Longo Ciprelli	FRA	2:05.02
	Monique Knol	HOL	2:05.03
1996	Jeannie Longo Ciprelli	FRA	2:36.13
	Imelda Chiappa	ITA	2:36.38
	Clara Hughes	CAN	2:36.44

Olympic Points Race

1896–1992	event not held		
1996	Nathalie Lancien	FRA	24
	Ingrid Haringa	HOL	23
	Lucy Sharman Tyler	AUS	17

Olympic Individual Cross-Country (32 km)

1896–1992	event not held		
1996	Paola Pezzo	ITA	1:50.51
	Allison Sydor	CAN	1:51.58
	Susan DeMattei	USA	1:52.36

Olympic Individual Match Sprint

1896–1984	event not held	
1988	Erika Salumäe	EST
	Christa Rothenburger Luding	GDR
	Connie Young	USA
1992	Erika Salumäe	EST
	Annett Neumann	GER
	Ingrid Haringa	HOL
1996	Felicia Ballanger	FRA
	Michelle Ferris	AUS
	Ingrid Haringa	HOL

Olympic 3000m Individual Pursuit

1896–1988	event not held		
1992	Petra Rossner	GER	3:41.753
	Kathryn Watt	AUS	3:43.438
	Rebecca Twigg	USA	3:52.429
1996	Antonella Bellutti	ITA	3:33.595
	Marion Clignet	FRA	3:38.571
	Judith Arndt	GER	3:38.744

CANOE AND KAYAK, SCULLS, YACHTING

HISTORY

Boats, some of the earliest vehicles developed by man, reached a level of sophistication early in history. Well before the birth of Christ, while the chariot was still the land vehicle of choice, ocean-going vessels were already engaged in exploration, conquest, and commerce. A measure of the craftsmanship and engineering involved is suggested in this fact: except for the introduction of newer, lighter, and tougher synthetics, the basic design of man-powered craft such as the native American kayak has changed little over the centuries. And though we think of crewed shells as a product of the late Victorian era, the proto-type model—the Viking dragon ship—dates back more than a thousand years.

The first known all-female regatta was held in 1493. It was one of many events staged to celebrate the arrival of Beatrice d'Este in Venice, and involved fifty peasant girls clad in short skirts. The pageant was a vivid success, and the young women in their costumes completely upstaged the men's regatta that followed.

Though informal races and contests were probably always engaged in, formalized contests stem from the affluence and ease of British upper-middle-class Victorian culture. Early contests were part athletic event, part ritual spectacle. Boys from Eaton and other schools wore crowns of flowers as they rowed, and form was paramount over speed. Boating also benefited from the physical fitness movement of the late nineteenth and early twentieth centuries, when a serious effort was made to establish sports within the college curricula. In the mid-1890s one of England's leading Chaucer scholars, Dr. Furnival, made a campaign of encouraging college women to row for health and exercise. A popular British novel of 1899, *Miss Cayley's Adventures,* celebrates an athletically minded coed who, among other sports, rows competitively. The first collegiate rowing club for women was established at Wellesley in 1875. As with early European versions of the sport, spectacle was the keynote rather than speed, and the season's culmination, Float Night, featured sweet-voiced women, lit by lanterns, rowing gently to their own chorus of song. Yachting similarly got off to a gentle start, with country club regattas serving more as social than competitive events. In the United States, Vassar and Wellesley led the way in introducing rowing. Although early regattas were more pageant than sport—Wellesley women were judged on grace and form rather than speed—competition soon entered the picture. By 1898 Wellesley women were so intent on training that they worked out on rowing machines when inclement weather kept them indoors.

Outside the college campus, boating also gained popularity as a sport for women. The sport was especially popular in Scandinavia and Germany. A Berlin rowing club held a canoe race for women as early as 1895, and an all-women's club was established six years later. Other women's clubs were formed in Copenhagen, Oslo, and Warsaw. In 1919 the several separate women's clubs in Berlin and other parts of Germany came together to establish a national rowing club for women.

THE MODERN ERA

Women's boating didn't become an international sport until after World War II. Although rowing for men became part of the Olympic roster in 1900 and yachting was added in 1920, events for women were not added until 1976 and 1988 re-

spectively. The first Olympic boating event for women, kayak, was added to the first Olympic Games held after the war, twelve years but just one Olympiad after men's kayaking became an event. Prior to 1988, all women's races were rowed on a 1,000-meter course. From the 1988 games on, the course was extended to 2,000 meters, the same length used by men.

Despite the fact that Americans Allison Jolly and Lynne Jewell won the inaugural 470 yachting competition in 1992, boating sports in general have not captured American attention. Rowing especially has been dominated by the women of Europe and the old Soviet bloc. The first American woman to win a single sculls medal was Janet Lind, who took the silver in 1976.

Several factors may contribute to boating's lack of popularity in America. Few Americans have participated in any of the sports, compared to the millions of Americans who have firsthand knowledge of baseball, basketball, tennis, and other sports. Another factor may be that in celebrity-oriented America, boating—with the exception of single sculls—is a team event, and all three boating categories offer a welter of odd-sounding and frequently changing events and lack the "big game" drama of other sports. Finally, coverage of Olympic boating events has tended to be sporadic at best, making it difficult for even devout fans to follow their favorite contests.

To most Americans, the best-known boating event is not an Olympic contest but the Americas Cup, a five-month sailing contest. Although the event began before the Civil War, women did not become involved until recently. In 1992 self-made millionaire and amateur sailor Bill Koch of Kansas entered the race with a radically new top-secret design. As Americas Cup enthusiasts know, radical new hush-hush designs are the rule rather than the norm for racing, but Koch's boat, the *Mighty Mary,* lived up to its hype and won the event, despite having a less experienced crew than other entrants. The next year Koch did something even more radical. He announced that he was putting his boat, his research, and several million dollars in seed money in the hands of women. In 1995 the *America*[3] crew would become the first all-woman crew in sailing history. Six hundred and fifty women applied for the twenty-four available slots, and would-be sailors included several Olympic rowers and one well-toned star from *American Gladiators*. Although the crew suffered from lack of training time and failed to make it past the defense finals in 1995, their showing was good enough to prove that women, either alone or crewing with men, definitely do have a future in the Americas Cup.

Governing Bodies and Organizations

U.S. Sailing
Box 1260
Portsmouth, Rhode Island 02971
Phone: 401/683-0800

U.S. Rowing Association
Pan American Plaza
Suite 400
201 South Capitol Avenue
Indianapolis, Indiana 46225
Phone: 317/237-5656

Major Olympic Competitions

Rowing
Single sculls
Double sculls
Quadruple sculls
Coxless pairs
Coxless fours
Coxed eights
Discontinued Events
Coxed quadruple sculls
Coxless pair-oared shell
Coxed pairs

Yachting
Women's Events
Mistral (windsurfer)
Europe (single-handed dinghy)
470 (two-person dinghy)
Open Events
Laser (centerboard dinghy)
Tornado (two-person multihull)
Soling (keelboat/match racing)
Star (two-person keelboat)

Canoe/kayak
Singles 500 meters
Pairs 500 meters
Fours 500 meters
Slalom singles

✳ ✳ ✳ BIOGRAPHIES ✳ ✳ ✳

CAROL BROWN b. Philadelphia, Pennsylvania

Brown was a member of several U.S. teams in the late 1970s, when events for women began to be included in international competitions. Most notably, she was on the eight-oared crew that won a silver medal at the 1975 World Championships, America's first medal in rowing. She was also on the '86 Olympics bronze-medal team. Chances for a second Olympic medal were spoiled by the United States' decision to boycott the 1980 games.
Selected championships and honors: Two silver medals, 8-oared crew, World Championships, 1975 and '81; bronze medal, 8-oared crew, Olympic Games, 1976; bronze medal, 8-oared crew, World Championships, 1979.

BIRGIT FISCHER SCHMIDT b. ca. 1962, East Germany

The most decorated woman on the world canoe/kayak stage, Fischer competed in five consecutive Olympics, beginning with the 1980 games. At Moscow she was the youngest person to ever win a gold medal in Olympic canoe/kayak, taking the 500-meter kayak singles when she was just eighteen. She did not have a chance to defend her title, due to East Germany's boycott of the '84 games, but won two more medals in the event in '88 and '92. She has also won medals in kayak pairs and fours.
Selected championships and honors: Two gold medals, 500m kayak singles, Olympic Games, 1980 and '92; silver medal, 500m kayak singles, Olympic Games, 1988; gold medal, 500m kayak pairs, Olympic Games, 1988; gold medal, 500m kayak fours, Olympic Games, 1988; silver medal, 500m kayak fours, Olympic Games, 1992; silver medal, 500m kayak pairs, Olympic Games, 1996.

VIRGINIA GILDER b. United States

Turned down by coaches who felt she was too small, Gilder finally made the U.S. Olympic team in 1980—and never got to compete. She went on to compete in elite single and double and single and quad scull. A broken rib kept her from making the next Olympic single scull squad, but she made the coxed quad scull team despite her injury—and finally got her Olympic medal, a silver.

Selected championships and honors: Bronze medal, single scull, World Championships, 1983; silver medal, coxed quad scull, Olympic Games, 1984.

MARCIA INGRAM JONES (*aka Marcia Smoke*)
b. July 18, 1941, Oklahoma City, Oklahoma
One of the best kayak champions America has ever produced, Ingram dominated the national singles competitions throughout the 1960s. A graduate of the University of Michigan, Ingram won the national kayak singles competition from 1963 to 1973. At the 1964 Olympics she brought the United States its first medal in women's kayak by winning the bronze in her event. She competed in the 1968 games as well, finishing in fourth place.

Selected championships and honors: Bronze medal, 500m kayak singles, Olympic Games, 1964.

RITA KOBAN b. 1965, Budapest, Hungary
Perhaps the top woman kayaker of the 1990s, Koban began as a junior champion in her native Budapest. Her first wins in senior competition came at the 1985 World Championships, where she took home a silver (pairs) and a bronze (fours). Her first international gold came at the 1992 Olympic Games, where she was on the winning fours squad. She also earned a pairs silver. She has been virtually unbeatable ever since, especially at the World Championships. In her singles win at the 1995 championships, Koban posted the biggest margin of victory ever.

Selected championships and honors: Gold medal, kayak fours, Olympic Games, 1992; silver medal, kayak pairs, Olympic Games, 1992.

SILKEN LAUMANN b. ca. 1965, Mississauga, Ontario, Canada
One of the most dramatic stories in Olympic rowing belongs to Canadian Silken Laumann, the 1991 world champion. Ten weeks before the Barcelona Olympics, Laumann's shell was accidentally rammed by the German coxless pair's shell. A piece of splintered wood was driven through Laumann's leg, shattering bone and severing muscles and ligaments. The accident was so brutal that, after getting Laumann to safety, both German rowers fainted. Though doctors told Laumann to take six months off to recuperate, Laumann

refused to give up her Olympic dream. She did, however, scale back her expectations. Realizing she had no real chance at winning, she made it her personal goal to compete and to finish ahead of at least one competitor. Laumann did compete, and she rowed to an amazing bronze-medal finish, a full second ahead of America's Anne Marden. At the '96 games she came back to claim a silver in the same event.

Selected championships and honors: Bronze medal, single sculls, Olympic Games, 1992; silver medal, single sculls, Olympic Games, 1996.

BRIGIT PETER b. ca. 1965, Potsdam, East Germany
One of the great rowers of all time, Peter dominated the 1980s and is regarded as technically near perfect, with a smooth, balanced technique that makes the most of each stroke. In World Championship and Olympic competition, Peter has won gold in singles, pairs, and quadruple sculls.

Selected championships and honors: Gold medal, double sculls, Olympic Games, 1988; gold medal, single sculls, World Championship, 1990; gold medal, quadruple sculls, Olympic Games, 1992.

THERESA ZABELL b. ca. 1965, Ipswich, England
Though born in England, Zabell is a longtime resident of Spain and very much part of that country's illustrious yachting success. In addition to a dozen national titles in her specialty, the 470 class, Zabell has won three World Championships and two Olympic gold medals. Her partner for both Olympic performances was Begona Via Dufresne. Appropriately enough, Zabell currently lives in an apartment that was part of Barcelona's Olympic Village and overlooks the spot where she won her first gold medal in 1992.

Selected championships and honors: Two Olympic gold medals, 470-class yacht, 1992 and '96.

Kayak

Olympic Singles 500 Meters

Year	Medalists	Country	Time
1896–1936	event not held		
1948	Karen Hoff	DEN	2:31.9
	Alida van der Anker-Doedens	HOL	2:32.8
	Fritzi Schwingl	AUT	2:32.9

Kayak (continued)

Olympic Singles 500 Meters

Year	Medalists	Country	Time
1952	Sylvi Saimo	FIN	2:18.4
	Gertrude Liebhart	AUT	2:18.8
	Nina Savina	RUS	2:21.6
1956	Yelizaveta Dementyeva	RUS	2:18.9
	Therese Zenz	GER	2:19.6
	Tove Soby	DEN	2:22.3
1960	Antonina Seredina	RUS	2:08.08
	Therese Zenz	GER	2:08.22
	Daniela Walkowiak	POL	2:10.46
1964	Lyudmila Khvedosyuk	RUS	2:12.87
	Hilde Lauer	ROM	2:15.35
	Marcia Jones	USA	2:15.68
1968	Lyudmila Pinayeva (Khvedosyuk)	RUS	2:11.09
	Renate Breuer	GER	2:12.71
	Viorica Dumitru	ROM	2:13.22
1972	Yulia Ryabchynska	UKR	2:03.17
	Mieke Jaapies	HOL	2:04.03
	Anna Pfeffer	HUN	2:05.50
1976	Carola Zirzow	GDR	2:01.05
	Tatiana Korshunova	RUS	2:03.07
	Kiara Rajnai	HUN	2:05.01
1980	Birgit Fischer	GDR	1:57.96
	Vania Gesheva	BUL	1:59.48
	Antonina Melnikova	BLR	1:59.66
1984	Agneta Andersson	SWE	1:58.72
	Barbara Schuttpelz	GER	1:59.93
	Annemiek Derckx	HOL	2:00.11
1988	Vania Gesheva	BUL	1:55.19
	Birgit Schmidt (Fischer)	GDR	1:55.31
	Izabella Dylewska	POL	1:57.38
1992	Birgit Schmidt (Fischer)	GDR	1:51.60
	Rita Koban	HUN	1:51.96
	Izabella Dylewska	POL	1:52.36
1996	Rita Koban	HUN	1:47.65
	Caroline Brunet	CAN	1:47.89
	Josefa Idem	ITA	1:48.73

Olympic Pairs 500 Meters

Year	Medalists	Country	Time
1896–1956	event not held		
1960	Maria Chubina/ Antonina Seredia	RUS	1:54.76
	Therese Zenz/ Ingrid Hartmann	GER	1:56.66
	Klara Fried-Banfalvi/ Vilma Egresi	HUN	1:58.22
1964	Roswitha Esser/ Annemarie Zimmerman	GER	1:56.95
	Francine Fox/ Gloriane Perrier	USA	1:59.16
	Hilde Lauer/ Cornelia Sideri	ROM	2:00.25
1968	Roswitha Esser/ Annemarie Zimmerman	GER	1:56.44
	Anna Pfeffer/ Katalin Roznyoi	HUN	1:58.60
	Antonia Seredina/ Lyudmila Pinayeva (Khvedosyuk)	RUS	1:58.61
1972	Lyudmila Pinayeva (Khvedosyuk)/ Kateryna Nahima-Kuryshko	RUS	1:53.50
	Ilse Kaschube/ Petra Grabowski	GDR	1:54.30
	Maria Nichiforov/ Viorica Dumitru	ROM	1:55.01
1976	Nina Gopova/ Galina Kreft	RUS	1:51.15
	Anna Pfeffer/ Kiara Rajnai	HUN	1:51.69
	Barbel Koster/ Carola Zirzow	GDR	1:51.81
1980	Carsta Genauss/ Martina Bischof	GDR	1:43.88
	Galina Alexeyeva (Kreft)/Nina Trofimova (Gopova)	RUS	1:46.91
	Eva Rakusz/Maria Zakarias	HUN	1:47.95
1984	Agneta Andersson/ Anna Olsson	SWE	1:45.25
	Alexandra Barre/ Susan Holloway	CAN	1:47.13
	Josefa Idem/ Barbara Schuttpelz	GER	1:47.32

Kayak (continued)

Olympic Pairs 500 Meters

Year	Medalists	Country	Time
1988	Birgit Schmidt (Fischer)/ Anke Nothnagel	GDR	1:43.46
	Vania Gesheva/ Diana Paliiska	BUL	1:44.06
	Annemiek Derckx/ Annemarie Cox	HOL	1:46.00
1992	Ramona Portwich/ Anke von Seck (Nothnagel)	GER	1:40.29
	Susanne Gunnarsson (Wiberg)/ Agneta Andersson	SWE	1:40.41
	Rita Koban/ Eva Donusz	HUN	1:40.81
1996	Agneta Andersson/ Susanne Gunnarsson	SWE	1:39.32
	Ramona Portwich/ Birgit Fischer	GER	1:39.68
	Katrin Borchert/Anna Wood	AUS	1:40.64

Olympic Fours 500 Meters

1896–1980	event not held		
1984	Agafia Constantin (Buhaev), Nastasia Ionescu, Tecla Marinescu, Maria Stefan	ROM	1:38.34
		SWE	1:38.87
		CAN	1:39.40
1988	Birgit Schmidt (Fischer), Anke Nothnagel, Ramona Portwich, Heike Singer	GDR	1:40.78
		HUN	1:41.88
		BUL	1:42.63
1992	Eva Donusz, Kinga Czigany, Rita Koban, Erika Meszaros	HUN	1:38.32
		GER	1:38.47
		SWE	1:39.79
1996	Ramona Portwich, Manuela Mucke, Birgit Fischer, Anett Schuck	GER	1:31.07
		SWI	1:32.70
		SWE	1:32.91

Olympic Slalom Singles

1896–1968	event not held		
1972	Angelika Bahmann	GDR	364.50
	Gisela Grothaus	GER	398.15
	Magdalena Wunderlich	GER	400.50
1976–1988	event not held		
1992	Elisabeth Micheler	GER	126.41
	Danielle Woodward	AUS	128.27
	Dana Chladek	USA	131.75
1996	Stepanka Hilgertova	CZE	169.49
	Dana Chladek	USA	169.49
	Myriam Fox-Jerusalmi	FRA	171.00

Yachting

Olympic Mistral/Sailboard

			Pts
1896–1988	event not held		
1992	Barbara Kendall	NZE	47.8
	Zhang Xiaodong	CHN	65.8
	Dorien de Vries	HOL	68.7
1996	Lee Lai-Shan	HKG	16
	Barbara Kendall	NZE	24
	Alessandra Sensini	ITA	28

Olympic 470

1896–1988	event not held		
1992	Allison Jolly/ Lynne Jewell	USA	26.7
	Marit Soderstrom/ Birgitta Bengtsson	SWE	40
	Larysa Moskalenko/ Iryna Chunykhovska	UKR	45.4
1996	Theresa Zabell/ Begona Via Dufresne	SPA	25
	Yumiko Shige/ Alicia Kinoshita	JPN	36
	Ruslana Taran/ Olean Pakholchik	UKR	38

Olympic Europe Class

1896–1988	event not held		
1992	Linda Andersen	NOR	48.7
	Natalia Via Dufresne Perena	SPA	57.4
	Julia Trotman	USA	62.7
1996	Kristine Rough	DEN	24
	Margriet Matthijsse	NET	30
	Courtenay Becker-Dey	USA	39

Rowing

All women's races are rowed on a 2,000-meter course. Before 1988, they were rowed at 1,000 meters.

Olympic Single Sculls

Year	Medalists	Country	Time
1976	Christine Scheiblich	GDR	4:05.56
	Joan Lind	USA	4:06.21
	Yelena Antonova	RUS	4:10.24
1980	Sanda Toma	ROM	3:40.59
	Antonina Makhina	RUS	3:41.65
	Martina Schroter	GDR	3:43.54
1984	Valeria Racila	ROM	3:40.68
	Charlotte Geer	USA	3:43.89
	Ann Haesebrouck	BEL	3:45.72
1988	Jutta Behrendt	GDR	7:47.19
	Anne Marden	USA	7:50.28
	Magdalena Georgieva	BUL	7:53.65
1992	Elisabeta Lipa (Oleniuc)	ROM	7:25.54
	Annelies Bredael	BEL	7:26.64
	Silken Laumann	CAN	7:28.85
1996	Ekaterina Khodotovich	BLR	7:32.21
	Silken Laumann	CAN	7:35.15
	Trine Hansen	DEN	7:37.20

Olympic Double Sculls

Year	Medalists	Country	Time
1896–1972	event not held		
1976	Svetla Otsetova, Zdravka Yordanova	BUL	3:44.36
	Sabine Jahn, Petra Boessler	GDR	3:47.86
	Leonora Kaminskaite, Genovaite Ramoskiene	LIT	3:49.93
1980	Yelena Khloptseva, Larissa Popova (Aleksandrova)	USSR	3:16.27
	Cornelia Linse, Heidi Westphal	GDR	3:17.63
	Olga Homeghi, Valeria Racila-Rosca	ROM	3:18.91
1984	Marioara Popescu, Elisabeta Oleniuc	ROM	3:26.75
	Greet Hellemans, Nicolette Hellemans	HOL	3:29.13
	Daniele Laumann, Silken Laumann	CAN	3:29.82
1988	Birgit Peter, Martina Schroter	GDR	7:00.48
	Elisabeta Lipa (Oleniuc), Veronica Cogeanu	ROM	7:04.36
	Violeta Ninova, Stefka Madina	BUL	7:06.03
1992	Kerstin Koppen, Kathrin Boron	GER	6:49.00
	Veronica Cochelea (Cogeanu), Elisabeta Lipa (Oleniuc)	ROM	6:51.47
	Gu Xiaoli, Lu Huali	CHN	6:55.16
1996	Marnie McBean, Kathleen Heddle	CAN	6:56.84
	Cao Mianying, Zhang Xiuyun	CHN	6:58.35
	Irene Eijs, Eeke Van Nes	NET	6:58.72

Quadruple Sculls

Year	Medalists	Country	Time
1896–1984	event not held		
1988	Kerstin Forster, Kristina Mundt, Beate Schramm, Jana Sorgers	GDR	6:21.06
		USSR	6:23.47
		ROM	6:23.81
1992	Kerstin Muller, Sybille Schmidt, Birgit Peter, Kristina Mundt	GER	6:20.18
		ROM	6:24.34
		RUS	6:25.07
1996	Jana Sorgers, Katrin Rutschow, Kathrin Boron, Kerstin Koeppen	GER	6:27.44
		UKR	6:30.36
		CAN	6:30.38

Lightweight: Double Sculls

Year	Medalists	Country	Time
1896–1992	event not held		
1996	Constanta Burcica, Camelia Macoviciuc	ROM	7:12.78
	Teresa Z. Bell, Lindsay Burns	USA	7:14.65
	Rebecca Joyce, Virginia Lee	AUS	7:16.56

Rowing (continued)

Pairs without Cox

Year	Medalists	Country	Time
1896–1992	event not held		
1996	Megan Still, Kate Slatter	AUS	7:01.39
	Missy Schwen, Karen Kraft	USA	7:01.78
	Christine Gosse, Helene Cortin	FRA	7:03.82

Eight-Oared Shell with Coxwain

Year	Medalists	Country	Time
1896–1972	event not held		
1976	Viola Goretzki, Christiane Knetsch, Ilona Richter, Brigitte Ahrenholz, Monika Kallies, Henrietta Ebert, Helma Lehmann, Irina Muller, Marina Wilke	GDR	3:33.32
		USSR	3:36.17
		USA	3:38.68
1980	Martina Boesler, Kersten Neisser, Christiane Kopke (Knetsch), Birgit Schutz, Gabriele Kuhn (Lohs), Ilona Richter, Marita Sandig, Karin Metze, Marina Wilke	GDR	3:03.32
		USSR	3:04.29
		ROM	3:05.63
1984	Shyril O'Steen, Harriet Metcalf, Carol Bower, Carie Graves, Jeanne Flanagan, Kristine Norelius, Kristen Thorsness, Kathryn Keeler, Betsy Beard	USA	2:59.80
		ROM	3:00.87
		HOL	3:02.92
1988	Annegret Strauch, Judith Zeidler, Kathrin Haacker, Ute Wild, Anja Kluge, Beatrix Schroer, Ramona Balthasar, Uta Stange, Daniela Neunast	GDR	6:15.17
		ROM	6:17.44
		CHN	6:21.83
1992	Kirsten Barnes, Brenda Taylor, Megan Delehanty, Shannon Crawford, Marnie McBean, Kay Worthington, Jessica Monroe, Kathleen Heddle, Lesley Thompson	CAN	6:02.62
		ROM	6:06.26
		GER	6:07.80
1996	Anca Tanase, Vera Cochelea, L. Gafencu, Doina Spircu, I. Olteanu, Ellsabeta Lipa, M. Popescu, Doina Ignat, E. Georgescu	ROM	6:19.73
		CAN	6:24.05
		BUL	6:24.44

EQUESTRIAN

◆ *Beautiful to watch, equestrian events are the only Olympic contests in which men and women compete on a wholly equal basis.*

HISTORY

While medieval peasants played stoolball and folk football, the lady of the manor rode, hunted, and hawked with the men. As a result women became excellent horsewomen, even when encumbered by long, heavy skirts and perched precariously on sidesaddles. Women in the American colonies became excellent horsewomen as well, although their style was less genteel than that of their English sisters. British visitors were impressed with their ability and hardiness, but were somewhat taken aback by their eagerness to ride over rough terrain and the ease with which they challenged each other to impromptu, highly competitive races.

Horse racing became common in England during the Restoration, though contests were waged against the clock rather than a field of competitors. By 1721 races were measured in seconds, and the first stopwatches were introduced a decade later. First jockey honors are often attributed to twenty-two-year-old Alicia Thornton, the wife of Colonel Thomas Thornton and a member of Yorkshire's upper crust. In August 1804 she challenged her sister's husband, Captain William Flint, to race for a stake of 1,000 guineas. Alicia won and, two years later, challenged a professional jockey and five-time Derby winner to a two-mile race. This time the stakes were 700 guineas and a gold cup. The event drew a large crowd, and Alicia, riding sidesaddle, won by a neck. She was the toast of York until it became known that she was Colonel Thornton's mistress, not his wife, and upper-crust opinion turned decidedly against her.

THE MODERN ERA

Although women have long ridden, women did not begin to compete with men until relatively recently. Women were first allowed to enter Olympic equestrian events in 1952, competing equally with men. Today, women are well represented in dressage, in which the horse and rider execute a preset roster of halts, paces, direction changes, and figures; in jumping, in which horse and rider attempt to finish a course of obstacles with as few faults in the briefest time possible;

Major Events and Competitions

Olympic and **World Championship** competitions award both individual and team medals for a variety of events, including:

Individual
Three-day event
Jumping
Dressage

Team
Three-day event
Jumping
Dressage

Open to the Public

Training headquarters for the U.S. Equestrian Team are located in New Jersey, off Route 512 just west of Route 206 between Gladstone and Pottersville. The center is open to visitors Monday to Saturday, 9 A.M. to 1 P.M. The Gladstone Center recommends calling ahead of time to determine what activities will be going on the day you intend to visit. Their number is listed below.

---

and in three-day events, in which horse and rider compete in dressage, jumping, and an endurance run over a long course studded with obstacles.

Women have also made incursions into the previously all-male world of thoroughbred racing. In 1968 **Kathy Kusner** became the first licensed female jockey in the United States. Twenty-five years later, **Julie Krone** became the first woman to win a Triple Crown event. Although women jockeys are still rare, they no longer provoke a tidal wave of news coverage.

Governing Bodies and Organizations

U.S. Equestrian Team
Pottersville Road
Gladstone, NJ 07934
Phone: 908/234-1251

American Horse Shows Association (AHSA)
220 East 42nd Street
New York, New York 10017-5876
Phone: 212/972-2472

---

* * * BIOGRAPHIES * * *

LESLIE BURR HOWARD b. October 1, 1956, Westport, Connecticut

Between 1979 and 1984 Burr rode on two winning Nations Cup teams and a gold-medal U.S. Olympic team and set a record for consecutive Grand Prix wins (three in a row, in 1983)—this despite the fact that her winning mount, Chase the Clouds, died and she had to train three new horses. Aboard one of the new horses, Albany, Burr rode on the 1984 team that brought America its first Olympic gold in jumping. She continued to ride on U.S. teams throughout the next decade.

Selected championships and honors, team: Gold medal, jumping, Pan American Games, 1983; gold medal, jumping, Olympic Games, 1984. Mercedes Rider of the Year, 1983.

DIANE CRUMP b. ca. 1949

At Hialeah on February 7, 1969, Crump became the first woman jockey to ride at a pari-mutual track. Mounted on a 48-to-1 long shot, Crump finished in tenth place. The next year Crump became the first female jockey ever to ride in the Kentucky Derby. Her mount, Fathom, finished in fifteenth place.

HILDA GURNEY b. September 10, 1943,
   Moorpark, California

Gurney initially competed in eventing, then switched to dressage, which became her forte. Her best-performing mount was Keen, whom she rode at the 1976 Olympics when the United States took the team bronze. She also rode Keen at the 1979 Pan American Games, when the United States won top team honors in dressage and Gurney took the individual gold. She rode her second mount, Chrysos, at the Pan American games in 1983, and the United States again took the team gold. Gurney and Keen again competed together in the 1984 Olympics but failed to medal.

Selected championships and honors, individual: Gold medal, dressage, Pan American Games, 1979. *Team:* Bronze medal, dressage, Olympic Games, 1976; two gold medals, dressage, Pan American Games, 1979 and '83.

LIS HARTEL b. 1921, Denmark

Hartel was young, pregnant, and one of Denmark's top riders in 1944 when she was stricken with polio. Although she gave birth to a healthy daughter, the paralysis lingered, and Hartel spent months regaining use of her arms and upper legs. Although she never regained use of her legs below the knee, Hartel realized her goal of riding again and won a silver medal at the 1952 Olympics, helped on and off her horse, then helped onto the victory platform by Swedish gold medalist Henri Saint Cyr. Hartel's courage became one of the enduring memories of the Helsinki games. She earned a second silver in the 1956 games.

Selected championships and honors: Two silver medals, dressage, Olympic Games, 1952 and '56.

VIRGINIA HOLGATE LENG b. February, 1955,
   Great Britain

Daughter of a British military officer, Holgate grew up in locales that included Singapore, the Philippines, and Cyprus. Wherever she went, there were horses, and Holgate began riding long before she began kindergarten. Her specialty has always been the three-day event, the most grueling of competitions. A fall during such an event in 1975 almost resulted in amputation of her arm, which had been broken in twenty-three places. During the 1988 Olympics she rode with a bad ankle, only later discovering that the ankle was broken and required surgery. In addition to her Olympic and World Championship wins, Holgate won several British and European championships.

Selected championships and honors, individual: Two bronze medals, three-day event, Olympic Games, 1984 and '88; two gold medals, three-day event, World Championships, 1982 and '86. *Team:* Two silver medals, three-day event, Olympic Games, 1984 and '88.

JULIEANNE (JULIE) KRONE MUZIKAR
   b. July 24, 1963, Benton Harbor, Michigan

In 1993 Krone became the first female jockey to win a Triple Crown race. Hardly an unknown, Krone had been a professional jockey for more than ten years and was well known to thoroughbred racing enthusiasts. Her first win, at a county fair horse show, came when Krone was five. By the time she was thirteen, she had set her sights on becoming a professional jockey. She rode her first winner in 1981 and over the next fifteen years became one of the best female jockeys in history, winning purses worth more than $50 million. Her career—and her life—almost came to a tragic halt in 1993, when she suffered a shattered lower leg, cut elbow, and bruised heart in a fall. Krone underwent grueling rehabilitation and returned to the track in May 1994. The next year Krone rode a full card at Saratoga just hours before her evening wedding to TV sports producer Matthew Muzikar.

Selected championships and honors: Became all-time winningest female jockey in U.S. history in 1988; won Belmont Stakes aboard Colonial Affair, 1993.

KATHRYN (KATHY) KUSNER b. March 21, 1940,
   Gainesville, Florida

Kusner mixed two sports that seldom see any crossover—dressage and thoroughbred racing. A rider from the age of ten, Kusner became the first person ever to win the International Grand Prix two years in a row aboard the same mount. After her second Grand Prix victory, she applied for a jockey's license and was turned down. Kusner took her cause to the press and to court. In 1968 a judge found the Maryland Racing Commission guilty of sex discrimination and ordered them to reverse their decision, making Kusner the first American woman to receive a jockey license. Kusner's jockey career was hampered first by a broken leg and later by problems making the stringent weight limits. She continued dressage riding, and continued to medal as a member of U.S. teams.

Selected championships and honors, individual: Two International Grand Prix wins, 1967 and '68. *Team:* Gold medal, three-day event, Pan American Games, 1963; two silver medals, three-day event, Olympic Games, 1964; silver medal, jumping, Olympic Games, 1972.

LISELOTT LINSENHOFF b. Germany

Linsenhoff finished eighth in individual dressage in the 1968 Olympics, then came back four years later aboard the same mount, Piaff, to become the first woman to earn a gold in the event. Finishing behind Linsenhoff was Yelena Petushkova of the Soviet Union.

Selected championships and honors, individual: Gold medal, dressage, Olympic Games, 1972. *Team:* Two silver medals, dressage, Olympic Games, 1956 and '72; gold medal, dressage, Olympic Games, 1968.

KAREN STIVES b. 1951, Wellesley, Massachusetts

In one of the great dramas of the 1984 Olympics, Stives was the last rider in the three-day event. With both an individual medal and a U.S. team gold on the line, Stives knew the margin of error was minimal—more than one knockdown, and the team gold would go to Great Britain. One knockdown was exactly what she had—enough to secure a silver for herself and help the United States to gold.

Selected championships and honors, individual: Silver medal, three-day event, Olympic Games, 1984. *Team:* Gold medal, three-day event, Olympic Games, 1984.

NICOLE UPHOFF b. January 25, 1967, Duisberg, Germany

With first-place finishes in 1988 and '92 Olympic dressage, Uphoff became the first woman to win the event twice. Only one other person had won back-to-back golds, Sweden's Henri Saint Cyr.

Selected championships and honors, individual: Two gold medals, dressage, Olympic Games, 1988 and '92. *Team:* Two gold medals, dressage, Olympic Games, 1988 and '92.

ISABELL WERTH b. 1975, Germany

Perhaps the top female dressage rider of the 1990s, Werth was just twenty-three when she won her first Olympic medal. Going into the '96 games, her chief rival was Anky van Grunsven of the Netherlands, who had split World Championship events with Werth. Although Werth made initial mistakes that put van Grunsven in the lead, she recovered to finish first.

Selected championships and honors, individual: Silver medal, dressage, Olympic Games, 1992; gold medal, dressage, Olympic Games, 1996. *Team:* Two gold medals, dressage, Olympic Games, 1992 and '96.

Photo credit: Bongarts/Mark Sandten

FENCING

◆ *Though still struggling for acceptance in the United States, fencing remains a high art form in many parts of Europe.*

HISTORY

Swordplay began on the battlefield with weapons so crude and heavy that one didn't so much seek to strategically wound the enemy as to simply hack him to death. As weapons grew more refined, swordsmanship became more a matter of skill and less a matter of luck. Knowing how to wield a sword became part of any well-bred young man's education. It's no accident that Shakespeare's vision of Renaissance Italy, visible in the opening scenes of *Romeo and Juliet,* pits the wealthy Montagues against the equally wealthy

Capulets in a show of swordplay. Such small frays were commonplace—as, undoubtedly, one-on-one challenges were—and it is probably from the custom of dueling that fencing derives. The invention of the button tip in the seventeenth century provided a measure of safety, and protective gear eventually followed.

Women's entrance into the sport is especially worth noting. Unlike archery, which drew on skills women acquired as they hunted small game for their families, or other sports drawing on natural skills such as running or weight throwing, women would have had to go out of their way to learn swordsmanship. There is some evidence that women's fencing was a carnival activity in Florence during the Renaissance. A 1725 match pitted a well-known female fencer from Ireland against an equally well-known English woman. In all probability these women were not well-off but came from the lower classes, and their willingness to participate in such an unladylike sport placed them on a footing with the female wrestlers of today.

With the advent of the gun, it seemed the sword might become a casualty of technology. Ironically, the opposite eventually proved true. As the gun became the utilitarian weapon of choice, the sword acquired a shimmer of romance and respectability it had not known before. Like archery, the sport was valued for its sheer pageantry. By the middle of the nineteenth century fencing was thoroughly acceptable for upper-class women. Of the hundreds of clubs that flourished throughout England, France, Hungary, Austria, Italy, and Spain, most had sections for women.

THE MODERN ERA

In America, fencing was introduced as a sport for college students. As a varsity sport it had several advantages. Students could pair off in twos, providing everyone with an equal measure of exercise. Moreover, the sport could be played indoors, even during the worst months of the year. By the early 1900s fencing was a women's sport in colleges throughout the East. Although fencing has never been widely pursued in the United States, it has remained popular with European women, who still dominate the sport. Fencing was one of

---

Foil or Épée?

Foil and épée matches involve two different implements and somewhat different rules. The **foil** has a flexible blade with a blunt tip, and only touches on the trunk of the body (between shoulders and hips) are legal. The blade of the **épée** is rigid, and the point is covered with a barb-tipped cone. In épée events, touches may be made anywhere on the body.

---

the earliest sports added to the Olympics as a women's event, making its debut in 1924. World Championships for women date from that same year. World Championships are not held in Olympic years, when the Olympic medalist is considered the world champion. Until recently, Olympic competition featured foil events only. For the 1996 games, individual and team épée were added.

Governing Bodies and Organizations

U.S. Fencing Association (USFA)
1 Olympic Plaza
Colorado Springs, Colorado 80909
Telephone: 719/578-4511

✳ ✳ ✳ BIOGRAPHIES ✳ ✳ ✳

ILONA ELEK. *See Ilona Schacherer-Elek, below.*

MARIA CERRA TISHMAN b. New York, New York
Cerra, the U.S. national foil champion in 1945, represented the United States at the 1948 Olympics. Although she didn't win a medal, she did finish in fourth place, becoming the first American woman ever to achieve that position.

MARION LLOYD VINCE b. April 16, 1906, Brooklyn, New York; d. November 2, 1969

A two-time national champion in foil, Lloyd was the first American woman to make it to the finals of a major international competition. At the Los Angeles Olympics in 1932 she made her way to an eighth-place finish. Her husband, Joseph Vince, was also a national champion during the 1920s and '30s.

HELENE MAYER b. 1911, Offenbach, Germany; d. October, 1953
Mayer made her Olympic debut in 1928, when she was seventeen, and went home with a gold medal. Daughter of a Christian mother and Jewish father, Mayer was

allowed to compete at the 1936 games because she had two non-Jewish grandparents. Mayer won the silver medal and saluted Hitler from the victory platform, although neither the gold medalist, **Ilona Schacherer-Elek,** who was also Jewish, nor the bronze medalist, **Ellen Preis,** did. Mayer settled in the United States after the games and won eight U.S. national championships. Tall (5'10"), strong, and extremely competitive, Mayer is considered the greatest fencer of the twentieth century by some. In addition to her Olympic medals, she won three World Championships.

Selected championships and honors: Gold medal, foil, Olympic Games, 1928; silver medal, foil, Olympic Games, 1936; three World Championships, 1929, '31, and '37.

ELLEN OTTILIA OSIIER b. 1891, Denmark

The first female Olympic medalist in fencing, Osiier was thirty-three when she cruised through the 1924 games, winning all of her bouts. Her teammate, Grete Heckscher, won the bronze.

Selected championships and honors: Gold medal, foil, Olympic Games, 1924.

ELLEN PREIS MÜLLER b. Austria

Preis competed in five Olympics, an achievement made even more remarkable by the fact that her streak was interrupted for twelve years by World War II. Preis made her first Olympic appearance at the Los Angeles games in 1932, and her final Olympic appearance twenty-four years later, at the 1956 games. Her last major international win was at the 1950 World Championships, when she tied France's Renee Garhile for the title.

Selected championships and honors: Gold medal, foil, Olympic Games, 1932; two bronze medals, foil, Olympic Games, 1936 and '48; three World Championships, 1947, '49, and '50.

ILDIKÖ REJTÖ UJLAKI SAGINE b. May 11, 1937, Hungary

Due to the inclusion of women's team foil in 1960, Rejtö is one of the most decorated fencers in Olympic history, with two individual and five team medals. Rejtö, who began fencing at age fourteen, was born

without hearing. Although communicating with her coaches was cumbersome, her impairment may have helped her ignore distraction during competition. She won the World Championships in 1963 and took the Olympic gold medal the next year. In addition to her individual medals, she was part of five Olympic medal-winning Hungarian teams.

Selected championships and honors, individual: World Championship, 1963; gold medal, foil, Olympic Games, 1964; bronze medal, foil, Olympic Games, 1968. *Team:* Three silver medals, foil, Olympic Games, 1960, '68, and '72; gold medal, foil, Olympic Games, 1964; bronze medal, foil, Olympic Games, 1976.

ILONA SCHACHERER-ELEK b. May 17, 1907, Budapest, Hungary

Had World War II not canceled the 1940 and '44 Olympics, left-handed fencer Schacherer-Elek would probably have spun out an unparalleled thread of Olympic gold. She won her first gold at the Berlin games in 1936 and, after an interruption of twelve years, won another gold at the postwar games in 1948. She won her final Olympic medal, a silver, at the 1952 Helsinki Olympics, when she was forty-five. Schacherer-Elek's greatest rival was Germany's **Helene Mayer.** Both won several World Championships, and each defeated the other in major competitions.

Selected championships and honors: Gold medal, Olympic Games, 1936; gold medal, Olympic Games, 1948; silver medal, Olympic Games, 1952; five World Championships, 1934–35 and '51.

JANICE LEE YORK ROMARY b. August 6, 1928, California

No American woman has medaled in Olympic fencing, but York, a member of six Olympic teams (1948–68), arguably ranks as the best female fencer the United States has ever produced. At the 1952 and '56 games she finished fourth, becoming only one of two American women (along with **Maria Cerra Tishman**) to achieve that position. Between 1950 and 1968 she took ten national championships, and at the 1968 Mexico City games she was the first woman to carry the American flag in an Olympic ceremony.

Fencing

Olympic Team Épée

Year	Medalists	Country
1896–1992	event not held	
1996	Sophie Moresse-Pichot	FRA
		ITA
		RUS

Olympic Individual Épée

1896–1992	event not held	
1996	Laura Flessel	FRA
	Valerie Barlois	FRA
	Gyoengyi Szalay Horvathne	HUN

Olympic Individual Foil

Year	Medalists	Country
1896–1920	event not held	
1924	Ellen Osiier	DEN
	Gladys Davis	GBR
	Grete Heckscher	DEN
1928	Helene Mayer	GER
	Muriel Freeman	GBR
	Olga Oelkers	GER
1932	Ellen Preis	AUT
	Heather "Judy" Guinness	GBR
	Erna Bogathy Bogen	HUN
1936	Ilona Elek	HUN
	Helene Mayer	GER
	Ellen Preis	AUT
1948	Ilona Elek	HUN
	Karen Lachmann	DEN
	Ellen Preis Mullen	AUT
1952	Irene Camber	ITA
	Ilona Elek	HUN
	Karen Lachmann	DEN
1956	Gillian Sheen	GBR
	Olga Orban	ROM
	Renee Garilhe	FRA
1960	Heidi Schmid	GER
	Valentina Rastvorova	USSR
	Maria Vicol	ROM
1964	Ildikö Rejtö Ujlaki	HUN
	Helga Mees	GER
	Antonella Ragno	ITA
1968	Yelena Novikova	BLR
	Maria del Pilar Roldan	MEX
	Ildikö Rejtö Ujlaki	HUN
1972	Antonella Ragno-Lonzi	ITA
	Ildikö Bobis	HUN
	Galina Gorokhova	USSR
1976	Ildikö Schwarczenberger	HUN
	Maria Consolata Collino	ITA
	Yelena Belova (Novikova)	BLR
1980	Pascale Trinquet	FRA
	Magda Maros	HUN
	Barbara Wysoczanska	POL
1984	Luan Jujie	CHN
	Cornelia Hanisch	GER
	Dorina Vaccaroni	ITA
1988	Anja Fichtel	GER
	Sabine Bau	GER
	Zita-Eva Funkenhauser	GER
1992	Giovanna Trillini	ITA
	Wang Huifeng	CHN
	Tatyana Sadovskaya	RUS
1996	Laura Badea	ROM
	Valentina Vezzali	ITA
	Giovanna Trillini	ITA

Olympic Team Foil

1896–1956	event not held	
1960	Tatyana Petrenko, Valentina Rastvorova, Lyudmila Shishova, Valentina Prudskova, Aleksandra Zabelina, Galina Gorokhova	USSR
		HUN
		ITA
1964	Ildikö Rejtö Ujlaki, Katalin Juhasz-Nagy, Lidia Sakovics-Domolky, Judit Mendelenyi-Agoston, Paula Foldessy Marosi	HUN
		USSR
		GER
1968	Aleksandra Zabelina, Yelena Novikova, Galina Gorokhova, Tatyana Samusenko (Petrenko), Svetlana Tsirkova	USSR
		HUN
		ROM
1972	Yelena Belova (Novikova), Alexandra Zabelina, Tatyana Samusenko (Petrenko), Galina Gorokhova, Svetlana Tsirkova	USSR
		HUN
		ROM

Fencing (continued)

Olympic Team Foil

Year	Medalists	Country
1976	Yelena Belova (Novikova), Olga Kniazeva, Valentina Sidorova, Nailya Gilyazova, Valentina Nikonova	USSR
		FRA
		HUN
1980	Brigitte Latrille-Gaudin, Pascale Trinquet, Isabelle Boeri-Begard, Veronique Brouquier, Christine Muzio	FRA
		USSR
		HUN
1984	Christiane Weber, Cornelia Hanisch, Sabine Bischoff, Zita-Eva Funkenhauser, Ute Wessel	GER
		ROM
		FRA
1988	Sabine Bau, Anja Fichtel, Zita-Eva Funkenhauser, Anette Klug, Christiane Weber	GER
		ITA
		HUN
1992	Diana Bianchedi, Francesca Bortolozzi, Giovanna Trillini, Donna Vaccaroni, Margherita Zalaffi	ITA
		GER
		ROM
1996	Francesca Bortolozzi Borella, Giovanna Trillini, Valentina Vezzali	ITA
		ROM
		GER

COMBAT SPORTS

◆ *Though wrestling, boxing, and other combat sports have long been pursued by men, they truly represent the last frontier for women.*

HISTORY

Women in Britain and France both boxed and wrestled in the nineteenth century, but their activities were more spectacle than sport. In Britain especially, women provided living soft-core pornography tableaux by climbing into the ring stripped to the waist. Although stripping wasn't widespread in France, matches were conducted in rather risqué outfits—bloomers and low-necked chemises—and conducted in music halls and caberets. In America, a much-advertised boxing match took place between Nell Saunders and Rose Harland at Hill's Theater in New York, a popular venue for men's boxing matches. A silver butter dish went to the victorious Saunders, but the match proved little more than a novelty. Until very recently, women's combat sports occupied the same giggle-and-jiggle place in the twentieth century that they did in the nineteenth. Women's wrestling was a popular oddity on 1950s television, while bars made money with such innovations as mud wrestling in the 1970s. In the last few decades, however, things have begun to change. In addition to World Championships for women who are serious wrestlers, there are also Golden Gloves and professional boxing opportunities for women who are serious boxers.

JUDO

The best-accepted and most widely pursued combat sports for women are the Asian martial arts, perhaps because they are thought of as appropriately "self-defensive." Judo, which already had a World Championship competition, became a full medal Olympic sport in 1992. Women's judo is played by the same rules as men's and, like the men's version of the sport, requires strength as well as agility and speed. Women's matches last four minutes (not counting referee's breaks or stoppages), compared to the five minutes of men's matches. Both World Championship and Olympic rules divide competitors into the seven weight classes listed below:

Division	Weight
Extra lightweight	Up to 106 lbs.
Half-lightweight	Up to 114.6 lbs.
Lightweight	Up to 123 lbs.
Half-middleweight	Up to 134.5 lbs.
Middleweight	Up to 145.5 lbs.
Half-heavyweight	Up to 158.5 lbs.
Heavyweight	Over 158.5 lbs.

Governing Bodies and Organizations

USA Wrestling
6155 Lehman
Colorado Springs, Colorado 80918
Phone: 719/598-8181

United States Judo (USJ)
Box 10013
El Paso, Texas 79991
Phone: 915/565-8754

* * * BIOGRAPHIES * * *

YAEL ARAD b. Israel
A native-born Israeli, Arad was eight when she began taking judo lessons with her brother. She caught on quickly and soon began winning national championships in her age group. Just four months after a knee operation, Arad found herself competing in the Barcelona Olympics. She faced France's **Catherine Fleury** in a scoreless final match, losing to her on a decision. Though Arad was disappointed not to have won the gold, it hardly mattered to her countrymen. As the first Israeli athlete to win an Olympic medal, Arad was regarded as a national heroine. She dedicated her medal to the Israeli athletes who'd been slain in Munich two decades earlier, and since her win has founded the Yael Arad Foundation to promote and support the participation of Israelis in athletic competition.
Selected championships and honors: Silver medal, judo, half-middleweight division, Olympic Games, 1992.

MIRIAM BLASCO SOTO b. ca. 1964; Spain
When judo made its Olympic debut at the 1992 Barcelona games, there was much grumbling about "hometown" judges. Blasco, however, seemed to earn her medal the old-fashioned way. Competing in the lightweight division, Blasco earned a yuko at the midway point in the match, then survived a massive attack by her opponent, Nicola Fairbrother of Great Britain, to win the gold.
Selected championships and honors: Gold medal, Olympic Games, 1992.

KAREN BRIGGS b. Great Britain
One of the greats in women's judo, Briggs was a four-time world champion and a gold-medal favorite headed into the 1992 Olympics, marking the premier of judo as a medal sport for women. Briggs's chief threat in the extra-lightweight division was thought to be France's **Cécile Nowak,** who had defeated her in the previous year's World Championships. The match between Nowak and Briggs never took place, as Briggs suffered a dislocated shoulder in a semifinal match with **Ryoko Tamura** of Japan. Amazingly, Briggs attempted to finish the match despite her injury but was eventually disqualified for passivity. It was her last competitive match, and despite her grit, Briggs went home without a medal.

CATHERINE FLEURY b. France

In 1989, Fleury won a world judo championship in the half-middleweight division. Although she remained active in the sport after her win, she struggled over the next three years and did not make it to the finals of a single major competition. Fleury made a big comeback at the 1992 Olympics, when defending world champion Frauke Eickoff fell to fifth place. Fleury advanced to the final with Israel's **Yael Arad,** who had defeated Eickoff. The match was a scoreless one, and the judges' decision was split. The referee cast his decision in favor of Fleury.

Selected championships and honors: Gold medal, Olympic Games, 1992.

KIM MI-JUNG b. Korea

Kim, Korea's first judo Olympic medalist, won a world championship in the half-heavyweight division in 1991. She was unstoppable at the '92 Barcelona games, where two of her four wins took ten seconds or less, and the remaining two took a combined total of under six minutes.

Selected championships and honors: Gold medal, Olympic Games, 1992.

JILL MATTHEWS b. ca. 1963, New York, New York

In the mid-1990s, women's boxing suddenly became *hot,* and one of the people turning up the heat was Matthews. A native New Yorker from a Jewish working-class background, Matthews has dubbed herself the "Zion Lion" and takes pride in her aggressive, all-New-York-all-the-time attitude. One reason for her pride may be that, a decade ago, lack of attitude cost Matthews a role in her chosen sport, gymnastics. Although she had the physical skills and potential, lack of self-confidence kept her from being a top contender. After giving up gymnastics, Matthews took up boxing just to stay in shape. However, when Golden Gloves initiated competition for women in 1995, Matthews decided to enter. Competing at 106 pounds, Matthews won the flyweight division in a final bout that lasted just one minute and eleven seconds. With her victory, Matthews found herself suddenly in possession of the self-confidence and will to win that had previously been missing. Since turning pro in 1995, Matthews has become a buzzword in boxing circles and is the first woman ever to gain name recognition in the sport.

CÉCILE NOWAK b. France

Nowak won a world judo championship, extra-lightweight division, in 1991 by defeating Britain's **Karen Briggs.** Everyone expected a rematch from the 1992 Olympics, but Briggs was injured in a semifinal match against **Tamura Ryoko** and had to withdraw from competition. Nowak faced Tamura, an excellent technician, in the final and earned a gold.

Selected championships and honors: Gold medal, Olympic Games, 1991.

TRICIA SAUNDERS b. United States

Women's freestyle wrestling doesn't get much press, but if it did, Saunders would be much better known than she is. In additional to her 1993 national championship, Saunders was the key factor in helping the U.S. women's team triumph in several international meets. At the 1993 women's World Championships, she turned in a second-place finish, the highest ever for an American woman. The same year she was named Woman Wrestler of the Year by USA Wrestling.

TAMURA RYOKO b. ca. 1976; Japan

In judo circles, Tamura will long be remembered as the contender who ended the career of British champion **Karen Briggs.** Although Tamura did inflict a serious shoulder injury on her opponent, she did it in the course of legitimate fair play and did not take advantage of Briggs's injury when she attempted to continue the match. The smallest contender in the extra-lightweight division, 4'8" Tamura is a master of technique, known in her homeland as "Yawara Chan" (loose translation, "Miss Martial Artist"). Although some thought her silver medal win in '92 was a fluke, abetted by Briggs's withdrawal, Tamura earned a second silver at the '96 games as well.

Selected championships and honors: Two silver medals, Olympic Games, 1992 and '96.

Judo

Olympic Extra-Lightweight

Year	Medalists	Country
1896–1988	event not held	
1992	Cecile Nowak	FRA
	Tamura Ryoko	JPN
	Amarilis Savon Carmenaty	CUB
1996	Kye Sun	PRK
	Tamura Ryoko	JPN
	Yolanda Soler	SPA
	Amarilis Savon	CUB

Judo (continued)

Olympic Half-Lightweight

Year	Medalists	Country
1896–1988	event not held	
1992	Almudena Munoz Martinez	SPA
	Noriko Mizoguchi	JPN
	Li Zhongyun	CHN
1996	Marie-Claire Restoux	FRA
	Hyun Sook-hee	KOR
	Noriko Sagawara	JPN
	Legna Verdecia	CUB

Olympic Lightweight

1896–1988	event not held	
1992	Miriam Basco Soto	SPA
	Nicola Fairbrother	GBR
	Driulis Gonzalez Morales	CUB
1996	Driulis Gonzalez	CUB
	Jung Sun-yong	KOR
	Isabelle Fernandez	SPA
	Marisbell Lomba	BEL

Olympic Half-Middleweight

1896–1988	event not held	
1992	Catherine Fleury	FRA
	Yael Arad	ISR
	Yelena Petrova	RUS
1996	Yuko Emoto	JPN
	Gella Van de Caveye	BEL
	Jung Sung-sook	KOR
	Jenny Gal	HOL

Olympic Middleweight

1896–1988	event not held	
1992	Odalys Reve Jimenez	CUB
	Emanuela Pierantozzi	ITA
	Kate Howey	GBR
1996	Cho Min-sun	KOR
	Aneta Szczepanska	POL
	Claudia Zwiers	HOL
	Wang Xianbo	CHN

Olympic Half-Heavyweight

1896–1988	event not held	
1992	Kim Mi-jung	KOR
	Yoko Tanabe	JPN
	Irene de Kok	HOL
1996	Ulla Werbrouck	BEL
	Yoko Tanabe	JPN
	Ylenia Scapin	ITA
	Diadenis Luna	CUB

Olympic Heavyweight

1896–1988	event not held	
1992	Zhuang Xiaoyan	CHN
	Estela Rodriguez Villanueva	CUB
	Natalina Lupino	FRA
1996	Sun Fu Ming	CHN
	Estela Rodriguez	CUB
	Christine Cicot	FRA
	Johanna Hagn	GER

Wrestling

World Championship Weight 97

Year	Champion	Country
1989	Shoko Yoshimura	Japan
1990	Shoko Yoshimura	Japan
1991	Xiue Zhong	China
1992	Pan Yan Ping	China
1993	Shoko Yoshimura	Japan
1994	Shoko Yoshimura	Japan

World Championship Weight 103.5

1989	Ming Haiu Chen	Taipei
1990	Asa Petersen	Sweden
1991	Miyuu Yamamoto	Japan
1992	Xiue Zhong	China
1993	Xiue Zhong	China
1994	Misho Kamibajashi	Japan

World Championship Weight 110

1989	Anne Holten	Norway
1990	Martine Poupon	France
1991	Martine Poupon	France
1992	Tricia Saunders	USA
1993	Anna Gomis	France
1994	Miyuu Yamamoto	Japan

World Championship Weight 116.5

1989	Sylvie Van Gucht	France
1990	Sylvie Van Gucht	France
1991	Xia Zhang	China
1992	Wendy Yzguirre	Venezuela
1993	Line Johansen	Norway
1994	Akemi Kawashashi	Japan

Wrestling (continued)

World Championship Weight 125.5

Year	Champion	Country
1989	Gudrun Hoie	Norway
1990	Gudrun Hoie	Norway
1991	Olga Lugo	Venezuela
1992	Riyoto Sakamoto	Japan
1993	Gudrun Hoie	Norway
1994	Line Johansen	Norway

World Championship Weight 134

1989	Jocelyn Sagon	France
1990	Brygette Sieffert	France
1991	Brygette Sieffert	France
1992	Ine Barlie	Norway
1993	Nikola Hartmann	Austria
1994	Nikola Hartmann	Austria

World Championship Weight 143

1989	Emmanuelle Blind	France
1990	Akiko Lizima	Japan

1991	Akiki Iljima	Japan
1992	Wang Chaoli	China
1993	Chao-Li Wang	China
1994	Yayoi Urano	Japan

World Championship Weight 154

1989	Georgette Jean	France
1990	Rika Iwama	Japan
1991	Yayoi Urano	Japan
1992	Xiomara Guevarra	Venezuela
1993	Yayoi Urano	Japan
1994	Christine Nordhagen	Canada

World Championship Weight 165

1989	Miyako Shimizu	Japan
1990	Yayoi Urano	Japan
1991	Liu Dong Feng	China
1992	Liu Dong Feng	China
1993	Liu Dong Feng	China
1994	Mit Funakoshi	Japan

U.S. National Freestyle Championships

Weight	Year	Champion	Runner-Up
97	1990	Marie Ziegler	Debby Weiss
	1991	Lauren Wolfe	Marie Ziegler
	1992	Cheryl Meyer	Marie Prado
	1993	Debby Weiss	Jackie Hileman
	1994	Vickie Zummo	Marie Prado
103.5	1990	Afsoon Roshanzamir	
	1991	Tricia McNaughton (Saunders)	Lisa Whitsett
	1992	Afsoon Roshanzamir	Lisa Whitsett
	1993	Tricia Saunders	Cheryl Meyer
	1994	Afsoon Roshanzamir	Margaret LeGates
110	1990	Tricia McNaughton (Saunders)	Asia DeWeese
	1991	Shannon Williams	Afsoon Roshanzamir
	1992	Tricia Saunders	Shannon Williams
	1993	Shannon Williams	Lisa Whitsett
	1994	Tricia Saunders	Lori Leon
116.5	1990	Jennifer Ottiano	Shannon Williams
	1991	Jennifer Ottiano	Phoebe Smith
	1992	Jennifer Ottiano	Andrea Carstens
	1993	Miyuu Yamamoto	Andrea Carstens
	1994	Miyuu Yamamoto	Shannon Williams
125.5	1991	Kristy Schultz	Andrea Carstens
	1992	Lee Ann Gonzales	Susan Howard
	1993	Atina Bibbs	Jessica Hobbs
	1994	Brenda Day	Cheryl Meyer
143	1991	Grace Jividen	
	1992	Grace Jividen	Carol Hamilton

Photo credit: Courtesy of PCH Sports Marketing Inc.

TRIATHLON

One of the world's newest sports, triathlon began in California as a publicity event. In the late 1970s, cycling had plenty of participants but a definite lack of public following. In an effort to attract more attention, California bike clubs began teaming road races with other sports, usually running and swimming. The timing couldn't have been better. After a decade of running and other forms of conditioning, people were ready for a new challenge and psychologically ready to push the endurance envelope. In 1978, Navy commander John Collins created the Ironman Triathlon, a combination of three already existing races—the Waikiki Rough-Water Swim, the Oahu Bicycle Race, and the Honolulu Marathon. The name "Ironman," evocative and instantly memorable, put the sport on the map once and for all. Since then, numerous triathlons have

been organized around the world, though none has ever gained the prominence or the cachet of the original Ironman, which is now officially known as the Ironman Triathlon World Championship.

Although no women competed in the first Ironman, twenty-seven-year-old Lyn Lemaire of Boston entered the 1978 race, and her finishing time (12:55:38 to swim 2.4 miles, bike 112 miles, and run a 26.2-mile marathon) was good enough for fifth place, a strong showing that encouraged other women to train and compete. The race got another publicity boost in 1981 when thousands of TV viewers watched Julie Moss's dramatic finish. The exhausted Moss collapsed a few yards from the finish and crawled the last few yards to win second place in the women's division, completing the course just 29 seconds behind first-place winner Kathleen McCartney. Moss's never-give-up performance gained even more recognition for the sport.

Over the years, triathlon has become a truly international sport. The first non-U.S. woman to win the Ironman was Sylviane Puntous of Canada in 1983. Eastern European women have also arrived on the scene, and two of the sport's greatest athletes, Paula Newby-Fraser and Erin Baker, are from Zimbabwe and New Zealand respectively.

Though the Ironman is a firmly established and well-sponsored event, there is some worry about the future of the sport as a whole. Ironically, triathlon's popularity may have been hurt by the increased attention paid to the sport it was designed to save—cycling. Once, cycling had to combine with other sports to attract a following. That isn't the case today and cycling, at least for the time being, has eclipsed triathlon in popularity. However, triathlon will be on view as a demonstration sport at the 2000 Summer Olympics. Enthusiasts hope this will fuel a new surge of popularity for the sport.

Governing Bodies and Organizations

Triathlon Federation USA
3595 East Fountsin Boulevard
Suite F-1
Colorado Springs, Colorado 80910
Phone: 719/597-9090

* * * BIOGRAPHIES * * *

ERIN BAKER; b. May 23, 1961, Kaispoi, New Zealand

When it comes to triathlon, Baker is one of the fastest in the world. Her first Ironman World Championship, in 1987, came with a record-setting performance of 9:35:25. In the course of winning her second title, in 1990, she set a course marathon record for women of 3:04:13—a benchmark that still stands. A terrific competitor, Baker would undoubtedly have won even more titles had her career not coincided with that of Paula Newby-Fraser, who was even faster.

Selected championships and honors: Two Ironman World Championships, 1987, '90.

PAULA NEWBY-FRASER b. June 2, 1962, Zimbabwe

If Newby-Fraser insisted they change the name of the world's most famous triathlon to the Ironwoman, she'd have plenty of ground to stand on—a seven-time winner of the Kona classic, no one to date, male or female, has won more Ironman Triathlon World Championships than she has. Newby-Fraser tried the sport for the first time in 1985. Accompanying her triathlete boyfriend to a short-course event, her spur-of-the-moment decision to enter the race ended in victory. Included in the prize was a ticket to Hawaii and a berth in the World Championship. Although Newby-Fraser finished in second place, the first-place finisher was later disqualified for drafting her bike. Newby-Fraser's subsequent victories were more satisfying—and far more spectacular. In 1988, she became the first woman to complete the bicycle course in under five hours, and in 1992 she became the first woman to finish the entire course in under nine hours. Newby-Fraser broke the nine-hour-barrier again in 1993, an achievement no woman has matched. In fact, the five fastest World Championship times all belong to Newby-Fraser, and the best time of her closest competitor, Erin Baker, is almost 13 minutes slower. Newby-Fraser's last Ironman World Championship was in 1995, when she came in fourth—the lowest finish of her spectacular career.

Selected championships and honors: Seven Ironman World Championships, 1986, '88, '89, and '91–'94; Ironman Hall of Fame.

SYLVIANE PUNTOUS b. December 28, 1960, Montreal, Canada

When Puntous became serious about triathlon competition, she didn't have to look far for a training partner—her twin sister, Patricia, not only trained with her but entered races as well, and the two became famous for tying each other at the finish line. Both entered the Ironman World Championship in 1983, and

when a punctured tire cost Patricia six precious minutes, Sylviane finished first, becoming the first Canadian to win the women's title and setting a women's course record of 10:43:36. The next year, Californian Jennifer Hinshaw swam the open-water leg of the race in a spectacular 50:31, a record that still stands, but Puntous outdid her overall and again won the women's division, becoming the first woman ever to win back-to-back titles.
Selected championships and honors: Two Ironman World Championships, 1983 and '84.

KAREN SMYERS b. October 6, 1965, Corey, Pennsylvania

Smyers, who finished second in 1994, looked forward to the 1995 Ironman with confidence and trepidation—to win the race, she would have to beat the seemingly invincible Paula Newby-Fraser. The contest became one of the most exciting in triathlon history. Smyers and Newby-Fraser completed the first leg of the event, the open water swim, in a dead heat. During the second leg, Smyers saw victory slip from her grasp as Newby-Fraser took a commanding lead on the bike. With the marathon left to run, Newby-Fraser led by a full twelve minutes. Smyers turned on the heat, running seven-minute miles to Newby-Fraser's seven-and-a-half-minute ones. Feeling the pressure, Newby-Fraser elected to skip her last water break. The decision took its toll. Exhausted and dehydrated, Newby-Fraser struggled through her last mile. With less than a quarter-mile to go, Smyers overtook her rival and won her first world championship title.
Selected championships and honors: Ironman World Championship, 1995.

Triathlon

World Championship

Year	Winner	Time	Country
1989	Erin Baker	2:10.01	NZ
1990	Karen Smyers	2:03.33	USA
1991	Joanne Ritchie	2:02.04	CAN
1992	Michellie Jones	2:02.08	AUS
1993	Michellie Jones	2:07.41	AUS
1994	Emma Carney	2:03.19	AUS
1995	Karen Smyers	2:04.58	USA
1996	Jackie Gallagher	1:50.52	AUS

Ironman Championship

Year	Winner	Time	Runner-up	Site
1978	no women competed in this year			Waikiki Beach
1979	Lyn Lemaire*	12:55		All Moana Park
1980	Robin Beck	11:21.24	Eve Anderson	Kailua-Kona
1981	Linda Sweeney	12:00.32	Sally Edwards	Kailua-Kona
1982	Kathleen McCartney	11:09.40	Julie Moss	Kailua-Kona
1982[†]	Julie Leach	10:54.08	Joann Dahlkoetter	Kailua-Kona
1983	Sylviane Puntous	10:43.36	Patricia Puntous	Kailua-Kona
1984	Sylviane Puntous	10:25.13	Patricia Puntous	Kailua-Kona
1985	Joanne Ernst	10:25.22	Liz Bulman	Kailua-Kona
1986	Paula Newby-Fraser	9:49.14	Sylviane Puntous	Kailua-Kona
1987	Erin Baker	9:35.25	Sylviane Puntous	Kailua-Kona
1988	Paula Newby-Fraser	9:01.01	Erin Baker	Kailua-Kona
1989	Paula Newby-Fraser	9:00.56	Sylviane Puntous	Kailua-Kona
1990	Erin Baker	9:13.42	Paula Newby-Fraser	Kailua-Kona
1991	Paula Newby-Fraser	9:07.52	Erin Baker	Kailua-Kona
1992	Paula Newby-Fraser	8:55.29	Julie Anne White	Kailua-Kona
1993	Paula Newby-Fraser	8:58.23	Erin Baker	Kailua-Kona
1994	Paula Newby-Fraser	9:20.14	Karen Smyers	Kailua-Kona
1995	Karen Smyers	9:16.46	Isabelle Mouthon	Kailua-Kona
1996	Paula Newby-Fraser	9:06.49	Natascha Badmann	Kailua-Kona

*Lyn Lemaire was the only woman in the race.

[†]The Ironman Championship was contested twice in 1982.

Photo credit: Culver Pictures

FIGURE SKATING

◆ *Yes, men skate too, but in this sport it's the women who get the ink. From Sonja Henie to Katarina Witt, few athletes have sparkled with the glamour that figure skaters have.*

HISTORY

Figure skating owes its birth to an unlikely midwife: political unrest. When members of the house of Stuart were exiled to Holland, the Dutch taught them the sport they had long practiced on their canals. Eventually the Stuarts were allowed to return to England, and they brought their new sport with them. Unlike the Dutch, the British did not have long canals to skate on. In Britain and Scotland, ponds and small lakes were more numerous,

forming natural rinks rather than tracks. The British shortened their skate blades to accommodate the smaller area, making it easier to turn in tight quarters. In time the British became so good at executing turns and patterns that they pointed with pride to the precise tracings—or "figures"—their blades made in the ice.

The World Championships, which began in 1896, were assumed to be a men-only event until British champion **Madge Cave Syers** entered in 1902. Since competition rules made no mention of women and did not specifically bar them, she could not be prevented from entering. The judges, flustered and disgruntled, reluctantly awarded her a silver, and many privately hinted that she should in all fairness have been awarded the gold. To prevent future embarrassments, the rules were amended to prohibit women from entering. Two years after the 1902 debacle, World Championships for women were established. In 1908 figure skating was added to the Olympic roster, featuring singles competition for men and women as well as a pairs event. Ice dancing, a world championship event since 1950, wasn't added to the Olympics until 1976.

Although many credit Sonja Henie with popularizing figure skating as a theatrical event, the true honors go to Charlotte Oelschlagel. Born around the turn of the century, Oelschlagel, daughter of a Berlin furniture manufacturer, was a musical prodigy who by the age of seven was already appearing with the Berlin Philharmonic. Unfortunately, the pressure took its toll, and Oelschlagel had a nervous breakdown. She took up skating as a form of therapy and by ten was appearing as a skater in Berlin theaters. As Oelschlagel grew, her popularity increased. An uncommonly attractive teenager with memorable flowing tresses, Oelschlagel and her producers recognized the theatrical potential of skating and capitalized on it, setting routines to music and conjuring up costumes worthy of a Maxfield Parrish fantasy. Oelschlagel made her first New York appearance in 1915. She was signed to a six-week stint at the Hippodrome, a show so popular that her contract was extended another six years, during which Oelschlagel performed twice a day to packed audiences. Though some historians have dismissed Oelschlagel as an actress with minimal skating ability, fellow skaters have argued in her defense. Oelschlagel's most memorable act was "The Dying Swan," for which she was coached by the great Russian ballerina Anna Pavlova.

Oelschlagel repositioned skating in the American mind, transforming it from a rather boring technical sport to one that provided ample room for theater. Into this niche stepped **Sonja Henie,** who was to become the sport's first great superstar. Henie united dynamic athleticism with the grace, drama, and costume audiences yearned for. Although American champion **Tee Weld** had skated in short skirts, Henie transformed the short, free-floating skirt into an indispensable costume. She chose her colors well and for theatrical

effect and may have been the first skater to wear boots dyed to match her tights.

After Henie retired from competition, she remained in the United States, skating with her own show and starring in a string of popular skate-based movies. Henie undoubtedly served as an inspiration to hundred of little girls throughout North America, for as the generation that grew up on Henie flowered into their teens and twenties, U.S. and Canadian skaters began to claim their first world medals.

THE MODERN ERA

If figure skating got its first push on the big screen, it got its second on the small one. The addition of television during the 1960 Olympic Games changed the sport forever, setting it on a path toward glitz, glamour, huge ratings, and ever-rising standards of performance. Television made 1960s gold medalist **Carol Heiss** a star, just as it later did **Peggy Fleming** and **Dorothy Hamill,** with high visibility and commercial appearances. Most of all, television made a star of women's figure skating. As network number crunchers are fond of saying, it's the only women's sport that can pull its own weight in prime time. The final night of the women's 1994 Olympic competition, featuring the free skate, was the sixth-most-watched television event of all time, and the most-watched U.S. television event in more than a decade.

Undoubtedly, the 1994 ratings got a boost from the much-publicized **Nancy Kerrigan**–Tonya Harding incident, which began months before the Olympics when Harding's associates bashed Kerrigan in the knee in an effort to vault Harding to the gold. As it happened, neither American took the gold, but the soap opera laid bare the high stakes involved. Even without a gold, Kerrigan was offered millions of dollars in product endorsements, while the ostracized Harding got virtually nothing.

The Kerrigan-Harding episode wasn't the first time television's Faustian effect had come under the gun. As screens grew larger and black and white turned to color, officials became concerned

Major Events and Competitions

Singles, pairs, and ice dance are all offered in:

World Championships
Olympic Games
U.S. Nationals
North American Championships
European Championships

that figure skating was becoming less like a sport and more like a Las Vegas floor show. For both men and women, costumes became skimpier and more revealing. Props, from hats to fur boas, were introduced as part of the act. Alarmed, the Olympic committee formalized a new and more

restrictive dress code. Effective as of 1988, men were no longer permitted to wear tights, while women's costumes were required to adequately cover the hips and derriere with a skirt or skirt-like decoration. Scaled-to-the-hip swimsuit-style costumes were banned, as were extraneous props, with the result that figure skating, at least so far as the Olympics are concerned, has retained a refreshing modesty and hewed to its ballet roots rather than putting down new ones in American Gladiators territory.

Governing Bodies and Organizations

U.S. Figure Skating Association (USFSA)
20 First Street
Colorado Springs, Colorado 80909
Phone: 719/578-4567

* * * BIOGRAPHIES * * *

TENLEY ALBRIGHT b. July 18, 1935, Newton Center, Massachusetts

The first American woman ever to skate to world and Olympic victories, Albright treated spectators to a seamless interweaving of the sport's most valued elements—athletic skill and artistic grace. A skater from the age of nine, Albright won several juvenile, novice, and junior titles before taking her first national championship at the age of sixteen. From 1952 through 1957 she dominated American figure skating, winning five consecutive national titles, two World Championships, and two Olympic medals. On the ice and off, Albright was ambitious, gritty, and tenacious. A few months after winning the first of two World Championships (1953 and '55), she began premed studies at Radcliffe. Determined to follow in her surgeon father's footsteps, Albright maintained high grades despite a daily 4–6 A.M. practice schedule and ballet lessons to improve her grace and artistic expression. She won her first Olympic medal, a silver, in 1952 and was a favorite in the 1956 games. Just a few weeks before the competition, she hit a rut in the ice and fell, one blade slashing her ankle to the bone and severing an artery. Albright's father flew to Cortina, the site of the games, and operated to repair the damage himself. Albright skated through the competition

on the unhealed ankle, masking the pain beneath an elegant performance. Ten of eleven judges gave her top marks, and she took the gold, finishing ahead of the woman who was to be America's next skating star, **Carol Heiss.** Heiss defeated Albright in the World Championships later that year, but in the final competition of her career, Albright defended her national title against Heiss. Albright went on to become a surgeon and expert in the field of sports medicine. In 1979 she became the first woman to serve as officer on the U.S. Olympic Committee.

Selected championships and honors: Two gold medals, World Championships, 1953 and '55; silver medal, Olympic Games, 1952; two silver medals, World Championships, 1954 and '56; gold medal, Olympic Games, 1956; International Women's Sports Hall of Fame.

TAI BABILONIA b. September 22, 1960, Mission Hill, California

When **Irina Rodnina** and husband Aleksandr Zaitsev took 1978–79 off to have a baby, relinquishing a ten-year hold on the pairs crown, the skating world craned their necks to see who the new champions would be. The U.S. duo of Babilonia and partner Randy Gardner emerged, and became the first Americans to win a world pairs championship since Karol and Peter Kennedy in 1950. Fresh and energetic, Babilonia had been skating with Gardner for more than a decade, since she was ten and he was twelve. Rodnina and Zaitsev returned from their hiatus to train for the 1980 Olympics, and pregames publicity hyped the event as a dual between the old masters and the new kids on the block. Unfortunately, Gardner suffered a serious groin injury just before the competition. Painkillers weren't enough to compensate for the mishap, and after Gardner fell four times during the short program warmup, the couple was forced to withdraw. Their disappointment, as much for each other as for themselves, cemented their popularity with Americans, and they later skated professionally to huge American audiences.

Selected championships and honors: World Championships, pairs, 1979.

OKSANA BAIUL b. November 16, 1977, Dnieperpetrovsk, Ukraine

Off the ice she was another teenage skater, thinner and gawkier than most, and wearing the florid blue eye shadow long favored by Soviet fashion. On the ice, she skated with a passion that was almost painful to watch. Few who watched Baiul's 1994 Olympic performance comprehended her past. Abandoned by her father and raised by her mother and grandparents, Baiul was first taught to skate by her grandmother. Her grandparents died, and then, when Baiul was thirteen, her mother died of ovarian cancer. Alone in the world, Baiul for a time slept on a cot at the skating center where she trained. Then her coach vanished without notice, seizing a chance at a job in Canada. Baiul moved to Odessa, 250 miles away, to train with coach Galina Zmievskaya. Zmievskaya took Baiul into her small apartment, providing home and family as well as training. Baiul soon began placing high in Soviet and European competitions, then took a World Championship at age fifteen, the youngest winner since **Sonja Henie.** At the 1994 Olympics, Baiul was overshadowed by the **Nancy Kerrigan**–Tonya Harding imbroglio—but the real drama was Baiul's performance as she skated to a gold despite receiving stitches for an injury just hours earlier. Since her win, life has been happier for Baiul, who is a popular international performer and has used her earnings to live and train in the United States.

Selected championships and honors: Gold medal, World Championships, 1993; gold medal: Olympic Games, 1994.

LYUDMILA BELOUSOVA PROTOPOPOV
b. November 22, 1935, USSR

Belousova was already married to husband Oleg Protopopov, three years her senior, when they won the first of their two Olympic golds in 1964. They were already well known in the Soviet Union, where they had been national pairs champions since 1961, a title they would hold through 1968. North Americans had never seen anything quite like them, however, and were enthralled by the passionate, almost balletic style that distinguished not only the Protopopovs but the Soviet school in general.

Selected championships and honors: Two gold medals, pairs, Olympic Games, 1964 and '68; four gold medals, pairs, World Championships, 1965–68.

FLORENCE MADELEINE (MADGE) CAVE
SYERS b. 1881, England; d. September 1917

In 1900 Cave skated with her coach, Edgar Syers, to win one of the first international pairs competitions in history, held in Berlin. The couple later married, and continued to skate both individually and in singles competitions. In fact, Cave Syers defeated her husband in the 1904 British national championships, which were open to both men and women. In 1902 Cave Syers gave the skating world a jolt when she entered the World Championships—the first woman ever to do so. She took the silver, finishing behind Swedish champion Ulrich Salchow. The championships acted to bar women from future competitions, and separate championships for women were established four years later. In addition to two World Championships and two Olympic medals, Cave Syers was a champion swimmer and equestrian. Tragically, her health declined after the 1908 Olympics, and she died of heart disease in 1917.

Selected championships and honors: Silver medal, World Championships, 1902; two gold medals, World Championships, 1906 and '07; gold medal, singles, Olympic Games, 1908; bronze medal, pairs, Olympic Games, 1908.

CHEN LU b. 1977, China

Chen learned to skate from her father, a hockey player. Unfortunately, in northeastern China, she had

> I skate how I feel. I think it must be a gift from God.
> —Oksana Baiul, in *Newsweek,* 1994

no access to coaches, training, or indoor rinks. Even obtaining a proper pair of skates proved a challenge. Realizing he had a potential star on his hands, Chen's coach watched hundreds of videos of major competitions in an effort to help train his pupil. At her first Olympics, in 1992, Chen skated to a sixth-place finish—a respectable showing for a fifteen-year-old with no experience in world competitions. At the next Olympics, in Lillehammer, Chen worked her way into the medals, and the following year she finished first at the all-important World Championships.

Selected championships and honors: Bronze medal, Olympic Games, 1994; gold medal, World Championships, 1995.

CECILIA COLLEDGE b. November 28, 1920, England

Winner of eight British championships and an Olympic silver medal, Colledge is less revered for her medals than for her innovative contributions to the sport. She was the first to perform a camel, a layback, a one-foot axel, and a double jump. Although she is also often credited with being the first to perform to music, that honor in fact seems to belong to **Lily Kronberger.** At eleven, Colledge was the youngest competitor in the 1932 Olympic Games, and twice in her career she narrowly lost gold medals to **Sonja Henie**—once in the 1935 World Championships and again in the '36 Olympics, where she lost by one-tenth of a point. After immigrating to the United States in 1951, she worked for the Skating Club of Boston for a quarter of a century.

Selected championships and honors: Silver medal, World Championships, 1935; silver medal, Olympic Games, 1936.

SJOUKJE DIJKSTRA b. January 28, 1942, the Netherlands

Most people never saw Dijkstra's best performance—an untelevised but near-perfect completion of the compulsory figures at the 1964 Olympics, which gave her an insurmountable lead and, ultimately, the gold medal. It was Dijkstra's third Olympics and second medal, but the first gold her country had ever received at a winter Olympics. Dijkstra had also won the World Championship the three previous years.

Selected championships and honors: Bronze medal, World Championships, 1959; silver medal, Olympic Games, 1960; gold medal, Olympic Games, 1964; three gold medals, World Championships, 1962–64.

PEGGY FLEMING b. July 27, 1948, San Jose, California

In 1961 the United States and Peggy Fleming suffered an immense loss when a plane carrying the national team crashed in Belgium. The country's entire figure skating team—including skating great **Maribel Vinson Owen**—was killed. Fleming's coach was on

All That Jazz— Or, Who Picks the Music?

As more and more emphasis has been put on the free-skate portion of the program and compulsory figures have diminished in importance, the theatrical trick of coordinating athletic skills and expressive performance has become a crucial element of the program. Have you ever wondered who picks the music and builds the skater's routine around it? Not surprisingly, today's skaters work with professional skating choreographers. Many choreographers have been skaters themselves and have an intimate personal knowledge of the sport. Sandra Bezic, a former world-class pairs medalist, is one of the best-known specialists working today. If you saw the 1994 Olympic performances of Brian Boitano or **Katarina Witt,** you saw Bezic's work on ice. Since her program grows out of her knowledge of a skater's individual style, strengths, and capabilities, conflict of interest is not seen as a problem, and Bezic often works with more than one skater at a time. To create a routine, Bezic begins with a piece of music, carefully editing it to provide a full canvas for the skater's program. This can take weeks, and promising pieces are often rejected because they lack a passage for a particular needed element. Working with the skater, Bezic tailors the program carefully. Since skaters go through streaks, the program may be amended to accommodate a particular move the skater is performing flawlessly, or to allow inclusion of a newly learned skill.

the ill-fated plane, and the loss was devastating for the young skater. Eventually, Fleming regained her desire to skate. Her family relocated to Colorado to facilitate her training, and her mother designed and sewed her skating costumes. Fleming won the first of five consecutive national competitions in 1964 and the first of three consecutive World Championships a year later. Her spotlight moment as an amateur, however, didn't come until 1968. Four years earlier, Fleming had skated to a sixth-place Olympic finish. By the time the Grenoble games arrived, Fleming's style had matured into a seamless blend of expressive artistry, technical ability, and athleticism. Millions of Americans watched on television as she skated to instant fame, bringing home the United States' only gold that winter. Fleming relinquished her amateur standing soon after the Olympics, skating with both the Ice Follies and Holiday on Ice and starring in several television specials. She also worked as a skating commentator for the ABC Television network.

Selected championships and honors: Bronze medal, World Championships, 1965; three gold medals, World Championships, 1966–68; gold medal, Olympic Games, 1968; Associated Press Female Athlete of the Year, 1968; International Women's Sports Hall of Fame; Olympic Hall of Fame.

LINDA FRATIANNE b. August 2, 1960,
   Northridge, California

On a good day, Fratianne could dazzle crowds and judges alike with her combination of showmanship, gutsy jumps, and electric spins. On other days, her performance could seem choppy and artless. Inconsistency—and the fact that she often had to compete against Germany's accomplished **Anett Pötzsch**—kept her from true international fame. However, those who watched the 1980 Olympics saw her at her peak, when she outskated Pötzsch in the free skate program. Unable to overcome the commanding lead Pötzsch had taken in the compulsories, Fratianne settled for the silver.

Selected championships and honors: Two gold medals, World Championships, 1977 and '79; two silver medals, World Championships, 1978 and '80; silver medal, Olympic Games, 1980.

EKATERINA GORDEEVA b. ca. 1971, Moscow,
   Russia

Gordeeva won her first World Championship gold medal in 1986, skating pairs with Sergei Grinkov, the man who would become her friend and, later, her

A Sequin Here, a Rhinestone There— The High Cost of Suiting Up

Peggy Fleming may have had made-by-Mom costumes, but for today's skaters it's a whole new world—and usually an expensive one. Since costumes are first and foremost athletic suits, they need to fit well, allow freedom of movement, and be durable enough to last through performances, spills, and bumps across the ice. They also need to be showstoppingly glamorous, designed to capture the camera's eye with bold slashes of line and color or the glitter of hand-sewn rhinestones. It isn't unusual for an outfit worn in Olympic competition to cost $10,000 when all is said and done, and while established skaters may attract designers who will contribute their services, young skaters working their way up usually have to dig deep into the family coffers. Aside from the costume itself, there are numerous sundry incidentals, like tights, and the key ingredient, the skates themselves. Competition-quality skating boots cost around $600, while blades—which don't last long due to the constant sharpening required—come in at around $500 per pair. This doesn't count the cost of lessons, choreographers, or travel expenses involved in pursuing a competitive career. Skating may be one of the most beautiful sports to watch, but it's one of the most expensive to participate in.

husband. Over the next ten years, Gordeeva and Grinkov won three more World Championships and two Olympic golds, and took their place beside other great Russian pairs. They turned professional, moved to the United States, and were skating together during a practice in late 1995, when suddenly Grinkov collapsed and died of heart failure at the age of twenty-eight. Within a year Gordeeva made the decision to return to the ice, a process that involved a difficult transition from pairs habits to solo techniques. Among her most difficult challenges, Gordeeva told a

Newsweek reporter in 1996, was learning to connect directly with the audience. While many skaters have begun as soloists and adapted to the demands of pairs, Gordeeva is the only world-class pairs champion who has attempted the transition from pairs to singles.

Selected championships and honors: Four gold medals, pairs, World Championships, 1986, '87, '89, and '90; two gold medals, pairs, Olympic Games, 1988 and '94.

DOROTHY HAMILL b. July 26, 1956, Chicago, Illinois

Long before Nadia's perfect 10, Hamill scored a perfect 6—in the short program of the 1976 Olympics. Nearsighted and uncomfortable with contacts, Hamill skated without the glasses she wore to complete her compulsories. She dispensed with her glasses again in the free-skate program and turned in a performance good enough to snatch the gold from the Netherlands' Dianne de Leeuw, who'd beaten her at the World Championships the year before. Hamill was the last woman to win a figure skating gold without a triple jump, but she compensated with a move of her own—the "Hamill camel," a standing spin that turns into a sit-spin. She was an immensely popular champion, and in the wake of her win thousands of young women had their hair cut in her signature bobbed style. A month after the Montreal games, Hamill won the World Championship. She then retired from competition and skated professionally with the Ice Capades.

Selected championships and honors: Two silver medals, World Championships, 1974 and '75; gold medal, Olympic Games, 1976; gold medal, World Championships, 1976; Olympic Hall of Fame.

CAROL HEISS JENKINS b. January 20, 1940, New York, New York

When Heiss was seven years old, her skating instructor told her mother that Carol could be the world champion in ten years. For several years it looked like he was wrong, and Heiss seemed destined to be many times a bridesmaid but never a bride. From 1953 to 1956, Heiss finished second to **Tenley Albright** in ten major competitions, including the World Championships and the Olympics. Finally, two weeks after losing the Olympic gold, Heiss defeated Albright to win the World Championship. It was Albright's last competition, and the first of many titles for Heiss, who went on to win four United States and five World

Championships as well as three North American titles. When her mother was dying of cancer in late 1956, Heiss promised her she would keep skating until she won an Olympic gold medal. She fulfilled the promise in 1960, at the Squaw Valley games, where she became the first woman to perform a double jump in competition. Heiss retired from competition later that year, and in 1961 she married fellow skater Hayes Alan Jenkins.

Selected championships and honors: Silver medal, World Championships, 1955; silver medal, Olympic Games, 1956; five gold medals, World Championships, 1956–60; gold medal, Olympic Games, 1960.

SONJA HENIE b. April 8, 1912, Oslo, Norway; d. October 12, 1969

Many people know Henie best as the petite blond skater in Busby Berkley–esque movie extravaganzas. It would be a shame if that was the *only* way they knew her, for Henie was a brilliant competitive skater, an innovative pioneer, and ultimately, the woman who made skating a popular spectator sport. Henie's competitive career began early and spanned four Olympiads. She won the first of six Norwegian national titles when she was nine years old and probably performed her first single axel—the first woman skater to do so—before she was ten years old. Henie attended her first Olympic Games in 1924 at age eleven, and won the first of ten consecutive World Championships in 1927. Though she failed to medal in her first Olympics, she came home from each of the next three with gold medals. Henie was perhaps the first woman to see figure skating's potential to dazzle the eye and captivate huge audiences. Trained in ballet, Henie melded skating with dance. She dispensed with long skirts in favor of showy costumes that afforded freedom of movement. After retiring from competition in 1936, she formed the Hollywood Ice Revue, in which she starred. She also starred in ten films and skated her way to a fortune. As a businesswoman, Henie was both shrewd and generous. She assembled a fabulous art collection, which she later bequeathed to her country. A lifelong Norwegian citizen, Henie was worth $47 million when she died of leukemia in 1969.

Selected championships and honors: Silver medal, World Championships, 1926; ten gold medals, World Championships, 1927–36; three gold medals, Olympic Games, 1928, '32, and '36; International Women's Sports Hall of Fame.

MIDORI ITO b. August 13, 1969, Japan

A disciplined if somewhat solemn skater, Ito was the first woman ever to land a triple axel in major competition, at the 1989 World Championships, which she won. Those who only saw Ito in Olympic competitions failed to appreciate her brilliance and fearlessness, as she was frequently outdazzled by **Kristi Yamaguchi,** whose freer, more expressive American style of skating captured the audience's heart.

Selected championships and honors: Gold medal, World Championships, 1989; silver medal, Olympic Games, 1992.

NANCY KERRIGAN b. October 13, 1969, Stoneham, Massachusetts

Many were unaware of Kerrigan until January 1994, when an accomplice of skating rival Tonya Harding bashed her on the knee in hopes of ruining her Olympic chances. He didn't, and Kerrigan claimed her second Olympic medal at the Lillehammer games. (Her first, a bronze, had come two years earlier at Albertville.) Although Kerrigan's naturally elegant looks led many to believe she came from a privileged background, that wasn't the case. Kerrigan's working-class parents made numerous sacrifices, as did Kerrigan herself, who often had to practice in ill-fitting skates because there was no money for new ones. Unwittingly, the Harding-inspired attack touched a nerve of toughness. Angered that the United States did not ban Harding from the games, Kerrigan skated her personal best at Lillehammer, outperforming everyone except gold medalist **Oksana Baiul.**

Selected championships and honors: Bronze medal, Olympic Games, 1992; silver medal, Olympic Games, 1994.

LILY KRONBERGER b. ca. 1885, Budapest, Hungary

The next time you enjoy a free-skate program, think of Kronberger—she was the first to skate to music, an innovation that transformed skating forever. At the first World Championships, held in 1906, Kronberger won the bronze, and finished third again the next year. From 1908 through 1911, however, she came in first.

Selected championships and honors: Two bronze medals, World Championships, 1906 and 1907; four gold medals, World Championships, 1908–11.

MICHELLE KWAN b. 1980, Torrance, California

The daughter of immigrants from Hong Kong, Kwan had her first ice experience at a rink at the local mall. The setting was pedestrian, but the magic was pure, and Kwan soon began taking private lessons. Kwan has been competing at the senior level since 1993, and in 1996 she won her first U.S. national title, then went on to win the World Championships. Disciplined and athletic, Kwan is one of only a few world-class skaters strong enough to put back-to-back triple jumps in her program, and barring injury she is a likely hopeful for the 1998 Olympics.

Selected championships and honors: Gold medal, World Championships, 1996.

BEATRIX LOUGHRAN b. June 30, 1900, New York, New York; d. December 7, 1975

Though Loughran never won a gold medal in Olympic competition, she did win three medals in three consecutive games—something no other American figure skater has accomplished. Her first two medals were in singles competition, and her last, at the 1932 games, was in pairs with partner Sherwin Badger.

Selected championships and honors: Silver medal, singles, Olympic Games, 1924; bronze medal, singles, Olympic Games, 1928; silver medal, pairs, Olympic Games, 1932.

JANET LYNN. *See Janet Lynn Nowicki, below.*

JANET LYNN NOWICKI b. April 6, 1953, Chicago, Illinois

Lynn dropped her surname early in her career and has been known to the public simply as Janet Lynn since she made her international debut at the 1972 Olympics. By then she had already won four of her five consecutive U.S. national titles and was favored to contend for gold. Unfortunately, she fell during her free-skating program, a misfortune that again befell her at the World Championships the next year. Despite the falls, Lynn performed well enough to win medals each time. Lynn turned pro in 1973 and signed a three-year contract with the Ice Follies. Unfortunately, chronic respiratory problems forced her to retire after just a few seasons. Years later, doctors discovered that the respiratory problems were caused by allergies. Lynn underwent treatment and at age thirty came out of retirement to win the first U.S. pro skating championship in 1983.

Selected championships and honors: Bronze medal, Olympic Games, 1972; silver medal, World Championships, 1973.

HERMA PLANCK SZABO b. February 22, 1902, Vienna, Austria; d. May 7, 1986

Had World War I not interupted and delayed Szabo's entrance on the world figure skating stage, she would probably have ranked with **Sonja Henie** in the number of medals accumulated. As it was, Szabo didn't begin competing until 1922, an age at which today's skaters are nearing retirement. Innovative, daring, and athletic, Szabo nevertheless won five consecutive World Championships in singles competitions, an Olympic gold medal, and, with partner Ludwig Wrede, two world pairs titles.

Selected championships and honors: Five gold medals, singles, World Championships, 1922–26; gold medal, Olympic Games, 1924; two gold medals, pairs, World Championships, 1925 and '27; silver medal, World Championships, 1927; U.S. Figure Skating Association Hall of Fame.

ANETT PÖTZSCH b. ca. 1960, Karl-Marx-Stadt, East Germany

For four years, from 1977 through 1980, two women ruled the figure skating world—Pötzsch and America's **Linda Fratianne.** They took two World Championships apiece and met at the 1980 Lake Placid Olympics, where Pötzsch edged her rival for the gold. An innovative performer who charmed the crowd by spinning with one foot held above her head, Pötzsch was the first East German figure skater to win a gold for her country.

Selected championships and honors: Two gold medals, World Championships, 1978 and '80; two silver medals, World Championships, 1977 and '79; gold medal, Olympic Games, 1980.

LYUDMILA PROTOPOPOV. *See Lyudmila Belousova Protopopov, above.*

IRINA RODNINA ZAITSEV b. September 12, 1949, USSR

Arguably the greatest pairs skater of all time, Rodnina skated for ten consecutive World Championship golds, a feat equaled only by **Sonja Henie.** Unlike Henie, who only had herself to worry about, Rodnina's performance depended on her partner. After winning several World Championships and one

Olympic gold with Alexsei Ulanov, Rodnina had to find a new partner when Ulanov married after the 1972 Olympics. The Soviet Union held a nationwide talent search, and hundreds of men auditioned for the chance to skate with the incomparable Rodnina. Aleksandr Zaitsev won, though it was by no means certain whether the two would find the chemistry of talent and personality needed to make a championship duo. They did, both on the ice and off. Rodnina and Zaitsev won the next World Championships without a hitch, and eventually married. After taking 1978–79 off to have a child, Rodnina and Zaitsev returned for what became their last major international appearance, the 1980 Olympics. The games promised dramatic competition between Rodnina and Zaitsev and Americans **Tai Babilonia** and Randy Gardner, who had won the World Championships in the Soviet couple's absence. Unfortunately, Gardner sustained a serious injury. The Americans had to withdraw, and the much-hyped competition failed to come off. Nevertheless, Rodnina and Zaitsev skated brilliantly, making their final bow on the world stage one of their best.

Selected championships and honors: Ten gold medals, World Championships, 1969–78; three Olympic gold medals, 1972, '76, and '80.

BARBARA ANN SCOTT b. May 9, 1928, Ottawa, Ontario, Canada

A prodigy who won a silver in the Canadian nationals at age twelve, Scott was the first North American skater to win a world singles championship. At the 1948 Olympics she and America's Dick Button symbolized North America's hopes of breaking a longstanding European lock on the sport. In those pre-Zamboni days, the ice had been badly rutted by earlier hockey games, and Scott was scheduled to skate early. Fortunately, Eileen Seigh of the United States skated before Scott and provided her with a verbal map of the rutted ice. Scott was able to adjust her program, avoid the worst patches, and skate to a first-place finish. On the ice, Scott was noted for an ability to meld delicate precision with athletic power. Her good looks and on-ice feats made her a role model for thousands of young girls, and she was one of the first athletes ever to have a doll marketed in her honor.

Selected championships and honors: Gold medal, World Championships, 1947; gold medal, Olympic Games, 1948.

ROSALYNN SUMMERS b. April 20, 1964, Palo
  Alto, California

Though born in California, Summers grew up in
Washington State, where she began to skate at the age
of six. In competition, Summers was consistent as well
as stylish. Unfortunately, her competitive career coincided with that of one of the supreme skaters of the
age, **Katarina Witt.** Twice Summers competed
against Witt in a major international competitions, and
both times she came away with silver instead of gold.
Selected championships and honors: Silver medal,
Olympic Games, 1984; silver medal, World Championships, 1984.

MADGE SYERS. *See Florence Madeleine Cave
  Syers, above.*

DEBI THOMAS b. March 25, 1967, Poughkeepsie,
  New York

Thomas became fascinated with skating while watching Mr. Frick, a famous ice clown. She began taking
lessons and discovered she had a natural talent for the
sport. Talent and love of skating aside, Thomas continued to study throughout her career, with an eye to
entering medical school. Her greatest moment came
in 1986, when she became the first woman of African
descent to win a gold medal in world competition. In
that competition, she also became the first woman
ever to defeat **Katarina Witt** in world competition.
Two years later Witt evened the score in the famous
"Battle of the Carmens" at the 1988 Olympics. Both
skaters had chosen Bizet's music, and Witt's beauti-
fully artistic but somewhat conservative program won
the day over Thomas's riskier but less elegant routine.
Thomas retired from competition after the games,
finished her undergraduate degree, and entered
medical school in 1991.
Selected championships and honors: Gold medal,
World Championships, 1986; bronze medal, World
Championships, 1988; bronze medal, Olympic
Games, 1988.

JAYNE TORVILL b. October 7, 1957, England

Ice dance, a World Championships sport since 1950,
was introduced to the Olympics in 1976—but no one
gave it much respect until Torvill and her partner
Christopher Dean got hold of it. After four consecutive World Championships, they became *the* ice story
of the 1984 Sarajevo Olympics, creating a wave so
strong people who'd previously dismissed the event
became almost instant fans. They weren't disap-

pointed. Torvill and Dean won the world professional
championship the next year and, after the rules ban-
ning professionals from Olympic competition were
relaxed, were popular favorites as they danced to a
bronze-medal finish at the 1994 games.
Selected championships and honors: Four gold medals,
World Championships, 1981–84; gold medal, Olympic
Games, 1984; bronze medal, Olympic Games, 1994.

JILL TRENARY b. August 1, 1968, Minneapolis,
  Minnesota

In 1987, Trenary upset reigning World Champion
Debi Thomas to win the first of her three U.S. National championships. In 1990, she again upset a
reigning champion—Midori Ito—to win the world
singles title. Trenary turned pro after her amateur career and won the 1992 U.S. Open championship. She
has worked as a network commentator and toured the
world with several professional skating troups, including Torvill and Dean. Some skaters find traveling in-
compatible with personal life but Trenary, married to
fellow skater Christopher Dean, finds it a perfect fit.
Selected championships: Bronze medal, World Championship, 1989; Gold medal, World Championship,
1990.

MARIBEL VINSON OWEN b. October 12, 1911,
  Winchester, Massachusetts; d. February 15, 1961

Though she never won an international gold medal,
Vinson was an enormously important figure in American figure skating. Between 1928 and 1937 she won
nine national titles, missing only 1933, the year she
graduated from Radcliffe and went to train in Europe. After retiring from competition in 1937, she
turned professional and for a time toured with her
own ice show. She later became a coach, numbering
among her pupils **Tenley Albright** and her own two
daughters, Maribel and Lauren Owen. Tragically,
Vinson and both daughters were among the eighteen
U.S. skating team members killed in a 1961 plane
crash near Belgium.
Selected championships and honors: Silver medal,
World Championships, 1928; bronze medal, World
Championships, 1930; bronze medal, Olympic Games,
1932; U.S. Figure Skating Association Hall of Fame.

THERESA (TEE) WELD BLANCHARD
  b. August 21, 1893, Brookline, Massachusetts;
  d. March 12, 1978

At the age of twelve, Weld began taking lessons at the
Skating Club of Boston, where her father—an avid

skater himself—was a charter member. The club was a formative influence on Weld and on American figure skating in general, encouraging a style that was graceful and free-flowing over the formal, carefully mannered British style. Weld had to wait for the sport to catch up with her, and she was twenty-one by the time organized national competitions were held in the United States. She encountered further difficulties when judges deducted points for jumps they considered "unladylike," and had just begun to compete when World War I intervened. Nevertheless she had a long and impressive career, winning six U.S. singles championships as well as nine U.S. pairs and four national dance titles with partner Nathaniel Niles. She won the United States' first winter Olympics medal, a bronze, at the 1920 games. That same year she married and continued to compete, under her married name, for the next fourteen years. In 1923 Weld and Niles founded *Skating* magazine, which eventually became the official publication of the U.S. Figure Skating Association. A lifelong enthusiast of the sport, Weld sat on the USFSA board for thirteen years and frequently served as judge in world competitions.

Selected championships and honors: Bronze medal, Olympic Games, 1920; International Women's Sports Hall of Fame; Figure Skating Hall of Fame.

KATARINA WITT b. December 3, 1965, Karl-Marx-Stadt, East Germany

The most memorable skater of the 1980s and '90s, Witt also had one of the longest careers. Between 1984 and '88 she won four World Championships, missing only 1986, the year she lost to American **Debi Thomas.** She competed in three Olympiads (1984, '88, and '94) and won golds in the first two, a feat no skater had achieved since **Sonja Henie.** On the ice, Witt's physical appeal blended well with her emphasis on artistry rather than high-powered athleticism. Always popular with crowds, she won her first gold medal to a medley of American show tunes. Her second Olympic gold medal program, skated to music from Bizet's *Carmen,* ranks as one of the most expressive in skating history. That year, American **Debi Thomas** also skated to Bizet's music, but had trouble landing her first jump and skated without Witt's fire. Although Witt turned pro after the '88 games, a rule change prior to the '94 games dropped the traditional ban on professionals. Witt competed one more time, again thrilling audiences despite a seventh-place finish.

Selected championships and honors: Four gold medals, World Championships, 1984, '85, '87, and '88; two gold medals, Olympic Games, 1984 and '88.

KRISTI YAMAGUCHI b. July 12, 1971, Hayward, California

Before she could skate, Yamaguchi had to face an even bigger challenge—walking. Born with feet that turned abnormally inward, as a baby she wore plaster casts laced with metal rods to force her feet outward. When the casts came off, she had to wear corrective shoes. To help her catch up developmentally, Yamaguchi's mother encouraged her daughter to explore dancing, skating, and other activities. Yamaguchi was good at skating and became passionate about it while watching **Dorothy Hamill** in the 1976 Olympics. Until 1982, Yamaguchi trained both as a singles and a pairs skater, then dropped pairs to concentrate on her real love, singles competition. Small (5' and less than 100 pounds) and not heavily muscled, Yamaguchi owes her strength as a skater to her ability to turn a rigorous routine into a sparkling, seemingly effortless performance. Her on-ice élan energizes crowds and has helped her forge a postcompetitive career as a professional skater.

Selected championships and honors: Gold medal, World Championships, 1991; gold medal, Olympic Games, 1992.

ELAINE ZAYAK b. April 12, 1965, Paramus, New Jersey

Skating stood at a great divide—and Zayak was the skater who became the deciding force. Originally conceived of as a sport that emphasized grace above all, women's skating over the years acquired more and more athleticism. Enter Zayak in the early 1980s, a skater short on artistic impression but long on strength, daring, and pure athletic power. In 1982 she won the World Championships with a program that included seven triple jumps. In the wake of her win, skating's international governing body imposed what became known as the "Zayak rule," barring women from including more than three triple jumps in a routine. Although Zayak continued to compete until turning pro after the 1984 Olympics, injury and an inability to do well on the then-important compulsories kept her from winning more medals.

Selected championships and honors: Silver medal, World Championships, 1981; gold medal, World Championships, 1982.

Figure Skating

Olympic Individuals

Year	Medalists	Country
1908	Florence "Madge" Syers	GBR
	Elsa Rendschmidt	GER
	Dorothy Greenhough-Smith	GBR
1920	Magda Julin-Maurey	SWE
	Svea Noren	SWE
	Theresa Weld	USA
1924	Herma Planck Szabo	AUT
	Beatrix Loughran	USA
	Ethel Muckelt	GBR
1928	Sonja Henie	NOR
	Fritzi Burger	AUT
	Beatrix Loughran	USA
1932	Sonja Henie	NOR
	Fritzi Burger	AUT
	Maribel Vinson	USA
1936	Sonja Henie	NOR
	M. Cecilia Colledge	GBR
	Vivi-Anne Hulten	SWE
1948	Barbara Ann Scott	CAN
	Eva Pawlik	AUT
	Jeannette Altwegg	GBR
1952	Jeannette Altwegg	GBR
	Tenley Albright	USA
	Jacqueline du Bief	FRA
1956	Tenley Albright	USA
	Carol Heiss	USA
	Ingrid Wendl	AUT
1960	Carol Heiss	USA
	Sjoukje Dijkstra	HOL
	Barbara Roles	USA
1964	Sjoukje Dijkstra	HOL
	Regine Heitzer	AUT
	Petra Burka	CAN
1968	Peggy Fleming	USA
	Gabriele Seyfert	GDR
	Hena Maskova	CZE
1972	Beatrix Schuba	AUT
	Karen Magnussen	CAN
	Janet Lynn	USA
1976	Dorothy Hamill	USA
	Dianne de Leeuw	HOL
	Christine Errath	GDR
1980	Anett Pötzsch	GDR
	Linda Fratianne	USA
	Dagmar Lurz	GER
1984	Katarina Witt	GDR
	Rosalynn Summers	USA
	Kira Ivanova	USSR
1988	Katarina Witt	GDR
	Elizabeth Manley	CAN
	Debra Thomas	USA
1992	Kristi Yamaguchi	USA
	Midori Ito	JPN
	Nancy Kerrigan	USA
1994	Oksana Baiul	UKR
	Nancy Kerrigan	USA
	Chen Lu	CHN

Olympic Pairs

Year	Medalists	Country
1908	Anna Hubler/Heinrich Burger	GER
	Phyllis Johnson/James Johnson	GBR
	Florence "Madge" Syers/ Edgar Syers	GBR
1920	Ludovika Jakobsson-Eilers/ Walter Jakobsson	FIN
	Alexia Bryn-Schoien/Yngvar Bryn	NOR
	Phyllis Johnson/Basil Williams	GBR
1924	Helene Engelmann/ Alfred Berger	AUT
	Ludovika Jakobsson-Eilers/ Walter Jakobsson	FIN
	Andree Joly/Pierre Brunet	FRA
1928	Andree Joly/Pierre Brunet	FRA
	Lilly Scholz/Otto Kaiser	AUT
	Melitta Brunner/Ludwig Wrede	AUT
1932	Andree Brunet (Joly)/ Pierre Brunet	FRA
	Beatrix Loughran/ Sherwin Badger	USA
	Emilia Rotter/Laszlo Szollas	HUN
1936	Maxi Herber/Ernst Baier	GER
	Ilse Pausin/Erik Pausin	AUT
	Emilia Rotter/Laszlo Szollas	HUN
1948	Micheline Lannoy/ Pierre Baugniet	BEL
	Andrea Kekessy/Ede Kiraly	HUN
	Suzanne Morrow/ Wallace Diestelmeyer	CAN
1952	Ria Falk/Paul Falk	GER
	Karol Kennedy/Michael Kennedy	USA
	Marianna Nagy/Laszlo Nagy	HUN
1956	Elisabeth Schwartz/Kurt Oppelt	AUT
	Frances Dafoe/Norris Bowden	CAN
	Marianna Nagy/Laszlo Nagy	HUN
1960	Barbara Wagner/Robert Paul	CAN
	Marika Kilius/ Hans-Jurgen Baumler	GER
	Nancy Ludington/ Ronald Ludington	USA

Figure Skating (continued)

Olympic Pairs

Year	Medalists	Country
1964	Lyudmila Belousova/ Oleg Protopopov	USSR
	Marika Kilius/ Hans-Jurgen Baumler	GER
	Debbi Wilkes/Guy Revell	CAN
1968	Lyudmila Belousova/ Oleg Protopopov	USSR
	Tatyana Zhuk/Aleksandr Gorelik	USSR
	Margot Glockshuber/ Wolfgang Danne	GER
1972	Irina Rodnina/ Aleksei Ulanov	USSR
	Lyudmila Smirnova/ Andrei Surakin	USSR
	Manuela Gross/Uwe Kagelmann	GDR
1976	Irina Rodnina/Aleksandr Zaitsev	USSR
	Romy Kermer/Rolf Osterreich	GDR
	Manuela Gross/Uwe Kagelmann	GDR
1980	Irina Rodnina/Aleksandr Zaitsev	USSR
	Marina Cherkosova/ Sergei Shakrai	USSR
	Manuela Mager/ Uwe Bewersdorff	GDR
1984	Yelena Valova/Oleg Vasilyev	USSR
	Caitlin "Kitty" Carruthers/ Peter Carruthers	USA
	Larissa Selezneva/Oleg Makarov	USSR
1988	Yekaterina Gordeyeva/ Sergei Grinkov	USSR
	Yelena Valova/Oleg Vasilyev	USSR
	Jill Watson/Peter Oppegard	USA
1992	Natalya Mishkutenok/ Artur Dmitriev	USSR
	Yelena Betchke/Denis Petrov	USSR
	Isabelle Brasseur/Lloyd Eisler	CAN
1994	Katerina Gordeeva/ Sergei Grinkov	RUS
	Natalia Mishkutienok/ Artur Dmitriev	RUS
	Isabelle Brasseur/Lloyd Eisler	CAN

Olympic Ice Dance

Year	Medalists	Country
1924– 1972	event not held	
1976	Lyudmila Pakhomova/ Aleksandr Gorshkov	USSR
	Irina Moiseyeva/ Andrei Minenkov	USSR
	Colleen O'Conner/James Millns	USA
1980	Natalya Linichuk/ Gennady Karpono	USSR
	Krisztina Regoczy/ Andras Sallay	HUN
	Irina Moiseyeva/ Andrei Minenkov	USSR
1984	Jayne Torvill/ Christopher Dean	GBR
	Natalya Bestemianova/ Andrei Bukin	USSR
	Marina Klimova/ Sergei Ponomarenko	USSR
1988	Natalya Bestemianova/ Andrei Bukin	USSR
	Marina Klimova/ Sergei Ponomarenko	USSR
	Tracy Wilson/Robert McCall	CAN
1992	Marina Klimova/ Sergei Ponomarenko	USSR
	Isabelle Duchesnay-Dean/ Paul Duchesnay	FRA
	Maya Usova/Aleksandr Zhulin	USSR
1994	Oksana Gritschuk/ Evgeni Platov	RUS
	Maya Usova/Aleksandr Zhulin	RUS
	Jayne Torvill/Christopher Dean	GBR

World Championship Ladies Singles

Year	Medalists	Country
1906	Madge Syers	GBR
	Jenny Herz	AUT
	Lily Kronberger	HUN
1907	Madge Syers	GBR
	Jenny Herz	AUT
	Lily Kronberger	HUN
1908	Lily Kronberger	HUN
	Elsa Rendschmidt	GER
1909	Lily Kronberger	HUN
1910	Lily Kronberger	HUN
	Elsa Rendschmidt	GER
1911	Lily Kronberger	HUN
	Opika von Horvath	HUN
	Ludowika Eilers	GER
1912	Opika von Horvath	HUN
	Dorothy Greenhough	GBR
	Phyllis Johnson	GBR
1913	Opika von Horvath	HUN
	Phyllis Johnson	GBR
	Svea Noren	SWE
1914	Opika von Horvath	HUN
	Angela Hanka	AUT
	Phyllis Johnson	GBR

Figure Skating (continued)

World Championship Ladies Singles

Year	Medalists	Country
1915–1921	not held	
1922	Herma Planck Szabo	AUT
	Svea Noren	SWE
	Margot Moe	NOR
1923	Herma Planck Szabo	AUT
	Gisela Reichmann	AUT
	Svea Noren	SWE
1924	Herma Planck Szabo	AUT
	Ellen Brockhofft	GER
	Beatrix Loughran	USA
1925	Herma Planck Szabo	AUT
	Ellen Brockhofft	GER
	Elisabeth Bockel	GER
1926	Herma Planck Szabo	AUT
	Sonja Henie	NOR
	Kathleen Shaw	GBR
1927	Sonja Henie	NOR
	Herma Planck Szabo	AUT
	Karen Simensen	NOR
1928	Sonja Henie	NOR
	Maribel Vinson	USA
	Fritzi Burger	AUT
1929	Sonja Henie	NOR
	Fritzi Burger	AUT
	Melitta Brunner	AUT
1930	Sonja Henie	NOR
	Cecil Smith	CAN
	Maribel Vinson	USA
1931	Sonja Henie	NOR
	Hilde Holovsky	AUT
	Fritzi Burger	AUT
1932	Sonja Henie	NOR
	Fritzi Burger	AUT
	Constance Samuel	CAN
1933	Sonja Henie	NOR
	Vivi-Anne Hulten	SWE
	Hilde Holovsky	AUT
1934	Sonja Henie	NOR
	Megan Taylor	GBR
	Liselotte Landbeck	AUT
1935	Sonja Henie	NOR
	Cecilia Colledge	GBR
	Vivi-Anne Hulten	SWE
1936	Sonja Henie	NOR
	Megan Taylor	GBR
	Vivi-Anne Hulten	SWE
1937	Cecilia Colledge	GBR
	Megan Taylor	GBR
	Vivi-Anne Hulten	SWE
1938	Megan Taylor	GBR
	Cecilia Colledge	GBR
	Hedy Stenuf	USA
1939	Megan Taylor	GBR
	Hedy Stenuf	USA
	Daphne Walker	GBR
1940–1946	not held	
1947	Barbara Ann Scott	CAN
	Daphne Walker	GBR
	Gretchen Merrill	USA
1948	Barbara Ann Scott	CAN
	Eva Pawlik	AUT
	Jirina Nekolova	CZE
1949	Aletta Vrzanova	CZE
	Yvonne Sherman	USA
	Jeannette Altwegg	GBR
1950	Aletta Vrzanova	CZE
	Jeannette Altwegg	GBR
	Yvonne Sherman	USA
1951	Jeannette Altwegg	GBR
	Jacqueline du Bief	FRA
	Sonya Klopfer	USA
1952	Jacqueline du Bief	FRA
	Sonya Klopfer	USA
	Virginia Baxter	USA
1953	Tenley Albright	USA
	Gundi Busch	FRG
	Valda Osborn	GBR
1954	Gundi Busch	FRG
	Tenley Albright	USA
	Erica Batchelor	GBR
1955	Tenley Albright	USA
	Carol Heiss	USA
	Hanna Eigel	AUT
1956	Carol Heiss	USA
	Tenley Albright	USA
	Ingrid Wendl	AUT
1957	Carol Heiss	USA
	Hanna Eigel	AUT
	Ingrid Wendl	AUT
1958	Carol Heiss	USA
	Ingrid Wendl	AUT
	Hanna Walter	AUT
1959	Carol Heiss	USA
	Hanna Walter	AUT
	Sjoukje Dijkstra	HOL
1960	Carol Heiss	USA
	Sjoukje Dijkstra	HOL
	Barbara Roles	USA
1961	not held	
1962	Sjoukje Dijkstra	HOL
	Wendy Griner`	CAN
	Regine Heitzer	AUT

Figure Skating (continued)

World Championship Ladies Singles

Year	Medalists	Country
1963	Sjoukje Dijkstra	HOL
	Regine Heitzer	AUT
	Nicole Hassler	FRA
1964	Sjoukje Dijkstra	HOL
	Regine Heitzer	AUT
	Petra Burka	CAN
1965	Petra Burka	CAN
	Regine Heitzer	AUT
	Peggy Fleming	USA
1966	Peggy Fleming	USA
	Gabriele Seyfert	GDR
	Petra Burka	CAN
1967	Peggy Fleming	USA
	Gabriele Seyfert	GDR
	Hana Maskova	CZE
1968	Peggy Fleming	USA
	Gabriele Seyfert	GDR
	Hana Maskova	CZE
1969	Gabriele Seyfert	GDR
	Beatrix Schuba	AUT
	Zsuzsa Almassy	HUN
1970	Gabriele Seyfert	GDR
	Beatrix Schuba	AUT
	Julie Holmes	USA
1971	Beatrix Schuba	AUT
	Julie Holmes	USA
	Karen Magnussen	CAN
1972	Beatrix Schuba	AUT
	Karen Magnussen	CAN
	Janet Lynn	USA
1973	Karen Magnussen	CAN
	Janet Lynn	USA
	Christine Errath	GDR
1974	Christine Errath	GDR
	Dorothy Hamill	USA
	Dianne de Leeuw	HOL
1975	Dianne de Leeuw	HOL
	Dorothy Hamill	USA
	Christine Errath	GDR
1976	Dorothy Hamill	USA
	Christine Errath	GDR
	Dianne de Leeuw	HOL
1977	Linda Fratianne	USA
	Anett Potzsch	GDR
	Dagmar Lurz	FRG
1978	Anett Potzsch	GDR
	Linda Fratianne	USA
	Susanna Driano	ITA
1979	Linda Fratianne	USA
	Anett Potzsch	GDR
	Emi Watanbe	JPN
1980	Anett Potzsch	GDR
	Dagmar Lurz	FRG
	Linda Fratianne	USA
1981	Denise Bleilmann	SWI
	Elaine Zayak	USA
	Claudia Kristofics-Binder	AUT
1982	Elaine Zayak	USA
	Katarina Witt	GDR
	Claudia Kristofics-Binder	AUT
1983	Rosalynn Sumners	USA
	Claudia Leistner	FRG
	Elena Vodorezova	URS
1984	Katarina Witt	GDR
	Anna Kondrashova	URS
	Elaine Zayak	USA
1985	Katarina Witt	GDR
	Kira Ivanova	URS
	Tiffany Chin	USA
1986	Debi Thomas	USA
	Katarina Witt	GDR
	Tiffany Chin	USA
1987	Katarina Witt	GDR
	Debi Thomas	USA
	Caryn Kadavy	USA
1988	Katarina Witt	GDR
	Elizabeth Manley	CAN
	Debi Thomas	USA
1989	Midori Ito	JPN
	Claudia Lsistner	FRG
	Jill Trenary	USA
1990	Jill Trenary	USA
	Midori Ito	JPN
	Holly Cook	USA
1991	Kristi Yamaguchi	JPN
	Tonya Harding	USA
	Nancy Kerrigan	USA
1992	Kristi Yamaguchi	JPN
	Nancy Kerrigan	USA
	Chen Lu	CHN
1993	Oksana Baiul	UKR
	Surya Bonaly	FRA
	Chen Lu	CHN
1994	Yuka Sato	JPN
	Surya Bonaly	FRA
	Tanja Szewczenko	GER
1995	Chen Lu	CHN
	Surya Bonaly	FRA
	Nicole Bobek	USA
1996	Michelle Kwan	USA
	Chen Lu	CHN
	Irina Slutskaya	RUS
1997	Tara Lipinski	USA
	Michelle Kwan	USA
	Vanessa Gusmeroli	FRA

Figure Skating (continued)

World Championship Pairs

Year	Medalists	Country
1908	Anna Hubler/Heinrich Burger	GER
	Phyllis Johnson/James Johnson	GBR
	A. L. Fischer/ L. P. Popowa	RUS
1909	Phyllis Johnson/James Johnson	GBR
	Valborg Lindahl/Nils Rosenius	SWE
	Gertrud Strom/Richard Johanson	SWE
1910	Anna Hubler/Heinrich Burger	GER
	Ludowika Eilers/Walter Jakobsson	FIN
	Phyllis Johnson/James Johnson	GBR
1911	Ludowika Eilers/Walter Jakobsson	FIN
	—	
	—	
1912	Phyllis Johnson/James Johnson	GBR
	Ludowika Jakobsson/Walter Jakobsson	FIN
	Alexia Schoyed/Yngvar Bryn	NOR
1913	Helene Engelmann/Karl Mejstrik	AUT
	Ludowika Jakobsson/Walter Jakobsson	FIN
	Christa von Szabo/Leo Horwitz	AUT
1914	Ludowika Jakobsson/Walter Jakobsson	FIN
	Helene Engelmann/Karl Mejstrik	AUT
	Christa von Szabo/Leo Horwitz	AUT
1915-1921	not held	
1922	Helene Engelmann/Alfred Berger	AUT
	Ludowika Jakobsson/Walter Jakobsson	FIN
	Margaret Metzner/Paul Metzner	GER
1923	Ludowika Jakobsson/Walter Jakobsson	FIN
	Alexia Bryn/Yngvar Bryn	NOR
	Elna Henrikson/Kaj af Ekstrom	SWE
1924	Helene Engelmann/Alfred Berger	AUT
	Ethel Muckelt/John Page	GBR
	Elna Henrikson/Kaj af Ekstrom	SWE
1925	Herma Planck Szabo/Ludwig Wrede	AUT
	Andree Brunet/Pierre Brunet	FRA
	Lilly Scholz/Otto Kaiser	AUT
1926	Andree Brunet/Pierre Brunet	FRA
	Lilly Scholz/Otto Kaiser	AUT
	Herma Planck Szabo/Ludwig Wrede	AUT
1927	Herma Planck Szabo/Ludwig Wrede	AUT
	Lilly Scholz/Otto Kaiser	AUT
	Else Hoppe/Oscar Hoppe	CZE
1928	Andree Brunet/Pierre Brunet	FRA
	Lilly Scholz/Otto Kaiser	AUT
	Melitta Brunner/Ludwig Wrede	AUT
1929	Lilly Scholz/Otto Kaiser	AUT
	Melitta Brunner/ Ludwig Wrede	AUT
	Olga Orgonista/Sandor Szalay	HUN
1930	Andree Brunet/Pierre Brunet	FRA
	Melitta Brunner/Ludwig Wrede	AUT
	Beatrix Loughran/Sherwin Badger	USA
1931	Emilie Rotter/Laszlo Szollas	HUN
	Olga Orgonista/Sandor Szalay	HUN
	Idi Papez/Karl Kwack	AUT
1932	Andree Brunet/Pierre Brunet	FRA
	Emilie Rotter/Laszlo Szollas	HUN
	Beatrix Loughran/Sherwin Badger	USA
1933	Emilie Rotter/Laszlo Szollas	HUN
	Idi Papez/Karl Kwack	AUT
	Randi Bakke/Christen Christensen	NOR
1934	Emilie Rotter/Laszlo Szollas	HUN
	Idi Papez/Karl Kwack	AUT
	Maxi Herber/Ernst Baier	GER
1935	Emilie Rotter/Laszlo Szollas	HUN
	Ilse Pausin/Erich Pausin	AUT
	Lucy Gallo/Rezso Dillinger	HUN
1936	Maxi Herber/Ernst Baier	GER
	Ilse Pausin/Erich Pausin	AUT
	Violet Cliff/Leslie Cliff	GBR
1937	Maxi Herber/Ernst Baier	GER
	Ilse Pausin/Erich Pausin	AUT
	Violet Cliff/Leslie Cliff	GBR
1938	Maxi Herber/Ernst Baier	GER
	Ilse Pausin/Erich Pausin	AUT
	Inge Koch/Gunther Noack	GER
1939	Maxi Herber/Ernst Baier	GER
	Ilse Pausin/Erich Pausin	AUT
	Inge Koch/Gunther Noack	GER
1940-1946	not held	
1947	Micheline Lannoy/Pierre Baugniet	BEL
	Karol Kennedy/Peter Kennedy	USA
	Suzanne Diskeuve/Edmond Verbustel	BEL
1948	Micheline Lannoy/Pierre Baugniet	BEL
	Andrea Kekesy/Ede Kiraly	HUN
	Suzanne Morrow/Wallace Diestelmeyer	CAN
1949	Andrea Kekesy/Ede Kiraly	HUN
	Karol Kennedy/Peter Kennedy	USA
	Anne Davies/Carlston Hoffner	USA
1950	Karol Kennedy/Peter Kennedy	USA
	Jennifer Nicks/John Nicks	GBR
	Marianne Nagy/Laszlo Nagy	HUN
1951	Ria Falk/Paul Falk	FRG
	Karol Kennedy/Peter Kennedy	USA
	Jennifer Nicks/John Nicks	GBR

Figure Skating (continued)

World Championship Pairs

Year	Medalists	Country
1952	Ria Falk/Paul Falk	FRG
	Karol Kennedy/Peter Kennedy	USA
	Jennifer Nicks/John Nicks	GBR
1953	Jennifer Nicks/John Nicks	GBR
	Frances Dafoe/Norris Bowden	CAN
	Marianne Nagy/Laszlo Nagy	HUN
1954	Frances Dafoe/Norris Bowden	CAN
	Silvia Grandjean/Michel Grandjean	SWI
	Elisabeth Schwarz/Kurt Oppelt	AUT
1955	Frances Dafoe/Norris Bowden	CAN
	Elisabeth Schwarz/Kurt Oppelt	AUT
	Marianne Nagy/Laszlo Nagy	HUN
1956	Elisabeth Schwarz/Kurt Oppelt	AUT
	Frances Dafoe/Norris Bowden	CAN
	Marika Kilius/Franz Ningel	FRG
1957	Barbara Wagner/Robert Paul	CAN
	Marika Kilius/Franz Ningel	FRG
	Maria Jelinek/Otto Jelinek	CAN
1958	Barbara Wagner/Robert Paul	CAN
	Vera Suchankova/Zdenek Dolezal	CZE
	Maria Jelinek/Otto Jelinek	CAN
1959	Barbara Wagner/Robert Paul	CAN
	Marika Kilius/Hans Baumler	FRG
	Nancy Ludington/Ronald Ludington	USA
1960	Barbara Wagner/Robert Paul	CAN
	Maria Jelinek/Otto Jelinek	CAN
	Marika Kilius/Hans Baumler	FRG
1961	not held	
1962	Maria Jelinek/Otto Jelinek	CAN
	Ludmila Belousova/Oleg Protopopov	URS
	Margret Gobl/Franz Ningel	FRG
1963	Marika Kilius/Hans Baumler	FRG
	Ludmila Belousova/Oleg Protopopov	URS
	Tatiana Zhuk/Alexandr Gavrilov	URS
1964	Marika Kilius/Hans Baumler	FRG
	Ludmila Belousova/Oleg Protopopov	URS
	Debbi Wilkes/Guy Revell	CAN
1965	Ludmila Belousova/Oleg Protopopov	URS
	Vivian Joseph/Ronald Joseph	USA
	Tatiana Zhuk/Alexandr Gorelik	URS
1966	Ludmila Belousova/Oleg Protopopov	URS
	Tatiana Zhuk/Alexandr Gorelik	URS
	Cynthia Kauffman/Ronald Kauffman	USA
1967	Ludmila Belousova/Oleg Protopopov	URS
	Margot Glockschuber/Wolfgang Danne	FRG
	Cynthia Kauffman/Ronald Kauffman	USA
1968	Ludmila Belousova/Oleg Protopopov	URS
	Tatiana Zhuk/Alexandr Gorelik	URS
	Cynthia Kauffman/Ronald Kauffman	USA
1969	Irina Rodnina/Alexsei Ulanov	URS
	Tamara Moskvina/Alexsei Mishin	URS
	Ludmila Belousova/Oleg Protopopov	URS
1970	Irina Rodnina/Alexsei Ulanov	URS
	Ludmila Smirnova/Andrei Surakin	URS
	Heidemarie Steiner/Heinz Walther	GDR
1971	Irina Rodnina/Alexsei Ulanov	URS
	Ludmila Smirnova/Andrei Surakin	URS
	JoJo Starbuck/Kenneth Shelley	USA
1972	Irina Rodnina/Alexsei Ulanov	URS
	Ludmila Smirnova/Andrei Surakin	URS
	JoJo Starbuck/Kenneth Shelley	USA
1973	Irina Rodnina/ Alexandr Zaitsev	URS
	Ludmila Smirnova/Andrei Surakin	URS
	Manuela Gross/Uwe Kagelmann	GDR
1974	Irina Rodnina/ Alexandr Zaitsev	URS
	Ludmila Smirnova/Andrei Surakin	URS
	Romy Kermer/Rolf Osterreich	GDR
1975	Irina Rodnina/Alexandr Zaitsev	URS
	Romy Kermer/Rolf Osterreich	GDR
	Manuela Gross/Uwe Kagelmann	GDR
1976	Irina Rodnina/Alexandr Zaitsev	URS
	Romy Kermer/Rolf Osterreich	GDR
	Irina Vorobieva/Alexandr Vlasov	URS
1977	Irina Rodnina/Alexandr Zaitsev	URS
	Irina Vorobieva/Alexandr Vlasov	URS
	Tai Babilonia/Randy Gardner	USA
1978	Irina Rodnina/Alexandr Zaitsev	URS
	Manuela Mager/Uwe Bewersdorff	GDR
	Tai Babilonia/Randy Gardner	USA
1979	Tai Babilonia/Randy Gardner	USA
	Marina Cherkosova/Sergei Shakhrai	URS
	Sabine Baess/Tassilo Theirbach	GDR
1980	Marina Cherkosova/Sergei Shakhrai	URS
	Manuela Mager/Uwe Bewersdorff	GDR
	Marina Pestova/Stanislav Leonovich	URS
1981	Irina Vorobieva/Igor Lisovsky	URS
	Sabine Baess/Tassilo Theirbach	GDR
	Christina Riegel/Andreas Nischwitz	FRG
1982	Sabine Baess/Tassilo Theirbach	GDR
	Marina Pestova/Stanislav Leonovich	URS
	Caitlin Carruthers/Peter Carruthers	USA

Figure Skating (continued)

World Championship Pairs

Year	Medalists	Country
1983	Elena Valova/Oleg Vasiliev	URS
	Sabine Baess/Tassilo Theirbach	GDR
	Barbara Underhill/Paul Martini	CAN
1984	Barbara Underhill/Paul Martini	CAN
	Elena Valova/Oleg Vasiliev	URS
	Sabine Baess/Tassilo Theirbach	GDR
1985	Elena Valova/Oleg Vasiliev	URS
	Larisa Selezneva/Oleg Makarov	URS
	Katherina Matousek/Lloyd Eisler	CAN
1986	Ekaterina Gordeeva/Sergei Grinkov	URS
	Elena Valova/Oleg Vasiliev	URS
	Cynthia Coull/Mark Rowsom	CAN
1987	Ekaterina Gordeeva/Sergei Grinkov	URS
	Elena Valova/Oleg Vasiliev	URS
	Jill Watson/Peter Oppegard	USA
1988	Elena Valova/Oleg Vasiliev	URS
	Ekaterina Gordeeva/Sergei Grinkov	URS
	Larisa Selezneva/Oleg Makarov	URS
1989	Ekaterina Gordeeva/Sergei Grinkov	URS
	Cindy Landry/Lyndon Johnston	CAN
	Elena Bechke/Denis Petrov	URS
1990	Ekaterina Gordeeva/Sergei Grinkov	URS
	Isabelle Brasseur/Lloyd Eisler	CAN
	Natalia Mishkutenok/Artur Dmitriev	URS
1991	Natalia Mishkutenok/Artur Dmitriev	URS
	Isabelle Brasseur/Lloyd Eisler	CAN
	Natasha Kuchiki/Todd Sand	USA
1992	Natalia Mishkutenok/Artur Dmitriev	URS
	Radka Kovarikova/Rene Novotny	CZE
	Isabelle Brasseur/Lloyd Eisler	CAN
1993	Isabelle Brasseur/Lloyd Eisler	CAN
	Mandy Woetzel/Ingo Steuer	GER
	Evgenia Shishkova/Vadim Naumov	RUS
1994	Evgenia Shishkova/Vadim Naumov	RUS
	Isabelle Brasseur/Lloyd Eisler	CAN
	Marina Eltsova/Andrey Bushkov	URS
1995	Radka Kovarikova/Rene Novotny	CZE
	Evgenia Shishkova/Vadim Naumov	RUS
	Jenni Meno/Todd Sand	USA
1996	Evgenia Shishkova/Vadim Naumov	RUS
	Mandy Woetzel/Ingo Steuer	GER
	Jenni Meno/Todd Sand	USA
1997	Mandy Woetzel/Ingo Steuer	GER
	Marina Yeltsova/Andrei Bushkov	RUS
	Oksana Kazakova/Artur Dmitriev	RUS

World Championship Ice Dancing

Year	Medalists	Country
1952	Jean Westwood/Lawrence Demmy	GBR
	Joan Dewhirst/John Slater	GBR
	Carol Peters/Daniel Ryan	USA
1953	Jean Westwood/Lawrence Demmy	GBR
	Joan Dewhirst/John Slater	GBR
	Carol Peters/Daniel Ryan	USA
1954	Jean Westwood/Lawrence Demmy	GBR
	Nesta Davies/Paul Thomas	GBR
	Carmel Bodel/Edward Bodel	USA
1955	Jean Westwood/Lawrence Demmy	GBR
	Pamela Weight/Paul Thomas	GBR
	Barbara Radford/Raymond Lockwood	GBR
1956	Pamela Weight/Paul Thomas	GBR
	June Markham/Courtney Jones	GBR
	Barbara Thompson/Gerard Rigby	GBR
1957	June Markham/Courtney Jones	GBR
	Geraldine Fenton/William McLachlan	CAN
	Sharon McKenzie/Bert Wright	USA
1958	June Markham/Courtney Jones	GBR
	Geraldine Fenton/William McLachlan	CAN
	Andree Anderson/Donald Jacoby	USA
1959	Doreen Denny/Courtney Jones	GBR
	Andree Anderson/Donald Jacoby	USA
	Geraldine Fenton/William McLachlan	CAN
1960	Doreen Denny/Courtney Jones	GBR
	Virginia Thompson/William McLachlan	CAN
	Christine Guhel/Jean Paul Guhel	FRA
1961	no Competition held	
1962	Eva Romanova/Pavel Roman	CZE
	Christine Guhel/Jean Paul Guhel	FRA
	Virginia Thompson/William McLachlan	CAN
1963	Eva Romanova/Pavel Roman	CZE
	Linda Shearman/Michael Phillips	GBR
	Paulette Doan/Kenneth Ormsby	CAN
1964	Eva Romanova/Pavel Roman	CZE
	Paulette Doan/Kenneth Ormsby	CAN
	Janet Sawbridge/David Hickinbottom	GBR
1965	Eva Romanova/Pavel Roman	CZE
	Janet Sawbridge/David Hickinbottom	GBR
	Lorna Dyer/John Carrell	USA
1966	Diane Towler/Bernard Ford	GBR
	Kristin Fortune/Dennis Sveum	USA
	Lorna Dyer/John Carrell	USA
1967	Diane Towler/Bernard Ford	GBR
	Lorna Dyer/John Carrell	USA
	Yvonne Suddick/Malcolm Cannon	GBR
1968	Diane Towler/Bernard Ford	GBR
	Yvonne Suddick/Malcolm Cannon	GBR
	Janet Sawbridge/Jon Lane	GBR

Figure Skating (continued)

World Championship Ice Dancing

Year	Medalists	Country
1969	Diane Towler/Bernard Ford	GBR
	Liudmila Pakhomova/Aleksandr Gorshov	URS
	Judy Schwomeyer/James Sladky	USA
1970	Liudmila Pakhomova/Aleksandr Gorshov	URS
	Judy Schwomeyer/James Sladky	USA
	Angelika Buck/Erich Buck	FRG
1971	Liudmila Pakhomova/Aleksandr Gorshov	URS
	Angelika Buck/Erich Buck	FRG
	Judy Schwomeyer/James Sladky	USA
1972	Liudmila Pakhomova/Aleksandr Gorshov	URS
	Angelika Buck/ Erich Buck	FRG
	Judy Schwomeyer/James Sladky	USA
1973	Liudmila Pakhomova/Aleksandr Gorshov	URS
	Angelika Buck/Erich Buck	FRG
	Hilary Green/Glyn Watts	GBR
1974	Liudmila Pakhomova/Aleksandr Gorshov	URS
	Hilary Green/Glyn Watts	GBR
	Natalia Linichuk/Gennadi Karponosov	URS
1975	Irina Moiseeva/Andrei Minenkov	URS
	Colleen O'Connor/Jim Millns	USA
	Hilary Green/Glyn Watts	GBR
1976	Liudmila Pakhomova/Aleksandr Gorshov	URS
	Irina Moiseeva/Andrei Minenkov	URS
	Colleen O'Connor/Jim Millns	USA
1977	Irina Moiseeva/Andrei Minenkov	URS
	Janet Thompson/Warren Maxwell	GBR
	Natalia Linichuk/Gennadi Karponosov	URS
1978	Natalia Linichuk/Gennadi Karponosov	URS
	Irina Moiseeva/Andrei Minenkov	URS
	Krisztina Regoeczy/Andras Sallay	HUN
1979	Natalia Linichuk/Gennadi Karponosov	URS
	Krisztina Regoeczy/Andras Sallay	HUN
	Irina Moiseeva/Andrei Minenkov	URS
1980	Krisztina Regoeczy/Andras Sallay	HUN
	Natalia Linichuk/Gennadi Karponosov	URS
	Irina Moiseeva/Andrei Minenkov	URS
1981	Jayne Torvill/Christopher Dean	GBR
	Irina Moiseeva/Andrei Minenkov	URS
	Natalia Bestemianova/Andrei Bukin	URS
1982	Jayne Torvill/Christopher Dean	GBR
	Natalia Bestemianova/Andrei Bukin	URS
	Irina Moiseeva/Andrei Minenkov	URS
1983	Jayne Torvill/Christopher Dean	GBR
	Natalia Bestemianova/Andrei Bukin	URS
	Judy Blumberg/Michael Seibert	USA
1984	Jayne Torvill/Christopher Dean	GBR
	Natalia Bestemianova/Andrei Bukin	URS
	Judy Blumberg/Michael Seibert	USA
1985	Natalia Bestemianova/Andrei Bukin	URS
	Marina Klimova/Sergei Ponomarenko	URS
	Judy Blumberg/Michael Seibert	USA
1986	Natalia Bestemianova/Andrei Bukin	URS
	Marina Klimova/Sergei Ponomarenko	URS
	Tracy Wilson/Robert McCall	CAN
1987	Natalia Bestemianova/Andrei Bukin	URS
	Marina Klimova/Sergei Ponomarenko	URS
	Tracy Wilson/Robert McCall	CAN
1988	Natalia Bestemianova/Andrei Bukin	URS
	Marina Klimova/Sergei Ponomarenko	URS
	Tracy Wilson/Robert McCall	CAN
1989	Marina Klimova/Sergei Ponomarenko	URS
	Maia Usova/Alexander Zhulin	URS
	Isabelle Duchesnay/Paul Duchesnay	FRA
1990	Marina Klimova/Sergei Ponomarenko	URS
	Isabelle Duchesnay/Paul Duchesnay	FRA
	Maia Usova/Alexander Zhulin	URS
1991	Isabelle Duchesnay/Paul Duchesnay	FRA
	Marina Klimova/Sergei Ponomarenko	URS
	Maia Usova/Alexander Zhulin	URS
1992	Marina Klimova/Sergei Ponomarenko	CIS
	Maia Usova/Alexander Zhulin	CIS
	Oksana Grishuk/Evgeny Platov	CIS
1993	Maia Usova/Alexander Zhulin	RUS
	Oksana Grishuk/Evgeny Platov	RUS
	Anjelica Krylova/Vladimir Fedorov	RUS
1994	Oksana Grishuk/Evgeny Platov	RUS
	Sophie Moniotte/Pascal Lavanchy	FRA
	Susanna Rahkamo/Petri Kokko	FIN
1995	Oksana Grishuk/Evgeny Platov	RUS
	Susanna Rahkamo/Petri Kokko	FIN
	Sophie Moniotte/Pascal Lavanchy	FRA
1996	Oksana Grishuk/Evgeny Platov	RUS
	Anjelica Krylova/Oleg Ovsiannikov	RUS
	Shae-Lynn Bourne/Victor Kraatz	CAN
1997	Oksana Grishuk/Evgeny Platov	RUS
	Anjelica Krylova/Oleg Ovsiannikov	RUS
	Shae-Lynn Bourne/Victor Kraatz	GER

Photo credit: Ken Regan/camera 5

SPEED SKATING

◆ *Although figure skating has overshadowed speed skating in the United States, this may be changing. An increase in the number of training facilities and homegrown superstar Bonnie Blair have focused new attention on the sport.*

HISTORY

Speed skating grew out of necessity, as prehistoric hunters strapped carved animal bones to their feet and raced to keep up with their quarry. Primitive skates have been found throughout Scandinavia and northern Europe and, from the fourteenth through the nineteenth centuries, when the climate was unusually cold, were an important means of transportation. The first contact many of us had with speed skating was through the children's classic *Hans Brinker and the Silver Skates.* The story was set in the Netherlands—an appropriate locale, for if Scandinavia gave us the skate, Holland gave us speed skating as we know it today. Throughout the Middle Ages and Renaissance, both men and women skated the frozen canals to bring all manner of goods to the Amsterdam market. Women also skated for pleasure. An early seventeenth-century painting by Avercamp shows women skating recreationally. A print from the same era shows female skaters in masks to protect their faces—not just a measure of the severe cold of middle Europe at the time but an indication that women spent enough time on the ice or skated with enough speed to make wind and weather a concern. The first races were organized in the eighteenth century, and the first recorded race for women was held at Leeuwarden in 1805. Among other things, the Dutch gave us the double-track system in use today. Although World Championships began in 1889, there were none for women until 1936. Olympic speed skating, a men's event since 1924, added events for women in 1960.

THE MODERN ERA

At the first women's World Championships, held in 1936, the all-round title went to American Kit Klein. It would be four decades before another North American woman won the title. During those years, world speed skating was essentially a European franchise, with the women of Finland, Norway, the Netherlands, and especially the Soviet Union holding sway. Competition began to open up in the 1970s, when East Germany became a force in skating. Dresden, known for its delicate porcelain, produced three of the best-known champions of the era—**Karin Enke, Andrea Mitscherlich Schöne,** and **Christa Rothenburger.** The 1970s also saw a new interest in speed skating in North America. In a rare three-way tie for second place in the 500-meter sprint, three American women—**Dianne Holum,** Jennifer Fish, and Mary Meyers—all received silver medals at the 1968 Olympic Games. In 1972 Holum and teammate **Anne Henning** came back from Sapporo with golds. In 1976 Canadian Sylvia Burka won the all-round World Championship, and three years later American **Beth Heiden** followed in her tracks.

While Heiden and her brother, Eric, helped draw attention to the sport in the United States, speed skating still lacked two things needed to truly popularize the sport: training facilities and that all-American commodity, a superstar. As David Wallechinsky has pointed out in his books on the Olympics, in 1980 there were over 1,200 Olympic-size speed skating rinks in the USSR,

SPEED-SKATE BASICS: LONG TRACK VS. SHORT

One reason North American women have been slow to medal in Olympic Games and World Championships has to do with different skating traditions. Until recently, all major international races were contested on a long track—a 400-meter oval on which competitors, teamed in pairs, skate against the clock rather than against each other. Most North American women begin as short-track skaters, switching to European-style skating in order to compete internationally. Since the two traditions involve different rules, strategies, and equipment, switching from one to another can take years of effort. A short track is almost one-fourth the size of a long track, with a circuit of just 111 meters. Unlike the long oval, which has long straightaways, the tight loop of the short track generates more centrifugal force as the skater takes sharper and more frequent curves. To facilitate the turns, skate blades are shorter than long-track blades and are set off center to create greater lean. Instead of competing against the clock, short-track skaters compete in a pack, with the pack being consistently thinned through quarterfinals, semifinals, and finals. Though the races are sprint distances of 500 and 1,000 meters, the short-track skater must have terrific stamina to make it through her elimination heats to the final. Because she competes with her rivals, she must also have a flair for strategy. In this sense, short-track skating resembles track events, with some contestants going out fast in an attempt to intimidate and burn out their opponents while others save the juice for the final laps. In the close jockeying for position and the tumultuous speed at which corners are taken, spills are a commonplace occurrence, and short-track skaters wear protective knee- and shinguards as well as helmets. As might be imagined, the combination of speed, flashing blades, a full pack, and a small space make short-track skating a terrific sport to watch.

Major Events and Competitions

World Championships
Olympic Games

Long-track events offered for women include races of 500, 1,000, 1,500, 3,000, and 5,000 meters. Short-track skating, which made its international debut at the 1992 Olympics, offers individual events of 500 and 1,000 meters and a 3,000-meter team relay.

at the 1988 Olympics, her repeats in '92 and '94, and her engaging personality made her one of America's most popular athletes. Just as Carol Heiss and Peggy Fleming had inspired earlier generations of girls to try on figure skates, Blair has undoubtedly inspired girls to try on long blades for the first time. Although the United States still has far to go to equal the number of facilities found in Europe, America more than doubled its number of Olympic-size facilities during the first half of the 1990s.

Governing Bodies and Organizations

U.S. International Speedskating Association (USISA)
Box 16157
Rocky River, Ohio 44116
Phone: 216/899-0128

while the United States had only two. But it also had something else—a superstar in the making. No one had heard of **Bonnie Blair** in 1980 when, like other American hopefuls, she headed for Europe to train. But Blair's gold-medal debut

* * * BIOGRAPHIES * * *

JEANNE ASHWORTH b. July 1, 1938, Burlington, Vermont
A nine-time national indoor and outdoor champion in the late 1950s, Ashworth was one of America's first world-class skaters, and in 1960 she became the first American woman to earn an Olympic medal in the sport. She participated in the '64 Olympics as well, finishing fourth in the 500-meter event.
Selected championships and honors: Bronze medal, 500m, Olympic Games, 1960.

BONNIE BLAIR b. March 18, 1964, Cornwall, New York
With six Olympic medals for speed skating, Blair is the winningest American athlete in winter games history. Blair began short-track skating—a sport not then recognized as an Olympic event—as a teenager in Champaign, Illinois. She switched to classic Olympic-style speed skating in 1980 but badly needed European experience to hone her skills. When Blair was unable to raise money for a trip overseas, her hometown police department held a series of fund-raisers and bake sales. Blair returned from her European tour to take several United States, North American, and world titles. She won her first gold medal at the

1988 Olympics, skating the 500 meters with a world record time of 39.10. She repeated the victory in the 1992 and '94 Olympics, years in which she also won the gold medal at 1,000 meters. Her wins made her the first skater, male or female, ever to win consecutive golds in the 500 meters. She won the same distances later that year at the World Sprint Championships, and set another world record at one of her final competitions, skating 500 meters in 38.99 at the 1994 World Championships in Calgary. The record books will remember Blair as someone who won more Olympic gold medals than any other U.S. woman. Those who watched her will remember her as an unusually engaging champion whose abilities and enthusiasm helped put American speed skating on the map.
Selected championships and honors: Three gold medals, 500m, Olympic Games, 1988, '92, and '94; gold medal, sprint, World Championships, 1989; two gold medals, 1,000m, Olympic Games, 1992 and '94; two gold medals, 1,000m, World Championships, 1992 and '94; gold medal, 500m, World Championships, 1994; Sullivan Award, 1992; Associated Press Female Athlete of the Year, 1994; United Press International Female Athlete of the Year, 1994; Sports Illustrated Sportsman of the Year, 1994.

JACQUELINE BÖRNER b. East Germany
Just weeks after winning the all-round World Championship title, Börner became the victim of a devastating hit-and-run incident. Börner and her teammates were cycling in a suburb of East Berlin when a car clipped two of the male cyclists. Insults were exchanged, and the car wheeled around and deliberately ran Börner down. The damage: head injuries, a broken foot, and torn knee ligaments. The driver escaped and was never brought to justice. Börner spent the next eight months in hospitals and rehab centers. Finally able to skate again, she returned to competition at the end of 1991. Her first outing, at the World Cup, brought a third-place finish, but Börner wouldn't give up her Olympic dream. Barely two months after her return to the ice, Börner won her Olympic gold.
Selected championships and honors: Gold medal, all-round, World Championship, 1990; gold medal, 1,500m, Olympic Games, 1992.

CONNIE CARPENTER PHINNEY. *See entry under Cycling.*

KARIN ENKE BUSCH KANIA b. June 20, 1961, Dresden, East Germany
Enke literally outgrew her chosen sport of figure skating to become one of the best speed skaters ever to take the ice. During her teenage years, when she shot up to a healthy 5'9" and 158 pounds, she crossed over to the speed-skating track and discovered a natural affinity for the sport. Enke took her last bow as a figure skater in 1977 and entered the speed-skating winner's circle just three years later, when she won her first World Sprint Championship. A week later, at the Lake Placid Olympics, she skated a world record time in the 500 meters to win a gold medal. She set another world record—in the 1,500 meters—at the next Olympics and came home from Sarajevo with two golds and two silvers. Because Enke has skated under a variety of names—including Karin Enke, Karin Busch, Karin Enke-Busch, Karin Kania-Enke, and Karin Kania—her dominance is not always obvious from a casual glance at the charts. Her total of eight Olympic and thirteen world championship medals are indeed enough for several women—but Enke won them all.
Selected championships and honors: Gold medal, 500m, Olympic Games, 1980; four gold medals, sprint, World Championship, 1980, '81, '83, and '84; silver medal, sprint, World Championship, 1982; two silver medals, all-round, World Championships, 1981

and '83; five gold medals, all-round, World Championships, 1982, '84, and '86–88; gold medal, 1,000m, Olympic Games, 1984; gold medal, 1,500m, Olympic Games, 1984; silver medal, 500m, Olympic Games, 1984; silver medal, 3,000m, Olympic Games, 1984; silver medal, 1,000m, Olympic Games, 1988; silver medal, 1,500m, Olympic Games, 1988; bronze medal, 500m, Olympic Games, 1988.

ELIZABETH (BETH) HEIDEN b. September 27, 1959, Madison, Wisconsin
Sometimes overshadowed by her brother Eric, Heiden is a phenomenal athlete in her own right and winner of events in three separate sports—speed skating, cycling, and cross-country skiing. Her first record came in yet another sport, running, when as a teenager she set a national age group record for the mile. In 1979 she won the world all-round speed-skating championship, winning individual championships at all four distances. The only other American woman to hold a world all-round title was Kit Klein, who won in 1936. She was favored to win multiple golds at the 1980 Olympics, but an ankle injury forced her to settle for a single bronze. Ironically, Heiden had a better season cycling than skating in 1980, winning the U.S. and national road race championships as well as the Coors International Classic. The following year, while attending the University of Vermont, she took up cross-country skiing. In 1983, when the NCAA initiated cross-country competition for women, Heiden took the championship.
Selected championships and honors, skating: Gold medal, 500m, World Championship, 1979; gold medal, 1,000m, World Championship, 1979; gold medal, 1,500m, World Championship, 1979; gold medal, 3,000m, World Championship, 1979; gold medal, World All-Around Championship, 1979; bronze medal, 3,000m, Olympic Games, 1980. *Cycling:* U.S. Road Race Championship, 1980; National Road Race Championship, 1980; Coors International Classic, 1980.

ANNE HENNING b. September 6, 1955, Raleigh, North Carolina
A spectacular sprinter, Henning won the 500 meters in both the World Championships and World Sprint Championships in 1971. The next year, favored to win Olympic gold, she was paired in the 500-meter finals with Canada's Sylvia Burka. At the crossover point Henning slowed to avoid a collision with Burka and lost valuable time. Nevertheless she won in 43.70, an

Olympic record. Burka was disqualified and Henning was allowed to reskate the distance alone, this time finishing in 43.33. Unfortunately, the second run may have been too taxing. Also favored for a gold in the 1,000 meters, Henning could do no better than third place, and later commented that her legs had felt dead throughout the event.

Selected championships and honors: Gold medal, 500m, World Championships, 1971; gold medal, 500m, World Sprint Championships, 1971; gold medal, 500m, Olympic Games, 1972; bronze medal, 1,000m, Olympic Games, 1972.

DIANNE HOLUM b. May 19, 1951, Chicago, Illinois

In 1966, at age fourteen, Holum became the youngest skater ever to compete in the World Championships. She went on to win four medals in two Olympic games and win several World Championships. Her most exciting race may have been the 500 meters in the 1968 Olympics, when she and two other Americans finished in a three-way tie for the silver medal. A key figure in the revitalization of women's speed skating in America, Holum retired from competition in 1973 and became a coach. One of her pupils, **Beth Heiden,** also became a world champion.

Selected championships and honors: Silver medal (tie, with Jennifer Fish and Ann Meyers), 500m, Olympic Games, 1968; bronze medal, 1,000m, Olympic Games, 1968; gold medal, 1,000m, World Championships, 1971; gold medal, 500m, World Championships, 1972; gold medal, 1,000m, World Championships, 1972; gold medal, 1,500m, Olympic Games, 1972; silver medal, 3000m, Olympic Games, 1972.

GUNDA KLEEMAN NIEMANN b. ca. 1970, Germany

Kleeman exploded on the world speed-skating scene like a rocket, winning the World Championship all-round in 1991 and taking golds in both the 3,000 and 5,000 meters at the Olympics the next year. Kleeman's powerful stride and phenomenal endurance make her one of the all-time best, though many Americans—caught up in Bonnie Blair fever—failed to appreciate her Olympic performances. Through 1995 Kleeman had won four all-round World Championships, making her second only to **Karin Enke.**

Selected championships and honors: Four gold medals, all-round, World Championships, 1991, '92, '93, and '95; two gold medals, 3,000m, Olympic Games, 1992 and '94; two gold medals, 5,000m,

Olympic Games, 1992 and '94; silver medal, 1,500m, Olympic Games, 1992.

ANDREA MITSCHERLICH SCHÖNE b. 1960, Dresden, East Germany

After a promising start as a teenager, winning an Olympic silver when she was just sixteen, Mitscherlich suffered a series of disappointments. At her next Olympics, in 1980, she finished out of the medals in the 1,500- and 3,000-meter events. So Mitscherlich finished training as a nurse, married, and had a child—but instead of settling down, she made a roaring comeback in her sport, winning the first of two World Championships in 1983. The next year she set world records at 1,500 and 3,000 meters and won three medals at the 1984 Sarajevo Olympics.

Selected championships and honors: Silver medal, 3,000m, Olympic Games, 1976; gold medal, 3,000m, Olympic Games, 1984; silver medal, 1,000m, Olympic Games, 1984; silver medal, 1,500m, Olympic Games, 1984; two gold medals, all-round, World Championships, 1983 and '85.

GUNDA NIEMANN. *See Gunda Kleeman Niemann, above.*

JEANNE OMELENCHUK b. March 25, 1931, United States

In an era when women's speed skating didn't get much attention in the United States, Omelenchuk was one of the best. Between 1957 and 1965, she won a total of ten U.S. and North American championships, and she ranks as one of the first American women to excel at the sport.

Selected championships and honors: Five North American outdoor championships, 1957–59, '62, and '63; four U.S. National outdoor championships: 1958, '59, '62, and '65; U.S. Open outdoor championship, 1965.

LEAH POULOS MUELLER b. October 5, 1951, Berwyn, Illinois

In a sport where a millimeter's lean one way or the other can mark the difference between victory and defeat, the words "self-taught" seldom apply. They do to Poulos, though, who learned "technique" by falling, getting up, and fine-tuning her natural talent. Before marrying fellow U.S. speed skater Peter Mueller in 1977, Poulos won a World Sprint Championship and an Olympic silver medal. Then she left competition in order to support her husband while he trained. Poulos began training again in 1978, won another World Championship in 1979, and took two silver medals at the Lake Placid Olympics the following year.

Selected championships and honors: Two gold medals, World Championships, 1974 and '79; two silver medals, 1,000m, Olympic Games, 1976 and '80; silver medal, 500m, Olympic Games, 1980.

CHRISTA ROTHENBURGER LUDING

b. ca. 1960, Dresden, East Germany

When Rothenburger's coach, Ernst Luding, suggested she take up cycling in the off-season, Rothenburger was reluctant. The speed and tactics of sprint cycling intimidated her. But she learned quickly and, more importantly, discovered that cycling improved her skating performance. She won a gold at the 1984 winter Olympics and wanted to try her hand in cycling competitions as well. Initially denied permission by East German sports officials to participate in both events, she eventually got her way. In 1988 Rothenburger won three Olympic medals—a gold and silver in speed skating and a silver in cycling, becoming the first person to win medals in both the winter and summer Olympics in the same year. Since the games are now staggered, no one will repeat her feat. After the 1988 winter games, Rothenburger married the coach who had encouraged her to take up cycling in 1980.

Selected championships and honors, skating: Gold medal, 500m, Olympic Games, 1984; gold medal, 1,000m, Olympic Games, 1988; silver medal, 500m, Olympic Games, 1988. *Cycling:* Gold medal, World Championships, 1986; silver medal, World Championships, 1987; silver medal, 1,000m match sprint, Olympic Games, 1988; bronze medal, 500m, Olympic Games, 1992.

ANDREA SCHÖNE. *See Andrea Mitscherlich Schöne, above.*

LYDIA SKOBLIKOVA b. March 8, 1939, Zlatoust, Chelyabinsk, USSR

For most Americans, *the* woman to watch at the 1960 winter Olympics was figure skater **Carol Heiss.** Speed skating was a barely a blip on the radar, and most Americans missed seeing Lydia Skoblikova, a psychology student from the USSR, take the first two of her eventual six gold medals. Four years later, at the Innsbruck games, Skoblikova became the first (and to date the only) woman to win all four distances at an Olympics. Skoblikova, who became a teacher after finishing her degree, also won two World Cham-

pionships and set several world and Olympic records. One of the sport's all-time best, Skoblikova competed for the last time at the 1968 Olympics, in which she skated to an eleventh-place finish in the 1,500 meters.

Selected championships and honors: Two gold medals, 1,500m, Olympic Games, 1960; two gold medals, 3,000m, Olympic Games, 1960; gold medal, 500m, Olympic Games, 1964; gold medal, 1,000m, Olympic Games, 1964; two gold medals, all-around, World Championships, 1963 and '64.

CATHY TURNER b. 1963, Michigan

Tough competitor or skating bad girl? Survivor or head case? During her fractured career as a short-course skater, Turner garnered both compliments and complaints. A child prodigy who felt pushed by her coach/father, Turner won the national short-track championship at sixteen and stopped skating the next year. She didn't skate for another eight years, returning to training while studying computer science at the University of Michigan. When short-track events were added to the Olympics in 1992, Turner won a gold in the 500 meters and defended her victory two years later, when the winter games shifted to its new schedule. Although two other skaters complained about Turner's tactics on the track, judges saw no disqualifying moves in her performance, and Turner herself dismissed the complaints as sour grapes. Turner retired from competition after the 1994 games.

Selected championships and honors, individual: Two gold medals, 500m short-track, Olympic Games, 1992 and '94. *Team:* Silver medal, 3,000m short-track relay, Olympic Games, 1992; bronze medal, 3,000m short-track relay, Olympic Games, 1994.

SHEILA YOUNG OCHOWICZ b. October 14, 1950, Detroit, Michigan

Young's father, a Michigan state cycling champion, taught his daughter both cycling and skating as a child. Young eventually had careers in both, and in 1973 she became the first person ever to hold simultaneous World Championships in two different sports. If cycling had been an Olympic sport in the 1970s, Young might have won double medals as well. It wasn't, and Young had to win all her medals as a skater. After missing a bronze by .08 of a second at the 1972 games, Young came back in '76 to become the first American to win three medals at a winter Olympics, taking home a gold, a silver, and a bronze. That same year she married fellow cyclist Jim Ochowicz, and soon retired to have her first child.

Young had two more winning seasons as a cyclist, in 1981 and '82. Since retiring from competition, Young has served on boards for both the U.S. Cycling Federation and the U.S. Olympic Committee.

Selected championships and honors, skating: Three gold medals, sprint, World Championships, 1973 and '76; gold medal, 500m, Olympic Games, 1976; silver medal, 1,500m, Olympic Games, 1976; bronze medal, 1,000m, Olympic Games, 1976. *Cycling:* Three gold medals, World Sprint Championships, 1973, '76, and '81; silver medal, World Sprint Championships, 1982.

Speed Skating

Olympic 500 Meters

Year	Medalists	Country	Time
1960	Helga Haase	GDR	45.9
	Natalya Donchenko	USSR	46.0
	Jeanne Ashworth	USA	46.1
1964	Lydia Skoblikova	USSR	45.0 OR
	Irina Yegorova	USSR	45.4
	Tatyana Sidorova	USSR	45.5
1968	Lyudmila Titova	USSR	46.1
	Jennifer Fish,	USA	46.3
	Dianne Holum,	USA	46.3
	Mary Meyers	USA	46.3
	Elisabeth van den Brom	HOL	46.6
1972	Anne Henning	USA	43.33 OR
	Vera Krasnova	USSR	44.01
	Lyudmila Titova	USSR	44.45
1976	Sheila Young	USA	42.76 OR
	Cathy Priestner	CAN	43.12
	Tatyana Averina	USSR	43.17
1980	Karin Enke	GDR	41.78 OR
	Leah Mueller (Poulos)	USA	42.26
	Natalya Petruseva	USSR	42.42
1984	Christa Rothenburger	GDR	41.02 OR
	Karin Enke	GDR	41.28
	Natalya Chive	USSR	41.50
1988	Bonnie Blair	USA	39.10 WR
	Christa Rothenburger	GDR	39.12
	Karin Kania (Enke)	GDR	39.24
1992	Bonnie Blair	USA	40.33
	Ye Qiaobo	CHN	40.51
	Christa Ludwig (Rothenburger)	GER	40.57
1994	Bonnie Blair	USA	39.25
	Susan Auch	CAN	39.61
	Franziska Schenk	GER	39.70

Olympic 1,000 Meters

Year	Medalists	Country	Time
1924–1956	event not held		
1960	Klara Guseva	USSR	1:34.1
	Helga Haase	GDR	1:34.3
	Tamara Rylova	USSR	1:34.8
1964	Lydia Skoblikova	USSR	1:33.2 OR
	Irina Yegorova	USSR	1:34.3
	Kaija Mustonen	FIN	1:35.7
1968	Carolina Geijssen	HOL	1:32.6 OR
	Lyudmila Titova	USSR	1:32.9
	Dianne Holum	USA	1:33.4
1972	Monika Pflug	GER	1:31.40 OR
	Atje Keulen-Deelstra	HOL	1:31.61
	Anne Henning	USA	1:31.62
1976	Tatyana Averina	USSR	1:28.43 OR
	Leah Poulos	USA	1:28.57
	Sheila Young	USA	1:29.14
1980	Natalya Petruseva	USSR	1:24.10 OR
	Leah Mueller (Poulos)	USA	1:25.41
	Silvia Albrecht	GDR	1:26.46
1984	Karin Enke	GDR	1:21.61 OR
	Andrea Schöne (Mitscherlich)	GDR	1:22.83
	Natalya Petruseva	USSR	1:23.21
1988	Christa Rothenburger	GDR	1:17.65 WR
	Karin Kania (Enke)	GDR	1:17.70
	Bonnie Blair	USA	1:18.31
1992	Bonnie Blair	USA	1:21.90
	Ye Qiaobo	CHN	1:21.92
	Monique Garbrecht	GER	1:22.10
1994	Bonnie Blair	USA	1:18.74
	Anke Baier	GER	1:20.12
	Ye Qiaobo	CHN	1:20.22

Olympic 1,500 Meters

Year	Medalists	Country	Time
1924–1956	event not held		
1960	Lydia Skoblikova	USSR	2:25.2 WR
	Elwira Seroczynska	POL	2:25.7
	Helena Pilejczyk	POL	2:27.1
1964	Lydia Skoblikova	USSR	2:22.6 OR
	Kaija Mustonen	FIN	2:25.5
	Berta Kolokoltseva	USSR	2:27.1

Speed Skating (continued)

Olympic 1,500 Meters

Year	Medalists	Country	Time
1968	Kaija Mustonen	FIN	2:22.4 OR
	Carolina Geijssen	HOL	2:22.7
	Christina Kaiser	HOL	2:24.5
1972	Dianne Holum	USA	2:20.4 OR
	Christina Baas-Kaiser	HOL	2:21.05
	Atje Keulen-Deelstra	HOL	2:22.05
1976	Galina Stepanskaya	USSR	2:16.58 OR
	Sheila Young	USA	2:17.06
	Tatyana Averina	USSR	2:17.96
1980	Anne Borckink	HOL	2:10.95 OR
	Ria Visser	HOL	2:12.35
	Sabine Becker	GDR	2:12.38
1984	Karin Enke	GDR	2:03.42 WR
	Andrea Schöne (Mitscherlich)	GDR	2:05.29
	Natalya Petruseva	USSR	2:05.78
1988	Yvonne van Gennip	HOL	2:00.68 OR
	Karin Kania (Enke)	GDR	2:00.82
	Andrea Schöne (Mitscherlich)	GDR	2:01.49
1992	Jacqueline Börner	GER	2:05.87
	Gunda Niemann (Kleemann)	GER	2:05.92
	Seiko Hashimoto	JPN	2:06.88
1994	Emese Hunyady	AUT	2:02.19
	Svetlana Fedotkina	RUS	2:02.69
	Seiko Hashimoto	JPN	2:06.88

Olympic 3,000 Meters

Year	Medalists	Country	Time
1960	Lydia Skoblikova	USSR	5:14.3
	Valentina Stenina	USSR	5:16.9
	Eevi Huttunen	FIN	5:21.0
1964	Lydia Skoblikova	USSR	5:14.9
	Han Pil-hwa	PRK	5:18.5
	Valentina Stenina	USSR	5:18.5
	Klara Nesterova (Guseva)	USSR	5:22.5
1968	Johanna Schut	HOL	4:56.2 OR
	Kaija Mustonen	FIN	5:01.0
	Christina Kaiser	HOL	5:01.3
1972	Christina Baas-Kaiser	HOL	4:52.14 OR
	Dianne Holum	USA	4:58.67
	Atje Keulen-Deelstra	HOL	4:59.91
1976	Tatyana Averina	USSR	4:45.19 OR
	Andrea Mitscherlich	GDR	4:45.23
	Lisbeth Korsmo	NOR	4:45.24
1980	Bjorg Eva Jensen	NOR	4:32.13 OR
	Sabine Becker	GDR	4:32.79
	Beth Heiden	USA	4:33.77
1984	Andrea Schöne (Mitscherlich)	GDR	4:24.79 OR
	Karin Enke	GDR	4:26.33
	Gabi Schonbrunn	GDR	4:33.13
1988	Yvonne van Gennip	HOL	4:11.94 WR
	Andrea Schöne (Mitscherlich)	GDR	4:12.09
	Gabi Zange (Schonbrunn)	GDR	4:16.92
1992	Gunda Niemann (Kleemann)	GER	4:19.90
	Heike Warnicke	GER	4:22.88
	Emese Hunyady	AUT	4:24.64
1994	Svetlana Bazhanova	RUS	4:17.43
	Emese Hunyady	AUT	4:18.14
	Claudia Pechstein	GER	4:18.34

Olympic 5,000 Meters

Year	Medalists	Country	Time
1924–1984	event not held		
1988	Yvonne van Gennip	HOL	7:14.13 WR
	Andrea Schöne (Mitscherlich)	GDR	7:17.12
	Gabi Zange (Schonbrunn)	GDR	7:21.61
1992	Gunda Niemann (Kleemann)	GER	7:31.57
	Heike Warnicke	GER	7:37.59
	Claudia Pechstein	GER	7:39.80
1994	Claudia Pechstein	GER	7:14.37
	Gunda Niemann	GER	7:14.88
	Hironi Yamamoto	JPN	7:19.68

Speed Skating (continued)

500 Meters/Short Track

Year	Medalists	Country	Time
1924–1988	event not held		
1992	Cathy Turner	USA	47.04
	Li Yan	CHN	47.08
	Hwang Ok-sil	PRK	47.23
1994	Cathy Turner	USA	45.98 OR
	Yanmei Zhang	CHN	46.44
	Amy Peterson	USA	46.76

1,000 Meters/Short Track

Year	Medalists	Country	Time
1994	Chun Lee-Kyung	KOR	1:36.87
	Nathalie Lambert	CAN	1:36.97
	Kim So-Hee	KOR	1:37.09

3,000-Meter Relay/Short Track

Year	Medalists	Country	Time
1992	Angela Cutrone, Sylvie Daigle, Nathalie Lambert, Annie Perreault	CAN	4:36.62
	Darcie Dohnal, Amy Peterson, Cathy Turner, Nikki Ziegelmeyer	USA	4:37.85
	Yulia Allagulova, Natalya Ishahova, Viktoria Taranina, Yulia Vlasova	RUS	4:42.69
1994	Lee-Kyung Chun, So-Hee Kim, Yoon-Mi Kim, Hye-Kyung Won	KOR	4:26.64 OR
	Christine-Isabel Boudrias, Isabelle Charest, Sylvie Daigle, Nathalie Lambert	CAN	4:32.04
	Amy Peterson, Cathy Turner, Nikki Ziegelmeyer, Darcie Dohnal	USA	4:39.34

Speed Skating World Records

Short Track

Event	Time	Competitor	Country	Site	Date
500m	45.25	Isabelle Charest	CAN	The Hague	3/2/96
800m	1:25.29	Bonnie Blair	USA	Kobe	4/16/83
1,000m	1:34.07	Nathalie Lambert	CAN	Hamar	11/7/93
1,500m	2:25.17	Yoon-Mi Kim	KOR	Harbin	12/2/95
3,000m	5:02.18	Lee-Kyung Chun	KOR	Gjovik	3/19/95
3,000m Relay	4:21.50	Marinella Canclini, Katia Colturi, Mara Urbani, Barbara Baldissera	ITA	The Hague	3/3/96

Long Track

Event	Time	Competitor	Country	Site	Date
500m	38.69	Bonnie Blair	USA	Calgary	2/12/95
1,000m	1:17.65	Christa Rothenburger	GDR	Calgary	2/26/88
1,500m	1:59.30	Karin Kania	GDR	Medeo	3/22/86
3,000m	4:09.32	Gunda Niemann	GER	Calgary	3/25/94
5,000m	7:03.26	Gunda Niemann	GER	Calgary	3/26/94
500/1,000/500/1,000m	156.435 pts	Bonnie Blair	USA	Calgary	2/11–12/95
500/1,500/1,000/3,000m	163.901 pts	Annamarie Thomas	HOL	Calgary	3/22–23/96
500/3,000/1,500/5,000m	167.282 pts	Gunda Niemann	GER	Hamar	1/7–9/94

Speed Skating (continued)

Short Track World Championships

500 Meters

Year	Winners	Country
1993	Yanmei Zhang	China
	Isabelle Charest	Canada
	Angela Cutrone	Canada
1994	Marinella Canclini	Italy
	Nathalie Lambert	Canada
	Yang Yang	China
1995	Chunlu Wang	China
	Isabelle Charest	Canada
	Yoon-Mi Kim	S. Korea
1996	Isabelle Charest	Canada
	Annie Perrault	Canada
	Marinella Canclini	Italy
1997	Yang Yang	China
	Isabelle Charest	Canada
	Marinella Canclini	Italy

1,000 Meters

Year	Winners	Country
1993	Nathalie Lambert	Canada
	Lee-Kyung Chun	S. Korea
	Xiuian Wang	Canada
1994	Nathalie Lambert	Canada
	So-Hee Kim	S. Korea
	Ryang-Hee Kim	S. Korea
1995	Chunlu Wang	China
	Lee-Kyung Chun	S. Korea
	So-Hee Kim	S. Korea
1996	Marinella Canclini	Italy
	Lee-Kyung Chun	S. Korea
	Isabelle Charest	Canada
1997	Yang Yang	China
	Hye-Kyung Won	S. Korea
	Lee-Kyung Chun	S. Korea

1,500 Meters

Year	Winners	Country
1993	Nathalie Lambert	Canada
	Lee-Kyung Chun	S. Korea
	Xiuian Wang	Canada
1994	So-Hee Kim	S. Korea
	Nathalie Lambert	Canada
	Ryang-Hee Kim	S. Korea
1995	Lee-Kyung Chun	S. Korea
	So-Hee Kim	S. Korea
	Chunlu Wang	China
1996	Lee-Kyung Chun	S. Korea

	Hye-Kyung Won	S. Korea
	Dandan Sun	China
1997	Lee-Kyung Chun	S. Korea
	Hye-Kyung Won	S. Korea
	Yang Yang	China

3,000 Meters

Year	Winners	Country
1993	Nathalie Lambert	Canada
	Lee-Kyung Chun	S. Korea
	Xiuian Wang	Canada
1994	Nathalie Lambert	Canada
	Ryang-Hee Kim	S. Korea
	Yang Yang	China
1995	Lee-Kyung Chun	S. Korea
	Yoon-Mi Kim	S. Korea
	Radanova	S. Korea
1996	Hye-Kyung Won	S. Korea
	Lee-Kyung Chun	S. Korea
	Dandan Sun	China
1997	Lee-Kyung Chun	S. Korea
	Hye-Kyung Won	S. Korea
	Yang Yang	China

3,000 Meter Relay

Year	Winners	Country
1993	Christine Boudrais, Isabelle Charest, Angela Cutrone, Sylvie Daigle Nathalie Lambert	Canada
		China
		S. Korea
1994	Christine Boudrais, Isabelle Charest, Angela Cutrone, Sylvie Daigle Nathalie Lambert	Canada
		China
		S. Korea
1995		China
		Korea
		Canada
1996	Marinella Canclini, Katia Colturi, Mara Urbani, Barbara Baldissera, Marta Capurso	Italy
		China
		USA
1997		Canada
		Korea
		Japan

Photo credit: Ken Regan/camera 5

SKIING

♦ *Though long dominated by the northern Europeans, North Americans have begun to pose a serious challenge, especially in Alpine events.*

HISTORY

Skis, along with sleds, evolved in the cold climates of the last ice age. Not only skis and poles but primitive snow goggles dating back thousands of years have been found in Scandinavia and northern continental Europe. Early skis were strictly utilitarian, designed for cross-country transportation, and were used by men, women, and children. Essentially unchanged except for innovations such as breakaway mountings and the use of synthetic materials, the cross-country ski has been in continuous use for at least 10,000 years. Mastery of

Nordic ski technique has long been a part of military training throughout Scandinavia, and Nordic know-how was one reason Roald Amundsen's expedition made it to the South Pole and back while the Scott expedition perished.

Alpine skiing, performed on a steep slope, also began as a form of vital transportation. For people living in the mountainous regions of Europe, skis provided a way to visit neighbors at lower elevations. However, a swift descent also meant a tedious trek home. Because of this, Alpine skiing did not flourish as a sport until the industrial age provided transportation up the mountain as well as down.

Ski clubs flourished in Europe in the late nineteenth century and gave rise to the first organized competitions for both men and women. A 400-meter cross-country competition for women, held at Mürzzuschlag in 1893, was won by Mizzi Angerer. Angerer must have been one of the leading athletes of her day, for she also won an early form of slalom a dozen years later.

In America, skiing's popularity was initially inhibited by topography. Immigrants to the New World, settling in the eastern half of the country, found themselves presented with a vast forest that stretched all the way to the Mississippi River, and East Coast mountains, unlike the clean slopes of the Alps, were carpeted with hardwood and evergreen. Mountains tall enough to clear the tree line lay thousands of miles to the west, and a century of settlement in the future. Competitions for women were not organized until the 1920s, under the aegis of the Lake Placid Club, and included cross-country race, slalom, and downhill events.

THE MODERN ERA

Women have competed in World Championship events, sponsored by the International Ski Federation, since 1931. Although Nordic ski competition for men was introduced at the 1924 Olympics, cross-country events for women were not added until 1952.

Inquiring Minds Want to Know— Why Can't Women Jump?

Since skiing was first introduced as an Olympic sport for women in 1936, there was been an inexorable move toward event parity in all categories but one—jumping. Women's balance, agility, and ability to land on both feet is regularly showcased in gymnastics, diving, and a host of other sports. Moreover, newer forms of skiing, such as aerials and moguls, have automatically included events for women. Why have women never had an international jumping competition to call their own? We don't know the answer, but maybe it's time to look for one.

Major Events and Competitions

Alpine
Olympic, World Championship, and World Cup events for women include:

> Downhill
> Slalom
> Giant slalom
> Super G (super giant slalom)
> Combined

Nordic
Olympic and World Championship competitions include:

> 5k   Combined pursuit
> 15k   4 × 5k relay
> 30k

Freestyle
Olympic competition for women includes:

> Aerials
> Moguls

Alpine ski for both men and women was introduced at the 1936 winter games with the Alpine combined event, which features a downhill race for speed and a slalom race for technical skills. Alpine skiing received a major boost when it became a major professional sport in the late 1960s. Today's World Cup tour features over thirty women's events in venues stretching from North America to Europe and Scandinavia, and points accumulated determine overall seasonal winners as well as winners in each event category.

THE AGE OF INNOVATION: FREESTYLE SKIING

America, never a dominant force in Alpine or cross-country skiing, may have solved its problem by inventing a form all its own, freestyle. Freestyle skiing actually includes three different events— moguls, aerials, and ballet—all made in the U.S.A. Freestyle got its start sometime in the 1960s, and the first official competition took place in 1966 in Attitash, New Hampshire. The Federation Internationale du Ski recognized freestyle in 1979, and during the 1980s both World Championships and a World Cup circuit were inaugurated. Mogul skiing became an Olympic sport for both men and women in 1992, with aerials added in 1994. In the mogul event, skiers compete over a course filled with high-speed turns and giant snow bumps (moguls). Skiing off the moguls launches the skier into the air, and while airborne, contestants perform any of a variety of moves. The names of the moves—which include the daffy, the back scratcher, and the mule kick—suggest the freewheeling atmosphere of the event, which is performed to raucous rock music. The aerial competition combines ski jumping with acrobatics, with skiers performing moves like backward triple somersaults before they hit the snow. Despite the party-on atmosphere of freestyle skiing, its athletic requirements shouldn't be overlooked—it takes a lot of skill to land with your skis straight.

If born-in-the-USA freestyle was a plot to help America crack the European lock on ski events, it may have worked. In 1992 America's Donna Weinbrecht skied through a near blizzard to win the first Olympic medal in moguls. Two years later another American, Liz McIntyre, picked up a silver.

Governing Bodies and Organizations

U.S. Skiing
Box 100
Park City, Utah 84060
801/649-9090

* * * BIOGRAPHIES * * *

DEBBIE ARMSTRONG b. December 6, 1963, Salem, Oregon

Armstrong began skiing competitively in 1980 and was named to the U.S. downhill team in 1982. She broke her leg on a training run and made a satisfactory but unimpressive recovery, with no major wins to her credit when she was picked for the 1984 Olympic team. Nevertheless, Armstrong retained her pure enthusiasm for the sport. "I'm just going to have fun out there," she told teammate **Christin Cooper** at the top of her second run. She did—and won the first gold of the Sarajevo games. Armstrong also skied for the United States at the 1988 Olympics.

Selected championships and honors: Gold medal, giant slalom, Olympic Games, 1984; national championship, giant slalom, 1987.

CLAUDIA BOYARSKIKH b. ca. 1944, Siberia

Growing up in Siberia, Boyarskikh learned to cross-country ski almost as soon as she learned to walk. After getting a degree in teaching, she remained in Siberia and continued skiing competitively. At the 1964 Olympics, the first to include individual cross-country events for women, Boyarskikh swept all the medals on offer. In addition to her individual golds, she helped her team win its first gold in women's cross-country relay.

Selected championships and honors, individual: Gold medal, 5k, Olympic Games, 1964; gold medal, 10k, Olympic Games, 1964. *Team:* Gold medal, 3 × 5k, Olympic Games, 1964.

SUSAN (SUZY) CHAFFEE b. 1947, Rutland, Vermont

An accomplished Alpine skier who captained the 1968 U.S. Olympic team, Chaffee's real love was freestyle skiing. A tireless enthusiast and pioneer, Chaffee did much to lift it from "hot dog" status to a legitimate sport. When freestyling went professional in 1971, there was no women's division. Chaffee joined the men's tour and won three consecutive World Championships. The message was loud and clear, and a women's division was promptly added. Appointed to the U.S. Olympic Committee's board of directors in 1976, Chaffee began her battle all over again, and was again successful in having freestyle skiing added to the list of events in 1992.

Selected championships and honors: Three gold medals, freestyle, World Championships, 1971–73.

BARBARA ANN COCHRAN b. January 4, 1951, Claremont, New Jersey

Cochran was practically born with skis on her feet. Her father, an avid Alpine skier, taught his children to ski and was so successful that in 1973 all four of them were on the U.S. national team, which he coached. Three of the group competed for the U.S. in the '72 Olympics, but it was Barbara who won the gold. The slalom run at Sapporo, Japan, was so difficult that only nineteen of the forty-two entrants completed both runs. Cochran won the event by .02 seconds, attributing her win to a technique her father had taught her—putting her body in motion in the starting gate a split second before starting the timer. Cochran later became a journalist and wrote a book on her sport—*Skiing for Women.*

Selected championships and honors: National championship, giant slalom, 1969; national championship, slalom, 1971; gold medal, slalom, Olympic Games, 1972.

DEBORAH COMPAGNONI b. ca. 1970, Italy

Alberto Tomba may be the superstar of the Italian team, but Compagnoni can certainly lay claim to the title of super-grit. And in Italy, where toughness is at least as admired as style, Compagnoni is a national heroine. By 1990 Compagnoni had already overcome several severe knee injuries. Then, in October, she was seized by severe abdominal pains and rushed to the hospital. Doctors performed life-saving surgery and removed almost two feet of intestines. Since abdominal surgery severs stomach muscles, Compagnoni had to work hard to get back in shape for the upcoming Olympics, but triumphed with a gold-medal win in the super G. Then, just 24 hours later, she fell in the giant slalom and tore ligaments in her left knee. Compagnoni worked her way through another cycle of recovery and rehab, and came back to win the event two years later.

Selected championships and honors: Gold medal, super G, Olympic Games, 1992; gold medal, giant slalom, Olympic Games, 1994.

CHRISTIN COOPER b. California

A national champion and World Cup competitor, Cooper won three national downhill titles in 1980 and skied for the United States on the 1980 and '84 Olympic teams. Sidelined by surgery on a broken leg throughout the 1983 season, she made a strong comeback in '84 and won the Olympic silver in the giant slalom behind teammate **Debbie Armstrong.** Cooper retired at the end of the '84 World Cup season.

Selected championships and honors: Silver medal, slalom, World Championships, 1982; silver medal, giant slalom, World Championships, 1982; bronze medal, combined, World Championships, 1982; silver medal, giant slalom, Olympic Games, 1984.

CHRISTEL CRANZ b. Germany

In 1936, when Alpine skiing for women was added to the Olympics, there was only one event, the slalom and downhill combined. Though Cranz had won World Championships in both events separately, she had a disappointing performance and finished in sixth place. However, both of her slalom runs blew the competition out of the water. In a sport where victory is measured in hundredths of seconds, Cranz finished a full 4 seconds ahead of the pack on her first run and 7.2 seconds in front on her second. The outbreak of World War II put an abrupt end to world competition and to Cranz's career.

Selected championships and honors: Three gold medals, downhill, World Championships, 1935, '37, and '39; four gold medals, slalom, World Championships, 1934 and '37–39.

MANUELA DI CENTA b. Italy

Although Italy has produced dozens of world-class Alpine skiers, it had never produced a medalist in cross-country events—until Di Centa arrived on the scene at the Lillehammer Olympics in 1994. The first Italian woman to earn a cross-country medal, Di Centa went home with five of them, two individual golds, two silvers, and a team bronze. Even the all-time cross-country champion **Raisa Smetanina** never captured so many medals in a single Olympics, fueling expectations for Di Centa's future and the future of Italian cross-country.

Selected championships and honors, individual: Gold medal, 15k, Olympic Games, 1994; gold medal, 30k, Olympic Games, 1994; silver medal, 5k, Olympic Games, 1994; silver medal, 10k, Olympic Games, 1994. *Team:* Bronze medal, 4 × 5k relay, Olympic Games, 1994.

LYUBOV EGOROVA b. 1967, Tomsk, Siberia, USSR

Her career isn't over yet, but when it is, Egorova will likely be judged the best female cross-country skier of all time. A gifted child skier, Egorova was fifteen when she left her parents and home in Siberia to train in St. Petersburg, at one of the best cross-country courses in the world. Ten years later she was ready for the Olympics. Egorova competed in both the '92 and '94 Olympic Games, entering nine races and coming away with a medal in each. She plans to enter the

'98 games in Nagano, Japan. At thirty-one years old, she'll just be hitting her peak as a cross-country skier. *Selected championships and honors, individual:* Silver medal, cross-country 5k, Olympic Games, 1992; two gold medals, cross-country pursuit, Olympic Games, 1992 and '94; gold medal, cross-country 15k, Olympic Games, 1992; silver medal, cross-country 30k, Olympic Games, 1992; gold medal, cross-country 5k, Olympic Games, 1994. *Team:* Two gold medals, 4 × 5k relay, Olympic Games, 1992.

MICHELA FIGINI b. ca. 1966, Switzerland
Some skiers have to wait their whole careers for an Olympic medal. Figini got hers at the start, just two weeks after winning her first World Cup event. With her first-place finish in the 1984 slalom, the Swiss seventeen-year-old became the youngest skier ever to go home with an Olympic gold. She went on to win two World Cup overalls and several individual titles. On the slopes her strength was speed, and Figini was the queen of downhill racers throughout the late 1980s.
Selected championships and honors: Gold medal, downhill, Olympic Games, 1984; two World Cups, overall, 1984 and '88; four World Cups, downhill, 1985 and '87–89; gold medal, downhill, World Championship, 1985; World Cup, giant slalom, 1985; World Cup, super G, 1988; silver medal, super G, Olympic Games, 1988.

FRASER, GRETCHEN. *See Gretchen Kunigk Fraser, below.*

CHRISTINE and **MARIELLE GOITSCHEL**
b. 1944 and 1945, Val d'Isère, France
Alpine skiers from the heart of France's ski region, the Goitschel sisters dominated the 1964 winter Olympics. Marielle, who'd won the first of three overall World Championships when she was only sixteen, was at age eighteen the youngest medal winner at the 1964 games. Both sisters skied for France at the games, and both came home with one gold medal and one silver medal, each having lost a gold to the other. Christine didn't compete in the 1968 Olympics, but Marielle did—and won a gold in the event her sister had bested her in four years earlier.
Selected championships and honors, Marielle: Gold medal, giant slalom, Olympic Games, 1964; silver medal, slalom, Olympic Games, 1964; gold medal, slalom, Olympic Games, 1968; three World Championships, overall, 1966–68; World Cup, downhill, 1967; two World Cups, slalom, 1967 and '68; gold medal,

Gold Medal, Shmold Medal, We Want to Know, *Who Are You Dating?*

Ever since women joined the Olympics, they've been deluged with questions men usually don't have to put up with. *Do you cook? Who's your dream date? Do you have plans to marry? How many children would you like to have?* Fed up with the press, **Marielle Goitschel** found a way to hoist reporters on their own petard. At the 1964 Innsbruck games, she told a throng of reporters she was "very much in love" and had just become engaged to a skier from her own hometown—heartthrob celebrity Jean-Claude Killy. She played her lines so straight the press stampeded off in search of Killy, and Goitschel and her sister **Christine** sat back and laughed.

slalom, Olympic Games, 1968. *Christine:* Gold medal, slalom, Olympic Games, 1964; Silver medal, giant slalom, Olympic Games, 1964.

NANCY GREENE b. May 11, 1943, Ottawa, Canada
Greene, a Canadian with four U.S. Alpine titles to her credit, won the first women's World Cup competition ever held, in 1967, and repeated her victory in 1968. She also went to the Olympics that year, bringing home a gold and a silver.
Selected championships and honors: Two World Cups, overall, 1967 and '68; gold medal, giant slalom, Olympic Games, 1968; silver medal, slalom, Olympic Games, 1968.

MARJA-LIISA HÄMÄLÄINEN b. ca. 1955, Simpele, Finland
Hämäläinen had everything a cross-country ski champion should have. She was tall, swift, and strong, and she had been skiing since childhood. The only thing missing was a winning record. Though she began competing in 1971 and made the Finnish Olympic team in 1980, she had no major wins to show for ten years of effort. Discouraged, she was about to quit, but her fiancé and fellow skier Harri Kirvesniemi encouraged her to stay with it. She did—and began to win; first a

World Cup title in 1983, then a three-medal gold rush at the 1984 Olympics. At the games, she also skied anchor for Finland's bronze-medal relay team.
Selected championships and honors, individual: Gold medal, 5k, Olympic Games, 1984; gold medal, 10k, Olympic Games, 1984; gold medal, 20k, Olympic Games, 1984. *Team:* Bronze medal, 4 × 5k relay, Olympic Games, 1984.

ERIKA HESS b. ca. 1962, Switzerland
Casual observers, who watch Alpine competition only during the Olympics, missed Hess at her best. A bronze-medal winner in the 1980 games, she failed to win any medals at all at Sarajevo in 1984. Sandwiched around those showings were Hess's best performances—eight solid-gold performances in world-class competitions.
Selected championships and honors: Bronze medal, slalom, Olympic Games, 1980; three World Cups, slalom, 1981–83; two World Cups, overall, 1982 and '84; gold medal, slalom, World Championships, 1982; gold medal, giant slalom, World Championships, 1982; gold medal, overall, World Championships, 1982.

PETRA KRONBERGER b. February 21, 1969, Pfarrwerfen, Austria
Kronberger's father taught her to ski when she was two, and from the age of ten on she attended schools devoted to nurturing and training athletic prodigies. Despite her early promise on the slopes, Kronberger wasn't a phenom. She had to work hard, and when she was a teenager, injuries threatened to close her career before it began. She made the Austrian Olympic team in 1988 but didn't medal. Two more years of hard work paid off, and in 1990 Kronberger became the first woman ever to win at least one competition in each of skiing's five events: slalom, giant slalom, super G, downhill, and combined. That same year, she won the first of three consecutive World Cup overall championships. The season ended with an injury that forced her off the slopes for several months. Although she came back to win two more World Cup titles and two Olympic golds, the injury forced her to retire from skiing at the end of the 1991–92 season.
Selected championships and honors: Three World Cups, overall, 1990–92; gold medal, slalom, Olympic Games, 1992; gold medal, combined, Olympic Games, 1992.

GALINA KULAKOVA b. ca. 1942, Izhevsk, USSR
At her first Olympic Games, in 1968, Kulakova had

the misfortune to start ahead of her closest rival, Sweden's Toni Gustaffson. Gustaffson, knowing exactly what time she had to beat, rallied in the final kilometer to finish first, and Kulakova had to settle for second. The story was different four years later. Now a physical education teacher and a far more experienced skier, Kulakova won both individual events and helped the Soviets to a victory in the relay.
Selected championships and honors, individual: Gold medal, 5k, Olympic Games, 1972; gold medal, 10k, Olympic Games, 1972. *Team:* Two gold medals, 3 × 5k relay, Olympic Games, 1972 and '76; silver medal, 3 × 5k relay, Olympic Games, 1980.

GRETCHEN KUNIGK FRASER b. February 11, 1919, Tacoma, Washington; d. February 18, 1994
Fraser's best-known achievement—bringing home the first U.S. women's Olympic gold in Alpine skiing—might have come eight years earlier had not World War II intervened. Born Kunigk, Fraser married fellow skier Don Fraser in 1939 and with him was named to the 1940 Olympic team. War halted all international competitions, so Fraser settled for national titles in 1941 and '42, then retired from competition. Encouraged to come out of retirement by her husband, Fraser made the 1948 Olympic team. Although she led the field after her first run, she had to wait at the starting gate for seventeen minutes while technical difficulties were corrected. Numb with cold, she still managed a best-of-field time to win the medal.
Selected championships and honors: National Championship, combined, 1941; National Championship, slalom, 1941; gold medal, slalom, Olympic Games, 1948; silver medal, combined, Olympic Games, 1948.

HILARY LINDH b. Juneau, Alaska
Going into the 1992 Olympics, Lindh had never finished higher than sixth in a World Cup event, and no one expected her to medal. The women's downhill course at Albertville, said to be one of the most difficult ever designed, featured a drop of 828 meters over a 1⅗-mile course, making it the steepest course women had ever competed over. It was no place for unknowns, especially with weather conditions that included intermittent fog and an impending snowstorm. But the day went to the underdogs, and Lindh finished just six-hundredths of a second behind Kerrin Lee Gartner of Canada, also an outsider.
Selected championships and honors: Silver medal, downhill, Olympic Games, 1992.

TAMARA McKINNEY b. October 16, 1962, Lexington, Kentucky

Originally told that, at 5'4" and 117 pounds, she was too small to make it as an Alpine skier, McKinney went on to become one of the best the United States has yet produced. She was born into a skiing family, and her brother Steve and sister Sheila were her companions on the junior circuit. When McKinney was fourteen, Sheila crashed during a race and nearly died. The injury left McKinney without her friend and rival, and she thought of giving up the sport. Nevertheless, she became a full-time member of the World Cup circuit the next year. Plagued by injuries on the slope and losses at home (McKinney's father, mother, and older brother McLane died within a few years of each other), McKinney always managed to do her best on the slopes, especially in World Cup competition. In 1983 she became the first American woman ever to win an overall World Cup title. McKinney retired at the beginning of the 1990s.

Selected championships and honors: World Cup, giant slalom, 1981; World Cup, overall, 1983; two bronze medals, combined events, World Championships, 1985 and '87.

ANDREA MEAD LAWRENCE b. April 19, 1932, Rutland, Vermont

After the 1948 Olympics, at which she failed to medal in Alpine ski, Mead's approach to the sport had become so dead serious that her coach suggested she take a one-year hiatus. Mead stayed on the slopes, but worked to find the zest and enthusiasm she had once possessed. She began finishing in the medals and, at the 1952 Olympics, won the giant slalom by over two seconds, an eternity in ski time. In the slalom a few days later, she caught a gate on the first run and came back with a fast second run to take the medal. Her win made her the first American ever to earn two golds in Alpine skiing.

Selected championships and honors: Gold medal, giant slalom, Olympic Games, 1952; gold medal, slalom, Olympic Games, 1952.

ROSI MITTERMAIER b. August 5, 1950, Reit im Winkel, West Germany

In the mid-1970s, Mittermaier was a competent Alpine skier who, after nearly a decade of World Cup competition, was still struggling for the big win. Suddenly she came alive, and 1976 became her year. In World Cup competition she took titles in the overall and slalom. At the Innsbruck Olympics, she almost became the first woman to triple-medal in Alpine. After taking golds in the downhill and slalom, she mistimed a gate on the giant slalom and came in second to Canada's Kathy Kreiner.

Selected championships and honors: World Cup, overall, 1976; World Cup, slalom, 1976; gold medal, downhill, Olympic Games, 1976; gold medal, slalom, Olympic Games, 1976; silver medal, giant slalom, Olympic Games, 1976.

MARIE-THERES NADIG b. March 8, 1954, Tanneboden, Switzerland

Nadig went to her first Olympics as a relatively unknown seventeen-year-old, never having won a single World Cup event. In the downhill, she defeated World Cup champion **Annemarie Pröll,** and defeated her again a few days later in the giant slalom. Nadig attributed her spectacular performance to being an underdog and the unbelievable low crouch she was able to maintain throughout the downhill. It was the start of a spectacular career for Nadig, and over the next ten years she and Pröll were the Martina Navratilova and Chris Evert of the ski world. Nadig's showing in the next Olympics, in 1976, was hampered by illness, and at the 1980 games she finished third behind Pröll and **Hanni Wenzel.**

Selected championships and honors: Gold medal, downhill, Olympic Games, 1972; gold medal, giant slalom, Olympic Games, 1972; two World Cups, downhill, 1980 and '81; World Cup, giant slalom, 1981; World Cup, combined, 1981; bronze medal, downhill, Olympic Games, 1980.

CYNTHIA (CINDY) NELSON b. August 19, 1955, Austin, Minnesota

Nelson joined the U.S. ski team at age fifteen and between 1973 and 1978 won a total of five national titles in downhill, slalom, and Alpine combined events. Despite her skill and promise, injuries hampered her career and spoiled her Olympic chances. She sat out the '72 games with a dislocated hip and, skiing with a brace on her knee at the '84 games, could finish no higher than seventeenth. Nevertheless, Nelson was able to win a bronze at the '76 games, finishing behind Germany's **Rosi Mittermaier** and Austria's Brigitte Totschnigg. Injuries forced Nelson to retire after the '84 games.

Selected championships and honors: Bronze medal, downhill, Olympic Games, 1976.

PENELOPE (PENNY) PITOU b. 1941, New Hampshire

As a teenager, Pitou made the boys' high-school ski team but was soon barred from competition. No matter, she made her first U.S. Olympic team at age fifteen and at age nineteen earned a silver medal in Olympic downhill competition. After her skiing career, Pitou became the first woman bank director in her native state of New Hampshire.

Selected championships and honors: Silver medal, downhill, Olympic Games, 1960.

ANNEMARIE PRÖLL MOSER b. March 27, 1953, Austria

When Pröll won her first World Cup overall title, in 1971, she was the youngest winner ever. Her repeat win the next year proved to anyone with doubts that Pröll was indeed the real thing. But Pröll was bitterly disappointed at the '72 Olympics, with two second-place finishes behind archrival **Marie-Theres Nadig** of Switzerland. The losses were a blow to Pröll, and although she had impressive wins after the games, she retired from competition in 1975. Pröll sat out the '76 Olympics but returned to the slopes later that year. Soon she was back on track, racking up World Cup victories that eventually put her in the record books as the winningest woman ever in World Cup competition. Pröll had one more chance at the Olympics at Lake Placid in 1980—and this time she won her gold.

Selected championships and honors: Six World Cups, overall, 1971–75 and 1979; seven World Cups, downhill, 1971–75, '78, and '79; two World Cups, slalom, 1971, '72, and '75; silver medal, downhill, Olympic Games, 1972; silver medal, giant slalom, Olympic Games, 1972; World Cup, giant slalom, 1975; World Cup, combined, 1979; gold medal, downhill, Olympic Games, 1980.

ANFISA REZTSOVA. *See entry under Biathlon.*

DIANN ROFFE STEINROTTER b. March 24, 1967, Austria

In 1985, when she was only seventeen, Roffe won the World Cup giant slalom season title. Then, as with many another youthful phenom, her hot streak ended. Roffe headed into the '92 Olympics with a six-year drought behind her. She tied Austria's Anita Wachter for a silver medal in the giant slalom, finishing just three-hundredths of a second behind Sweden's Pernilla Wiberg. Due to the shift to a staggered Olympic schedule, Roffe only had to wait two years for another try at Olympic gold. This time she won by nearly a third of a second.

Selected championships and honors: World Cup, giant slalom, 1985; silver medal, giant slalom, Olympic Games, 1992; gold medal, Olympic Games, 1994.

JEAN SAUBERT b. May 1, 1942, Roseburg, Oregon

In 1963 and '64 Saubert, an Alpine skier, dominated U.S. skiing, winning a total of six national titles. At the 1964 Olympics Saubert tied for second place with **Christine Goitschel** in the giant slalom and finished behind both **Goitschel** sisters in the slalom to win the bronze. Saubert could easily have continued skiing but retired from competition to focus on her college education.

Selected championships and honors: Silver medal, giant slalom, Olympic Games, 1964; bronze medal, slalom, Olympic Games, 1964.

VRENI SCHNEIDER b. 1966, Elm, Switzerland

Over the course of three Olympic Games, Alpine skier Schneider won three gold medals, one silver, and one bronze. Schneider, who grew up in a small Alps village, has been an avid skier since age three. As a coach once pointed out, Schneider never has to force herself onto the slopes—she enjoys each run as if it were her first. One of her most amazing victories came during her first Olympic appearance in 1988, when she won the slalom on the strength of a lightning second run that gave her the gold by a huge 1.68-second margin. Schneider had an equally spectacular '88–89 World Cup season, winning fourteen events to break Ingemar Stenmark's old record of thirteen. Despite being the hands-down best Alpine skier of her generation, Schneider prefers life as a noncelebrity. She still makes her home in Elm, population 800, where she runs her own sporting goods shop.

Selected championships and honors: Two gold medal, slalom, Olympic Games, 1988 and '94; gold medal, giant slalom, Olympic Games, 1988; three World Cups, overall, 1989, '94, and '95; silver medal, combined, Olympic Games, 1994; bronze medal, giant slalom, Olympic Games, 1994.

KATJA SEIZINGER b. ca. 1972, Eberbach, Germany

One of the top Alpine skiers of the 1990s, Seizinger came within a hair's breadth of winning the World

Cup overall title in 1992, when she was twenty years old. A skier who combines speed with technical ability, Seizinger excells at both downhill racing and super giant slalom events.

Selected championships and honors: Three World Cups, super G, 1993–95; gold medal, super G, World Championships, 1993; gold medal, downhill, Olympic Games, 1994.

RAISA SMETANINA b. February 29, 1952, USSR
In the annals of winter sports, Smetanina isn't nearly as famous Peggy Fleming, Gretchen Fraser, or Bonnie Blair. Nevertheless, Smetanina holds the record for most medals earned at the winter Olympics. A member of the formidable Soviet cross-country ski team in five consecutive winter Olympics (1976–92), Smetanina won seven individual medals and three in team relay. She retired after the 1992 games at Albertville.

Selected championships and honors, individual: Silver medal, 5k, Olympic Games, 1976; gold medal, 10k, Olympic Games, 1976; gold medal, 5k, Olympic Games, 1980; two silver medals, 10k, Olympic Games, 1984 and '88; silver medal, 20k, Olympic Games, 1984; bronze medal, 20k, Olympic Games, 1988. *Team:* Gold medal, 3 × 5k relay, Olympic Games, 1976; two silver medals, 3 × 5k relay, Olympic Games, 1980 and '92.

PICABO STREET b. ca. 1972, Triumph, Idaho
With her unusual name, effervescent personality, and flower-child parents, Street was a walking press release. In fact, as her teen promise failed to flower, some suggested she was all press release. It wasn't that Street wasn't talented—she had natural talent to spare, but lacked focus and dedication. After being dropped from the U.S. team in 1990, Street had to decide whether to give up competitive skiing or work to get back in shape. She took the second option and rejoined Team USA in 1991. In 1993 Street won a silver medal in the World Championships downhill combined event. The next year, at Lillehammer, her downhill performance was good enough for an Olympic silver medal. Focused and motivated, Street was unstoppable. In 1995 she became the first American ever to win the World Cup season title in downhill racing.

Selected championships and honors: Silver medal, combined, World Championship, 1993; silver medal, downhill, Olympic Games, 1994; World Cup, downhill, 1995.

HANNI WENZEL b. December 14, 1956,
  Germany
Though she was born in Germany, Wenzel's family moved to Liechtenstein when she was just one year old, and she was granted official citizenship in 1974. Two years later she enjoyed her first major international success by finishing third in the slalom at the Calgary Olympics. The gold medal that year went to the dynamic **Rosi Mittermaier,** and at the next winter games Wenzel equaled Mittermaeir's feat by winning two golds and a silver. Her brother Andreas, skiing for the men's team, won a silver in the slalom. Beyond the Olympics, 1980 proved Wenzel's year as well, when she won the World Cup overall title.

Selected championships and honors: Gold medal, slalom, World Championship, 1974; bronze medal, slalom, Olympic Games, 1976; two World Cups, overall, 1978 and '80; gold medal, slalom, Olympic Games, 1980; gold medal, giant slalom, Olympic Games, 1980; silver medal, downhill, Olympic Games, 1980.

PERNILLA WIBERG b. Sweden
In the 1970s Sweden fielded one of the best male skiers on the slopes, Ingemar Stenmark. But the sports-minded Swedes had no female Alpine champion until Wiberg arrived on the scene in the 1990s. Swift and technically superb, Wiberg was world champion in the giant slalom going into the 1992 Olympics. She defended her title with a gold-medal performance, then came back two years later to collect a gold in the combined event.

Selected championships and honors: World Championship, giant slalom, 1991; gold medal, giant slalom, Olympic Games, 1992; two World Cups, combined, 1994 and '95; gold medal, combined, Olympic Games, 1994.

Skiing

Olympic Alpine Downhill

Year	Medalists	Country	Time
1924–1936	event not held		
1948	Hedy Schlunegger	SWI	2:28.3
	Trude Beiser	AUT	2:29.1
	Resi Hammer	AUT	2:30.2
1952	Trude Jochum-Beiser	AUT	1:47.1
	Annemarie Buchner	GER	1:48.0
	Giuliana Minuzzo	ITA	1:49.0
1956	Madeleine Berthod	SWI	1:40.7
	Frieda Danzer	SWI	1:45.4
	Lucile Wheeler	CAN	1:45.9
1960	Heidi Biebl	GER	1:37.6
	Penelope Pitou	USA	1:38.6
	Traudl Hecher	AUT	1:38.9
1964	Christl Haas	AUT	1:55.39
	Edith Zimmerman	AUT	1:56.42
	Traudl Hecher	AUT	1:56.66
1968	Olga Pall	AUT	1:40.87
	Isabelle Mir	FRA	1:41.33
	Christl Haas	AUT	1:41.41
1972	Marie-Theres Nadig	SWI	1:36.68
	Annemarie Pröll	AUT	1:37.00
	Susan Corrock	USA	1:37.68
1976	Rosi Mittermaier	GER	1:46.16
	Brigitte Totschnigg	AUT	1:46.68
	Cynthia Nelson	USA	1:47.50
1980	Annemarie Moser-Pröll	AUT	1:37.52
	Hanni Wenzel	LIE	1:38.22
	Marie-Theres Nadig	SWI	1:38.36
1984	Michela Figini	SWI	1:13.36
	Maria Walliser	SWI	1:13.41
	Olga Charvátová	CZE	1:13.53
1988	Marina Kiehl	GER	1:25.86
	Brigitte Oertli	SWI	1:26.61
	Karen Percy	CAN	1:26.62
1992	Karin Lee-Gartner	CAN	1:52.55
	Hilary Lindh	USA	1:52.61
	Veronika Wallinger	AUT	1:52.64
1994	Katja Seizinger	GER	1:35.93
	Picabo Street	USA	1:36.59
	Isolde Kostner	ITA	1:36.85

Olympic Alpine Super Giant Slalom

Year	Medalists	Country	Time
1988	Sigrid Wolf	AUT	1:19.03
	Michela Figini	SWI	1:20.03
	Karen Percy	CAN	1:20.29
1992	Deborah Campagnoni	ITA	1:21.22
	Carole Merle	FRA	1:22.63
	Katja Seizinger	GER	1:23.19
1994	Diann Rolfe-Steinrotter	USA	1:22.15
	Svetlana Gladischeva	RUS	1:22.44
	Isolde Kostner	ITA	1:22.45

Olympic Alpine Giant Slalom

Year	Medalists	Country	Time
1924–1948	event not held		
1952	Andrea Mead Lawrence	USA	2:06.8
	Dagmar Rom	AUT	2:09.0
	Annemarie Buchner	GER	2:10.0
1956	Ossi Reichert	GER	1:56.5
	Josefine Frandl	AUT	1:57.8
	Dorothea Hochleitner	AUT	1:58.2
1960	Yvonne Rüegg	SWI	1:39.9
	Penelope Pitou	USA	1:40.0
	Giuliana Chenal-Minuzzo	ITA	1:40.2
1964	Marielle Goitschel	FRA	1:52.24
	Christine Goitschel	FRA	1:53.11
	Jean Saubert	USA	1:53.11
	Christl Haas	AUT	1:53.86
1968	Nancy Greene	CAN	1:51.97
	Annie Famose	FRA	1:54.61
	Fernande Bochatay	SWI	1:54.74
1972	Marie-Theres Nadig	SWI	1:29.90
	Annemarie Pröll	AUT	1:30.75
	Wiltrud Drexel	AUT	1:32.35
1976	Kathy Kreiner	CAN	1:29.13
	Rosi Mittermaier	GER	1:29.55
	Danièlle Debernard	FRA	1:29.95
1980	Hanni Wenzel	LIE	2:41.66
	Irene Epple	GER	2:42.12
	Perrine Pelen	FRA	2:42.41
1984	Debbie Armstrong	USA	2:20.98
	Christin Cooper	USA	2:21.38
	Perrine Pelen	FRA	2:21.40
1988	Vreni Schneider	SWI	2:06.49
	Christa Kinshofer-Güthlein	GER	2:07.42
	Maria Walliser	SWI	2:07.72
1992	Pernilla Wiberg	SWE	2:12.74
	Diann Rolfe	USA	2:13.71
	Anita Wachter	AUT	2:13.71
	Ulrike Maier	AUT	2:13.77
1994	Deborah Compagnoni	ITA	2:30.97
	Martina Ertl	GER	2:32.19
	Vreni Schneider	SWI	2:32.97

Skiing (continued)

Olympic Alpine Slalom

Year	Medalists	Country	Time
1924–1936	event not held		
1948	Gretchen Fraser	USA	1:57.2
	Antoinette Meyer	SWI	1:57.7
	Erika Mahringer	AUT	1:58.0
1952	Andrea Mead Lawrence	USA	2:10.6
	Ossi Reichert	GER	2:11.4
	Annemarie Buchner	GER	2:13.3
1956	Renée Colliard	SWI	1:52.3
	Regina Schöpf	AUT	1:55.4
	Yevgenia Sidorova	USSR	1:56.7
1960	Anne Heggtveigt	CAN	1:49.6
	Betsy Snite	USA	1:52.9
	Barbara Henneberger	GER	1:56.6
1964	Christine Goitschel	FRA	1:29.86
	Marielle Goitschel	FRA	1:30.77
	Jean Saubert	USA	1:31.36
1968	Marielle Goitschel	FRA	1:25.86
	Nancy Greene	CAN	1:26.15
	Annie Famose	FRA	1:27.89
1972	Barbara Cochran	USA	1:31.24
	Danièlle Debernard	FRA	1:31.26
	Florence Steurer	FRA	1:32.69
1976	Rosi Mittermaier	GER	1:30.54
	Claudia Giordani	ITA	1:30.87
	Hanni Wenzel	LIE	1:32.20
1980	Hanni Wenzel	LIE	1:25.09
	Christa Kinshofer	GER	1:26.50
	Erika Hess	SWI	1:27.89
1984	Paoletta Magoni	ITA	1:36.47
	Perrine Pelen	FRA	1:37.38
	Ursula Konzett	LIE	1:37.50
1988	Vreni Schneider	SWI	1:36.69
	Mateja Svet	YUG	1:38.37
	Christa Kinshofer-Güthlein	GER	1:38.40
1992	Petra Kronberger	AUT	1:32.68
	Annelise Coberger	NZL	1:33.10
	Bianca Fernandez Ochoa	SPA	1:33.35
1994	Vreni Schneider	SWI	1:56.01
	Elfriede Eder	AUT	1:56.35
	Katia Koren	SLO	1:56.61

Olympic Alpine Combined

Year	Medalists	Country	Pts
1924–1932	event not held		
1936	Christl Cranz	GER	97.06
	Käthe Grasegger	GER	95.26
	Laila Schou Nilsen	NOR	93.48
1948	Trude Beiser	AUT	6.58
	Gretchen Fraser	USA	6.95
	Erika Mahringer	AUT	7.04
1952–1984	event not held		
1988	Anita Wachter	AUT	29.25
	Brigitte Oertli	SWI	29.48
	Maria Walliser	SWI	51.28
1992	Petra Kronberger	AUT	2.55
	Anita Wachter	AUT	19.39
	Florence Masnada	FRA	21.38
1994*	Pernilla Wiberg	SWE	3:05.16
	Vreni Schneider	SWI	3:05.29
	Alenka Dovzan	SLO	3:06.64

*Beginning in 1994, scoring was based on time.

FIS World Alpine Ski Championship Downhill

Year	Champion	Country
1931	Esme McKinnon	Great Britain
1932	Paola Wiesinger	Italy
1933	Inge Wersin-Lantschner	Austria
1934	Anni Roegg	Switzerland
1935	Christel Cranz	Germany
1936	Evie Pinching	Great Britain
1937	Christel Cranz	Germany
1938	Lisa Resch	Germany
1939	Christel Cranz	Germany

FIS World Alpine Ski Championship Slalom

Year	Champion	Country
1931	Esme McKinnon	Great Britain
1932	Rosli Streff	Switzerland
1933	Inge Wersin-Lantschner	Austria
1934	Christel Cranz	Germany
1935	Anni Roegg	Switzerland
1936	Gerda Paumgarten	Austria
1937	Christel Cranz	Germany
1938	Christel Cranz	Germany
1939	Christel Cranz	Germany

Skiing (continued)

World Alpine Ski Championship Downhill

Year	Champion	Country
1950	Trude Beiser-Jochum	Austria
1954	Ida Schopfer	Switzerland
1958	Lucile Wheeler	Canada
1962	Christl Haas	Austria
1966	Erika Schinegger	Austria
1970	Annerosli Zyrd	Switzerland
1974	Annemarie Moser-Pröll	Austria
1978	Annemarie Moser-Pröll	Austria
1982	Gerry Sorenson	Canada
1985	Michela Figini	Switzerland
1987	Maria Walliser	Switzerland
1989	Maria Walliser	Switzerland
1991	Petra Kronberger	Austria
1993	Kate Pace	Canada

World Alpine Ski Championship Slalom

1950	Dagmar Rom	Austria
1954	Trude Klecker	Austria
1958	Inger Bjornbakken	Norway
1962	Marianne Jahn	Austria
1966	Annie Famose	France
1970	Ingrid Lafforgue	France
1974	Hanni Wenzel	Liechtenstein
1978	Lea Solkner	Austria
1982	Erika Hess	Switzerland
1985	Perrine Pelen	France
1987	Erika Hess	Switzerland
1989	Mateja Svet	Yugoslavia
1991	Vreni Schneider	Switzerland
1993	Karin Buder	Austria

World Alpine Ski Championship Giant Slalom

1950	Dagmar Rom	Austria
1954	Lucienne Schmith-Couttet	France
1958	Lucille Wheeler	Canada
1962	Marianne Jahn	Austria
1966	Marielle Goitschel	France
1970	Betsy Clifford	Canada
1974	Fabienne Serrat	France
1978	Maria Epple	W. Germany
1982	Erika Hess	Switzerland
1985	Diann Roffe	USA
1987	Vreni Schneider	Switzerland
1989	Vreni Schneider	Switzerland
1991	Pernilla Wiberg	Sweden
1993	Carole Merle	France

World Alpine Ski Championship Combined

1982	Erika Hess	Switzerland
1985	Erika Hess	Switzerland
1987	Erika Hess	Switzerland
1989	Tamara McKinney	USA
1991	Chantal Bournissen	Switzerland
1993	Miriam Vogt	Germany

World Alpine Ski Championship Super G

1987	Maria Walliser	Switzerland
1989	Ulrike Maier	Austria
1991	Ulrike Maier	Austria
1993	Katja Seizinger	Germany

Olympic Freestyle Skiing Moguls

Year	Medalists	Country	Points
1924–1988	event not held		
1992	Donna Weinbrecht	USA	23.69
	Yelizaveta Kozhevnikova	USSR	23.50
	Stine Lise Hattestad	NOR	23.04
1994	Stine Lise Hattestad	NOR	25.97
	Liz McIntyre	USA	25.89
	Elizaveta Kojevnikova	RUS	25.81

Olympic Freestyle Skiing Aerials

1924–1992	event not held		
1994	Lina Cherjazova	UZB	166.84
	Marie Lindgren	SWE	165.88
	Hilde Synnove Lid	NOR	164.13

Olympic Nordic Skiing 5 Kilometers (Classical)

Year	Medalists	Country	Time
1924–1960	event not held		
1964	Claudia Boyarskikh	USSR	17:50.5
	Mirja Lehtonen	FIN	17.52.9
	Alevtina Kolchina	USSR	18.08.4
1968	Toini Gustafsson	SWE	16:45.2
	Galina Kulakova	USSR	16.48.4
	Alevtina Kolchina	USSR	16:51.6

Skiing (continued)

Olympic Nordic Skiing 5 Kilometers (Classical)

Year	Medalists	Country	Time
1972	Galina Kulakova	USSR	17:00.50
	Marjatta Kajosmaa	FIN	17:05.50
	Helena Sikolova	CZE	17:07.32
1976	Helena Takalo	FIN	15:48.69
	Raisa Smetanina	USSR	15:49.73
	Nina Baldycheva	USSR	16.12.82
1980	Raisa Smetanina	USSR	15:06.92
	Hikka Riihivuori (Kuntola)	FIN	15:11.96
	Kvetoslava Jeriova	CZE	15.23.44
1984	Marja-Liisa Hämäläinen	FIN	17:04.0
	Berit Aunli (Kvello)	NOR	17:14.1
	Kvetoslava Jeriova	CZE	17:18.3
1988	Marjo Matikainen	FIN	15:04.0
	Tamara Tikhonova	USSR	15:05.3
	Vida Venciene	USSR	15:11.1
1992	Marjut Lukkarinen	FIN	14:13.8
	Lyubov Egorova	USSR	14:14.7
	Yelena Vialbe	USSR	14:22.7
1994	Lyubov Egorova	RUS	14:08.8
	Manuela Di Centa	ITA	14:28.3
	Marja-Liisa Kirvesniemi	FIN	14:36.0

Olympic Nordic Skiing 10 Kilometers (Classical)

1952	Lydia Widemen	FIN	41:40.0
	Mirja Hietamies	FIN	42:39.0
	Siiri Rantanen	FIN	42:50.0
1956	Lyubov Kosyreva	USSR	38:11.0
	Radya Eroshina	USSR	38:16.0
	Sonja Edstrom	SWE	38:23.0
1960	Maria Gusakova	USSR	39:46.6
	Lyubov Baranova Kosyreva	USSR	40:04.2
	Radya Eroshina	USSR	40:06.0
1964	Claudia Boyarskikh	USSR	40:24.3
	Eudokia Mekshilo	USSR	40:26.6
	Maria Gusakova	USSR	40:46.6
1968	Toini Gustafsson	SWE	36:46.5
	Berit Mördre	NOR	37:54.6
	Inger Aufles	NOR	37:59.9
1972	Galina Kulakova	USSR	34:17.8
	Alevtina Olunina	USSR	34:54.11
	Marjatta Kajosmaa	FIN	34:56.45
1976	Raisa Smetanina	USSR	30:13.41
	Helena Takalo	FIN	30:14.28
	Galina Kulakova	USSR	30:38.61

1980	Barbara Petzold	GDR	30:31.54
	Hilkka Riihivuori (Kuntola)	FIN	30:35.05
	Helena Takalo	FIN	30:45.25
1984	Marja-Liisa Hämäläinen	FIN	31:44.2
	Raisa Smetanina	USSR	32:02.9
	Brit Pettersen	NOR	32:12.7
1988	Vida Venciene	USSR	30:08.3
	Raisa Smetanina	USSR	30:17.0
	Marjo Matikainen	FIN	30:20.5
1992	event discontinued		

Olympic Nordic Skiing 15 Kilometers (Classical)

1928–1988	event not held		
1992	Lyubov Egorova	USSR	42:20.8
	Marjut Lukkarinen	FIN	43:29.9
	Yelena Vialbe	USSR	43:42.3
1994	Manuela Di Centa	ITA	39:44.5
	Lyubov Egorova	RUS	41:03.0
	Nina Gavriluk	RUS	41:10.4

Olympic Nordic Skiing 10 Kilometers (Freestyle)

1924–1988	event not held		
1992	Lyubov Egorova	USSR	40:07.7
	Stefania Belmondo	ITA	40:31.8
	Yelena Vialbe	USSR	40:51.7
1994	Lyubov Egorova	RUS	41:38.1
	Manuela Di Centa	ITA	41:46.4
	Stefania Belmondo	ITA	42:21.1

Olympic Nordic Skiing 20 Kilometers (Freestyle)

1984	Marja-Liisa Hamalainen	FIN	1:01:45.0
	Raisa Smetanina	USSR	1:02:26.7
	Anne Jahren	NOR	1:03:13.6
1988	Tamara Tikhonova	USSR	55:53.6
	Anfisa Reztsova	USSR	56:12.8
	Raisa Smetanina	USSR	57:22.1

Olympic Nordic Skiing 30 Kilometers (Freestyle)

1928–1988	event not held		
1992	Stefania Belmondo	ITA	1:22:30.1
	Lyubov Egorova	USSR	1:22:52.0
	Yelena Vialbe	USSR	1:24.13.9
1994	Manuela Di Centa	ITA	1:25:41.6
	Marit Wold	NOR	1:25:57.8
	Marja-Liisa Kirvesniemi	FIN	1:26:13.6

Skiing (continued)

Olympic Nordic Skiing 4 × 5 Kilometer Relay

Year	Medalists	Country	Time
1924–1952	event not held		
1956	Sirkka Polkunen, Mirja Hietamies, Siiri Rantanen	FIN	1:09:01.0
		USSR	1:09:28.0
		SWE	1:09:48.0
1960	Irma Johansson, Britt Strandberg, Sonja Ruthström (Edström)	SWE	1:04:21.4
		USSR	1:05:02.6
		FIN	1:06:27.5
1964	Alevtina Kolchina, Eudokia Mekshilo, Claudia Boyarskikh	USSR	59:20.2
		SWE	1:01:27.0
		FIN	1:02:45.1
1968	Inger Aufles, Babben Damon-Enger, Berit Mördre	NOR	57:30.0
		SWE	57:51.0
		USSR	58:13.6
1972	Lyubov Moukhatcheva, Alevtina Olunina, Galina Kulakova	USSR	48:46.15
		FIN	49:19.37
		NOR	49:51.49
1976	Nina Baldycheva, Zinaida Amosova, Raisa Smetanina, Galina Kulakova	USSR	1:07:49.75
		FIN	1:08:36.57
		GDR	1:09:57.95
1980	Marlies Rostock, Carola Anding, Veronika Hesse (Schmidt), Barbara Petzold	GDR	1:02:11.10
		USSR	1:03:18.30
		NOR	1:04:13.50
1984	Inger Helene Nybraten, Anne Jahren, Brit Pettersen, Berit Aunli (Kvello)	NOR	1:06:49.7
		CZE	1:07:34.7
		FIN	1:07:36.7
1988	Svetlana Nageikina, Nina Gavrylyuk, Tamara Tikhonova, Anfisa Reztsova	USSR	59:51.1
		NOR	1:01:33.0
		FIN	1:01:53.8
1992	Yelena Vialbe, Raisa Smetanina, Larissa Lazutina, Lyubov Egorova	USSR	59:34.8
		NOR	59:56.4
		ITA	1:00:25.9

Olympic Nordic Skiing Freestyle Mogul

Year	Medalist	Country	Pts
1992	Donna Weinbrecht	USA	23.69
1994	Stine Lise Hattesad	Norway	25.97

Olympic Nordic Skiing Freestyle Aerial

Year	Medalist	Country	Pts
1994	Lina Cherjazova	Uzbekistan	166.84

Photo credit: Nancie Battaglia

BIATHLON

♦ *Though women have long participated in both shooting and cross-country skiing, biathlon, which combines the two, is a relatively new sport for women.*

HISTORY

Biathlon, which combines cross-country skiing and rifle shooting, probably began as something altogether different, when Nordics strapped on skis and followed game with spears and bows thousands of years ago. The pursuit of game was traditionally a man's job, but in cold climates women skied as well, and many probably hunted small game from skis. With the advent of the industrial age, hunting from skiis was no longer a necessity. However, it became a standard part of

military training in countries such as Norway, Sweden, and Russia and gradually evolved into a sport. The first known ski-and-shoot competition took place in Norway in 1767. Because biathlon was absorbed into military life, women have little place in its history.

THE MODERN ERA

The first modern biathlon competition was organized by members of the Norwegian military in 1912. Gradually the sport was pursued in non-military venues, and the first World Championships were held in 1958. The inclusion of women's biathlon in the world sports scene grows out of a single idea: "We ski, we shoot—there's no reason not to try biathlon." In 1984 the

RULES OF THE GAME

Because biathlon hasn't been traditionally popular in North America, few Americans understand the sport well enough to appreciate the skill required to excel. Biathlon requires both superior cross-country endurance and a marksman's expert eye. It isn't just a matter of "stop and shoot" but "stop, shoot, and be accurate," as each missed shot results in a time penalty. A measure of how costly each miss is can be seen in the case of Bulgaria's Nadezda Aleksieva. At the 1992 Olympics, she was in first place after making 18 of her 20 total shots. She missed the next-to-last shot, for which she received a one-minute penalty. Instead of bringing her country its first gold medal in winter sports, Aleksieva finished in fifth place. The format of each event is described below.

7.5k. The 7.5-kilometer race involves two shooting stops. After skiing 2.5 kilometers, each skier stops and makes five shots from a prone position. For each missed shot, the skier must ski a 150-meter penalty loop. After this phase of the competition, the skier continues another 2.5 kilometers and stops at the 5-kilometer mark to make five shots from a standing position. Again, each missed shot results in a 150-meter penalty loop, costing the skier valuable time.

15k. This race features four shooting stops, two to shoot five prone shots, at 3.75 and 10 kilometers; and two to shoot five standing shots, at 6.25 and 12.5 kilometers. A minute for each missed shot is added to the skier's time.

3 × 7.5k. In the relay event in biathlon, the shooting rules differ from those in the individual events. Each skier shoots twice, once standing and once prone, and has eight chances to make five shots. However, as only five cartridges can be loaded at once and each additional cartridge must be loaded separately, missing on the initial round means losing time to reload. If the skier fails to make five hits, she must ski a 150-meter penalty loop for each miss.

Major Events and Competitions

Olympic Games
World Championships

World Championships expanded to include women's events, and women's biathlon became an Olympic sport in 1992. Oddly enough, everything about women's biathlon is three-quarters the size of men's. The short race is 7.5 instead of 10 kilometers, the long is 15 kilometers instead of 20, and even the relay team features three athletes instead of the four found on most relay teams.

Governing Bodies and Organizations

U.S. Biathlon Association
421 Old Military Road
Lake Placid, New York 12946
Phone: 518/523-3836

✱ ✱ ✱ BIOGRAPHIES ✱ ✱ ✱

MYRIAM BEDARD b. ca. 1969, Loretteville, Quebec, Canada

Bedard began as a figure skater but abandoned the sport because the cost of competitions, lessons, and costumes was burdensome to her family. Trading her blades for skis, she took up biathlon and became the first North American woman to win major international competitions, claiming her first World Championship in 1993. A solitary person by nature, Bedard can—and has—trained in virtual seclusion, with little outside attention or help. Her ability to focus in competition, to tune out distractions, and to ignore fatigue are unmatched. At Lillehammer in 1994 she swept both races, the first woman in the short history of Olympic biathlon to do so.

Selected championships and honors: Bronze medal, 15k, Olympic Games, 1992; gold medal, World Championships, 1993; gold medal, 15k, Olympic Games, 1994; gold medal, 7.5k, Olympic Games, 1994.

ANTJE MISERSKY HARVEY b. October 5, 1967, Oberhof, East Germany

In East Germany, where people take their skiing seriously, a dispute over technique can cause a nationwide uproar. In 1985, when the country's sports establishment decided to favor the gliding "skate" stride over the more traditional "diagonal" stride, Miserksy's father, an unyielding proponent of the diagonal technique, lost his position as coach of the cross-country team. Misersky, a national cross-country champion, resigned from the sport in protest. She didn't return to sports until 1989, when she took up biathlon. She won—presumably using the diagonal technique.

Selected championships and honors, individual: Gold medal, 15k, Olympic Games, 1992; silver medal, 7.5k, Olympic Games, 1992. *Team:* Silver medal, 3 × 7.5 relay, Olympic Games, 1992.

ANFISA REZTSOVA b. ca. 1964, Sverdlovsk, Russia

The first woman ever to win Olympic gold medals in two winter sports, Rezstsova began as a cross-country skier. At the Calgary games, she took an individual silver and helped her team to gold in the relay. When Reztsova retired from cross-country to have a baby, her husband, coach of the men's biathlon team, encouraged her to try that sport instead. She took the challenge and won the Olympic's inaugural event for women.

Selected championships and honors, individual cross-country: Silver medal, 20k, Olympic Games, 1988. *Biathlon:* Gold medal, 7.5k, Olympic Games, 1992. *Team cross-country:* Gold medal: 4 × 5k relay, Olympic Games, 1988. *Team biathlon:* Bronze medal, 3 × 7.5k relay, Olympic Games, 1992.

Biathlon

Olympic 15 Kilometers

Year	Medalists	Country	Time
1924–1988	event not held		
1992	Antje Misersky Harvey	GER	50:47.2
	Svetlana Pecherskaya	RUS	50:58.5
	Myriam Bedard	CAN	50:15.0
1994	Myriam Bedard	CAN	52:06.6
	Anne Briand	FRA	52:53.3
	Ursula Disl	GER	53:15.3

Olympic Spring 7.5 Kilometers

1924–1988	event not held		
1992	Anfisa Reztsova	UT	24:29.2
	Antje Misersky Harvey	GER	24:45.1
	Yelena Belova	UT	24:50.8
1994	Myriam Bedard	CAN	26:08.8
	Svetlana Paramygina	BLR	26:09.9
	Valentyna Tserbe	UKR	26:10.0

Olympic 3 × 7.5-Kilometer Relay

1992	Corinne Niogret, Veronique Claudel, Anne Briand	FRA	1:15:56.6
	Uschi Disl, Antje Misersky Harvey, Petra Schaaf	GER	1:16:18.4
	Yelena Belova, Anfisa Reztsova, Yelena Melnikova	UT	1:16:54.6
1994	Nedejda Talanova, Natalia Snytina, Louiza Noskova, Anfisa Reztsova	RUS	1:47:19.5
	Uschi Disl, Antje Misersky Harvey, Simone Greiner-Petter-Memm, Petra Schaaf	GER	1:51:16.5
	Corinne Niogret, Veronique Claudel, Delphyne Heymann, Anne Briand	FRA	1:52:28.3

World Championship Individual

Year	Winner	Country
1984	V. Tchernichova	USSR
1985	Kaya Parve	USSR
1986	Eva Korpela	Sweden
1987	Sanna Groenlid	Norway
1988	Anne Elvebakk	Norway
1989	Petra Schaaf	Germany
1990	Svetlana Davidova	USSR
1991	Petra Schaaf	Germany
1993	Petra Schaaf	Germany
1995	Corinne Niogret	France

World Championship Sprint

1984	V. Tchernichova	USSR
1985	Sanna Groenlid	Norway
1986	Kaya Parve	USSR
1987	Jelena Golovina	USSR
1988	Petra Schaaf	Germany
1989	Anna Elvebaak	Norway
1990	Anna Elvebaak	Norway
1991	Grete Nykkelmo	Norway
1993	Myriam Bedard	Canada
1995	Anne Briand	France

World Championship Relay

1984	USSR
1985	USSR
1986	USSR
1987	USSR
1988	USSR
1989	USSR
1990	USSR
1991	USSR
1993	Czech Republic
1995	Germany

World Championship Team

1989	USSR
1990	USSR
1991	USSR
1993	France
1995	Norway

World Cup Overall

1988	Anna Elvebaak	NOR
1989	Elena Golobina	USSR
1990	Jirina Adamichkova	CZE
1991	Svetlana Davidova	USSR
1992	Anfisa Reztsova	RUS
1993	Anfisa Reztsova	RUS
1994	Svetlana Paramygina	BLR
1995	Anne Briand	FRA

LUGE

♦ *One of the more dangerous winter sports, luge is also one of the most thrilling, with sleds barreling through an icy tunnel at speeds in excess of 80 miles an hour.*

HISTORY

Virtually all snowbound cultures, from the earliest times on, invented some form of sled. The innovation came from necessity, as sleds provided a way to transport goods, food, and children across frozen terrain. Prehistoric sleds may have consisted of little more than bone runners and a stretched hide, which could be loaded with gear and easily pulled. In North America and Siberia, the sled quickly evolved into an aerodynamic marvel. Made primarily of wood, early sleds are remarkably complex, consisting of numerous specially sculpted parts. These early sleds taper at the front both horizontally and vertically, thereby reducing resistance. Forward runners curve up to meet the frame, a shock-absorbing feature. A variation on the sled, the toboggan, owes its invention and its name to natives of North America. Designed as a utilitarian object, the sled probably did not have long to wait until its recreational worth was discovered and appreciated. Early sleds carried many items, including children, who would undoubtedly have enjoyed rapid descents down icy inclines. We know from the records and letters of early explorers that Native American youngsters had sleds of their own, and enjoyed sledding and tobogganing as standard winter fare.

The form of sledding known as luge (the French word for "sled") was developed in Europe, probably in the reaches of Switzerland and Austria. The first international competition, which drew competitors from seven nations, took place on a four-kilometer stretch of road near Davos, Switzerland, in 1883.

THE MODERN ERA

Despite North America's long history of sledding and tobogganing, luge was unknown here until relatively recently. Soldiers stationed in West Germany after World War II learned the sport from the Germans. Skiers who trained in Austria also learned the sport, and both groups brought the art of luging home to America. By the 1950s luge had established itself in America, and American women were competing in both singles and doubles national competitions. In international events, only a singles event is provided for women, both in the World Championships, which began in 1955, and the Olympics, which added

---

Major Events and Competitions

World Championships
Olympic Games

---

luge for both men and women in 1964. From its earliest days, the sports has been dominated by the women of Russia, Germany, and Austria. North American women have yet to finish in the medals, though Cammie Myler turned in a heads-up fifth-place finish at the 1992 winter Olympics.

Governing Bodies and Organizations

U.S. Luge Association (USLA)
Box 651
Lake Placid, New York 12946
Phone: 518/523-2071

---

* * * BIOGRAPHIES * * *

ORTRUN ENDERLEIN b. December 1, 1943, Trunzig, Germany

Winner of the Olympic's inaugural competition for women, Enderlein also won three World Championships. She was positioned to take a second Olympic gold in 1968 but was disqualified, along with teammates **Anna-Maria Müller** and Angela Knösel. The East German women aroused suspicion when they showed up at the last minute for each run. Officials checked the runners and concluded they had been heated, a violation of rules. Although East German authorities tried to bill the brouhaha as a capitalist frame-up, the disqualification stuck.

Selected championships and honors: Gold medal, Olympic Games, 1964; three gold medals, World Championships, 1964, '65, and '67.

STEFFI MARTIN WALTER b. ca. 1963, Schlema, East Germany

Martin, one of the best women lugers of all time, became the first to defend an Olympic championship in her sport, winning golds in 1984 and '88. In 1984, when she was the reigning world champion, any of

her four times would have secured the medal. Her next Olympic win was far more challenging. Martin had taken the 1987 season off to have a baby, and initially had a hard time making the team. In view of her past wins, officials gave her an extra three weeks to prepare. Martin brought her times up, made the team, and was part of a dynamic East German sweep of events.

Selected championships and honors: Two gold medals, Olympic Games, 1984 and '88.

ANNA-MARIA MÜLLER b. February 23, 1949, East Germany

Müller was devastated when she and her teammates were disqualified for illegally heating their runners in the 1968 Olympics. Avery Brundage, then president of the IOC, encouraged Müller and her friends to train hard, come back, and try again. Müller followed his advice, and four years later found herself in a hard-fought battle for gold. Just thirty-six hundredths of a second separated the first-place finisher from the third, but Müller came out on top and went home with her medal.

Selected championships and honors: Gold medal, Olympic Games, 1972; World Championship, 1972.

DORIS and **ANGELIKA NEUNER** b. ca. 1971 and 1973, Innsbruck, Austria

The Neuner sisters pulled off an Olympic first, taking first and second places in the same event. Twenty-year-old Doris finished the first run with a two-tenths-of-a-second lead—a decisive gap by luge standards. Although she did not lead in either of the other runs, no one was able to catch her, including her older sister Angelika, who finished the competition little more than seven-hundredths of a second behind her.

Selected championships and honors, Doris Neuner: Gold medal, Olympic Games, 1992. *Angelika Neuner:* Silver medal, Olympic Games, 1992.

MARGIT SCHUMANN b. ca. 1955, East Germany

At the 1972 Olympics Schumann finished just .36 seconds slower than teammate **Anna-Maria Müller,** and that made the difference between a gold and bronze medal. It was the last time Schumann, a lieutenant in the East German army, would be defeated for some time. Over the next four years she won five consecutive World Championships and earned a gold medal at the Innsbruck Olympics.

Selected championships and honors: Bronze medal, Olympic Games, 1972; five World Championships, 1973–77; gold medal, Olympic Games, 1976.

BONNIE WARNER b. April 7, 1962, Mount Baldy, California

Warner, an outstanding field hockey goalie, was exposed to luge at the 1980 Lake Placid Olympics. The sport so fascinated her that she stayed on after the games to begin training. Three years later, she was good enough to win the first of five national championships. Four years later, she was good enough to make the Olympic team. At the games she stood in seventh place after her first two runs—at the time, the highest standing ever achieved by an American woman. Unfortunately, Warner crashed into the wall on her third run and finished in fifteenth place. Warner, who continued to play field hockey throughout her luge career, felt the two sports were an ideal cross-training matchup.

Luge

Olympic Single

Year	Medalists	Country	Time
1924–1960	event not held		
1964	Ortrun Enderlein	GDR	3:24.67
	Ilse Geisler	GDR	3:27.42
	Helene Thurner	AUT	3:29.06
1968	Erica Lechner	ITA	2:26.66
	Christa Schmuck	GER	2:29.37
	Angelika Dünhaupt	GER	2:29.56
1972	Anna-Maria Müller	GDR	2:59.18
	Ute Rührold	GDR	2:59.49
	Margit Schumann	GDR	2:59.54
1976	Margit Schumann	GDR	2:50.621
	Ute Rührold	GDR	2:50.846
	Elisabeth Demleitner	GER	2:51.056
1980	Vera Zozulya	USSR	2:36.537
	Melitta Sollmann	GDR	2:37.657
	Ingrida Amantova	USSR	2:37.817
1984	Steffi Martin	GDR	2:46.570
	Bettina Schmidt	GDR	2:46.873
	Ute Weiss	GDR	2:47.248
1988	Steffi Walter (Martin)	GDR	3:03.973
	Ute Oberhoffner (Weiss)	GDR	3:04.105
	Cerstin Schmidt	GDR	3:04.181
1992	Doris Neuner	AUT	3:06.696
	Angelika Neuner	AUT	3:06.769
	Susi Erdmann	GER	3:07.115
1994	Gerda Weissensteiner	ITA	3:15.517
	Susi Erdmann	GER	3:16.276
	Andrea Tagwerker	AUT	3:16.652

Photo credit: Archive Photos/Nordisk

SLED DOG RACING

◆ *Many people think sled dog racing comes down to one event, the Iditarod. In fact, there are numerous, albeit less well-known, events.*

Dogsledding began as a utilitarian activity. Racing was equally utilitarian, with early mushers vying not with each other but against the hostile elements of snow and ice. In Siberia, Alaska, and northern Canada, where dogs were heavily relied on, having a fast sled and spirited team could spell the difference between life and death. For the lone traveler, dogs also saved the day as portable heating units. With their thick fur and radiant heat, dogs made it possible to stop for the night, dig into a bank of snow, and survive. The vast distances involved made roads and railroads impractical, and sleds served as the primary means of transport of goods, people, and mail

until well into the twentieth century. One of the most memorable sled dog events in history, the so-called Race for Life, highlights the importance of dogs in the North. In late January of 1925, Nome was stricken with a sudden outbreak of diphtheria. Diphtheria serum could be freighted to Nenana by train, but there the tracks ended— and Nenana, south of Fairbanks, was 700 miles west of Nome. A relay system was quickly organized, and mushers pressed their teams into service. Eventually twenty pounds of serum arrived in Nome, and the epidemic was halted.

Although races were long conducted informally, life in the North left little time for formalized events. The first organized sled dog race was the All-Alaska Sweepstakes. Run over a seven-mile course, the inaugural race took place in 1908 and soon became an annual event. We don't

◆ ◆

WHO ARE THESE DOGS, ANYWAY?

Don't expect to find an Alaskan sled dog in a book on pedigrees. There is no such breed, but devoted mushers—and informed enthusiasts—know them at a glance. Sled dogs may be the most carefully selected mongrels in history, and breeders search for the right mix with the thoroughness of a chef creating a master recipe. Today's sled dog is likely to incorporate strains of native-bred husky, malamute, and hound. Aside from health, body strength, a protective thick coat, and sound paws, a good dog must possess speed. As pups mature and are turned out to run, the potential of each is carefully evaluated. In addition to physical attributes, the dog must also display heart and zest, a love for running, and an interest in learning. Pups who don't make the championship cut go into the pet pool or are sold to those who sled for fun. Many northerners who don't have the time, resources, or dedication to race do keep dogs for skijoring, the Scandinavian-born sport in which one or two dogs pull a rider on skis.

One of the persistent myths about sled dogs is that forcing them to run miles through the snow is somehow cruel. Sledding can be cruel if an owner is careless and exploitative—just as being a pet can be cruel if a dog is unlucky in its owner. But the vast majority of mushers enjoy their dogs and take excellent care of them. Maintaining a team is a phenomenal investment of time and money—just ask Susan Butcher, who met her husband, Dave Monson, because she was deeply in debt to the dog food company he represented. The estimated cost just to run the Iditarod is $7,000, not counting the training and preparation leading up to it. Since underfed, uncared-for, or mentally stressed dogs will never perform well, there's no point in racing a team that is not in good physical and mental condition. Accidents do occasionally occur, as in 1985, when two of Susan Butcher's dogs were killed by a pregnant moose. Such losses are rare, and responsible mushers take every possible step to keep their dogs safe and healthy. To discourage those who might be tempted to exhaust their dogs in hopes of winning, most races—including the Iditarod—set standards for dog maintenance and automatically disqualify anyone who loses a dog, even if the death was wholly accidental. The Iditarod also gives a special humanitarian award to the musher who takes the best care of his team.

Another popular myth is that a team of dogs is little more than a snarling mass of half-tamed wolves. Hardly. Susan Butcher, who maintains her own kennels and breeding program, devotes a huge share of her time simply to bonding with her dogs, talking to them, encouraging them, and getting to know each as an individual. All of her dogs—and there may be as many as 150, depending on the season—have names, and it's said that Butcher can identify the bark and cry of each one. Even mushers who don't maintain their own breeding kennels spend hours bonding with their teams and helping dogs work together. Well-fed and well-managed dogs are sociable to their owners and to each other, and the barks some think of as "wild" or "wolflike" are the dogs' signals of eagerness and enthusiasm.

know exactly when women began competing as mushers, but a photo taken at an early Ladies' Day race is dated 1913. Sledding lost its importance with the arrival of the airplane, but racing never quite lost its appeal or romance. The tradition was revived on a grand scale in 1973, when the first Iditarod was run. Nicknamed "The Last Great Race on Earth," the Iditarod is a grueling 1,000-plus mile feat of endurance. Raced along the traditional Iditarod Trail, the link from Anchorage to Nome, the race encompasses a variety of terrain and weather that ranges from pleasantly below freezing to blizzard conditions and temperatures of −50° F. The first race took twenty days to complete. Today, nine is more like it. In addition to being the last great race, the Iditarod is the world's only great race in which men and women compete as equals. Women have

> When I'm out there racing, I'm racing as much as anybody to win. But I'm also out there because I enjoy being with my dogs. . . . What I love about my dogs is they tend to be more personable and have a little better manners than others.
> —Libby Riddles, interviewed in *Women's Sports & Fitness*

never been excluded from the Iditarod, and for one phenomenal four-year stretch, 1985–88, the title was won by two women, **Libby Riddles** and **Susan Butcher.** Their feats popularized a best-selling T-shirt bearing the legend ALASKA—WHERE MEN ARE MEN AND WOMEN WIN THE IDITAROD. There are numerous other races in the North, with picturesque names like the John Beargrease and the Kusko 300, but to most of us outside the Arctic, the Iditarod remains synonymous with the sport itself.

Governing Bodies and Organizations

Iditarod Trail Committee
Box 870800
Wasilla, Alaska 99687
Phone: 907/376-5155

* * * BIOGRAPHIES * * *

SUSAN BUTCHER MONSON b. December 26, 1954, Cambridge, Massachusetts

Many people think Butcher was the first woman to win Alaska's grueling, 1,000-plus-mile Iditarod. She wasn't—**Libby Riddles** beat her to the honor in 1985. However, Butcher was the first woman to enter the race, making her first run in 1978, and the first woman to finish in second place, which she did in 1982 and 1984. Her 1982 performance was especially remarkable. After her sled crashed into a tree and she suffered bruises, a blizzard obliterated the trail. Butcher went ten miles off course and was stranded for over two days by howling winds and thirty-foot-high drifts. Her ability to come back and finish second put her on the map, and many began to feel it was only a matter of time until her utter devotion to the sport ended in a first-place finish. Butcher won her first Iditarod in 1986 and repeated her victory for the next two years. No musher before or since has won three consecutive Iditarods. Butcher's fourth win, in 1990, was run in 11 days, 1 hour, and 53 minutes, a record that stood until 1994. Butcher often refers to herself as merely a "coach," and insists that her dogs are the real athletes of the sport.

Selected championships and honors: Four Iditarod Trail championships, 1986–88 and 1990.

LIBBY RIDDLES b. April 1, 1957, St. Cloud, Minnesota

Though not as famous as **Susan Butcher,** Riddles was the first woman to win the Iditarod. She did it in 1985, on her third try. Riddles, who grew up in Minnesota, finished high school early and moved to Alaska. She became involved in sled dog racing almost immediately and ran her first Iditarod in 1980, finishing eighteenth. The next year she finished two rungs lower, and didn't try again until 1985. No one picked her as a likely winner. By the tough standards of the race, Riddles was still considered an amateur, far too inexperienced to even finish in the top ten. In her book *Race Across Alaska*, Riddles offers a glimpse of the unexpected events that can occur over the course of 1,200 miles. Riddles had stopped to rest her team and give them a snack, tying them to a tree with a rope. When another team raced by, her dogs tried to follow them, pulling the rope taut. Since Riddles couldn't untie the rope and didn't want to cut it, she began chopping down the tree. As soon as the tree gave way, the team took off. Riddles scrambled, caught the end of the tree, and was pulled facedown through the snow until she finally let go. She set off on foot, got a ride with another musher, and eventually discovered her team, tied to a tree by a musher who'd spotted them and taken time to corral them for their owner. At the next checkpoint, Riddles was in seventeenth place in a field of sixty-three, but she eventually made up the time and came in first.

Selected championships and honors: Iditarod Trail championship, 1985.

Appendix

◆ ◆ ◆

* * * FANTASTIC FIRSTS * * *

ca. 600–400 B.C. Pherenice of Rhodes becomes the first woman to see the Olympics and live to tell about it. Although women were barred from the games on pain of death, the plucky Pherenice disguised herself as a man and took over as coach to her boxer son after her husband's unexpected death. She was found guilty but, as the mother of an Olympic champion, allowed to live.

1567. The first known woman golfer is Mary Queen of Scots. History notes that she was seen on the greens shortly after the death of her unlamented husband, Lord Darnley.

1607. America's first acrobat of record, Pocahontas, challenges the boys of Jamestown settlement to compete with her at handsprings.

July 26, 1745. The earliest recorded women's cricket match is played between the women of Hambledon and Bramley, England.

July 11, 1788. Miss S. Norcross becomes the first woman on record to score a century in cricket (100 runs in a single match). We do not know if her team, the Maids of Surrey, won or not.

August 25, 1804. Alicia Thornton, the first woman jockey, rides against Captain Flint in a four-mile race in York, England. She won two more York races in August 1805.

1810. First recorded women's golf match is held at Musselburgh, Scotland.

ca. 1860s. Croquet becomes the first sport played outside by women, and the first game in which men and women compete equally.

1866. Vassar girls form baseball teams and take to the diamonds.

1867. The Ladies' Golf Club, the first golf club for women, is formed at St. Andrews, in Scotland.

1869. First women's croquet championship held in England. Won by a Mrs. Joad.

1876. Maria Spelterina is the first woman to cross Niagara Falls on a cable.

March 16, 1876. First women's boxing match held in the United States, at Hill's Theater. Nell Saunders defeats Rose Hartland to win a silver butter dish.

1884. Singles competition for women debuts at Wimbledon. The first event is won by Maud Watson, who will win again in 1885.

1886. Mary ("Carlotta") Myers, first woman to pilot her own balloon, sets four-mile altitude record without using her oxygen equipment.

1887. The first U.S. women's singles tennis championship is held at Newport, and is won by Ellen Hansel.

1894. Australia initiates national golf championships for women.

1895. First U.S. Golf Association's Women's Amateur Championship game held, at the Meadowbrook Country Club in Westbury, New York. Thirteen women played nine holes in the morning and nine in the afternoon. Mrs. C. S. Browne won.

January 6–11, 1896. First marathon bicycle race for women, held at Madison Square Garden in New York. The race was a six-day marathon, won by Frankie Nelson, who pedaled 418 miles.

April 4, 1896. First intercollegiate women's basketball game, Stanford over Berkeley, 2–1.

April 10, 1896. Denied the chance to compete officially in the first modern Olympic marathon, Melpomene of Greece competes unofficially and completes the course in four and a half hours.

1898. First woman to compete in an automobile race, a two-day drive from Marseilles to Nice, France. Mme Laumaille finishes fourth, two places ahead of her husband.

July 5, 1898. Lizzie Arlington, the first woman signed to a contract with a men's minor league baseball team, pitches in an all-male regular season game.

May–October 1900. Women participate in events officially designated part of Paris Olympics. The events include golf, tennis, and yachting, but the games are so poorly organized that many of the women competing do not realize the contests are considered part of the Olympic roster.

October 1901. The first magazine devoted to women's sports is published—*Hockey Field,* published by the Ladies' Hockey Association of England.

August 1904. Archery for women is included in the St. Louis Olympics, but does not appear again until 1972.

August 1908. Women's figure skating is added to the Olympics.

1910. Annette Kellerman shocks Boston by swimming in her own, specially designed suit, the revolutionary one-piece.

Blanche Scott becomes the first woman to fly solo in an airplane, taking off and landing from an airstrip in Dayton, Ohio.

February 1912. Femina Sport, one of the first modern clubs exclusively for women, is founded in France.

August 1912. Swimming and diving debut as Olympic events for women.

1915. Regret, ridden by Joe Notter, becomes the first filly to win the Kentucky Derby. A filly didn't win again until 1980.

July 5–September 12, 1916. Adelina and Augusta Van Buren, sisters, become the first women to cross the country by motorcycle.

1920. Ethelda Bleibtrey of the United States becomes the first woman to win three Olympic gold medals, sweeping all three swimming events for women at the Antwerp games.

The birth of international women's sports competition in the United States occurs when an American women's field hockey team sails to England to play against an English women's team.

Early 1920s. Sonja Henie is the first female skater to perform a single axel.

May 1921. The first Jeux Olympiques Féminines du Monde is held for women in Monaco. The games have no official connection to the Olympics, but grow out of frustration over the sparse number of events open to women in the games. Three hundred women from five countries compete in basketball as well as track and field events. The Jeux Olympiques are held again in 1922 and 1923.

1923. In the United States, the first AAU outdoor track and field meet for women is held.

February 1924. At the first modern winter Olympics, held in Chamonix, France, eleven-year-old Sonja Henie makes her first appearance on the international stage.

August 1924. At the first modern summer Olympics, fencing for women is added to the program.

With her Olympic backstroke performance, Sybil Bauer becomes the first woman to beat an existing male swimming record.

Aileen Riggin becomes the first person ever to win Olympic medals in both swimming and diving, adding a bronze backstroke medal to diving gold and silvers.

June 11, 1925. Phyllis Green of Britain is the first woman to clear five feet in the high jump, at a meet in London.

1926. Miniature golf is invented by a woman, Frieda Carter, part owner of a resort. Carter's idea is an almost-instant hit, and over 25,000 courses are built over the next four years.

August 6, 1926. Gertrude Ederle of the United States is the first woman to swim the English channel, from Cap Gris-Nez to Dover. Her time, 14 hours and 39 minutes, beats the existing male record. For her efforts, she becomes the first female athlete to receive a New York ticker tape parade.

1927. Violet Cordery becomes the first woman to drive around the world, covering 10,266 miles across five continents in a three-liter Invicta. Her average speed is 24 mph.

1928. The Olympic Games inaugurate track and field events for women.

Gymnastics for women make their Olympic debut.

Martha Norelius of the United States becomes the first woman to win a gold medal for the same event at two successive modern Olympics. Her event is the 400-meter freestyle swim, won in 1924 and 1928.

1929. Rose Jacobs is the first woman to bowl a perfect 300 game, in Schenectady, New York.

1931. The first Alpine ski championships for women are held at Muren, Switzerland. Both the Alpine and slalom events are won by Esme McKinnon.

The first woman to sign a baseball contract is seventeen-year-old Jackie Mitchell, joining the Memphis Lookouts of the Southern Association. In an exhibition game against the Yankees, she strikes out Babe Ruth, Lou Gehrig, and Tony Lazzeri before being pulled. Despite Mitchell's efforts, the Lookouts lose 14–4.

The World Championships sponsored by the International Ski Federation add events for women.

June 23, 1931. Lili de Alvarez becomes the first woman to wear short trousers at Wimbledon.

1932. Helen Madison of Seattle is the first woman to swim 100 yards in a minute.

January 1932. Speed skating for women is a demonstration sport at the Lake Placid Olympics.

August 1932. At the Los Angeles Olympics, Babe Didrikson becomes the first women to win medals in three different events.

January 1936. Alpine skiing for women is added to the Olympic Games.

May 27, 1936. Sally Stearns of Rollins College in Winter Park, Florida, is the first woman coxswain of a men's rowing team, in a race against Marietta College.

September 4, 1937. First U.S. women's bicycling championship. The one-mile race is held in Buffalo, New York, under the auspices of the U.S. National Amateur Bicycling Association. Doris Kopsky of Belleville, New Jersey, wins with a time of 22.4 seconds.

1939. Esther Yates wins the women's all-round at the first waterskiing championships, held in Long Island, New York.

May 2, 1940. Belle Martell becomes the first woman to referee boxing, officiating eight matches in San Bernardino, California.

May 19, 1942. Mrs. W. Driver becomes the first person ever to score two holes in one in a single round, on the third and eighth holes, at Balgoelah Club in New South Wales, Australia.

April 27, 1943. Judy Johnson of Britain is the first woman jockey to ride in the United States, racing in a steeplechase at Pimlico, in Baltimore. She finishes tenth in a field of eleven.

1944. Swimmer Ann Curtis is the first woman to win the Sullivan Award.

ca. 1946. Edith Houghton becomes the first woman to scout for a major-league baseball team, the Philadelphia Phillies.

1948. At the winter Olympics in St. Moritz, Alpine ski events for women make their debut.

August 1948. Fanny Blankers-Koen of the Netherlands is the first woman to win four track and field gold medals in a single Olympics, in the 100- and 200-meter runs, the 80-meter hurdles, and as a member of the 400-meter relay team.

Alice Coachman of the United States wins the high jump to become the first woman of color to win an Olympic gold medal.

1950. Eighteen-year-old Joan Pfluger is the first woman to win the Grand American Trapshoot, in Vandalia, Ohio. The only woman competing, she breaks 100 clay pigeons in a row, then wins a 75-bird shootoff against four men.

1951. The first women's parachute jumping competition is held at Lesce-Bled, Yugoslavia. Monique Laroche of France wins the overall title.

August 1952. Equestrian sports and individual gymnastics join the Olympics as women's events.

1953. Toni Stone becomes the first and only woman to play in the segregated Negro American League.

Maureen Connolly of the United States is the first woman to win the tennis grand slam.

May 18, 1952–August 13, 1953. Ann Davison of Britain is the first woman to make a solo transatlantic crossing, in a 23-foot sloop called the *Felicity Ann.* She leaves from Plymouth, England, and finishes in Miami, Florida.

August 1956. At the Melbourne Olympics, Juliana Clemenol Minuzzo becomes the first woman to recite the Olympic oath.

By repeating her 1952 double-gold victory in the springboard and platform competitions, Pat McCormick of the United States becomes the first diver to win both events in two successive Olympics.

1957. Marion Ladewig is the first woman named International Bowler of the Year.

Marie Wadlow becomes the first woman elected to the National Softball Hall of Fame.

1958. Maria-Teresa de Filippi is the first woman to race in a Grand Prix auto race. She competes in three Grand Prix races all together, and her top finish is in tenth place.

October 18, 1958. Iolanda Balas of Rumania is the first woman to clear six feet in the high jump, at a meet in Bucharest.

August 1959. An all-woman mountain climbing team, composed of eleven women from five countries, sets out from Katmandu to climb Nepal's "Turquoise Goddess," the world's eighth-tallest mountain and one of the most treacherous. Two of the women, Belgian skier Claudine van der Strate-Pronhoz and French sportswear designer Claude Kogan, die with their guide when they are caught in a blizzard.

January 1960. Women's speed skating becomes a permanent Olympic sport.

Carol Heiss of the United States becomes the first woman to perform a double jump in competition.

1962. Greta Andersen becomes the first person to swim fifty miles, completing a solo crossing of Lake Michigan.

1963. The final round of the LPGA tournament is televised for the first time.

1964. Donna Mae Mims becomes the first woman driver to win the Sports Car Club of America Championship. She beats thirty-one men in the Class H production category for imported two-seaters.

January 1964. Olympic luge for women debuts at the Innsbruck games.

August 1964. Women's volleyball joins the Olympics.

Dawn Fraser of Australia becomes the first swimmer to win gold for the same event in three successive Olympics, repeating her 1956 and 1960 victories in the 100-meter freestyle.

Gymnast Larissa Latynina becomes the first woman to win nine Olympic gold medals, adding to previous victories in the 1956 and 1960 games.

1965. Canadian figure skater Petra Burka is the first woman to land a triple jump in competition.

Donna de Varona becomes the first woman sports commentator on a television network.

April 19, 1966. Disguised as a man, Robin Gibb Bingay is the first woman to compete in the Boston Marathon. She doesn't win, but she does finish ahead of most of the men.

1967. At the Pan American Games, American Doris Murdock sets a world record in small-bore rifle competition by shooting a score of 391. This is the first time in sports history that a women's record has surpassed a men's record.

1968. Kathy Kusner is the first woman to receive a jockey's license in the United States.

January 1968. Gender testing for women is introduced to the Olympics.

August 1968. Norma Enriqueta Basilio Satelo is the first woman ever to carry the Olympic torch, completing the last leg of the journey into the Mexico City stadium to light the Olympic flame and open the summer games.

American Wyomia Tyus defends her 100-meter Olympic medal, thus becoming the first man or woman to win two straight Olympic sprint titles.

Donna de Varona is the first woman to do television commentary on the Olympics.

Debbie Meyer of the United States is the first swimmer to win three gold medals in three individual swimming events in a single Olympics, winning the 200-, 400-, and 800-meter freestyles.

February 7, 1969. Twenty-year-old Diane Crump is the first woman to jockey at a pari-mutuel track.

February 22, 1969. Barbara Jo Rubin becomes the first woman jockey to win at a U.S. track, riding a horse named Cohesion at Charles Town, West Virginia.

May 10–July 24, 1969. Sharon Sites of the United States is the first woman to make a solo crossing of the Pacific, in a 25-foot sloop.

May 2, 1970. Diane Crump is the first woman to jockey in the Kentucky Derby, riding Fathom to a fifteenth-place finish.

June 13, 1970. Chi Cheng of Taiwan is the first woman to run 100 yards in 10 seconds, in Portland, Oregon.

1971. Shane Gould of Australia is the first female swimmer to hold world records in every freestyle category from 100 to 1,500 meters.

Billie Jean King becomes the first woman in any sport to earn more than $100,000 in a season, with winnings of $117,400.

June 30, 1971. Mary Bacon becomes the first woman jockey to win 100 races, with a victory at Thistledown Race Track in Cleveland, aboard California Lassie.

1972. Billie Jean King is the first woman named Sportsman of the Year by *Sports Illustrated* magazine.

Marie-Theres Nadig of Switzerland is the first woman skier to win Olympic gold medals in both the downhill and the giant slalom.

April 17, 1972. The Boston Marathon officially opens competition to women. Nina Kuscsik of New York City wins with a time of 3:08:58.

June 1972. Bernice Gera is the first woman to umpire a minor-league game, overseeing the Auburn Phillies and the Geneva Rangers. She made a bad call and retired from umpiring after the game.

1973. Sheila Young becomes the first athlete in history to hold simultaneous world championships in two different sports, world sprint titles in speed skating and cycling, a feat she repeats in 1976.

Golfer Marilyn Smith becomes the first woman to work as a television commentator for a men's pro event.

March 1, 1973. Robyn Smith is the first woman jockey to win a major stakes race, garnering

$27,450 in the Paumanauk Handicap at the Aquaduct, New York City, aboard North Sea.

1973. The U.S. Open becomes the first major tennis event to offer equal prize money to men's and women's singles champions. As of 1997, it was still the only event to do so.

1974. The International Volleyball Association (IVA) is the first association ever to organize a professional coed sport. The attempt fails after one season.

May 1974. The first international women's yachting competition is held at Quiberon, France. Eighty women from eleven countries participate.

June 12, 1974. Little League Baseball announces that girls will now be allowed to play on teams.

July 1974. Carol Polis is the first woman licensed to judge boxing matches, by the New York State Athletic Commission.

1975. Shirley Muldowney becomes the first woman licensed to drive top fuel dragsters.

First Women's World Cup gymnastics competition is held, in London. Lyudmila Tourischeva wins all five gold medals.

May 16, 1975. The first woman to reach the peak of Mount Everest, the world's tallest mountain, is thirty-five-year-old Junko Tabei of Japan.

March 28, 1976–March 26, 1978. Krystyna Choynowska-Liskiewiez of Poland is the first woman to sail solo around the world, in a 32-foot sloop.

August 1976. Basketball, handball, and rowing join the Olympic program for women.

Karin Smith becomes the first woman to throw a javelin more than 200 feet, with a throw of 203 feet, 10 inches.

Nadia Comaneci is the first gymnast ever to receive a perfect 10 score in Olympic competition. She received a total of seven perfect scores in the course of the games.

Kornelia Ender becomes the first woman to win four gold medals at a single Olympiad, with three individual medals and one team win in swimming.

Judy Rankin becomes the first woman golfer to crack the $100,000 season winnings mark, with $150,734.

1977. Jan Todd becomes the first woman to lift more than 1,000 pounds in three power lifts: a bench press of 176.25 pounds, a dead lift of 441 pounds, and a squat lift of 424.25 pounds.

Lucy Harris is the first woman to be drafted by an NBA team, the New Orleans Jazz.

March 5, 1977. Betty Cook, a grandmother, is the first woman to win a major offshore power-boat competition, the Bushmills Grand Prix off Newport Beach, California.

May 1977. Janet Guthrie is the first woman to compete in the Indianapolis 500. She completes 27 laps.

May 29, 1977. Sue Press becomes the first person to shoot holes in one on two consecutive holes, the 13th and 14th, at the Chatswood Golf Country Club in Sydney, Australia.

September 7–8, 1977. Cynthia Nicholas, a nineteen-year-old Canadian, is the first woman to complete a round-trip swim of the English Channel. Her time, 19 hours and 55 minutes, beats the existing male record by more than 10 hours.

1978. First International Women's Driving Tournament for harness racers. Women from eight countries compete in sixteen races. Bea Farber of the United States wins, and Agnese Palagi of Italy is runner-up.

Nancy Lopez is the first woman to win Rookie of the Year and Golfer of the Year in the same season.

September 1978. In a case filed against the New York Yankees by *Sports Illustrated* reporter Melissa Ludtke Lincoln, federal judge Constance Baker Mostley rules that female reporters cannot be banned from locker rooms.

December 9, 1978. Debut game of the Women's Professional Basketball League, played between the Chicago Hustle and the Milwaukee Does. The Hustle wins, 92–87.

August 30, 1979. Ann Meyers is the first woman to sign an NBA contract. The contract, for

$50,000, is for one year with the Indiana Pacers. She never appears in a game.

August 1980. Women's field hockey makes its debut at the boycotted Moscow Olympics, giving Zimbabwe its first gold medal.

1981. The first figure skating triple-triple combination is performed by Midori Ito of Japan, done at the World Junior Championships.

April 4, 1981. Sue Brown, coxswain for Oxford, is the first woman to compete in the Oxford-Cambridge race. Oxford rows to an eight-length victory.

1982. For the first time, all four rounds of a woman's golf tournament, the Nabisco Dinah Shore, are televised.

1983. The first NCAA women's championship in cross-country skiing is held. Beth Heiden wins.

1984. Connie Carpenter Phinney becomes the first woman to take part in both the winter and summer Olympics when she wins the inaugural 79-kilometer pursuit race. Twelve years earlier, she was on the U.S. speed-skating team.

With her eighty-fifth career win, golfer Kathy Whitworth breaks Sam Snead's record to become the winningest pro golfer in history.

August 1984. Valerie Brisco-Hooks becomes the first runner to win both the 200 and 400 meters at a single Olympics.

For the first time, the Olympic Games feature a marathon for women.

1985. Lynette Woodard is the first woman to play for the Harlem Globetrotters.

March 2–20, 1985. Libby Riddles becomes the first woman to win Alaska's Iditarod dogsled race.

1986. Playing for the Springfield, Massachusetts, franchise in the short-lived U.S. Basketball League, Nancy Lieberman becomes the first woman to play in a men's pro league.

July 7, 1986. Jackie Joyner-Kersee becomes the first woman to break the 7,000-point mark in heptathlon.

1987. Nancy Lieberman becomes the first woman to play with the Washington Generals, the team that tours with the Harlem Globetrotters.

1988. China's Gao Min becomes the first woman ever to break the 600-point barrier in springboard diving—a feat she performs at three separate meets that year.

For the first time, the *Sporting News* Man of the Year is a woman—Jackie Joyner-Kersee.

East Germany's Christa Rothenberger becomes the first—and only—person to win medals in both a winter and summer Olympics in the same year, taking home medals in speed skating and cycling.

July 1988. After a long absence, women's tennis reappears at the Olympics.

1988–89. A woman, Switzerland's Vreni Schneider, breaks Ingemar Stenmark's old record of thirteen World Cup wins in a season by skiing to her fourteenth Alpine victory.

1989. The first triple axel by a woman is performed by Midori Ito of Japan at the World Figure Skating Championships.

1991. The first women's soccer World Cup is held, with the United States defeating Norway for the championship.

1992. Margaret Wade becomes the first woman to receive the James Naismith Basketball Trophy for lifetime contribution to the sport.

Lyn St. James is the first woman to race on the IndyCar circuit, and is named Rookie of the Year.

January 1992. Biathlon becomes an event for women at the winter Olympics.

July 1992. Triathlete Paula Newby-Fraser becomes the first woman to break the nine-hour barrier in the Ironman Triathlon in Hawaii.

Derartu Tulu wins the 10,000-meter race to become the first black African woman to win an Olympic gold medal.

Judo debuts as a full medal sport for women at the summer Olympics in Barcelona.

May 1993. Julie Krone wins the Belmont Stakes aboard Colonial Affair, becoming the first woman ever to win a Triple Crown race.

1995. Linda Wallace is the first woman ever to bowl in the ABC Masters tournament.

Kerri-Ann McTiernan becomes the first woman to coach a men's college team when she takes over

Brooklyn's Kingsborough Community College team.

June 24, 1995. Suzyn Waldman is the first woman to broadcast a network baseball game, over the radio Baseball Network, covering the Texas Rangers and the New York Yankees.

January 1996. Judy Bell, a former golfer, becomes the first female president of the United States Golf Association.

April 15, 1996. Uta Pippig becomes the first woman to win the women's division of the Boston Marathon three years in a row.

June 4, 1996. Pam Davis becomes the first woman to pitch in the minor leagues, hurling one relief inning to win the game.

July 25, 1996. With a gold-medal win in the 200-meter backstroke, Krisztina Egerszegi of Hungary becomes the first swimmer ever to win five individual gold medals.

July 26, 1996. Amy Van Dyken becomes the first female swimmer to win four gold medals in a single Olympic Games, two individual and two team.

May 12, 1997. Susie Maroney is the first person to swim from Cuba to Florida.

Index

♦ ♦ ♦